WALTHER EIC...

EZEKII

WALTHER EICHRODT

EZEKIEL

A Commentary

SCM PRESS LTD

Translated by Cosslett Quin from the German
Der Prophet Hesekiel
(Das Alte Testament Deutsch 22/1–2)
1965–1966
published by Vandenhoeck and Ruprecht, Göttingen

334 00443 8
First published in English 1970
by SCM Press Ltd
58 Bloomsbury Street, London WC1
Third impression 1980

Printed and bound in Great Britain by
Redwood Burn Limited
Trowbridge and Esher

CONTENTS

ABBREVIATIONS

ANET	*Ancient Near Eastern Texts*, ed. J. B. Pritchard (2nd ed., 1955)
AOB²	*Altorientalische Bilder zum Alten Testament, gesammelt und beschrieben von G. Gressmann* (2nd ed., 1927)
AOT²	*Altorientalische Texte zum Alten Testament*, ed. H. Gressmann (2nd ed., 1926)
ARW	*Archiv für Religionswissenschaft*
AThANT	Abhandlungen zur Theologie des Alten und Neuen Testaments
BH	Biblia Hebraica, ed. R. Kittel (3rd ed., eds. A. Alt and O. Eissfeldt)
BWANT	Beiträge zur Wissenschaft von Alten und Neuen Testament
BZAW	Beihefte zur Zeitschrift für die alttestamentliche Wissenschaft
JBL	*Journal of Biblical Literature*
LXX	Septuagint
MT	Massoretic text
Pesh.	Peshitta, Syriac version of the Old Testament
RGV	*Religionsgeschichtliche Volksbücher*
RHPR	*Revue d'histoire et de philosophie religieuses*
SVT	Supplements to *Vetus Testamentum*
THR	*Theologische Rundschau*
Th.St.Kr.	*Theologische Studien und Kritiken*
ThT	*Theologischi Tjdschrift*
ThZ	*Theologische Zeitschrift*, Basel
V	Vulgate
VDOG	*Veröffentlichungen der Deutschen Orientgesellschaft*
VT	*Vetus Testamentum*
VTS	Supplements to *Vetus Testamentum*
ZAW	*Zeitschrift für die alttestamentliche Wissenschaft*
ZThK	*Zeitschrift für Theologie und Kirche*

BIBLIOGRAPHY

Commentaries cited in the text

Auvray, E., *Ezéchiel*, 1947

Bertholet, A., *Das Buch Hesekiel*, Kurzer Handkommentar zum AT, Abt. XII ed. K. Marti, 1897 = Bertholet[1]

Bertholet, A., *Hesekiel*, Handbuch zum AT, 1.Reihe, 13, 1936 = Bertholet[2]

Brunner, R., *Ezechiel*, Prophezei, Schweizerisches Bibelwerk für die Gemeinde, 1944

Bewer, J. A., *The Book of Ezekiel*, vols 1 and 2, Harper's Annotated Bible, nos 8 and 9, 1954

Calvin, J., *Praelectiones in Ezechielis prophetae viginti capita priora*, Corpus Reformatorum, vol. LXVIII, 1889

Cooke, G. A., *A Critical and Exegetical Commentary on the Book of Ezekiel*, International Critical Commentary, 1936

Cornhill, C. H., *Das Buch des Propheten Ezechiel*, 1886

Fohrer, G., *Ezechiel*, Handbuch zum AT, 1.Reihe, 13, 1955

Heinisch, P., *Das Buch Ezechiel übersetzt und erklärt*, Die heilige Schrift des AT VIII, 1, ed. Feldmann und Herkenne, 1923

Henne, E., *Ezechiel*, Die heilige Schrift des A und NT, 1936

Herrmann, J., *Ezechiel übersetzt und erklärt*, Kommentar zum AT, ed. E. Sellin, vol. XI, 1924

Krätzschmar, R., *Das Buch Ezechiel*: Göttinger Handkommentar, ed. W. Nowack III.3, 1900

May, H. G., *The Book of Ezekiel*, The Interpreter's Bible, vol. 6, 1956, pp. 41–338

von Orelli, C., *Das Buch Ezechiel ausgelegt*, Kurzgefasster Kommentar zu den heiligen Schriften des A und NT, ed Strack-Zöckler, A.5, 1, Hälfte, 1896[2]

Rothstein, J. W., *Das Buch Ezechiel*, Die hl. Schrift des AT, ed. A. Bertholet, 4.Auflage, vol. 1, 1922, pp. 868–1000

van den Born, A., *Ezechiel uit de Grondtekst vertaald en uitgelegd*, De Boeken van het Oude Testament, Deel XI, Boek 1, 1954

Zimmerli, W., *Ezechiel*, Biblischer Kommentar, AT ed. M. Noth, XIII, fascicules 1–17, 1954ff.

Other works, cited only under the name of the authors

HÖLSCHER, G., *Hesekiel. Der Dichter und das Buch. Eine literarkritische Untersuchung*, BZAW 39, 1924

KLOSTERMANN, A., 'Ezechiel. Ein Beitrag zur besseren Würdigung seiner Person und seiner Schrift', *Theologische Studien und Kritiken* (1877), pp. 391ff.

KUHL, C., 'Die "Wiederaufnahme"—ein literarkritisches Prinzip?', *ZAW* 64 (1952), pp. 1ff.

INTRODUCTION
THE PROPHET EZEKIEL AND HIS BOOK

THE PROPHET IN THE HISTORY OF HIS TIMES

STATEMENTS IN THE BOOK of Ezekiel which we may regard as reliable (1.1–3 and 29.17) place the prophet's period of activity between 594 and 571 BC. He received his call to be a prophet when he was a young man, probably at the age of thirty (cf. below the commentary on 1.1–3, pp. 51f.). So his youth fell in the period of the reformer king Josiah (639–609), and was greatly influenced by the great political and cultic reformation undertaken by that king in the year 621. Josiah had aimed at strengthening his people and state, worn out as the result of vassalship to Assyria, with the forces of a purified faith in Yahweh, so as to be able to lead them to a better future. Considering the sympathy such a man as Jeremiah showed towards this undertaking, we may safely assume that it must have found even more decided supporters among the temple priesthood. At that time the young priest, the son of Busi, a member of the priesthood in the Jerusalem temple, newly arrived at adulthood, must have been profoundly impressed by the religious aspects of the reform, as he saw the temple being cleansed of the heathen filth that had settled in it, and the original forms and laws of Yahweh worship being put into force. This must have aroused his enthusiasm at the thought of the greatness of the task that this would lay upon the shoulders of the temple priesthood. The renewal of the covenant between Israel and her God, sworn to by king and people in a solemn act of state, must have seemed to bring back the ideal period of David, and bold extensions of the boundaries of the kingdom in the north seemed likely also to revive the nation as a political force.

This only seemed to intensify the disillusionment when the young monarch's life came to an untimely end, as, trying to defend his country's newly won independence against Pharaoh Neco, he met his death at Megiddo. This disappointed the hopes occasioned by his work, and wrested the reins from the hands of the triumphant champions of the reform. Jehoahaz, the younger son of Josiah, was raised

to the throne by the free citizens of Judah, who passed over his elder
brother Eliakim, probably because it was thought that he could be
better depended upon to carry on his father's policy. But he was
thrown into prison (II Kings 23.33f.; Jer. 22.10) by Neco, who,
being overlord of Syria, regarded such decisions as infringements of
his prerogative.

Eliakim, who seemed a more suitable instrument for Neco's purposes, was selected to be king, and his name changed to Jehoiakim
as a token of his subjection to the great king. From the political point
of view he proved in practice to be a docile vassal of the Pharaoh,
ruthlessly extracting from his subjects the large tribute that had to be
paid to Egypt, and giving free rein to his despotic inclinations by
employing forced labour in erecting his palaces (II Kings 23.35; Jer.
22.13ff.). In the religious sphere, he returned to the syncretism of
Manasseh, which had barely been suppressed. True, he did not make
any state enactment to repeal the covenant pledged by his father; the
strict prohibitions against the worship of foreign gods still stood on
paper, but in actual practice the way was left open for heathen cults
to spring up in such a way that Jeremiah could speak of a conspiracy
against Yahweh, which turned its back on the nation's true Lord
while cloaking itself in the mantle of legal fidelity to the covenant
(Jer. 11.9ff.). His brutal suppression of any criticism of his decisions
by prophets, resulting in the execution of the prophet Uriah and the
proscription of Jeremiah, gave a particularly revealing example of
how opposed the aims of his reign were to those of his father. The
adroitness with which he switched over from vassalage to Egypt to
being a satellite of Babylon, once Nebuchadrezzar had driven Neco
back into Egypt and put an end to his few years of apparent successes,
left Jehoiakim's position on the throne undisturbed and seemed to
justify his policy.

This violent change in Judah's whole condition must necessarily
have seemed to those faithful to Yahweh to be a breach of faith and a
departure from their beliefs. Such flagrant defiance of the covenant
God must have presented the temple priesthood in particular with
very serious problems of conscience. The cleavage which must have
divided them and have been deepened further by the passionate way
in which the prophets reacted against the tyrant, must have borne
heavily upon one like Ezekiel. The tension between the opposing
demands of religion and politics will have grown to breaking-point,
and his mind must have felt more and more the weightiness of the

problem of the serious decision that he must himself make. This will have been further intensified by the warm sympathy with which he followed Jeremiah's struggle and the way in which, as his own preaching shows in more than one passage, the message of Jeremiah appealed to the deepest feelings of his heart.

The prophet's struggle against the oppressor was soon justified by events. When Jehoiakim repudiated his position as a vassal of Babylon in 602 (II Kings 24.1), he returned once more to the old political manoeuvre practised by the Syrian states, according to which they seized the first opportunity to throw off such a galling yoke, and tried to have their own way by playing off the rival powers of the Euphrates and the Nile against each other. Nebuchadrezzar reacted slowly, launching a sort of guerilla war against him with the assistance of Edom, Moab and Ammon, Jehoiakim's chief competitors in Palestine, which may have done no more than strengthen the king of Judah's confidence in his ability to overcome his opponents. But in about 598 a more serious Babylonian attack took place. A Babylonian army appeared before Jerusalem and began to besiege it. At that critical moment, Jehoiakim was swept away, either by the sword of his enemy or else by the sickness with which Jeremiah (Jer. 22.18f.) had threatened him. His son Jehoiachin, only just eighteen years old, had to suffer punishment for his father's guilt. The hopeless position of his capital led him to the right conclusion and so he yielded up the walls to the besiegers after a reign of only three months, in order to deliver his subjects from all the horrors that would have followed its storming. This seems to explain why Nebuchadrezzar treated the city with forbearance. The palace and temple were indeed plundered, and the king and royal family led off into captivity in Babylon, and along with them large numbers of the upper and artisan classes of the country. At that time, young Ezekiel was one of those who underwent the bitter fate of deportation, which prevented him from taking up his priestly office, and annihilated all natural hopes. But Jerusalem was not destroyed, nor did Judah become a Babylonian province. It continued to subsist as an independent state with a king of its own from the house of David, Mattaniah, an uncle of Jehoiachin's, whose name was changed to Zedekiah as a sign of his position of vassalage. At that time, of course, the southern part of the land may have been taken away from Judah and handed over to Edom (Jer. 13.18f.). Ezekiel must have regarded this as comparatively generous treatment, seeing that it allowed the country to survive (Ezek. 17.5f.). The treatment of

4

those led into captivity also seemed to be more like a temporary measure, since they were not settled in a province of the empire to add a new stratum to the population, but were put in Babylonia itself for the purpose of restoring the economy of strips of land that had gone out of cultivation. They were allowed to order their own affairs by means of elders chosen by themselves, and were not prevented from holding firmly to the worship of their own God, although this could only take shape in a very limited way under the new conditions (cf. below, p. 53). So they did not have to face a sudden break in the whole of the pattern of their life or give up everything to which they had previously been accustomed, but were able to preserve a certain degree of continuity, making it easier to bear the yoke of exile. We see here, therefore, no strict imprisonment or permanent confinement under continuous hardships at the hands of brutal jailors, as scholars were earlier inclined to assume, under the influence of certain passages in Lamentations and Deutero–Isaiah (Lam. 3.34; Isa. 47.6). Jeremiah could counter the refusal of the exiles to make the best of their lot with a summons to build houses, plant gardens and found new families (Jer. 29.5f.). Nevertheless, the exiles found that their status was that of serfs to the state without right of appeal. It depended entirely on the caprice of circumstance, on the situation of the time, on the increasing needs of the government, and the more or less hostile attitude of officials. Sometimes the pressure exercised upon them remained tolerable; sometimes it turned into downright oppression and ill treatment. It need not therefore surprise us that conditions were not uniformly the same everywhere and all the time, but that captivity in a foreign land displayed its more painful and oppressive side, as well as its more endurable aspects.

It remained significant that the king and his family were given lodgings in a wing of the royal palace in Babylon, and were allowed to provide for their own household arrangements, and that, as Babylonian records inform us, supplies of food were issued to them by the state. Everything seemed to indicate that neither those at home nor those in exile need regard the state of affairs as final, but could count on these being purely temporary measures, soon to be followed by a return home. It is obvious that this brought about an unsettled excited state throughout the whole nation, and reduced them to a condition of fanatical unteachability.

In face of this optimistic view of the situation, supported as it was by promises from nationalistic prophets of victory, it was completely hopeless to appeal to people to adopt a different view. All that Ezekiel, like Jeremiah, could do was to be obedient to the task committed to him and proclaim that Yahweh had decided otherwise, putting up with the enmity and spiteful contempt which this aroused among his fellow countrymen, while at the same time what he observed of matters at home drove him to condemn those in power and their followers with increasing sharpness. He saw the future take on ever darker colours. Complete independence of popular opinion, such as could be won only after severe inward struggles, was the prerequisite for any power to provide genuine help, when the day of reckoning would dawn.

Even if Nebuchadrezzar had been still intending to reserve to himself the final decision as to the fate of Judah, his experiences with Zedekiah, the puppet king he had placed on the throne, led him to different decisions, which sealed the fate of that unfortunate nation. It seems that the Jerusalemites were unwilling to accept any improvement in their conditions from the hands of a heathen overlord, and further, that the return of Jehoiachin and the former governing class associated with him would be anything but welcome to the supporters of Zedekiah. Blinded by wishful thinking, they preferred to have a rapprochement with Egypt and Tyre, and then to take up arms in order to win independence. As early as 594, secret negotiations took place for an anti-Babylonian pact between the small states of Palestine, but as yet they did not dare to take any really decisive steps, a hesitancy towards which the strong opposition put up by Jeremiah may have contributed (cf. Jer. 27). Zedekiah, who was not entirely insensitive to the word of the prophet, and who evidently had some personal misgivings over the daring game his counsellors were playing, was unfortunately not a man capable of carrying through any strong policy of his own. His wavering character was powerless in face of the pressure brought upon him by the party of independence, which brought him step by step closer to the despairing fight for freedom, until he had gone so far as to make it impossible to turn back.

So in 589, an open breach took place with the Babylonian overlord, which was partly induced by the hope of considerable assistance from Egypt (Ezek. 17.15). Ezekiel condemned such breaking of the oath of allegiance by a vassal with rigid severity. The fight to the death on which his native land now began led his prophecy to take the shape of a biting proclamation of judgment, which might tear the bandage from the eyes of his countrymen and bring them to a true knowledge of their God. But he could also see Judah's heathen allies under divine retribution, and he could proclaim their subjection to the mighty one who alone ruled the world. It was he who had selected Nebuchadrezzar to carry out his plans; the people of the world were his and he asserted his lordship in face of all opposition. The prophet therefore saw the destiny of Jerusalem reaching its fulfilment under two different aspects. Yet deeply as he suffered as he watched the final accomplishment of the ruin of his native country, he was not filled with bitter despair. The storming and destruction of the capital city of Judah in the year 587, the burning down of the temple, the ruthless execution of Zedekiah and his family (II Kings 25.7) and of the responsible political leaders, the carrying off of the population (II Kings 25.8ff.) into exile did make him suffer severely because of his love for his people and country; yet at the same time he saw the break-up of the hard core of resistance by his people to his message, and the resultant possibility of leading them out of the hopeless despair they felt at having been so misled, towards a new hope.

It also served his turn that the outward circumstances of the exiles did not undergo any change for the worse, even after their numbers had been swelled by the survivors of the catastrophe. Nothing was done to change the regime for a severer one; the comparative freedom of movement in the prisoners' colony and its self-government by its own elders was maintained, so that the gatherings for worship with prayer and singing, priestly instruction and prophetic word went on more or less as before, making it possible for the remnants of the ruined nation to preserve its spiritual identity. The prophet must have recognized the fixing of these forms of common prayer as the special task that was to occupy the remaining years of his life. The disciples, too, who gathered around him, the group which collected, copied out and edited his writings, facilitated the development of a fixed tradition which would supply a protective outward shape for the life that still pulsated here. The fact that their old native land had not been occupied by settlers of foreign blood, but still remained in the hands of its own inhabitants, reduced in numbers though they were, made the country still seem home, even for the exiles. The appointment of a man of Judah, Gedaliah, a member of the family of Shaphan, as governor to administrate the little province, was only a passing gleam of light to summon up hopes for new possibilities of development for the land. His assassination by a prince of the Davidic dynasty who had escaped to Ammon, and who must have acted partly out of jealousy, partly out of savage hatred towards everything associated with Babylon, soon nipped this new growth in the bud. Whether in spite of this bloodthirsty deed any further effort was made to provide Judah with an administration of its own in order to bring the land back under cultivation by planned resettlement (cf. Ezek. 33.24), or whether from then on it sank into being a part of the province of Samaria, we do not know.

Quite apart from this, Nebuchadrezzar's attention was given to the unruly states of Syria for many more years: soon after the fall of Jerusalem he set off on another punitive expedition against the second of the main centres of resistance to his hegemony, and endeavoured to force the hitherto impregnable island fortress of Tyre to make an unconditional surrender (cf. ch. 26). But after a thirteen-year-long siege, from 586/5 to 573/2, he found himself forced to consent to a compromise. This was a very disappointing outcome for a struggle conducted with such extreme ferocity, and the last dated prophecy by Ezekiel in 29.17–21 deals with it. Calmly and deliberately it acknowledges that the prophet's threat that the city would be completely annihilated has not taken effect, and replies to it only the more proudly, affirming the unlimited control exercised by his God over the powers of the world, and that this control cannot be thwarted by any transitory success for its opponents. He knows that God's hands are capable of bringing his plans for the world to their goal, and that he need not recant any part of his message.

OTHER VIEWS OF THE PLACE AND TIME OF THE PROPHET'S MINISTRY

This picture of the historical situation suggested by the dates given in the book and by various statements by the author has in fact been questioned by many scholars, at any rate in the last few decades. They find themselves compelled to take a totally different view of the time and place of Ezekiel's work, based upon a fresh analysis of the book. Their point of departure consists in the offence taken at the fact that large portions of the prophet's preaching are explicitly aimed at Jerusalem and its inhabitants, and do not enter into the conditions of the exiles, which do not seem to be taken into consideration until the promises of salvation which begin after 587. Therefore, instead of a 'prophet without people' in Babylon, addressing himself at long range to his fellow countrymen in Jerusalem, it seemed to them more appropriate to posit *a bearer of the prophetic message working in Palestine*, whose posthumous writings were only subsequently given an exilic stamp by his disciples.[1] However, the difficulty of explaining large sections of the prophetic book on the basis of this exilic revision brings out only too clearly how very one-sided this theory is. It was hoped to overcome this problem by postulating that the prophet worked not only in Palestine but also in Babylonia, and this made it possible to make the heavily overloaded prophetic discourses, with all their repetitions and postscripts (as, for example, in ch. 8–11), intelligible by relating them to different places and conditions. In Germany it was above all Bertholet who worked out the possibilities of this in an instructive and attractive way in his commentary (1936). According to his view, Ezekiel worked in Jerusalem until the fall of the city, then, after a short stay in an unknown place in Palestine, he emigrated to Babylonia, where he subsequently received a second call and developed a second period of prophetic activity. Of course, the lack of any appropriate tradition makes it possible for the theories held to vary very considerably, as can be seen from the writings of the numerous supporters of this hypothesis. Some of them posit that Ezekiel, having been deported to Babylon and having worked there, returned to Jerusalem once more as the result of a divine call. They then make him return to Babylon again, either at the beginning of the siege or during the pause when the siege was lifted or only after the destruction of the city. Beside this we have a theory that Ezekiel had to break off his first period of activity in Jerusalem because of the strength of the hostility to him there; Yahweh willed to deliver his prophet from it by giving him a command in the fifth year (1.2), after the first deportation, to flee to Babylonia and settle among the *golah* (captivity) there.[2]

This unsatisfactory fluctuation in the theories is no mere matter of chance; it is the necessary result of all the difficulties encountered by any attempt to work out such a fundamental theory on the basis of a text which states the exact opposite. Whenever they do not fit in with the theory, the established pieces of information about dates and geographical locations must now be accepted, and again dismissed

[1] V. Herntrich, *Ezechielprobleme*, BZAW 61, 1932, whose thesis has been taken up and developed further by a whole series of other critics.
[2] Cf. in this connection C. Kuhl, 'Neuere Hesekiel-Literatur', *ThR*, NF 20 (1952), and 'Zum Stand der Hesekiel-Forschung', *ThR*, NF 24 (1956/7), 1.

as doubtful, without any reliable methodological basis for the conclusions. There is also a readiness to take those elements of the tradition that are difficult to accommodate to this interpretation, and either make them mean something else or else try to eliminate them by critical methods. Doubt is thus cast on large portions of the book such as the oracles to the nations, creating a very suspicious element of uncertainty. The alleged double character of the accounts, which are supposed to be made up of two strands which have to be disentangled, is solved much more satisfactorily by a penetrating interpretation of the text which demonstrates the firm and significant interweaving of the different parts, as in the vision of the call, the unity of which is so often challenged. Here, of course, the later history of the text must be carefully taken into account, so as to follow accurately the way in which the original tradition has been refashioned to a considerable extent by the disciples of the prophet, who are also transmitters of his message, not only by the addition of numerous glosses but also by the insertion of sections which serve to bring out its full implications and also to explain its meaning. In this subsequent rehandling we can distinguish two lines of thought, one prophetic and the other priestly. The first can be traced in the pronouncements of judgment, addresses to the nations and promises of salvation. The second attains most prominence in the sections connected with the temple, e.g. ch. 10; 40–48. In this situation, form- and traditio-historical criticism may be able to give us new insights into the way in which the preaching of Ezekiel was conditioned by contemporary history.

Thanks to this, many individual difficulties are satisfactorily explained, but at the same time all the inner weakness of the basic theory of the 'prophet without a people' begins to emerge. For it is so obvious as to be a certainty that Ezekiel was first and foremost a prophet for the exiles, and that his influence upon the homeland was entirely secondary. It is a fact rightly emphasized that his proclamations of judgment are aimed exclusively against Jerusalem. But this does not mean that he gave no thought to the needs of the exiles; on the contrary, it means that he was showing a radical realization of the burning problem presented by the existence of that portion of the nation. It was precisely the destiny in store for Jerusalem with its temple and its inhabitants which constituted the cardinal problem for the exiles, a problem which had decisive significance for their attitude towards their own destiny and relegated to the background the hardships immediately connected with their deportation. It was Jerusalem that constituted the guarantee of the continued existence of the nation, and its preservation or non-preservation would decide whether what was happening to the exiles themselves would prove to be a transitory visitation or whether it would have to be regarded as a mortal blow at their very roots. So attempts were made to maintain their close ties with the homeland and to keep in touch with events there by means of messages which passed to and fro, in the way of which Jer. 29.25ff. gives testimony. When, therefore, Ezekiel spoke of the destiny of Jerusalem, he could be sure of finding his exilic audience full of attention and of tense expectation. By the strong 'no!' with which he met their feverish hopes, he also led them at the same time towards responsibility for the attitude they took up towards the God who was exercising judgment; for they, too, belong to the 'house of rebelliousness' and are as much 'Israel' as the other members of the nation who are still in the homeland, and the same word of God goes out to them bringing judgment or blessing. Israel continues to form a single spiritual whole, whether it exists in Palestine or in Babylonia, and to count up the number of passages applying the honorific title of 'the nation' to the exiles or to the Jerusalemites and then try to deduce from the difference in the number that one or the other portion of the people is more important, is just as senseless, and has as little relation to the material facts, as to speak of a 'prophet without a people'.

The same holds true in regard to the thesis of a thoroughgoing transformation of the original writing of the prophet by a redactor who took the alleged testimonies to a double sphere of activity for Ezekiel and wove them together so as to claim them to be testimonies of his working among the exiles. Such a thesis is loaded with difficulties. For the suppression of his preaching in the holy land, so as to transpose it into the unclean land of exile, a process which would leave aside a considerable number of the testimonies which really do come from there, is such an extraordinary thing that it is very difficult to make it credible that by this means one would have claimed a continuous succession of Yahweh prophecies for the exiles from 598, the first year of the exile. The fifth year of the exile at any rate remained unaltered as that of the time when Ezekiel began to prophesy.

In view of the insuperable difficulties with which the prophetic book confronts any attempt to interpret it from the assumption that Ezekiel had a double sphere of activity, we find that there has been an attempt at a still more radical solution. This has been stated by C. C. Torrey, following some precursors who remained unnoticed, at frequent intervals since 1925, and has been received by many with acclamation. Torrey has found a large number of adherents to his theory, which tries to *account for this prophetic book by explaining it as pseudepigraphic.* According to him, the kernel of the book originated about 230, and contained prophetic discourses which were set by the author in the seventh century, and disguised as prophecies of the abominations of Manasseh and of the punishment which they met. Soon after, it was worked over, ascribed to the prophet Ezekiel, and furnished with appropriate dates. This theory presents so many points of attack that attempts to revive it have taken several different forms. One ascribes a part of the book to a prophet called Ezekiel who first appeared at the end of the fifth century, but was furnished by a redactor with a great number of additions, dating the appearance of the prophet one hundred and fifty years earlier. Another theory is that the many points of contact of the book with post-exilic texts, especially those belonging to Priestly literature, are due to an author of the period of Ezra and Nehemiah, whose autobiographical work was worked over and enriched at the time of Alexander the Great. In both of these versions the origin of the book takes on a fortuitous and capricious character. So another attempted solution tries to specify a strong motive for an author in the question of the messianic future which had been obscured in his time by a great uncertainty. This redactor belongs to the Judahites deported to the Black Sea in the fourth century, and gave the book the cryptic character beloved of apocalyptic by means of references to earlier dates and events, with the inevitable result that both the figure of the writer and the historical circumstances remain in a very uncertain light. All these widely divergent theories serve to illustrate the danger of throwing away what this book testifies to in regard to itself, because it only leads to fleeting speculations which, in spite of all their cleverness, cannot arouse any confidence in their results.

THE FORM TAKEN BY THE PROPHET'S MESSAGE

Exegetical work during the last few decades has a different story to tell. It displays increasing certainty in penetrating to the original text and understanding its context out of the beginning of the exile. The numerous questions and deliberations about the traditional wording of the book have not been overlooked, but have been worked out afresh from new perspectives. The way in which the present text has been distorted by numerous glosses and additions, the widely varying peculiarities of each of which must always be kept in view, has been the subject of increasingly thorough research, which has succeeded above all in laying down a basis by which to explain the prose portions of the text. The assistance received in this from the ancient versions, especially the Greek, is always of value here, as in other parts of the Bible, but especially important in the case of Ezekiel, because of the neglected state of its text. Thus, for example, the evidence of the Septuagint shows that the additional epithet Adonai, 'almighty Lord', which we find added to the divine name Yahweh in the traditional Hebrew text, is a subsequent addition, not found in the original Hebrew. The divine name *Kyrios* of the LXX should not be regarded as a translation of Adonai, as was formerly assumed; it was originally the rendering of Yahweh, and exercised a strong influence on those who transmitted the Hebrew text at the time when their reluctance to pronounce aloud the holy name of God was making them look out for a suitable substitute. This makes it necessary to restore the divine name in its original isolation everywhere in the translation, except where, in the vocative, it is accompanied by the honorific addition 'my Lord'. Thus in this, as in numerous other instances, the terser Septuagint text guides us to an older recension of the Hebrew text, more reliable than the Massoretic text. We ought not, however, to overvalue the capacities for guidance of these older testimonies to the text; internal criticism is always required in addition for recognizing supplements to the text. In this work, Fohrer has made important contributions.[1]

It is here that traditio-historical research has become important, since it has demonstrated a relationship between the prose passages of Ezekiel and the priestly style of sacral law, as with old prophetic literature, and has thus opened up new possibilities of understanding, without doing anything to interfere with the highly characteristic peculiarity which marks the prophetic text. The well-justified objections raised by Hölscher to the prose parts of the text in his widely recognized work[2] may therefore be given all the value they deserve, and the acuteness of his arguments receive due recognition, though at the same time his one-sided limitation of the prophetic message to the poetical passages, which is as far from providing a genuine solution of

[1] Cf. G. Fohrer, 'Die Glossen im Buch Ezechiel', *ZAW* 63 (1951), pp. 33–53; *Die Hauptprobleme des Buches Ezechiel*, BZAW 72, 1952, pp. 78–100.
[2] *Hesekiel, Der Dichter und das Buch*, BZAW 39, 1924.

the difficulties as Duhm's similar attempts in Jeremiah, is not acceptable. Whether, like Fohrer, one can go still further and attain the original form of the prose-addresses by introducing a metrical system of short verses with only two or three stressed syllables, arranged together in a series of strophes of similar construction, remains a very doubtful point, in view of the difficulty of establishing any fixed rules determining the existence of such verses or the way they fit together. This leaves far too much room for elements that are purely subjective. In the commentary, therefore, we shall speak of sections as poetical only where the well-known longer verses occur, especially the *qinah*, the elegiac form, and where the form can be stressed in print.

The text achieved by critical research must undoubtedly be regarded as being in the main that committed to writing by Ezekiel himself. The accounts of the prophet's speeches and actions are almost entirely in the first person singular, leaving no room for doubt that the prophet himself saw to their being written down either before or after delivering them orally. Many sections, such as, for example, the longer poems in the oracles to the nations, may have existed solely in written form from the beginning. The writer's characteristics are inimitable and quickly recognized: in the visions we are clearly shown the intensity with which the prophet entered into the visionary events. The beginning of the vision transports him directly into an event not of his own making, as the spirit or hand of Yahweh overpowers him. He is summoned to play an active part in the event which is now initiated, and has to co-operate, whether in action or in suffering. The conclusion of the vision leaves behind strong influences upon his spiritual and bodily make up. This distinguishes him sharply from his predecessors, especially Jeremiah, but the formulation of his vision exercises a wider influence on Zechariah and Daniel. One cannot maintain that there is any close mutual correspondence between all the visions. There is indeed a mutual correspondence between the two temple visions in ch. 8 and 11 and the revelation of the new temple in ch. 40ff., where we see the sanctuary fall in judgment and then created anew. But the vision in which the prophet receives his call has a function all of its own. At most, it can be regarded as presenting the prerequisite for divine action in judgment, by portraying the sovereign majesty of the lord of the universe. Chapter 37 stands all by itself; the date prefixed to all the other visions is lacking. We do, however, have to consider the possibility that the text has been damaged at a later date (cf. the commentary below, pp. 298ff.).

Just as the accounts of the visions have a fixed introduction consisting in the stereotyped formula telling how the hand of Yahweh came upon the prophet, so the accounts of his receiving the word are marked by a phrase showing how the word of God came to the messenger who was to deliver it. This form of phrase departs from the simple one employed in earlier days: 'Yahweh spoke to me' (Isa. 7.3; 8.1) and also from the formula employed by Jeremiah: 'And the word of Yahweh came to me.' The object is evidently to assert the objectivity of the word of God given to the prophet, and to affirm that it is a manifestation which forms an integral part of the historical event (described by Zimmerli as 'word-event'), thus certifying the authenticity of what the prophet proclaims and the source from which it is derived in face of all the unbelief and insinuations expressed by his audience.

Associated with this as a regular rule is the title 'Ben-adam', son of man, by which the prophet is addressed instead of by his proper name. Such a regular use of the term is quite unique, and imparts a special stamp to Ezekiel's prophecy. That this form of address indicates the weakness and lowliness of the creature over against the world-filling glory of the God of Israel is taken for granted by all interpreters. The prophet is thus continually reminded how he is dependent on a gift of special spiritual power, in order to fulfil the task to which God has called him in his prophetic activity. The condescension by which God bows down to one born of the dust and makes him worthy to serve as his messenger accentuates the wonder of the approach of his grace in the midst of judgment. He alone directs his words by specifically naming the person to whom they are addressed, and supports the accuracy of his proclamation by pieces of information and declarations of what his hearers and opponents are actually thinking, their hearts being transparent to him. At the same time he gives the prophet warning of the trials in store for him, and assures him that he will overcome them (12.21–28; 33–33). His appearance on the scene thus takes place within the framework of this direct divine guidance, and it also prescribes the form that his speech is to take, whether that of a sentence of judgment, a poem or a picture.

The consciousness of this continuous guidance, based on the experience of his vocation (3.1ff.), gives a stamp to the carefully chosen words with which each section is introduced. But that does not prevent the development of an astonishingly rich variety of forms in the traditional methods of proclamation which he takes over and develops independently. So when the prophetic word tells of the future in some announcement of judgment and grace, it is enriched and made to fit the situation by a broader statement of its causes and a stronger consideration of the subjective results of divine intervention. In this way it can sometimes swell to considerable dimensions, especially in moving forward to a general reckoning; as in ch. 13 and 20, where we are impressed by the skilful architecture of the construction, or in ch. 16 and 23, where he seeks to compass the history of Israel in the form of a parable. A point of particular importance is the frequency of references to the objective of God's action, which is to confer a new knowledge of himself. Generally it takes the stereotyped form 'And they shall know that I am Yahweh', but it can also appear in all sorts of variations. We find this statement already in the Mosaic tradition, particularly in the Priestly writing, but it is also prominent in the older narrative writings, and it is used again in Deuteronomy. It states that the object is the recognition of the all-prevailing almighty power and the exclusive rights of the divine Lord, but also points to obedience to his will, and is a feature which is also prominent in earlier prophecy (I Kings 20.13, 26). It bases the knowledge of God upon God's saving acts, like his bringing Israel out of Egypt and some of the individual wonders, as also on God's execution of his sentences of judgment upon his enemies, and thus always carries it back to its source in some historical action by Yahweh, by means of which he wills to make himself known. But because Ezekiel's preaching always keeps in view this object of God's action, to prove his own existence to a humanity estranged from him, he creates a hitherto unknown type of speech which we may with Zimmerli call a 'word of proof', in order to bring out its special nature.

The word of warning, on the other hand, is very noticeably less prominent, as is perfectly in accordance with the general tendency of the prophet's proclamation, which cannot expect any results from mere human action. On the other hand, another form of the word dealing with the future undergoes considerable development. This is the death lament, or elegy, which comes to the fore in ch. 19 and in the oracles to the nations, where it extends into poems of considerable length. These poems are full of the magic of a unique form of imagery, and in the mighty motion of the world they make our eyes look and see the providence of God, hidden in the background, and yet exercising its control in a decisive fashion. The prophet also tries by means of the enigmatic saying to catch the attention of his audience and guide them, not to a rational solution of the paradoxical situation he has shown them, but to the inward connection between guilt and punishment, or the impossibility of escaping the coming judgment (15.2–5; 17.2–10; 20.46–49). In his hand the hymn also becomes an instrument played by a master, so as to impress unforgettably upon his audience the awful depth of suffering under judgment (23.32—34) or the furious rage of battle (21.8–17), the madness of which breaks out in the surging passion of the sword dance.

As well as applying and developing further the usual forms of speech, Ezekiel takes up the didactic statement, already used by Jeremiah on a few occasions, and thus introduces a hitherto unknown method of preaching into the prophetic message. Here he makes use of the forms of speech belonging to sacral law, well known from their use in the priestly law, in order to take up certain themes the importance of which he has realized from discussions with his audience, and state them at full length. The very act of taking over such material has exposed him to the severest condemnation, since it has led many to regard him as a priest-prophet who descends to juridical formality and triviality, one who backslides from pure prophetic cognition into priestly and legalistic pietism. But if we are more accurate in our examination, we shall come to a very different verdict. Admittedly, when it borrows the terminology of priestly law the message moves forward ponderously, weighted down by all the repetitions by which the lawyer tries to give full technical expression to the excellence of his advice. But on the other hand, a theme stated in this legal form can develop every one of its aspects, and lead on with logical precision to a verdict which is hard to refute, and whose weighty formulations state the irrevocability of the divine will, which allows no possibility of appeal, so that human pretexts and excuses are useless. One may also add that when Ezekiel shows this preference for the style of sacral law, he totally refuses to let himself be carried back into priestly legalism. On the contrary, he makes a masterly use of a means thus available to him, in order to unfold a prophetic message of great independence, one which in our opinion is very sharply opposed to the general tendency of the priestly tradition, but which is at the same time capable of subjecting even the prophet on his side to the norm of God's will as expressed in the covenant, impressing upon him how great his responsibility is. Thus, for example, the answer given to the idolatrous elders (14.1–11) seeks the support of the law of the sanctuary in order to work out a statement of the punishment which holds for all members of the people of the covenant and is possessed of absolute validity; yet it also leaves room for an appeal to repentance, and places the prophet who says what is pleasing to the idolaters under the same threat of judgment as them. In conclusion, taking over a central thought from Deuteronomy, it is pointed out how the final objective of salvation may be hidden by God's severity, but is still guaranteed by his faithfulness (cf. below, p. 186). A similar movement occurs in the answer to the question whether the children of godly parents are to receive exceptional treatment in the divine judgment (14.12–20), as first a scholastic disputation makes a list of the different cases, and then the prospect of special treatment for Jerusalem is posited in opposition to the conclusion just established, and it is shown that this really serves to corroborate the guiding principle, silencing all revolt against God's judgment. However, this type of style reaches its most effective development in the forcible piece of instruction on the subject of divine retribution in ch. 18. In spite of being shaped as a scholastic disputation with definitions and lists of typical cases, it develops no new theory about the solution of that agonizing problem; instead, an astounding offer of salvation is made, transmitted cultic forms of speech are fused and reapplied, and the community of exiles, upset and perplexed by the blows of judgment, is given new ground to stand on and shown the possibility of entering into the fellowship of a new covenant. In significant association with it in 33.10–20, a further appeal is made to the exiles to carry their inward conversion to a complete decision by turning towards the goal promised by God. Here the juridical style is relaxed even more than in ch. 18, by repeated allusions to words directly spoken by Yahweh himself.

Thus in these and other similar passages, the genre of sacral law is put to serve the prophet in his task and thus made to enrich the possibilities of his preaching. To this we may add the numerous symbolic actions (ch. 4f.; 12.1–11, 17–20; 24.3–5, 15–17; 37.15–17), and we see opening out a wide variety of forms of preaching, which testify not only to the width of the prophet's mental horizon but also to the unwearying efforts he made to utilize every method of proclamation available to him.

THE FORMATION OF THE PROPHETIC BOOK

In view of what has been said so far, it would not be surprising if
Ezekiel had collected his writings and arranged them in order to
make them into a book. This is first of all indicated by the exact dates
scattered all through the book, and marking certain sections. They
seem by nature to point to a series of notes set down in chronological
order. Seeing that we find a set of memoirs composed by the prophet
himself in the case of Isaiah, Jeremiah and, in a later day, Zechariah,
the same assumption is equally probable in the case of Ezekiel. However, the dates given by him are arranged in a curious fashion: for
example, in ch. 26–32, which contain the oracles to foreign nations,
there are as many as in the rest of the book, that is to say, seven. These
prophecies embrace a period longer than the two years of the siege
of Jerusalem, so most of them are dated and thus set apart from the
rest to form an integral whole. The position of this collection within
the whole book, however, suggests that it was not originally connected with its present context. It was not possible to put it in its
present place without making a ruthless break in the connection
between 24.26f. and 33.21f., which tell first of the announcement and
then of the fulfilment of the promise made specially to Ezekiel, and
which cannot have been separated from each other by more than six
months. In addition to that, the date given in 33.21 is more than a
year earlier than that of the latest of the oracles to the nations. These
circumstances compel us to conclude that the book was already
complete in itself before this insertion was made by some other hand.
That makes inevitable the assumption that the dates in the book of
Ezekiel are divided between two independent collections, one of
which was a collection of proclamations of judgment against foreign
nations, the coincidences of which with important stages in the siege
and conquest of Jerusalem must have been so important to the
prophet that he recorded them on the day when he delivered them.
Along with that, the prophet must have composed a second collection giving particulars of what he preached about Jerusalem and
Judah, in order to bear witness to his activities when in exile.

The dates given extend over a period of more than twenty years,
from the prophet's call to the close of his activity, but on each occasion they apply only to the section to which they are immediately
attached. So they are evidently meant to mark occurrences which are
to be regarded as forming the milestones along that lengthy road. In

fact, that will be found to be true of most of them. For example, in
1.1–3.15 we are told of the calling and commissioning which lies at
the basis of the prophet's life; in 3.16a; 4 and 5 we are informed of
how he begins his activities by performing symbolic actions and
explaining what they mean, after which ch. 8–11 describe two temple
visions, which were of decisive importance to his prophetic effectiveness. Chapter 20 tells of a perilous plan to build a temple in Babylon
and of the strong objection he expresses to such a course; ch. 24 deals
with the beginning of the siege of Jerusalem; 33.21f. with the arrival
of a fugitive from the captured city and the prophet's deliverance
from his state of paralysis. Finally, ch. 40ff. give visions of the new
temple. It is impossible to doubt that what is described in this way
forms a complex of events which develop in an important way along
a definite line, and that its components are mutually applied to each
other. Thus the vision of the call, revealing the Lord of the universe
in his sovereignty over against and apart from Israel and his own
temple, forms a point of departure for the revelation of God's action
in judgment and grace, the most important manifestations of which
can be read out of what happens to the temple. While the symbolic
actions in ch. 4f. point to the approaching judgment upon the holy
city, ch. 8f. show the temple being profaned and thus given up to
destruction, and then ch. 20 forbids all human attempts at self-help,
as seen in the effort to set up a place of worship in an unclean land.
Only in the place which has been chosen once and for all is it
possible to have a new temple, and we see that beginning to happen
in ch. 40ff., through a miraculous act performed by Yahweh.

The question now arises whether the contents of this prophetic
autobiography should be limited to the passages directly associated
with dates. This, however, seems doubtful. One cannot say that the
connection that has been demonstrated, which is provided by four or
five of the dates given, requires any such limitation. Neither the
parabolic action at the beginning of the siege (24.3ff.), nor the
freeing of Ezekiel from his state of paralysis (33.21f.) have any direct
connection with the fate of the temple. Undoubtedly they mark
important dates in the progress of the actualization of the prophet's
prediction. But is this not true also of the vision in 37.1ff., the importance of which has already been emphasized by the solemnity of the
introduction, in which there are some signs of the original presence of
a date? If it is said to be an important point that dates are used
solely to introduce events, but never speeches, then we have to ask

why the symbólic actions in 12.1ff. and 37.15ff. should not have been
part of the memoirs. They may be described as counterparts with
special connections with each other (the first describes the fall of the
last king, the second gives a vivid picture of the rise of the new David).
In the same way, the deliberate contrast between the curse and the
blessing upon the mountains of Israel in ch. 6 and 36.1–15 is immediately obvious, and may be regarded as one of the clamps holding
together the different parts of the memoirs. Also, the dramatic reply
given to the idolatrous elders by Yahweh in 14.1–11 clearly goes
beyond the speeches which 'transcend space and time' (Eissfeldt). If
one reflects a little on the important part played in the prophet's
memoirs by such passages either left undated or deprived of a date
through some chance, it is hardly possible to deny that also such
deeply moving events as the sudden death of the prophet's wife
(24.15–27) or his installation into the new office of spiritual director
in ch. 33 could have found a place in this first collection of matters of
importance to Ezekiel's work. The principle of the reference to the
temple or the account of events, by which a certain guide line for the
content of Ezekiel's consecutive description could be obtained, cannot therefore be applied in formal exclusiveness; room must be left
for other considerations, so that the prophet's narrative may be
allowed to display a richer variety in its material. Besides, at many
points the final decision, at any rate, may be left to individual
judgment.

We may, however, take it as established that, as their purpose
demanded, the memoirs were characterized by a very definite line of
events and descriptions which became a standard for the structure
and development of the prophet's activity. This gives a reason for
excluding from the first memoir, with reasonable certainty, contro-
versies over principles, didactic accounts, diffuse parables and
summary proclamations of judgment, as, for example, ch. 13 with its
basic and all-embracing denunciation of false prophets, ch. 18 and
33.10–20 with their carefully constructed discussion, ch. 16 and 23
with their allegories embracing the whole history of Israel, the threats
in ch. 21f. with their exhaustive catalogues of sins, and the enigmatic words in ch. 15; 17; 21. At the same time, it is impossible to
make an exhaustive selection, since too few points of view of general
application are available for such a purpose. As a result, room is left
for differences of opinion over many points.

There are, in any case, good reasons for asserting that a considerable number of passages which go back to Ezekiel himself were not included in the collections of his speeches which he himself left behind. They may have been transmitted independently for a long time, but their value was realized when the two prophetic passages were combined into one so as to provide a place for all extant records where they might be preserved from dispersion. That this redactional work cannot be ascribed to Ezekiel himself is already clear from the inorganic way in which the oracles to the nations have been inserted, so as to interrupt the series of proclamations of judgment against Israel. As we read we become aware of how this led to revolutionary displacements and to new interweavings of what were originally independent addresses; striking examples of this are the way in which 3.24–26 and 4.4–8 have been moved from their original position in ch. 24 in order to connect them with the beginning of the prophet's activity (see below, pp. 76f.; 83ff.), the transposition of 33.7–9 in the form of 3.16b–21 with the same object (cf. below, p. 75), the way in which ch. 10 and 11.14–21 have been worked into ch. 8–11 and the resultant insertion of 1.15–21 in the vision at the call, which has also led to an alteration of the wording in vv. 8b and 9 and other minor additions. We may also recall the extensive additions to ch. 16 and 23, and in general the other elaborations made with a prophetic or priestly bias which are dealt with in detail in the commentary. This process has also led to the working in of large sections not belonging to the original prophetic tradition, and which are most important and extensive in the addresses to the nations in ch. 38f., and in ch. 40–48, the last main division of the book. We see therefore that this prophetic book as we now have it is the result of a complicated process of remodelling, elaborating and supplementing. It is only natural to expect that under the circumstances many problems must be left unsolved, such as the reason for the separation of ch. 17 from ch. 19 by the insertion of ch. 18. But throughout the whole book the unique and characteristic style of the parts composed by Ezekiel is so strong and dominant that it has not undergone any material change through the work of redaction, extensive though that has been, and it still continues to be the decisive factor which determines the whole.

The book was given its final shape by being arranged in three large sections: the pronouncements of judgment upon Israel in ch. 1–24, the prophecies concerning foreign nations in ch. 25–32, and the portrayals of the time of salvation in ch. 33–48, a structure also found in the books of Isaiah and Jeremiah, and visible on a smaller scale in other prophetic books. By this means we can see the prophet's mighty forward march from judgment to salvation, and the arrangement also reflects the way in which the community understood the movement of the history of salvation as displayed in his word.

THE PERSON AND MESSAGE OF EZEKIEL

I

Two spheres intersect in the person of Ezekiel, the life of the priest and that of the prophet, so his life is filled with strain and tension between the tradition he inherited and the demands of his call to be a prophet. As a member of the Zion priesthood, he grew up amid the proud traditions of a priesthood where a unique conception of history was combined with a conception of God of a deeply spiritual character full of inner greatness and other-worldly sublimity. So for him, fidelity to the commandment of the law and preservation of the priestly ideal of purity were as much a matter of course as the spiritual discipline and self-control which, aware of the closeness of the holy presence of God in the temple, subjected every inward movement to strict control and held back all expressions of passion or self-will. The exercise of pronouncing and interpreting the law had trained him to express his ideas with extreme precision of thought and terminology, and had also taught him to present his views in an architectonic construction and to give full consideration to all their various aspects. In expressing his thoughts he likes to make use of the scholastic lecture, enumerating each different case and the conclusions resulting from it, which gives his manner of speech the slow repetitious flow of the pedagogue and educationalist, but also the carefully chosen terms and weighty formulations of attained results. This intellectualist training had been combined with the acquiring of great learning, which shows an acquaintance not only with the past history of his own nation, its literature and the problems of its government and political development, but also such understanding of the life of the neighbouring nations as made it possible for him to criticize both their religious beliefs and their political activities. He thus came to be familiar with the realm of the mythical; he even seems to have taken pleasure in the bizarre images and learnt to apply them with a sure touch. The breadth of his mental horizon is especially noticeable in the addresses to the nations. This gives a great spaciousness and serene acceptance of the factual both in his life and in his preaching, and prevents him from any stiff doctrinaire systematizing of his opinion by narrow-minded categorical statements.

This rationally consistent cultivation of intellect and volition is blended with strength of emotion, usually repressed, but which can surge up and grow passionate in a way which shows how lasting an influence his environment exercised upon his psychology. This receptive side of his nature fertilizes his poetic gift and gives us, in addition to his prose speeches, a wealth of short enigmatic and allegorical poems, long-drawn-out parables and stirring death laments, so excellent that little can be found in the Old Testament to rival them. There is no sign in them of the cool matter-of-fact manner of the legal expert; these poetic creations follow their own laws and tower up into images and metaphors that are often daring, yet always enthralling, or burst out in some unmeasured explosion of indignation and emotion, which is at once painfully offended and extremely irritated by ugly and disgusting manifestations of the wild lawlessness of unfettered sensual instinct. In the proclamation of judgment this often leads to trenchant irony and bitter mockery of a nation which, despite all warnings, still maintains its short-sighted complacency. Yet the speaker is not the cruel remorseless judge whom many have often thought to be implied by the rigid realism and coldness of the verdict he expresses, but a human being in a state of profound disturbance and excitement, who hides his embarrassingly sensitive feelings behind the mercilessness of his accusation, for fear of being misled into any secret sympathy. This tension was already present in the make up of his character, and after he was uprooted from the priestly soil in which he had grown up it must have led to a severe inward conflict, during which the prophetic activity to which he was destined gradually emerged and became a dominant certainty. To know that he was being given over to a new divine reality, which put a question mark over against all in which he had hitherto believed, meant a final break with the familiar past relationship to God and its glorification of the whole of national life. Instead, Ezekiel felt himself transferred into another reality consisting in a judgment which embraced all departments of human life and unmasked their refractoriness to the divine. Even the well-organized pastoral care for the congregation with its ancient and sacred institutions and its watchful regulation of the communication with God, fitting into every occasion in life, found itself confronted with a will of utterly inconceivable otherness, so as to show it to be completely useless in the critical times which had now begun, and announce its inevitable annihilation. A harmonious union of the world, built on unshakable foundations and satisfying to human longings for security, was to be replaced by a questioning of the whole present condition of the chosen people. The one fixed point in a world torn apart by centrifugal forces remained the divine majesty high above all human reach, with its claim of lordship which demanded that all life should undergo radical reorganization.

We may well imagine that Ezekiel felt some misgivings as he faced this destructively revolutionary element in the prophetic proclamation, as a whole, but as a result of his obvious acquaintance with the writings of the earlier prophets and with the living judgments of Jeremiah, he was aware of it and took it seriously into his inner reckonings. Yet, however much he may have sympathized and agreed with it at many points, he still had a long way to go before identifying himself with it. So the hour of his calling confronted him with the problem whether he could go on clinging to his previous spiritual home or whether he must give it up as a sacrifice to the unconditional claim of that all-dominating will, which was leading him towards an uncertain future.

In actual fact, it has been thought often enough that it was the priestly side of Ezekiel that was the victor in this debate. He is therefore charged with having allowed his prophetic mission to be influenced profoundly and altered by his priestly inheritance. He has been labelled the father of Judaism, or the first apocalyptist, and it has been asserted that he confined the uninhibited flow of the prophetic message by specifically priestly ideas, and held it within legal banks until the channel was silted up. The observations on which this view is based ought certainly to be taken seriously, and we will deal with them in due course (cf. below pp. 28ff.). But they must not be allowed to prevent us from realizing what a thorough-going reorientation the priest actually did undergo, under the influence of the experience of his vocation, which shook him to the very depths of his being.

At that moment Ezekiel did indeed see a new world opening up to him, which was henceforward to lay a continual claim on him, and give a new direction and objective to his thought. It tore him away from the old links binding him to his people and called him to unlimited service to the sovereign Lord, whose majesty fills the world and is not tied to Israel. Here there is no room for any compromise, no assurance in the possession of ancient and holy traditions, no room for anything but utter submission to the God who calls and commissions, and who severs this man, overwhelmed by his glory, from the way in which his people are walking and compels him to go obediently along a way determined by him and known by him alone. By humbly accepting his commission, as is symbolized in his vision by his swallowing of a parchment roll, Ezekiel surrenders unconditionally to the will of his Lord. At the same time, he has experience of how merciful that lordly will can be by having vouchsafed to him a special endowment of strength, through which his inward weakness and defencelessness find the help and protection they need against the threats of a merciless environment. So he now feels himself equipped to face the violent opposition that he will encounter, and to meet the stony obtuseness of his fellow countrymen with the adamantine impetus of his message (3.8f.). These words are often mistakenly taken as testifying to the character of his own disposition, but that is not so; on the contrary, they indicate a highly sensitive and emotional temperament, which does not feel capable of standing up to furious counter-attacks or to cold hatred, and needs to be hardened and toughened, in order to endure such an unequal combat.

That is not to say that Ezekiel was henceforth invulnerable against all dangers arising from his own nature and heredity. Although he generally accepts the divine commands without a word of protest, there is now and then a sudden exclamation which bursts out to show that he has come to the limit of what he can endure, the point when all his priestly training and self-discipline cannot any longer restrain him from, as it were, catching at God's arm and trying to hold back the hand after it has been lifted up to strike a blow (4.14; 9.8; 11.3). He was also profoundly affected by the death of his wife, and the way in which he speaks of it, brief though it is, betrays his longing for human warmth and intimacy, now that his last chance of having it has been cut off (24.15ff.). The psychological disturbances arising out of his vocation, which had very severe effects on his strong sensitivity, lead more than once to a breakdown of his bodily resistance, which results in paralysis and dumbness (1.28; 3.14f.; 12.17ff.; 21.6; 24.16, 27; cf. 4.4–8 and 3.25f.). But he learns how to take these depressing experiences and make them part of the work of expressing his message, so they do not lead him to complain or assert his rights against God, in the way we see Jeremiah do, but come to be regarded by him as a summons to place himself and all that he has and is at the service of God's cause.

Thus self-surrender to the firm leadership of the God who calls him is transformed into an inward willingness to take all the forces which in the past strove in another direction, and to subject them to the new order of his life's task, and thus find a way out of division into unity in his inward life. During a seven-day-long period of critical dumbness and paralysis (3.15), his being was as it were melted down and recast, so as to protect him from the strong influences of his childhood and environment and, by completing his links with the sources of his guidance, to enable him to find a sure way between the abysses that lay on all sides in a period during which the world seemed to be falling to pieces.

Never at any point in this history of so radical an inward transformation do we find any trace of mental abnormality or even disease. In spite of all his frequently bizarre symbolic actions and the often overstrained excitability of his speech, Ezekiel's message is everywhere seen to be well thought out and directed towards a single end, which is in keeping with his conception of God, of the world, and of human nature. The attempt by Karl Jaspers[1] to explain Ezekiel as a paranoiac affected by schizophrenia, like the suggestion advanced by others that he suffered from catalepsy, is one for which no convincing proofs can be given, and does not contribute towards any genuine understanding of the prophet. The statements made in the prophetic book used to supply evidence for this thesis have been satisfactorily accounted for in other ways in recent research.

II

The conflicts into which Ezekiel was led as a result of taking up his prophetic task are very clearly shown for the first period of his activity during the seven years preceding the fall of Jerusalem. As an exile, he found himself occupying a totally different position in the crisis of national life from those who had stayed at home. He was compelled to experience the dissolution of old restraints, which seemed only too likely to render the exiles an easy prey to their heathen environment. He himself was forced to deprive these for-

[1] 'Der Prophet Hesekiel. Eine pathographische Studie', *Festschrift für K. Schneider*, 1947, pp. 77–85. Compare also the study by H. Heimann referred to on pp. 72f., note.

saken remnants of the last anchorage which, they felt, attached them to their home and called up their hopes. Since his calling had already manifested to him a Lord of the universe independent of Zion and of every other earthly limitation, therefore now Jerusalem and its temple, that guarantee in stone of the election of Israel, both could be and must be devoted to utter destruction through his symbolic actions, through his visionary description of the conditions prevailing there and of the way in which they aroused the wrath of God, and by his predictions of the inevitability of the approach of judgment. The severity of this message, which seemed unfeelingly to ignore all the anxieties and troubles of the exiles and to see nothing but the wrath of a world-God now grown alien to Israel being poured out in judgment, must have aroused passionate resistance in his audience. Indeed, it comes as a shock to a modern reader. At first sight he feels that he can see nothing but a fanatical love of righteousness, which leads to cold ferocity, unless he recalls the extreme fellowship with his people which the prophet always displays and never repudiates.

There does therefore in fact exist a wide common foundation of faith binding him to his fellow countrymen and never called in question by his ruthless repudiation of all their hopes. That Israel has been chosen and exalted to be the covenant people by the unsearchable love of God, that Jerusalem occupies a peculiar position among the nations of the world, that the temple should offer a special possibility of personal meeting and fellowship with the divine Lord of the covenant, that is to say, the articles of faith on which the whole people (including the exiles) based their consciousness of their own identity, these were things which the messenger of God not only did not impugn, but took for granted as the premises on which his faith in God was based (5.5f.; 8; 16.1–14; 20.5f.; 23.4). It is only by a 'strange deed' and 'alien work' (Isa. 28.21) that Yahweh, after watching his chosen people patiently for a long time and postponing their punishment, now turns on them to eliminate them from the face of the earth.

Yet this irrevocable reckoning, as Ezekiel and his predecessors always endeavour to show, does not constitute any contradiction to Yahweh's acts of salvation. His audience thinks that it does, and answers with a 'never!' But actually it arises out of the ordinances of the covenant with the same logical necessity which makes that covenant the source of the grace and the preference shown to Israel above other nations. The basis upon which their relationship to God was founded, the exclusive worship of Yahweh demanded by the fundamental command of the covenant, had been abrogated in public and barefaced fashion (ch. 8), and similarly the mutual obligations demanded by the solidarity of the human partners in the covenant one with another, proclaimed through the second table of the Decalogue, had been transgressed through lust for power and wealth, and replaced by the very opposite (cf. 33.25f.). That was enough to reveal Israel's inability to fulfil the covenant. Her worship of God had become a hypocritical mummery, and the solemn recital by the mouth of the priest at the great covenant festivals proclaiming her election as people of God with all the privileges and honours that that involved, had become a blasphemy of the covenant God. In face of facts such as these, the passionate protest against the message of judgment, as if it were a godless blasphemy against the solemnly guaranteed saving acts of Yahweh, had to be unmasked as the grandiose piece of self-deception that it was. The patient love, which had hitherto repeatedly pardoned Israel's apostasy and striven to correct by chastisement or by forgiveness and re-acceptance, was faced by the complete failure to respond to salvation in a people which sought in their unbridled lust for life to find satisfaction by some easier means than genuine surrender to God's will. By turning to the mysteries of the heathen nature-gods, they surrendered to the temptation to deify their own basic vital forces, and had necessarily to be dismissed as incapable of personal communion with the divine will which controls history. The dissolution of the covenant relationship and the surrender of the covenant people, who had become a house of rebellion instead of being the house of Israel, to the heathen power of the world, is the inevitable result of a history of sin. They have no epoch of glory that deserves fame, but have shown themselves from the very beginning to be a generation infected with heathenism at their very roots, who have squandered and dissipated their glorious heritage by wild outbreaks of self-will. Here we see revealed what forms the sharpest antithesis to the beliefs cultivated and proclaimed by the priesthood, and the question arises whether Ezekiel did succeed in going consistently along those lines, or whether, as many hold, he was gradually compelled by his specifically priestly ideas to come to a compromise.

In his statements concerning God, in which the majesty and absolute transcendence of Yahweh is emphasized as inviolable to all earthly powers, so that the inexorable judge at times seems completely lacking in any trace of compassionate condescension or patient understanding, we see an unmistakable similarity to priestly descriptions of the divine nature: he is throned in his inaccessible otherness high above all earthly affairs in light inapproachable and vouchsafes to let the sign of his revealed presence, the light of divine glory, or *kābōd*, gleam forth only now and then, in exceptionally holy places. This *kābōd* occurs also in Ezekiel at an important point (1.28),[1] where the description of the throne of God is undoubtedly influenced in many of its features by the holy ark in which the holiness of the temple of Zion has its centre.

The temple therefore comes to possess great importance for the prophet. It is the sign chosen by Yahweh of his presence in the midst of his people, not only in the present, when his people's whole attitude towards him illustrates abundantly their ripeness for judgment, but also in the future, when, given anew in God's fulfilment of salvation, it forms the guarantee of God's intimate fellowship with his people. This is in agreement with the idea we find both in Ezekiel and in the Priestly writing, that the recognition of worshipping God in Israel must succeed in finding expression primarily by obedience to God's control of human life. As a result of this we find a somewhat priestly type of ritual purity retaining its place more or less as a matter of course in the following of the will of God (4.14; 18.6, 11, etc.), and priestly terminology in calling idols *gillulim* and acts of disobedience 'abominations', as also in the use of old traditional cultic forms of speech, such as the appointed mode of confession and the formulas for blessings and curses (ch. 18), all of which seem to come in quite naturally.

These are important considerations, which guarantee with sufficient clarity how strongly and permanently the prophet was rooted in the priestly mentality. But they are not enough to prove that the prophet should be estimated as an incongruous figure because his thought-world was divided into two conflicting sets of rigid principles (cf. above, pp. 24f.). On the contrary, his newly won certainty in regard to God's method and objectives was frequently found to contradict the innate ideals and beliefs of the priest, and the consequence was that these inherited elements in his mentality were in part transformed or in part retained so as to function in a new way, by being absorbed into or subjected to the new task, or even by making

[1] Cf. also 3.12; 43.2–5 and W. Eichrodt, *Theology of the Old Testament*, II, 1967, pp. 29f.

a positive contribution towards fulfilling it more effectively. In the
case of the traditional cultic forms of speech, we have already seen
above, (pp. 15f. and 22) the remarkable way in which they were
utilized towards this end. In Ezekiel's testimony to the majesty of
God, moreover, the very closeness of its relationship with priestly
elements only served to add to our awareness of a fundamental
difference. The transcendent God of Ezekiel's vision does not
manifest his presence solely in a sphere which is sharply severed from
the profane world, but enters the field of vision of the man he favours
even in a heathen land, and his throne, blazing with supernatural
splendour, casts a shadow over the Jerusalem sanctuary. He does not
remain hidden, as in the Priestly writing, in a formless glory of light,
but makes himself known, as he made himself known to Isaiah, as the
Lord on his throne addressing his word to the man whom he has
called. The description in ch. 8f., too, of his form surrounded with
brightness like fire, is in complete contradiction to priestly assertions about divinity, which aim at being completely other-worldly. A
description of such an encounter with any degree of adequacy needs
the anthropomorphic language of one overwhelmed by the power of
God in an ecstasy of vision; that is, conceptual completeness in
speaking about God must give way to the language of direct appre-
hension, in which his static position high above the world recedes in
favour of his dynamic intervention as the Lord of this world in
earthly events (in this connection, see also below, p. 44). So we find
a second term used alongside *kābōd* to sum up the revealed glory of
God, that of the *šem*, or name of God, which has such an important
place in Deuteronomic theology, and illustrates how inclusive is the
sweep of Ezekiel's thought.[1]

Thus even the temple is divested of its inviolable sanctity: judgment does not respect it; it is a place so shamed and disgraced that it
must be given up to desecration and destruction by its own occupants.
Yet the hope of salvation includes the expectation of a new temple,
which is exhaustively described, though not in terms conforming to
the priestly ideal. But that, again, is not foreign to prophetic thought,
as is sufficiently shown by Isa. 2, in which a piece of the tradition of
Zion is woven in to form part of the prophets' picture of salvation.

At most, then, it can be said that in order to make it possible to
know who are righteous and who are ungodly, recourse is had to lists of

[1] Cf. Ezek. 20.44; 36.20–23; 43.7 and W. Eichrodt, *Theology of the Old Testament*, II, 1967, pp. 30f.

commandments cited to provide examples. The noticeable Levitical element in this might seem to impose a limitation to the genuine prophetic conviction, which elsewhere with such unwearying insistence makes the central point consist in sincerity of personal commitment. The all-important point, however, is whether we are to take it that Ezekiel's introduction of these commands indicates a legalistic system which has caught devoutness and bound it in fetters, or whether the fundamental covenant commandments are being recalled to mind in the same way as we find in Hos. 4.2; Micah 6.1–12 and Jer. 7.9. So we can give serious consideration only to the second of these alternatives (cf. below the exposition of ch. 18 and 22). When the commandments refer to ritual purity, we need to realize that they are being used as weapons of warfare against heathen beliefs in alien forces.[1]

The prohibition against the consuming of blood occurs among other commandments in ch. 18. It must have been aimed against one element of foreign religious practice, to the dangers of which the position of the exiles at the time particularly exposed them. The sacrificial meals on the high places (22.9) must also be regarded as manifestations of the rank syncretism which had come to predominate in the local Palestinian cults. Strict observation of the sabbath, as the sign of the covenant which needed to be kept holy, supplies the most important argument in favour of the claim that Ezekiel confined the ordinances of God within priestly limits. But this point has lost its importance as a result of more accurate researches into the relevant passages in ch. 20 and elsewhere, which have made it particularly clear that here is one of the elements added by the priests in their revision of the prophetic book (cf. below, p. 41, and the commentary on ch. 20). In Ezekiel's protests against the breaking of God's commandments and in his expectations of the reconstitution of the people of God, the central all-determining factor is in any case personal faithfulness towards the covenant God and brotherly solidarity between all the people.

This does not constitute any attempt to deny that Ezekiel's theology has a special colour of its own as a result of his priestly origins. But what is really exciting and dramatic is that the whole complex of priestly conceptions breaks down, being a world which must be given up as destined to pass away. The fixed constitutions and ordinances of the community can no longer be regarded as guaranteeing the

[1] Cf. W. Eichrodt, *Theology of the Old Testament*, I, 1961, pp. 134f.

undisturbed continuance of the existence of that community, nor can the covenant be said to be everlasting. The community does indeed recognize that disobedience must suffer chastisement, but it witnesses to a belief that Israel's greatness must be preserved undimmed through all the dark periods of her history, for the salvation of mankind.

In spite of this proclamation of the radical neglect of his faithless people by the world-God, there are preparations, as the prophet proceeds further in preaching judgment, for a gradual approach by God's messenger to his fellow countrymen, since he can tell of a history of God's dealing capable of including the despised remnants of the people who have been led into captivity. We find not only repeated queries addressed to the prophets by the elders of the community of exiles, with requests of divine decisions over certain matters (14.1ff.; 20.1ff.), followed, despite severe rebukes, with answers which give guidance, but occasional dialogue sayings which refute all objections and assert that what the prophet has seen will soon come to pass (12.21–28) or certify the righteousness of God to those who doubt it (14.22). There are even clear calls to repentance, as though there were still a possibility of it (14.5f., 11), and in addition, hints of an ongoing establishment of the community in exile, which may lead to further developments (13.9, 22; 20.33ff.). Even taking into account postscripts added at a later stage by Ezekiel himself, or changes produced by later passages added by those who finally edited the book, the oracles to the nations composed for the most part before the fall of Jerusalem do go to show that one of the prophet's concerns was to convince a community which had to face the severest stroke of all in the demonstration of Yahweh's righteous judgment throughout the whole world, that there was purpose behind the divine action and that it extended even to the enemies of Israel. Here and there various groups come into view among the exiles, whose questions and objections Ezekiel thinks are worth going into. Here, too, we see a further sign that his prophetic activities were beginning to have more of an impact upon the exiles.

It is, however, in making his own bodily weakness and frailty part of his message that the prophet achieves the most immediate departure from an uncommitted attitude which is offensive in its unapproachability. By the address 'son of man', God has already made him the anonymous messenger, divested of all earthly claims, who stands in profoundest lowliness before the only exalted one. Only through the call which has gone out to him has he been raised above the *massa perdita* of his people. It is by virtue of his very weakness that he is to act as the instrument of the Lord, whose will it is to reveal through him the unlimited divine power. Ezekiel's solidarity with human misery is shown even more clearly by the bodily suffering imposed upon him. He is attacked by convulsive shaking in taking food (12.18) or overcome by grief so suddenly as to lose his self-control and break out into moans of misery (21.6), or, at the point when the last remaining consolation in his earthly existence, his wife, is snatched away by sudden death, he becomes completely dumb in a motionless coma of grief and carries out none of the rites prescribed for the dead (24.15–17), or lies paralysed and without moving for whole months in his bed (4.4–6.8). At such times he has become a prophetic symbol of his people even in his bodily life, as it were submerged in their dying, overwhelmed by the destructive power of the divine wrath which he himself proclaimed, anticipating the punishment of his fellow countrymen by willingly bearing their guilt, and by his total dumbness representing the severance of every link with the ruthless judge and avenger of all guilt. This active self-involvement in the coming ruin, by which what has only been an expectation is now announced in its terrifying realism, must more than anything else have made it possible to believe that the messenger of God was one with his message and therefore profoundly and closely bound to those whom he threatened. In this way it served to reveal that the nature of the God to whom he bore witness had quite other sides beside that of the impartial judge.

The fall of Jerusalem brings all these first beginnings which can already be detected to their full development, so we can take it as initiating a fresh period of prophetic activity. This is because once the prophecy of judgment has been fulfilled the prophet's work takes on more and more the new shape of an effort to give a new form to the community in exile. One of the most important testimonies to this change is the new offer of salvation, which the prophet is instructed by God to announce to the exiles, and by which he refutes the bitter accusations brought against the just retribution of their God by a generation which has fallen into completely false ideas about divine righteousness (ch. 18). Freed from the paralysing pressure of a hereditary guilt which forbids all escape from the doom of death, even those of the nation who are burdened with a sinful past are graciously accepted; now that the decision for the will of God that demands obedience and which had been required by the prophet is actually taking place, those who have fallen into despair over Israel's destiny face what is actually a totally new situation. What is now stated in scholastic style in the traditional priestly forms of speech is not a mere recapitulation of old admonitions for consistent legal piety, by means of which a man can at any time show himself to be an unblemished member of the covenant people and appeal to God's promises; it is an invitation to seize by faith the great moment at which God is dispensing his grace, by willingly taking one's place and entering into the mutual obligations of a community which is directed towards a new future. In this appeal for obedience to the command of God in all its concreteness, the decisive element is a new inner attitude to the giver of the command. This is shown by the admonition to the people to create within themselves a new heart and a new spirit, i.e. to respond to the divine offer of salvation by surrendering their will to it, knowing that they are freed from the compulsion of their earlier bad disposition by the love of God and are summoned to a new way of life. Thus inward renewal can be presented here as the objective at which those who are called are to aim, to open themselves to the newly creative power of God, which, through its demand, arouses in them consciousness of the great all-embracing transformation and at the same time bestows the will and power to bring it about (36.26f.). For God's will to redeem disposes all who follow his call, and here, in the midst of their heathen environment, unites them into a new community living together as brethren, in which his promise of life becomes a reality. This promise includes not only power to prosper in the unclean land of exile, but a share in Israel's coming salvation, in which God's gift of full life is at last given. It is therefore a brotherhood which moves forward to meet the approaching fulfilment, which is to be founded by God's new offer of salvation. It is never to be regarded as the end itself, but solely as the transitions towards that end, the fulfilment towards which it is God's will to lead his people.

In the interim period, they are to experience fully the way in which God turns towards them in their state of humiliation. Here the new commission to Ezekiel, to take on the office of watchman over the house of Israel (33.1–9), represents a decisive step forward towards awakening the banished ones from their lethargy and moral paralysis. For in this way a watchful care becomes effective for the individual members of the new community, which takes up the battle against doubt and despair as well as against self-righteous complacency or indifference with pastoral words of both admonition and promise.

Thus the expectation of the full accomplishment of a salvation prepared by God is kept alive. What the priest had hitherto been able to do in giving the community general guidance from the law is now greatly surpassed by the personal presence of an adviser and helper, who enables the individual to become conscious of the importance of the decision he now makes. By this means, the nearness of the divine judge is displayed repeatedly in the face of all forms of self-righteous arrogance or indifference. Alongside the divine judgment carried out upon the whole nation, there therefore goes a second phase of the judgment, retribution overtaking the individual if he shuts himself off from the saving purpose of his God (30.10–20). This keeps conscience awake to all the possibilities of being misled. In this context, the representative mediation of the prophet, already glimpsed here and there (cf. above, p. 33), comes clearly into the foreground. He himself shares in the punishment of those who have become guilty through his negligence. This asserts his ultimate identification with his people, and liberates his work of spiritual direction from all external compulsion or constraint and makes possible help and encouragement to put men on their feet and lead them forward.

Of course, to anyone looking for the reinstatement of the people in their homeland, the word spoken by the prophet offers a narrow door, through which none can enter but the man who is obedient to God's call: it is the purifying judgment that is to come upon the whole people who have been invited to return home. God's faithfulness to the choice he has made once for all is revealed in the way in which this new saving act forms an antitype to its own earlier stages, that series of events which had impressed themselves upon the consciousness of the nation and had been continually commemorated at the feasts as summing up the meaning of its history: the exodus from among the nations must be followed by a period in the wilderness with its revelation of God, bringing blessing and judgment (20.34–38). In this way the last efforts of the rebellious or apostate at resistance will be cut off, and only then can the people be led into the land of promise and to the holy mountain there, which once more has upon it the sign of God's presence with his people in the shape of a temple worthy to replace the former one.

It is therefore emphasized with very strong language that what is said about new salvation does not mean simply resuming the past, or ignoring the unbridgeable chasm between the past and the future. If those who have survived in Judah want to appeal to the old covenant promises to receive sanction for their undertakings through God's blessing, without submitting to him inwardly before his judgment, their action can only meet with a rebuke and a cutting word of condemnation against all such self-willed claims to the inheritance of old blessings (11.15, 21; 33.24–29). This is because the God who causes a new Israel to spring up out of the ruins of the nation is performing the miracle of recreation out of death, to which no access may be had except by an unqualified 'yes' to his death-dealing judgment. This is suggested by the vision of the resuscitation of a huge field of dead bones (37.1–14) vouchsafed to Ezekiel in response to the cry raised by the exiles when sunk into a state of utter lifelessness, in which they compare themselves to dried-up bones. This makes it an eloquent symbol of the character of the saving event that he is awaiting. We see what no human power can bring about, a bestowal by God of a grace leading out of death into life, since he can put to flight all earthly forces of death by his life-giving spirit. The prophet would have us understand all the great images of salvation in this light, as he portrays the goal of fulfilment for which the congregation of exiles, looking for deliverance and kept under discipline by God, are being prepared.

For as compared with the present state of the exiles, God's great saving acts in the future represent the revelation of a new world which will reflect the fullness of the divine glory. This constitutes the main difference between it and the present, and stamps it with a purely eschatological character. This emerges even more clearly with Ezekiel than with his predecessors, as his eye is fixed not on this or that particular fact, but on salvation as a world-embracing and all-transforming fact. Only those who endeavour to take the additions contained in ch. 40–48, which are based on presuppositions totally different from those of the preceding chapters, and force them into an amalgamation with the prophet's views, can try to make out that his statements refer to a purely earthly sort of world, freed of its ranker excrescences, but not materially altered in other respects.

Any such idea has already been basically called in question by Ezekiel's adoption of the old prophetic hope of salvation. What characterizes it is not only the undisturbed possession of the promised land after it has been made a safe home for a favoured people by the removal of all oppressors and the introduction of just ordinances, but also the prince of peace, to whom Yahweh imparts a special divine glory and authority, and who does not appear until the accomplish-

ment of a world-embracing judgment, to inaugurate the new age and
to be a personal embodiment of the highest gift of grace, the sovereign
reign of God. His appearance is closely connected with the conclusion
of a covenant of salvation, through which all forces menacing to life,
like wild beasts and armed oppressors, will be rendered harmless, and
undisturbed enjoyment of the overflowing gifts of nature will be thus
secured. Other prophets clothe this blessing in a garment of myth
(cf. Hos. 2.18; Isa. 11.6–8; 32.15ff.), but Ezekiel does not. Instead,
he employs formulas in the priestly style. But this does not alter the
fundamental otherness of the new aeon; it simply transfers the mythical element to the appearance and operation of the new sanctuary,
with which the description of salvation concludes.

It becomes evident that the prophet is especially interested in
something far wider than the familiar features of the old future hope,
for he names new miracles by the covenant God through which the
fulfilment takes on a tone all of its own. For example, special emphasis
is laid on the way in which the spirit is imparted to all the members of
the new people of God, who display their inward renewal by their
joyful assent and obedience to the law of the covenant. Along with this
fundamental new creation goes the rebuilding of the structure of the
state. The divided kingdoms, which have vanished from the face of
the earth, having contributed to their downfall by assimilation to
heathen kingdoms and their politics of hostility to God, rise again and
are indissolubly united; now, through the second David, they are to
be the material embodiment of that divine law through which Israel
was originally intended to be a light to the nations. Above this inwardly and outwardly re-created nation rises the sanctuary bestowed
anew by God, upon Zion, now exalted to be the chief mountain of
the world, into which God now makes his entry, so that direct communion with him may sanctify and preserve the whole existence of
his people. The spring proceeding from the temple becomes a river of
paradise, transforming even the terrible wilderness and filling it with
the divine powers of life. In his reuse of these images based on primal
traditions, the prophet discovers a means of making visible a spiritual
and moral reality pervading all creation and leading on towards
perfection.

This new form of the fulfilment of salvation is not anchored to any
soteriological motivation, such as God's goodness or fidelity to his
covenant, his sworn promises to the patriarchs or his general condescension towards the weakness of his creatures, but finds a firm

theological basis in God's own nature. Thoughts of the covenant so
shamefully broken by Israel can obviously no longer supply any
grounds for hope. It is not that, but God's faithfulness to his own holy
will to reveal himself which makes the hope that he will accomplish
his work of salvation so sure that nothing can shake it. This involves
severe repudiation of any attempt by sentimental self-pity to tie the
hope of salvation to the restoration of Israel's dignity among the
nations, as if her reinstatement were an obligation imposed upon God
by his earlier covenant promise (36.22, 32). We see how far this is
from being true by the fact that his people only begin to be filled with
shame and self-disgust after receiving his grace (36.31; 20.43; cf.
16.54, 61, 63, which is a subsequent addition by one of the prophet's
disciples). God's bestowal of grace is completely independent of the
sphere of nationalistic sensitivity which confounded the honour of
Israel with the honour of God. What is really at stake is the honour of
God's name which has been put to shame before the nations, because
the chosen people have had to be punished for their unfaithfulness
towards their own mission, by being cast out of their homeland. As a
result, the hope for the miracle of God's saving act can only be based
on the certainty that his will to reveal himself will reach its goal in
spite of all human opposition, and that its holiness will receive all the
recognition and worship to which it is entitled. Here we find a
foundation independent of all men's wishes and aspirations, already
visible in Isaiah's appeal to God's *qin'a*, his jealousy, that is to say his
will to give full self-expression to his nature, which Ezekiel now preserves from being misunderstood in any way by his words about God's
redeeming love (18.23, 32).

This, too, is the viewpoint from which one can rightly understand
the purpose of God's dealings with Israel and the nations which
dominates Ezekiel's whole message, and finds its proper expression in
the objective explicitly stated in the statement of design, 'they shall
know that I am Yahweh'. The phrase 'I am Yahweh' which is used
to describe the content of this knowledge is a formula which points
back to a cultic event, God's own affirmation of the incomparableness
of his own nature, as he makes himself known in concluding the
covenant. The knowledge envisaged here is not therefore instruction
about a timeless truth, but an inward realization of God's will to
reveal himself in a direct encounter with his action in history, which
lays claim to man and brings him to the point of decision. When the
prophetic interpretation of the inmost meaning of historical events is

in terms of this ever-renewed self-manifestation of Yahweh, it regards the object of human knowledge not as some external matter but as the encounter with Yahweh's manifestation of himself; it seeks to lead men to worship and yield in obedience to the will of the God who reveals himself and takes man into full fellowship with himself (20.26, 42, 44; 24.24; 34.30; 37.13, 14, etc.). If, on the other hand, man refuses, there is nothing left for him but the terrible realization of his error when he feels God strike the blow which is to destroy him (6.7, 13, 14; 7.9, 27; 12.20; 33.29; 35.15, etc.). The world is governed, not by some impenetrably mysterious fate, but by the God who comes out of his hiddenness to reveal himself by his name. In wrath and judgment, as in grace and renewal, he seeks to enter into personal relationship with individuals and with nations, and to bring them into his presence through his actions.

Here light is also thrown as it were on the inward side of the great saving acts by which God sanctifies his name. They do not exhaust all their meaning in the *mysterium stupendum* of his might, nor yet in the more fascinating mystery of his overflowing kindness, but in the revelation of his hidden being, which contains within itself the pledge of the possibility of full fellowship with him. This throws fresh light not only on God's covenantal relationship with Israel, but also on his relationship to the nations. Ezekiel, like the earlier prophets, asserts their general obligation to serve the Lord of the world (5.6f.), and threatens them with judgment for their rebelliousness against his stature by divinizing their own strength and despising the majesty of God (25.3f.; 28.2, 6, 9; 29.3; 31.10f.; 32.18). In their relationship to Israel, however, despite their own guilt they have a just claim to see good faith preserved and to be trusted, so they are given the rank of partners with Israel, whose rights are protected by God (17.13, 15, 19; cf. below the commentary on the whole passage). In contrast to this, the behaviour of Israel's political leaders, who, instead of obeying the divinely given·standards by which men ought to live together, indulge in a deceitful and treacherous policy and think that the meaning of the highest political office consists in exercising unlimited power rather than in establishing law and justice (19.3, 6f.), appears as a betrayal of the divinely determined duties of kingship. This destroys the contribution that Israel ought to make to international life. What is prepared for in this prophetic critique comes into effect in the accomplishment of the divine salvation. The fact that the future of the nations is not gone into in detail only serves the more to display how they are brought out into the light of his revelation as a result of what he does with his people. The witness Israel is to bear before them is to come into effect in the new creation of his people which God is carrying out. Albeit passively, Israel now receives the witness to the God whose claim to lordship over the whole world is exercised not only by actions, which display his outward might, but also by a self-disclosure of his being, which summons not only Israel but also the nations to a new future (36.23, 36; 37.28).

The special feature in this far-reaching future promise consists in the fact that it is not entrusted to a small circle of disciples but to a community which does not have an uncommitted attitude towards it but is already preparing the way towards its fulfilment by being engaged in the task committed to it. Ezekiel knew that, unlike his predecessors, he had been summoned to awaken to life as a community of God the remnant exempted from the judgment, and now appointed to be receivers of Yahweh's full promise of life. Even beforehand this community had been a living nucleus within the nation, but now they were summoned to develop independently of it. In that they are living out the personal relationship with God which has been entrusted to them, they are stretching out for the central gift and endowment of the era of salvation, the new birth of each individual through the spirit as the mysterious centre without which neither people nor world can be reshaped.

Thus at the very time when old Israel was moving towards its final doom, the beginnings of a community life was coming into existence in Babylonia under the influence of the prophet's preaching. Here the appeal which Ezekiel uttered as watchman over Israel with admonition and warning was transformed into the corresponding practical action. Meetings had already been held before in places of prayer by the riverside or in the houses of leading teachers of the law (cf. below, p. 53). The noteworthy words of 11.16 had said that by means of them Yahweh could only become a sanctuary for the exiles to a little extent (cf. below, p. 145). But now, by the prophet's rousing message, an awakening to a new lease of life could gain ground. Undoubtedly this development first took place in the prophet's own house, where the elders (8.1; 12.9; 14.1; 20.1; 24.19) and other members of the colony in Babylon (33.30ff.) gathered, in order to hear some word from Yahweh or to obtain advice about various problems. Many were superficial and merely came out of curiosity, but that did not prevent the prophet from finding some who responded to his appeal for a decision and carried his words out to reach others. As a result, in meetings hitherto held in order to keep up and preserve inherited spiritual possessions, a movement began to be aroused in which the prophetic hope became a spark which brought to life new expectations and resolutions. Among such people, Ezekiel must have increasingly come to be recognized as a teacher sent by God, whose statements about the vision of a new world were captivating while at the same time free from any fanatical exaggeration, since they fixed and limited the new hope of the future within the permanent God-given norms of human life.

We know nothing of the details of how this might have come about. But, as has been repeatedly pointed out in the commentary, the later history of the text of the book shows that its message was accepted as the authoritative record of the preaching of a prophet who had been sent by God, while at the same time it had necessarily to be subjected to a process of interpretation, addition and elaboration through which its original purity was broken and refracted by the various media through which it was passed on. Some additions had no influence in this direction; they were interested only in adding further matter illustrating what the prophet had said. Among these is the exhaustive description of the world-wide trade of Tyre (26.9b–25a) or the expansion of the prophet's announcements of judgment by a detailed enumeration of the strong points of the nation to which they were addressed, as in 30.13–19, or words emphasizing or restating the offence committed by it or the punishment executed upon it. These often get lost among the details and have only a remote connection with the prophet's basic train of thought (16.17–21, 25b–29, 30–34). There are, on the other hand, many contributions added by disciples of the prophet which show a deep understanding of their teacher's thought, and give an independent interpretation of his message, or enrich it by bringing forward surprising new aspects (12.12–14.16; 16.44–58; 22.15f., 23–31; 26.9b–16; 28.6b–16). Here we see advances in religious knowledge resulting from Ezekiel's activity. Yet at the same time we see failures to catch up with his interpretation of the nature and basis of God's actions, as in the case when his specific charges are turned into Deuteronomic generalizations and reduced to a polemic against idolatry (20.31, 39; 23.28–30), or when they are twisted round to point to other breaches of the law which the redactor took more to heart, such as the breaking of the sabbath, which was particularly offensive to priests (20.12f., 16, 20f., 24; 22.8; 23.38).

Here the concerns of a particular situation or religious group have forced their way in. At the same time, however, an effort can be made to gain a comprehensive general view of the nation's history, or to give some passing prophecy of misfortune a wider application within the context of world-judgment, which intimates a closer relationship to the threats of the prophet (23.35–49; 28.20–24).

More serious interference with the fundamental lines taken by the prophet's message can be seen in the attempts to extend his sentence on the neighbouring nations by the addition of particular individual threats; for this inevitably leads to an attempt to put additional emphasis on the particular sin against Israel which provides a reason for the judgment. Thus the prophet's threats, which had been aimed at the central religious offence, came to be narrowed down to satisfy mere nationalistic feelings (26.6f., 8–17; 28.24). In this way, Israel's responsibility can seem reduced by the assertion that the temptation came from outside (29.6, 7, 16), and the eschatological aspect can be forced into the background (32.9, 10). These elaborations of the text, which in the main go back to the prophet's disciples, attain the character of an independent composition in ch. 38f., which were written after the return of the exiles, when Yahweh had still as yet failed to be recognized by the Gentiles. This constituted an agonizing problem, for which a solution had to be sought, and it was found in the mighty juridical punishment executed upon Gog, the prince from the north, and upon his hosts. Here was to be manifested to all peoples that the world was controlled by the power of God. In this passage, the prophetic proclamation of judgment already clothes itself in apocalyptic forms, the speculative character of which is clearly brought to light. The author explicitly wishes to be regarded as the correct interpreter of prophetic words not as yet fulfilled (38.17; 39.8), and is therefore evidently thinking chiefly of the enemy from the north expected by Jeremiah (Jer. 4–6). The sections inserted into this little apocalypse, evidently by a priestly hand, are full of an anxiety to see the laws of ritual purity enforced in the holy land.

This revision of Ezekiel has taken on considerable dimensions in two passages, in ch. 10 and the elaborations of ch. 1 (cf. pp. 112ff.) which have taken place from there, and in ch. 40–48 (cf. below, the commentary on pp. 530ff.). Both passages show an obvious concern to take a prophecy which departs from the priestly line of thought or does not show sufficient regard for it and to assimilate it to the redactor's own point of view. So the throne of God in ch. 1 is changed into a chariot throne, which agrees better with the ark sanctuary in the temple of Zion, and the sketch outlining the new sanctuary, which says nothing of the community of God's people and their festivals, is made serviceable to priestly interests in carrying out the cult by the addition of descriptions of various structures and communications of cultic laws. Again, the boundaries of the promised land and its division between the twelve tribes is dealt with in a way which displays some resemblance to Priestly writing found in Numbers and Joshua, but is at the same time forced into obedience to an artificially symmetrical plan. Here, as in 16.59–63, which is concerned with the thorough enforcement of a priestly conception of the eternal covenant, we see an attempt to arrive at an understanding of the prophetic message which shows full awareness of the inconsistency between the latter and important ideas of priestly piety, and tries as far as possible to assimulate the inheritance left by the prophet to its own particular type of piety. Even though the prophetic message as a whole is not subjected to any profound transformation, since its linguistic and stylistic peculiarities exclude this, and impose unsurmountable boundaries to any such efforts, it is still possible to see clearly the direction from which it was threatened. Here we see a process of assimilating a foreign body not only to the old traditional piety of the community, but also to fresh currents of fanaticism within it, which block the cleansing and enlightening influence of prophecy, preventing it from enforcing its own special aim or from effecting a complete breakthrough. It does not need to be demonstrated how important it was under these circumstances that the prophetic text on the whole was accurately transmitted apart from some more or less inevitable changes of wording. It is clear, too, that the Christian community of today, which inherits the legacy left by the prophets, is faced with the task of fighting to secure an intact version of their message, and with that of freeing it from the additions which distort the news of the judgment and deliverance of the covenant God. In this way, the source of new creative knowledge, rising from here, may flow freely to fertilize and regenerate the people of God.

III

Now that we have reviewed the prophet's preaching, it still remains for us to carry out the task of giving a brief recapitulation of the theological ideas upon which it is based and which determine it. We see with perfect clarity how the prophet's vision carries the stamp of God's supernatural majesty, and this makes visible at an important point the priestly elements in Ezekiel's theological statements. The action of this God embraces the whole of the world which he is subjecting to his lordly will. So, whereas priestly proclamation tries to limit the appearance of supernatural glory, the *kābōd* of Yahweh, to the dwelling place of the Zion sanctuary, we find that in Ezekiel the manifestations are not tied to any place, and are actually present in the unclean land of exile. The choice of the man made worthy of beholding that glory as its ambassador means first of all that God has not dismissed from his service those who have been banished from the homeland, but rather that he has brought them into the presence of the judge who can find the fallen wherever they may go and make them acknowledge the justice of his sentence. The vision does indeed recall the former place where he was enthroned in Jerusalem, but it is completely free from any tie to that place; it bears witness to the sovereign freedom of the Lord of the universe in revealing himself and renders impossible any complacent answer to the question whether the complete rejection of the 'rebellious house' is the concluding act of repudiation of his former obligations, seeing that the other nations also belong to him and can be called into his service, or whether the harsh turning away from Israel conceals a mystery which for the moment must remain undisclosed.

The aim of Ezekiel's commission to preach is seen to be the revelation of God by word and deed, leading to the knowledge 'that I am Yahweh', i.e. a will to universal lordship aiming at world-recognition of this lordship. Such a divine declaration belongs to a dimension different from all contemplative ways of representing God, and from all metaphysical statements regarding his nature; it is the statement of a fact demanding recognition and surrender. By going beyond Israel and including the Gentiles, it frees God's act of revelation from being imprisoned within a dogma of election tying him indissolubly to a single nation, obliging him to give it the first place among the nations and to impart himself to it alone.

This attitude towards an Israel which tries to seize God's election as its own prey is further asserted in the words which promise salvation, when they state that their ultimate motive is not love or compassion or any bond of affection whatsoever, but the sanctification of the name of God which has been profaned in the world. This name, which is God's disclosure of his nature, entrusted to a community which serves him, makes the originating cause of God's saving action consist in the assertion of his own nature by the holy God in faithfulness to himself, and serves to protect supernatural majesty from being anthropomorphized in any way.

Yet it is this God and no one else who institutes the covenant with Israel. The fire of consuming holiness that surrounds him does not render questionable that central statement of faith, but from the outset rules out any indissoluble obligation for the divine founder of the covenant, let alone any mutual partnership in which both sides have equal rights, and the inexpressible miracle of the giving of grace which is characteristic of divine election is put in a dominant position in the foreground. So it is not a God who keeps accounts and drives hard bargains who now comes to meet the chosen people, but a gracious Lord and master, whose will is to make a people the place of his self-disclosure in history, and who also bestows upon it by his commandments the means by which it may live and thrive, so one must naturally expect such an offer to be seized upon with joy and thanksgiving.

But the self-seeking will of man resists and rejects that offer, and there is the enigma which turns this gift of life into a bringer of cursing and destruction, and perverts what God willed should be the history of salvation into a history of sin. Like his predecessors, Ezekiel here stands face to face with the same dilemma and describes it in the same or similar terms, with the exception that cultic sins, being regarded as treachery against the unique divinity of Yahweh, are given more space. Yet his indictment is severer than any previous proclamation of judgment: his remorseless analysis of the nation's history does not leave behind any trace of any proving and surrender, not even in an ideal period at the beginning, let alone any pretext for self-glorification or complacency; it leaves no room for anything but horror at the hostility and alienation pervading all human nature in the face of the efforts of the covenant God's attempts to seek and to win it. Only the unfathomable patience of God, who keeps faith with a nation which has faithlessly broken his covenant, makes it possible still to discern within the history of corruption a history of salvation, which celebrates the praise of the compassionate Lord of the covenant.

The people as a whole had been shattered by their encounter with God in all his holiness, and that threw a completely new light on the importance of the individual. The prophet knows that among the universal destruction there are still some surviving members of the people who sigh and groan at the abomination committed by Jerusalem (9.4) and who are capable of being termed righteous (14.12ff.). But as parts of such a whole they are helpless, and can only be snatched out like brands from the burning by the divine judge, who even in judgment keeps a just account of what is due. Only after God's judgment has been accomplished and the new creation begun can they start to act. That is not to say that they now constitute an élite, whom God employs to build something new. Nowhere in the whole of this prophetic book are the 'righteous' spoken of, as if they had merited a new gift of salvation or occasioned a new hope. The prophet with his unerring eye knew too much about the caprices of human trustworthiness to be capable of suggesting anything of the sort. God's new creation shows its greatness by being poured out over righteous and unrighteous alike, and summoning them to decide in the face of his offer of salvation. Both alike may here stumble and fall; indeed, there would seem to be more danger of resistance from those who have been strict supporters of the old traditional ordinances than from those who have been guilty of offences against God's command (18.19, 25, 29). Yet the full will of the redeeming God to save is aimed at these latter; it is they who receive most benefit when men are liberated from the violence and lust for power of their oppressors (34.11ff., 17ff.). If only they understand the signs of the times, it is possible for them to become genuine witnesses to God's preparation of a new Israel.

That indeed is the position of all who hear the word of the prophet; they are called to take part in a resurgence, made possible by the general amnesty declared by God for the sins of past and present generations. Only the person who here and now finds himself able to turn back from his previous course and join the new people which is to wait for God's final act of salvation can have a share in the future of the new Israel, as they are shaped by the creative power of the spirit and attain to the destined goal fixed by God's faithfulness to his decree of election. Only when these conditions are fulfilled can man be a creation of God's good pleasure.

The statements about the law guiding man, the decision required of him and the fellowship into which he is admitted, only at last fall into their proper context when seen in association with this picture of man. What we have here is not a religion of ethical humanism, to be put into effect in any and every country and context, and which is completely divorced from the special position of Israel, which would be as much as to say that the ultimate solution of the problem of how a people of God is to exist is to be found in the atmosphere of a clear, uncomplicated legal ethic. That would be in flagrant contradiction to the permanent significance possessed by the holy land in the dealings of the world-God, and to the particular road along which it is his will to lead the exiles towards a new salvation. Instead, everything hinges on the ever to be renewed struggle to stand in faith before the God who, by making known his indescribable gift of grace, removes the threatening mystery of death which overhangs the covenant breaker and leads the remnant of the people, delivered from the annihilating judgment, into a new relationship of service and faithfulness in which they are guaranteed life and a future by that will of his which shapes all history.

Now this implies a willingness to walk obediently along the road of history, where God makes salvation ripen into fulfilment, a road along which the prophet, now become a watchman and spiritual director, accompanies those entrusted to his guardianship. This way leads through the great judgment of the nations, in which the resistance of the human creations of power and culture, directed by hybris and self-deification against the great moral rules according to which God has formed the world, are shattered. This opens the way for a recognition of the mysterious rule of the power that governs history. It also brings to fulfilment a new people of God, in whom the great creative and saving purposes of the covenant God take shape, and bear witness to the living God before the whole universe. Here the old images of hope taken over by Ezekiel from his predecessors and used for ends of his own take on a profounder meaning through their close association with the community originating in the exile. They are not meant to picture any return of the good old days, but are a demonstration of the power of those norms of life which serve to constitute the community and to transform a world alienated from God. Israel is the first nation to experience their reality within itself.

This introduces a great deal of tension into the life of the community in exile, preserving it from every sort of complacency and preventing it from ever finding satisfaction in a world-renouncing autarchy. It is also forbidden to try to anticipate the future by any fanatical extravagance. The hope that it possesses does not enable it to hover in a celestial vacuum, but insists firmly on its duty of realizing earthly fellowship. It is this same tension also which generates such power within it that disillusionment and defeat do not cause it to lose sight of the goal, since there comes an inner drive and flexibility, preventing spiritual life from becoming stagnant and keeping it receptive and well fitted to take on new shapes.

COMMENTARY

Chapter i.1–28

The vision in which the prophet receives his call

1 In the thirtieth year, in the fourth month, on the fifth day of the
month, as I abode among the exiles by the river Chebar, the heavens were
opened and I saw visions of God, 2on the fifth day of the month (it was the
fifth year of the exile of king Jehoiachin), 3the word of Yahweh came to
Ezekiel the priest, the son of Buzi, in the land of the Chaldeans by the
river Chebar.a The hand of Yahweh [. . .]b was upon mec there, 4and I
looked: behold, a stormy wind came out of the north, [and]d a great cloud
with fire flashing hither and thither [. . .]e and out of the midst of it there
was a gleam as of bronze [. . .]f 5and from the midst of it appeared what
looked like four living creatures, who were in form like men to look upon;
6each had four faces and each four wings.g 7Their legs were straighth and
the soles of their feet were round,i and they sparkled like burnished bronze.
8They had human handsj under their wings on their four sides [. . .].k
10As for the likeness of their faces: [all four] had the face of a man [in
front],l all four had the face of a lion on the right side, all four had the face
of an ox on the left side, and all four had the face of an eagle [inwards].m
11And [all four]n had their wings spread out above, two always touching
each other,o while two covered their bodies. 12And each went straight
forward; wherever the spirit made them go, there they went, without
turning as they went.13And [between]p the living creatures was what
lookedq like burning coals of fire, like torches moving to and fror among
the living creatures, and the fire was bright, and out of it went forth
lightning [. . .]s
22 And over the heads of the living creatures there was the likeness of a
vaultt shining like crystal,u spread out at the top above their heads.
23And under the vault their wings were stretched out straight, one towards
another [. . .]v 26And above the vault over their heads could be seen
something like a sapphire, like a throne in appearance; andw above the
likeness of the throne at the top was a form like that of a man.27And I saw:
something like gleaming bronzex upwards from what had the appearance
of his loins; but downwards from what had the appearance of his loins I
saw the appearance of open fire; and there was brightness round about

the form. ²⁸Like the bow that appears in the cloud on the day of rain, such was the brightness to be seen round about. Such was the image of the glory of Yahweh to behold. And when I saw it, I fell upon my face. And I heard the voice of one speaking.

ᵃFor vv. 2 and 3 see commentary.

ᵇMT: 'there' is lacking in LXX, and was only required after the subsequent insertion of v. 3a.

ᶜMT: 'over him'; assimilation to v. 3a.

ᵈInserted from LXX.

ᵉMT: *wᵉnōgaḥ lō sabīb*, a gloss from the end of v. 27b.

ᶠMT: *mittōk hāʾēš*; additional explanatory phrase made necessary by previous gloss.

ᵍSee BH.

ʰRead *yᵉšārōt* with LXX for *regel yᵉšārā*.

ⁱMT: 'their soles like the soles of a calf'. We read instead, with Aquila, simply *ᶜagullā*.

ʲSee BH.

ᵏMT: '8b and their faces and their wings with all four, ⁹their wings touched one another; they did not turn as they went; each went straight forward'. These words are evidently a mistaken anticipation of vv. 11f. with the principal words distorted by dittography.

ˡThe words stating the position of the first face are lacking in MT, and must be supplied from those relating to the other three.

ᵐMT has *ūpᵉnēhēm* as the first word of v. 11. It should be changed to *lipᵉnīmā* and put at the conclusion of v. 10 (Wellhausen, Bertholet).

ⁿFor MT *lᵉīš* read *lᵉʾarbaᶜtan* with LXX.

ᵒ⁻ᵖSee BH.

ʳMT: *hīʾ mithalleket*. Read with LXX *mithallᵉkōt*.

ˢVerse 14: 'And the living creatures darted to and fro like the appearance of "lightning"' is a gloss with a misinterpretation of v. 13, cf. BH.

MT: '¹⁵And I looked (at the living creatures) and behold, one wheel was on the earth (or 'on the ground'=below?) beside the living creatures, for each of the four. ¹⁶The appearance of the wheels ('and their construction': not in LXX) was like the gleaming of chrysolite; and the four had the same form ('and their appearance': not in LXX) and their construction was, as if there were one wheel inside another. ¹⁷('When they went': not in LXX), they could go in all four directions without turning as they went. ¹⁸(The first four words are untranslatable, cf. BH.) And their rims were all four full of eyes. ¹⁹When the living creatures went, the wheels went beside them; when the living creatures rose from the earth the wheels rose also. ²⁰Wherever the spirit drove them (wherever the spirit to go: meaningless dittography) there the wheels also went, and they rose along with them, for the spirit of the living creatures was in the wheels. ²¹When those went, these went, and when those stood, these stood, and when these rose from the earth, the wheels rose with them, for the spirit of the living creatures was in the wheels.' For an explanation of how this section is a subsequent insertion into ch. 1 under the influence of ch. 10, see commentary on ch. 10.

ᵗSee BH. The word may also be translated 'firmament' or 'plate'. It is used in Gen. 1.6–8 to denote the vault of heaven.

ᵘWe omit the additional adjective 'awesome', not in LXX, and alien to the context.

ᵛMT: '²³ᵇeach had two covering its body' (see BH). ²⁴And I heard the roar of their wings like the roar of great waters, like the voice of the Almighty, when they went, the sound of tumult like the roar of a host. When they stood, they let down their wings. ²⁵And there came a voice from the place above the firmament which was above their heads. When they stood, they let their wings hang loose.' The second half of v. 23 is a repetition from v. 11; v. 24 gives a description of the noise of the wings contradicting the rest of the vision; v. 25 is not found in certain MSS and does not fit in with the context.

ʷSee BH.

ˣMT: 'as fire appears, which is enclosed round about'; a gloss not found in the LXX, and without any apparent meaning.

The superscription of the whole book is to be found in vv. 1–3, incorporated in the opening of the description of the vision. Verse 1 has its direct continuation in v. 3b. Verse 2 is somewhat clumsily associated with the day of the month in the thirtieth year, mentioned in v. 1, and seeks to fix it by connecting it with some well-known event. Then v. 3a provides a title in the proper sense of the word. All this leads to a suspicion that the present beginning of the book is the final result of a complicated process, in which others besides the prophet had a share. Undoubtedly the employment of the first person singular in the vision narrative must be attributed to him. Verse 2 must come from a different writer, who furnishes a precise explanation of the thirtieth year, of which originally it did not stand in need. When v. 3 was added the result was a title like those in the prophetic books of Haggai and Zachariah. As in them, we are told the prophet's name, and the time at which he received the word of Yahweh, but this passage also adds his dwelling-place, which could easily be inferred from the previous statements in v. 1.

[1] If this insertion of a title into the original prophetic text points to the work of a later redactor, it seems likely that the wording of v. 1 was not left intact. The disconnected mention of a thirtieth year, introduced in order to date a decisive event in the prophet's life, is quite unparalleled, and hardly explicable unless there has been some serious interference with the old prophetic narrative. Attempts to relate this statement of time to a well-known fixed point, either king Josiah's reform of the cult, or Nebuchadrezzar's accession, or the year of king Jehoiachin's exile as in v. 2, cannot be carried out

without arbitrarily altering the number thirty, quite apart from the improbability of such a vague statement by Ezekiel, who elsewhere invariably dates his years from that in which Jehoiachin was carried into exile. So we are more or less forced to conclude that the particulars relevant to it have been either lost or deliberately suppressed. Explanations of the number thirty must therefore be conjectural. Most probably it states the age of the writer; an assumption which has had its champions ever since the days of Origen (Klostermann, Bewer, etc.). That the prophet was carried into exile in the twenty-fifth year of his life can be deduced to have been stated in a lost portion of the text. This must have had a special significance for him as a priest. Judging by the analogy of the traditional regulations for Levites (Num. 8.24; 4.3, 30ff.), a man would also have entered upon the priesthood at that age. So, at the age at which he would under other circumstances have entered priestly office, Ezekiel was transplanted into unclean heathen soil, experiencing the first major disappointment of his life. The judgment which threatened his people first struck him, thus beginning at the house of God. The mention of this event, so important to his own life, also throws a peculiar light upon all the subsequent events. We may well regard it as having served to introduce the vision in which he received his call. Its erasure by subsequent redactors of the book has parallels in the erasure of similar biographical details in Isaiah, Hosea, Micah, etc.[1]

[2] Ezekiel had his vision in the year 594. So v. 2 states, and there is no reason for doubting it. The prophet was among the exiled Jews, carried off to Babylonia along with king Jehoiachin in the year 598, and settled along the river Chebar. According to Babylonian contracts of the fifth century discovered in that same district, the river is to be identified with the *nār Kabāri*, a navigable channel of the Euphrates south-east of Babylon, which is thought to be the same as the present *Šatt-en-nīl*. The king himself, along with his family, his retinue, and a few nobles, was kept in imprisonment in Babylon. (Lists of persons receiving rations from the royal storehouses have been discovered in the southern zone of Babylon, containing his name for the years 595–570). Most of the other exiles were settled in country districts south of Babylon, as colonists in separate villages, whose task it was to till wastelands belonging to the state. They might

---

[1] Cf. K. Budde, 'Eine folgenschwere Redaktion des Zwölfprophetenbuches', *ZAW* 39 (1922), pp. 218ff., and B. Duhm, *Das Buch Jesaia*[3], 1914, on Isa. 7.1.

carry on their internal government through· their own system of elders, but had to pay tribute and do forced labour as subjects of a heathen state. It might make its yoke heavier or lighter as it thought fit, but they could never forget their position. The first captivity had mainly affected the better-off classes in Judah, and men inured to healthy mountain air must have suffered considerably from the hard work they had to do in the sweltering marshlands of Babylonia.

In these villages of colonists exiled priests would naturally assist such religious activities as might still go on, at the places of prayer by the waterside, or at meetings conducted by men learned in the scriptures, or in their houses (cf. Ps. 137 and Acts 16.13). In the absence of temple worship, teaching on the distinction between clean and unclean and instruction in the moral law were still not only possible but necessary, if the exiles were not to lose their last foothold, thanks to which they could still call their souls their own even in that foreign land. There must have been men enough with a sense of responsibility to make them take up such a task, even though many of the exiles must have either sunk into dull resignation or grown hard and defiant, and been very unreceptive.

There can be no doubt that Ezekiel was one of these men; we can see indications on every side of his deep feeling of responsibility for his own people. Besides that, he was a hereditary member of the priesthood of the temple of Zion, a class which, in spite of all the corruption, must have had in its ranks a greater number who stood for the great traditions of the holy people than could be found among the country-priests. But all the time one dreadful doubt made his work difficult. Was there any sense in taking such trouble over a few scattered remnants in a foreign land, seeing that meanwhile the whole destiny of the people to whom they belonged was on the point of being decided at Jerusalem, and that, if the catastrophe which was threatening that place were to come, the whole existence of Israel would inevitably come to a terrible end? He was excluded from the fierce struggles for the deliverance of the holy city, in which Jeremiah was wearing himself out, and giving vent to utterances expressed in speech or writing which stirred up the mind of the exiles in Babylon; he was one of the men dismissed by those at home as long since rejected by God; he was far from Yahweh's presence in the sanctuary, leading a shadowy existence in a lost world where there was not even the faintest glimmer of a hope of liberation: all that must have weighed heavily upon the heart of the young priest and brought out with redoubled sharpness all the darker sides of the life of the exiles, with their religious superficiality and lack of receptiveness, and their moral degeneracy and readiness to submit to the heathen influences all round them. There in that unclean land there was nothing to hope for, and no improvement could be effected. Jerusalem was the only place from which any light came. If that light were to be put out, then Israel would sink into the hopeless night of total alienation from God, and be wiped off the face of creation.

So the young priest had to pass through a waiting period of agonizing tension in which hope and fear alternated. Then something took place to deliver him from doubt and despair and give him new firm ground upon which he could stand. [1] He could find no better description of this miraculous transformation than the statement that the heavens were opened, and that he was granted a wonderful glimpse into the divine world. This expression has a far wider connotation than the usual suggestion of the windows of heaven being opened for gifts or judgments to be sent out (Ps. 78.23; Mal. 3.10; Deut. 28.12; Gen. 7.11; Isa. 24.18), yet its employment is proper to the occasion. There are genuine parallels only in the New Testament (e.g. Rev. 4.1; Acts 7.56), and its being used once only serves to indicate the powerful breaking through of a new reality into Ezekiel's life, where up to that point all his prayers and hopes had seemed to beat in vain against a brazen heaven. While including the perception of things formerly unknown, it was also inseparably associated with a painful paralysis of every human endeavour at self-determination or self-assurance. The hand of God, the power not his own which compels a man, came down upon Ezekiel, just as it had forced Isaiah on to a new career (Isa. 8.11), and torn Jeremiah away from the company of the merrymakers (Jer. 15.17). It overpowered his thoughts and feelings, so as to make them serve a vision different from everything before. This is undoubtedly the same experience which the ancient Israelite prophets called being seized by the hand of Yahweh, the ecstasy in which, according to one ancient description (I Sam. 10.6), a man becomes a different person. Ezekiel therefore possesses an unshakable certitude, that the indescribable vision which he has been found worthy to see does not proceed from his own spiritual power, but that God in person is introducing him into a new dimension of reality, the strangeness and terrifying sublimity of which far transcend all that is imaginable to man.

He is quite right in thinking so, even though the picture of God which follows may be indebted to contemporary conceptions as a whole, and in many of its details. The meaning of that picture is not conveyed merely by the outward imagery, but consists chiefly in the concentrated pressure of its inward testimony. God, under the form of the ruler upon his throne, was seen by others also (cf. Isa. 6 and I Kings 22.19ff.). [5] The bizarre 'living creatures', also called cherubim, as in ch. 10 of this book, are known all over the ancient East, under a similar form, as throne-bearers or guardians of temple or palace thresholds.[1] The half-human, half-bestial shape and attributes load them with all the powers of both species, and express how awe-inspiring such guardians of holy things must be.

[6–8] The order followed in the description, which moves on from the faces and wings to the feet and hands both in vv. 6–8 and vv. 10–12, but in fact describes only the details of the faces and wings, may seem strange. It may suggest that v. 11b comes immediately after v. 6, and that the details in vv. 7–11a are to be set aside as a subsequent elaboration (so Zimmerli). Yet we must also recall how the prophet, having insisted in v. 5b on the human form of the living creatures, needs to bring out this resemblance to man in detail. After the general impression conveyed in v. 6, he describes in v. 7 the upright stance of the feet, thus clearly distinguishing them from the quadrupeds combining the characteristics of two species, the serpent-griffons, and lion-men or ox-men of Babylonia and Assyria. Then the mention of the hands in v. 8 supplies another circumstantial indication of their human shape. [10–12] Only in vv. 10ff. does he begin to do full justice to the characteristics of the faces and wings, derived from the animal realm, but once more with the human face set in front. These last peculiarities of the living creatures also make intelligible for the first time the emphatic statement in v. 12b that they do not have to turn round in order to move, since they front all the points of the compass, and show themselves to be an indispensable part of the whole context. The oscillation between masculine and feminine suffix forms is far from clear in its meaning, as is shown by v.10 with its abrupt alternations between them. In our opinion no counter-argument against our interpretation can be built upon them; their variations must be ascribed to the scribal transmission of the

[1] Cf. the illustrations in H. Gressmann's *Altorientalische Bilder zum AT*, 1927, nos. 370–81, and in the *Bilderatlas zur Religionsgeschichte* [6], ed., H. Haas, 1925, nos. 17ff. For the general picture, cf. H. Bietenhard, *Die himmlische Welt im Urchristentum und Spätjudentum*, 1951, pp. 63ff.

text, as has been shown by E. Hoehne.[1] To ascribe to Ezekiel, on the basis of an appeal to Isa. 6, the authorship of only one comment on the wings of these creatures, part human, part animal, and to deny his responsibility for all that is original in the description of them, is excessively to exaggerate the significance of the traditional style of prophetic composition. Fohrer's attempt at restoring the original form of the vision-description by arranging its metrical construction in ten strophes with seven short lines each is not convincing, as the formation of these short verses is too much dependent on subjective judgment.

[22] The living creatures bear the vaulted platform on which the throne of God stands, so that they exercise the same function as the cherubim associated with the holy ark, on which Yahweh has his throne, according to I Sam. 4.4; II Sam. 6.2; II Kings 19.14f. The way in which they are associated with the seat of the throne is best illustrated by the two Phoenician thrones of Astàrte, where the seat is upheld by two winged beings standing to the right and the left. The cherub throne of Ishtar on the Assyrian rock-relief of Maltaia displays a similar arrangement (cf. the works referred to above). This passage expresses in terms of actual experience what was originally a concept of nature-mythology, in which the cherub was symbolized by the storm-cloud upon which Yahweh rode. This is made probable by the role of the cherub in Ps. 18.11 and Gen. 3.24. [4] This provides us with the basic conceptions behind the way in which the living creatures in Ezek. 1 are associated with storm and cloud, and with masses of fire which dart out like lightning from between them (v. 13). This does not, of course, mean that Ezekiel's description is the result of a conscious and calculated piece of construction out of traditional elements, such as is attributed to him in many commentaries. Such a pedestrian type of criticism is utterly blind to the freedom with which this picture makes use of the traditional ideas. It fails to see how in it a familiar world of imagery naturally springs to life, and how a tremendously impressive spiritual content is thus provided with the form which best suits it, without there being any deliberately calculated purpose to follow any previously determined aim. [5] Thus mixed beings of human shape and upright stance are less commonly found in ancient representations than four-footed ones, and heads with [6] four different faces are quite unparalleled.[2]

---

[1] *Die Thronwagenvision Hesekiels*, 1953, pp. 80–84.

[2] An old Babylonian bronze statuette does show a god with four faces, but these

[7] The peculiar formation of the feet, which seem to run together into a rounded pillar, serves to bring out the bearer-function exercised by the living creatures. [8] If the human hands, under the wings emphasize similarity to human shape, [11] the wings are the typical feature of the mixed beings, and are a feature which is entirely lacking in the angels which figure in the Old Testament. Here, along with the two which cover the body, another pair of wings is extended on either side, evidently introduced in order to cover the space under the vaulted roof, without any thought of their being used for flight. It is quite different in Isaiah, where the Seraphim have a third pair of wings so as to be able to fly. In this, apparently, we find a further motive for the introduction in vv. 15–21 of wheels under the throne seen in the vision; this is the way in which its forward motion is symbolized. It is the only element to betray signs of an artificial construction; however, as ch. 10 will show, it belongs to a later expansion of the vision-picture, which is one that has evidently aroused to a remarkable extent the theological interest of copyists and interpreters. [12] For the prophet himself the power to move is derived solely from the might of the Spirit, by which the cherubim are made to 'walk', or 'go', i.e. to move through the air. What is envisaged is not progress along the surface of the earth, but hovering among the clouds, which form the brightly shining background against which the figures are seen. They have no will of their own, but are ruled by the might of the Spirit streaming through them. Because they face to all four points of the compass, it is unnecessary for them to turn, and thus they always appear as if seen from the front.

Ezekiel himself was evidently more aware of the differences between his own conceptions and those of the idols and images of the ancient East than of the similarities. He purposely abstains from the use of the word 'cherub' in order to distinguish the bearers of God's unique glory from the throng of Babylonian monsters. Being servants of the great world-God, they carry in themselves some of the uniqueness of Yahweh. [22] The vault or firmament which they carry is the copy of that vault of heaven which the Creator, according to Gen. 1.6, set up to separate the earthly from the heavenly waters, and

---

are all human. Cf. H. Schmoekel, *Ur, Assur und Babylon* (Grosse Kulturen der Frühzeit, ed. H. T. Bossert), 1955, Plate 67, following H. Frankfort, *More Sculpture from the Diyala Region*, 1943, which also gives an illustration of a goddess of a similar type.

above which he is enthroned. The four living creatures are thus shown to be the representatives of the four corners of the earth, and therefore of the world-embracing sovereignty of him who is enthroned upon them, as is also suggested by their fourfold faces and wings. [26] While they are related to the world, the world-ruler has no dwelling within the world, but is enthroned in other-worldly glory above the dome of heaven. The heavenly brightness is represented by crystal (cf. the crystal sea of Rev. 4.6) and blue sapphire, just as in Ex. 24.10, the pavement under the feet of the God of heaven already appears to be light blue and gleaming like sapphire. [27] Of the figure to be perceived upon the throne we get only a vague outline. Isaiah, too, shows a similar restraint in his description. It is clad in a garment of fire, which burns above in the calm gleam of heavenly brightness, and below in the menacing might of licking flames. [28] Yet its glittering image is surrounded by the gentler hues of the rainbow like a gleaming aureole: it is the sign of the covenant with the human race (Gen. 9.12ff.), qualifying the vision of the super-worldly God by his divine faithfulness to that which he has created. But this sign points to the God of the whole world; one can no longer suggest any special reconciliation with Israel. On the contrary, the Almighty power, whose wonders unfold before the prophet's eyes, turns towards the nations, and no thought of Israel is involved.

The cumulative effect of all the details of the vision is clearly evident to the consciousness of the prophet. It serves in very fact to raise him from his present state, and the oppressive feeling of being without any expedient, by showing him the power hidden behind the curtain of earthly reality. At this very moment, that power is expressing its will to carry through its inconceivable activity in the face of all opposition. Divine perfection, power and authority are themselves impressively symbolized by the glittering vision with all its gleaming colours. They make a deep impression upon this outcast in a heathen land. To what he has seen he applies the widely used term kābōd, i.e. the glorious form assumed by the divine presence. This, according to the priestly view, dwelt only in the tabernacle, or in the holy of holies of the temple at Zion (Ex. 40.34; Lev. 9.6, 23; Num. 14.10; 16.19; I Kings 8.11; II Chron. 7.1). But now he sees that it is not indissolubly tied to those places, but is manifesting itself, by preference, to a lost and banished one like himself. Yet this reflected image of the heavenly glory of Yahweh, which as the ἀπαύγασμα τῆς δόξης αὐτοῦ (Heb. 1.3) imparts a revelation of him, shows, not the national

God of Zion to whom Israel lays an exclusive claim, but the Lord, free from all earthly limitations, and able to command the whole universe. He comes from the north, i.e. from the divine dwelling place which lies inconceivably far away, into the world of the lost. Thus he shows that the end of the chosen people does not involve the end of his dominion, but rather opens all sorts of new and undreamed-of possibilities for a power as almighty as his to set up its kingdom. Hi being bursts all human measurements. Even in the vision, a mer copy or reproduction of the glory of his power, it is so overwhelming to weak human nature as to cast fainting to the ground the man upon whom it comes. Yet at the same moment it is showing beyond all possibility of doubt that since the judgment of the Flood, God's will has never ceased to operate for the benefit of mankind.

Yet God does not give convincing testimony of this will of his to man until he lifts him up out of the dust and addresses his word to him. So the 'vision of God' attains its objective only when, from amid the flames ablaze around him, the Lord of this world and of all worlds speaks to the man whom he has reduced to such a state of dissolution.

CHAPTER 2.1–3.15

The commissioning by God

1 And he said to me, 'Son of man, stand upon your feet, that I may speak to you.' ²Then Spirit entered into me [. . .]ªand set me upon my feet, and I heard him speak to me. ³And he said to me, 'Son of man, I will send you to the houseᵇ of Israel, to the rebelliousᶜ people [. . .].ᵈ They and their fathers have transgressed against me to this very day. ⁴[. . .]ᵉ And you shall say to them: "Thus says Yahweh." ⁵Whether they hear or refuse to hear—for they are a rebellious house—they will recognize that a prophet has arisen among them. ⁶But you, son of man, be not afraid of them, nor be afraid of their words, if [they attack and revile you]ᶠ and you must live among scorpions [. . .].ᵍ ⁷Speak my words to them, whether they hear or refuse to hear; for they are a rebellious house.

8 'But you, son of man, hear what I say to you: be not rebellious, like the rebellious house. Open your mouth and eat what I give you.' ⁹And I looked, and behold a hand was stretched out to me, and behold, it held a written scroll. ¹⁰And he spread it before me, and it had writing on the

front and on the back, and there were written on it words of lamentation and mourning and woe. 3 1ᵃAnd he said to me, 'Son of man[. . .],ʰ eat this scroll.' ²So I opened my mouth and he gave me the scroll to eat ³ᵃand he said to me, 'Son of man, let your body eat and fill your stomach with this scroll that I give you, ¹ᵇand go, speak to the house of Israel!' ³ᵇThen I ate it, and it was in my mouth as sweet as honey.

4 Then he said to me, 'Son of man, go, get you to the house of Israel and speak my words to them. ⁵For you are not sent to a people of foreign speechⁱ [. . .]ʲ ⁶nor to many foreign peoples [. . .]ᵏ whose speech you cannot understand. If I sent you to such,ˡ they would listen to you. ⁷But the house of Israel will not listen to you, for they are not willing to listen to me; because all the house of Israel are of a hard forehead and of a stubborn heart. ⁸Behold, I have made your face hard like their faces, and your forehead hard like their foreheads. ⁹Like diamond, harder than rock, do I make your forehead; fear them not nor be dismayed before their face, for they are a rebellious house.' ¹⁰Moreover he said to me, 'Son of man, all my words that I speak to you, receive in your heart, and hear with your ears. ¹¹And go, get you to the exiles, to the children of your people, speak to them and say, whether they hear or refuse to hear, "Thus says Yahweh!" '

12 Then Spirit lifted me up, and I heard behind me a great noise, as the glory of Yahweh arose from its place.ᵐ ¹⁴But Spirit lifted me up and took me away, and I went lifted up in the airⁿ and greatly moved in spirit, the hand of Yahweh being strong upon me. ¹⁵So I came to the exiles at Tel Abib,ᵒ where they dwelt, and I sat there overwhelmed among them seven days.

ᵃMT: 'when he spoke to me'; a gloss according to LXX.
ᵇMT: 'son'; read 'house' with LXX.
ᶜCf. BH.
ᵈ'Who have rebelled against me'; a gloss.
ᵉMT: 'And the sons are of an impudent countenance and hard heart—I send you to them'; a gloss quoted from 3.7.
ᶠThus with LXX. MT: 'nettles and thorns with you'.
ᵍMT: 'Be not afraid of their words, nor be dismayed at their looks, for they are a rebellious house'; originally catchword glosses to v. 6a, which have been wrongly transferred from the margin into the text.
ʰMT: 'What you find, eat'; gloss after Jer. 15.16, not found in LXX.
ⁱ'And of a hard tongue; expansion under the influence of Isa. 33.19, and introducing an extraneous idea.
ʲ'To the house of Israel'; superfluous explanation.
ᵏ'Of foreign speech and of a hard tongue'; a repetition from the previous verse.
ˡMT: 'If I did not send you'; a slip of the pen.
ᵐVerse 13: 'And the sound of the wings of the living creatures, as they touched

one another, and the sound of the wheels together with them and a great noise' is an explanatory gloss, which has been inserted at the wrong point in the text.

ⁿThus with J. Herrmann, as suggested by the word μετεωρος in the LXX *hex.* MT reads 'bitter'.

ᵒMT here inserts: 'who dwelt by the river Chebar'. The way this phrase is attached is bad. Moreover, Ezekiel is already beside the river, and goes from there to the settlement, which is apparently on higher ground.

A messenger to rebels: 2.1–7

The liberating new assurance of God's nearness, imparted to Ezekiel through the vision which he had experienced, was not a gift upon which he could repose and which he could enjoy in the manner of the mystics, but a means by which he might actively serve this glorious God. God might have denied him priestly office, but he had now bestowed upon him the far more responsible office of acting as his plenipotentiary. God had determined to act through this very situation of exile and apparent separation from God so as to communicate himself to this man in a new way, and thus bring to nought all human speculations about what constitutes nearness to or distance from God.

[1] The choice of this particular man as a prophet in itself runs counter to practically every human presupposition. The title 'son of man' by which he is addressed is one frequently employed in this book. But it is found nowhere else in the Old Testament except Dan. 8.17, which is derived from the present passage. Now that title already expresses, in the same words and manner as Ps. 8.5, the weakness of the creature to whom the mighty Lord shows such condescension. When the man addressed by such a title is bidden to stand up and come before his Lord, to receive his Lord's commands, [2] it must be made possible for him to do so through the power of the Spirit. The Spirit, the breath of divine life, will penetrate his feeble body, in the same way as it gives new life to all created things, or returns to bestow new life upon that which its departure has menaced with death (Ps. 104.29f.; Job 34.14; Judg. 15.19; I Sam. 30.12). God must therefore at every step continue to aid and support by his gifts the man upon whom he has imposed such a task.

[3] No secret is made of the burdensome nature of the task; this message to the house of Israel is like one from an exiled king to his rebellious subjects. [5] The honourable title of 'house of Israel', which Judah had so proudly monopolized after the fall of the Northern kingdom, must now, with bitter mockery, be changed to 'house of

rebelliousness'. All illusory hopes of acting successfully must be given up. [6] The messenger of God must be prepared to encounter hostility, contempt, and actual bodily injury, all painful as the sting of a scorpion. [7] He is not to make any room in his heart for the fears only too natural to man, but to concentrate his whole attention on being a faithful messenger who duly delivers the message entrusted to him. He is not to feel any anxiety about success. [5] His commissioner guarantees this one thing, and it alone: that no resistance will be able to prevent the emergence of a recognition that a prophet has arisen among the exiles, i.e. that the veritable Lord of this people is causing his royal right to rule to be proclaimed aloud in the very place where everyone thought it had died out and been abolished. However resistance may flame up, nothing will be able to silence that word. It will prove itself stronger than all who resist it.

Commissioning for service: 2.8–3.3

The difficulty of the task is brought out in the particular way in which the messenger is commissioned for service. [8–10] His commission is expressed by an unusual, and almost grotesque, transaction; he is to consume, as though it were food, a scroll announcing the approach of grave disasters, inscribed not on the usual one side, but on both sides. The exact significance of this curious procedure will be misunderstood if we fail to pay enough attention to its precise context in the tradition and see it as expressing the way in which revelation takes place through Ezekiel, in other words, as a theory of prophetic inspiration. For such a view, the word revealed to the prophet is already extant as a ready-made whole, fixed in a written form; it is thus thought of as a sort of 'objective material', already existing beforehand, the assimilation of which was only a passive, mechanical sort of process. What is involved here is rather, on the one hand, a proof of the obedience of the person who has been chosen and, on the other hand, an assurance that the message with which he is entrusted is independent of his own subjective judgments, and is divine in origin. That he sees this under the form of a written scroll has no connection with Deuteronomy or with the 'book-religion' alleged to have arisen out of it. It points to the preaching of the prophets, already at that time frequently recorded in writing, the most influential example of which is the collected words of Jeremiah dictated to Baruch. That writing, which had appeared ten years before and had attracted great attention, was without doubt known to and revered by Ezekiel as a record of divinely authorized prophetic speech. Most of its contents consisted of severe threats of God's judgment. For the delivery of a scroll to be a symbol to him of the way in which he could be sure that he had been entrusted with God's strange message to his people, quite independent of any feelings or personal opinions of his own, is an idea that is perfectly intelligible in its own context, and has nothing to do with any theories of inspiration.

This becomes still more evident when we recall the spiritual conditions of that age. The attraction of the satellite states towards the syncretistic world-culture sponsored by Assyria to a large extent dissolved the traditional bonds of local independence, and threw the individual back on his own resources. His critical attitude towards all traditional influences made him also resistant to the objective authority of the prophetic word, and undermined all self-assurance on the part of God's ambassador by asserting that his enthusiasm had its source in his own inward feelings. Ezekiel's predecessors ever since the time of Isaiah had been troubled by efforts to find a divine legitimation for their words, and this, further intensified by the rise of nationalistic prophecy, had reached a climax in Jeremiah. Distrust, not only of his rivals but also of his own heart and its deceptions, had become a torturing accompaniment to the experience of being a prophet, and threatened to destroy all prophetic self-assurance. The more consciously a prophet felt his responsibility, the more he needed a conviction, stronger than that of his predecessors, of the objectivity of the word with which he had been entrusted as something other than, and distinct from, his own inward feelings. Jeremiah was therefore assured that the word of God was being imparted to him by God's hand touching his lips, while Ezekiel received a similar assurance through the delivery of a written scroll, containing words already inscribed there without his knowledge. This obviously has no connection with any past pre-existence of the prophetic word, or any future power of drawing upon an inexhaustible supply of divine words. So Ezekiel, like Jeremiah, must have gone on all through his life depending on the ever-renewed inspiration supplied by his God. [3.2] That alone, of course, does not explain why Ezekiel eats the scroll. [3a] Still less does it explain the highly realistic terms which the prophet, evidently intentionally, employs, as he speaks of having to take this unusual food into his mouth, to eat it and to fill his body and stomach with it. A symbolic interpretation of the phenomenon will, of course, at once suggest itself: that Ezekiel is to be fully united with the word committed to him, that it is, as it were, to enter into his very flesh and blood. But if that is all, then the way of expressing it is too extreme and too contradictory of all bodily experience. Two other things ought really to be taken into account. First of all, there is the great importance of compulsive experiences, which plays so large a part in Ezekiel's life, in such a way as to invade the physical sphere; he, more intensively than any other prophet, finds his experience as a prophet claiming and controlling his body. This has led to an opinion, not of course susceptible of conclusive proof, that he must have been delicate in physique, or even an invalid, as a result of cataleptic fits. Even were it possible to prove that this was the fact, it would not give us any generic understanding of the nature of his prophetic consciousness, as the illness must be regarded as the result, not the cause, of his soul-shaking experience.

From another aspect, unusual sensations of eating and drinking appear to be typical of certain types of trance, as is shown by descriptions from Arabia and Jewish mystics.[1] The ecstatic experience of eating a book-scroll is therefore far from being an isolated occurrence in the ancient world; such things are referred to in Egyptian accounts. [1] But even though such analogies may serve to illustrate it, the precise significance of this particular piece of visionary experience to Ezekiel himself will not become intelligible to us until we become aware of the point of view from which the whole matter is presented. The complete renunciation of the attitude of his community on the part of the man who has been called by God must be expressed by a decisive act, closely associated with his task; their rebelliousness is to be offset by his unqualified obedience, and what the entire people should achieve is to be realized in the one son of man who is their representative. Complete adoption of, and incorporation into, the alien divine will is to become a law of life for the whole man, even to the extent of his overcoming even the natural reluctance of his physical body. No other prophet ever expressed with such strength and consistency as did Ezekiel the manner in which, in actual event, even his corporeality is over mastered by the all-embracing claim of God. He is to go forth and speak to the house of Israel in this particular way, and there is no other way in which he could do it.

[1] Cf. G. Widengren, *Literary and Psychological Aspects of the Hebrew Prophets*, 1948, pp. 100ff.; T. Andrae, *Die Person Mohammeds in Lehre und Glauben seiner Gemeinde*, 1918, pp. 376ff.

[3b] In the final feature of the visionary occurrence, we also find a bodily experience corresponding to a spiritual phenomenon; the inner liberation bestowed by the carrying out of obedient action is mirrored in the sweet taste of the strange food. To see a hint here of the sweetness of the divine word in general would be allegorical distortion of the powerful symbolism of this experience, of which there is no indication in the occurrence. It is much more probable that it points to our experience that even strange and apparently unintelligible demands on the part of God, when they are once fulfilled by us, bestow an inward satisfaction which takes away all their bitterness.

Equipping and sending: 3.4–15

[4] The test of obedience once passed, the call may become a sending. But the order to depart introduces a new element which is significant for the activity that is now to begin. The deepest roots of the resistance which Israel is likely to put up must be recognized, if prophetic preaching is to be kept from taking the wrong road. **[5]** If men refuse to give the prophet a hearing, it will not be because they find it difficult to understand what he is saying. So it is not his chief concern to adapt his message to the understanding of his audience; such a process might only too easily lead to his softening down and misstating its offensive content. **[7]** The rejection of his words has a deeper basis: it is the result of alienation from the God who sends him. '[They] will not listen to you, for they are not willing to listen to me.'

[6] The external conditions necessary towards establishing contact with his audience were already granted, since he and they spoke the same language. We cannot miss the allusion to Isa. 28.11. There Isaiah's opponents mock at his speech as unintelligible muttering, and so Isaiah threatens them with a message from God, in an unintelligible foreign language, that of their Assyrian conquerors, about the meaning of which there can be no possible doubt. Ezekiel may also have the impression that he is speaking a different language to his hearers. But that has so little to do with their resistance that the remark is ventured that he would find a hearing, even were he sent to peoples speaking foreign languages. Isaiah's thought is therefore reversed, by being applied in such a way as to demonstrate how in itself the prophet's message is intelligible even to heathen speaking a foreign language. This expresses the hardest possible judgment upon the stubbornness of Israel, who, while enjoying all the best possible conditions, far exceeds the heathen in her inability to understand. No external compromise is possible with the rock-hard imperviousness of heart and spirit shown by such a people; the inevitable result must be a head-on collision. **[8f.]** God's messenger need have no fear of that; he will be given a hardness like that of a diamond, so as to meet the closed hearts with ruthless unbreakable strength. **[10]** Only one thing matters, that he should always accept the word of God as it comes to him, with pure and utter openness.

It is important to compare this account of the special equipping of the messenger with the similar promise at the sending of Jeremiah (Jer. 1.17f.). We may conclude that the unqualified severity with which judgment was to be preached was no more self-evident to Ezekiel than it had been to Jeremiah, and that it corresponded neither with his natural inclinations nor with his original convictions. He, in striking contrast to Jeremiah and his loud laments, conceals his feelings beneath tough armour, in which he seldom lets a single chink appear. But one may see in that a symptom of a nature even more tender and sensitive than Jeremiah's, which even priestly self-discipline could repress only with great difficulty. For the same reason, as the burden grows heavier, this characteristic can sometimes change to a rigid insensitivity, or even into a real attempt to wound others with chilly mockery. Only those who miss the subtle touches in Ezekiel's narrative referring to this point can arrive at the unconvincing theory of his having been a grim insensitive character, who derived a pleasure bordering on sadism from destructive mockery of his opponents. To explain away his severity in delivering his message, a severity demanded and caused by God himself, as merely a previously existing characteristic of the man is a theory which cannot be reconciled with any serious evaluation of his witness about himself.

[12] God appears amid storm and tempest, and disappears in the roar of a thunderstorm. **[14]** Meanwhile the seer feels that, by the power of the divine spirit, his apparently paralysed body is being lifted up and rendered capable of a peculiar soaring movement. Here is another manifestation familiar to mystic experience, save that, in the case of Ezekiel, it is accompanied by sensations not of liberation but of overmastering compulsion. Once again Yahweh's hand falls heavily upon him, making him feel the power of a will superior to his own, in spite of all his inward resistance. Like one bemused, he must sit among his fellow exiles, and probably be regarded by them with suspicious curiosity as a man at whom God's finger has pointed. They do not realize that this mighty irruption into the life of their comrade will also cause a disturbance in their own, from which they will not be able to defend themselves.

[15] At this point we get the first reference to the prophet's dwelling-place. Tel Abīb is not to be translated according to Hebrew as 'hill of ears' (of corn). It is to be connected with *til abūbi*, which often occurs in Accadian, meaning 'the hill of the rain flood', or 'deluge', and frequently applied to a heap of ruins. The Jewish exiles among whom Ezekiel was living had settled upon such a hill of debris, probably in light huts which they had themselves constructed.

A glance back over the whole narrative of the call of Ezekiel will bring out its internal unity and compactness. To explain away the account of the vision as a later expansion of the account of his call made by the prophet himself (Herrmann), or to reject it as an addition by another hand (Hölscher, Herntrich), provides no real solution to the enigma of the picture of the vision, full though it may admittedly be of textual distortions, and encrusted though it may be with later additions. It may be impossible to tell exactly how far the picture has been overpainted and touched up, but after all the unavoidable critical operations have been applied, it still remains clear and recognizable in all its main outlines, and can, without the least friction, be fitted in with the prophetic tradition in general and with the attitude of Ezekiel in particular. To cut it off from the account of the call proper in ch. 1 and 2, as an 'information-vision' not in need of any completion from elsewhere,[1] does not accord with its clear connections with Isa. 6 and I Kings 22.19ff.; such a theory appeals too much to secondary features, and relies on an exaggerated estimate of the importance of the parallel account in ch. 10. To appeal to Jer. 1 in order to justify the view that the vision of God is an element extraneous to the commissioning[2] overstresses Ezekiel's dependence on Jeremiah, instead of appreciating how the differences in their accounts of the commissioning are due to differences in the mentality of the two prophets. The most obvious solution is that the vision of God in Ezek. 1 finds its culmination in the call of the prophet in ch. 2 and 3.

It will be found that these statements are confirmed at every point

---

[1] E. Baumann, 'Die Hauptvisionen Hesekiels', *ZAW* 67 (1955), pp. 56ff.

[2] *Ibid.*, p. 62; C. Kuhl, 'Zum Stand der Hesekiel-Forschung', *ThR* NF24 (1956/7), p. 21.

by the account of the calling. Some assert that the text is overloaded with intolerable accretions, and try in some way or other to play 3.4–9 off against 2.4–7. They do so partly through failure to notice glossatory elaborations and redactional transpositions, and partly as a result of inaccurate exegesis, which fails to do justice to the actual aim of the narrator. Some attempt to simplify the present text by reducing it to parallel recensions (e.g. Bertholet, 1936 ed.). Others pick out one or the other portion as solely original, either 3.4–9 (May, Baumann) or 2.8b–10; 3.2 (Hölscher). Or again the text is divided into two separate accounts of a call, one in Jerusalem (2.8ff.) and one in Babylonia (3.10–15). All these hypotheses alike fail to provide a convincing solution to the textual problem. They fail to work out any lucid principle accounting for the way in which the text has been dealt with. All cancel each other out by their mutual contradictions.

A deeper motive underlies all these merely formal objections. It is the prejudice against a call during exile, producing a prophet without a people, which seems a contradiction in terms. Large portions of Ezekiel's preaching are aimed at Jerusalem and its inhabitants, which excites still stronger doubts. However, this prejudice does not afford sufficient grounds for the theory of a double activity on Ezekiel's part in both Jerusalem and Babylon. This thesis, ever since Herntrich's influential adoption of it (*Ezechielprobleme*, 1932), has received the approval of a whole host of critics, and the facts are correctly stated. But they must be accounted for in some other way than by transferring Ezekiel's first public appearance to Judah. We are struck by the way his early preaching ignores the troubles of exile and aims at Jerusalem. But there is a more probable explanation of why this happens. Any theological argument between Ezekiel and the exiles must have its focus in the fate of the mother-city. There, as always, lies the centre of their life, which still receives its orientation from what happens in and around Jerusalem. The continued existence of city and temple is a fact to be taken into consideration in assessing the situation even in Babylonia. The Jews there had by no means ceased to be interested in the homeland. They had tidings of every major event through the messengers who passed to and fro. They even tried from abroad to influence what was decided at home, as the book of Jeremiah clearly shows (cf. Jer. 29.25ff.). So it is not surprising to see that the fate of Jerusalem has a tremendous influence on the words and deeds of the prophet of the exile. He quite agrees with his contemporaries that it is there that the fate of the people is being decided. Yet he expresses this conviction still more profoundly by his suggestion that God is personally encountering them and dealing with them in what is happening there, and that God has not let exile sever the links uniting them with his people, but makes them bear their share, as responsible members of the body, in the judgment upon the holy city. Exiles and residents in the homeland are alike addressed as the 'house of Israel', and as such are regarded as a 'rebellious house', i.e. they possess the same spiritual nature as the rest of the people, past and present. The division of the people does not destroy the unity of Israelite history. Still less does the fact that it is now uttered in Babylonia cast any doubt on the unity of the word of God, addressed to the people as a whole. That word must be for the whole people, and must reach the great goal towards which God intends it to go, as is expressed all through the book in the impressive monotony of the phrase: 'That they may know that I am Yahweh.' Nevertheless, as we study this prophetic book, we shall at various points have to consider the theory that Ezekiel worked in two different places.

Jewish rabbis and church fathers alike, when evaluating Ezekiel's account of his calling, one-sidedly stress the fascinating picture given in the throne vision, and regard it as a treasury of deep insights into the hidden mysteries of the divine being. Within Judaism there was an attempt by that means to reach conclusions about the nature of God and the world of heavenly spirits. It resulted in such questionable speculations that it led in the Mishnah to the exclusion of the first chapter of Ezekiel from the synagogue lectionary. Within the Christian Church, it was thought that the appearance of an anthropomorphic figure on the cherubic throne contained revelations of the pre-existence of Christ and the mysteries of the Trinity. So attempts were made to extract statements upon these subjects from the picture-language of the vision.

The Jewish rabbi Hananiah ben Hiskiah in the first century AD is said to have blocked the way to speculative estimates of the chapter. Calvin, too, while expressing all due respect for the authority of the church fathers, denied that there was any essential connection between the throne vision and the mystery of Christ or the dogma of the Trinity. He applied all the statements in the description of the vision to the power and wisdom with which God rules the world.[1]

[1] *'Hinc autem colligimus, ubi simplex fit Dei mentio, intellegi totam essentiam, quae*

This sober estimate of the amount of actual revelation contained in the vision, which has now come to be almost universally accepted,[1] does in fact correspond to the fundamental lines of the message of the Old Testament. It agrees especially with that of the prophets, who show us not God as he is in himself, in his mysterious transcendence, but God in his saving action towards mankind, and would have us recognize his nature solely from the revelation of his will.

We do none the less find here an indication of how a Christian may find satisfaction for his fully justified concern for a clearer insight into the relationship between the Old Testament salvation-history and God's imparting of himself in the 'fullness of time' (Gal. 4.4). Analogical solutions, which expound allegorically the pictorial representation and thus force out of it the desired conclusions, do not really bring out its meaning. The only way is to plunge deeply into the here and now of divine revelation, and to focus one's attention on the transparency of the Old Testament saving event, in which we see its tendency towards fulfilment in the New Testament. So in Ezek. 1 we must make it our sole object to apprehend the encounter with God in which that prophet was involved, in its once for all meaning at that particular historical moment; and in this way to be aware of its position and function in the vast context, both historical and political, which links together the Old and New Testaments.

In many details, as well as in the underlying meaning which gave all its effectiveness to his work, the task imposed on Ezekiel recalls that of his great prophetic predecessors. Suddenly to be uprooted from his former life, and confronted by a terrifying new reality; to look forward to a life full of struggle and fruitless effort, yet nevertheless embraced by the gift of an unheard-of certainty; to have been given a glimpse into the plans of the world-God, and to have been accredited as his ambassador and herald; all that is as characteristic of Ezekiel's hour of call as it was of either Isaiah's or of Jeremiah's. Yet one cannot fail to see the further feature peculiarly characteristic

---

communis est filio et spiritui sancto cum patre. Nam sub nomine Jehovah absurdum est intelligere solum Christum.' 'From this therefore we conclude, that when God only is mentioned, we are to understand the whole divine essence, common to the Son and Holy Ghost with the Father. For it is absurd to understand only Christ as meant by the name Jehovah' (*Corpus Reformatorum*, vol. 68, col. 55).

[1] E. Henne in 'Die hl. Schrift des Alten und Neuen Testaments', *Ezechiel*, 1936, still expounds it as referring to the incarnation of Christ; R. Brunner, *Ezekiel* 1, 1944, p. 24, still remains undecided.

of Ezekiel's experience. It is not just the historical situation of the exile, where the reality and nearness of God as he emerges from his hiddenness achieves a quite epoch-making significance for the total understanding of God's work in Israel (cf. above, p. 62). Rather it is the new experience of how the divine Lord claims man, in which the paradox of God and man walking together is accentuated to almost intolerable intensity. There is nothing to relieve the stark contrast between the other-worldly glory of the divine world and the weakness and transience of humanity. The blazing perfection and purity of the Lord of the universe impinges upon a miserable lump of human flesh. The current of divine power lifts him up out of the dust, enabling him to hear and take in the message addressed to him. This particular man, who is always addressed as 'son of man', meaning born of dust, reveals, at the very moment when he is entrusted with the divine word, what an inadequate vessel human nature is for the divine treasure which it has to hold. God's object is to effect a complete union between the man he has called and his will made known to him by the word. Ezekiel, by obediently swallowing the written scroll presented to him, expresses his desire to do nothing else but communicate the word, now made a part of his own being. So, when he records what he has preached, we later on see him use, with a hitherto unprecedented regularity, 'and the word of Yahweh came to me' as the formula expressing reception of the word, and 'and the hand of Yahweh was upon me' as the formula expressing the experience of a vision. His object is to characterize the content of his preaching as the effect of an event within time and history, in which God's word met him and took him into its service.[1] Thus, with remorseless consistency, he guards against all self-willed desires or thoughts, and renounces every temptation to treat divine truth as if he could himself manipulate it, making it his aim to be the mere instrument of one higher than himself, and to remember with each fresh proclamation of his message[2] that it has its source in God himself.

This unification of the word with the person of its bearer may well

[1] Zimmerli would therefore like to term this introduction to prophetic sayings a 'word-event formula'. It occurs fifty times in Ezekiel. This, even though it may in some case be due to redactors, must be regarded as characteristic of Ezekiel, in comparison with only ten instances in Jeremiah.

[2] Cf. the thorough description and evaluation of this phenomenon in K. von Rabenau, 'Die Entstehung des Buches Ezekiel in formgeschichtlicher Sicht' (Wiss. Ztschr. der Mart. Luther-Univ. Halle-Wittenberg, Gesellschafts-u. sprachwiss. Reihe, Jg. V,H.4), 1956, pp. 659ff.

remind us of the one in whom the same mysterious process lifted all human life up on to a higher plane and made it the centre of the whole revelation of God, so that the Christian Church, taking up the words of John 1, called him the Logos, or Word of God in the full sense. For God's freely sent Word to enter into the limited earthly reality of a single human life and to do away with the independence of that life in favour of its sole control is a bliss-giving and terrifying mystery of which, evidently, Ezekiel had deep experience. Yet he never thought of it as implying any deification of man. Rather, the Word thus imparted, even after choosing an earthly carrier, at the same time remains a completely other-worldly word. Here, once more, we find the exact opposite of the incarnation of the Word. In the incarnation of the Word, of which the New Testament speaks, the most important thing is the historical person with his words and deeds. But here that is least important, and is a mere instrument without any will of its own, through which the call from above makes its voice heard upon earth.

It is still more impressive to see how near and yet how far Ezekiel appears to be to the one through whom God has spoken 'in these last days' (Heb. 1.2), as his self-surrender to God starts him on a way of suffering, the beginnings of which we have already glimpsed in the history of his commissioning. From the very start, the prophet finds that to serve this Word is to enter upon a path of shame and pain. What is already hinted at in Jeremiah, provoking, as his confessions reveal, a violent counter-attack from the human feeling that he has a right to a life of his own, becomes an agonizing reality to Ezekiel as he first encounters his new task. The weak human vessel always threatens to burst asunder under the pressure of the divine fullness that has come to dwell within it. He can only break down before the glory of heavenly power, as it forces its way into him. This follows the test of obedience imposed upon his resisting body and the paralysis by the hand of Yahweh, breaking down his inward resistance, and leaving him incapable of doing anything for days so that he brooded in helplessness and impotence among his fellow exiles. During the period which follows, too, mental and physical pain continue to haunt him. As a result, the diagnosis of a severe illness attempted by some scholars must inevitably be attractive to those who do not note the agonizing mental breakdown which occurs at this point in Ezekiel's life.[1] We may get a better insight into the matter if we note

[1] For the question of an illness suffered by the prophet, most likely schizo-

that the prophet's disciples regarded his suffering as so characteristic a feature of his whole call that they felt they ought to emphasize it and place it at the beginning of his prophetic autobiography (3.24ff., cf. below, p. 76). They have thus interpreted correctly the omission of the prophet's own name, and his being addressed as *ben adam*, son of man. It means that he, as a weak human being, must always share all the human sufferings of his time, and that he is under an obligation to be one with his fellows and to share in the troubles destined for them. At the same time, he imparts an exemplary significance and a representative character to this suffering of his, through his call to prophesy to a people who have frittered away their birthright as the elect, and have been thrown into a state of alienation from God (cf. below, on 4.4–8, pp. 83ff.; on 11.13, pp. 138ff.; on 12.17–20, pp. 153f., and also 24.15ff., pp. 341ff.). This son of man is stripped by God of all the pretensions of his birth and position. He has to descend into the depths of humiliation in order that, by his work of mediation, a new work of salvation may begin and a new people of God come into being. He thus comes remarkably near to the servant of God in Isa. 53, and can only be understood fully within his own historical context and significance, when the line on which he stands is extended towards the Son of Man in the New Testament. That title, the exalted name of the eschatological saviour, may seem to contrast him sharply with the son of man of this book. Yet the name 'son of man' as employed by Jesus does of necessity include the idea of humiliation,[1] as is already implied by the word throughout the Old Testament, and particularly in Ezekiel. In that this son of man shares in the weakness of humanity in a representative way, he is bringing to fulfilment something already sketched in outline in the special sufferings of the prophet. Jeremiah's relationship to Jesus is much more generally recognized, both because of popular expectation (Matt. 16.14) and because of the way in which his prophecy is worked into the last testament of the Servant of God at the moment when he determines to follow the road leading to his death (Luke 22.20). But we must recognize, in Ezekiel no less than in Jeremiah, a living inward connection with the greatest

phrenia, cf. the excellent study by Hans Heimann, *Prophetie und Geisteskrankheit*, Berner Universitätsschriften, vol. 11, 1956.

[1] Cf. O. Cullmann, *The Christology of the New Testament*, 1963, pp. 160ff.

of all prophets, or, with the words of Calvin, a *praeludium eius mysterii*.[1]

CHAPTER 3.16–27

The office of watchman and the prophecy of dumbness

16 And at the end of seven days, the word of Yahweh came to me: [17]'Son of man, I make you a watchman for the house of Israel. Whenever you receive a word from my mouth, you shall give them warning from me. [18]If I say to the wicked, "You shall surely die", and you give him no warning[. . .][a] in order to save his life, then [that] godless man[b] must die for his iniquity, but his blood I will require of you. [19]But if you have warned the godless, and he does not turn from his wicked way, then [that godless man][c] must die for his iniquity, but you have saved your life. [20]And if a righteous man turns from his righteousness and commits iniquity [. . .],[d] and you do not warn him, then he must die for his sin, [. . .][e] but his blood I will require of you. [21]Nevertheless if you have warned the righteous man not to sin [. . .][f] and he has not sinned, then he shall surely live, and you will have saved your life.'

22 And the hand of Yahweh came [. . .][g] upon me, and he said to me: 'Arise, go out into the plain, and there I will speak with you.' [23]And I stood up and went out into the plain. And, lo, the glory of Yahweh stood there, like the glory which I had seen by the river Chebar, and I fell on my face. [24]And Spirit entered into me and put me upon my feet. Then he spoke with me and said, 'Go home, shut yourself within your house. [25]And you, O son of man, cords will be placed upon you, and you shall be bound with them, so that you cannot go out among the people. [26]And I will make your tongue cleave to the roof of your mouth, so that you shall be dumb and unable to reprove them; for they are a rebellious house. [27]But when I speak with you, I will open your mouth, so that you may say to them, "Thus says Yahweh!" He that will hear, let him hear, and he that will refuse, let him refuse; for they are a rebellious house.'

---

[a]'And do not speak, to warn the wicked from his wicked way'; an elaborating gloss.

[b]–[c]Thus with LXX.

[d]'And I lay a stumbling block in his way, so that he must die'; an addition giving a theological explanation.

[1] Calvin's words in reference to the throne vision in Ezek. 1 in his *Commentary on Ezekiel* (*Corpus Reformatorum*, vol. 68, col. 53).

e'And his righteous deeds, which he has done, shall not be remembered'; an additional expansion.

fMT: 'the righteous'; explanatory gloss.

gMT: 'there'; delete with LXX.

The present section is one of the most difficult in the book of Ezekiel, in spite of the good condition of the text. Verses 16–21 bring up the problem of their relationship to 33.7–9, which is verbally identical with vv. 16–19. But then vv. 22–26 make it very hard to understand not only what precedes, but what follows, without making bold hypotheses. With regard to the first of these problems, it may be remarked that the assumption that the prophet was for a second time solemnly invested with the office of a watchman after the fall of Jerusalem obviously fails to provide an adequate explanation. One would, in this case, expect some reference to the first time this had occurred. Also, the wording of 33.1ff. seems to announce this new duty for the first time, and suggests that it is the original passage from which the other was copied. This latter adds nothing, except for a casuistical piece of special pleading in 3.20f. in the case of the righteous man who falls away. A further consideration is that such activities, aimed entirely at individuals, while not altogether impossible at the beginning of the prophet's career, become more probable after all the hopes of the exiles had collapsed than during their period of proud inaccessibility. We see here a new conception of his office, distinguishing Ezekiel from other prophets. It is easier to assume that the passage from ch. 33 was quoted here at the beginning of his work than that the reverse process has taken place. It therefore seems better to understand the section 3.16–21 (with the exception of v. 16a, the content of which is connected with Ezekiel's first appearance) as the product of the final redaction of the prophetic book. For a full consideration of its content, see below the commentary on ch. 33, pp. 441ff.

It is far more difficult to explain the circumstances of vv. 22–27. It is plain that this section, too, did not form part of the original text.[1]

We are forced to this conclusion by the hopeless contradiction between the statement in v. 26 that Ezekiel was struck dumb at the commencement of his career, and God's command that he is not to be held back from carrying out his commission in full (2.4ff. and

[1] According to K. von Rabenau, *op. cit.*, p. 664, it appears to be a fragment; all attempts so far made to reconstruct a meaningful context have been unsuccessful.

3.4ff.). For v. 27, in which the prophet's dumbness is explained as merely involving longer or shorter periods of silence, broken from time to time when Yahweh specially intervenes with one of his commands to speak, can only be considered a laboured and not altogether convincing attempt to explain away the incongruity between these passages and v. 26. The latter describes the ending of the prophet's proclamation by word as a single definite event, called forth by the antipathy of his audience. If one tries to overcome the difficulty, by assuming that before being struck dumb, Ezekiel had been vigorously active, and thus encountered strong and finally physical opposition (v. 25), and that this again led to his being suspended as a prophet as a punitive measure on the part of Yahweh (as do the older commentators, e.g. C. von Orelli, Bertholet), then there will have to be considerable manipulation of the text, and in ways not to be justified by any critical canon. Besides, the description of the prophet's preaching in vv. 4–24 never suggests that his activity was hindered in any such way. On the other hand, we do meet, in 24.15ff. and 33.21f., with a symbolic period of dumbness imposed upon the prophet shortly before the fall of Jerusalem, the long duration of which is ended by the arrival of the news that the city of God has been taken. It is reasonable to conjecture that his disciples, who saw their teacher's work as an integral whole and tried to make it intelligible as a whole, regarded this silencing of the prophet in his preaching as a recurrent sign to the unbelieving people. Because it emphasized the decisive character of his message from the start, it was placed at the beginning of the book, like the call to be a watchman.

It has already been pointed out more than once, that vv. 24f. have a special connection with the symbolic action reported in 4.4–8, and a comparison with 4.8 makes this particularly clear. A study of that section (cf. below, pp. 83ff.) will show us that the parabolic action reported there is in such distinct contrast with its surroundings that it cannot have taken place during the prophet's early ministry. Its transposition to the present context must be secondary. Like 3.26, it was probably given its present position during the final redaction of the book and for similar reasons; i.e. the association of such a proceeding with the outset of the prophet's career amounts to a statement that his vocation from the beginning involved him in severe suffering. The symbolic action in 4.4–8 then illustrates this in expressive terms. It also fits in easily with the statement that the prophet was struck dumb, and thus helps to render more intelligible the anticipatory announcement in vv. 24f. To isolate one element, the prophet's locking up his own house (v. 24b), and to regard it as an extract from his own autobiography, speaking of a sort of seclusion inflicted upon him, but not preventing him from preaching (Zimmerli), seems a questionable procedure. The statement that he was shut up in his house does not refer so much to the place of his preaching as to his seclusion from the public.

These elements cannot be immediately connected either with the history of the commissioning or with ch. 4f. So the words introducing them take the shape of a particular prophecy by Yahweh to the prophet, and an occasion is found for them in a second appearance of the divine glory. As ch. 8–11 will show, the appearance of the *kābōd* has, for special reasons, also been employed in other secondary passages, for the purpose of combining later additions with the original text (cf. below, pp. 114f.). In 3.22f., the setting down of the divine throne in the flat part of the valley seems remarkably lifeless compared with the dynamic motion of ch. 1. It is linked to the earlier appearance by a brief reference, exactly as in 8.4; 10.15, 20, 22. There is also a word-for-word repetition from 1.28 and 2.2, recounting the effects felt by the prophet. All of these features suggest the literary character of this theophany. It gives assurance of the unity of the will of God even in the apparently contradictory forms under which the prophet makes his first appearance. The one original element in this revision of the prophet's as yet not fully stated task is the mention of a flat part of the valley, evidently some other place than that named in 1.1, but only vaguely described as part of the wide Babylonian plain, situated near the settlement of the exiles. *bik'a*, the word employed for it, occurs elsewhere only in 37.1. So Bertholet's suggestion that there is a connection between the two passages should not be rejected out of hand. The monumental representation in ch. 37 of the creative triumph of Yahweh over death is brought into a well-thought-out contrast with God's first commissioning of Ezekiel, which seemed to his disciples to be a way leading to death. Zimmerli may be right in regarding this complicated redactional process as no purely literary activity on the part of later writers, but as an attempt by the prophet's disciples to adapt their master's picture to the understanding of the community by accentuating or underlining certain features in his message. We see here a striking example of the way in which the prophetic word continued to work within the Jewish community, and how they did not regard it, any more than they did the law of Moses, as something untouchable, which had reached its final literary fixation; on the contrary, those of whom it had taken hold were called to play their part in bringing out its meaning.

CHAPTER 4.1–5.17

Symbolic actions and their meaning

1 'And you, son of man, take a brick and lay it before you, and portray upon it a city [. . .],ᵃ ²and construct a wall against it, and build a bulwark against it, and throw up an embankment against it, and construct camps against it, and plant battering rams against it round about. ³Then take an iron pan and make of it an iron wall between you and the city and set your face steadfastly towards it; so it shall be put in a state of siege, and you shall blockade it. It shall be a sign to the house of Israel.

4 *But you shall lie upon your left side, and I will lay the guilt of the house of Israel upon you. As many days as you lie upon it, you shall bear their guilt.* ⁵*And I assign to you a number of days, one hundred and ninety days,*ᵇ *equal to the years of their imprisonment in their guilt; so long shall you bear the guilt of the house of Israel.* ⁶*And when you have completed the days, lie down upon your right side* [. . .]ᶜ *and bear the guilt of the house of Judah for forty days; I assign you one day for each year.* ⁷*And you shall set your face steadfastly towards the siege of [the city]*ᵈ *with your arm bared, and you shall prophesy against it.* ⁸*And behold, I put cords upon you so that you cannot turn from one side to the other, until you have fulfilled the days of your affliction.*

9 And you, take wheat and barley, beans and lentils, millet and spelt, and put them into a single vessel, and make yourself bread of them [. . .].ᵉ ¹²And you shall eat it as a barley cake, and you shall bake it upon human dung in their sight.'ᶠ ¹⁴Then I said, 'Ah Lord Yahweh! Behold, I have never defiled myself, from my youth up until this day I have never eaten a beast that had died of itself or that was torn, and no sacrificial flesh that had become unclean has ever come into my mouth.' ¹⁵Then he said to me, 'See, I will let you have cow's dung instead of human dung, on which you may prepare your bread. ¹⁰And [you shall eat your food by weight]ᵍ twenty shekels a day; day by day shall you eat it. ¹¹And water also you shall drink by measure, a sixth part of a hin; from one day to another you shall drink it [. . .].ʰ

5 1 And you, son of man, take a sharp sword, use it as a barber's razor

and pass it over your head and your beard; then take a pair of scales and divide them: 2a third you shall burn to ashes in the midst of the city [. . .],[i] and [. . .][j] another third you shall strike with the sword round about it, and the other third you shall scatter to the wind and [unsheathe the sword after them].[k] 3Then take from there a small number and bind them in the skirts of your robe.[l] 4And of these again take some and cast them into the midst of the fire and burn them.

[Then say][m] to the whole house of Israel: 5Thus says [. . .][n] Yahweh: This is Jerusalem! I have set her among the nations, and [the][o] countries round about her. 6But she was rebellious against my ordinances in greater wickedness than the nations and against my statutes more than the countries around her; for they despised my ordinances and did not walk in my statutes. 7Therefore [. . .][p] thus says Yahweh: because you were more [rebellious][q] than the nations round about you, and have not walked in my statutes or kept my ordinances, and have not even done according to the ordinances of the nations round about you, 8therefore [. . .][r] assuredly I will now lay my hand upon you and will execute judgments in the midst of you in the sight of the nations; indeed I will do with you what I have never yet done, and the like of which I will never do, because of all your abominations. 10Therefore in the midst of you fathers shall eat their children and children shall eat their fathers [. . .],[s] and all of you who survive I will scatter to all the winds. 11Wherefore, as I live, says [. . .][t] Yahweh, surely, because you have defiled my sanctuary with all your detestable things and with all your abominations, therefore I will clip close, and will not look on you mercifully nor pity you. 12A third of you shall die of pestilence and be brought down by hunger in the midst of you, a third shall fall by the sword round about you, and a third will I scatter to all the winds and unsheathe the sword after them. 13[. . .][u] 14And I will make you [with your daughter cities][v] round about you a desolation in the sight of all that pass by. 15You shall be a reproach and a mockery, a warning and a horror to the nations round about you, when I execute judgment upon you [. . .][w] with my furious chastisements. I, Yahweh, have said it [. . .].'[x]

[a]MT: 'Jerusalem'; a gloss anticipating what will be explained later.

[b]Thus with LXX; MT: 390.

[c]MT: 'a second time'.

[d]MT: 'of Jerusalem': a correct, but premature explanation.

[e]MT: 'corresponding to the number of the days that you lie on your side, you shall eat of it for 390 days'; a gloss connecting it with what goes before. For vv. 10f., see after v. 15.

[f]Verse 13: 'And Yahweh said, "Thus shall the Israelites eat their bread unclean, among the nations whither I will drive them" '; an anticipatory interpretation which also refers the symbolic action to the exile.

ᵍMT: 'your food which you shall eat'.

ʰVerses 16, 17: 'And he said to me, "Son of man, behold, I break the staff of bread in Jerusalem, so that they shall eat bread only by weight and in fearfulness and drink water by measure and with dismay, so that they may lack bread and water and may be destroyed one like another and perish in their sins." ' Like v. 13, a prematurely inserted explanation of the symbolic action.

ⁱMT: 'when the days of the siege are at an end'; incorrect indications of time.

ʲMT: 'and you shall take'; elaborative gloss.

ᵏMT: 'and I will unsheathe', etc.; a mistaken transition to the interpretation of the symbolic action.

ˡSee BH.

ᵐThus with LXX, MT: 'Fire shall proceed from him'; a gloss occasioned by 19.14.

ⁿSee BH.

ᵒThe article to be inserted following LXX.

ᵖSee BH.

 qMT: 'because of your turbulence'; a scribal error.

ʳMT: 'Thus says the Lord Yahweh'; a wrong repetition from v. 7.

ˢMT: 'and I will execute judgment upon you'; a repetition from v. 8.

ᵗSee BH.

ᵘVerse 13: 'And my wrath shall consume and my rage shall satisfy itself upon them and give me vengeance, and they shall know that I Yahweh have spoken in my jealousy, when I satisfy my rage upon them.' The verse betrays itself as an insertion, perhaps a quotation from another speech, by the confusing transition from addressing Jerusalem to speaking about some unnamed majority, and also by its vague generalities in the midst of concrete detail.

ᵛThus following LXX. MT: 'for a reproach among the nations'; an error in transcription under the influence of the following verse.

ʷMT: 'in anger and fury', rightly omitted by LXX.

ˣVerses 16 and 17: 'Then I loose against you the deadly arrows of hunger, to destroy—I will shoot them, so as to destroy you—and also bring famine upon you, when I shall break the staff of bread and send forth hunger and wild beasts against you, so that they shall rob you of your children, and pestilence and murder will pass through you, and I will bring the sword upon you. I, Yahweh, have spoken it.' After the concluding formula of v. 15 no continuation is to be expected; there is also a change in person, the text is evidently much overloaded and its phraseology does not ring true. It seems to be an attempt to combine the four well-known plagues.

The introduction to the present section seems to have been omitted because of the previous insertions. So now there is nothing to serve as a transition between the manifestation of God in the flat part of the valley and the acts performed by the prophet in the community of the exiles. If the indication of time in 3.16a is to be regarded as having originally belonged to ch. 4 (cf. above, p. 75), then Ezekiel, after the seven days of inactive waiting in the community of the exiles at Tel Abīb, was called upon by his God to commence his activity by performing a number of symbolic actions, so as to give a sign to the people of Israel (v. 3).

Such actions had also been used by earlier prophets as a means of expressing their message.[1] We are inclined to regard such actions as mere ornaments to a prophetic discourse, which do no more than illustrate and drive home its meaning. So we feel some surprise to see Ezekiel begin his work with them. But in actual fact a symbolic action on the part of a prophet is more than a mere accompaniment to his discourse. It is an independent means of preaching, which can on occasion take the place of the word, and its presence first makes possible the effective delivery of the message.

The basis for that consists in the close connection between word and action in Hebrew thought. The word *dābār* means not only 'word' but also 'deed'. 'The word is the highest and noblest function of Man and is, for that reason, identical with his action.'[2] Seeing that word and deed form a unity, a prophetic action is not just an appendage, but a powerful means of proclamation of God's will.

This assignment of a high value to the prophetic act is made still more intelligible by a consideration of the connection between the symbolic action and the magic rite. It can be conclusively proved that there is a remarkable resemblance to a magical act, not only in the construction, nature and method of the symbolic action but also in the belief that it will prove effective once it is accomplished. Indeed, it is quite possible to regard it as a mere survival in Israelite faith of the old magical way of looking at things. The strongly compulsive character taken on at times by symbolic action also recalls the psychical compulsion so often felt in the sphere of witchcraft.

That may indeed help us to realize why there is so general a belief in the peculiarly effective power of human actions. But it is equally clear that we must not affix the label magical to the prophetic act. The close relationship between the prophet's activity and the divine Lord of the people lifts this whole complex of ideas on to a higher plane. This is because the compelling power of the symbolic action is not based upon its mechanical performance. The reason for carrying it out is that Yahweh has so commanded, and it is from him that it receives its meaning. It is Yahweh's consent which confers

---

[1] In regard to what follows, cf. the excellent treatise by G. Fohrer, *Die symbolischen Handlungen der Propheten*, 1953.

[2] T. Boman, *Hebrew Thought compared with Greek*, 1960, p. 65.

authority, which supplies the basis for faith in the irresistible effective might of the prophetic action. That makes it now an effectual symbol of what God purposes to do in the future, and so the revelation of the hidden will of God is both the foundation on which it stands and the objective at which it aims.

That makes it impossible to explain it as an unconscious compulsive act performed by the prophet when in a state of ecstasy, for which his subsequent reflections provided an interpretation; nor can it be reduced to a mere illustration of his thoughts chosen by the prophet himself. Even though the drive to perform the symbolic act entered directly into the prophet's consciousness and exercised its compelling power to overcome his resistance, so that he carried it out under psychic compulsion, it was nevertheless deliberately performed in order to serve as a proclamation of the mighty will of God. That is why there is no reflection on the scandalous or even damaging character of the symbol, and why there is no thought of the rebuke it may attract. We may come to welcome what is striking or even repulsive in an action, when we see it as a means of arousing or disturbing the indifferent. Or one may seek a deeper explanation, and say that it is directly related to the enigmatic way in which God acts, incomprehensible to the traditional conception of God. Knowing that he is called to proclaim just that, strange and obscure reality, the prophet, faced with human guilt and hardness of heart, is forced to grasp at such apparently alien auxiliary means and expedients.

The prophet's symbolic action, therefore, strikingly expresses the wonderful nature of his God, and goes far beyond being merely a visible illustration of the message he gives with his lips. It is itself an integral part of his preaching. As the anticipatory representation and actualization of a real event, it guarantees, establishes, or serves to indicate the fact that God acts. It involves the spectator and makes him become an actor, and thus directly confronts him with the God of whom he is the instrument.

Enactment of a siege: 4.1–3

Ezekiel's first action is striking because it is so unusual. The prophet enacts a siege, scratching a sketch-plan of a city on a brick of soft sunbaked clay. This was the usual building material in Babylonia. So he is employing a material always available in Mesopotamia, but not in Palestine. He is also adopting the Babylonian practice of representing a thing by a drawing. [2] Round about it he builds (whether by drawing, or by arranging miniature models is not stated) a circumvallation, a fort and a bank running straight up to the city wall, such as was used for an assault on the walls; he also puts in position the battering-rams for breaching the wall.

[3] But that is not enough. The prophet's demeanour must be such as to show that the siege which he is portraying is no mere passing danger for the city, but has behind it a will determined to make an end of it. Turning his face steadfastly towards the city is evidently a gesture representing the attitude taken up by his divine Lord. The implacable, impassioned way in which he pursues his goal is brought out by the placing of an iron plate between the prophet and his model. There is no chance of influencing that will.

It must have at once been obvious to the spectators that Ezekiel was engaging in something more than a childish game. Nor can there have been any doubt about just what he meant. The only possible question was: to what city were they to apply the things represented? There is nothing to say that it must be Jerusalem rather than any other place. Had not Nahum proclaimed the destruction of Nineveh in words of flame? Might not this young priest perhaps be trying to anticipate the deepest wishes of the exiles, by representing in effectual actions the fate of the proud world-city, which was laying its heavy yoke upon the nations? With what fascination they must have followed the actions performed by their companion in misfortune, as one new symbol succeeded another.

Bonds: 4.4–8

This symbolic action beyond all others has contributed to the opinion that many, indeed most, descriptions of these prophetic actions are not to be taken literally but to be regarded as a poetical way of expressing their message in parabolic or pictorial form. It has been thought incredible that Ezekiel lay absolutely still for one hundred and ninety days in order to give a sign. Were this so, would not one be compelled to pronounce him a sick man and to accept the diagnosis of catalepsy arrived at by many critics? But it is difficult to justify such suspicions. Appeals to physical impossibility are not justified by what we know of the powers of Indian Yogis and fakirs to enter into a sustained trance. It is hardly necessary to adopt the expedient of taking these as symptoms of catalepsy. We would have to attribute the onset of such symptoms to the disturbance suffered by Ezekiel's physical constitution, as conditioned by his visionary experience. Such assertions do not cast any doubt on his prophetic character, but are rather suspicious because of the rarity of such paralytic seizures in his case. The unusualness of this and similar symbolic actions does not, however, supply grounds for doubting their actual occurrence; to suggest this is to apply a false measure to prophetic methods of acting.

[4] It is easier to demonstrate that the prophet was in fact bound than to prove clearly what it meant. Some claim that the guilt which the prophet was told to bear was that of the years of Israel's (= Judah's) sin, which the prophet was to represent by a similar number of days. Others think of years of punishment for sin, the bitter sufferings of which are symbolized by the complete paralysis of the prophet. In the former case one can take the bonds as applying to the days of the siege and see in them a symbol of the complete encirclement and immobilization or 'paralysing' of the besieged. But it is impossible to supply convincing proof that the days of the siege corresponded with the years of guilt, which leaves it a quite arbitrary assumption. It is no less impossible to apply it to the forty years of Judah's guilt, as that number would be much too low. As a result of this interpretation we would, to be consistent, have to delete v. 6 (Herrmann), without any convincing reason to give for the later insertion of the verse. The fact that this symbolic action would represent a past event instead of a future one, as elsewhere, also tells against this interpretation. It is much more probable that we ought to think of the years of guilt as standing for liability, and that we should see in the binding of the prophet a symbol of punishment which in that case can only be interpreted as consisting in the imprisonment of the exile. The number of years this punishment is said to have lasted need not, of course, be taken as chronologically exact.

[5] True, one can assume the forty years of Judah's punishment to be included in the one hundred and ninety years of Israel's punishment, so that both sentences run concurrently and terminate on the same date. One may then reckon backward the remaining one hundred and fifty years of Israel from 586, the year of the destruction of Jerusalem, and thus come to 736, only two years before 734, the ill-fated year of Israel's first exile at the hands of Tiglathpileser III, which also saw the tearing away of the Israelite provinces of Galilee and Transjordania. But the fact that the State of Israel did not really come to an end till the fall of Samaria twelve years later leaves this calcula-

tion a doubtful one. **[6]** The forty years for Judah stand for one generation and are evidently to be regarded as a round number; this makes it likely that we should assume the same of the one hundred and fifty years for Israel. The three hundred and ninety years of the Hebrew text may be derived from a later calculation, seeing that they and Judah's forty years add up to four hundred and thirty, the exact figure given in Ex. 12.40 for Israel's stay in Egypt, with which the new period of servitude is meant to correspond.

If the prophet is a type of Yahweh in his first action, he evidently represents Israel in the second. The guilt of his people oppresses him and casts him down to the ground, like a heavy burden. **[8]** This makes him feel as if Yahweh himself was binding him with cords, i.e. taking away all his power to break out of his painful state of immobility. Plunged in a period of suffering lasting over seven months, he experiences to the full in his own body the inflictions of the punishment which breaks in unremittingly over his unrepentant nation, whom he represents in the same way as a sacrificial animal (Lev. 10.17; 16.22). Death on a huge scale is to come. It sets its mark on his whole existence, making him confront his contemporaries as a soul-stirring wordless sermon on the severity of the divine judgment awaiting them (cf. 9.8; 11.13; 12.17ff.; 24.16ff.).

A final difficulty in exposition is how to make this sign action fit in with the surrounding parabolic actions. **[7]** The mention in v. 7 of the lifting of the bared arm, as a warrior in battle pulls back his upper garment, and of the delivering of threatening prophecies is not easy to reconcile with the description of a paralysing of the body. As a result, many insert the verse after v. 3 to form a conclusion to the first symbolic action. Even if one accounts for the raising of the arm as one of the symptoms of a paralytic seizure, one cannot do the same with the prophesyings. The same must be said of the actions next described, which do not contain any hint of any such seizure, and are connected with it only by the gloss in v. 9b. If one is not to transform the state of complete paralysis into a mere temporary attack, depriving it of its symbolic power, one must probably abandon v. 7.

The contents of the episode of the binding also make it difficult to see how it is to be attached to the other parabolic actions. These are all unambiguously symbolic of siege, as v. 13 is not original. If one is to find exile symbolized here, one would expect to find it at the end, without the limitation expressed by the numbers, with the hopeful suggestion which they contain. Moreover, the exhaustive explanation

of the prophetic actions given in 5.5ff. conspicuously omits any
reference to this parable. So it is easy to conjecture, as has been often
done of late, that we have here a parabolic action which took place
at a later time, which actually belongs near the events related in
24.15ff. When the book was compiled it was detached from similar
subject matter, taking 3.22ff. with it (cf. p. 75). This is a matter to
which we shall have to return at a later point.

Siege rations: 4.9–15

The representation of the hardships of the besieged is directly associated with the symbolism of the siege. The prophet has to typify
by his own daily ration the uncleanness and paucity of their diet.
[9] He prepares his meal from a mixture of different kinds of grain
and pulse, such as a man will use only when reduced to very short
commons. As the law forbade such mixtures (Deut. 22.9ff.; Lev.
19.19), this represents legally unclean food. [12] The method of
cooking must serve to intensify the uncleanness of the food, since
human dung, [14] only replaced by cow's dung after an earnest
request by the prophet, is to be employed as the fuel. The whole
transaction makes one think of the methods of baking still known
among Bedouins and Palestinian peasants. [15] According to this
primitive method of baking without utensils, the dough is baked
by being laid either on a hot stone or directly in the glowing ashes, so
that the bread thus produced can only roughly be cleansed of the
marks of the ashes.[1] This supplies a further reason for the frightened
protest by the prophet, appealing to the pattern of cleanness demanded by his office and conscientiously maintained by himself (cf.
Ex. 22.30; Lev. 11.39f.; 17.15f.; 22.8; Deut. 14.21; as also Lev.
7.18ff.; 19.6f.). The use of cow's dung permitted to him, however
much it may be taken for granted in the timber-denuded Orient of
today, does not altogether take away the uncleanness. [10f.] This
unappetizing bread is restricted to a daily ration of about half a
pound, along with a correspondingly scanty water-dole of one and
three-quarter pints per day, making a very realistic picture of the
agonizing lack of the necessities of life within the besieged city. A
special explanation was as unnecessary for it as it was for the staging
of the siege.

---

[1] Cf. G. H. Dalman, *Arbeit und Sitte in Palästina*, IV: *Brot, Öl und Wein*, 1935,
pp. 29ff.

Shearing and dividing: 5.1–4

The fate of the besieged city is sealed. [1] Isaiah 7.20 also employs the image of shearing to denote slaughter and the laying waste of the country by a foreign conqueror. Ezekiel must act the parable in his own person by shaving off his hair and beard with a sword, the symbol of military force. The city will thus suffer the reproach of being deprived of its inhabitants, like a dignified personage who is shaved bald (II Sam. 10.4f.). In a cynically mocking process (who would ever want to weigh hair in scales?), the shaved-off hair is weighed to represent the threefold fate of the citizens. [2] The third part burnt on the brick signifies liquidation by starvation and pestilence, the third part cut down all round it denotes those who fall in the battle for its defence, the third part scattered to the wind stands for the survivors who escape by flight or by being carried into exile, all giving only too true a picture of the horrors of defeat. [3f.] The remarkable epilogue, in which some of the scattered hairs are gathered again and carefully preserved, only for some of them again to be subsequently burnt, has often been regarded with disfavour as a theological gloss, intended to bring out how unerringly retribution falls on individuals. But it is not calculated to fulfil that purpose; it is more probably aimed at the destruction of all hope of surviving the judgment with a whole skin. Even those who feel assured of being preserved by a higher hand (cf. I Sam. 25.29) are not thereby guarded against destruction. We obviously have no right to expect a particular detail like that to be included in the general interpretation.

The interpretation: 5.5–15

One must consider this as a whole, without looking for detailed interpretation of the actions preceding it. Such things are only expected by subsequent readers who are inclined to think that each individual detail has some special reference. This is why we have rejected the interpretations in 4.1, 13, 16f., since they would only have served to bring to a premature end the tension felt by the audience. The prophetic picture-language stood in no need of further elucidation at that point. The sole question left unanswered was the name of the city that was being represented. So the answer to that question takes the central place in the prophet's interpretation.

[5] The terse phrase 'This is Jerusalem' cuts off at a single stroke all the hopes that the menacing symbolic acts must be aimed against

the tyrant city of Babylon. This sentence of God's wrath is gathering
over that other lofty city in which the exiles place all their pride and
all their hopes. The same cries of 'Impossible!' which greeted Jeremiah's threats of doom also greet this sinister predictor of misfortune
among the exiles and open up a deep gulf between him and the others
who share the same fate. So the prophet, along with his interpretation,
gives the reason why Jerusalem's greatness is so closely associated
with her ruin.

For this purpose, he makes use of the widespread idea of the 'navel
of the earth' (38.12).[1] In Babylon, Greece, Rome, and even in China,
it was employed as a proud expression of national self-importance. In
Ezekiel it has many associations besides that of a primitive geographical conception ministering to national vanity. It is the central importance possessed by that city in the world God's plan of salvation
which makes him speak of Jerusalem as the centre of the earth. It is
God's will for the world to have its pivot there, but not because her
power or culture could claim world-dominance, nor yet because she
was the dwelling place of the world-God, but because it had been
entrusted with a new system of law. This law (according to the
underlying thought, given its most striking formulation by Isaiah, cf.
Isa. 1.21ff.; 2.2ff.) was to shine out thence over the world. [6f.] The
chosen city has, however, surrendered this position in an inconceivable blindness, inasmuch as she has cast away the law of God
entrusted to her out of open dislike for its giver, and has even disregarded the justice which the very heathen nations rate so high, in her
determination to lead a life of self-will. Instead of being a pattern of
goodness she has become a temptress to evil. So she has not only
disobeyed God's orders, but done the exact opposite. Such extreme
guilt calls for an extreme punishment, and this provides the terrifying
fulfilment of the prophet's symbolic actions. [8–10b] The mock siege,
.with God inexorably taking his vengeance, finds fulfilment in the
general announcement of the beginning of the judgment, the unclean
diet forced on the besieged is interpreted and supplemented by the
statement that men will be slaughtered and devoured like beasts,
even when they ought to be protected by the closest ties of blood,
while the shaving off of the hair stands for the annihilation of the
population and the laying waste of the city and of all Judah with her.
The prophet's references to the actions just performed are in words

[1] Cf. in this connection, W. A. Roscher, *Omphalos*, 1915 (Abhandlungen der
Sächsischen Gesellschaft der Wissenschaften, 29.9 and 31.1).

that are at first loose-knit, then terse, then exhaustive, as they rise in an impressive *crescendo*, which is not destroyed by long repetitions, and culminate in the final words stating the irrevocability of the Judge's decision. [10c, 12] How radical this pronouncement of judgment is is seen in the way it excludes all thought of surviving it. Some prophets use the large or small group of the population who survive even the worst catastrophes of war as a bridge to promises of salvation (cf. Amos. 5.15; Isa. 7.3; 8.18; Zeph. 3.12f.), but Ezekiel employs vv. 10c and 12, which interpret the symbolic action of 5.1–3 by the total annihilation of the population, as a means of expressing utter annihilation. [11] In the same way, further emphasis is added to the pronouncement of doom by Yahweh's oath 'as I live'. It re-echoes from now on in Ezekiel's threats. The reality of God's nearness, of which the people had so lost sight, is thus made visible and tangible, in violent contrast to the way they had taken it for granted, and wished to be assured of it by miraculous blessings.

In v. 11 the pollution of the temple by heathen abomination seems to be introduced in such a way as to supply an entirely new motive for judgment. We shall see later how this disregard of the place in which Yahweh has intended to grant his people the grace of free access to him is, in fact, considered by Ezekiel to be the core of the alienation from God which made them ripe for judgment. Yet the present context compels us to ask whether the term 'sanctuary' does not here possess a wider connotation, so as to include the whole area of the holy city, which Isaiah (1.26) calls a city of righteousness and identifies with Zion (2.3) and the holy mountain (11.9). Here, as at the outset, we see the city of righteousness being deconsecrated by the abomination of iniquity which is without reverence for the holiness of God. Those who insist that the verse applies solely to the temple are inclined to regard it as a later expansion of the sentence of judgment, which tried to account for the terrible judgment solely by the profanation of the temple, and had already before it the temple vision of ch. 8f. The unexpected reintroduction of this reasoning by Yahweh's oath could in any case be regarded as confirmation from a formal point of view.

[14f.] In v. 14 the shearing of Jerusalem denotes the laying waste not only of the capital but also of its daughter cities. In v. 15 the sentence of judgment finds its climax in an energetic summary of all the individual acts of judgment, stating that Jerusalem's blessed position in the centre of the earth, purposed by God, has been so perverted that it has been transformed into the embodiment of God's curse, from which the nations shudder and turn their faces. That means that Yahweh's retribution has reached its goal: the Lord of the world has passed his sentence, and an irrevocable decision has taken place.

It will be noticed how, even in this first address of his, the prophet Ezekiel brings the heathen nations into the picture. They are not just the admiring chorus, which Israel's pride had looked for, who now turn away in disgust and who are introduced to form a particularly bitter element in her punishment. It is much more that the prophet regards them as having been brought into a direct relationship with Yahweh, by having come to possess some of the world-God's legal ordinances and to be under an obligation to uphold them, an axiom also assumed in Amos 1 and 2 and in Jer. 2.10f. But this means more to Ezekiel than it did to his predecessors. He sees that they are called not only to the same responsibility before Yahweh as Israel, and to serve as instruments of judgment upon her; their relation to Israel's destiny becomes a deeper one, seeing how they must come under some positive influence from a people with such a knowledge of the law of God.

Ezekiel sums this up later in his concept of the new knowledge of Yahweh, a subject to which we will return in due course. This much, however, is already evident: Israel's external relationship to the nations has come to the point where it is turning into an internal one. So the portrayal of it by the Noachian covenant in the Priestly writing (Gen. 9), which in other respects expresses an outlook closely akin to Ezekiel's, is remoulded by him at one decisive point. It is no mere accident that this should happen at the exact moment when the destruction of all that makes her a nation has made all external exclusiveness towards foreign nations finally impossible to Israel, and brought the demand for an intense spiritual effort to reach an understanding with them. Ezekiel's views have often been misunderstood, but he has done no small service in this respect, since it was he who first brought the nations into the picture, in such a way that Deutero–Isaiah could build further on the same foundation in a decisive way. The disgust and derision, along with profound horror, which the heathen show (v. 15), is far from being the prophet's final word about them. But all the function they fulfil here is to provide a contrast to the original blessing which it was Israel's task to bring them, but which she had refused to bring.

An awareness of the special responsibility of the elect is one of the fundamental elements in the preaching of the prophets from the very outset (cf. Amos. 3.2). Jesus himself takes it up, and Luke 12.48 gives it classic expression: 'Everyone to whom much is given, of him will much be required; and of him to whom men commit much they will demand the more!' His denunciations of the 'children of the kingdom', who have so misused their prerogatives that notoriously wicked places like Tyre and Sidon, Sodom and Gomorrha must appear as witnesses piling up evidence against them, re-echoes other prophetic passages (cf. Ezek. 16.48ff.) and cuts no less deeply than they. In both passages we see the special danger which overhangs the God-given gift of grace. It is that false security, which prides itself upon its privileged position, making it into a pillow for human sloth and selfishness to slumber on. God's free gift ought to be regarded as a call to service; it does not at all satisfy man's lustful desires, but it does open to the human will a new possibility of union with God's saving will. But man instead soothes himself with irrevocable assurances of the divine good pleasure, so as to save himself from having to make any efforts, and to make him the proprietor of a divine domain specially reserved for him alone to enjoy. This refusal to make the right response to the question which lies in God's gift can have no other outcome but disregard for the 'statutes and ordinances' 5.6f.: (the means for setting up a new order for life). Since the 'royal law' (James 2.8) has thus been forced to yield to human self-will, the possibility of repentance is also shut out, producing that caricature of a genuine trust in God's forgiveness, which Paul, no less than Ezekiel, threatens with judgment (Rom. 3.5ff.).

Ezekiel brings out this sentence of doom in all its severity by pointing to God's world-wide purpose of salvation and showing how it forms the background to the election of Israel. It is by her resistance to God's plan for the whole world that Israel has thrown away the position she was intended to occupy and made her own rejection inevitable. The church of Christ becomes subject to the same guilt and brings upon herself a similar fate, when she forgets the 'new commandment' of love (John 13.34) or the 'law of liberty' (James 2.12), which has been entrusted to her in order that through them her life may take on the shape demanded by her office as a herald. God's people and the order of his kingdom are two things which belong together and cannot be separated from each other, in the New Covenant just as in the Old.

Chapter 6.1–14

Threat to the mountains of Israel

1 And the word of Yahweh came to me: [2]'Son of man, set your face against the mountains of Israel and prophesy against them, [3]and say, You mountains of Israel, hear the word [. . .][a] of Yahweh! Thus says [. . .][b] Yahweh:[c] Behold, I am bringing the sword upon you and destroying your holy heights. [4]Your altars shall become desolate, and your incense altars all be broken; and I am casting down your slain before your idols! [. . .][d] [7b]Thus you shall come to know that I am Yahweh!

8 *And I will leave some of you alive among the nations*[e] *who escape the sword, when you are scattered through the countries,*[f] [9]*and those of you who escape will remember me among the nations where they are carried captive. And I will break their wanton heart,*[g] *which has departed from me, and their eyes, which have looked wantonly after their idols; and then they shall be loathsome in their own eyes for all the evils which they have committed [by]*[h] *all their abominations,* [10]*and they shall know that I, Yahweh, have not threatened in vain to bring this evil upon them.'*

11 Thus says [. . .][i] Yahweh: 'Clap your hands and stamp your foot and say: Woe! because of all[j] the abomination of the house of Israel;[k] by sword, famine and pestilence shall they fall. [12]He that is far off shall die of pestilence, and he that is near shall fall by the sword; and he [. . .][l] that is shut in shall die of famine. Thus shall I fulfil my fury wholly upon them, [13]and [they shall know][m] that I am Yahweh.

When their slain lie among their idols round about their altars upon every high hill, on all the mountain tops and under every green tree and under every leafy terebinth, where they offered the pleasing smell of sacrifice to all their idols, [14]then will I stretch out my hand against them and make the land [from the steppe to beyond Riblah][n] utterly waste throughout all their habitations. Then they shall know that I am Yahweh.'

[a–b]See BH.

[c]MT: 'To the mountains and the hills, to the ravines and to the valleys'; an addition, intended to include the unlawful places of worship situated in the valleys; but ignored in the passage which follows.

[d]'[5] I will lay the dead bodies of the Israelites before their idols and scatter your bones round about your altars. [6]In all your dwelling places the cities shall be waste and the holy heights ruined, so that your altars shall be waste and ruined, your idols broken and destroyed, your incense altars cut down and your works wiped out. [7a]And the slain shall fall in the midst of you'; an addition, which may in part include quotations from other speeches, but which in the main takes the form of an address to the Israelites, repeating what has just been said in other words without

introducing any fresh ideas. The last phrase takes up the conclusion of v. 4, and may well be the catchword under which the addition originally stood in the margin.

eMT provides two readings to choose from, one of which has been adopted above, and the ⌐ .her of which is: 'when you have among the nations some who escape the sword. . . .'

ᶠSee BH.

ᵍSee BH. We must delete *'ašer*, with LXX, and read the past consecutive.

ʰ⁻ⁱSee BH.

ʲMT: 'evil' is not found in the LXX.

ᵏMT attaches the phrase with a relative; which goes against the LXX.

ˡMT: 'that is left and . . .'; a gloss, explaining the following word incorrectly as 'preserved', and not found in LXX.

ᵐ⁻ⁿSee BH.

The chapter falls into three sections, loosely connected together, and displaying considerable accretions to the original text.

Judgment upon the mountains of Israel: 6.1–7

[3] The prophet turns away from the capital of Judah to address the mountains of his native land. Just as Yahweh gives commands and imposes his laws upon all creation, including inanimate nature (Isa. 5.6; Job 37.12; Ps. 148.6; etc.), so, too, he communicates his judgments to it. Man feels himself linked in such close fellowship with the surrounding created world that he even thinks of it as hearing God's decisions. This is intensified by the fact that God's lordship over nature is thought to consist not so much in an unalterable system as in a series of ever new acts of creation and displays of power, and thus God's control of nature is thought to be a very immediate one. So, too, the words addressed by Yahweh to the mountains of Israel are no mere poetic form of expression: nature, by virtue of the way in which God has made it subserve human life, comes to be a part of what men do and to share in their punishment.

[4] Besides this, Israel's alienation from her God had been made visible in a most revolting fashion upon these very mountains of Canaan. They were the sites of the *bāmoth* or high places, taken over from Canaanite religious practice. Through them customs associated with the worship of Baal had come to be naturalized in the Yahweh-cult, and the Israelite conception of God had been assimilated to that of the inhabitants of the land with their nature-god. With nature's mysterious life-force coming to occupy the foreground, the content of the relationship with God shifted to being the communication of

superhuman life to those who visited the sanctuary; the mystery of fellowship with the divine was made perceptible to the senses in an ecstatic feeling of *joie de vivre*. An inexhaustible stream of life seemed to break forth, sustaining threatened human existence and assuring it of its unbreakable solidarity with the divine ground of all life. But at the same time the will of the sovereign God was dimmed. His covenant no longer expressed an unmerited election to moral communion but the bond between God and his land and people, of which he was reminded. It assured man that he was indissolubly united with a divinity which existed for no other purpose than to pour out its gifts upon him. So these holy places, in which the nature of Yahweh has been travestied and his will made unknowable, come in for the sharpest attacks from the prophets beginning from Amos. They supply a name for the accursed syncretism which has taught Israel to forget her own God. These sanctuaries had originally been exclusively employed for the worship of Yahweh, but the way in which they are associated, or rather identified, in this passage with incense altars and idols shows what dangerous doors they became into overt heathenism. The little incense altars, generally placed on top of an altar of sacrifice,[1] which only emerged in the period of the later kings, seem to have come to be used in the cult of the goddess Astarte, just as the cult-tree, called Asherah, which is much more frequently mentioned and banned as a heathen requisite, is derived from the cult of the mother goddess. This transition to heathenism took place quite boldly when Judah was overwhelmed by foreign influences in the seventh century, and heathen gods were thought of as taking their place beside Yahweh in the picture of God. Excavations and the customs of the countries surrounding Palestine show little metal figures kept in a movable cult-shrine as the form which this idea was permitted to take. In all this the God of Israel had come to be put on the same level as the heathen idols and had to share his people's worship with them.

So the curse of Yahweh falls upon the mountains which are as it were in league with men in granting recognition and right of citizenship to a foreign god in a place where the lordship of Yahweh alone should hold sway. The sword of the conqueror will effect what Israel herself has failed to do; the places of false idolatrous worship will be destroyed, the altars of incense and of sacrifice smashed to pieces, the

---

[1] Cf. in this connection, K. Elliger, 'Chammanim = Masseben?' *ZAW* 57 (1939), pp. 256ff.

idolaters smitten and cast down before their idols. Yahweh thus gives a tangible proof of the powerlessness of the idols which become helpless spectators of the ruin which overtakes their worshippers. [7] Through their fall, those upon whom retribution comes are to recognize the terrible delusion, of which they have been the victims, and give Yahweh, the Almighty Lord, his due.

In his threatening words addressed to the mountains of Israel, Ezekiel is renewing under a particular form a complaint voiced by earlier prophets. He does not mention the concomitants of nature-worship, like the partly orgiastic and partly gruesome practices which are so characteristic of the polemic of Hosea (2.2ff.; 4.13ff.; 9.10) and Jeremiah (2.23ff., 33f.; 3.2, 13; 5.7f.; 13.27). He puts the emphasis on the innermost falsification of a man's picture of God, which occurs when he thinks he has found a direct road to God by surrendering to the mystery of natural life with all its overflowing richness of gifts and forces. God's revealing word, that ever-fresh miracle, calls man not only to personal fellowship but also to obedience and to an inward readiness to accept him. In its place we see an unconditional access to the divine life-force which gives promise of satisfying a man's own longings for life, but makes the sovereign Lord vanish behind a plurality of holy forces, symbols and images. The alluring possibility which opens up here of an assurance of unconditionally belonging to the divine world lends its special attraction to such nature-worship. It has come up in every age as the chief antagonist of the revealed faith and has its adherents even today. Yet the facts bear out the truth of all the prophet's words. When the acid test is applied, at the great breaking-points of history which remove all man's feelings of security, that type of religion forsakes him and leaves him to his own perplexity. One may well ask if the bankruptcy described by Ezekiel is not repeating itself today, as we see the educated modern man turn away in disillusionment from every type of natural religion. So the thorough-going secularization of all the different spheres of life is accompanied by an equally thorough-going doubt whether life has any meaning at all. Such an outcome is quite inevitable where the Creator himself is ignored and where more attention is bestowed on the forces of creation.

The survivors: 6.8–10

The preceding section closes with the inexorable ruin of the idolaters who know nothing of God save in the bitter final account they have

to render for an ill-spent life. **[8]** These verses, however, speak of
those escaped from the sword after Israel has been scattered through
the other lands, so they are connected more with 5.10 and 12. Yet
there is one striking contrast: the lot of the fugitives does not serve,
as there, to supply an illustration of how inexorably the wrath of
Yahweh pursues them. The terms in which it is described suggest a
new development. **[9]** As Herrmann rightly points out, 'remembering'
here does not mean the 'bare functioning of the faculty of recollection'. It holds within it a new openness to, and inquiry after, the
long-forgotten God of Israel. Already we see that judgment has borne
fruit. Yahweh is already at work among these contrite ones. The tone
in which this is described is very similar to 36.26, 31. The hardening
and alienation from God is completely broken, leading to a profound
attitude of self-condemnation. The 'recognition' of the effectual power
of Yahweh's word takes on a highly positive sense, of which v. 7 was
still ignorant. All this goes to suggest that the redactors of the book
have here inserted some portion of a note recorded by Ezekiel at a
much later period. Undoubtedly it does the reader a service in helping him to look beyond the gloomy threats of judgment to the ultimate
goal of salvation. Yet the interests of an accurate knowledge of the
first period of the prophet's work demand its restoration to its proper
position, for fear of confusing the order he followed in his preaching.

Confirmation of the threat of disaster: 6.11–14

[11f.] With excited gestures the prophet is to utter a cry of woe to
conclude his threats against his own city and native land, giving a
brief hint of all that is to happen. Ezekiel's task claims body as well
as spirit, and we are gripped by the impassioned way in which he
throws himself into it. His outcry of grief is given a psychophysical
expression, as he jerks his body, claps his hands and stamps his feet.
He is thus able to find a vent for the excitement piling up within him,
while in other respects paralysed by the oppressiveness of the vision.
He must proclaim and thus propitiate the rage of his God which
exhausts itself in destruction (v. 12).

The gestures here described show a general resemblance to 25.6.
So they have been regarded as symptomatic of sadistic delight, and a
slight alteration of the word for 'Woe' has transformed it to the
mocking 'Aha' which also occurs in Ezekiel. This is as much as to
say that the prophet has been instructed to enact the part of the
envious neighbouring nations rejoicing over Israel's ruin. Against

such a view is the fact that the outcry is explicitly related to the abominations committed by the house of Israel, not the fate of the sinners, in whose sufferings alone it might be possible to find pleasure. The reading 'Woe' gives a better sense. In addition to this, the language of gesture can be expressive of very various feelings. One can appeal to ancient rites of lamentation as an accompaniment to the mourners' cries. But in 21.14 this gesture makes the avenging sword of Yahweh come a second and a third time, and in 22.13 Yahweh claps his hands together so as to reduce to nothing the gains won by Israel's whoredoms. So it is more probable that we should think of this as an originally magical gesture which could make a misfortune firm and irrevocable, and even increase its power. Whether it still carried this meaning or whether, as has been assumed above, it was a mere symptom of excitement is a matter upon which it is impossible to decide with certainty.

[13a] Here again the catastrophe displays the hitherto ignored God who shows himself to be the true one. But the recognition of this is not lit up by any saving gleam of light. It is the grim conclusion drawn from the inevitability of the chastisement that is to come.

[13b, 14] In spite of this explicit conclusion, the threats are taken up once more in vv. 13b and 14. This is evidently the outcome of a desire to emphasize the unbroken completeness of the chastisement, as in 5.16f. and 6.5–7. So v. 14 carries us far beyond the mountains originally addressed and speaks of vengeance coming over the whole land. The mention of Riblah as the northern boundary is probably influenced by II Kings 23.33 and 25.6f. It does not occur elsewhere in Ezekiel and could not have occurred to him till a much later period. The Babylonian position of the speaker is explicitly maintained here. He points to the homeland as if it were very far away (cf. especially v. 5), and thus makes certain of moving the hearts of his companions in misfortune.

CHAPTER 7.1–27

The end

1 And the word of Yahweh came to me:
2 'And you, son of man, say:ª Thus says [. . .]ᵇ Yahweh to the land of Israel:

An end comes, the end comes^c over the four corners of the earth.

3a Now the end comes upon you,^{d 5}[. . .]^e disaster [upon]^f disaster shall surely come.

6 An end comes, the end comes, it has awakened, that it may fall upon you, surely it already comes.

7 [Your turn comes],^g O inhabitant of the land!
The time comes, the day draws near, [it does not hesitate nor tarry]^h.

8 Now, I will soon pour out my wrath upon you
and my rage shall take effect against you.
I will judge you according to your conduct and bring upon you all your abominations.

9 My eye shall not look upon you with mercy and I will not spare you;
[for]ⁱ I will pay you back for your conduct
and your abominations shall have their effect in the midst of you,
and [you shall]^j know that I am Yahweh [. . .].^k

10 Behold, the day! Behold, [. . .]^l it has commenced its course, the staff blooms, pride buds,

11 [. . .]^m the staff of wickedness [withers]ⁿ [it is cast down, its pomp cannot subsist] [. . .].^o

12 The time has come, the day has drawn near; he who can afford to buy need not rejoice, and he who is forced to sell need not mourn [. . .].^p

13 For the seller shall not be able to return back to the property he has sold [. . .],^q
[and the buyer cannot have secure possession of his property].^r
For wrath^s comes upon all their pomp,^t and because of his iniquity none of them shall be able to deliver^u his life.

14 [Blow aloud the trumpet and make mighty preparations],^v
yet no man shall go forth to battle! [. . .]^w

15 The sword (rages) outside, pestilence and famine within:
He that is in the field falls by the sword, he that is in the city is swept away by famine and pestilence.

16 And a few of them escape [. . .]^x on the mountains like [moaning doves],^y
[thus they shall all die],^z each because of his own iniquity.

17 All hands are feeble and all knees drip with water.^{aa}

18 Men gird themselves with sackcloth and cover themselves with horror; shame is upon all faces and all their heads are shorn bald.

19 They cast out their silver into the streets, and their gold is counted an abominable thing [. . .],^{bb}
they cannot by it satisfy their appetite or with it fill their belly [. . .].^{cc}

20 For [their]^{dd} beautiful ornament they have used for vainglory, and

their detestable images [. . .]ee have theyff made out of it [. . .].gg

21 Therefore do I give it away to foreigners for a prey, to the wicked upon earth as a booty [. . .].hh

22 And I turn my face away from them, for they have profaned my jewel.
Therefore robbers shall break in [there]ii
and profane [it]jj 23 and [spoil all in it even to the foundations].kk
For the land is full of [bloodshed]ll and the city full of violence.

24 [Therefore I bring the worst of the nations;
they shall take possession of their houses].mm
And I make an end of their [strong] pride,nn
and [their sanctuaries]oo shall be profaned.

25 Anguish of deathpp comes,qq and if they seek for deliverance, there is none to be found.

26 Disaster comes upon disaster, terrifying rumour meets terrifying rumour,
and the vision of the prophet is [put to shame],rr and teaching perishes from the priest [. . .].ss

27 [. . .]tt The prince shall wrap himself in despair
and the hands of the common people shall be paralysed by terror.
According to their own conduct I will do with them and according to their own judgments do I judge them,
and they shall know that I am Yahweh.'

a–cSee BH.

d 3b'I will let loose my wrath upon you and will judge you according to your conduct and bring upon you all your abomination. 4My eye shall not look upon you with mercy and I will not spare; for I will pay you back for your conduct, and your abominations shall have their effect in the midst of you, and you (LXX: second person singular for MT second person plural) shall know that I am Yahweh.' A comparison of these verses with vv. 5–9 will show them to be an inferior variant of the same passage, which should be replaced by the better-preserved text of vv. 5–9.

eMT: 'thus says (the Lord) Yahweh'; a repetition of the formula for the delivery of a message, necessitated by the insertion of vv. 3b and 4.

fSee BH.

gThe word ṣᵉpīrā is also found in Isa. 28.5 with the meaning of 'garland'. Here we can perhaps accept the suggestion of T. H. Gaster ('Ezekiel and the Mysteries', JBL 60 (1941), p. 298) on the basis of the Arabic and Ugaritic so as to give it the meaning of the 'revolution' (of fate), literally 'the revolution reaches thee'. J. A. Bewer ('On the Text of Ezekiel 7.5–14', JBL 45 (1926), p. 231) reads habbāṣīr, 'the gathering of the vintage'.

hThe completely unintelligible wording of the MT has been reconstructed from the LXX.

iSee BH.

[j]MT: second person plural; read second person singular with LXX.

[k]MT: 'who smite'; an addition to the present concluding formula.

[l]MT: 'has come'; insertion assimilating to v. 7.

[m]MT: 'iniquity'; delete with LXX as an explanation of the staff previously mentioned.

[n]Read *qāmal* for *qām l^e*.

[o]MT piles up words without meaning (see BH). *hunaḥ lō yāqūm ḥ^amōnām* is a conjecture adopted merely to give some idea of what is to be expected in this context.

[p]MT: 'for wrath will come over all their pomp'. This phrase also returns in vv. 13 and 14 with a slight change. It looks like a refrain, the function of which has been obscured by the now confused context. That it is wanting in the LXX is not a sure proof of its secondary origin. So also Bewer, above note [g].

[q]MT has three unintelligible words, see BH.

[r]Cornill's emendation, see BH. This conjecture is based on the parallelism, but textually unsupported. So it is only to be used with due qualifications.

[s]MT: 'vision'; evidently a scribal error.

[t]Read third plural suffix for third singular.

[u]MT: 'establish himself'; read with LXX *yaḥ^azīq*.

[v]It is generally accepted that the first two words should be read as imperative: *tiqʿū tāqōʿa*. They correspond to the parallel section *hākīnū hākēn*.

[w]MT: 'for my wrath comes over all their pomp'; an inferior variant of the refrain, which cuts v. 14 off from v. 15 and is thus betrayed as an addition in the wrong place.

[x]MT: 'and tarry' is not found in LXX and makes the line too long.

[y]Read *hōgiyyōt* for MT *haggēʾāyōt* with the majority of textual evidence.

[z]See BH.

[aa]A coarse expression indicating overmastering terror, cf. 21.12 and also II Kings 18.27.

[bb]MT: 'their silver and their gold shall not be able to deliver them in the day of Yahweh's wrath'; a quotation from Zeph 1.18, which does not suit a speech by Yahweh.

[cc]MT: 'for it became a snare for their guilt'; a prose gloss.

[dd]Cf. BH.

[ee]MT: 'their detestable things'; a familiar phrase explaining the previous unusual expression.

[ff]Cf. BH.

[gg]MT: 'therefore I have made it filth to them'; a gloss supplying a theological reason.

[hh]MT: 'that they may profane it'; obviously a lame insertion. Cf. v. 22 conclusion.

[ii–jj]Cf. BH.

[kk]A conjectural restoration of the unintelligible Masoretic text 'make the chain', after Cornill's *ʿārō ūbāqōq*.

[ll]MT: 'judgment'; alter slightly and read 'bloodshed': *mišpak dām*.

[mm]This portion of the verse is not in LXX.

[nn–oo]See BH.

ppFor the hap. leg. *qᵉpādā* Herrmann conjectures *pᵉqwddā*, 'visitation', cf. Ezek. 9.1, which seems very appropriate.

qqCf. BH.

rrMT: 'and they shall seek', *wᵉhōbīš* fits in better with the parallel phrase.

ssMT: 'and counsel from the elders'; an expansion after Jer. 18.18, which makes the line too long.

ttMT: 'the king shall mourn' is lacking in LXX. The word 'prince' is frequent in Ezekiel in the sense of 'king'; but the glossator takes it as meaning a subordinate to the king, so he adds the king, too.

This chapter has come down to us in such a hopeless textual condition that it can only be restored partially, and very cautiously, by means of well-confirmed conjectures. Yet in spite of its sadly mangled form it reveals unusual poetic power. The uncanny approach of the tempest of destruction, against which all human efforts to deliver are vain, is described in heavily loaded forward-sweeping phrases, in such a way as to be almost physically present and perceptible to the audience. Pictures drawn with a few swift strokes show dramatically how tribulations grow in dramatic intensity till the terrible climax.

The general announcement: 7.1–3a, 5–9

Amos 8.2 supplies the theme, 'the end has come'. Amos states that in one brief, bulky menacing phrase. Our prophet shapes the same theme into a fugue, a piece of music circling round in mighty sweeps, and again and again returning to the one theme. Verses 2 and 6 reiterate, like heavy hammer strokes, 'an end comes, the end has come', and vv. 7, 12 and 26 reassert that dismal assurance under another shape, indeed a warning not to make a fresh poem begin in v. 10. [2] But it is not merely the chastisement of a small nation like Israel that is here present to the poet's vision; the end comes upon the four corners of the earth. A comparison with Isa. 11.12, and with the 'four world-regions' of the Assyrian royal inscriptions, shows that this means that the end comes over all mankind. This is a world-catastrophe, such as we find in the mythological expectations of disaster of the ancient oriental nations and such as Israel associated with the coming of Yahweh the world-judge. The people of the covenant claimed exceptional treatment for themselves in that world-overthrow. But the prophets insisted that God would make them give an account, and that it would be the goal and climax of that all-embracing judgment (Cf. Amos 1 and 2; Isa. 2.12ff.; 3.13f.; 8.9; 17.12; Jer. 1.10; 4.23ff.; 25.15f., 31ff.; Micah 1.2–4; Zeph. 1f., etc.).

To allege that such passages show signs of post-exilic editing is to
fail to appreciate the prophet's universalism. He makes Israel form up
along with the other nations who are ripe for judgment. That spells
a very effective attack upon the pride of the chosen people, who
throw away their preferential position through the contempt they
show for their God. The end is pictured as like a wild beast awakened
from slumber and about to go out in search of a victim. [7] As in
Amos 5.18, it is no occasion for joy, as though liberation were near,
but a cause for deep terror; nothing can hold back the approaching
disaster, and it, unlike earlier strokes, will complete the final reckoning. [8f.] Hitherto God has waited patiently and restrained his wrath,
but now he lets it have free course and says good-bye to all pity, that
all may see the atrocities of an unrepentant people. Israel's apostasy
had so far been veiled, as it were, to keep it from exercising its
damning effects, but now it must come into activity and produce
annihilation. It is striking how, in order to give concrete shape to the
picture, an old conception of sin as a substance of sinister power is
employed, while at the same time it loses its impersonal and mechanical character by having its power to work a curse subordinated to the
control of Yahweh. Even it is forced to aid towards the recognition
that Yahweh alone is mighty, and that it is his will that men should
recognize him as the Incomparable One who stands out in distinction
from all idols.

The judgment upon all pomp: 7.10–13

Judgment is pronounced upon concrete misdoings in the four shorter
sections which follow. [10] The idea first mentioned in v. 7 is taken
up again; the notion, peculiar to ancient oriental cosmology, of the
circular motion of the universe being applied in order to express the
inexorable approach of the destiny in store. The metaphor of the
root, which so quickly shoots up and blooms, and as quickly withers
and is trodden down, also seems to agree well with such a conception. [12] It is also supported by the phrase about the uselessness
of buying and selling. It does not constitute a special attack upon
commercial profit-making, but recalls ancient oriental ideas of the
time of the curse, and of the way it upsets all the relationships of life,
so as to take all meaning from the pride and ambition with which
men act. [11] The swelling pomp, which overweening arrogance
employed for its own self-glorification, will be consumed by Yahweh's
furious wrath. (We should here think in general of the newly-rich

class within the nation, of the doubtful means by which they had acquired their possessions and of the luxurious living to which they were prone. They were the object of the denunciations of earlier prophets, and not some unnamed prince, although the metaphor of the staff would by itself agree well enough with that, cf. Ezek. 19.) [13] The stress laid upon the righteous judgment of Yahweh blunts the point of the ancient conception of the cyclic movement of the universe, since it is not fate but sin which prevents every man from having a sure hold on life.

The judgment upon the preparations of war: 7.14–16

[14] In those days it was not possible to bring a military force on the field unless one could count on the support of allies. Isaiah also regarded reliance upon it as an extreme symptom of godless pride and threatened it with judgment (Isa. 2.7; 3.25; 22.2ff.; 30.16f.; 31.1ff.). In Ezekiel, Yahweh's wrath brings about a complete paralysis of the whole military system, so as to make victory easy for the enemy (as in Amos 2.13ff. and Isa. 8.9). [15] The effects of the threat of judgment by division into three parts, disclosed in ch. 5, still seem to linger on. [16] To say that every man must die for his own guilt gives an unexpected importance to the personal responsibility of every individual in the midst of the universal degeneracy. It introduces for the first time a theme which will be more and more strongly developed as we go on.

The judgment upon accumulated riches: 7.17–21

Reliance on the god Mammon, and hoping to defy with his aid the dangers which are to come, is another sign of alienation from God and of ripeness for judgment. [20] As well as being proud of their wealth, the rich are ensnared into misusing it for the showy idols they fabricate. [21] Now those possessions are to be seized by the very men to whom they thought themselves far superior, the godless of the earth. [17ff.] Such will be their terror at the ruin overwhelming them and their despair when hunger makes a mockery of their piled-up wealth, that they will let their silver and gold drop like a useless burden into the filth of the streets, and thus present the greatest contrast possible to their former adoration of Mammon. The terms in which the approaching plunderers are described in v. 21, and again in v. 24, can hardly be intended to express any special contempt for the Babylonians; it is more probable that Ezekiel sees in this rabble

of soldiers lustfully bent on booty the refuse of the nations, to whom
the chosen people are cast as a prey. Herrmann thinks the heathen
are reproached as godless and placed in opposition to the Israelites
who are the servants of Yahweh. But that would be an extraordinary
piece of inconsistency with the way in which Ezekiel condemns his
people for a sin which puts them on the same level of alienation from
God as the heathen.

The judgment upon the temple: 7.22–24

[22] If we are to take it that Yahweh's jewel means the temple rather
than the whole holy land (the profanation of the sanctuaries [v. 24]
may argue in favour of the latter), then we see there the heaviest
blow struck by the wrath of God. [23] Bloodlust and violence have
profaned Yahweh's consecrated possession. It is significant to see how
the priest makes the main force of his condemnation fall not so much
on the degeneracy of the cult as upon the ruthless deeds which break
the brotherly solidarity between the members of the people of the
covenant! [22] 'Seeing' Yahweh's face is a regular synonym for a
visit to the temple. Yahweh must now turn away from Israel that
face which hitherto he had graciously turned towards her; [24] as a
result, the temple loses its dignity and, as Jeremiah says, becomes a
robbers' den (Jer. 7.11) and ceases to be under God's protection.

The notion, that it is horror at the thought of such a holy place
being handed over to the robbers who break in, which has led the
author to describe them as the worst of the nations (Bertholet), is
unjustifiable, in view of the way he insists that it is Yahweh himself
who wills its destruction and that it is he himself who strips Israel's
pride of its strongest protective coating. If Ezekiel really was thinking
of the Babylonians, then his words would be dictated by grim irony;
Yahweh chooses precisely those men who are most infected with guilt
as the executioners who carry out his sentence, so as to repay
thoroughly the human profanation of his jewel and to strike at Israel's
overweening pride in its very tenderest spot. In this case, the judgment upon Babylon has a prototype in that in Isa. 10 upon Assyria
and is re-echoed in Deutero-Isaiah (Isa. 47).

The Finale: 7.25–27

[26] The strokes of disaster succeed one another without a break,
with the result that the former interpreters of God's will are silenced,
showing that they are self-deceived deceivers. [27] This unmasking

perishes for ever the last hopes for prince and people. God's righteousness triumphs now in the way in which those who, as judges of their own people, showed them no mercy and coolly sacrificed them to their own utility are now forced to experience the unmitigated severity of divine justice. Even in their fall they have to recognize that that same righteousness which they trod under foot is the dominant power in this world, and must learn to bow before it.

Chapter 6 saw the punishment of the countryside, and now ch. 7 sees that of the proud capital and metropolis, for having turned away from the living God to serve idols. There it was the powers of nature, here it is human achievements, which try to usurp the position which belongs to God alone. The secularized attitude of mind associated with urban culture makes economics (v. 13), military force (v. 14), wealth (v. 19), or skilled leadership (vv. 26f.) into holy things, in which man is to put his trust. For 'anything you give your heart to and put your trust in is really your God' (Luther). A world which has turned its back on the source from which it derives its life is on the very brink of ruin. We see the writing on the wall wherever men try to deify culture in the East or in the West.

CHAPTER 8.1–11.25

The temple vision

1 In the sixth year, in the fifth[a] month, on the fifth day of the month, as I sat in my house and the elders of Judah sat before me, the hand of Yahweh came[b] there upon me, 2and I beheld, and lo a form that had the appearance of a man;[c] down from his loins[d] was fire, and upwards from his loins was what appeared like heavenly brightness, as the gleam of bronze. 3And he stretched out what appeared to be a hand and took me by a lock of my head, and wind[e] lifted me up and bore me between earth and heaven and brought me to Jerusalem [. . .][f] to the entrance of the northern door of the inner court [. . .].[g] 5And he said to me: 'Son of man, lift up your eyes now to the north.' So I lifted up my eyes to the north, and behold to the north of the door stood the altar of the image of pleasure[h] [. . .].[i] 6And he said to me: 'Son of man, do you see what they are doing? They are committing great abominations here[j] to drive me far from my sanctuary. But you will see still greater abominations.'

7 And he brought me to the entrance to the court [. . .][k] 8and said to

me: 'Son of man, look closely at it.'[1] So when I looked in closely, lo, there was a door. [9]And he said to me: 'Go in and see the[m] abominations which they commit there.' [10]So I went in and looked, and lo there were all kinds of forms of reptiles and animals, monsters, [. . .][n] scratched upon the wall round about. [11]And before them stood seventy men of the elders of the house of Israel, among them [. . .][o] also Jaazaniah, the son of Shaphan, and each had his censer in his hand, and the scent of[p] the incense went up. [12]And he said to me: 'Son of man, do you see what [. . .][q] they are doing here [while each chooses an idol for himself]?[r] For they say: Yahweh does not see [. . .][s] it; Yahweh has forsaken the land!' [13]And he said to me: 'You will see still greater abominations which they commit.'

14 And he brought me to the entrance of the north gate of the temple of Yahweh; and behold, there sat there women,[t] weeping for Tammuz. [15]And he said to me: 'Have you seen this, son of man? You will see still greater abominations than these.'

16 And he brought me to the inner court of the temple of Yahweh, and behold, at the entrance to the temple of Yahweh, between the porch and the altar, were about twenty men[u] with their backs to the temple of Yahweh and their faces turned to the east worshipping the sun.[v] [17]And he said to me: 'Do you see this, son of man? Is it too little for the house of Judah to commit the abominations they commit here, since they have filled the land with violence and provoked me to anger yet further? Behold, now they are forcing their stink up my nostrils.[w] [18]Therefore I will deal in wrath, my eye will not look with pity nor will I spare [. . .].'[x]

9. 1 And he cried in my ears with a loud voice: 'Draw near,[y] you who are to execute judgment upon the city [. . .].'[z] [2]And lo, six men came from the direction of the upper gate, which faces north,[aa] each with his destroying weapon in his hand; and among them was a man clothed in linen with writing materials at his side. They came and stood beside the bronze altar. [3][. . .].[bb] And he called to the man in linen clothing with the writing materials at his side [4]and said[cc] to him: 'Go[dd] through the midst of Jerusalem and put a mark upon the foreheads of the men who sigh and groan over all the abominations that are committed in it.' [5]But to the others he said in my hearing: 'Pass through the city after him and smite them down! You shall not look mercifully nor shall you spare. [6]Slay and destroy old men and young men and maidens, little children and women, but do no harm to any one who has the mark upon him. Begin at my sanctuary!' So they began with the men [. . .][ee] who stood before the temple. [7]Then he said to them: 'Defile the temple, and fill the courts with the slain! Then go forth[ff] and smite within the city!' [8]While they were smiting here and I was left alone, I fell there upon my face and cried out and said: 'Ah Yahweh, wilt thou destroy all that remains of Israel, that thou pourest out thy wrath upon Jerusalem!' [9]Then he answered me: 'The

guilt of the house of Israel[gg] is exceedingly great, and the land is filled with bloodshed and the city full of injustice; but they say, Yahweh has forsaken the land, Yahweh does not see it. [10]And therefore my eye will not look with pity nor will I spare, but I will requite their deeds upon their heads.' [11]And lo, the man clothed in linen with the writing materials by his side came and reported: 'I have done as thou didst command me.'

10. 2 And[hh] he said to the man clothed in linen[ii]: 'Go in [. . .][jj] and fill both your hands with burning coals [. . .][kk] and scatter them over the city.' And he went in before my eyes [. . .].[ll] [7]And he[mm] stretched out his hand [. . .][nn] to the fire [. . .][oo] and took some of it and came out again[pp] [. . .].[qq]

11. 1 And the spirit of power lifted me up and brought me to the door of the temple of Yahweh which faced east [. . .].[rr] And behold, in the entrance of the door stood twenty-five men, among whom I saw Jaazaniah, the son of Assur, and Pelatiah, the son of Benaiah, princes of the people. [2]And Yahweh[ss] said to me: 'Son of man, these are the men who devise iniquity and who give wicked counsel in this city, [3]who say: "Have not the houses lately been rebuilt?[tt] It is the cauldron and we the flesh." [4]Therefore prophesy against them, prophesy, O son of man!' [5]Then the spirit of power[uu] fell upon me, and he said to me: 'Say, thus says Yahweh: So you have said, O house of Israel, for what has come into your mind, that I know well. [6]You have slain many of your fellow citizens in this city and filled its streets with the slain. [7]Therefore thus says Yahweh: Those slain by you, whom you have laid in the midst of it, they are the flesh, and it is the cauldron; but you I will take forth out of it[vv] and deliver to foreigners and execute judgments upon you. [10]You shall fall by the sword [. . .][ww] and you shall know that I am Yahweh.' [11, 12][. . .].[xx]

13 And it came to pass, while I was prophesying, that Pelatiah, the son of Benaiah, died. Then I fell upon my face and cried aloud and said: 'Ah Yahweh, thou wilt really make a full end of the remnant of Israel.'

14 And the word of Yahweh came to me thus: [15]'Son of man, your brethren [. . .],[yy] your fellow exiles[zz] [. . .][aaa] of whom the inhabitants of Jerusalem say, "They are far[bbb] from Yahweh, it is given to us [. . .][ccc] to possess." [16]Therefore say, "Thus says [. . .][ddd] Yahweh: Though I have removed them far off among the nations and scattered them among the countries, and am a sanctuary to them only a little in the countries to which they have come. [17][. . .].[eee] But I will gather them[fff] out of the nations and assemble them out of the countries, where they have been scattered, and will give them the land of Israel. [18]And when they come there, they will remove from it all its detestable things and all its abominations. [19, 20][gg] [21]But as for those, whose[hhh] heart goes after their detestable things and their abominations, I will requite their deeds upon their own heads, says[iii] Yahweh." ' [22, 23][. . .][jjj] [24]And a storm wind[kkk] lifted me

up and brought me again to Chaldaea to the exiles [. . .].[111] And the vision which I had seen went up from me, [25]and I told the exiles all the words of Yahweh, which he had revealed to me in the vision.[mmm]

[a]Thus LXX. MT: 'in the sixth month' seems to be an attempt to correct the original statement to conform with the 390 days of 4.5.

[b]MT: 'fell' is an expression nowhere else employed of the hand of God. LXX preserves the more usual one.

[c]MT: 'like the appearance of fire'; the words have been misread. See BH.

[d]MT: 'from what appeared to be his loins'. See BH.

[e]The word 'wind' may also be translated 'spirit'.

[f]MT: 'in visions of God'; a mistaken attempt at further description.

[g]MT: 'where was the seat of the image of jealousy, which provokes wrath'; a mistakenly anticipatory gloss, cf. v. 5. Verse 4: 'And behold there stood the glory of the God of Israel, like the vision I had seen in the plain'; an insertion in connection with 9.3. Cf. pp. 114ff. below.

[h]miṣāpōn laššaʿar mizbaḥ sēmel. MT: 'north of the altar-gate stood the image of jealousy'; but there is no reference anywhere else to an altar-gate.

[i]MT: 'it stood in the entrance'; unintelligible, not in LXX.

[j]MT: 'that the house of Israel' (commit); not in LXX.

[k]MT: 'and I looked, and behold, there was a hole in the wall'; an explanation, occasioned by a misunderstanding of the verb in the following verse.

[l]The verb ḥātar used here can also mean 'to dig through'; this had led a scribe to insert twice over the words 'through the wall', which are not found in LXX. Cf. G. Fohrer, 'Die Glossen im Buch Ezechiel', ZAW 63 (1951), p. 38.

[m]MT: 'vile'; not in LXX.

[n]MT: 'and all the shameful idols of the house of Israel'; a generalizing gloss.

[o]MT: 'stood'; an unnecessary elaboration, not found in LXX.

[p]MT adds to the rare word ʿatar (better spelt ʿaṭar), scent, the words 'of the cloud', explaining it wrongly.

[q]MT: 'the elders of the house of Israel in the dark'; an explanatory gloss.

[r]MT: 'each in his room of pictures'; an obviously corrupt text, which can only be conjecturally restored; read with Bertholet[1] boḥēr bemaskītō.

[s]According to 9.9, 'us' should not be inserted here.

[t]Cf. BH.

[u]This is meant to be a rough estimate of the number present, so twenty-five is as improbable as estimating the weight of a stone at 5½ lb. Probably the original number twenty was brought into conformity with the twenty-five of 11.1 (for the exactness of which there are special reasons, see p. 135). This change has not been consistently made in all the MSS, cf. BH.

[v]MT: 'to the east'; unnecessary repetition. mištaḥavītem; a scribal error, see BH.

[w]The translation is uncertain owing to the difficulty of interpreting the word zemōra, here rendered 'stink' following the medieval Jewish exegetes. Cf. Köhler-Baumgartner, Lexicon s.v. zemōrā and BH.

[x]'Though they cry in my ears with a loud voice, I will not hear them'; a mistaken anticipation of the first words of the following sentence; not found in LXX.

[y]MT points for perfect tense; read imperative.

[z]MT: 'each with his destroying weapon in his hand'; an anticipation of v. 2.

[aa]Cf. BH.

[bb]MT: v. 3a: 'Now the glory of the God of Israel had gone up from the cherub, on which it had rested, to the threshold of the temple'; a similar insertion to 8.4 made in connection with ch. 10, cf. commentary *ad loc.*

[cc]Cf. BH.

[dd]MT here inserts 'through the midst of the city', which is rightly omitted by LXX.

[ee]MT: 'the elders'; a mistaken assimilation to 8.11, not made in 8.16. See BH.

[ff]In MT the following phrase is 'and they went and smote'. The translation follows the Peshitto.

[gg]MT: 'and Judah' is added from a wrong assumption that Israel means the Northern kingdom.

[hh]10.1: 'And I looked, and behold, on the firmament that was over the heads of the cherubim was something resembling a sapphire stone, like a throne' ('that appeared above them' is not in the LXX). Here begins the great piece of additional embroidery in connection with the cherub-throne, see commentary.

[ii]Cf. BH.

[jj]MT: 'among the whirling wheels underneath the cherubim' is a part of this embroidery, as are also the portions of text given below.

[kk]MT: 'from between the cherubim'.

[ll]MT: '[3]Now the cherubim were standing on the south of the temple, as the man went in, and the cloud was filling the inner court. [4]Then the glory of Yahweh went up from the cherub to the threshold of the temple, and the temple was filled with the cloud, and the court was full of the brightness of the glory of Yahweh. [5]And the noise of the wings of the cherubim was to be heard as far as the outer court, like the thunder of the Almighty, when he speaks. [6]And when he commanded the man clothed in linen, "Take fire from between the whirling wheels, from between the cherubim," he went in and stood beside the wheel.'

[mm]MT: 'the cherub'; further embroidery.

[nn]MT: 'from between the cherubim'; a mistaken gloss, not found in LXX.

[oo]MT: 'that was between the cherubim'; an embroidery.

[pp]The conclusion seems to be incomplete; nothing is said of the scattering of the handful of red-hot coals.

[qq]MT: '[8]The cherubim appeared to have something like a human hand under their wings. [9]And I looked, and behold, there were four wheels beside the cherubim, one beside each cherub, and the appearance of the wheels was like the sparkling of a chrysolite. [10]As for their appearance—all four were the same shape—it was like one wheel inside another. [11]When they went, they could go in all four directions, without turning as they went; for in whatever direction the front wheel turned, the others followed, without turning as they went. [12] (And all their bodies) and their backs and hands and wings, and also the wheels, were all full of eyes round about in all four (the wheels which they had). [13] As for the wheels, they were called Galgal (wheelwork or whirlwind) in my hearing. [14] And each had four faces: the first (cf. BH) was the face of an ox (MT: 'face of a cherub', cf. BH), the second (cf. BH) the face of a man, the third the face of a lion, the fourth the face of an eagle. [15] And the cherubim mounted up. These were the living creatures that I had seen beside the river Chebar. [16]When the cherubim went, the wheels

also went beside them, and when the cherubim beat with their wings, to lift themselves up from the earth, the wheels did not turn from beside them. [17]When they stood still, these stood still, and when they lifted themselves up, these lifted themselves up with them; for the spirit of the living creatures was in them.

[18]And the glory of Yahweh went forth from the threshold of the temple, and took up its position once more above the cherubim. [19]Then the cherubim beat their wings and lifted themselves up from the earth in my sight, and as they went away the wheels were with them (cf. BH). But at the entrance of the east door of the temple of Yahweh they stood still, while the glory of the God of Israel was above them. [20]These were the living creatures that I had seen by the Chebar beneath the God of Israel. And I knew that they were cherubim. [21]Each had four faces and each four wings, and what resembled human hands were under their wings. [22]And as concerns the form of their faces, they were the very faces which I had seen by the river Chebar (their appearance); each went straight forward.'

1.15–21 may be appended here so that it may be compared with ch. 10: '[15]And I looked (at the living creatures) and behold, each wheel was on the earth (or 'on the ground' = below?) beside the living creatures, for each of the four. [16]The appearance of the wheels ('and their construction': not in LXX) was like the gleaming of chrysolite; and the four had the same form ('and their appearance': not in LXX) and their construction was, as if there were one wheel inside another. [17]('When they went': not in LXX) they went in all four directions without turning as they went. [18](The first four words are untranslatable) and their rims were all four full of eyes. [19]When the living creatures went, the wheels went beside them; when the living creatures rose from the earth, the wheels rose also. [20]Wherever the spirit drove them (wherever the spirit to go: meaningless dittography) there the wheels also went, and they rose along with them, for the spirit of the living creatures was in the wheels. [21]When those went, these went, and when those stood, these stood, and when those rose from the earth, the wheels rose with them, for the spirit of the living creatures was in the wheels.'

[rr]MT: 'to the east'; a redundancy.

[ss]Cf. BH.

[tt]MT: 'Not in a short time to build houses!' LXX reads as above.

[uu]MT: 'the Spirit of Yahweh', but the name of God is not found in the LXX, cf. phrasing in 2.2; 3.14.

[vv]MT: '[8]You fear the sword, and I will bring the sword upon you, says the Lord Yahweh. [9a]I will bring you out of the midst of it.' We see, from the way the end of v. 7 is taken up and continued in v. 9a, that v. 8 with its extraneous suggestions has been put in between, and is a later insertion, which betrays itself by the premature prophetic closing formula.

[ww]MT: 'I will judge you at the border of Israel'; a further detail subsequently added from II Kings 25.6f., 18ff.

[xx]MT: '[11]It shall not be the cauldron for you, nor shall you be the flesh in it. At the border of Israel I will judge you. [12]And you shall know that I am Yahweh, in whose statutes you have not walked, and whose ordinances you have not observed; but have rather acted according to the ordinances of the nations round about you.' These verses either interpret or repeat what has already been said. They end with an ungainly relative phrase, formed after the analogy provided in 5.6, but which we would not naturally expect to follow the concluding formula of

v. 10. They do not seem to have formed part of the text before the LXX translators, so they must be one more example of the repetition and embroidery of what has been previously stated, which makes the MT so excessively long.

ʸʸMT has a second *'aḥeykā*: dittography. Bertholet[1]'s emendation, *'aḥayyeh*, 'I suffer to live', presupposes an impossible position for the verb and offers no explanation of the present text. An emphatic repetition of *'aḥeykā*, as is suggested by F. Horst ('Exilsgemeinde und Jerusalem in Ez. VIII–XI', *VT* III [1953], pp. 337–39), is not justified by the context, which does not set out to suggest relationship to the prophet, so much as remoteness from the land which is Yahweh's inheritance.

ᶻᶻMT: *geʾullātekā* 'your blood-relations', apparently occasioned by the abnormal writing of *gāʾluteka = gāluteka*.

ᵃᵃᵃMT: 'And the whole house of Israel, all of them.' But Ezekiel does not describe the exiles elsewhere exclusively as the 'house of Israel'. It must therefore be an insertion by a reader who regarded it as improper for the prophet's audience to be restricted to his relations.

ᵇᵇᵇSee BH.

ᶜᶜᶜMT: 'the land', to clarify the *hī'* originally referring to Jerusalem, and which when spoken *viva voce* stood in no need of explanation. It is worth noting that the LXX omits *hī'* and reads only *hāʾāreṣ*: the easier reading has been adopted!

ᵈᵈᵈSee BH.

ᵉᵉᵉMT: 'Therefore say, thus says the Lord Yahweh'; stylistically impossible after the words with which v. 16 opens; probably it serves to emphasize the first great promise of salvation for the exiles.

ᶠᶠᶠMT here consistently reads second person plural, whereas the LXX retains the third person plural, for all four pronouns in this verse; see BH.

ᵍᵍᵍThe verses omitted above read: '19And I will give them one (LXX 'another', see BH) heart and put a new spirit within you ('them' in another tradition) and will take the stony heart out of their flesh and give them a heart of flesh, 20that they may walk in my statutes and observe my ordinances and carry them out. And they shall be my people and I will be their God.' These verses are an almost word for word, but careless and simplified repetition of 36.26f. The second person plural has been transformed into the third person plural (though the scribe's pen has apparently slipped back once into the second person at the 'within you' of 36.26). It is more than probably a marginal note by a reader well versed in the scriptures, who knew from ch. 36 how in Ezekiel's prophecies of salvation 'possession of the land' is the precursor of 'inward purification', and has in consequence been led to introduce the second blessing of salvation as well as the first. If, however, we note the opposition between the population of Jerusalem at that time and the exiles, from whom the section, asserting their claim to possession of the holy land, is derived, we cannot with the majority of exegetes regard vv. 17, 18, 21 as a later insertion, seeing how they express God's decision over who is to possess the land. On the contrary, vv. 19 and 20 must be explained as a quotation by a reader showing how the promise of salvation is to be fulfilled. We are also saved from having to explain the insoluble problem of why Ezekiel should here indulge in a direct and premature anticipation of his greatest promise.

ʰʰʰMT: 'to the hearts of their detestable things'; see BH.

ⁱⁱⁱSee BH.

ʲʲʲ22And the cherubim beat their wings, and the wheels (moved) together with

them, while the glory of the God of Israel was upon them above. [23]And the glory
of Yahweh went up from the midst of the city, and stood upon the mountain to the
east of the city.' This text is obviously entirely dependent upon 10.19 and may have
been added here in association with the introduction of the great section in ch. 10
introducing the moving throne. Cf. commentary.

[kkk]Here also as in 8.3 it is equally possible to translate 'the spirit of power'.

[lll]MT: 'In a vision, by the spirit of God'; an unusual piling up of terms previously employed, meant to insist on the supernatural source of the prophet's
experience, and rightly regarded (with Fohrer) as an explanatory gloss. Cf. on
8.3 (p. 108). Bertholet[2] wishes to retain only 'in the vision of God', whereas
Herrmann and Zimmerli prefer to adhere to the unaltered MT text.

[mmm]Literally: 'which he had made me to see'.

The problem of the composition of Ezekiel: 8–11

The problem of the composition of the book of Ezekiel is a difficult
one. The series of chapters from 8 to 11 provide us with a particularly
instructive sample of these difficulties. The reader finds an account
of visionary experiences of the prophet, with clear distinguishing
features and several elements which bind it together. It is a carefully
calculated composition dealing with one self-contained event. But
even to state that much already shows how the problems begin to
pile up. We cannot accept as satisfactory the extant text in the form
in which it has come to us. We have to face the problem of what parts
have been written by Ezekiel himself, and what parts are the work of
his disciples.

It is in ch. 10 that the doubtfulness of the traditional text is most
obvious to the eye. The facts are such that even those untrained in
textual criticism cannot fail to see them. The picture of the visionary
occurrence was being drawn in one bold stroke after another, as the
vision developed itself in successive events—only to be suddenly
interrupted by a chaotic and long-winded description of the throne
of God. It is obviously connected in some way with the other description of that throne in ch. 1. A problem arises which we are
compelled to face. What is the purpose of it all? Why repeat what has
been said before? Why do it here? Why do it so wordily and so
vaguely?

The first step towards solving the problem is to be aware of the
fact that there is a sudden interruption in the narrative at 10.1.
Chapter 9 ended with the angelic scribe reporting the completion of
one task to his heavenly commander. In 10.2 he is entrusted with
another task. But now something occurs, which, at this point at least,
is totally unexpected. The prophet apparently loses interest in the

breath-taking event that is going on all round him, and brushes it all
aside to tell of the results of some detailed observations he then made
of the throne of God. This is all the more surprising as the description
does not go beyond that of the sapphire throne of 1.26a, and only the
cherubim are introduced as a new feature which in fact remains un-
explained. Seeing that 10.2 answers our expectations, aroused by
9.11, of a fresh command being issued to the angelic scribe, 10.1, at
least, must be out of place. The detailed description of the throne of
God is not proceeded with till vv. 8.17. First we get a brief remark
about the hand of the cherubim, then a description of the system of
wheels beneath them, of their faces, and of the way in which they
move forward. This shows a general similarity to 1.10 and 15.21, but
also has some variations peculiar to itself. This further piece of description also interrupts the events of the vision which had been continued in v. 2 and v. 7, since it cuts short the angelic scribe's fulfilment
of the command given to him in 10.2 after the first few words relating
to it. It seems only natural to conclude that a descriptive passage like
this, so injurious in its effect on the account of the vision and so
uncalled for after ch. 1, cannot possibly have formed an integral part
of the original temple vision.

Beside this static description we find, in 10.3–6 and 18–20, a more
dynamic description of the cherubic throne in its forward movement,
which is brought into closer association with the event of the vision
and seems to fit in better with it. In it we see the appearance of the
glory of Yahweh move in a quite unprecedented way from one
position to another. In 10.3 we had been told that it had taken up its
position immediately south of the temple on a movable cherubic
throne which had come to rest there, whereas one would naturally
have expected it to appear in the midst of the holy of holies in the
temple. We see the throne there and the form of the one who sits
upon it surrounded by cloud and blazing fire. Then we see him rise
from the throne and step upon the threshold (or according to an
alternative rendering of the word, upon the pedestal)[1] at the entrance

---

[1] Following a suggestion by Winkler, G. Gerlemann has given this explanation
(*Zephania textkritisch und literarisch untersucht*, 1942, pp. 9f.), which Köhler has adopted
in his *Lexicon Veteris Testamenti*. It is, however, impossible to state the object of such
a pedestal at the entrance to the temple (unless perhaps it was for placing the ark
upon when it was used in processions?). In any case it must mean some sort of
elevation in front of the temple, from which Yahweh fills the court with the fire
amid which he appears. A description of a similar object can be found in W. F.

to the temple, stand there until the angelic scribe has carried out his orders, and then ultimately return to his former position, and move forward out of the east door of the temple. The reason for this altera- tion of position can only be to obviate any unseemly approach by the angelic scribe to God sitting on the throne. The next step towards which the narrative is moving must be for him to procure the burning coals that are to provide the destroying fire from between the cheru- bim which bear up the throne in 10.2b and 6b. This new development may possibly have been suggested by the description of the bright and blazing fire in 1.13. But in any case it involved his going right in under the plate which held up the throne of God and underneath the one who sat upon the throne. An approach so little consonant with reverence had to be prevented. So an otherwise totally purposeless movement of the vision of God has been inserted, and then, to give it some sort of plausible content, a description is added of how the holy majesty gleamed out in an alternation of a new cloud and sparkling light. At one point the description betrays itself to be mere specula- tion, not interpretation of an immediate perception. This is shown by the statement in 10.5 that the sound of the wings of the cherubim could be heard as far as the outer court, a matter the truth of which Ezekiel could not have verified standing in the inner court. In addition, the identification of noises made by wings and the voice of El Shaddai is evidence of a very curious comparison of heavenly sounds, and of an attempt to reduce the mysteries of the super- natural world to mere human measurements. We are moving in an entirely different realm to a prophet gripped by a vision he has actually seen and following it stage by stage as it unfolds. The way in which v. 2 is taken up in v. 6 shows that vv. 3–5 must be an insertion in an originally shorter text. The excessive verbiage in vv. 2 and 6, caused by the parallel statements about the space between the whirl- ing wheels and between the cherubim, is unmistakable.

We have established the existence of a speculative element, which also comes to view in vv. 2 and 7. 'The' cherub is suddenly introduced to give the coals of fire to the angelic scribe. This leads to extra- ordinary complications in the operation prescribed in v. 2, and serves as the occasion for an explanatory gloss in v. 8. It, too, seems to have

---

Albright, *Archaeology and the Religion of Israel*, 3rd ed., 1953, pp. 152ff. where the king of Ugarit is depicted standing on a chest or tub, apparently of metal and provided with a lid, to worship the storm-god Baal.

been dictated by reflection upon the unapproachability of the all-holy one. *All these points compel one to ask if the role played in this vision by the cherubic throne is not an entirely extraneous element.* The quite unique way in which Ezekiel is caught up in 8.1–3 has no reference to the complicated cherubic conveyance. The following verse, 8.4, places it in the temple in Jerusalem, but introduces it with the words 'in that very place' in a very passing and indeterminate fashion which permits no concrete visualization. 9.3a is inserted equally abruptly into the context, and anticipates 10.4 in a very clumsy manner.

How or why the chariot-throne of God takes up position to the south of the temple (10.3) is nowhere stated. The original account in ch. 8 and 9 tells quite simply how Yahweh spoke and acted with the prophet yet veils in mystery the manner in which the world-God appears. Compared to that, the ceremonious pomp with which Yahweh enters, borne upon the cherubim, brings the divine judge into the visible realm in a manner which it is very difficult to reconcile with the preceding narrative, but finds a parallel in the repetition of the theophany of ch. 1 in 3.23. As 11.1–21 is clearly the insertion by a redactor of a passage which should be put later (see below), removal makes quite certain that the conclusion of the vision of the chariot-throne is also the work of a redactor. For the verbal repetitions in 10.19 and 11.22f. could never have occurred in immediate succession to each other. 10.20, which attributes the identification of the cherubic conveyance with the cherubic throne of ch. 1 to the prophet himself, is an intensification of 8.4; 9.3 and 10.15. It certainly occurs too late, since the appearance of the glory of Yahweh is on the point of making its departure. It betrays how the final redactors felt the need to legitimate the acceptance of a passage like ch. 10, so remarkably parallel to ch. 1, into the temple vision.[1] Now this means that the vision of God on the cherubic throne has been used by one of the prophet's disciples as a *leit-motif* in the composition of ch. 8–11. This made it possible to take elements which did not originally belong in this context and weld them with the temple vision into a powerful unity, for which an imposing conclusion is provided by the withdrawal of the glory of Yahweh, first, in 10.19, from the temple, and finally, in 11.22f., from the city. Another subsidiary interest could also be

[1] 10.21f. is a collection of fragments, evidently derived partly from ch. 1 and partly from 10.14 They may be marginal glosses subsequently introduced into the text by some scribe; but they do not fulfil any special function in the whole scheme.

satisfied by preventing any creaturely approach to the divine glory. Some elements in 10.3–7 may also subsequently have found their way from the description of the appearance into that of the departure e.g. vv. 3 and 5.

Less conscious aims have dominated the composition of the account of the vision in 10.1, 8–17. Of course, there can be no possible doubt of where its chief interest lay: it was in the system of wheels, which is now made visible beneath the cherubim and is evidently an important item for the movement of the cherubic throne over the earth. We have already seen in ch. 1 (see above p. 57) that this means of progression, which gives the cherubic throne the appearance of a chariot, does not fit in with the imagery of the original vision, but introduces an alien, rational and technical element: the manifestation of the throne, moved entirely by the spirit of God, soars through the air, and does not roll like a chariot over the earth. It is associated with a system of wheels which is very hard to visualize in detail (the exact construction of the wheel within a wheel, making it possible to move in any direction without having to turn (10.10, cf. 1.16), remains obscure). It can only be explained as a recollection of another vehicle, which played a part in the cultic theophany of Yahweh in the temple, namely the chariot upon which the ark of God, usually out of sight within the holy of holies, was brought out in processions. The existence of such an object is assured by various indirect references (cf. Pss. 47.5; 65.11; 68.4, 17; II Sam. 6.3ff.; I Chron. 28.18; I Sam. 6.7ff.).[1] As the ark, itself adorned by cherubim, was regarded as a throne for Yahweh,[2] it already provides a movable throne of God. The destruction of the temple, which also meant the destruction of the ark, brought up the tormenting problem of how God could find a throne, as is shown by Jer. 3.16. What could be more probable than that an attempt was made in priestly circles to solve that problem by identifying the throne of God in Ezek. 1 with the idealized temple apparatus? Without that, it was probably impossible to conceive that the manifestation of the *kābōd* of Yahweh granted to the prophet could be essentially different from the *kābōd* which used to dwell in the temple. The imagery of the vision in Ezek. 1 made it possible to regard the object standing in the holy of holies as a mere outward

[1] Cf. also H. Schmidt, 'Kerubenthron und Lade', *Eucharisterion für Gunkel*, 1923, pp. 135ff., and H. Torczyner, *Die Bundeslade und die Anfänge der Religion Israels²*, 1930, pp. 11f., 45.
[2] Cf. W. Eichrodt, *Theology of the Old Testament* I, 1961, pp. 107ff.

shadow of a transcendental reality, the δόξα of which was not touched by earthly catastrophes, but could, when the temple was destroyed, be taken up into the heavenly sphere.

The speculations in ch. 10 about the wheels under the throne of God therefore probably serve this bold attempt to combine the ark sanctuary with the throne of God in the vision. It did not come into its present form in a single stage, but as the result of repeated insertions. This is shown by the extreme disorder of the text, in which it is still possible to identify the points of juncture between layers of insertions. Thus, for example, v. 12 provisionally served to conclude the description of the system of wheels,[1] until it attracted vv. 14f., and vv. 16f. were also added to take further the picture of the chariot. Verse 13 seems to have been inserted in order to bring the static and dynamic visions into conformity with one another. It explicitly identifies the wheels in the former with the 'system of wheels' (*Galgal*) in the latter, showing that the two accounts were originally independent of each other, before it became necessary to try to bring them into conformity.

A realization that the chapter has been gradually filled out in several stages, each with a different motive, makes the present state of the text more or less intelligible. But many points, like the description of the faces of the cherubim and its inconsistency with 1.10, must still remain enigmas. (The omission in 1.10, cf. the translation, may in any case have occasioned the misunderstanding in 10.14.) All attempts made so far at a detailed explanation of each successive stage are anything but satisfactory. It is particularly hard to work out in detail how ch. 1 and 10 have influenced each other, clear as it may be that such influences came into play after the cherubic vehicle was

---

[1] In this verse the description seems to extend to the forms of the cherubim, stating, in extraordinary contradiction to 1.18, that not only the wheels, but also the bodies of the twofold beings are covered with eyes. It may, however, be noticed that *gabbēyhem* may also be translated 'their rims' and designate a part of the wheels, in analogy with 1.18. Two courses are then possible. Either we may see here a description of the individual details of the wheels obscured by subsequent misinterpretation (so Bertholet[1]: 'all their hubs and rims and sockets and axles were full of eyes') or, if we shrink from textual emendations, we may explain the transfer of the eyes to the bodies of the cherubim as a result of a misinterpretation of *gabbēyhem* to mean 'their backs'. In this case, the transfer of the technical expression to the bodies of the twofold beings led to a further elaboration of the picture, in which not only the backs, but also the whole body, hands and wings are covered with eyes. It is thus patently obvious that the text has been interfered with.

introduced into ch. 10.[1] Only one point does seem really probable, namely that 1.15–21 was inserted in its present position under the influence of ch. 10. Here Sprank[2] is right in insisting on the utter impossibility of reconciling the system of wheels with the throne of God travelling through the air borne up by the spirit of power. The latter is no mere portable cult-requisite native to the temple at Jerusalem, as the theologians of ch. 10 make it out to be. It is an integral element of the imagery of the prophet's vision, presenting a visual symbol of the limitless power and glory of the world-God (cf. pp. 57f.). But the insertion of 1.15–21 introduced by the same theoretical statement as 10.1, which is so inappropriate to a visionary event, makes the symbol of God's unrestricted power a sacred chariot rolling along the ground (1.15), such as might be seen in temple worship. It would also be difficult to see how the beauty and order of 1.15–21 could ever have given rise to ch. 10 with all its disorder which points to its construction in successive stratifications. The fact that in this deliberate insertion into ch. 1 the often-noticed fluctuation between masculine and feminine suffixes is kept to a minimum is easily understood. The attempt to clarify the state of the text by literary criticism with the aid of the feminine suffixes, which are grammatically correct for the *ḥayyōt*, the living creatures, in ch. 1, and the masculine ones, which are correct only for the cherubim of ch. 10, is a risky business. It cannot be carried through without assuming editorial alterations and scribal errors which are difficult even to define. This is enough to show that the present text does not present any secure grounds for any such conclusions (cf. above, p. 56). It is also exactly what we ought to expect, in view of the obvious fact that ch. 1 and 10 began to affect each others' text at a late period, when, owing to the influence of Aramaic, the distinction between masculine and feminine suffixes had ceased to be a rigid one.

At first sight, it seems extraordinary that a text first composed by the prophet should have the complicated history that we have seen from ch. 10. The position is clearly illuminated by ch. 11. For here we find two narratives, neither of which originally fitted to the other or to what preceded them. The section, 11.1–13, tells of twenty-five men, assembled to take counsel together at the east door of the temple, and smitten by God's sentence of condemnation. But it so

---

[1] A comparison between Sprank, *Studien zu Ezekiel*, BWANT III, 4, 1926, and Zimmerli, *Ezekiel, ad. loc.*, makes this perfectly clear.

[2] *Op. cit.*, pp. 52ff.

clearly clashes with 10.19, and comes so late, after God has completed his judgments on the temple and city, that suggestions that it ought to be inserted at some earlier point, either after 8.15 (with Rothstein) or after 8.18 (with Bertholet[2], May, etc.) are quite comprehensible. But that would not do justice to the introduction in 11.1 which runs parallel to 8.3, nor are there convincing reasons for picking out a piece originally belonging to ch. 8 and putting it in after ch. 10. 11.1, in fact, points clearly to a vision like the previous one. So here, too, sections similar in character and tendency have been welded into a single whole by the redactors of this prophetic book.

The following section, 11.14–21, is different in type. It is introduced by the same formula about receiving the word that Ezekiel employs elsewhere for independent visions. Sentence is pronounced upon some unnamed inhabitants of Jerusalem for their complacent assumption of their own superiority to their exiled fellow countrymen. It is evident that here we are referred back to a period prior to the second captivity (see commentary). But the passage has been lifted out of its proper position and put in its present one so as to help the reader to solve a problem with which he has just been faced. As a result of the despairing observation in 11.13, he may be wondering whether, after all, the 'remnant of Israel', that surviving fraction of the people for whom the future can hold some hope even after the greatest disasters, is not going to be wiped out altogether.[1] This gives the temple vision with its shattering message of judgment a climax which points beyond it and eases the task of the later community as it tries to make the prophet's word its own.

In 11.22f. the cherubic vehicle is transferred from the edge of the sanctuary to the Mount of Olives. This completes the linking up of these two sections with ch. 10. The vision thus comes to an end, and the proclamation of its message to the exiles in 11.24 serves as a conclusion to the whole composition, and demands that hearers and readers shall regard the whole narrative with that expectancy and receptiveness which a message from God deserves.

Ezekiel is transported: 8.1–3

The importance of such a powerful visionary experience for the early preaching of Ezekiel corresponds to its accurate dating. Chapters 4 and 5 had brought his message before the eyes of the exiles by means

[1] Cf. exposition below, and W. C. Mueller, 'Die Vorstellung vom Rest im Alten Testament', dissertation, Leipzig, 1939.

of impressive symbolic actions. Here clairvoyant powers lay bare its inner springs and initial realization. Assurances from God himself to his prophet about what is to come take the form of the active contemplation and intervention of the messenger of God in a world that has risen in rebellion against him. Full of trembling, he goes through a tremendous experience of God's judgment, and his witness makes his audience immediate participants in it.

It must be freely admitted that this is an event quite unique in all prophetic literature. We can understand why some have been so struck by the uniqueness that they feel the details of the prophetic vision to be an apocryphal invention and reject it as secondary. They prefer to think of a visit by the prophet to the temple while he was either still living in Jerusalem under divine compulsion (Herntrich, pp. 86ff., Bertholet[2]) or else on a visit to Jerusalem from Babylonia.[1] However, as Zimmerli rightly insists, they have failed to notice how frequent and well known are such experiences of transportation, not in the writing prophets, but in the narratives of the groups of nebiim. One need only think of Elisha, sitting in his house and hearing what the king is saying on the city wall (II Kings 6.32f.) or following his servant Gehazi and seeing what he is doing on his way to Naaman, already travelling home (II Kings 5.26). Furthermore, though this may be the most striking, it is not the only account given by Ezekiel of his transportation (cf. 3.12, 14; 37.1; 40.1) and the only satisfactory conclusion is that in our prophet there emerged once more a capacity for psychic experiences which most of the writing prophets had eliminated, in spite of its frequency among earlier prophets. For a person to be lifted up by a lock of hair is quite without parallel in the rest of the Old Testament. But it has often been remarked how close is its general agreement with the apocryphal addition to the book of Daniel (Bel and the Dragon, 36) and with fragment 2a of the Gospel to the Hebrews. Both of these seem to testify to the further extension of a form of experience hitherto peculiar to Ezekiel. Nevertheless, an instance of a man being caught up by a lock of hair by a god is already to be found in an account by an Assyrian king of how he went down to hell to visit Nergal.[2] The experience of soaring through the air is comparable to the accounts of levitation given by Arab Mevlevis and other such mystics.[3]

[1] R. H. Pfeiffer, *Introduction*², 1948, p. 537.

[2] E. Ebeling, *Tod und Leben nach den Vorstellungen der Babylonier*, 1, 1931, p. 6.

[3] G. Widengren, *Literary and Psychological Aspects of the Hebrew Prophets*, 1948, pp.

[1] The date of the month given in 8.1 varies in the two different texts. It seems best to follow the Greek, and fix on the fifth month. The postponement to the sixth month may very well be occasioned by recollections of the statement in 4.5 that the prophet stayed motionless for three hundred and ninety days, whereas no reasonable cause can be given for moving the date forward from the sixth to the fifth month. This means that approximately one year and three weeks have passed since the date mentioned in 3.16. But it does not necessarily mean that no prophetic communications took place during that period, since there must certainly be some gaps in the account which we possess.

The elders of Judah assembled in the prophet's house were evidently continuing the ancient institution of leading the tribes by esteemed men, and in the Babylonian captivity served as organizers of such internal self-government as was still allowed to the exiles in Babylonia (cf. Jer. 29.1; Ezek. 14.1; 20.1). Their assembling in the prophet's house seems undoubtedly to show that he had come, in the intermediate period, to possess a certain amount of influence. He may have been regarded as the person best qualified to settle disputes, a duty quite often associated with priestly office. Alternatively he may have owed his influence to the prophecies he disclosed (cf. II Kings 6.32). But 2.6f. describes how much hatred and how much hostility was shown towards him. So we must look on such recognition as he received as either unwilling toleration which their troubles compelled them to give or else that mixture of curiosity and horror one feels towards a lunatic. Did the elders wish to consult him on the problem of what was going to happen to Jerusalem (Fohrer, etc., cf. Jer. 37.17)? There is nothing to suggest any such thing, least of all the subject of the subsequent vision. Indeed, that, like his other threatening prophecies (cf. 14.1ff.; 20.1ff.), seems to be deliberately framed in such a way as to be directly opposed to the requests and wishes of his audience.

Whatever it was that brought them, they became witnesses of the severe ecstatic seizure of dumbness which cut off the man of God from any association with the outside world, until such time as returning consciousness made it possible for him to pass on his mysterious experiences to others.

106ff.; there the reader is also referred to C. H. Richet, *Traité de Métapsychique*, 1922, pp. 622ff.; and S. Lindquist, *Siddhi und Abhinna, Eine Studie über die klassischen Wunder des Yoga*, 1935, pp. 57ff.

[2] The prophet's eyes are riveted upon what has appeared to him. It is the fiery shape of a man, described in the same words as the one that sits upon the throne in 1.27, and probably to be identified with him. But this time no word sounds in his ears. [3] A lordly hand draws him up by the hair of his head. At the same time he feels himself being swept away by a whirlwind, rushing away through the air, till he is set down in his far-away native land at the northern entrance of the temple at Zion.

The profanation of the sanctuary: 8.5–18

The cult of the Asherah: 8.5–6

[5] In this place, which he knows so well, the first thing he hears is a word from his mysterious guide, telling him to look round before going in through the door. As a result of this, he turns north, and his eye falls upon an altar, set up before the image of a deity. The Accadian loan-word *semel* provides a name for this pillar-image. It is referred to as the (familiar) 'image of jealousy', as if the expression would have an intelligible meaning for everyone who heard it. The gloss in v. 3b understands this 'jealousy' as the wrathful jealousy of Yahweh, which would blaze out at the sight of such an image. Yet Herrmann must be right in preferring to give the word the alternative meaning of 'passionate love', which serves to indicate that the image is that of Asherah, the goddess of love. This is in perfect agreement with the statement that an image of Asherah was set up in the temple by king Manasseh (II Kings 21.7), and in the parallel account in Chronicles (II Chron. 33.7) the same name *semel* is given to it. II Kings 23.6 tells how the image was removed by Josiah during his reform of the cult. Evidently it was restored by one of his successors, as a part of that quiet ignoring of the law of reform since Jehoiakim which Jeremiah denounced as a conspiracy against Yahweh (Jer. 11.9). We shall probably be correct in identifying Asherah with the queen of heaven of Jer. 7.18; 44.17ff. As the service of her altar did not simply take place somewhere outside the temple on the street, and indeed all the statements we have quoted speak of her image being set up in the temple, according to 8.3, we find ourselves not before the great wall encircling the royal palace (Bertholet, Fohrer, etc.) but already within it, at the door giving access to the temple court proper.

[6] The fact that visitors to the chief sanctuary of the God of the covenant are, at the very entrance to that sanctuary, met by the goddess of love, and invited to worship her, from the very outset puts

the being of Yahweh under a false light. He claims to be absolutely unique and allows no other divinity to share in his royalty. Above all, any bisexuality is repudiated so as to assert that his being is complete in itself, and as a result the word 'goddess' does not once occur in the Old Testament. But now he has apparently to put up with the presidency of the ancient eastern queen of heaven as the female guardian over his threshold. She is thus the go-between who can obtain admission to an audience with the divine Lord, just as Tanit, the consort of the Phoenician Baal at Carthage, was styled 'the countenance of Baal', and was regarded as acting as his representative and mediating his grace. Sexual desire and pleasure, hitherto excluded from the picture of God, are now introduced into it. Yahweh is thus degraded to the level of a nature-god, with an ambivalent moral will, inclusive of evil as well as good.

The expression in v. 6 is somewhat ambiguous. But the most probable interpretation of 'to drive me far from my sanctuary' is that Yahweh is being driven out of the place consecrated to him. This also states the ultimate result of the heathenism which has secured a lodgment within his temple. For we here meet with *tōʿēbōt* or abominations, or, in other words, with heathen practices which ought to be regarded with loathing. The word was already used in the language of the ancient law to denote whatever would profane the people of God by taking away their consecrated character, and is therefore to be utterly rejected. Here the phrase 'still greater abominations' is first employed, to be constantly repeated as the profanation spreads over everything holy, and finally becomes so intolerable that every listener can see that nothing can avert the stroke of the inevitable judgment.

A clandestine Egyptian cult: 8.7–13
[7f.] In obedience to a divine command, the prophet turns his back on the altar of Ashera, and looks once more towards the door. This does not mean a mere entrance-gate, but a whole complex of buildings with two wings containing rooms of various sizes.[1] He is, apparently by some door concealed in it, to make his way to a room of considerable size, in which there are seventy men (v. 11). The description in its present form speaks of a hole in the wall and of breaking through a partition, so it seems somewhat confused. If there was a hole in the wall, it would not have been necessary to break through the partition to uncover the door; while, on the other hand, if the

---

[1] Cf. the ground-plans in R. Galling's *Biblisches Reallexicon,* 1937, p. 523.

door was then opened up for the first time, there was some other entry which afforded the seventy men access, and no reason is given us why the prophet should not also have used it. One can hardly appeal to the bizarre and inconsistent features we experience in a dream as an argument for the preservation of the present text. So we must follow Balla[1] and Fohrer[2] in their explanation of what has occurred.

It is very likely that the verb *ḥāpar* 'discover' has been mistakenly read as *ḥātar* 'violently break through'. Alternatively, *ḥātar* has been given its alternative meaning of 'investigate', 'search for', and then subsequent misunderstanding turned it into the action of breaking through the wall. The command issued to the prophet thus did no more than direct him to search for an appropriate door which had been deliberately concealed, showing that whatever went on behind it was done in secrecy. What actually presents itself to the eyes of the person who enters is indeed strikingly unusual. **[9f.]** Pictures of animals are sketched or carved on the walls, like graffiti or bas-reliefs. **[11]** Incense is solemnly offered to them, so they evidently stand for divine beings worshipped by those present, whose complete participation is emphasized. It is further specified that these pictures are of cattle and creeping things, clearly indicating that they follow Egyptian prototypes; in Egypt more than anywhere we find gods in animal shape, whether as crocodiles, snakes and dung-beetles or as oxen, sheep and cats. Babylonia, on the other hand, can offer only a few isolated examples of images of demons with animal's heads or bodies, which is not enough to satisfy our specifications. The fact that this foreign cult was practised in secret provides additional confirmation. In this connection, H. Schmidt rightly observes that 'at that period of Jerusalem's history, Babylonian gods did not need to go into hiding'. The policy of Zedekiah and of the upstarts who gained control under him was completely pro-Babylonian. On the other hand, for the members of the old ruling class, now deprived of all power, only a fraction of whom had been carried into exile by Nebuchadrezzar, all political intrigue and all hope of regaining power was centred upon, and dependent on, Egypt. By the designation 'elders', they are publicly recognized as belonging to the patrician families of Jerusalem, in which qualifications for leadership had been

---

[1] 'Ezek. 8.9–9.11; 11.24, 25', *Festschrift für Rudolf Bultmann*, 1949, p. 8.

[2] 'Die Glossen im Buch Ezekiel', *ZAW* 63 (1951), p. 38, and *Hauptprobleme des Buches Ezechiel*, 1952, p. 59.

hereditary from ancient times. The cult in which we now find them engaged was little more than an alternative way of expressing their political programme. But it also showed how they ignored Yahweh, who, in the prophet's eyes, ought to have the deciding voice in Israelite politics, as in everything else. The bitter disillusionment of 598 had left them homeless, religiously speaking, as well as in other respects. It had seemed to them that their national God had neither the will nor the power to assert his lordship against the gods of the great powers. [12] Their behaviour is summed up by their slogan: 'Yahweh does not see it; Yahweh has forsaken the land.' They have already made up their minds that the destinies of their native land, of Israel, are controlled by other powers, and that everything depends on making them turn out favourably. These other powers are the gods of the kingdom on the Nile, to whose magical and mantic sphere of influence they have now unconditionally surrendered. They have thus given up one of the most sacred convictions of Israel's faith: they have ceased to recognize that Israel is Yahweh's inheritance, the land whose destinies he alone has the right to control, that the people of Israel once received the land of Israel from him, and, year by year, at the great festivals, have it bestowed by him upon them anew. So the link between Yahweh and his own land is severed, severed, as it were, under the very eyes of the divine Lord of that land and in his temple, severed in favour of those very gods out of whose sphere of influence Yahweh had once brought his own people when he led them to this land, and severed by the former leaders of the people who had solemnly sworn to be faithful. At the reform of Josiah, the last attempt to restore the people of God to its ancient purity and greatness, they had still promised faithfulness; even Jaazaniah, a member of the house of Shaphan (II Kings 22.3ff.) who had played a leading part in those efforts at reform, is to be seen, to the dismay of the prophet, among this group whose actions express their denial of God as an actual authority. [13] Yet, even here, it can be said: 'You will see greater abominations than these!'

The adoration of Tammuz: 8.14–15
[14] The prophet now leaves the chamber of clandestine worship to go on through the door leading into the temple court proper, where he comes upon the women weeping for Tammuz. Babylonian gods had thus been welcomed into the inner court, as had happened once before to *Ašur-Šamaš*, the chief god of the Assyrian empire (II Kings

23.11). Tammuz, or in Babylonian Dumuzi, was already well known in Sumerian times, and was one of the most popular deities of Mesopotamia. His myth represented the dying and reawakening of vegetation. When plant life died away in summer during the month which bore his name (June–July), the withering away of life was identified with his descent into the realm of the dead and lamented aloud with all the ritual of mourning.[1] Once his sister-consort Ishtar, the Sumerian Innina, has freed him from the underworld, the holy marriage takes place once more, to bring about the resurrection of life in the spring. As early as the days of Isaiah we find indications that this Babylonian cult has found its way into Israel (cf. Isa. 17.11; 1.29f.; 10.4, and O. Procksch's *Jesaia I, ad loc.*). The syncretistic wave of the seventh century served to naturalize it fully in Judah. When Judah was made a satellite state of Babylon, that favoured its further spread.

Here we see Yahweh being robbed of his right to control his land in yet another sphere. The mystery of life and fertility, upon which Israel's earthly existence depends, is no longer dominated by the mighty controlling power of the covenant God, to whom men offer the firstfruits of the harvest, as they humbly recognize his undeserved kindness and bring their petitions for his blessing (Deut. 26.1–15); it is torn away from him and handed over to a natural power, whose favour men hope to secure by the due performance of certain magical rites. The natural side of life had hitherto formed part of an integral whole, where at every point a fully loyal relationship was kept up with the Lord of the people. So even earthly possessions became signs of covenant fellowship with him, and harvest festivals were ways of proclaiming the will of the divine Lord as revealed in history. Now natural life was dissociated with all that, to be put under the control of powers which called men to the deification of life by mystical union, promising at once to satisfy religious yearnings and sanctify sensual instincts by allowing them to engage in orgies imitative of the reproductive forces of divinized nature. Thus here, too, the attack of paganism was carried into the innermost zone of the covenant fellowship between God and Israel.

The sun-worshippers: 8.16–18
Every step Ezekiel has taken has brought him nearer to the holiest

---

[1] The text of these laments is to be found in *Altorientalische Texte zum Alten Testament*[2] and in J. B. Pritchard, *Ancient Near Eastern Texts*[2], 1955, p. 109.

place of the public temple worship, the open space between the vestibule of the temple and the altar of burnt offering, which he now approaches by way of the inner court (v. 16). According to Joel 2.17, the priests stand in this place on a fast day, with their faces towards the temple door which led through the holy place to the holy of holies beyond it, so that they may offer intercessory prayer. Twenty-five men are now gathered in this same place in order to perform an act of worship. There is nothing to indicate that they are priests (Bertholet[2]). But they must be persons of distinction, in order to have been admitted to such an eminent place as this. These are very different persons from the elders of v. 11. They are most probably representatives of 'Zedekiah's proletarian government' (H. Schmidt), who are showing their loyalty to Babylon by engaging in her state-cult, the worship of Marduk-Šamaš. To support this view, we have the added fact (v. 17) that, on top of the contempt of Yahweh shown by their idolatry, they are accused of having filled the land with violence. That is exactly what 11.6 says is being done by those at present holding power.

It is characteristic that a contempt for the laws of the people expressed in violent deeds and a religious and cultic alienation go hand in hand, the one conditioning and accentuating the other. It is characteristic of the proclamation of God's will in Israel right from the days of Moses that these two things are seen together. [16] In this passage the cultic practice is a symbol of what has already actually taken place in the course of the practical exercise of governmental power, that is, of a thoughtless contempt for Yahweh's claim to lordship. As they worship the sun-god, the worshippers look towards the sunrise. By so doing they turn their backs on the temple and hence on the ark where Yahweh has his throne! It is an expression of their utter contempt for the holy God of Israel; it amounts to saying that they have actually dethroned him from being Lord of his people, to set up instead a foreign god, the mighty sun-god of the Babylonian empire. The real God is the one who has power and gives success! In the eyes of these persons, Yahweh has shown himself to be helpless, and can no longer be worshipped except as a subordinate divinity of merely national significance.

[17] A coarse word is used to make this inward attitude visible in an outward manifestation. The word $z^e m \bar{o} r \bar{a}$, which has been translated 'stink' here, elsewhere means 'tendril' (cf. Ezek. 15.2; Num. 13.24; Isa. 17.10; Nahum 2.3). It is rather far-fetched to try to

connect it with Persian or more recently Egyptian (Fohrer) cultic customs, according to which plants, portions of plants, or bunches of twigs were either used to cover the mouth in sign of reverence or held out as a life-giving symbol towards the divinity who was to be worshipped. Neither of these can be regarded as a particularly offensive gesture, or as a blasphemous insult thrown in the face of Yahweh, which might occasion an alteration in the text by the scribes. As the attitude of the sun-worshippers would not support a connection between the word and the male organ, to be found elsewhere in Jewish tradition (cf. Herrmann, *ad loc.*), one must either follow L. Köhler (see *Lexicon s.v.*), who appeals to *zumru*, the Accadian word for 'body', and explains the phrase as indicating an unseemly bodily posture, or, with the medieval Jewish exegetes (the details may be found in Herrmann), adopt the conjectural interpretation proposed in our translation, and apply it to the stench of farting. In actual fact this is the only way of understanding the exceedingly contemptuous and defiant attitude of the sun-worshippers, and of explaining the subsequent alteration of the coarse phraseology which does not occur elsewhere in Ezekiel.[1]

In any case it is not till this point that the shameless profanation of the sanctuary comes to a climax, in so far as it leads to a direct insult to Yahweh. It becomes clear, at the same time, how little the condemnation of all these cultic misdoings is concerned with the mere defence of an external ritual holiness of the place. The decisive factor is rather the actual inward detachment from that holy awe which is Yahweh's due and the foundation of all communion with him. We must, from the outset, dispute that the basic presupposition for the divine sentence of judgment is that his temple is meant to be the place of the real meeting between the people and its Lord, and see in the whole vision a ritualistic overvaluation of the outward forms of cultic piety which is impossible for us to reproduce. This ought to be an impossibility for anyone who recognizes that the gracious bestowal of the divine presence, promised to the Old Testament community in its celebrations, is the presupposition of worship. Only through a grotesque misunderstanding can this be perversely transformed into psychological experience resulting from cultic communal actions.

Once we have seen this, we can see the direct relevance of the

---

[1] MT reads 'in their nostrils' instead of the original 'in my nostrils', but gives an explicit indication that the scribes have here effected an alteration in the text.

Old Testament prophetic word for the community of God at all times. The object of the worship of the Christian Church is not the 'edification' of pious souls, nor even fellowship between a set of persons of like tastes, but a meeting with their Lord, who gives them a share in his resurrection life, and thus equips them to be witnesses to him in the world. Forgetfulness of what gives it all its meaning is the real danger to Christian liturgy; the infiltration of strange 'gods' into its worship as it tries to satisfy selfish desires pollutes the worship-in spirit and in truth. 'To be in Christ', this form of fellowship with God which aims at reaching full unity with his will (Gal. 3.28; I Cor. 1.30; II Cor. 5.17; Gal. 5.6), had to be defended by the early Church again and again against the misunderstandings of erotic mysticism and an experience of enthusiastic unity (Rev. 2.14, 20, 24; I Cor. 6.12ff.; 10.7ff.). There was an urgent need to insist that it was incompatible with any homage to other gods, or homage to Caesar, i.e. the homage claimed by political power (I Cor. 10.20f.; Rev. 2.13; 13.2ff.). In this connection, it is the consciousness of a real meeting with Christ in the Lord's Supper celebrated by the community which gives the strength to shut out all these heathen powers. In exactly the same way, the Old Testament prophet was led by the evidences of the presence of the holy God in the temple to the absolute rejection of all heathen syncretism. What asserted itself in the temple of Zion in the tangible form of ancient cultic practice remains for the Christian community the tempting power which falsifies the meaning and the force of its worship, and needs to be unmasked again and again by the prophetic ministry.

Yahweh calls in the destroyers: 9.1–2

[1] Ezekiel hears in a loud cry the command to the avenging angels to go about their work of annihilation. [2] So, along the same route by which the prophet himself has come, there approach six warriors, whom we are to imagine to be of gigantic size, each of whom carries in his hand 'his weapon', that is to say, the special weapon of slaughter he has been given to employ. As Yahweh fights his battles now with the bow, and now with the sword (Deut. 32.23; Ezek. 5.16; 21.3), as the Babylonian gods employ special weapons of their own, Hadad, the lightning and the axe, Marduk, the bow and the net, Sin, the scimitar, etc., so the avengers whom Yahweh calls in are equipped with terrible and irresistible instruments of slaughter. Their chief, who has other special duties beside that of leading them, is a dignified

personage, clad in a long linen robe and carrying not weapons but writing materials. These probably consist of a reed-pen and ink, in a wooden case, and he probably also has a penknife and sheets of parchment or papyrus in his girdle.[1] The number 'seven' of these supernatural beings suggests astral associations, as it recalls the gods of the seven planets; the last of them to appear on the scene confirms this impression by suggesting Nebo, the heavenly scribe of the Babylonian pantheon.[2] We must also compare the idea of seven demons working in association, which was a widespread one in Babylon. This is not to say that Ezekiel first became acquainted with such figures in Babylonia. It is probable, rather, that in view of its strong cultic and political connections with Mesopotamia, the Israelite conception had been coloured by various other notions, including Babylonian ones, which had previously been foreign to it. The *mal'ak Yahweh* also has elsewhere the characteristics of a heavenly vizier, who acts as Yahweh's representative when he judges and pronounces sentence (Zech. 3.1ff.; Mal. 3.1). The word for writing materials, *qeset*, is borrowed from Egyptian, and seems to point to influences from that quarter; so Zimmerli may be right in suggesting that this priestly scribe may have had some Egyptian prototype. How freely such traditional conceptions were used in Israel is shown by Zech. 1.20f., with its four heavenly smiths, who are to break down the power of the foreign nations.

It is at the brazen altar, north of the temple (cf. I Kings 8.64 with II Kings 16.14f.), that the little troop forms up and awaits the order to begin. Its supernatural origin makes it more formidable than the greatest earthly army. Against them all resistance, however heroic, is useless; and whereas the defenders are expecting the enemy on the walls, they start their work of annihilation at the temple of Zion, in the centre of the city! They are thus an overwhelming embodiment of the divine will, in face of which mere humanity is helpless. No information, of course, is here supplied as to the historical details of the fall of Jerusalem. What we are given here is the metaphysical background of it all.

The protective sign: 9.3–4

[3] The divine wrath is about to be outpoured upon the hapless city.

[1] Cf. R. Galling, *Biblische Reallexicon*, 1937, pp. 463ff.
[2] Cf. H. Gunkel, 'Der Schreiberengel Nabû im Alten Testament und im Judentum', *ARW* I (1898), pp. 294ff.

Before that happens, the divine Lord and Judge must set a limit to the operation of the disaster in such a way as to display his flawless justice even in the very act of chastisement. [4] The heavenly scribe is to mark with a sign the foreheads of all those who had experienced all the inward misery and agony of witnessing national apostasy without being able to avert it. This sign is designated as *tau*, the last letter of the alphabet, and probably took the shape of a sloping cross, the most archaic form of that letter. In this vivid procedure, analogous to that of fixing a mark of ownership on a piece of material property, the prophet is shown that the eye of the heavenly Lord still watches over those who remain faithful, just as he watched over his people when he punished the Egyptians long before, and provided them with a sign to protect them from the destructive forces then unloosed.

The slaughter of God's enemies: 9.5–7

[5] Next comes a command to the heavenly warriors. The guilty parties are to be mercilessly wiped out, together with all that belongs to them. Immediately before this an exception has been made. [6] But now wives and children are included. This shows that collective retribution is the principle according to which the matter is decided. The merciless law of the holy war in its most extreme form (cf. Josh. 6.17ff.; Judg. 20.48; I Sam. 15.3; Deut. 13.15ff.; 20.16ff.) is here enforced at the expense of Yahweh's own people. This shows what a mistake it is to assume that in Ezekiel there is any such thing as a transformation of the principle of collective retribution, which replaces it with a consistent theory of individual responsibility. The large-scale judgments which strike any community sweep away all who belong to it into ruin. For anyone to be excepted is a special sign of favour on the part of Yahweh (for Ezek. 18, see commentary below, pp. 234ff.). Such a view does greater justice to the character of a great historical catastrophe than any atomistic doctrine of individual retribution. It is also evidently based on an estimation of sin which regards it as the out and out disintegration of man's real destiny as determined by God. We see what is at stake. Where it is a question of putting a stop to its influence and giving men a healthy horror of its dreadfulness, no price is too great to pay. But what is most remarkable here is the way in which, at the very point where, according to the view of the universe current in the ancient East, the way lay open for complete pessimism and despair of any divine purpose to save, we are

not allowed to have any doubt that salvation is God's ultimate aim and that he really does will to bring men to life.

The full inexorability of the divine judgment becomes evident in the fact that the temple itself is the point at which it begins (v. 6b). The sanctuary loses all its old rights of asylum; even those who visit it are treated as outlaws. The sun-worshippers are the first to pay with their lives for an apostasy characteristic of the whole nation. [7] The next to follow are not those preceding them in the list of idolaters, but the whole of the temple staff. The court is filled with dead bodies. Even the holiness of the priest does not stay the destroying weapon; the numinous character of the whole place is trampled terribly in the dust—and by Yahweh himself in person. Such a stupendous act of judgment leaves no room for any doubt as to whether the command for the complete liquidation of all the inhabitants of the city will be carried out in full.

Vain intercession: 9.8–10

Now the emissaries of doom have gone. [8] The prophet is left in the temple court alone with the angry God, while cries and shrieks can be heard from the streets of the city. The whole mass of his nation's misery overwhelms the prophet. He finds it impossible to maintain his usual attitude of dumb obedience and silent acceptance of his Lord's decisions. He is forced to utter a cry of grief, and to address a question to the judge. Does he on his part realize that the sentence he has pronounced negates any future salvation? No 'remnant of Israel' will now exist. There will be no one to carry on the history of salvation, and therefore there will be no earthly possibility of setting up his lordship over Israel and over the nations. Hope in that remnant, who survive the disaster which overwhelms the nation and provide the means for a fresh beginning, was one which had come to possess importance for prophetic minds mainly because of the preaching of Isaiah (cf. Isa. 7.3, the son named 'remnant returns'; and 28.16, the congregation held together by faith which God will use as a cornerstone upon which to build in future days; 1.25ff.; 14.32; 29.18f.). They provided a possibility of emerging from the present darkness. To see this possibility lie dead and buried beneath the ruins of Jerusalem presents an extreme temptation to despair. After that, how can anyone keep faith in Yahweh's saving intentions?

[9] The prophet, however, receives no answer but a fresh confirmation of the sentence already pronounced by God. The end has come

for Israel in a way from which there can be no appeal. Her guilt has heaped up mountain high. The time for patience has now passed. The judge must sum up and pronounce the final sentence. Chapter 7 spoke of the end, but only now do we realize the full depth of the meaning of that word.

It may be surprising to find that v. 9, in summing up the reasons for this sentence, makes no further mention of the way the sanctuary has been profaned, but only of bloodguiltiness and perversion of justice. That serves to bring out still more clearly a point to which we have already referred, the close connection between cultic and social sin; the former is only a surface manifestation of the fundamental cause of the latter (cf. above, p. 127). Because man has ceased to possess any relationship to the holy being of Yahweh, all his relationships, including those with his fellow men, have been handed over to the demons of self-assertion. So one cannot speak of the one without also speaking of the other. It is impossible to evade this conclusion by assuming a passage to have here been inserted from some different context, since no seams appear in the fabric, and the whole context has a unity all its own.

The question (v. 8b), wrung from the prophet by his deep inward grief, is a hidden attempt at intercession, and meets with rejection. Yet even in this rejection we can still perceive how strong is the intrinsic bond between Yahweh and his people. [10] The very refusal to show mercy or to mitigate the punishment now threatening them points back to the forbearance and faithfulness which has characterized all that God has done up to now. His words are not the tones of a God delighting in indiscriminate destruction, but of a Father whose inclinations are still all for forgiving love (cf. 16.6f.), and who has to steel himself against the strongest instincts within him to carry out the long-deferred sentence. It is a faint echo of the unique witness of this innermost power of the divine nature of which Hos. 11.8f. and Jer. 31.20 bear such unique testimony. Here, of course, it is almost drowned by the thunders of judgment, but even then ears that are open for the subtle undertones of God's speech cannot miss this almost imperceptible hint of some mystery in God's way of acting still hidden but yet to be revealed, which is enough to prevent a lapse into hopeless despair.

Jerusalem burnt to the ground: 9.11; 10.2–7

[9.11] Is it a mere accident, that just when God has reached this point in what he has to say, the heavenly scribe should now appear to report that he has carried out his mission of rescue? [**10.2**] But it must be admitted that the next order issued to him serves only to show the complete ruthlessness with which judgment is executed. The man clothed in linen is to go into the temple (the original text must be thus interpreted, once it has been freed from the insertions by which it has been almost hidden). [**1**] There he is to fill both hands with red-hot coals, evidently from the altar of incense, and scatter them over the city, so that it may be utterly destroyed by a conflagration on top of the massacre. We can hardly be wrong in attributing a special destructive power to fire brought from such a holy spot; every available means is used to bring out the fact that Yahweh himself is transforming a fire kindled in his honour into the fire of his wrath, so as to annihilate his own city. The description of how the destruction comes to pass in a blaze reaching up to heaven is no longer extant, later editors having replaced this awful finale by the description of the cherubic throne. It is therefore impossible to say how it was originally connected with the vision of 11.1ff. All that can be done is to deal with each account separately on its own merits.

A second visionary experience: God's sentence upon the new ruling class in Jerusalem: 11.1–13

[**1**] The introduction recalls 8.3b. But a comparison between the two descriptions shows that this one has been abbreviated to a remarkable extent. The statement that the prophet was carried by the spirit of power and set down at the east door of the temple might, if need be, also indicate that the prophet was brought from where he was, inside the temple, and overwhelmed by his encounter with Yahweh in 9.8. That must also have been the intention of the person who attached ch. 11 to what precedes it and who gave it its present shape. As ch. 11 still retains its original independence (see above, pp. 118f.), the reference to a similar experience of transportation as in ch. 8 may have led to its being attached to the great temple vision. The fact that it speaks of the east door, and that 10.19 also refers to it, could serve as an additional link. Nevertheless, it was felt necessary to abbreviate it, so as to obviate the glaring repetition which showed up in comparison with the context. We cannot follow Bertholet[2] and Horst in assuming the transportation to be an editorial insertion, since that makes it harder, and not easier, to explain how it came to be connected with what precedes it. We must assume, instead, that

what was originally a richer description of a vision has been considerably cut down. It must have told of how the prophet was snatched up a second time and carried to Jerusalem, so that he might be an invisible participant in the council meeting held by the twenty-five men in the room at the east gate of the temple.

The description of the participants and the place where they meet alike point to the fact that they are an influential body, and that whatever they resolve decides the fate of Jerusalem for good or ill. The prophet knows the exact number of those who meet here, whereas the numbers in 8.11 and 16 are only approximate estimates.[1] This shows that he was able to identify them, and to know what they stood for, as soon as he had recognized their two presidents, Jaazaniah[2] and Pelatiah. They alone are called 'rulers of the people' (in Hebrew, *sārē hāʿām*), a title found in Neh. 11.1; I Chron. 21.2; and II Chron. 24.23, and one which evidently invests its possessors with a special dignity and power. So in them we are to see no mere leaders of political parties, but ministers of state, who preside over a 'council with full governmental authority' (Herrmann) whose numbers and composition are such as to be known even to the exiles. The verses which follow show that there is no limit to the powers which this college takes to itself, and that we will not be mistaken if we regard it as a sort of 'national council' which had gained control by the social and political revolution that followed upon the first exile of 598. The Babylonian overlords had allowed or perhaps even authorized their seizure of power, and under the protection of king Zedekiah they had to a very large extent taken over the executive power. All resistance on the part of the former aristocrats was ruthlessly suppressed. Suspicious characters were eliminated by summary executions, before they could spell any danger to the consistently pro-Babylonian policy of these new rulers. How slavishly they acted as assistant executioners on behalf of their foreign overlords was so notorious as to be known even to the exiles in Babylonia. This political situation makes it easy to see why the pro-Egyptian group carried on their cult in secret, whereas the worship of the Babylonian state-god Marduk-Šamaš had great

---

[1] The LXX shows a *kᵉ* to have been inserted before the number in 11.1. But this is a later attempt to modify the differences in the numbers, and therefore to be rejected (see above, p. 108, n.ᵗ).

[2] This Jaazaniah is not to be identified with the son of Shaphan mentioned in 8.11, nor with the prince referred to in Jer. 40.8, whose seal has been found at Tell en Nasbeh (cf. W. F. Bade, 'The Seal of Jaazaniah', *ZAW* 51 (1933), pp. 150ff.).

publicity, and was conducted by the official representatives of the satellite state of Judah (8.7ff. and 16ff.).

[2] In view of the despotism of this governing council, it is not surprising that its members should be called devisers of iniquity and givers of evil counsel 'in this city', meaning Jerusalem. The hint of their plans given in v. 6 is clear if we note that the perfect tense of the verb and the answering threat from Yahweh in v. 7, introduced with a *lāken*, therefore, make a reference to the future impossible, and that the word *ḥālāl* is far from being used solely of persons slain in battle. It is used just as often, particularly in Ezekiel, of the victim of a murder or an execution.[1] [3] Verse 3, on the other hand, contains a statement that is difficult to explain. The phrase about building houses is patient of many meanings, quite irrespective of whether one is to take it as expressing, under an affirmative form, a refusal to undertake some future building project; or again, with a slight emendation as in our translation, as a triumphant rhetorical question in reference to a building programme already carried out. Rejecting the translation of 'houses' by 'families' (in itself a perfectly possible course), and the assumption that building houses refers to a synoikismos, i.e. an increase in the numbers of the population by special rules of living together, mentioned in Neh. 7.4ff. (thus Horst), but quite improbable for the authorities mentioned here, we may best understand this enigmatically terse sentence to be self-glorification on the part of the speakers, who are boasting of all the successful work they have done for the reconstruction of Jerusalem and the repairing of war-damage, to justify their great self-importance. Very much the same thing is happening at this present day. Satellite régimes which have managed to gain power in defiance of the popular will keep boasting of their social progress, as if it were a thing which they alone could attain, and make that a reason for denouncing all who oppose them as enemies of the state. In the same way, the members of this committee of men of blood boast of all the benefits conferred by them upon the city, as if that conferred upon them a clear divine right to monopolize all government. Anyone who can report such success need not pay any heed to criticism, and may safely take for granted that he has a right to do as he likes and to make everyone obey his orders. The proverbial expression about the meat in the

---

[1] Cf. the exhaustive demonstration by O. Eissfeldt, 'Schwerterschlagene bei Hesekiel', *Studies in Old Testament Prophecy*, 1950, pp. 73ff. In face of this, the objections made by Horst, pp. 341f., and Zimmerli, p. 245, fall to the ground.

cauldron is undoubtedly intended to suggest both the high worth of Jerusalem's present rulers and also their security from all external dangers. Cauldrons are used to cook the more expensive articles of diet, on which their owners set a high value. When the population of a city are metaphorically spoken of as meat in a cauldron, it means that they are carefully guarded because they are an élite of the very highest quality. Here we find the same exaggerated estimate of self that Amos found in his contemporaries, when they styled themselves the notable men of the chief among the nations (Amos 6.1). Yet, on the other hand, we must not try to introduce any contrast between the valuable meat and the useless bones which are rejected as waste, and thus make out that the image is meant to express contempt for other sections of the people (Herrmann, Fohrer).[1] This idea, though central in the following section, is here quite marginal, and is not suggested by the imagery, as is shown by the way the same image is used in Ezek. 24.3ff. But there the threat to the contents of the cauldron is portrayed by the fire kindled under it and by its being emptied out. We find in it, therefore, only one more example of Ezekiel's characteristic habit of elaborating a simple parable, so that it may serve to express a new idea. We cannot therefore transfer any of these features to the present passage.

[4] God pronounces sentence on the boastful arrogance of the present lords of Jerusalem, who try to conceal their own wicked deeds by impudent self-advertisement. He does so by making his prophet announce the punishment which is in store for the assembled council. [5] The address 'house of Israel' corresponds to the self-importance of the rulers, who regard themselves as the legitimate successors and heirs to all the rights possessed by the people of God, since the whole Northern kingdom and considerable sections of the population of the south had gone off into exile, and had thus ceased to belong to that part of the nation with political rights. To realize that makes 11.13 become perfectly intelligible. It is remarkable that a prediction should take place within a vision. It will happen again only in ch. 37. According to v. 5, it is made possible by a fresh upsurge of the spirit of God's power, which here, unlike 8.3; 11.1 and 24, where the

---

1 To interpret 3a as giving positive reasons for refusing to build more houses, by suggesting that the present leaders have enriched themselves by confiscating the property of those socially weaker than themselves, as suggested by Fohrer, can indeed be established from the unamended MT, but only serves to make the passage mean exactly the same as 11.15, and thus cease to possess any point of its own.

transportation is attributed to it, includes divine authority to speak the word with full effect. One may nurse some suspicions (as do Fohrer and Zimmerli) about the originality of this saying, since its view of the Spirit is like that of the *nābī'*, and since there is nothing corresponding to it in the parallel passage already referred to in ch. 37. One therefore begins to wonder whether anything more is meant here than that the prophet receives the physical energy required to perform his task, as in 2.2; 3.12, 14, and is forced to leave the text with different effects of the spirit standing side by side (thus Horst, p. 341, n. 1).

Yahweh, as he pronounces sentence on these politicians, takes up their favourite slogan, and changes its meaning to a highly ironical one. The duplicity of these authorities is transparent to the judge. **[6]** They claim to be the rightful representatives of the 'house of Israel', i.e. of a people chosen and called to be of world-wide importance, yet at the same time they try to make their position secure by shedding innocent blood. This inconsistent behaviour now stands revealed.

The proverbial phrase about the flesh in the cauldron undergoes a gruesome transformation. **[7]** It is not they but the victims of their ruthless self-assertion who form the real élite and who deserve to be cherished within Jerusalem the holy city. What is probably to become of a city which is busy eliminating all the best of those within it by means of judicial murder is only too obvious, and does not need to be stated. **[9b–10]** The present holders of power will be dragged out of what they imagined to be a sure refuge, and have God's sentence executed upon them by foreigners. That will bring them out of their blindness, and make them, in the moment of their downfall, come to 'know Yahweh', e.g. come to an inward realization of that holy majesty of his, which hitherto they had so blatantly ignored (cf. 6.7).

[13] While Ezekiel is still proclaiming this divine judgment, he sees Pelatiah, one of the princes of the people named in v. 1, collapse and fall down dead in the midst of the assembled council. The simplicity of the wording makes it plain that both the death and the despairing cry it wrung from him were part of the vision which the prophet experienced. It is equally impossible to deny that there would have been no sense in writing such an account had it not been verified when, not long afterwards, the news had come to Tell Abīb of Pelatiah's sudden death in Jerusalem, to give staggering proof that the prophet's threat was already taking effect. We cannot take seriously any exegesis which tries to evade the actual facts, and to explain away things for which there is no rationalistic explanation, by declaring that the mention of the names of the two princes of the people in v. 1 and of the death of Pelatiah in v. 13 are later elaborations.[1]

Stories like this are undoubtedly unusual. But they are, of course, made harder to understand if elements are introduced which are not already present. There is, for example, no justification for saying that Pelatiah must have heard with his own ears what the prophet said to collapse in terror at it. There is not a word to suggest this, nor is any such assumption necessary in order to understand what happened. His sudden death can nevertheless be regarded as the effect of the pronouncement of prophetic judgment if we only remember how, according to the ancient and the Israelite way of thinking, such a threat was full of dynamic power and began to work as soon as it was expressed in speech, bringing disaster. Whether the object of the curse did or did not have this association of ideas present to his own consciousness has nothing to do with the case. It is therefore perfectly consistent to say that that death resulted directly from the word of judgment without trying to establish any psychological connection between them; such a view agrees precisely with the objectively destructive powers of a prediction made during a trance, and symbolized the beginning of its effect in a way which gives the prophet himself a severe shock. 'God's veto' (Horst, p. 342) to the plans of that national council is given vivid expression through the death of Pelatiah, first for the prophet himself, then for the exiles who accept as true his account of it, and for whose benefit he undergoes his trance (11.25). Despite its peculiarity, the event is closely connected with the Israelite conception of the prophet's word and cannot be dismissed as the workings of imagination. That visions seen in a trance cannot possibly be connected with anything which really happens (Fohrer) is far from axiomatic. In fact, to say so is to contradict all our available information in regard to such matters.

In view of all the facts presented to the world by the scientific literature of the last few decades, there can no longer be any doubt that there is such a thing as genuine clairvoyance. So we are forced to adopt a realistic attitude towards such manifestations.[2] Rationalistic

---

[1] Fohrer's appeal to a highly doubtful metrical scheme cannot be regarded as providing sufficient grounds for his going to such lengths.

[2] Cf. in this connection the clear and balanced arguments of R. Kittel (*Geschichte des Volkes Israel* III, 1, 1927, pp. 147f.; 152ff.), which are still valuable today over

explanations of the prophet's account thus seem antiquated, and do not deserve to be taken seriously, irrespective of whether they regard the account of the death of Pelatiah as a 'legendary anecdote' composed by later disciples of the prophet (Hölscher), or as a literary garb for the prophet's ideas of retribution without corresponding to any real experience (C. von Orelli), or turn the whole narrative upside down and make the death of Pelatiah, the news of which came to the prophet at Tell Abīb, the originating cause of the visionary experience,[1] or have Pelatiah deported to the elders in Babylonia to die there of fright at Ezekiel's disclosures about him,[2] or finally deny the visionary character of the whole event by deleting the relevant verses and then make use of the psychological difficulties in order to build up a case for an alleged activity of Ezekiel at Jerusalem, during which he denounced Pelatiah in the temple, and thus brought about his death (Herntrich, Bertholet and others). An impartial and scientific outlook cannot be associated with any such reconstructions. It must be recognized that here, as on other occasions (cf. 21.18–23; 24.1f., 15–27; 33.21f.), Ezekiel had clairvoyant powers to help him in his prophetic task and to support him in attacking the hard unreceptivity of his audience. It is this last fact, not the parapsychological manifestation of clairvoyance *per se*, which is of really decisive importance. Ezekiel is not a typical medium. He does not pride himself in any way upon his unusual powers. He accepts this faculty as being the means which Yahweh has bestowed upon him so that he may be of service to his people in this particular way.

How far the possession of such an unusual gift was from awakening any special feeling of superiority is shown by his reactions upon seeing the man fall dead. He sees that it is quite in line with the judgment brought about by his prediction, and in this way recognizes the significance of the event. The despairing cry with which he falls down is distinguished from the one recorded in 9.8, not only by a stronger expression for total annihilation 'to make a full end of', but also by

---

against Hölscher's verdicts, which have been determined by *a priori* presuppositions. G. A. Cooke (*The Book of Ezekiel*, 1936, p. 123) also decides in favour of an actual occurrence having been seen through second sight. For scientific examinations of the phenomenon, cf. A. Neuhäusler, *Telepathie, Hellsehen, Praecognition*, 1957; C. Richet, *Grundriss der Parapsychologie und Parapsychophysik*, 1923, pp. 65ff.; J. B. Rhine and J. G. Pratt, *Parapsychology*, 1962.

[1] D. N. Freedman, 'The Book of Ezekiel', *Interpretation* (1954), pp. 446ff.
[2] L. Finkelstein, *The Pharisees*, II, 1946, p. 688, n. 27, cited by Fohrer.

the affirmation of the irrevocability of the disaster. In 9.8, on the other hand, some sort of feeble attempt still remained in the shape of a question to stave off the final horror. One must therefore be cautious about assuming that there is a fixed form of prophetic style, which underlies both exclamations (Zimmerli). One must not always force Ezekiel to act under the compulsion of a traditional style, even if it is natural that he should employ literary forms familiar to him in order to recount his experiences. Pelatiah's death is more than a mere judgment upon one individual. It is a sign of what is in store for this Jewish rump-state. The coming judgment will not vindicate it. It is not destined to enjoy any resurgence which might lead to the restoration of the people of God, such as Jewish elements in Babylonia may be expecting. What awaits it is total annihilation which will leave no 'remnant of Israel' (see above, p. 119) to tell the tale. The rich history of salvation and hope, bound up with the name of Israel, has come to an end: there is not even the faintest glimmer of hope. And all this is not due to any change of mind on the part of Yahweh, but to the internal disintegration of a nation which has turned her back upon the one reason she has for her existence and dared to defy the will of her God.

This also serves to display what a hopeless position Jerusalem was in from the political point of view. The brutal self-aggrandisement and smug security of the new party in power in Judah may have seemed impressive to those Jews who were in exile, but were as symptomatic of hostility towards God as the foreign cults that had insinuated themselves into the sanctuary; in fact, they were no more than operations of that same alienation from God in public life. The indissoluble association between rank exuberance in public worship and disdain of God's will in matters of state, already explicit in 8.17 and 9.9, is here brought fully to light.

Yet the fit of despair which seizes the prophet only serves to bring to view how tenacious were the forces of hope that still lived on in him, in spite of all the messages of doom he had been given to bear. The death of the natural man, with all his impracticable claims and excuses for hoping on, does not take place all at once, but through one stage after another of an agonizing mental struggle, like the mortification (νέκρωσις) of which St Paul speaks in II Cor. 4.10.

Though in this continuous dying he is using his own body to portray the fate in store for his nation, as many other prophets before him had consciously endeavoured to do (one need only mention

Hosea and Jeremiah), he does not as yet know, and cannot tell us, how this death leads on through to a new life. On the contrary, he keeps sinking down into ever deeper darkness.

In this particular point he resembles Jeremiah, to whom he is in other respects so unlike (cf. Jer. 20. 14–18), except that he does not break out into loud laments, but in disciplined fashion represses his personal grief behind his devotion to duty, and thus brings upon himself a reproach which he does not deserve, and is called unfeeling. That, nevertheless, his was a νέκρωσις τοῦ Ἰησοῦ, that is, a mortification surrounded by the divine life of resurrection, was, of course, a thing which could not become evident to him till later on.

The elders had been waiting in a state of tense expectation for the prophet's ecstasy to come to an end (11.24ff.). When he communicated to them his great temple vision, its impact upon the exiles must have been discouraging. Ezekiel's second experience of ecstasy was of such a nature as to intensify these previous impressions and to add weight to his predictions of disaster. The resistance which many had opposed to the prophet's message hitherto may well have been changed to a feeling of profound terror, especially after the arrival of Tell Abīb of the news of the death of Pelatiah. Men must have recalled how, only two years before, the death of the false prophet Hananiah had fulfilled a prophesy of Jeremiah's, so similar to this of Ezekiel's. Now that such a salutary change had set in in the feverish hopes of the exiles, it was obviously highly undesirable to mitigate the process by such a promise as we find in 11.14. But it puts a different complexion on the whole matter if, as we saw above (p. 119), this section is really intended to assist not them, but later readers, to understand the prophet's message.

Postscript: the true Israel: 11.14–21

[14] The introductory formula about the coming of the word shows that this section does not belong to the vision experienced by Ezekiel, of which the preceding chapters have told. Through it the prophet learns the decision which his God has made about a claim set up by residents in Jerusalem, which must have been particularly hurtful for the exiles, seeing the way in which it treated them as persons who had been totally cast out of covenant fellowship with Yahweh. It has long been recognized that the controversial point dealt with here has no immediate connection with the message of judgment in the vision, but belongs to a different period. It has, however, been deliberately taken

and used to form an epilogue to ch. 8–11 in their final version. Critics claim almost universally that the passage dates from the time before the destruction of the temple. But the whole passage in general, and in particular the form in which residents in Jerusalem state their contested claim, displays such striking resemblances to 33.24ff. that it makes all contrary arguments quite unconvincing. The fact that Jeremiah shows no knowledge of any such hasty repudiation by the Jews remaining in the land of their deported fellow countrymen must tell against putting it at a date previous to 587. Some still lived on in Jerusalem, even subsequently to the conquest of that city. So one need not conclude from the mention of such inhabitants that the destruction had not yet taken place.

[15] The word of God thus committed to Ezekiel has as its objective the unlimited self-complacency shown by those still left in Jerusalem. They claim that they, not the exiles, are the rightful possessors of the city (this obviously includes its lands, which LXX misses, and consequently supplies). They assert that those who have been punished by exile have forfeited any claim to the hereditary land of Yahweh. But the terrible events of that time of judgment have shattered the old standard by which nearness to God was measured. So, although Canaan is still the land of Yahweh's inheritance, those who dwell there have moved further away from Yahweh's grace-giving presence than those who have been carried off into the unclean heathendom of Babylonia. And what at present is regarded as impossible, and too absurdly paradoxical even to imagine, is going to happen. The despised exiles will return home and repossess the land, that they may cleanse it of all those idolatrous heathen follies in which those who remained behind had persisted, in spite of all their bragging of being well-pleasing to God.

On the other hand, those who seem to have been spared judgment in Jerusalem are the very ones who are affected by the implacable divine retribution.

This course of reasoning is logically consistent in itself, as well as being firmly anchored in the saying quoted in v. 15b. When we give it due consideration we cannot fail to recognize the elements extraneous to the context in a text obviously full of later modifications (cf. above, p. 111, notes). That the blood-relations of Ezekiel, under an obligation to help him as their kinsman, who are introduced in the vocalization of MT, cannot play any part in the argument of this saying of God's is obvious. Kinship to the prophet is irrelevant in the question under discussion, which in fact deals with all those who are scattered over the lands (v. 16). The glossator inserted the words 'and all Israel' in his hurry to bring them in and associate them with all the rest who have been called to form part of the national community of Israel, thus making them only indirectly significant. The passage which follows is thus concerned not with a judicial but with a religious verdict.

Nor does the inward quality of the exiles have a part in this verdict. It is not as though they were 'inwardly faithful to Yahweh, in spite of all their refractoriness' and thus superior to the Jerusalemites (Fohrer). In any case, that hardly agrees with the other evidence supplied by Ezekiel (cf. 14.1ff.!). What we are concerned with here is the breaking down of that godless pride which refuses to admit the need of conversion, which swells up still even among the miserable remnant left in Jerusalem, and the thorough-going prosecution of the paradoxical divine economy of salvation, with its declaration that the rejected are in fact the chosen, 'that every mouth may be stopped, and that all the world may become guilty before God' (Rom. 3.19). The author of the marginal remarks which are now vv. 19f. shows that he understood this very well. He subjoins the promised inward transformation of the returning exiles, so as to render impossible any misunderstanding, which might imagine that their guilt was less extreme, or that they were in a closer inward relationship to God.

Here also we see the fundamental difference which marks off the prophet's word from the theology of his time and especially from Deuteronomy. The way in which he delivers Israel to out and out damnation, and can no longer see in her anything good or pleasing to God, so that she cannot even begin to exist again except by some incomprehensible new act of grace on the part of Yahweh, is quite alien to that theology. He maintains the prerogatives of Jerusalem. But that does not mean that he is inclined to any approach to or compromise with Deuteronomy, any more than the earlier prophets, who were just as convinced as he was of the unique significance of the city of God (Amos 9.11; Isa. 2.2ff.; 8.18; 28.16; 31.4, 9; Zeph. 3.12; Jer. 30.18, cf. 23.5). The language used here does not express any fetish-like adoration of the holy place, but a faithful believing adherence to a historical decision made by Yahweh himself, as we shall see in due course when we come to deal with the promises of salvation.

[16] Ezekiel gives us one significant glimpse of his thoughts about

what exile could contribute to the relationship of Israel with God in his remarkable statement that Yahweh has become a sanctuary 'only a little' for the exiles, in the countries to which they have been scattered (v. 16b). This statement is based upon the assumption that in the normal relations between God and people Yahweh does in reality become a sanctuary for those who truly belong to him; in other words, that he allows himself to be encountered in person in the temple services. In actual fact, what Ezekiel has to say elsewhere of the value of the temple, as we saw especially clearly in ch. 8, agrees in every particular with what is said by the earlier prophets.[1] One may even go so far as to follow Zimmerli (p. 250) in his conjecture that along with the well-known covenant formula 'I will be your God', priestly circles were in the habit of using the other equally stereotyped expression 'I will be your sanctuary.'

This connection of the gracious presence of God with the sanctuary seems to have been completely severed for the exiles now they have been deported to an unclean heathen land. So those who remain at home conclude that the exiles have, once for all, been deprived not only of covenant fellowship but also of the accompanying gift of the possession of the land. The prophet is commissioned to speak a word against such an unfeeling condemnation. Undoubtedly, the former fellowship has been broken off. But that does not mean that God has cut off those whom he is chastising from all association with him. Some signs of covenant fellowship are still left, even in a heathen land, and even though they have been greatly reduced. In this connection, we may recall the instruction still given about the law, the continued observance of the Sabbath and circumcision, and the assemblies for worship in the places of prayer (Ps. 137.1f.) or in the houses. In all these activities there were faithful priests served as advisers and instructors (cf. above p. 53). Another consideration of no less importance is the fact that prophets of Yahweh were sent to these *deracinés*.[2]

---

[1] Cf. M. Schmidt, *Prophet und Tempel*, 1948.

[2] An attempt has been made to make the peculiar expression 'only a little sanctuary' refer particularly to the synagogues in Babylonia. We find it in the Talmudic tradition, and in A. Menes, who follows that ('Tempel und Synagoge', *ZAW* 50, (1932), pp. 268ff.), associating it with the passage in Josh. 22 of the altar without a sacrifice. It is undoubtedly true that synagogue worship did take its origin in the state to which the exiles were reduced. But the further assertion, that such a 'little sanctuary', i.e. the synagogue as a place of cult without sacrifice, was at that time deliberately brought into existence, is one which the available evidence is plainly insufficient to establish.

The prophets unsparingly denounced them for their hardness of heart. But their presence witnessed to the fact that God's faithfulness still served as a basis for the link between him and those smitten by his judgment. Jeremiah had had very similar assumptions in mind when he wrote his memorable epistle to the exiles (Jer. 29). Jeremiah thinks that those presuppositions give him grounds for proclaiming 'a future and a hope' (29.11) for the exiles, and so also does Ezekiel. [17f.] The day will come when these godless and landless persons are restored to their old possessions. They will thus be put once more in material possession of the qualifications necessary towards full covenant fellowship with their God. It is that same majestic freedom of God, in absolute transcendence above all relative human judgments, which Paul in Rom. 11.17–24 contrasts with all arrogance, that will make his rod shatter upon those who are victims of this judgment. In Isa. 56–66, the struggle to enforce this divine decision plays a decisive part in the return of the exiles to Jerusalem.

Such a full promise of positive salvation is one which Ezekiel cannot begin to proclaim until the final catastrophe has come and smashed to pieces all remaining opposition to his message. Still, we can see why, when ch. 8–11 were brought into their present form, it was employed to state the ultimately decisive closing word. It is to show the community the 'thoughts of peace' (Jer. 29.11) which are in the background to the undiminished reality of God's wrath, and how, once the judgment is fully submitted to, they will become effective. Therefore 'do not become proud, but stand in awe' (Rom. 11.20).

CHAPTER 12.1–20

More symbolic actions showing the catastrophe that is to come upon Jerusalem

THE EXILE'S BAGGAGE 12.1–16

1 And the word of Yahweh came to me: ²'Son of man, you dwell in the midst of a rebellious house, who have eyes to see but see not, who have ears to hear but hear not, for they are a rebellious house. ³Therefore, son of man, prepare for yourself an exile's baggage [. . .]ᵃ by day in their sight, and go away from your dwelling place to another place in their sight;

perhaps they will see, though they are a rebellious house. ⁴You shall prepare your belongings [. . .]ᵇ by day in their sight in front of the house,
and you yourself shall go forth in the evening in their sight [. . .].ᶜ ⁵In
their sight break a hole in the wall of the house and go out through it.ᵈ ⁶In
their sight lay (the baggage) upon your shoulders; and when it has grown
dark, go out from there.ᵉ Cover your face, that you may not see the land.
For I have made you a sign for the house of Israel.'

7 Then I did as I had been commanded: I made ready my belongings
and brought them out by day like the baggage of an exile and in the
evening I made a hole in the wall of the house with a tent peg.ᶠ When it
grew dark, I went out, and laid it on my shoulders in their sight. ⁸The
next morning the word of Yahweh came to me: ⁹'Son of man, has not the
house of Israel, the rebellious house, said to you: "What are you doing?"
¹⁰Say to them: "[. . .]ᵍ ¹¹[. . .]ʰ I am a sign to you. As I have done, so
shall it be done to them: they shall go into exile."

12–14 [. . .].ⁱ ¹⁵And they shall know that I am Yahweh, when I disperse them among the nations and scatter them among the countries.
¹⁶[. . .].'ʲ

EATING AND DRINKING IN TREMBLING 12.17–20

17 And the word of Yahweh came to me: ¹⁸'Son of man, eat your
bread with quaking and drink your water with tremblingᵏ ¹⁹and say to
the people of the land: Thus says [. . .]ˡ Yahweh concerning the inhabitants of Jerusalem in the land of Israel: they shall eat their bread in
fearfulness and drink their water with dismay—because theirᵐ land is
stripped of its inhabitants on account of the violence of all those who dwell
in it. ²⁰And the inhabited cities shall be laid waste and the land shall thus
become a desolation, that you may know that I am Yahweh.'

TWO DISPUTED SAYINGS: 12.21–28

21 And the word of Yahweh came to me: ²²'Son of man, what is this
mocking proverb that you have about the land of Israel: the days grow
long and every vision comes to contempt! ²³Therefore say to them: "Thus
says [. . .]ⁿ Yahweh: I will put an end to this mocking proverb, so that
it may be no longer spoken in Israel; say to them rather: The days are at
hand and every vision [is coming into effect!]ᵒ ²⁴For there shall no more
be any worthless vision or deceitful prophecy in the house of Israel, ²⁵but
I, Yahweh, will speak: the word which I speak will be performed, and will
not any longer be postponed. Yes, in your days, O rebellious house, I will
speak a word and also perform it!" ' ²⁶And the word of Yahweh came to
me: ²⁷'Son of man, behold, the house of Israel says the vision which he
sees is for many days hence and he prophesies of times far off. ²⁸Therefore

say to them: Thus says [. . .]ᵖ Yahweh: None of my words shall be postponed any longer; the word which I speak will be performed, says [. . .]�q Yahweh.'

ᵃMT: 'and go forth'; an anticipation by dittography of what is to follow.

ᵇMT: 'like the baggage of an exile'; a further detail which v. 3 shows to be unnecessary, but inserted here word for word from v. 7.

ᶜMT: 'as men do who go into exile', or, with a slight alteration (see BH), 'like those who are led into exile'; a circumstantial explanation given without regard to the manner of departure prescribed in the words immediately following.

ᵈ⁻ᵉSee BH.

ᶠMT: 'with the hand'. Instead of omitting the word, we follow Krätzschmar in introducing a consonant and reading *yātēd*, which helps to complete the picture.

ᵍMT: 'Thus says [. . .] (see BH) Yahweh: This saying [concerns] the prince in Jerusalem and all the house of Israel that are in the midst [of it].' This passage has been restored, by adding the prepositions suggested by the LXX and altering the suffix, but it does not fit into the context. What follows is not the word of Yahweh, but the words of the prophet, and is not at first concerned with the prince, but with all the people of Jerusalem. It may perhaps be a footnote to 12.1-11 (Fohrer).

ʰMT: 'say'; a repetition of the first word of v. 10 added after the above insertion.

ⁱMT: '¹²The prince who is among them shall lift it upon his shoulders, in darkness shall he go forth (see BH), through the wall shall they (LXX: he) break a hole, that he may bring it out (LXX: go out) through it, he shall cover his face, because (LXX: so that) he does not see with an eye (LXX: is not visible to any eye) he himself the land (LXX: and he will not see the land). ¹³And I will spread my net over him, that he may be taken in my snare, and I will bring him to Babylon in the land of the Chaldeans, yet he shall not see it, and there he shall die. ¹⁴And all that are about him, his help (LXX: his helpers) and all his troops, I will scatter to every wind, and unsheathe the sword after them.' This application of the symbolic action to the prince (indicating Zedekiah, without favouring him with the name of king) takes the typical features of the leading into exile of the population of a city specified in vv. 3ff. as if they were particular details of what is to happen to Zedekiah. But some of them, such as the laying of the miserable exile's baggage upon his shoulders and going out through a breach in the city wall, are not suitable, in view of the fact that, according to II Kings 25.3ff., the king tried to escape to the Jordan district by a sortie on horseback out of the city gate. Other really unimportant details, like the hiding of the face in grief, are more or less violently applied to the blinding of the hapless prince, which made him unable to see the land to which he was banished. As v. 15 is connected with v. 11 and again speaks solely of the people, the verses inserted between will give an interpretation of the symbolic action made as a result of the shock and the impression of Zedekiah's fate, at a time when the simple symbolic act had suddenly seemed to show amazing depths of insight. Belief that even such a painful episode of the defeat as this was a part of Yahweh's irrevocably established plan has created, by the insertion of this passage into the prophet's prediction of the event, an impressive example for the education of the community. It can hardly be attributed to Ezekiel himself. But the punishments threatened by him in 17.20f., and here repeated almost word for word, certainly played some part in causing the symbolic act to be applied specially to Zedekiah.

jVerse 16: 'And I will let a few of them escape from the sword, from famine and pestilence, that they may confess all their abominations among the nations where they go, and so they will know that I am Yahweh.' The verse introduces the scattering among the nations, already mentioned in v. 15, as something new, and connects it with what is said in v. 14. It also takes over a saying of Ezekiel's preserved elsewhere in its proper context (14.21–23), and uses it to state the way in which Yahweh is vindicated before the heathen nations: the few who survive are themselves to see that their abominable apostasy is made known (whether by ostentatious boasting or by a humble confessing of their guilt is not said), so that the heathen world may know that their fate is a just punishment inflicted by the God whom they have defied. Thus Yahweh compels even those who insult him to bear witness to his honour. This is a glimpse into the future, which in its bold application of the idea of the remnant to Israel's self-condemnation is thoroughly worthy of Ezekiel, and shows how effective his influence was upon his disciples.

kMT further adds 'and in fearfulness', making a premature use of the words of the interpretation in v. 19 and destroying the regularity of the parallelism with it one verbal noun in each member.

l–mSee BH.

nMT: 'the Lord', see BH.

oMT: 'and the statement of every vision' is possible in itself, but too flat for so pointed a statement as this, and impossible because of the deliberate contrast with v. 22b. The emendation $w^e g\bar{a}bar$, proposed by Bertholet[2], involves the least change.

p–qMT: 'the Lord'; see BH.

The divine command: 12.1–6

Ezekiel's activities so far have attained success only at one point. They have served to bring out more clearly a fact already presupposed in the command which sent him out (in 2.1ff.), namely, the decided refusal of the people to accept his prophetic message. What manifests itself for Isaiah as a consequence of the divine commission to harden the hearts of his audience (Isa. 6.9ff.) is for Ezekiel already the basic attitude of his audience, and no efforts on his part can change it. [2] Before he is summoned to further action, this fact is noted by God, as it were in a retrospective glance, who then, however, continues immediately with a 'nevertheless'. This may reflect the state of exhaustion and despair which had taken hold of the prophet after he had been working for more than a year. God assures him that he knows his situation well and can see all the difficulties in it, but there is no reason here for abandoning his task. On the contrary, he must press home his attack upon this 'rebellious house'. And here a note of hope, never hitherto perceptible, rings out in the words 'perhaps they will see' (v. 3). The exiles have, apparently, lost the faculty to perceive what God is saying and doing. But evidently God still sees how it is possible to revive them by his continued knocking, as a crippled limb is revivified by an electric current, or a lifeless body rescued by an electric current, or a lifeless body rescued from the water and brought back to life by ceaseless efforts at artificial respiration. This may serve as a warning to us against taking too seriously our own pessimistic diagnoses of other people's sensitivity, or lack of it, and still more against assuming that their stubbornness is willed by God. The Deuteronomist, who wrote in the same period, saw more clearly that the power of Yahweh to give new life to dulled minds and despairing hearts was the really decisive factor in making Israel yield to the will of her God (Deut. 30.6), while at the same time showing no inclination to minimize man's guilt and responsibility. Ezekiel, too, is here called to be hopeful against all the appearances.

This is the more remarkable in view of the fact that the commands from God have so far said nothing of any such expectation. The hard words of the first commission sweep contemptuously aside all considerations of receptiveness or stubbornness (2.5, 7; 3.11). They suggest that the most that is to be expected will be a reluctant admission of the incontrovertible fact that a prophet is at work (2.5). We go on looking to, and moving in, a region far above the hearers until this present chapter. Now these hearers make their appearance on the stage with their reaction, such as it is. In the chapters which follow we find more and more speech and action undertaken with this deliberately calculated aim. So we may probably say, without being able to tell exactly why, that ch. 12 marks not only a new section of the book but also a new stage in the prophet's work.

[3] In accordance with the possibility hinted at in v. 3, the action prescribed for the prophet is now given added point with the almost tiresome insistence that it is to be performed 'in their sight'. What the prophet does is intended to be noticed; indeed, to demand attention. So a very realistic picture is drawn, and many details are given, of what exactly Ezekiel is to do. He is to prepare the baggage of an exile, such as would be required solely by the inhabitants of a city or a country district who had been marked out to suffer exile. It was limited to the very barest essentials. A little food, a water bottle, the necessary cooking utensils, perhaps some sort of bedding, a miserable bundle, small enough for a man to carry with him on a march lasting for weeks, such as is still to be seen with gruesome clarity in many an

ancient Eastern bas-relief.[1] **[4f.]** He is to lay down these articles in front of his house by daylight. In the evening he is to break a hole through the wall of the house, big enough for him to go out through it. This was not too exacting a task with a flimsy hut of sun-dried bricks, but it, too, was likely to attract notice. **[6]** When he has settled the baggage on to his shoulders as darkness sets in, he is to cover his head and set off for some other place. Evidently the darkness, which so quickly follows the twilight in the East, will not discourage the numerous spectators who have assembled to witness the prophet's extraordinary behaviour.

The execution of the command: 12.7

[7] These actions were unaccompanied by any words, and provoked inquisitive questions from the bystanders. It is evident that their meaning was not as unambiguous as most commentators assume. If it had been impossible to interpret it as anything but a symbol of a journey into exile, then it could not have evoked so many excited questions as to what it meant (v. 9). It is much more probable that here, as in ch. 4f., one should allow for the prophet's actions having a double meaning, which could lead to different conclusions. We know also from the book of Jeremiah of the feverish expectations of an early return home in which the exiles of 587 lived and of how those expectations were further stimulated by what prophets were saying. Ezekiel had made preparations for a long journey, and before setting off had begun to demolish his temporary dwelling—in such circumstances, why could that not be the signal for them to knock down their improvised adobe huts and start upon the longed-for journey home? Even the covering of his face could be fitted in with this interpretation as an indication of the secrecy which was to veil the preparations and the beginning of the undertaking. Anyone who has heard of the excitement aroused in prison camps during the last two world wars at the very faintest hint of imminent release and of how ready men were to jettison their most cherished possessions and reduce their baggage to absolute necessities will find this possibility of two alternative interpretations of Ezekiel's expedition a very probable one. The refusal, too, to provide any information about it till next morning must have helped to increase the excitement with which

---

[1] Cf. G. Gressmann, *Altorientalische Bilder zum AT*[2], 1927, plates 133 and 141; J. B. Pritchard, *The Ancient Near East in Pictures*, 1954, plates 10, 311, 365f.

men asked if this prophet of doom could possibly have changed his
mind, and come round to the views of other prophets.

The interpretation: 12.8–9, 11, 15

We can now imagine how utterly crushing Ezekiel's interpretation,
which would also take account of his return from his symbolic
journey, must have been for the tense spectators. **[11]** The prophet
calls himself a wonderful sign and token of the revelation of God, by
which Yahweh shows that his prophecies are true. He next explains
how his actions are intended to represent what will happen to the
inhabitants of Jerusalem. They, too, will have to face the journey into
exile which his audience know only too well. **[15]** By means of it their
eyes will at last be opened to the sole might of the God whom they
have so long denied. He alone takes them from their homes and
reduces them to the uncertain state of refugees without a country (cf.
6.7, 13). A clear distinction is drawn between those to whom the
prophesy of doom is addressed and those in Judea who form its
objective. Yet here, once again, we see how the exiles in Babylonia are
directly concerned in what happens at Jerusalem. Ezekiel, being a
'sign for the house of Israel' (v. 6), acts alike upon those at home and
those abroad. His prophecy helped the exiles in an inestimable way
to see how God himself was acting in what was happening to Jerusalem, slow and unwilling though they were to take in what he
preached to them. But his consistent preaching of doom also had to
be a sign of warning to the men of Jerusalem, to prepare those among
them who were ready to listen for the coming events. Just as Jeremiah's prophecies had come to be known in Babylonia (Jer. 29.24ff.),
so also the preaching of Ezekiel will have attracted notice in the homeland. The impact made in both places by the prophet's message was
further strengthened by the way it coincided with the warnings of
Jeremiah.

It is particularly noticeable how the interpretation of the symbolic
action, given in 12.11 and 15, refrains from going into detail, unlike
the later verses which try to apply it to the fate of Zedekiah. Even so,
at least the forced exit through the yawning gap in the wall of the
hut and the covering of the face suggest a departure through the
breach in the city wall and that grief-stricken gesture which avoids a
last look at the homeland and keeps off the inquisitive stares of
ruthless foes. A new point of reference for the action in vv. 12–14
may have led to an abbreviation of the text at this point; so, for

example, in v. 11 one would naturally expect 'the inhabitants of Jerusalem' to be mentioned by name and not merely indicated by a pronoun.

When we recall how symbolic action by a prophet was regarded as being not merely an illustration of his word, but an irresistible power operating to bring about the fulfilment of that word (cf. above, pp. 81f.), we can appreciate the full force of this attack on the hardened stubbornness of the exiles. We find another indirect testimony to its effectiveness in the subsequent history of the narrative. The fact that it came to be applied to Zedekiah heightened in a very striking way the underground influence of the simple prophetic action. [16] It is all the more impressive that the main view is that there remains a universal salvation which allows no brooding over a great national catastrophe, but tells of an action of God directed at still larger objectives (cf. commentary on 12.12–14, 12.16, notes ^{i} and ^{j}).

The prophet as an embodiment of panic: 12.17–20

Here we are told of a second command by Yahweh. It has a separate introduction of its own and so it is not advisable to attach this symbolic action too closely to the one preceding it, as if it drew a parallel between the fate of the deportees and that of those who were still left in Judea (Fohrer). This is unlikely, especially in view of the fact that the laying waste of the land is still regarded as being far from complete, and that we cannot speak of a repeated judgment (v. 20). But to appeal to 4.10f., 16f. and assume that the symbolism of eating refers solely to the anxious way in which those besieged in Jerusalem eat is to narrow down its meaning too much. It is much more probable that we ought to think of the consternation men feel when a calamity breaks in and takes them by surprise, and turns all their former security (cf. 11.3) into panic.

[18] The compulsive character of Ezekiel's trembling and quaking, which makes eating a torment, results from the divine command. It will only be understood properly if we consider it, like the transportation of his paralysed body by a higher power and then the day-long torpidity of 3.14f., as at least in part a result of the severe strain on his physical energy imposed by the trances and visions granted to him (thus also Zimmerli, who refers to Jer. 4.19f. and accounts of Mohammed). He can no longer control his limbs like a healthy man; he has to force them to do their work by a violent effort of will. But from the word of his God which comes to him he learns not to regard

the paralysis which comes upon him as something to react against strongly, as he had done at his first encounter with God at the river Chebar, but to recognize it as a part of his calling, [19] since that calling commands him to make use even of his suffering body to bear witness to God's will to execute judgment. Just as in leaving his house like a poor exile he embodied his hapless people, so, too, in his present condition he is a symbol of his fellow countrymen who are overtaken by judgment. [20] They, too, tremble with a consternation they cannot control, as they see their well-cultivated land laid waste, and its populous cities reduced to smoking ruins, since the lawless violence with which men in Israel have trodden down the helpless and shown contempt for God's command is now at the hands of Yahweh meeting with the retribution it deserves.

There is one special difficulty about this account of the transformation of the dumbly suffering prophet into an eloquent symbol. This is the way in which the 'people of the land' are addressed. This term, according to fixed usage, denotes the body of free landowners in a certain area capable of political action.[1] So one can see why Bertholet can find no meaning in such a title on Babylonian soil and see it as a reference to a stay of Ezekiel at that time in the land of Judah.

But in actual fact the direct mention of the audience in v. 19, with its 'say to the people of the land', can hardly refer to persons who are far away (Herrmann). Yet it is somewhat irresponsible to go on and strike out the words explicitly naming 'inhabitants of Jerusalem in the land of Israel' as the victims of the coming disaster (thus Herrmann, and also Fohrer). One must therefore look for the 'people of the land' among the exiles. Now in actual fact there seems to be a certain relationship between this address and the threats which follow, since those threats do not speak of the capital but of the country and of the country towns. And among the men of the upper classes of Jerusalem who had been led into exile there must have been many representatives of those very families who, by usury and perversion of the law, had come to own most of the landed property in the province of Judah. For this Isaiah (5.8ff.) and Micah (2.1ff.) had already rebuked them. In that case, there is extreme irony in calling them the 'people of the land' and thus addressing them by a title they are no longer qualified to bear. These men had but lately

[1] Cf. L. Rost, 'Die Bezeichnungen für Land und Volk im Alten Testament', *Procksch-Festschrift*, 1934, pp. 144f., and E. Würthwein, *Der 'amm ha'arez im Alten Testament*, BWANT 69, 1936.

become the sole landowners, and took a pride in feeling they were the representatives of the 'people of the land'. Now it is announced to them that their ill-gotten gains have lost all value, and that they have been reduced to 'people of the land' without land. Now the knowledge of Yahweh which this is meant to achieve has an immediate meaning. The God to whose repeated demands that they should protect the economically weak within their domains they had turned deaf ears is now revealed to them as the righteous vindicator, before whom they must humble themselves in the dust.

Against the sceptics: 12.21–25

We saw how in 12.3 a new concern became perceptible for the audience who listen to the prophetic word. We now see a surprising increase in it. As he preaches the prophet takes up some of his adversaries' retorts and considers them worth answering. True, we do not find an actual disputation, giving the arguments for and against, such as occurs later on in the book of Malachi. Yet in spite of the authoritative tone and the rebuttal which admits of no further discussion, the prophet is ready to take seriously the way in which his audience reacts and to allow that to be discussed. He has glimpsed the line the defence is taking, and selects an answer to penetrate that line of defence, and make it impossible for those who hear it to feel comfortable about the attitude of resistance which they have once again taken up. We find only a few isolated examples of this in the earlier prophets (cf. e.g., Isa. 30.15f.; Jer. 2.23), but in Ezekiel it becomes a favourite method of preaching (cf. 18.2f.; 25.29; 33.10, 17; 37.11).

[21] Here, as often, the remarkable word *māšal*,[1] which covers wisdom-sayings, legal precepts, formulas of cursing or blessing, oracles or lyrics, because it probably meant at first a powerful and therefore effective word, designates a pungent piece of mocking wit. It was put into circulation about the land of Israel, and everyone was discussing the fate which pursued the exiles at every turn. Prophetic words about the future of that land were self-contradictory. One moment they were promising salvation and freedom, and in the next breath they were announcing the coming of days of gloom and disaster. What was to be made of them? Which, if any, was more probably true? The exaggerated pictures of blessing drawn by

---

[1] Cf. in this connection O. Eissfeldt, *Der Maschal im Alten Testament*, BZAW 24, 1913; A. R. Johnson, 'מָשָׁל', *Wisdom in Israel and in the Ancient Near East* VTS, III, 1955, pp. 162ff.

professional prophets of salvation had not as yet been fulfilled any
more than had the descriptions of coming ruin sketched by their
opponents. Life had gone on through good and bad times. Even such
a disaster as the first captivity of 598 was not necessarily irretrievable;
some other great power might oust the one at present on top and
restore the former *status quo*. What was a sober realist to do but shrug
his shoulders at all the unverifiable forecasts to which the imaginations
of the prophets might give birth? The mere passage of time would
suffice to show their futility, provided one had patience to wait long
enough and refused to let oneself be upset by them: 'The days grow
long, and every vision comes to contempt.'

This mocking phrase asserts the general uncertainty of all prophetic
words, and uses that as an excuse to avoid having to decide in face of
a particular individual prophet. But Ezekiel, too, has been provided
with a saying which refutes this attempt to evade his word. The
prophet does not trouble to counter each individual argument. He
does not demonstrate the superficiality of treating all prophets alike,
or the difference between false prophets and genuine prophesy. [23]
He simply announces that it is God's intention to stop all this in-
decisiveness. He can therefore in full confidence transpose this mocking phrase into its opposite: 'The days are at hand, and every vision
comes into effect!' [24] God himself will show the would-be wisdom
of the sceptics to be foolishness. That will also give a mortal wound
to the deceitful predictions of the prophets who say that all will be
well. They will vanish out of Israel, since what they have said has
proved to be a lie.

It is thus admitted that false prophesy exists, and that since it
takes the same shape of 'vision' and 'soothsaying', it is almost impossible to distinguish from the true. So there we see full recognition of
the puzzled state to which Israel is reduced by these mutually contradictory words from her prophets. In ch. 13 Ezekiel goes exhaustively
into that problem. [25] Here, however, he makes it his object to
recall those who evade his word to their responsibilities, by confronting them with that word of Yahweh's which is now making itself
heard. That word is going out once more, and strongly asserting its
power to produce a real effect. Men are not to decry it by saying it is
reduced to nullity by the steady passing of time; that is not true, for
those who now hear it are to experience physically its overwhelming
effects on their own bodies.

So the prophet meets the scepticism of his hearers not by any such arguments as carry conviction to common sense but by referring them to that word of God which is now about to become event as a result of his proclamation of it. Anyone who finds this unsatisfying should recall how in this Ezekiel is, at this point, wholly in line with the earlier prophets. Amos, too, when his words were questioned, could do nothing but point to the fact that his preaching was brought about by an immediate inward compulsion, which again forced those who listened to him into an encounter with the one who had given him his commission and who stood behind him (Amos 3.3–6). Now this process by which prophecy authenticates itself is confirmed by none other than by Jesus himself. In the same way, he can do nothing with all the questions and demands for proof but make them refer to himself: 'From the beginning, I am he who speaks to you' (John 8.25, cf. 8.18, 28). Prophetic assurance, like all assurance of faith, cannot be comprehended or proved from any point outside itself, but carries its authentication within itself. It can do nothing but appeal back to itself and to the fact of its own existence, as a fact which calls for a decision about it, and advise men for once to begin to be really serious about what they see there. Yet this assurance has its source in a commission by a God who can control history, whose word intervenes in the course of the world and leads it into new paths. No scepticism can release anyone of his responsibility in face of that word.

Against the frivolous: 12.26–28

Attached to the previous passage, but given an independent formulation, we now find stated and refuted a second objection to the prophet's word. The striking agreement of the prophetic pronouncement in v. 28 with v. 25 should not mislead us into thinking that it is simply a parallel, either as another formulation by Ezekiel (Bertholet[2]) or else as a repetition of it, due to redactors (Kuhl). It is much more probable that it is aimed at another group of persons with different characteristics from the preceding one. [27] They, too, are trying to protect themselves against the demand made by the prophetic word, not by denying its credibility, but by associating it with a distant future, too far off to cause them any worry. These are the frivolous who live only for the moment and believe they can evade the menace of the prophetic word by saying '*Après moi le déluge*'. But Ezekiel refuses to accept any such 'eschatology', and here, one might point out, shows his agreement with his prophetic predecessors. His preaching does, of course, envisage an ἔσχατον, an ultimate, the conclusion of history. But this does not come in the shape of a far-off event that is not as yet a present actuality. It is something that has already begun: a radical questioning, a demand for accounts to be settled, and his very audience are affected. **[28]** What ch. 7 hammered home so emphatically is true of all the threats which come after it, and is in fact true of all the words of Yahweh (v. 28), which, Ezekiel sees, combine with his message to form one great integral whole for yesterday and today: they are already beginning to be realized. Prophetic expectation—and this is also true of the expectation of Jesus and of his disciples—is always a near expectation; it is born of a consciousness of being at the turn of the ages and can never go along with procrastination into a vague future. True 'eschatology' consists in such a power to live in the ἔσχατον, and not in describing a final event that has not yet come to pass, and which has no real meaning for this present time, and can therefore be employed to lull consciences to sleep in face of God's demands. Fundamentally, the dimension of time is not applicable to this expectation, since for it all times have taken on a new quality, the quality of belonging to the time of the end. But Israel doubts the seriousness with which the word of God pronounces judgment upon her. So Yahweh guarantees that what is proclaimed will come to pass in the nearest possible future. Jerusalem's day of reckoning came in 587 to prove that this warning, probably spoken only a few years previously, was true.

There is no need to specify in detail how the lesson which Ezekiel taught his particular audience can never go out of date, but impinges directly on all who listen to God's message in the Old and New Testaments. In the face of the Gospel, too, we see the man who yearns for security make the same attempt to evade the word of God as it comes to meet him, as II Peter 3 has long made clear.

But we are facing the God of revelation. He brings man into his presence by means of his word. No attempt at escape can be successful. One may try to barricade himself behind the alleged inconsistencies of the biblical message. Another may take the time of the end, which has broken in in Christ, and accommodate it to his own views of time-succession, and thus transform its menacing here and now into a far-off 'end of the times'. But in either case the message of the Lord who has come and will come again keeps breaking through all the defences man can put up against it, insisting upon his making a response, facing him with a question about which a decision must be made. And there is no solution to it but assent and obedience.

CHAPTER 13.1–23

Against false prophets and prophetesses

1 And the word of Yahweh came to me; 2'Son of man, prophesy against[a] the prophets of Israel, prophesy[b] and say [to them]:[c] "Hear the word of Yahweh!" 3Thus says [. . .][d] Yahweh: Woe to the prophets [who prophesy out of their own hearts][e] and according to that which they have not seen. 4Your prophets have become like foxes among ruins, O Israel! 5You have not gone up into the breach,[f] that you might build a wall to defend the house of Israel, so that it might hold firm in the battle on the day of Yahweh. 6[. . .].[g] 7Have you not seen deceiving visions and spoken lying oracles, and said of them: "A saying of Yahweh", while I had not spoken? 8Therefore, thus says [. . .][h] Yahweh: Because you have spoken delusions and seen lies, therefore will I in truth come upon you[i] says [. . .][j] Yahweh, and I am stretching out my hand against[k] the prophets, who see delusions and prophesy lies; they shall not abide in the fellowship of my people and they shall not be enrolled in the register of the house of Israel and they shall not come to the land of Israel. Thus you shall know that I am [. . .][l] Yahweh.

10 Because, yea, because they have misled my people,[m] by saying "salvation" where there was no salvation, and because, when they, the people, built a wall, they were busy daubing it with whitewash,[n] 11speak to those who daub with whitewash [. . .]:[o] Behold[p] [I will send][q] a deluge of rain, and hailstones shall fall, and a stormy wind shall break out. 12Then when the wall falls, will it not be said to you, "Where now is the plaster with which you covered it?" 13,14[. . .].[r] Then you shall know that I am Yahweh!

15, 16 [. . .].[s] 17And you, son of man, set your face against the daughters of your people, who prophesy out of their own hearts, and prophesy against them 18and say: Thus says [. . .][t] Yahweh: Woe to the women who sew magic bands for all [wrists][u] and head-veils for (persons of) every stature, in order to catch souls. Will you [kill][v] souls belonging to my people and keep others alive for your profit? 19You have profaned me among my people for a few handfuls of barley and pieces of bread, in order to kill souls which should not die, and keep souls alive that should not live, by lying to this people of mine, which listens so readily to lies. 20Therefore thus says [. . .][w] Yahweh: Of a truth, I am against your bands with which you catch souls,[x] and will tear them from your arms,[y] and will set free[z] the souls, which you[aa] try to catch, [. . .][bb] 21and I will tear your^{cc} veils and deliver my people from your power, so that they shall no more fall like prey into your hands. Thus you shall know that I am Yahweh.

22 Because you have troubled the hearts of the righteous by falsehood^{dd} although I had not troubled them, and you have strengthened the hands of the wicked, that he might not turn from his wicked way that I might save his life, ²³therefore you shall no more see delusions or prophesy lies,^{ee} but I will deliver my people out of your hand, and you shall know that I am Yahweh.'

^{a-b}See BH.

^cMT: 'to the prophets out of their own hearts' is a premature anticipation of what is to follow, so the briefer LXX text is to be preferred; cf. the evidently deliberate parallel v. 17.

^dSee BH.

^eMT: 'the fools who follow their own spirit' is an elaboration made necessary after v. 2 by the anticipation of the original text preserved in the LXX (Fohrer, Zimmerli).

^fRead singular instead of plural. See BH.

^gMT: 'They see vanity and false divination, who say, "a saying of Yahweh", but Yahweh has not sent them, and then they expect that he will fulfil the word.' An inferior variant of v. 7, betrayed by the way it falls into indirect speech and speaks of Yahweh in the third person.

^{h-l}See BH.

^mAramaic *ḥṭ'h* for Hebrew *ḥt'h*.

ⁿThe word employed here is *ṭāpēl*, which elsewhere means 'nonsense', 'idle chatter'. The identification of it with *ṭîaḥ*, the 'plaster' or 'daub' on the wall of a house, helps to establish the meaning, but sounds suspicious as the parallel root *ṭpl* mainly used to explain it means to 'smear' or 'soil'. Cf. G. Dalman, *Arbeit und Sitte in Pälastina*, VII, 1942, p. 28.

^oMT: 'and it will fall'; in spite of the good textual evidence in support, this must be a gloss on what follows.

^pRead *hnh* for *hyh*.

^qSee BH.

^{r'13}Therefore thus says [. . .] (see BH) Yahweh: I will make a stormy wind break out in my wrath, and a deluge of rain shall come through my anger, and hail stones in wrath for complete destruction. ¹⁴And I will break down the wall that you have daubed with plaster, and will bring it down to the ground, so that its foundation shall be laid bare. (Addition: 'and she shall fall and you shall perish in the midst of her'. As is shown by the third person feminine in the first verb, the metaphor is not kept up, and Jerusalem takes the place of the wall. It is in the midst of Jerusalem that the prophets shall perish, which could not be said of the wall.) This prosaic report of the carrying out of the threats previously given of the wrath and judgment to come can hardly be original, but is a typical example of the 'repetitions' with which we meet; cf. the systematic addition to the emphasis by means of well-worn phrases 'in my wrath . . . through my anger . . . in wrath', and the elaborated description of the wall being destroyed down to the foundation, which departs unnecessarily from the metaphor and the purpose for which it was used.

The concluding phrase of v. 14 is the only part to be retained, since it gives us the correct conclusion to vv. 10–12, cf. text.

ˢ¹⁵And I will spend my wrath upon the wall and upon those who have daubed it with plaster and will say (conj.: 'and it will be said') to you: the wall is gone (conj.: 'where is the wall'), and they have gone (conj.: 'where those are') who plastered it, ¹⁶the prophets of Israel who prophesied concerning Jerusalem and saw visions of salvation for her, when there was no salvation, says (the Lord) Yahweh.' Verse 15 is unexpected in view of the concluding formula which precedes it in v. 14. The two verses have been put together from vv. 10 and 12, in the course of which some copyists' errors have taken place (cf. the conjectures). They do not introduce any fresh ideas.

ᵗSee BH.

ᵘMT: 'for all my wrists'; copyist's error.

ᵛMT: it is better to replace 'catch' by 'kill', following Bertholet[1] and Fohrer, in view of v. 19 and other adjacent phrases.

ʷSee BH.

ˣMT: 'like a bird'; a word of Aramaic formation not used elsewhere. The way in which it is introduced with a *lᵉ* seems to involve a conception of the soul totally alien to Israel, and is very hard to explain as signifying no more than a comparison of souls with birds. Hence it is probably a later addition.

ʸRead feminine suffix for masculine.

ᶻSee BH.

ᵃᵃRead feminine pronoun for masculine.

ᵇᵇThe same word as in note x.

ᶜᶜRead feminine suffix for masculine.

ᵈᵈSee BH.

ᵉᵉMT: 'nor divine divination'. The very similar description of the false prophets in vv. 6–9 suggests that we should write *kāzāb* for *qesem* here.

Criticism of false prophets is only occasionally expressed by Ezekiel's predecessors (Amos 7.14; Isa. 28.7ff.; 30.10f.; Micah 2.11; 3.5–7). In Jeremiah it forms a conspicuous feature (5.31; 6.13f.; 8.10f.; 14.13ff.; 20.6) and culminates in an important discussion, in which the prophetic message is compared with, and distinguished from, its dark counterpart (23.9–32). Ezekiel, too, finds himself forced to state his view, but independently of the pattern set by Jeremiah. Although he is acquainted to a very considerable extent with Jeremiah's preaching and seems to presuppose it in many of his formulations, Ezekiel follows an independent line in the controversy, and mentions, in connection with false prophecy, phenomena not found in Jeremiah. The spiritual atmosphere prevailing in their times evidently forced the two prophets to give extra consideration to that sinister opposition, forming as it did the main obstacle to their preaching. That this was so is perfectly clear from Jeremiah's struggle with his personal rivals, as described in ch. 27–29 of his book. We see the same feature brought out clearly in Ezekiel. He, too, had practical experience of how he came into conflict with this counterfeit which wore the lineaments of genuine prophecy. It attempted to twist his best weapons out of his hand, it tried to discredit his claim to be a preacher of the word of God, it caused great trouble for his work as a spiritual adviser.

We ought not to forget this inner conflict and allow ourselves to be deceived by the systematic way in which this declaration of doom is constructed as merely one other instance of Ezekiel's love for symmetry of form and well-rounded periods. Zimmerli has very properly called our attention to the care expended on every detail of the arrangement and to the symmetry with which this pronouncement unfolds God's condemnation of the way in which his word is being perverted and brought to shame. There are two main sections on prophets and prophetesses. Both have similar introductions (vv. 2 and 17) and are connected together by a title common to both in v. 1. Each of these main sections is divided into two subsections, and each subsection shows the same threefold structure and serves the same object of making Yahweh known. One must allow for the possibility that the scheme has been followed up further and vigorously applied by some later hand. Nevertheless the general layout, and the way in which what is said in the first part of each main section is re-echoed in the second, gives a striking proof of owing its construction as a whole to Ezekiel himself. He had been charged with the duty of pronouncing condemnation. So he tried to give weight and effectiveness to what he said by such an architectural arrangement.

The deceit of false prophesy exposed and punished: 13.1–9

[1f.] First of all, vv. 1f. designate all that is to follow as a word uttered in obedience to a commission from Yahweh, and coming therefore from too high a sphere for men to try to justify themselves against it. [3] After that, a full weight of woe can be called down upon the prophets for their wanton behaviour. They are addressed as 'prophets of Israel'. So their claim to the title of prophet is not contested. They have a legitimate task to exercise on behalf of Israel, that is, for the people of God whether at home or in exile. But they have made an irresponsible use of their commission to that task. A messenger's duty is to transmit nothing more than the message he has received. But they have exceeded their commission, and given a message dictated by their own insight or caprice, without waiting to receive a vision. A genuine prophet is on his guard, and does not speak without a definite call. (We have only to recall the behaviour of Jeremiah, even on occasions when he stood in desperate need of a crushing retort, Jer. 28.11ff.: 42.4ff.) But these men to whom he is speaking have been in too much of a hurry. They have made up a message of their own, and labelled it 'thus saith the Lord', although Yahweh had never spoken to them (v. 7). So their messages can be rated as nothing more than 'deceiving visions and lying oracles'.

Ezekiel shows why he condemns them so severely. He draws two pictures of the whole attitude of those whom he is attacking, giving an accurate sketch of their characteristic behaviour, and thus prepares for the damning conclusion.

[4] First of all, he compares them to foxes in ruins. Many solutions have been proposed as to the meaning of this metaphor, most of them more enigmatic than the enigma itself. Among other suggestions are undermining and grubbing up (Herrmann), the destruction of loosely built vineyard walls (Zimmerli), their habit of always dodging questions which call for a decision[1] or how in popular supersitition the sight of a fox is an omen of ill luck.[2] But, on the one hand, all such suggestions excessively exaggerate the destructive powers of the fox, and illegitimately involve v. 5, while, on the other hand, no notice is taken of the way in which it is insisted that these foxes live among ruins.

So it is much more probable that the metaphor simply takes the natural habits of the fox, for which concealed cavities approached by difficult winding passages, such as are readily found among ruins, represent the ideal home, and uses them to describe how these prophets behave in face of the disaster and ruin which has overcome their nation. A fox makes a comfortable den among fallen ruins, and is in his element there. These prophets do not view Israel's inward and outward downfall as a calamity, the thought of which fills them with dismay, and which they try to dismiss by every means at their disposal. Quite the reverse! They feel perfectly at ease in this disaster, they enjoy it and even make themselves at home in it and exploit it! Never has the nation shown more readiness to be taken in by these tricksters, with their plausible behaviour and their glib patter to which Jeremiah refers (23.31, *wayyine'mū ne'um*), than in those days when its security was falling to pieces and its hopes were laid in ruins. It longed for a prophet who would regard it as his duty

---

[1] Quell, *Wahre und falsche Propheten*, 1952, p. 146, n. 1.
[2] A. Jirku, *Materialien zur Volksreligion Israels*, 1914, pp. 111ff.

to create *šālōm*, welfare and prosperity for both people and state, by means of the real effects which his word was capable of producing.[1] This, the guild prophets felt, was the very job they were meant to do; they were filled with conscious pride at their own indispensability, and showed no diffidence in supplying the demand for dignified and sonorous predictions of good things to come. Thus they soothed the fears of the populace and, conscious of duty well done, made sure of having money to jingle in their pockets.

They thus made unscrupulous use of the national catastrophe in order to add to the dignity of their own professional position as prophets. But behind that again, Ezekiel can discern another still more deeply rooted corruption of prophecy, which he describes in a second parable taken from the siege of a city. [5] When the besieger has succeeded in making breaches in the wall of the city which he is attacking, then everything depends on whether the besieged will be able to close the gap in their defences by an extemporized wall, to keep the enemy from breaking in, and whether they will succeed in doing so before the storming party mounts the breach. Such a duty calls for soldiers who have realized in time the danger which threatens and are determined at all costs to keep it out. In drawing this picture of the most perilous moment of a siege in order to show what it is a prophet's duty to do, and what these prophets ought to have done and have failed to do, Ezekiel makes it clear what a high regard he has for a prophet's calling. But what he really means can only be understood when one tries to see what the prophet thought was the danger which threatened Israel. The attacker by whom Israel seems about to be stormed and brought to ruin is not one of those earthly powers whom the people prepare to repel, and upon whom their eyes are wholly fixed, but Yahweh himself in person. To parry his threatened attack, repeated declarations that all will be well, made in imitation of the example given by the anti-Assyrian prophecies of the great Isaiah, are not enough. What is more urgently needed is, first, a clear eye to see what the present peril is, and then, a readiness to provide the people with the only means by which they can hold their ground in face of this particular danger. The day of Yahweh, the great day of judgment, is about to dawn. In this final settling of the account between the holy God and his sinful people, Israel's fate is already sealed, unless at this last moment it can be shown the way in

---

[1] For this part of a prophet's duties, cf. A. R. Johnson, *The Cultic Prophet in Ancient Israel*, 1944, pp. 50f., 63.

which it can be delivered. But that can happen only if prophecy itself is ready to confess Yahweh's great fundamental demands, and to impress them once more upon the hearts and consciences of the people. This understanding of the situation, and of the task arising from it, was a thing in which Ezekiel knew himself to be fully at one with his predecessors. But his opponents were completely blind to it. According to their wishful thinking the covenant God had power only to bless, and was incapable of actually destroying his people, even though he might perhaps punish their misdeeds. They could, of course, appeal to traditional elements in the faith which favoured such a view, especially those customarily proclaimed at the great covenant festivals[1] and demonstrated by ancient narrators in the history of the people of God. But they only gabble these phrases like schoolchildren; they show no feeling for the enormous gap between the ages, they shut their minds to every new insight. All this goes to show how utterly blind they are; they betray the fact that Yahweh has never spoken to them, but that their own heart is determining what they preach as the word of God.

So in the end it is the self-assurance with which the messenger exceeds his duty to say no more than he was told which makes them untrue to their prophetic calling. [6] One thoughtful reader of this section has therefore justly remarked in v. 6 on the folly of expecting the fulfilment of a favourable prediction which has no divine authority to support it: self-will grows into fanaticism which clings desperately to false hopes of salvation.

[7] In v. 7, the address to those under threat, which only began in v. 5, is continued with the vigorous question whether they themselves ought not to admit how false those visions and oracles are. This very probably implies that their message has been severely hit by the actual course of events, which has shown it up in all its inward hollowness. If the catastrophe of 587 had already come into sight, we can very easily understand such a question. But it is equally possible that some other blow preceding that ultimate collapse is being presented by Ezekiel to his opponents, to make them concede that Yahweh himself is stripping them of all their pretensions. One very suitable occasion would be provided by the collapse of the abortive attempt at a revolt against Babylonian supremacy by the vassal states in Palestine, which, according to Jer. 27, had been supported by predictions of success by the prophets.

[1] Cf. A. Weiser, *The Psalms*, 1962, pp. 35ff.

[8] So the invective comes to an end, and v. 8 uses the well-known 'therefore' to introduce a statement of what the sentence is to be. The delinquents are first of all directly addressed, and informed that Yahweh has already raised his hand against them. [9] Verse 9 continues in the third person, but that is no reason for regarding it as a fragment surviving from another denunciation (Fohrer). It is much more probable that the formulation of the sentence in precise legal terminology, together with explicit naming of the guilty parties and of the offence committed, has led to the change of person.

This becomes still more intelligible when one observes the sort of punishment to which they are sentenced. It is not stated that they will only perish, but that they will be excluded from community rights and struck off the roll of citizens. *Sōd*, the word used here for 'community', indicates the intimate way in which persons meet and talk together when linked by something they have in common. It may be the local community at the gate in their leisure-time, discussing all the local concerns, or it may be a merry group of young people (Jer. 6.11; 15.17); it may be an association of the ungodly secretly planning their next undertaking (Gen. 49.6; Ps. 64.3) or a meeting of the devout for the deepening of their spiritual life (Pss. 55.15; 111.1; Job. 19.9). When Ezekiel extends the connotation of the term so as to denote the whole community of the people of God, he is probably meaning to stress the inward loyalty which unites all those who belong to the chosen people.[1] But his employment of the word has made it more of an official term. The 'register of the house of Israel', to which he refers in the same breath, also fits this. It must be 'a sort of official register' or list of citizens,[2] such as we find also implied by Ezekiel's contemporary Jeremiah (Jer. 22.30).[3] For a man to have his name entered there is a sign of public recognition of his rights as a citizen of Israel. The punishment of the false prophets therefore consists in their being outlawed and excommunicated, by being excluded from their membership of the people of God. Their exclusion from any share in landed property is only too obvious a corollary. One may well ask, if this 'coming to the land of Israel',

---

[1] Cf. how this word is later used to refer to Yahweh's intimate communion with those who are faithful to him: Ps. 25.14; Prov. 3.32; Job 29.4.

[2] W. Rudolf, *Jeremia*, 1947, p. 124.

[3] The 'book of life' kept by Yahweh, often mentioned in this connection, has really nothing whatever to do with such earthly documents, which do no more than give a public guarantee of the legal claim to which they refer.

which introduces the return of the exiles as something obviously to be expected without any qualification, is not an extension of the sentence of judgment, added at some later date.

The self-willed way in which they have made just what they liked of the word of God in order to serve their own selfish purposes is matched by the dismissal of the disloyal messengers, and the deception and misguidance of the community committed to their leadership is matched by their exclusion from the number of those designated by God's election and blessed by him. The *ius talionis*, which made the punishment fit the crime as closely as possible, had long set the standard of ancient Israelite legislation. Here, as elsewhere in the prophets, it is transformed into an inner accord between crime and punishment, which forces the frivolous to see the inevitable consequences of ignoring the will of God.

The emptiness of hopes of salvation: 13.10–16

This second word against the prophets makes special mention of the content of their prophecies, to which so far we have only had an indirect reference. **[10]** The expression used here is taken from Jeremiah, and gives proof of Ezekiel's acquaintance with the preaching of his great contemporary. He says their characteristic theme is 'salvation when there is no salvation' (Jer. 6.14; 8.11). *Šālōm*, 'salvation', is a characteristic of Isaiah's hope of salvation (Isa. 9.5f.; 32.17), and has evidently been adopted as a slogan to express an optimistic faith. The guild-prophets could appeal to the great prophets of the time of trouble under Sennacherib, to counter every warning voice and thus attack any proclamation of judgment as lack of faith and capitulation to earthly powers. It was clearly very hard to counter such a type of prophecy, since it was apparently justified by what Isaiah had preached in all good faith. Ezekiel tries to expose the lack of sincerity with pathos with which it appeals to men's feelings by a picture which shows how it tells the people only what they like to hear, and glosses over their obstinate resistance.

In Palestine, we find solid outer walls to the houses, made of stones firmly bonded together with mortar. But we also find lightly built partition walls, made of dry stone put together without any of the clay which serves as mortar. Such walls serve for partitions between rooms inside the house, or to divide the inner court.[1] Well-constructed

---

[1] That the prophet does not think of an inner partition wall is shown by the subsequent implication that it is exposed to wind and rain.

walls were not always overlaid with plaster, and its use must have been still more unusual for such a flimsy partition wall. He who would cover such a roughly and hastily constructed wall[1] with the plaster usually reserved for a strong outer wall, and thus make it look like a solid piece of masonry, would be a foolish man indeed.

Ezekiel marks out the prophets of salvation as just such fools. The people are trying to stave off the dangers threatening them by roughly improvised walls, i.e. by utterly inadequate means. Here one must think first of all of superstitious trust in the temple and holy city as pledges of divine election and salvation, and of the zealous sacrificial worship which is regarded as the means of winning favour with God. Instead of revealing these ideas as mere illusions, the prophets encourage them. They cover over the wall the people have made, or as the prophet contemptuously says they 'smear'[2] it over: translating the metaphor, that means that they take the false hope of the people and make it look like the soundly based expectation of true faith by means of their deceitful promises of salvation. They thus degrade themselves into pledged supporters of every piece of wishful thinking. They evade any suggestion of moral commitment and encourage men who are alienated from God in their presumptuous claim to enjoy divine protection.

[11] Such prophecy falsifies God's will. So God himself gives it a shattering refutation by the thunderstorm of judgment which overthrows the makeshift wall, i.e. the false hopes of the people. This points to the sudden occurrence of some disaster, which can hardly have been anything but the fall of Jerusalem. So it is likely that this denunciation arose shortly before it. The collapse of the wall shows what absurd botching the whitewashing has been. [12] The mocking inquiry 'Where is it now?' is enough to give an impressive demonstration of the unmasking of the self-deceived deceivers. [14b] In this way, Yahweh forces them to bow in the dust and recognize the holiness of his being.

Denunciation of the magical charms of women soothsayers: 13.17–23

[17] Along with the word against false prophets goes another, introduced in similar phraseology to that of v. 2, against prophetesses who

---

[1] For such a wall Ezekiel uses the word *ḥayiṣ*. It is not found elsewhere in the Old Testament, but Jewish-Aramaic and Neo-Hebrew confirm its meaning.

[2] Dalman, *Arbeit und Sitte in Palästina*, VII, 1942, p. 28.

prophesy out of their own hearts. But the description of the activities in which these women engage makes us feel doubtful as to whether they really deserve the title of prophetesses, since all seems to belong to the 'domain of minor soothsaying and witchcraft' (Zimmerli). The Old Testament gives the honorific title of $n^e b \bar{i}' \bar{a}$ elsewhere to women such as Miriam (Ex. 15.20), Deborah (Judg. 4.4), Huldah (II Kings 22.14) and Noadiah (Neh. 6.14), who, like male prophets, dealt with matters concerning the people as a whole. It does not matter in the least, if the first two among them received their title posthumously and retrospectively from a later generation. But here, apparently, all that we are concerned with is a few women who deal in magic on the sly for the benefit of individual clients who pay in cash for their services.

Yet that does not allow for all that is involved in this phenomenon, which is not mentioned elsewhere in the Old Testament. One cannot account for every detail of the practices with which the objects of the denunciation are charged. But undoubtedly they point to magic arts which we know from Babylonia, and indeed from the world of the primitives. [18] The bindings round the wrist recall the magical knots and bands which have some prominence in the rich Babylonian library of incantations.[1] One may also refer to accounts of magical practices among primitive peoples or in popular superstitions, according to which ill luck is warded off by tying strips of palm-leaf, bark, or wool round the joints,[2] or diseases are cured by tying knotted thread to the groin, head, neck or limbs of the patient.[3] The rhyming prayers in Jewish ritual are frequently referred to in this connection, and rightly so, since they have magical powers, and serve as a protection against evil spirits (cf. φυλακτήρια, amulets, the Greek equivalent, Matt. 23.5) and are therefore a sort of prophylactic against magic. These $t^e pillīn$, or small capsules, containing pieces of parchment inscribed with texts from the Torah, are fastened with thongs on the forehead and half-way up the left forearm. According to the

---

[1] Cf. the various translations of the Maqlu and Šurpu series of incantations in: Morris Jastrow, *Die babylonisch-assyrische Religion*, I, 1905, pp. 288; 302ff.; B. Meissner, *Babylonien und Assyrien*, II, 1925, ch. 17: 'Die Magie', pp. 216; 223; 227ff., and especially the specimen of a healing-charm by means of a band of brightly coloured wool in G. Contenau, *La Magie chez les Assyriens et les Babyloniens*, 1947, p. 170.

[2] J. Barth, 'Zu dem Zauber des Umnähens der Gelenke', *Monatsschrift für Geschichte und Wissenschaft des Judentums* 57, 1913, p. 235.

[3] J. G. Frazer, *The Golden Bough*, III, 1911, pp. 303f.

prescription for attaching it to the arm, the thongs are wound seven times round the arm and then three times round the middle and the ring-finger, which is particularly reminiscent of the prescription for magical bindings. The head-veils evidently also covered the body, since they had to be adapted to fit the size of those who wore them. Here we are to compare the practice of wrapping the person who performs a magical operation in veils or cloths so as to envelop him in all the power concealed within it.[1] One may also recall the part played by Elijah's mantle in the calling of Elisha (I Kings 19.19), which shows some surviving remnant of a primitive belief in such practices. Furthermore, the transmission of the sacred power, through which priests ministered in the temple, by touching the robes in which they ministered, referred to in Ezek. 44.19 (which is not by the prophet Ezekiel) should here be referred to as a counterpart. That people tried by such practices to hunt or catch souls, i.e. to get others under their power, shows their unbounded confidence in the effectiveness of this art. So the prophet seems to be denouncing those who deliberately indulge in that type of magic for their careless and brutal conduct, in taking upon themselves either to kill or to keep alive. This does not mean that their magic aimed directly at bringing about the death of the victim. But the enchantresses did undoubtedly claim to be able by their magic powers to deliver those menaced by the powers of death, and left those who disdained their aid defenceless in face of death. Often, too, they were seriously harmed by the paralysing fear induced by the dark doings of the witches.

[19] What is strange here is the emphatic accusation of the prophet that this behaviour of theirs has 'deconsecrated', i.e. profaned, Yahweh, by degrading him to the level of the common and ordinary. Attempts have been made to explain this as meaning that the enchantresses snatched for themselves the decisions of life and death which belonged to Yahweh alone, and thus failed to recognize the holiness shown by him in his just treatment of the deportees (Bertholet[2], Fohrer). But is there no other way of establishing a connection between the peculiar phraseology employed by the prophet and the practice in question except by such a theological deduction? Here alone in the Old Testament do we find the profanation related directly to Yahweh himself. If we may identify it with the profanation of the name of Yahweh, a fairly frequent occurrence and one also

---

[1] Cf. *Handwörterbuch des deutschen Aberglaubens*, ed. H. Bächtold, 8, 1596f., 1602; 7, 1211ff., on veils as means of protection and healing; 5, 1583f., on the veil of Mary.

known to Ezekiel, what we have here is profanation by direct insults and contempt for Yahweh, the defiling of his sanctuary with pagan abominations (Lev. 18.21; 20.3; Amos. 2.7), disdain for the regulations concerning priests and sacrifices (Lev. 21.6; 22.2, 32), open idolatry (Ezek. 20.39), and swearing false oaths by the divine name (Lev. 19.12), by which this profanation happens. There is a stronger theological phrase only in Ezek. 36.20ff., where the reproach borne by the exiles is seen directly to shame the name of Yahweh before the heathen, who see in it a sign of Yahweh's powerlessness and unimportance. Jeremiah 34.16 is very illuminating; there the breaking of an agreement to free the slaves, made in the name of, and therefore involving, Yahweh (cf. 34.15), is described as a profanation of the name of God. Ought we not to assume the same to have taken place here? The name of Yahweh has been solemnly pronounced to give strength to the magic and to the effects expected from it. Such misuse of the name of God, as contrasted with the devout way in which it ought to be sanctified, plays a large part in magical practices down to the present day. To proclaim subsequently, in the name of Yahweh, that deliverance from the death has been effected through the magical practices, could also be called prophesying out of their own hearts. So from this point of view it is quite uncalled-for to draw any distinction between the witches of 13.18-21 and the prophetesses of vv. 22 and 23 (Bertholet[2] and Fohrer).

Probably on purpose, Ezekiel refrains from saying any more of this way of degrading the name of God, which people use to serve their own purposes, claiming by its employment to have gained full control of the life or death of the members of the people of God. But this alone shows how hostile to God such 'prophecy' is; it audaciously infringes upon the sovereign rights which belong to Yahweh alone, without inquiring what his will is, and treats him as if he were a confederate in black arts and selfish purposes. For here, too, the grand words and mysterious rites cover the naked self-seeking which, for a miserable pittance, places itself at the service of all comers. Amid the miserable circumstances to which these displaced persons are reduced, some of them thus try to preserve their own lives by exploiting those of others.

There can be no doubt that Ezekiel took for granted that these prophetesses could and did produce solid results. When he accuses them of deceiving Yahweh's people and says they gain credit with the people, because they are so afraid of the truth as to turn away from it, he is not suggesting that all they do is a mere ineffective fraud; what he is pointing to is the falsehood of their claim to be acting with God's commission or according to his will. We see at this point what dangerous rivals they are to genuine prophecy. Under the appearance of devoutness, they bring about the death of some who were destined to life, by misleading them to their ruin, or by frightening them to death by gloomy suggestions of coming destruction. Others, delivered over to death by sickness or accident in accordance with God's will, they preserve alive by exercising their magical powers. Such evil doings serve to lead the whole people astray, by obscuring for them the clear will of God which they ought to obey and by enslaving them to uncontrollable forces. Genuine prophecy finds itself caricatured and ousted by demonic soothsaying, which seems to work within a very limited sphere, and yet poisons the whole atmosphere.

[20f.] We can now appreciate the severity of the retribution with which they are threatened. God will himself destroy the magic snares and set his people free from them, or, substituting more literal language for the metaphor, a stronger power will cancel the operations of magical power, and show the people how to free themselves from such slavery to the demonic. Ezekiel tells how the power of truth comes on to the stage to uncover all the hidden winding ways followed by sinful selfishness, and thus rob them of their seductive power. Those overwhelmed by anxieties are brought back to the one power that really can deliver. The insolent woman soothsayers will have to bow before the true God. The prophet does not attempt any rational refutation of the absurdity of such superstition, but conquers it on its own ground by the demonstration of the spirit and of power. Again and again, as the biblical revelation of God has found itself face to face with heathen demonism, this has proved to be the one method capable of producing decisive results.

[22f.] As in dealing with the prophets in 13.10ff., this first longer denunciation has appended to it a second, briefer, one. It is chiefly distinguished from the first by the way in which it pays attention to the power to lead astray men's minds and spirits which stems from the enchantment aimed in the beginning at producing bodily effects. Two groups of people not previously mentioned now come clearly into view, whom the magic art chooses to victimize, one of which is termed righteous and the other ungodly. What exactly is meant by troubling the righteous is not, however, further explained. But as they are evidently attacked and injured, we should probably think of them as having their faith in the almighty power of Yahweh shaken, and thus losing their strongest support, whereas it actually is Yahweh's will to preserve them even in the severest disasters. But in comparison with the first saying, it is surprising to see what a completely different tone of voice is employed in speaking of the second group, the ungodly. In v. 19 they were simply described as men condemned by God who had forfeited their lives, so that to heal them was to contravene God's right to punish them. Here, on the other hand, they are described rather as the objects of God's mercy. The way to their conversion is said to be kept open, in that the sentence of death which menaces them brings with it an insistent demand to cut themselves loose from their evil past. But God's will to save them is frustrated by the enchantress who promises a way of deliverance by other means than through God, and thus encourages them to continue in their former evil ways.

We cannot be mistaken in feeling that the priest who gave pastoral care to the souls of the exiles is here speaking, and that he is drawing on his own experience, corroborated by the sentence of judgment with which he has been charged against those who are laying waste the congregation of God's people. God's will may assert itself inexorably at every point in judging men, but nevertheless his ultimate object is to deliver those who are at enmity with him. The prophet is actuated by this conviction in his work. But again and again he encounters a demonic adversary, who tries by lying speech and deceiving powers to make men forget the one thing they need to remember—that there is no way to deliverance except through recognition of divine retribution. These things take place in the twilight; they are private affairs and hard to see or control. But they endanger Israel's future quite as much as the promises of salvation which the false prophets proclaim aloud in the daylight. Experienced pastors have expressed their opinion that even in Christian congregations the hidden growth of the weed of magical belief and practice is one of the greatest obstacles to the progress of the message of the Gospel and the development of a healthy church life. So the breaking of such magic spells forms one very necessary part of the general offensive against false prophecy.

The problem of dating these denunciations does not present insurmountable difficulties. Measures against enchantress-prophetesses are conceivable at almost any period, but are most probable during the period of complete despair following the destruction of Jerusalem, when there would be a particularly strong inclination among the exiles to welcome such dubious messages of salvation. The metaphors of the first half of the chapter, on the other hand, more probably indicate the period before the final disaster. Then the urgent demand of the day was for the prophet to enter into the breaches which had already been made in the walls, and then Jeremiah also was encountering the work of false prophets, consisting in a similar legitimation of false hopes of better fortune soon to come. One may well ask whether v. 9 really tells to the contrary; one may either take the mention of a return to the holy land as a supplement introduced by someone at a later period, as has been suggested above (p. 167), or, if this is not admissible, one can always think of the formula as introduced by Ezekiel himself during the second period of his activity, when giving a final shape to his denunciation of the false prophets.

Here also it is clear that the inclination to take a positive interest in the prophet's audience, which we saw commencing in ch. 12, has developed a step further. A rampart is now to be overthrown which has been the chief cause for the refusal to accept God's word in the form in which Ezekiel had to preach it. The whole chapter evidently reflects the practical pastoral experience which the prophet must have acquired in the course of his labours. He sees his people under the influence of forces which cause an unhealthy increase in their naturally stubborn tendencies, and which try to oppose God's operations. But now it has ceased to be a matter of indifference 'whether they hear or refuse to hear' (2.5, 7). The people remain charged with their guilt, but nevertheless it is not God's will that they should be surrendered to these forces until they are completely hardened, in the way that Isaiah foresaw would be the outcome of his work (Isa. 6.9ff.). It is God's will that their chains should be broken, so that they could be capable of an unfettered decision in favour of the messenger he has sent and the message he brings. Quite of itself, one saving aim that lies on the other side of judgment comes into view. God is to set up his lordship over a new Israel, and to belong to that new Israel spells deliverance from death. Some of what is said may have been shaped by hopes which did not take definite form until later, and owing to the ruthlessness with which judgment has to be carried out, that aim is almost lost to sight in the darkness of the immediate future. Yet that aim remains an integral part of the prophetic message and stamps it with an affirmative character in spite of all its inexorability. Yahweh has not simply abandoned his people; humanly speaking they may seem a mere lost rabble, but it is his will to form out of them a new people who shall taste his salvation.

The sinister adversary of genuine prophecy is, in this context, dragged out of its natural twilight and exposed to the light. We see all the ambiguity of his manifestation which makes him so hard to grasp. That is why it is named, even in the New Testament, as one of the greatest temptations of the time of the end, and a temptation which cannot be overcome or eradicated until God himself directly intervenes (Matt. 7.15; 24.11, 24; Mark 13.22; I John 4.1; II Thess. 2.8f.; Rev. 13.11–13; 19.20). It is highly significant here that the proclamations of the Lord's parousia says nothing whatever of any unmistakable signs, marking off false prophets from true in a way visible to everyone. On the contrary, it is foreseen that even the elect will be in danger of being led astray. Only the greatest watchfulness and trust in God's election will serve as a protection for believers. Paul does indeed see some protective power in a firm hold on the instructions imparted by him to the community; but actual deliverance depends on their hearts being encouraged and strengthened by God himself (II Thess. 2.15–17). John alone pleads for one clear criterion by which false prophets may be detected, by pointing to faith in the miracle of the incarnation (I John 4.2f.). But this view of his seems to be conditioned by the special spiritual conditions of his day with its gnostic heresies. The signs of recognition named in the Apocalypse are expressed in the secret language of metaphor; only those whose names have been written since the beginning of the world in the Lamb's book of life (Rev. 13.8) have the possibility of being delivered.

The point so prominent there, the extreme elusiveness of false prophesy, is one that is quite as characteristic of the Old Testament. Ezekiel does mention in 13.4f., 10 some of the special peculiarities of the type of prophet he is denouncing (see above, pp. 162f., 167ff.). But these are inward criteria which indicate the direction only to one whose sight and hearing have been illuminated by the appeal of the words of the prophet. They say nothing to those who try to keep in step with the populace, and are still blind to the inward requirements of divine salvation, finding whatever is said by the prophet to the contrary nothing but a confusion and an offence. In 12.21ff., Ezekiel asserts that the threats he pronounces will be fulfilled in the future, and that that will prove them to be true. Here, of course, he agrees with what Deut. 18.21f. say of the criterion by which to recognize a genuine prophetic word. But neither he nor the Deuter-onomist provides us with any simple test by which to tell whether it is true or not at the present moment. The Old Testament refers else-where upon occasion to the moral blemishes which so cleave to false prophets as to be their typical stigma (Jer. 23.14; 29.21–23; Isa.28.7f.; Micah 3.5). Ezekiel does no more than to touch upon it (see on v. 4, above, p. 163). Destructive though it may be for those stricken by it, it has nothing to say about the most difficult cases, since it is not applic-able to all prophets. Nor does Ezekiel mention the external form un-der which the revelation is received, which Jeremiah uses in his criticism of the dreams and visions of his rivals as a criterion of a type of prophecy and which, if not actually false, is probably to be of inferior value (Jer. 23.16, 25ff.), in spite of the confident way he uses formulations taken from Jeremiah like 'a vision out of one's own heart' (Jer. 23.16) and 'saying peace, where there is no peace' (Jer. 6.14). So one must admit that there is no such thing as an exter-nal test by which to tell true prophecy from false, such as all reason-able persons may safely apply.

That is not to say that the believer is defenceless in face of false prophesy, merely because he cannot detect it. We saw above in discussing 12.21ff. (p. 157) that Ezekiel, like his predecessors and like Jesus himself, makes the man who is still uncertain fully responsible in face of the word which comes to him at this moment. Evidently the prophet is convinced that that word has, inherent in it, a power of self-authentication, which cannot be resisted by anyone who really does give it a fair hearing. He may not display all the joyous self-assurance of Micah, or the dogged forcefulness of Jeremiah (Micah 3.8; Jer. 23.29). But he does perfectly and definitely claim for his preaching all the direct spiritual authority and inward dynamic power that is inherent in the word of Yahweh. That implies that the hearer has an inner relationship with the divine source and giver of prophecy, and so it does anything but lead him to self-assurance. He feels himself ever and again called in question by the holy God. In contrast to all self-assurance, he does not feel that his salvation has made its home in him because a bargain has been made and the other party to that bargain is under a permanent obligation to him; rather, he realizes that salvation is an inextricable blend of grace and judgment, such as is inseparable from a meeting with the covenant God. This attitude becomes a possibility and an actuality, when first the prophet, and then his hearers, enter into the right relationship with all that God has so far revealed of himself in his covenant with Israel. Where God is brought down to the level of a Canaanite divinity, automatically beneficent, and is regarded as the protective divinity attached to Israel, instead of the sovereign Lord who is determined to enforce his holy will both upon this people and upon the whole world, prophetic preaching yields to the pressure of natural popular wishful thinking, and ceases to be capable of any valid enforcement of the infallible standard of the moral will of God which must dissipate all illusions about the real situation of Israel. Then the call for repentance can give place to a quite unconditional announcement of salvation for all. Then eyes are closed to the urgency of an hour that points to the day of Yahweh as the great final settling of accounts with all sinful resistance. In preference to that, the favourite theme harped upon is the unbreakable obligation under which God has placed himself to his people by making a covenant with them. Then all the past promises of salvation are misapplied in order to legitimate a fanatical nationalism without any feeling for truth or power of self-criticism, which refuses to let itself be sobered when it sees its promises fail to come true. Then all willingness and capability die away for taking the new roads along which God wishes to lead them, in face of all sorts of sinister changes in historical conditions both in the international world around and in the internal life of Israel. In short, we find a prophecy that is false, because it is false to its own proper task of acting as a mediator between God and people, having itself come to be a flagrant contradiction to the whole inward essence of the revelation of God in Israel. At isolated moments of crisis it can at times, thanks to its associations with great traditions, spread a delusive light round about it. But a faith that has been trained and disciplined to more sober expectations can see through it, and recognize the internal instability which makes it a 'vision out of one's own heart', which has no connection whatsoever with the real word in which God reveals his holiness.

Only faith can judge the truth or falsehood of prophecy, a faith to which all that God has said and is saying in the law and the prophets has struck home, and so has come to have a clear eye and a sharp ear for the deeds and words of the one shepherd of his people, a faith which cannot and will not 'obey the voice of a stranger' (John 10.5). The spiritual nature of this 'discernment of spirits' (διάκρισις πνευμάτων) reaches its clearest expression in the New Testament. Here once again the fulfiller of all prophecy is followed by the shadow of the false prophet. Right hearers of the word are described as 'those who are of God' (John 8.47), or those who 'are of the truth' (John 18.37). That is to say, they are in a direct relationship with God himself, and his influence gives them life. Those who deny or criticize the claim of Jesus, on the other hand, reveal that they are determined by the devil (John 8.37ff.), the 'father of lies' (John 8.44). So it is consistent with this for John and Paul to describe the 'being' of the believer as one determined by the Spirit of God (Rom. 8.9f., 20f.; I Cor. 3.16; 6.11, 19; II Cor. 3.3ff., 17f.; Eph. 2.22; II Thess. 2.13; John 7.39; 16.13–15; I John 4.13; 5.6). At this point, however, as we shall see in Ezek. 36, the Old Testament prophet has already received authority to bring his negative criticism of the spirits of error to its positive fulfilment in the new people of God. He describes that new people of God as having the Spirit of God within them, and being thus taken into ceaseless communion with the holy God himself, and enabled to overcome all the error that is natural to the human spirit.

CHAPTER 14.1–11

The man to whom the prophet has nothing to say

1 And there came[a] to me certain of the elders of Israel and sat down before me. 2And the word of Yahweh came to me: 3'Son of man, these men have turned their hearts once more upon their idols, and they look with pleasure upon that which makes them fall into guilt. Should I indeed let myself be inquired of by them? 4Therefore speak to them and say to them: Every man of the house of Israel, who turns his heart once more upon his idols, and who looks with pleasure upon that which makes him fall into guilt, and yet comes to the prophet, to him do I, Yahweh, offer myself in my own person[b] to answer him in spite of the multitude of his idols, 5for the sake of those of the house of Israel, who have estranged themselves from me for the sake of their idols, that I may lay hold of their heart [. . .][c]. 6Therefore say to the house of Israel: Thus says [. . .][d] Yahweh: Repent and turn from your idols [. . .].[e] 7For every man of the house of Israel, and of the foreigners who sojourn in Israel, who has estranged himself from me, and who turns his heart once more upon his idols, and looks with pleasure upon that which makes him fall into guilt, and yet comes to the prophet, to inquire of me for himself, to him will I, Yahweh, offer myself in person to answer him, 8by setting my face against such a man and

making^f him a sign and a byword^g and destroying him from among my people, that he may know that I am Yahweh.

9 But if the prophet lets himself be deceived and has anything to say, then I, Yahweh, have deceived that prophet, and I will stretch out my hand against him and destroy him from among my people Israel. ^{10}Thus they shall bear their guilt. As is the guilt of the inquirer, so shall the guilt of the prophet be, ^{11}that they of the house of Israel may go no more astray from me nor defile me any more by all their faithlessnesses, but that they may be my people and that I may be their God, says [. . .]^h Yahweh.'

^{a}See BH.

^{b}*bā* should be corrected to *bī*, according to the exact parallel in v. 7.

^{c}MT: *kullām* ('all of them') cannot be taken with the preceding plural 'idols'. It must refer to the 'house of Israel', who are here represented in the sense usual later, but in contradiction to what is stated by Ezekiel, as being all without exception idolatrous.

^{d}See BH.

^{e}MT: 'and from all your abominations turn away your faces'; an amplifying gloss striking because of its circumstantial repetition.

^{f}See BH.

^{g}For plural read singular, consistently employed in the idiomatic phrase 'make a byword', cf. Deut. 28.37; I Kings 9.7; etc.

^{h}See BH.

Idolaters ask the prophet for a word from Yahweh: 14.1–3

[1] Once more we find leading representatives of the exiles interviewing Ezekiel, this time with the express intention of addressing through him an inquiry to Yahweh. We are not informed what the inquiry was about, but the circumstances of the exiles make such a longing seem natural enough either before or after the fall of Jerusalem. It may have been a question about the fate of the homeland, or about whether there was any sign to give some hope to the exiles under their gloomy circumstances. The inquirers are here termed elders of Israel, and not of Judah, as in 8.1, although they will have been the same persons. Evidently the distinction is deliberate. This serves to emphasize from the start how they are responsible for the whole people and for their future.

[2f.] Ezekiel replies to the question put to him in a way which takes the inquirers by surprise. He discloses a serious offence which they have committed, that of idolatry. The expression employed is literally 'they have made their idols go up into their hearts', i.e. have given way to a hankering for them. It indicates that a practice which had once been customary, and had then been discontinued, has now been resumed. It also suggests that the cult was not practised in public, but confined to private life, or even deliberately kept secret. Secret longings for the aid of foreign gods have grown into actual goodwill towards them and reliance upon them (literary 'they have set them before their face'). They had thus allowed another into the place which belonged to Yahweh alone. We know well how often the nation had been overcome by that recurring temptation ever since they first settled in Canaan. The reform by king Josiah in 621 followed a century during which foreign deities had been introduced on a wide scale, even into the temple itself. An attempt was made by those at the helm to enforce a stricter exclusiveness in the worship of Yahweh. But old habits had reasserted themselves subsequently to the king's early death, in ways which Jeremiah's complaints and Ezekiel's temple vision serve to display. Separation from home and the profound impression of the severity of Yahweh's judgment caused by the first captivity must have made many of the exiles give up these customs, and Ezekiel's own activities and his zeal for Yahweh must have been enough to prevent any barefaced restoration of former practice. But as time went on the temptation to seek collateral securities and call in other helpers beside the now wrathful God of the people became too strong, and even the leaders began to give in to it. It is not clearly stated under what form this fresh apostasy asserted itself. But excavations in Canaan reveal large numbers of small statuettes of Babylonian and Egyptian divinities. This suggests that, during the exile also, such images and amulets as could easily be concealed came once more to find a home in the huts of the exiles. Of course, they did not think there, any more than in Judah, of making a public apostasy from the national God. But, adopting the prevailing pagan attitude of mind, they tried to combine a recognition of Yahweh's lordship with recourse to subordinate powers. As the prophet was a still more important source of help, of which they intended to make increased use, they tried to avoid any head-on collision with him.

The inward falsity of such an attitude needs to be attacked, and Ezekiel is summoned to do so by a command from God. There is no room for holding back for fear of losing such pastoral influence as he can still hope to exercise over men who set the tone for others; he must pronounce an unmistakable 'No!' to such a half-hearted recognition of his prophetic function. For what is vaunting itself once more will inevitably grow into 'the stumbling-block of their guilt', a phrase coined by the prophet that is unforgettable in its conciseness, and which suggests the stumbling and the fall into fresh guilt to which this will lead. And guilt—Ezekiel prefers such a severe word for denoting actions offensive to God—can have no result but to be cast away from before the face and cut off from the fellowship of one so holy. A further severity is added to the rejection, by its being declared solely in a dialogue between God and the prophet. The elders are not thought worthy of address, but have to stand by and listen like the unmasked traitors they are. The searching inquiry 'should I let myself be inquired of by them?' also makes the prophet conscious of how impossible it is for idolaters to receive any word from God. That no compromise is possible as long as God's majesty is despised is made searingly evident.

The divine judgment: 14.4–11

[4] The command in v. 4 for an answer to the inquiry which has taken place therefore comes as a surprise, both in form and in content. As has already been seen on the basis of comparisons with Lev. 17.3, 8, 10, 17; 20.2; 22.18, it imitates a formula customary in the law of the sanctuary, and thus raises an order applicable only in one particular context to a statute of common law, binding upon each member of the 'house of Israel', the holy people of God. What happens in this moment is so important to the continued existence of that people that it must take a form by which God shows his unalterable will to make it law, so the persons whose inquiry occasioned it are quite lost to sight.

The statement it contains surprises us by apparently contradicting all that has just been said in vv. 1–3. Yahweh now offers himself in reply to the inquiry addressed to the prophet. He presents himself under an especially solemn form, by coming into direct personal contact with the inquirer. [5] It is quickly added that in any case this answer, given in spite of his numerous idols, is vouchsafed not for his benefit but for that of the house of Israel. God's people are estranged from their Lord and have turned to other gods. But Yahweh shows that it is his will to touch their heart; Yahweh himself is ready to answer them. We begin to get some notion of how utterly overwhelming an answer that will be. In actuality, this answer does not stand in any relation to the curiosity of the inquirer, and does not need to be expressed in any words, since it will consist in God's execution of a sentence we can read out of v. 8. The judge will strike his blow, and the idolater who has dared to present himself in such self-confidence before the holy face of God will be destroyed out of the midst of God's people. This promise of an answer is therefore a bitter piece of irony, and only serves to confirm the prohibition against the prophet giving any answer. To turn to other gods was a crime worthy of death. That warning was clearly enough stated in the law already (Ex. 20.3–5, 23; Lev. 19.4; 26.1; Deut. 5.8; 12.3; 27.15). That lesson is soon to be burnt into Israel's heart and conscience by terrible judgments, so that they finally come to know who Yahweh really is.

[6] But the prophet must make a pause before proclaiming in the brazen language of law this decision made by God. A special message from God must go first to prepare the way for the sentence of judgment which is to follow, so that they may understand what it really means. God's answer must not be regarded as a cold legal decision mercilessly designating the transgressor for punishment. It is the very last appeal, which cannot possibly fall on deaf ears, from a God who is fighting to keep his people. He calls on them not to miss the chance of deliverance and to turn back, while there is still time, from the road they have once more taken. The call to conversion already appears in many different forms in Jeremiah's message and gives it a special tone. In Ezekiel we meet it here for the first time. It shows us, as nothing else could, that his preaching is taking on a new note, namely the progression from the ruthless punishment pronounced upon the reprobate to the hope of a new people of God. Strongly legalistic terminology is used to express how the guilty are handed over to the punishment they deserve. Yet that legal sentence comes not from a hard unfeeling judge but from a God who wills to save.

[7] So God's saving aim is first stated in convincing fashion, and only after that has been done can freedom of operation be given to the verdict that has to be pronounced upon those who have transgressed against God's most fundamental ordinance. Once again legal terminology is adopted to enumerate all who belong to the people of the covenant without exception (even foreigners who seek refuge in Israel belong to that people, just as in the law they are taken under God's protection: Ex. 22.21; 23.9, 12; Deut. 24.14, 17; 29.11).

[8] Then the action which has caused the guilt is defined in precise terms, and the punishment of God is announced as an example for all contemporaries. Elsewhere we find a general threat to the whole people, that their punishment will be a proverbial example of the righteousness of God (Deut. 28.37; I Kings 9.7; Jer. 24.9). Here we

find this applied to the individual. But what happens to him is called a 'sign' to show how it is used as a contribution towards Yahweh's revelation of himself. God eliminates the guilty person without any mediation by human agents. This is not so much a warning sign (Herrmann) or a sign by which God makes himself known (Zimmerli) for the benefit of idolaters. It is a sign evoking belief in the unlimited power of his will to assert itself, removing Israel from the sphere of influence of all foreign gods and attaching her exclusively to himself. This genuinely prophetic interpretation of the punishment established by law is matched by the conclusion, with its reference to the knowledge of God this brought about. What is involved here is not some particular paragraph of the penal code, but the new relationship between Israel and her God, which the idolater has brought into doubt.

[9] We find here something more than the comprehensiveness to be expected from a trained legal expert, when, following up the sentence of vv. 7 and 8, the accessory to the crime, i.e., the prophet, is subjected in the same way to the execution of the law. To be sure, external adherence to the sacred formulas of God's law does operate here, as Zimmerli has shown in an exhaustive piece of form criticism. But the main aim at this point is to exclude anything likely to cast doubt upon Yahweh's claim to his people. The prophet to whom an idolater addresses an inquiry stands under the same threat as his inquirer. Woe to that prophet, if in such circumstances he lets himself be induced by the wish to please or by a calculated compromise to make any communication in Yahweh's name, treating his client's deadly crime as if it were a venial weakness. He, too, would be destroyed out of the congregation, he would be eliminated as still more dangerous, since his influence gives him additional power to mislead. Indeed, such a lapse on the part of one commissioned to announce the will of God is particularly hard to understand in view of the clear divine prohibition. The only explanation is that it is a blindness caused by God himself, as he punishes sin by sin, and thus makes plain how those who thoughtlessly fall into guilt will have to face the inevitable consequences to which it leads. Deuteronomy 13.3 shows a similar outlook. It explains that if a miraculous sign takes place, by which a prophet tries to win people's faith when he is leading them into idolatry, then that sign has been brought about by God himself to tempt or test his own people. For the congregation, however, it serves as a stern warning of how very watchful they will

need to be in order not to be brought to grief by such a great temptation, in which we find an uncanny alliance between human sin and
God-sent blindness.

[10] In conclusion, v. 10 sums up the result which follows the order
of penalty just mentioned, again in a formulation which is customary
in the law, as 'bearing guilt' (Lev. 20.20; Num. 5.31), and one that
had long been current in the legislation of the ancient East (cf. the
examples furnished by Zimmerli). [11] The concluding verse makes
another emphatic return to the people of God. It renews the warning
call of v. 6 and reminds us of the chief aim of divine retribution: it is
in order that Israel may be brought back from where she has gone
astray, and cleansed from the apostasy by which she has become
unclean for Yahweh and been cast out of fellowship with him, and
thus—(here the announcement of the punishment is wholly transformed into a promise of salvation)—be united once more with her
Lord in God's covenant. The covenant formula marks the conclusion.
A couple of isolated testimonies (II Sam. 7.24; Hos. 1.9) show how it
was employed in the Deuteronomic period with a special emphasis,
in order to express Israel's privileged position among the nations.
The central principle of the Deuteronomic movement, basic also to
Jeremiah's analysis of the situation in which he and his people found
themselves (Jer. 7.23; 11.4; 24.7; 31.33), is vigorously affirmed and
taken for granted. But false reliance upon it as if it were an unalienable
possession is turned into a declaration that there is a goal which has
not yet been reached, and no guarantee of its being reached except
God's faithfulness. So those called to reach that goal are summoned
to make a total surrender such as will put to shame the half-hearted
loyalty shown by their leaders. To Israel in its present state, such a
demand must necessarily seem impossible to fulfil. It would have to be
dismissed as a mere illusion, but for something not explicitly stated,
standing behind it, something of which the prophet is not as yet
allowed to speak. His word of salvation is built up upon the terrifying
seriousness of his word of judgment, and stands or falls with the
authority of the God who commands him to speak. The same thing
happens in the Sermon on the Mount. The new life of the children of
God is proclaimed by one who is fully authorized and empowered to
do the work of the Messiah. He alone can make that new life into
something more than a mirage, can in fact make it into a recognizable
reality coming from another dimension.

The special way in which God deals with Jerusalem

12 And the word of Yahweh came to me: [13]'Son of man, when a land sins against me by acting faithlessly, and I stretch out my hand against it and break its staff of bread and send hunger upon it, to cut off from it man and beast, [14]even if these three men, Noah, Daniel and Job, were in it, then only they would be delivered for the sake of their righteousness, says [. . .][a] Yahweh. [15]Or else,[b] if I cause wild beasts to pass through the land, so that they depopulate it, and it becomes a waste, because no man goes through it because of the wild beasts, [16]and[c] these three men were in it, as I live, says [. . .][d] Yahweh, they would deliver neither sons nor daughters, but only they would be delivered, while the land would become a waste. [17]Or if I bring a sword upon that land, and say: Let the sword go through the land! to cut off from it man and beast, [18]though these three men were in it, as I live, says [. . .][e] Yahweh, they would deliver neither sons nor daughters, but they alone would be delivered. [19]Or if I send a pestilence upon[f] that land and pour out[g] my wrath upon it, to cut off from it man and beast, [20]and Noah, Daniel and Job were in it, as I live, says [. . .][h] Yahweh, they should deliver neither son nor daughter, only they should escape alive from it for their righteousness' sake.

21 For thus says [. . .][i] Yahweh: And yet, when I send my four sore acts of judgment; sword, famine, wild beasts and pestilence, against[j] Jerusalem, to cut off from it man and beast, [22]then there shall be survivors left in it, who shall lead out[k] sons and daughters. But when they come forth to you and you see their ways and their doings, you will be consoled for the evil that I have brought upon Jerusalem [. . .][l] [23][. . .][m] and you will come to know that I have not done in vain all that I have brought upon her, says[. . .][n] Yahweh.'

[a]See BH.

[b]MT: *lū*, 'if'. It is better to read instead '*ō*, 'or', as in vv. 17 and 19.

[c]–[f]See BH.

[g]MT: 'with blood, bloody' or 'because of bloodguilt'. The first of these senses goes better with the sword than with the pestilence; the second defines more closely, in a way not to be expected here, the breach of trust mentioned in v. 13. In 5.17 (a gloss) blood, meaning massacre, is put side by side with pestilence, but it cannot have that meaning here. Yet the insertion of *dām* at this point may be due to its influence.

h–kSee BH.

lMT: 'with regard to all that I have brought upon it'; a gloss.

mMT: 'And they will console you, when you see their ways and their doings';
a repetitive addition.

nSee BH.

God's just retribution is uniformly self-consistent: 14.12–20

[12] Yahweh now turns and directly addresses the prophet in four
paragraphs, three times finding their climax in an oath, and thus
assures him of the just but merciless retribution which awaits all
unfaithfulness towards him. This piece of instruction delivered with
such unusual emphasis, and with the deliberate recurrence of so many
phrases, is evidently aimed at some anonymous opponent who dares
to protest against the principle of retribution that has been laid down.
In spite of its somewhat didactic form, it is not a mere abstract expression of a theological idea, a thought which was troubling the
prophet's mind, and from which he 'tried to free himself by going
through the process of writing it down' (Herrmann). It is a deliberate
polemical attack, so it seems more proper to term it 'a word of discussion' (Fohrer). Now vv. 21–23 form a supplement to vv. 13–20,
and are purely prophetic in character, being also introduced by words
showing them to be a messenger's saying. To separate these two
sections as two completely autonomous and mutually independent
utterances by the prophet, and to justify this operation by their own
characteristics, shows itself upon closer examination to be a procedure
which tears apart things belonging to each other, and does not
facilitate the work of exegesis. In order to grasp fully the meaning of
vv. 13–20, one must read and interpret them in the light of vv. 21–23;
they disclose the objective at which the first section was aiming.

[13] The first lesson which needs to be impressed upon the
prophet's mind is the fundamental principle of a divine retribution
valid not only in the case of Israel but of any nation which has come
to merit chastisement. Each individual's accountability for his own
guilt is stated in legal terminology, first defining the case, and then
giving the corresponding penalty. This formulation of the divine will
resembles that in 14.4. It is repeated four times in almost identical
words. This is evidently to impress upon us how unbreakable is this
norm of which we are told. It is further emphasized by a thrice-
repeated oath on the part of God. That such is the intention becomes
still clearer when we observe that we have here not four materially

different cases, to which one norm is to be applied, as is elsewhere usual in law, but that the whole difference consists in the various methods of chastisement applied by Yahweh: famine, wild beasts, sword and pestilence. It is evidently taken for granted that there cannot be any alteration in the divine procedure, so the construction of the different 'cases' is artificial—one might even say that it is dictated by extreme irony. The expression in legal terms is an out-ward artifice of style, which tries by the sonorous tone of identical judgments and sentences to make clear the universal validity of what God enacts.

It is now important for us to see exactly what is meant to be ex-pressed. Evidently not simply individual retribution as such, as is so often asserted. For the climax of the account does not just point to the distinction between collective and individual retribution, so that the guilty nation is definitely a *massa perditionis* exposed to judgment, and to make an exception of the devout, and to spare them, is something which has to be defended. This line of reasoning, which comes up in ch. 18, is not adopted here; it is rather taken as a self-evident fact that genuinely righteous men will be expected from the general chastisement. That again is in exact agreement with the process of selection described in 9.4ff. Indeed, in punitive procedure according to Israelite law, children are not responsible for their parents' crimes, or parents for their children's; the penalty is always imposed upon the person immediately guilty. The contravention of this fundamental principle in such extraordinary cases as high treason or infringement of the ban (II Kings 9.26; Josh. 7.24f.) is sufficiently explained by the exceptional gravity of these crimes and by the probability of the family's complicity. So there was a basis for Ezekiel's assumption that individual responsibility could be taken for granted. According to cultic law, admission to the temple and congregation was a privilege determined by the special circumstances of each individual, and there could be no question of a transference of his ritual cleanness to another person. Zimmerli calls attention to this fact, and in view of the prophet's experience as a priest, it may have strengthened his attitude. The actual aim of the whole account, and the point where resistance is expected and will have to be met, is the question whether devout parents can, by virtue of their devoutness, succeed in having their guilty children spared from judgment. Evidently it was taken for granted among the exiles that this question was to be answered in the affirmative, but it is very doubtful whether we can regard this as

a corollary drawn from Deuteronomic theology (Fohrer). Deuteronomic historiography does indeed recognize that Judah is spared for the
sake of David (I Kings 11.12f.; 15.4; II Kings 8.19; 20.6) and
punished for the sake of Manasseh (II Kings 21.11ff.). But the first
case was not an application of the general principle of retribution,
but had behind it a particular promise made by God to David
(II Sam. 7.12ff.). In the second case, on the other hand, the sin of
the king had also become the sin of his people (II Kings 21.11). Now
precisely this notion of a solidarity of guilt between parents and
children is abrogated by Deuteronomic law (Deut. 24.16), and we
may safely take it for granted that the same applies to the allied
notion of the transference of merit.

It may seem likely, therefore, that in the circles in which Ezekiel
moved a claim was put forward that children of devout parents would
receive special consideration excepting them from the full effects of
divine retribution. But the motive which led to this came from another
source. We most probably find it in the dogma of election, with its
claim that Jerusalem, because of her temple, enjoyed a privileged
position in the divine judgment. It took the old conception of family
solidarity and appealed to it as support for the sparing of a remnant
when the city fell under judgment.

In view of all this, it is particularly significant that there is a
contrast between the line of argument followed in vv. 13–20 and that
found in Jer. 15.1, where Moses and Samuel, the two great inter-
cessors for the people of God, are named. Here, however, the special
relationship of Israel with God is disregarded; the case under consideration is that of any nation whatsoever which has offended
against the divine order, and is used by the prophet to illustrate the
justice of the divine retribution. Anyone who accepted such retribution as the general rule could still protest against that rule being
applied without qualification to Israel.

Nevertheless the process of divine retribution does already apply to
Jerusalem. We see it clearly implied in the fact that no exception is
made even in face of recognized representatives of faultless righteousness. [14] The examples given of such conduct of life pleasing to God
are not Israelites, but devout men belonging to foreign nations,
namely Noah, Daniel and Job. This goes without saying as far as
Noah and Job are concerned, but may seem surprising in the case of
Daniel; even though his being named between the two others points
to the fact that he was what each of them was, an ideal figure belong-

ing to a wider sphere. What started as a conjecture has subsequently been proved. Daniel is mentioned in the mythical texts of the North Syrian city of Ugarit, in which we see him figuring as a righteous ruler and judge of a human or semi-divine type, unable, in spite of all this, to protect his sons from the vengeance of the goddess Anat.[1] Ezekiel names him in 28.3 as well known in Phoenicia also as a possessor of exemplary wisdom. Probably, therefore, we ought to regard him as a figure belonging to Syria in general, and one to be distinguished from the hero of the book of Daniel. The biblical hero of the flood was also the first cultivator of the vine, and it is this latter occupation of his which lends him a place in Syrian tradition. We find his name as a constituent part in Accadian names dating from the nineteenth/eighteenth century BC, at the place where, in such names, a goddess was mentioned. So he may have figured as a god or demi-god in the realm of Syrian saga, although extra-biblical tradition has so far supplied no further information about him. Ezekiel, in agreement with Israelite prehistory, names him as an ideally devout man of primitive times, who was nevertheless unable to ward off disaster from his son, and was compelled to call down a curse on him for his misdeed. Finally we come to Job, who is described as an Edomite in the biblical book called after him. He, too, previously to his mention in literature, was a well-known figure in a wider sphere of tradition. That this was so is an old, and a correct, conclusion derived from the popular tale employed by the author of the book of Job. The popular tale stands quite independent of the problem-poetry of the teacher of wisdom, guaranteeing that its hero was an ideal figure belonging to more ancient times. He is connected with the two others by having undergone the same fate of helplessly seeing disasters come upon his own children.

[14, 16, 18, 20] The fortunes of these ideal embodiments of righteous life must help to refute any idea that God must give preferential treatment to guilty individuals out of regard for the merits of their devout fathers. Such an idea is an alien element which must be rejected as inconsistent with the principle of divine retribution, even though the instances are exceptional men, standing in a special relationship to God. In this way the prophet, by anticipation, prepares his hearers for a rejection of Israel's claim for special treatment in

---

[1] Cf. G. A. Barton, 'Daniel, a Pre-Israelite Hero of Galilee', *JBL* 60 (1941), pp. 213ff.; C. H. Gordon, *The Living Past*, 1941, pp. 149ff.; T. H. Gaster, *Thespis*, 1949, pp. 257ff. Additional literary data is to be found in Fohrer and Zimmerli.

view of her position in the covenant, even when judgment is being carried out. So one expects the conclusion that it is a frivolous illussion to hope that God will connive at the escape of guilty persons when he settles his final account with the ungodly capital city.

The special treatment received by Jerusalem: 14.21–23

At this point testimony to God's will to work retribution undergoes an unexpected change of direction. Verses 21–23 give us a glimpse of what God's retributive action is going to be. It is violently inconsistent with what has been so solemnly vowed in the preceding verses. The explanation given is that Yahweh has a special aim, for the sake of which, in this one unique case, he sacrifices what is otherwise his invariable procedure. **[22]** There are actually going to be some individual inhabitants along with their sons and daughters who are going to survive, and thus escape the foreordained destruction at God's hands, in this city that is destined to be so severely punished, where, more than anywhere else, God must display the justice of his retribution.

One can hardly do justice to the explanation of this inconsistency provided by Ezekiel himself by viewing it as a subsequent justification of an occurrence which he himself had not expected, and regarding it therefore as a sort of theodicy. If we are to suppose that the prophet indulged in such solemn asseverations in vv. 13ff. only to sweep them aside by a not altogether convincing piece of didacticism, which sounds very like a subsequent *ad hoc* correction to explain something that had happened, then we make him cause himself unnecessary difficulties in what he evidently regarded as his main task. So we will be better advised to take seriously the prophetic element in v. 22 and to see in it God announcing beforehand the unexpected way in which he is going to act. Yahweh is turning towards the exiles in a wholly personal manner and confronting them with his divine sovereign freedom, the factor they took least into account in objecting to his retribution.

What they object to is the seemingly blind doctrinaire uniformity of treatment, according to which Jerusalem, in spite of all the uniqueness of her history and the special task given to her in the international sphere, must meet with exactly the same doom as any heathen rebels against God's sovereignty. Now they are unexpectedly informed that God is taking their complaint seriously, and is willing to deliver a remnant from the destruction about to fall upon the doomed city. Is

God then saying a 'Yes!' to that assertion so often made by the exiles that Jerusalem has a special place in God's planning of history? The second part of v. 22 shows what a deep delusion such a notion is and reveals the bitter irony which appears again here. Those who are spared from annihilation will not form a remnant graciously invested with the rich promise of the future, but a sample of the immense corruption of Jerusalem and of its inhabitants. They, with their sons and daughters, will be led forth before the exiles, so that these may be forced to recognize that the punishment and judgment which has broken in upon the city of God just as if it were a heathen place is, as nothing else could be, an act of retribution worthy of the majesty of the covenant God as judge. So in the end this exception is not really an exception, but rather an irrefutable proof that the case of Jerusalem cannot be treated as exceptional. Assuredly, this is a bitter 'consolation' for Jerusalem's fall, a consolation by which, as in 14.5, God once more lays hold of their hearts, and subjects them to his holy will. This is not the didactic move of a clever teacher, but an attempt to convict the petulant rebelliousness which becomes evident when the people criticizes God's judgment, an attempt that we also find in ch. 18. Thus understood, what is said by the prophet anticipates the great refutation in Rom. 9 of all Jewish criticisms of the way in which Israel had been hardened in her unbelief, because of which the accomplishment of salvation is closely joined to a merciless judgment upon the ancient people of God. Only when man capitulates in face of a holy God's exercise of his sovereign power to judge can that criticism be silenced and man be brought to recognize the mystery of the decree of redemption, in which the faithfulness of God wins its eventual triumph by making him his elect.

CHAPTER 15.1–8

Useless vine wood

15 [1]And the word of Yahweh came to me: [2]'Son of man, what is the wood of the vine in comparison with all the trees [. . .]ª of the forest? [3]Is any of its wood taken, so that a tool can be made of it,ᵇ or do men take a peg from it, to hang any vessel on? [4]Truly, it is given up for the fire to eat; when the fire has consumed both of its ends, and it is charred in the middle, is it

then useful for any work? [5]Behold, when it was still whole, it could not be made into a tool; how much less, when the fire has consumed it and it is charred, can it ever be made into a tool.

6 Therefore [say]:[c] Thus says [. . .][d] Yahweh: Like the wood of the vine among the trees of the forest, which I have given up for the fire to eat, so do I make the inhabitants of Jerusalem, [7]when I set my face against them: they have escaped out of the fire, yet the fire shall consume them! And you shall know that I am Yahweh [. . .]'.[e]

[a]MT: 'the vine branch, which is among the trees'; an addition, which tries to reduce the comparison with the trees of the forest to a comparison with the shoots of brushwood there. So far as this goes Bertholet[1] is right in translating: 'above all the brushwood, that is among the trees of the forest'. Yet to assume this gloss as part of the text greatly weakens the whole force of the comparison, since the vine has many advantages as compared with brushwood, which it has not in comparison with large trees. Cf. also v. 6.

[b]'Tool' is here expressed by the word for 'work' in the sense of something produced by work. It would be easier to insert a *kaph* and read *kol-mᵉlāʾkā*: 'in order to do any kind of work'.

[c]Thus with LXX.

[d]See BH.

[e]MT: 'when I set my face against them. [8]And I will make the land desolate because they have acted faithlessly, says the Lord Yahweh.' After the concluding formula in v. 7 about the knowledge of God, we do not expect the repetition of v. 7a and the attempt to explain the chastisement by fire by transferring it to the land.

The parable: 15.1–5

[1f.] As in the preceding section, the prophet receives instructions from his God, from which come the words of the message which he is to deliver to the exiles. The opening words spoken to the prophet are different from 14.12ff., being expressed not in the style of a legal enactment but in that of a parabolic saying. This method of instruction was derived from the practice of the teachers of wisdom, who loved to impart their counsels and warnings under the guise of riddles and parables, thus raising them above the drab level of everyday speech, in order that the keen attention and readiness to learn which they demanded might impress them more deeply upon the mind. The Queen of Sheba tested the wisdom of Solomon by such riddles (I Kings 10.1), and of the sayings composed by that great king; the great majority seem to have been parables from the world of animals and plants (I Kings 4.33). Parables were also used by the prophets, in order to convince their hearers: II Sam. 12.1ff.; Amos 5.19; Isa.

5.1ff.; 28.26ff. So it is not surprising to find Ezekiel making use of this form of wisdom teaching. In Jer. 18.1ff., the prophet in very similar fashion receives instructions from Yahweh himself, conveyed by the way in which a potter works and an interpretation of it in the form of a parable.

As such wisdom sayings frequently take poetical form, it is natural enough to suspect that this passage follows a metrical scheme. But on closer examination, this assumption, made by many (Bertholet, Fohrer, Hölscher), proves untenable. The 'lines' have so irregular a form, some long and some short; the metre is so far from bringing out the main thought, that we must conclude that the prophet was quite indifferent about poetic form, even if we should suppose him to have used it at all. Even a translation as smooth and pleasant to read as that by Hölscher cannot disguise the fact that his German verse-lines hide from us how irregular the original is. In our translation we have therefore renounced any attempt to seek a metrical solution.

The parable of the useless vine wood may well seem forced, if not actually wide of the mark , if one looks at it in isolation. [3] There is nothing particularly natural or enlightening in the idea of judging a vine by the material value of its timber, and comparing it with a forest tree. No one has ever claimed that vine wood possesses any exceptional quality. Whether it is or is not suitable for making tools does not matter. The value of the vine does not depend upon that; it shows its value by its fruit. So when earlier prophets were rebuking the people of God for their corruption, they asserted that lack of fruit, or unexpectedly bad, diseased or unripe fruit, robbed the vine of Israel of possessing any value, and must inevitably lead to its rooting up (Hos. 10.1; Isa. 5.1ff.; Jer. 2.21). So one can hardly say that the prophet was appealing purely to the natural facts in comparing the vine with other trees (Fohrer). On the contrary, the comparison goes so obviously against all the natural facts as to make obvious the intention with which it was made. And once we see what that intention is, it becomes intelligible and effective. For it obviously aims at taking a favourite popular image expressive of the nobility and superiority of Israel and transmuting it into the exact opposite, so as to transform its boastful self-assertion into shame. The fact suggested by the passages quoted from the prophets is confirmed by Ps. 80; the vine was a favourite image in popular poetry for representing the beauty Israel was so conscious of possessing, her noble qualities and her proud bearing, and the act of implanting that vine in Canaan brought out how God himself had shown recognition of her value. Anyone who has actually seen the splendour of the vineyards of Judah and Samaria can, thanks to that experience, appreciate to the full all the beauty of the metaphor.

But the metaphor carried within it a dangerous temptation. One might see one's own national being in a false light which seemed to glorify it, and thus accentuate feelings of self-admiration, which led to no feeling but one of contempt for other nations, and thus try to 'give recovery to the world' by the essence of Israel's nature. Here was a process of replacing the gracious act of the Creator with the natural excellence of the creature, and setting up a would-be legal claim to possess as property what could only be honoured in profound humility as wonderful condescension on the part of the God of the covenant. The parable of the useless vine wood is intended to strike at such falsification of the consciousness of belonging to the elect; so the distortion of the beautiful image of the noble vine into a revelation of self-confessed shame cannot be taken in any sense but as a play of bitter irony, by which, in almost cynical fashion, a point of comparison not present in the usual version of the metaphor is given a central place, and the value of the vine decided by the quality of the timber it affords. Obviously the vine must come off badly in this way, since it can indeed be reasonably maintained that its wood is really unsuitable for the manufacture of tools. Anyone who sees his own nature reflected in that picture must confess his utter uselessness and valuelessness. But that is not enough; the comparison is carried on in a still more offensive way. [4] The question is now what use can be made, not of ordinary vine wood but of a charred piece of vine wood, which, for some reason or other, has been rescued out of the fire. Here the description of the two ends that have been destroyed by fire clearly points to Sargon's destruction of the Northern kingdom and Nebuchadrezzar's carrying Judah into exile and reducing its size, while the charred middle represents the still existing rump state along with its capital, Jerusalem. [5] To the mocking query as to what it is worth, the only possible answer must be 'nothing whatsoever'.

The interpretation of the parable: 15.6–7

[6] The lesson taught by the parable is not a general truth such as we usually have in wisdom teaching, but a verdict which has to be pronounced. The announcement that the vine is to be burned is not a

natural matter-of-fact conclusion from what it is by nature, it is what the judge has decided must be done with a useless nation: 'So do I make the inhabitants of Jerusalem!' It is Yahweh, who treats it as if it were useless vinewood. Here we begin to see that the parable owes its conclusiveness and strength not to the clearness of the comparison it draws but to the clear testimony it gives to Israel's position in the sight of God. Israel as a nation refuses to become an instrument in the hand of the divine craftsman, and therefore there is no way of correcting its boastful assertions that it is the vine, except by pointing out the uselessness of vine wood. In this way the fatalistic determinism which can so easily attach itself to a nature-parable is excluded. The natural uselessness of vine wood is used to serve as an illustration of the collective behaviour of a closed society, which repudiates serving its God, and thus empties of all meaning the advantage of having been chosen by God in preference to others. Israel has no natural superiority by which it can be of service in the hand of the ruler of the universe. Other nations may be like trees of the forest which produce valuable timber, and enrich the common life of the nations by martial valour, skilful adaptation of natural resources, model administration, highly developed industries, or by the cultivation of literature and art. Israel cannot boast of any such gifts, and so is left with nothing when she repudiates the one to whom she owes her special position. In pronouncing this verdict, Ezekiel is in entire agreement with the exhortations in Deuteronomy (cf. Deut. 7ff.), which teach us to regard Yahweh's election as the sole reason for Israel's existence. [7] God turns his face to his people, not, as formerly, in grace, but in wrath at their betrayal of his trust in them; even the remnant, up to now preserved from destruction by his patience, fall victim to the fire of judgment. It is once again declared that the fate of Jerusalem is irrevocably fixed. Yet out of all this a new knowledge of the God of the covenant will emerge for the exiles, since a humble acceptance of God's will to judge and to save is at once the prerequisite and instrumental cause of God's turning to his people.

Ezekiel thus turns our attention away from external misdeeds like idolatry and law-breaking towards that inward perversion of faith in Yahweh which is only too likely to render completely vain all appeals for repentance. It consists in the utilizing of a God-given position of privilege for the purpose of elevating the dignity and importance of one's own nationhood out of all due measure, without at the same time recognizing the seriousness of all the accompanying responsibilities and obligations. This deceptive counterpart to a genuine faith in Yahweh's call prevented the very individuals who held fast to Yahweh as the covenant God of Israel from understanding the contemporary situation and also served as a rich seed-bed for false prophecy. When we see it unmasked, we also see shown up every attitude of mind which exploits God's gift of grace to glorify and idolize a particular nationhood, forgetting its own responsibility in false contempt of others, whether it takes the form of Christian arrogance towards Jews or the apotheosis of a German, English, African or Indian type of Christianity. Here, blindness to one's own faults is combined with unwillingness for selfless service to others. What Ezekiel said to rebuke Israel, blinded by her self-esteem, is elevated by St Paul in Rom. 11.11–24 to a formula which possesses universal validity. A watchman is thus put in charge of the vineyard, to prevent those conscious of belonging to the elect of God from degenerating into useless vine wood, which must necessarily be judged and condemned by God.

CHAPTER 16.1–63

The unfaithful wife

1 And the word of Yahweh came to me: 2'Son of man, make known to Jerusalem her abominations 3and say: Thus says [. . .]ᵃ Yahweh to Jerusalem: Your origin and birth are of the land of the Canaanites; your father was anᵇ Amorite and your mother a Hittite. 4[. . .]ᶜ On the day you were born your navel string was not cut, nor were you washed with water [to cleanse you]ᵈ nor rubbed with salt, nor carefully swathed with bands. 5No eye pitied you, to do any of these things for you, out of compassion for you; but you were cast out in the open field, for you were abhorred [. . .].ᵉ 6Then I passed by you and saw you weltering in your blood,ᶠ and I said to you in your blood,ᵍ "Live, [. . .]ʰ 7and grow upⁱ like a plant of the field! [. . .]"ʲ And you grew up and became tall and arrived at [the time of ripeness];ᵏ your breastsˡ became firm and your hair grew, but you were naked and bare. 8And I passed by you and saw you, and behold, your time had come, the time for love. So I spread the skirt of my mantle over you and covered your nakedness. I plighted my troth to you and entered into a covenant with you,ᵐ says [. . .]ⁿ Yahweh, and you

became mine. ⁹I washed you with water [. . .]º and anointed you with oil.
¹⁰And I clothed you in bright garments and shod you in sandals of *taḥaš*
leatherᵖ and swathed you in byssus and covered you with delicately embroidered material. ¹¹And I decked you with ornaments, and put bracelets
on your arms and a chain on your neck. ¹²I put a ring on your nose, and
earrings in your ears and a beautiful crown upon your head. ¹³Thus you
could deck yourself with gold and silver and your raiment was of byssus
and of delicately-worked and gaily-coloured material. You ate fine flour,
honey and oil and grew exceedingly beautiful and came to regal estate.
¹⁴And your renown went forth among the nations because of your beauty,
for it was perfect because of my ornaments, which I had put upon you,
says [. . .]�q Yahweh.

15 But you trusted in your beauty, and played the harlot because of
your renown, you importunately solicited each passer-by like a harlot and
[became his].ʳ ¹⁶[. . .].ˢ

17 *And you took your splendid jewels, made out of my gold and my silver, which
I had given you, and made for yourself images of men and played the harlot with
them.* ¹⁸*You also took your brightly embroidered garments and clothed· them with
them, and set my wine and my incense before them.* ¹⁹*And my food which I had given
you—(I fed you with fine flour, oil and honey)ᵗ—you set before them for a pleasing
odour [. . .].ᵘ* ²⁰*And you took your sons and your daughters, whom you had borne to
me, and slaughtered them for them to eat. Was your harlotry so small a matter,*
²¹*that you should also slaughter my children and deliver them up, by making them
go to them through the fire?*

22 But [. . .]�v in all your harlotry you did not remember the days of
your youth, when you were naked and bare and weltering in your blood
[. . .].ʷ ²³And after all your wickedness,—woe, woe to you, says Yahweh—
²⁴you built a harlot's bedˣ for yourself and set up a lofty couchʸ in every
open square. ²⁵Yes, at the head of every street you built your lofty couch
and gave up your beauty to shame; and offered yourself to every passer-by.

And you increased your harlotry still more ²⁶*and you played the harlot with the
Egyptians, your lustfulᶻ neighbours, and thus increased your harlotry, so as to provoke me to wrath.* ²⁷*But behold, I stretched out my hand against you, and took away
from you the portion allotted to you, and I gave you up to the greed of your enemies,
the daughters of the Philistines, who were ashamed because of your wicked behaviour.*
²⁸*Yet you still played the harlot also with the Assyrians, because you had not yet been
satiated [by whoredom].ᵃᵃ Yet even after that you were not yet satisfied.* ²⁹*And you
further increased your whoredom towards the landᵇᵇ of the Chaldeans, and even after
that you were not yet satisfied.* ³⁰⁻³⁴ᶜᶜ

35 Therefore, you harlot, hear the word of Yahweh: ³⁶Thus says
[. . .]ᵈᵈ Yahweh: Because in your love-affairs you [made bare]ᵉᵉ your
shame and uncovered your nakedness before all your lovers, [. . .]ᶠᶠ
³⁷therefore assuredly I will bring together all your lovers, to whom you

were agreeable [. . .]gg and uncover your nakedness before them, that they may see all your shame, 38and I will judge you according to the legal decisions upon adultresses [. . .]hh and [bring upon you]ii wrath and jealousy. 39And I will give you into their power, that they may tear to pieces your harlot's bed and destroy your lofty couchjj and strip off your clothes and take away your jewels and leave you standing there naked and bare. 40And they will convoke an assembly of the people against you and stone you and cut you in pieces with their swords. 41[. . .]kk Thus shall they execute judgment upon you in the sight of many women [. . .].ll 42But I will satisfy my wrath upon you, until my jealousy departs from you, and I am calm and no more angry. 43Because you did not remember the days of your youth, but [provoked me to wrath]mm by all these things, therefore do I surely requite your deeds upon [your]nn head, says [. . .]oo Yahweh [. . .].pp

44 *Behold, every maker of mocking verses will sing of you, "Like mother, like daughter".* 45*You are the daughter of your mother, who loathed her husband and her children, and the sister of your [sisters]qq who loathed their husbands and children. Your mother is a Hittite, your father an Amorite.* 46*And your elder sister is Samaria, with her daughters, who lived to the left of you. And your younger sister, who lived to your right, is Sodom with her daughters.* 47*You did not walk in their ways or commit the same abominations as they; it was only a little while, before you were still worse than they in all your ways.* 48*As I live, says [. . .]rr Yahweh, Sodom and her daughters have not done as you and your daughters have done.* 49*Behold, this was the guilt of your sister Sodom: that she and her daughters enjoyed splendour, superfluity and secure ease, yet took no heed of the oppressed and the poor,* 50*but were haughty and committed abominations before me, so I removed them, as [you have seen].ss* 51*Samaria has not sinned half as much as you, you rather have committed far more abominations than they. So you have justified your [sisters]tt by all the abominations which you have committed.* 52*Bear therefore also your disgrace, you who by your sins have interceded for your [sisters]uu by acting more abominably than they, so that they are shown to be more righteous than you. So be you also ashamed and bear your disgrace, for you have justified your [sisters].vv*

53 *But I will restore their fortunes, the fortunes of Sodom and her daughters and the fortunes of Samaria and her daughters [. . .]ww* 53*that you may bear your disgrace and be ashamed of all that you have done, by becoming a consolation to them.* 55*And your sister Sodom and her daughters shall return to their former estate, and Samaria also and her daughters shall return to their former estate [. . .].xx* 56*Did you notyy pronounce the name of your sister Sodom continually as a term of abusezz in your mouth in the time of your pride,aaa* 57*before your wickedness was uncovered? [Now like her you are]bbb an object of reproach for the daughters of [Edom]ccc and all who dwell round about her, for the daughters of the Philistines, who despise you round about.* 58*For that lewdness and abomination of yours, you must now bear, says Yahweh.*

59 *For thus says* [. . .][ddd] *Yahweh:* [*I deal*][eee] *with you, as you have done, by despising the oath, and breaking* [*my*] [fff]*covenant.* 60*But I for my part will remember my covenant with you in the days of your youth and will establish an eternal covenant with you.* 61*And you will remember your ways and be ashamed, when I take both your elder and your younger sisters and give them to you as daughters, but not on account of your covenant.*[ggg] 62*Yes, I will establish my covenant with you, and you shall know that I am Yahweh,* 63*so that you may remember it and be ashamed and never open your mouth again for shame, when I make atonement for you in all that you have done, says* [. . .][hhh] *Yahweh.'*

[a]See BH.

[b]MT: 'the Amorite'.

[c]MT: 'and as concerns your origin'; dittography from v. 3.

[d]A completely uncertain word, lacking in the LXX and perhaps to be regarded as an addition.

[e]See BH.

[f]MT: 'on the day when you were born'; a repetition from v. 4. If one is to take the elements treated as additions here and in note[c] above as stylistic touches after the model of the priestly account of creation in Gen. 1 (Zimmerli), then one may well attribute them to the hand of the priestly transmitter of the text when working over it. Such traces are visible elsewhere in the book of Ezekiel and especially in this chapter.

[g]See BH.

[h]MT: 'and I to you in your blood: live'; dittography.

[i]See BH.

[j]MT: 'I have destined you'; a verb the insertion of which became necessary after the first word of v. 7 had been corrupted into 'a myriad'.

[k]MT: 'the richest ornaments'; an anticipation of what follows. Read instead *beʿēt ʿiddīm* 'at the time of the first menstrual periods, i.e. at puberty.'

[l–n]See BH.

[o]MT: 'and washed your blood off you'; this interpretation of the washing as being to remove menstrual blood is dominated by concern for ritual (cf. Lev. 20.18) and is therefore probably due to priestly scrupulosities when working over the text (thus Zimmerli).

[p]Especially valuable leather, employed for the outermost covering of the tabernacle according to the law of the tabernacle (Ex. 25.5; 26.14; 35.7; etc.), and interpreted as being either sea-cow or dolphin-skin.

[q]See BH.

[r]MT: 'it was his' has no meaning here. Unless it is a fragment displaced from some other context, the reading of the LXX is to be preferred, and has been adopted above.

[s]Verse 16: 'And you took some of your garments and made for yourself gaily striped high places and committed your harlotry there . . .' The last four words are unintelligible. This verse awkwardly departs from the terms of the parable and is out of keeping with v. 18.

[t]See BH.

[u]MT: 'and it was, says the Lord Yahweh'; unintelligible.

^vMT: 'in all your abominations and'; an addition occasioned by the previous insertion, not in LXX.

^wMT: 'you were'; inserted to lighten the sentence.

^{x-y}These words (lit. 'socket' and 'height') are difficult to render. Herrmann, first, going by the renderings in the LXX, V., and other ancient versions, conjectured them to be technical terms for places of prostitution. Sculptural designs from Assyria now leave no room for doubt that they originally referred to structures consecrated to the service of the goddess of love. They were high couches constructed of bricks, like the base of an altar, upon which the temple harlots who served the goddess of love gave themselves up to ritual prostitution. (Cf. W. Andrae, 'Die jüngeren Ischtar-tempel in Assur', *Veröffentlichungen der deutschen Orientsgesellschaft* 58, 1935, T. 45a, b, T. 46n). The names of these cult-requisites, which had probably already found their way into Israel in the time of Amos and Hosea (cf. Amos 4.7f.), seem already to be employed by Ezekiel as meaning public brothels, which are stated, with considerable exaggeration, to be set up 'at the head of every street'.

^zLiterally 'with the large member'; the exceptional lewdness of the Egyptians is thus intended to be expressed.

^{aa}MT: 'and you played the harlot with them'; it is better to omit the suffix and connect with what precedes.

^{bb}MT has *'ereṣ kᵉna'an* in the sense of 'land of merchants', cf. 17.14; however, the additional *kn'n* is lacking in the LXX.

^{cc}MT: '³³How fever-hot (cf. F. Stummer, אֲחֻכָה (Ez XVI 30A)' *VT* IV, 1954, pp. 34ff.) was your heart (text uncertain), says (the Lord) Yahweh, that you did all these things, even as a 'brazen harlot' (lit. 'an imperious whorish woman') would do, ³¹building yourself a harlot's bed (see BH) at the head of every street and setting up your lofty couch in every open square (cf. v. 33). Yet you were not at all like an ordinary harlot, because you despised the harlot's hire. ³²The adulterous wife takes to herself strangers instead of her husband. ³³Whereas men give hire to all harlots, you alone gave your dowry to all your lovers, and bribed them to come to you from every side, to commit whoredom with you.³⁴Thus you were different from other women in your harlotry, since no man ran after you, and you gave hire, while none was given to you, and thus you were different.' Cf. the exegesis *ad loc.*

^{dd}See BH.

^{ee}MT: 'poured itself out'; better read instead with Targum *hospēk*.

^{ff}MT: 'and all your abominable idols (in itself a correct interpretation of lovers) and because of the shed blood of your children, which you gave them'; a gloss because of the insertion of vv. 16–21.

^{gg}MT: 'and all you loved with all you loathed'; a meaningless heaping up of spectators at the judgment, so as to represent Israel as standing alone among the nations. 'And will gather them against you round about'; resumption after the insertion.

^{hh}MT: 'and murderesses'; see above, note ^{ff}.

ⁱⁱMT: 'and I will make you blood'; the original text can be only conjecturally restored; cf. BH.

^{jj}Read singular for plural with Hebrew variants and LXX.

kkMT: 'and they will burn down your houses' is already implied in v. 39 and was originally a gloss applying to it.

llMT: 'and I will put an end to your whoredom, and you will also give hire no more': inserted to leave nothing unsaid, in such a way as really to diminish the heaviness of the sentence.

mm–ooSee BH.

ppMT: 'you did not commit whoredom in addition to all your abominations'; this phrase does not fit in here, the statement it contains is doubtful, and it is evidently textually corrupt. Its original meaning can only be conjecturally restored, cf. Bertholet[1]: 'and I will not be sparing with you because of all your abominations'.

qqRead plural for singular, see BH.

rr–vvSee BH.

wwMT: 'and your fortunes also will I restore with theirs'; an assimilating marginal note made in view of vv. 59ff., but one which overlooks the fact that the restoration of the sisters spells a judgment upon Jerusalem.

xx–yyMT: 'And also you and your daughters, you shall return to your former estate'. See note ww.

zzLiterally: 'in proclamation'.

aaa–dddSee BH.

eeeStrike out the 'and' before the verb, and read a perfect with present sense instead of a consecutive perfect.

tttSee BH.

gggThe last five words are obscure. Evidently they are meant to state some limitation of Yahweh's actions, but it is impossible to state with any certainty what it is. It is usually taken as meaning: 'but not because you have kept the covenant', a sense which it must be admitted the words do not altogether convey. It may perhaps be a corrupt addition.

hhhSee BH.

General observations

Here, for the first time, we meet with one of this prophet's pronouncements which takes the form of a story. The bright colouring and attractive details make an immediate impression upon the hearer, and make him sensitive to the prophet's concern. This method of gaining attention had been repeatedly employed from Jotham's fable of the plants (Judg. 9) on (cf. II Sam. 14.5–16; II Kings 14.9). The prophets, too, did not disdain it when it suited their purpose. The early prophetic movement gives us the well-known fable related by Nathan to David (II Sam. 12.1ff.). Amos makes use of the folk-tale of the luckless man who escapes from one danger only to run the more headlong into another (Amos. 5.19). Isaiah illustrates Judah's guilt with the famous parable of the vineyard (Isa. 5.1ff.) and again alludes to the tool claiming precedence over the craftsman (10.15), in order to remind Assyria of its limitations. Jeremiah tells of the demonic sword, which consumes everything around in its bloodthirsty rage, as if it

had a life of its own (47.6; taken up by Ezekiel 21.14ff.), and of the
mother who feels for her children's fate while lying in the grave
(31.15f.). All these parable stories are in extremely brief form, and
some are no more than a brief allusion. Those of Ezekiel, on the other
hand, are considerably longer and have a solid accumulation of
details, showing a true story-teller's enjoyment of his subject. At the
same time, he is not content simply to stress a single striking feature.
His didactic aim makes him go further, and indulge in an interpretation of the details, almost transforming the parable into an allegory.
Making each part serve a purpose begins, however, to destroy the
poetic charm of the whole.

These peculiarities of Ezekiel's when telling a story are already
clear in the present chapter. In the first section, vv. 1–14, it is still
easy to recognize the widespread fairy-tale motif of the foundling
child who is preserved from disaster by the intervention of a beneficent power and brought to prosperity and happiness.[1] The colourful
details, which do not lend themselves to a didactic interpretation and
therefore are not taken advantage of by Ezekiel, betray the fact that
he did not himself construct the narrative, but took over a folk-tale
for his purpose. From v. 15 on we meet with an ever-increasing
number of interpretations referring to the cultic and political sins of
Jerusalem, which lose themselves in detail and can often be associated with the actual story only by a somewhat forced and artificial
process.

We have in any case to face the question how far the prophet himself should be considered responsible for this interpretation. There are
distinct indications that still later additions have been made in order
to intensify the didactic application of the passage, especially when
new features are inserted in the original working. Among these is the
sudden introduction of the sisters (vv. 44–58), a feature not to be
accommodated with the motif of the foundling child, and the absurdly
exaggerated lust of the harlot (vv. 30–34), which finds no support
whatever in the story. All this having been said, however, allegorical
interpretation still remains characteristic of Ezekiel. Hölscher goes
so far as to deny him authorship of vv.17–29, and is quite right in
feeling that it does not harmonize with the actual parable. On the
other hand, because of his ideal picture of what a poet-prophet ought

---

[1] Cf. in this connection H. Gunkel, *Das Märchen im Alten Testament*, Religions-
geschichtliche Volksbücher II, 23/26, 1917, pp. 113ff.

to do, he fails to do justice to the actual characteristics of the prophet with whom we have to deal.

It must, of course, be admitted that the question whether particular sections of this chapter should be attributed to the prophet or to his redactors is one which can only be answered with more or less probability, and even then plenty of room is left for subjective judgments. Yet even were we to suppose all such theories to be so many temporary expedients, it would remain true that they were demanded and justified by all the actual tensions and inconsistencies between the different sections that make up the chapter. We have in the main followed Fohrer's classification of the parts, with occasional recourse to his predecessors.

One must not lose sight of this complicated process of composition if one is looking for an answer to the question whether Ezekiel communicated his parable stories by word of mouth or whether he intended them from the very first to be circulated in writing. All that we have so far noted about his way of working undoubtedly suggests the former. But it also points to a much shorter parable, in a form still free from subsequent additions. Hölscher may well be fundamentally right in his attempt to settle the question by finding what parts conform to a metrical system. Nevertheless, the process of writing it down and the additions then made have so interfered with the original poetic shape as to make it impossible to effect even an approximate restoration. So it seems better not to make any such attempt in this work.

The rescue of the exposed infant: 16.1–14

[2] As the introduction states, the parable is intended to display the abominable way in which Jerusalem has behaved. The characteristics of the historical situation are reflected by the fact that the metaphor of Yahweh's bride is dressed to fit the city of God, and not the people of God as in Hosea and Jeremiah. That, however, does not rule out the latter from being included. Ezekiel, quite as much as Deutero–Isaiah, regards the city of God as standing for the people of God, whose manner of living owed its character to the holy city and temple, and would therefore be decisively influenced by anything happening to the city, as we have already seen. But the prophet had an additional reason for thinking the parable applicable to Jerusalem. It was the most striking of all possible ways by which to place even the origins of the people of God in that questionable situation in

which all earthly things find themselves, and to strip them of all
religious glamour. [3] Jerusalem actually did possess a heathen past.
At the time of Israel's entry into Canaan it was in the hands of a
population of mixed race, in which two elements had fused. The
Semitic substratum consisted of Amorites, as they are called by the
Elohistic narrator of the Pentateuch, using a collective term that had
grown to be colourless. The upper stratum was a mainly non-
Semitic feudal nobility confined to the cities. In being styled Hittite,
it is given the name of a people of Asia Minor whose leaders at least
were Indo-Germanic. Their fascinating rise during the second millennium BC into a great power contemporary with Babylon and Egypt
has only come to be known through the research work of the last fifty
years.[1] Yet it has not as yet been established from non-Israelite
records that any Hittite racial elements found their way into the
population of southern Palestine. The mention of them in Gen. 10.15;
23.10ff.; 26.34; Num. 19.23; I Sam. 26.6; II Sam. 11.2ff.; I Kings
11.1 may, apart from the naturalization of individual Hittites such as
Uriah, simply be the result of a confusion of identity common elsewhere. After the fall of the Hittite empire in about 1200, they were
mingled with the Hurrites, another non-Semitic people with a strong
admixture of Aryan elements, who had been expanding since 1600 BC
through Mesopotamia and Syria. They had played a considerable
part in establishing the alien Hyksos domination of Egypt and had
set up many small princedoms in the Syrian cities. Abdiḥepa, the
name of the king of Jerusalem in the Tell el Amarna letters of the
second half of the fourteenth century, seems to be of Hurrite provenance. So here we receive a surprising confirmation of the prophet's
statement that the city owed its origin to a Canaanite population of
mixed race.

This piece of information is ingeniously woven into the tale of the
foundling by the statement that its father and mother were representative of the different racial strains. [4f.] But these two parents
followed the hideous custom of eliminating unwanted children
(especially girls) by exposing them. This custom was widespread in
the ancient world.[2] In the letter from the Egyptian labourer Hilarion

[1] Cf. C. W. Ceram, *Enge Schlucht und schwarzer Berg. Entdeckung des Hethiterreiches*, 1955.
[2] Cf. H. Ploss, *Das Kind*[3], I, 1911, pp. 160ff.; B. Nyberg, *Kind und Erde* 1931, pp. 170–94; R. Tolles, *Untersuchungen zur Kindesaussetzung bei den Griechen*, Diss. Breslau, 1941, pp. 78–91.

to his wife, written at the beginning of our era, we see the heartless
way in which it is mentioned, as a matter not in need of explanation.[1]
Mohammed, too, found the custom deeply rooted among his countrymen, and had to fight against it. [6] So the infant was denied the
usual care given to new-born children[2] and would have perished
miserably had not a chance passer-by departed from the usual ruthlessness to rescue the hapless sprawling little creature. In the original
tale there will have been a magician who preserved the child's life
by his magic spells. In the prophet's version God himself plays this
part, acting as the bestower of all life, who by his creative word
recalls to life a creature dedicated to death. [7] However improper it
may be to interpret allegorically single details, such as casting out the
foundling to grow wild in the desert, there can be no doubt of the
intent of the parable: the city of God, and with it the people of God,
already owe their very existence to an act of grace which was not
grounded upon any superiority or merit on the part of the object of
that grace. Indeed, this origin from heathen blood presents a remarkable contrast to the dogmatic theory of being children of Abraham,
used by the rest of Israel as a proof of their claim to be a peculiar
people. On the contrary, it presupposes that there is already present
in the nature of the chosen people an original inclination towards
heathenism, which it has received as an inherited family failing, and
which cannot be expected to produce anything but bad results. Those
for whom the high merits of Jerusalem are an occasion of pride must
naturally regard such a reduction in her reputation as downright
belittlement.

Yet the story as it proceeds seems to accord once more a rightful
place to the fame of Jerusalem. [8] The little savage grows into a
young woman with whom her rescuer falls in love. At a second meeting, which takes place accidentally, the girl, who has nothing but
her natural beauty, is wooed and won by her benefactor, taken out of
her poverty and loneliness, and elevated to the status of a wife and
consort. He lovingly covers her nakedness[3] with his own garment,
and by a vow and contract[4] accords to her the full legal status of a

[1] Cf. A. Deissmann, *Light from the Ancient East*, 1927, p. 168.
[2] Cf. H. Granquist, *Birth and Childhood among the Arabs*, 1947.
[3] While such an action could perfectly well have a secondary legal significance,
that is not significant here, in view of the legal act which follows, cf. A. Jirku, *Die
magische Bedeutung der Kleidung in Israel*, 1914, pp. 14ff.
[4] The available Babylonian texts of marriage contracts, including two recently

wife, so that she is now joined to her husband by firm pledges and
has become his own. **[9–12]** Her princely benefactor further shows
his regard for her by himself preparing her for the wedding ceremony
by bathing and anointing her, and loading her with rich clothing and
costly jewels, among which the bridal crown, mentioned last of all,
gives her all the appearance of a bride being led to her wedding.[1]

Here Ezekiel is really speaking of a springtide of love, in other
words, of perfect mutual understanding between Yahweh and Israel.
[13] This is shown, not only by the preparations for the wedding, but
also by the further indulgence shown towards the bride, who in her
married state may still enjoy princely clothing and delicate viands
(as in Hos. 2.8f.). Such care is taken of her that she blooms into a
beauty who is queenly and attains a wide celebrity. **[14]** The joy her
husband takes in her high renown is further shown by the pleasure he
takes in giving her presents. It is therefore wrong to assert that
Ezekiel disagrees with Isa. 1.21 and does not know of any ideal period
for Jerusalem. What sets him apart is more his insistence that she
possessed an evil nature from the start which, after a short period of
happiness, must necessarily break out harmfully.

Repudiation of the unfaithful wife: 16.15–43

From this point on the prophet must have abandoned the original
story of the foundling and her good fortune, and continued in a
different way. There are indeed many stories telling of the insults
heaped on a woman thus unexpectedly raised to high station in consequence of some suspicion of unfaithfulness on her part, but they
usually make a shining proof follow the period of perils. Ezekiel,
however, accentuates this feature still more in the direction of the
real happening so as to lend full weight to his indictment. **[15, 22]** In
mistaken reliance on the power of her beauty, seduced by the flattering

---

discovered, have been collected by C. Kuhl in a general summary of the subject:
'Neue Dokumente zum Verständnis von Hos. 2.4–15'. *ZAW* 52 (1934), pp. 102ff.
Here we also find the suggestion that Israelite marriage law, which does not seem
to have possessed such a solemn legal ceremony for the marriage contract, may well
at an earlier stage have imposed a stronger tie upon the husband. Quite apart
from this, for Ezekiel the idea of Yahweh's divine covenant with Israel must have
exercised a perceptible influence upon the narrative.

[1] For marriage garments, cf. the description of customs in modern Palestine
by H. Granquist, *Marriage Conditions in a Palestinian Village* II, 1953, pp. 40ff.; and
also G. Rothstein in *Palästinajahrbuch* 6 (1910), pp. 109f.

attentions of the world around her, she who was so highly exalted forgets her past and her wonderful deliverance, and dishonours herself and her husband by surrendering as any harlot would to her adorers. [22, 25] Indeed, she sinks to being a common prostitute who serves the demands of the whole public. The parable thus changes into being an indictment against Israel for the cultic excesses of Canaanite nature-worship, and compares its high places, defiled as they were by cultic prostitution, to brothels set up at every street-corner.

In this description of so strangely and sudden a fall to such abysmal depths, the bright colours of the parable are already seriously faded. Then the parable is given up altogether in two separate descriptions of Israel's misbehaviour which are connected only loosely with the parable through the term whoredom, which had become a traditional image of unfaithfulness to Yahweh since the time of Hosea. Verses 17–21 describe the cultic unfaithfulness of idolatry, [17–19] with its idols decorated with gold and silver (the 'images of men' may well suggest phallic images, as large statues are unknown in Canaanite worship). These are hung with costly cloths and worshipped with votive gifts. The provision of garments for such idols is also to be presumed from II Kings 23.7, where the temple prostitutes weave garments for Astarte. [20f.] Verses 20f. add to this the sacrifices of children, also referred to by Jeremiah (2.34; 3.24; 7.31; 19.5; 32.35), which, as the most valuable offering in a time of special crisis, were also native to nature-religion. Such cultic practices were introduced into Judah during the eighth and seventh centuries when there was an influx of foreign, especially Phoenician,[1] religious customs. There was even a place of sacrifice in the valley of Ben Hinnom, where the national God was invoked as 'Melek' or 'King' (the vocalization of which was changed to Molek by the Masoretes) and took on all the gruesome attributes of a nature-god (cf. II Kings 16.3; 17.17; 21.6; 23.10). These habits in worship are resisted by the prophets as also by the law (Deut. 12.30f.; 18.10; Lev. 18.21; 20.1–5). They mark a climax of the surrender of the fundamental convictions of the ancient faith of Yahweh in favour of Canaanite heathenism.[2]

This picture of the religious unfaithfulness of Israel, in spite of all

[1] Cf. W. von Baudissin, *Kyrios*, III, 1929, pp. 101ff.
[2] On the whole question see W. Eichrodt, *Theology of the Old, Testament* I, 1961, pp. 148ff.

its excessive secondary detail, may be by Ezekiel himself, perhaps as he wrote down the parable in order further to illustrate and interpret his first brief indictment. Surely this is the case in vv. 25b–29, where the unfaithfulness begins to be called whoredom, and to be applied to the political self-abandonment of the people of God. The way in which she courts the favour of the two great powers of the Nile and the Euphrates also called forth the bitter mockery of Jeremiah (Jer. 2.14–19). It could well be likened to the immodest self-abandonment of a harlot, seeing that such political manoeuvring always worked in favour of importing the state-cult of the great power concerned and other foreign religious customs, and thus infringed the exclusive right of the covenant God. [27] Ezekiel regards as a warning against such practices the severe loss of territory to which Judah had to resign herself in 701, after she had attempted, with Egyptian help, to revolt against Assyria. Sennacherib tried to render the turbulent state powerless by partition, transferring a number of districts of Judah to the Philistines.[1] This is expressed in parable language by the statement that Yahweh took away from his wanton wife some of his rich presents, and gave her over to the greed of the 'daughters of the Philistines' (without the metaphor, the Philistine cities). The effects of the loss of these provinces must have been so painfully felt, even a century later, that a mere mention by Ezekiel was enough to recall the suicidal results of Judah's treachery.

[30–34] Verses 30–34 leave the general direction of the parable and bring out the ingratitude and unfaithfulness displayed by Israel towards her God. They try to stigmatize the faithless apostasy as a folly that makes sheer nonsense of itself, like the infatuation of a whorish wife who gives away all her dowry to her lovers, thus deriving no profit from her self-betrayal, except being a public laughing-stock. The bitter mockery of such a comparison accords well enough with Ezekiel's invective in general, but is inconsistent with the other two interpretative passages preceding it, so it may perhaps be right to follow Fohrer and attribute it to a disciple of the prophet's.

[35–43] However that may be, the pronouncement of the sentence, which we have been expecting ever since v. 25, does not come

---

[1] Cf. Sennacherib's account in the 'Taylor'-Cylinder, Col. III, lines 23–26 in *Altorientalische Texte*[2], 1926, p. 345. Eissfeldt may well be right to establish a connection between this portion and Ezekiel's denunciation (*Palästinajahrbuch* 27 (1931), pp. 58ff.).

till v. 35. **[36]** The guilty party is solemnly addressed and once more rebuked for the loathsomeness of her behaviour in trifling away her husband's protection and throwing herself into the arms of strangers. She thus brings about her own punishment by the merciless justice of those strangers. That they should sit in judgment upon a woman with whom they have been in the habit of taking their pleasure may easily be explained as the result of their indignation at the deceit of which she is guilty, and the way she plays off one lover against another. **[39]** They therefore try her and take a hideous vengeance upon her, demolish her brothels, tear the clothes off her body and spoil her of her ornaments, and make her stand naked for all to see her shame. **[40f.]** After the defendant has undergone mockery, she is tried before the assembly of the people, which proceeds to stone her as an adulteress; this punishment is accentuated further, with frightful thoroughness, when the body of the executed is cut in pieces, as an example to warn and frighten all the woman spectators of the execution.

The merciless judgment upon Jerusalem is made good. The punishment is that usual in ancient law,[1] but behind it stands God himself. **[37f.]** It is he who gathers the lovers to the trial, he who reveals the shame of the adulterous wife, he who sees that she is condemned to suffer the legal penalty for her adultery. In choosing this woman to be his wife he was not amusing himself, but fully committing himself to put his love into effect by founding a community, within which it was his will to enter into an intimate relationship with his people, and through it with all mankind. So the retribution demanded by such light-hearted disregard of his unheard-of graciousness is not merely a chilly withdrawal, nor yet a penalty enforced according to the letter of the law independently of any inward feeling, but a solemn act of calling to account, carried out in a fit of blazing indignation, to bring about a realization of what a grave thing it is to put his holy will to shame, and at the same time to show how seriously he takes his human partner. **[42f.]** The way in which expressions for God's wrath and jealousy are heaped up is to denote the inexorable, yet wholly personal, manner in which he reacts against every attempt to deny or ridicule his giving of himself in fellowship. Unless this is impressed with all possible seriousness upon

---

[1] Cf. Deut. 22.21–24; Lev. 20.10; Gen. 38.24; Codex Hammurabi paras. 129; 142f.; *Altassyrisches Gesetzbuch*, ed. Ehelolf, paras. 13–16; *Hethitische Gesetze*, ed. Zimmern, II, paras. 83f.

the conscience of the creature, its value would become doubtful, and the absolute will behind it ambiguous. What is finally at stake is whether or not we realize the existence of that divine majesty, apart from which the dignity of man is empty or non-existent.

Jerusalem has therefore been made to realize the horror of what she has done. So the objective stated at the commencement has been attained, and the subsequent sections possess either a vague connection or no connection at all with the reaching of that objective.

Once it has been freed of later accretions, the parable displays the prophet's appeals for repentance and utterances of threats in all their concentrated strength. Israel is brought face to face with her God and his wonderful will to love, and thus brought to recognition of the full depth of her guilt. In employing the symbol of marriage to express Israel's relationship to God, Ezekiel is, of course, standing on the shoulders of Hosea and Jeremiah. One may even doubt whether he would on his own initiative ever have chosen such a metaphor, or brought the Yahweh throned in other-worldly glory down into such positively disquieting proximity to human eroticism. But evidently the inward truth of this way of expressing God's enigmatical will to love made such a powerful impression upon the mind of the priest that in spite of the way he shrinks from all anthropomorphisms as degrading to the majesty of God, he is unable to resist employing so bold an image. He even accentuates it still further by some touches of almost crude realism, which his predecessors had not ventured to apply.

Some of these may, of course, be put to the credit of the old folktale. But the way in which they are taken over at this particular point is so striking that some have thought that we must explain it as derived from the ideas present in the old Canaanite fertility-religion which was accustomed to celebrate the wedlock between divinity and earth by a religious ceremony of a sacred marriage performed in a grossly realistic fashion (Fohrer). That, however, is most unlikely for the earlier prophets, as, in the rural rites, the divine marriage never had any special land or people, or even 'mother earth' as female partner. The fertilizing of the earth was made a process taking place in the divine world, so as to release and set working terrestrial powers. That those who were zealous believers in the divine election of a historical people would simply substitute that people for the goddess in the ἱερὸς γάμος, transforming a once-for-all historical demonstration of grace into a recurrent, typical event is not at all likely. In view of the fierce way in which they fought against a lure of God permeated by eroticism and the distortions of moral fidelity by the naturalistic misunderstanding of the covenant relating to God, we may regard such a notion as unthinkable for them.

This utilization of the marriage symbol was always confined to a few in Israel (including only Deutero–Isaiah in addition to those already named). Deuteronomic circles, though they also had absorbed prophetic ideals, rejected it in favour of the father-son relationship. So we must confine ourselves to the tangible facts of the historical evidence of the Old Testament and associate that symbol with the personal experience and conviction of a prophet who shows there the inimitable originality which marks all his other thoughts and words, namely Hosea. It was he who applied the symbol of marriage to God's relationship with Israel with a profundity reached by none of those who came after him.[1] But it is still significant for the general character of Yahwism that he had virtually to be forced into it by an experience which brought deep grief into his life and to interpret its meaning by a direct divine disclosure. Only after that did he venture upon such an hitherto unheard of step in interpreting the history of his people. Even in this situation, he did not, in mono-manic one-sidedness, take it upon himself to bring into this picture all the features of Israel's relation to God, but felt perfectly free to employ other metaphors alongside it, such as the father-son relationship, so intimately represented in Hos. 11.1ff. It is not altogether a matter of chance that those prophets who followed his lead were men who, like him, had undergone suffering and temptation almost to breaking-point with such intensity of feeling that it led to an utter shaking of their spiritual being. Against the customary view, we have already argued several times that Ezekiel, like Jeremiah, ought to be considered in this perspective. Both prophets lived to see Yahweh repudiate his people, and put an end to all their security. But that again led them to immerse themselves in that same God's wonderful assurance of his love, by which he had given himself in such unheard-of fashion to belong to his people on earth. That provided them with a sort of spiritual rallying-point, and made it possible for them to hold out in face of all the psychological tension they had to

---

[1] See W. Eichrodt, *Theology of the Old Testament* I, 1961, pp. 250ff.; II, 1967, pp. 290ff.

undergo. Ezekiel enjoys one additional advantage. Thanks to the extremely human way in which it represents love, the folk-tale which he uses as a model enables him to portray in a very strong and unreserved way what a revoltingly ugly thing it is to turn away so faithlessly from such a divine spouse. If here, and still more in ch. 23, he indulges in frantic exaggerations as he pictures the more indecent and disgusting features of harlotry, we must recognize that this is solely due to the fury of a mind in agony with unbearable suffering. It has seen smashed to pieces its most cherished possession, its ideal of a pure people of God; so it must heap mockery upon that picture and caricature it out of all recognition in order to avoid bleeding to death at its feeling of inward degradation. This is no mere abreaction of psychological repressions, as some who apply the methods of psychoanalysis to Hosea and Ezekiel have tried to prove (Häusermann, Jaspers); it is the explosion of a set of tensions which now exert unbearable pressure on belief in God, as all hitherto possible hopes of a sanctified people of God are broken to pieces, and perverted into the caricature of subhuman vileness.

Ezekiel marks the last and most extreme stage of the embitterment already perceptible in his predecessors at their people's alienation from God. In close conjunction with that, he also employs the history of his people in order to state the indictment against his own generation even more severely than his predecessors had ever done. As is evident from the Elohistic historical narrative, nebiism had already seen that social and religious life in Canaan was evolving in such a way as to arouse divine wrath because of the growing collective guilt of the nation. Amos and Isaiah added depth to this judgment by pointing to the divine education which had made itself manifest in many a crisis, but which, in face of the increasing hardening of the people, could only end in a final stroke of annihilation (Amos 4.6ff.; Isa. 9.7ff.). Hosea reviewed the whole history of Israel from the exodus from Egypt, and saw the faithful education given by God to the helpless child being destroyed by the obstinate way in which that same child kept turning away from him (Hos. 11.1ff.), which was as much as to say that the settlement in Canaan and the taking over of the culture of that country marked the decisive turning-point after which the people of the covenant began to be religiously and morally alienated from their God. Jeremiah also looks back again and again into the past, contrasting the continual unfaithfulness of the nation and God's attempts to educate it (Jer. 2; 6.16f.), and sees in their refusal to repent the reason for the judgment which is to come and destroy them. Ezekiel stretches this critical judgment of Israel's development upon the frame of his great historical conspectus, the statement of which is built up in three separate essays (ch. 16, 20, and 23) into one combined picture consisting of election, covenant breaking and judgment. The incurable nature of the disloyalty of the people to their God is thus brought to consciousness in a shattering way. We see the people of God, sunken even lower than the guilty nations of the world, move on towards its doom. It is sometimes, rather extraordinarily, suggested that Ezekiel modelled his view of history on that of Deuteronomy (Bertholet, Fohrer). But his historical criticism is very different. He ruthlessly exposes the instinctive enmity towards God which has from the very beginning been as it were a natural characteristic of the nation. In contrast to the optimism of Deuteronomy, he tries to make us realize what depths of alienation from God, defying all human efforts at improvement, are laid open by the breaking of a relationship of love and trust. The Deuteronomist, on the other hand, is more interested in working out a neat rational scheme calculating the external equivalent of guilt and punishment. Strange to say, in the prophetic indictment the nation as a collective whole is treated as the responsible agent guilty of behaviour hostile towards God. One can regard that as inconsistent with the prevailing 'individualism' of Ezekiel (Bertholet) only if one confounds such individualism with a doctrinaire theory in which every aspect of the relationship to God must necessarily be included (more on this subject in ch. 18).

As against all that, it is important to recall Jesus' judgment. He condemns 'this generation', who, he says, fill up the measure of their fathers by acting in the same way as those who murdered the prophets, and thus must share in solidarity in the same punishment which is to avenge all the innocent blood shed since Abel (Matt. 23.29ff.). The same alliance of the generations in resisting God's work of salvation is given in Acts 7, when Stephen concludes his great speech in his own defence by repeating the verdict of Jesus (Acts 7.51f.). This New Testament review of the sacred history of the old covenant, which serves to answer a contemporary problem, does not for nothing recall the wide-ranging view of Ezek. 20. It, too, warns us against taking demands for individual decision as entirely opposed to the collective responsibility of whole generations bound together by the possession of a common history.

The additions: 16.44–63

The three sisters: 16.44–58

The new comparison drawn here is to be distinguished from the preceding parable. We do not find the lively movement of a pictorial narrative, but a direct personification to denote Jerusalem's relationship to Sodom and Samaria, which makes it possible to compare together the conduct and the fate of each of those three cities, without seeking the aid of any further allegorical features. As we have already pointed out, the introduction of sisters into the story of the foundling child in the first half of this chapter strikes a discordant note, and cannot be anything but an artificial piece of additional elaboration (see below p. 202). A link has to be provided to tie the different motifs together. So a mocking reference to Jerusalem's heathen mother of v. 3 is recalled to attach other daughters to that mother. This destroys the aptly chosen relationship between the parents named in the parable and the unique and unrepeatable historical past of Jerusalem, and replaces it by the colourless stereotyped figure of a bad mother, but that does not disturb its author. So it is most improbable that Ezekiel himself added such a crude and ill-adapted extension to a parable already complete in itself. It will be an elaboration of a denunciation of Jerusalem by a disciple who wanted to add an idea he thought important to the picture of the adulteress.

To this end he makes a fresh complaint against the mother, inconsistent with Ezekiel's parable, saying that she has abhorred her husband and their children, and then quotes the proverb 'as the mother, so are the daughters' to prove that Jerusalem is a true daughter of her mother. Included again here is the fact that Jerusalem's trespass, strictly speaking, is not comparable to that of her mother, seeing that she was false to her earthly husband, the Amorite, whereas Jerusalem is unfaithful to Yahweh, her heavenly spouse. But the author does not regard this detail as being of any fundamental importance; he merely uses it as a connecting-link, by means of which to arrive at the sisters, whose notorious wickedness provides the proper point of comparison for Jerusalem's guilt. In any case the taking over of the parents from v. 3 does not fit in well with the sisters, and turns that pointed assertion into a colourless generalization. Samaria and Sodom are apparently capriciously chosen as the elder and younger sisters respectively. The terms 'left' and 'right' indicate that their homes are north and south of Jerusalem. Evidently the determining factor leading to this choice is not Judah's relationship to northern Israel, as it still is in Jer. 3.6ff., but the fact that the two 'sisters' have been punished by a judgment which has attracted notice, and stamped them as especially damnable transgressors in the eyes of the world. The passage in Jeremiah may very well have provided the model followed in this section, but the special didactic intention of Ezekiel's disciple makes him follow a different road. Even compared to Samaria, accursed as she seemed in the eyes of Judah, Sodom was a city with a still heavier load of guilt and was, in fact, the typical example of the heathen reprobate (Deut. 32.32). So Isaiah was already saying something highly offensive to his contemporaries when he denounced their princes as princes of Sodom and themselves as people of Gomorrah (Isa. 1.10). Jeremiah took over this stigmatization, replacing princes by prophets (Jer. 23.14). Here, however, Jerusalem is regarded as having sunk far lower than Sodom, whose sin is described not as the shameless perversity of Gen. 19 but as the godless self-security of a rich worldly city, which adds to its hybris a hard unsympathizing attitude towards those menaced by hunger and want, thus drawing down Yahweh's wrath and judgment upon itself. This characterization of Sodom is so audacious as to raise the question whether it does not presuppose a different tradition about the destruction of Sodom from the one in Gen. 19. In any case it cuts the ground from under the feet of the people of Jerusalem, who try to assert their own superiority by an attitude of self-righteous contempt towards Sodom. They have behaved even worse than that city which Yahweh singled out for exemplary punishment. They had been shown the seriousness of divine retribution, they enjoyed the gift of the divine covenant, and therefore their responsibility was incomparably greater. The same conclusion is drawn about Samaria, this time without going into a detailed description of her faults; she is a sort of colourless companion-piece to Sodom, like her the object of divine judgment, and equally despised by her sister city. So now we see that the infamy of Jerusalem is such as to excuse and even justify in the eyes of the divine judge those 'sisters' of hers, ever to be regarded as accursed and godless cities. As an outward sign of this, the punishment laid upon them is removed, and they are restored to their former condition, whereas Jerusalem has to take their place and sink into the depths of degradation, at the hands of her heathen neighbours to the east and west, the

Philistines and Amorites (cf. Ezek. 25.15; Lam. 4.21; Ezek. 35.12–14; Obad. 3.12f.). In this situation there is nothing for it but to recognize the righteous judgment of Yahweh and bow to it. 'You must bear your disgrace' is repeated again and again (vv. 52, 53, 58) in a significant variation of phrase from 14.10, showing that the object of all this extreme humiliation is to bring about a subjective recognition of the justness of the sentence. This casting down of the city of God, unillumined by any light of grace, to a place still lower than that of the proverbially notorious sinners was at an early stage found so unbearable that an insertion was made in vv. 53 and 55, adding the same pardon as that given to the sister cities—but this was done, of course, without realizing that it made impossible the shattering conclusion in vv. 57f. But the author of this insertion evidently felt himself justified by vv. 59–63 in indulging in such an anticipation. Nevertheless, the renunciation of such subsequent modifications enables us to see better the true inward greatness of this section, and the radical way in which it rejects all self-righteous illusions and fearlessly faces the bitterest consequences to which its remorseless logic leads. We here see revealed some of the fruits of Ezekiel's preaching of disaster, in the contrition which arose under the impact of the catastrophe of 587. It bids farewell to all self-pity and puts an end to all those vengeful side-glances at adversaries, which so often disfigure submission to God's judgment in the Jewish community

The eternal covenant: 16.59–63
This section is now an independent one, introduced by the usual verbal formula marking a prophetic utterance. It may, however, join v. 43, where we also find the idea of the time of youth. As v. 61 has such a significant relationship to vv. 44–58 that one can hardly delete it as an addition, it seems clear that it should be attached to this section. This section will then probably have been composed in the same period as the last, that is, during the first few years after the second captivity.

Its relationship to what precedes has made us doubt whether Ezekiel wrote it. The way in which it speaks of the new covenant raises that doubt to a practical certainty. Quite unlike the subsequent promises of a covenant by the prophet in ch. 34 and 37, it regards the old covenant as providing a basis for the new. In that God either establishes or upholds the eternal covenant (the word *heqîm* can have either meaning), he stresses the continuity of his regard for the covenant, which is so faithful to the first covenant with the chosen people as to give eternal validity to the relationship there set up, in spite of the injury done to it by human unfaithfulness. Thus the Sinai covenant has a valuation put upon it almost as high as that in the Priestly document in the Pentateuch, where, although it is ultimately no more than a confirmation of the covenant with Abraham, it remains valid for all ages and independent of all human behaviour, and is a centrally important divine establishment of grace proportionate to the inviolable majesty of its divine founder. Ezekiel, on the other hand, did not give central place to the covenant under its institutional aspect. He preferred to subordinate it to God's personal actions in glorification of his name. He even takes this broken covenant, evidently no longer valid as the indestructible foundation of future salvation, and sets over against it the new covenant of peace, by which an everlasting relationship of grace will be established between God and his people (34.25; 37.26).

The obvious difference in this prophetic conception may be enough to show decisively that we ought not to ascribe this section to Ezekiel. Its author tends more towards that priestly line of thought which regards the institution of the covenant as a symbol of the inalienable divine faithfulness. Along with this high valuation of the divine foundation, which remains the same throughout all ages, goes an equally deep understanding of the inward transformation and new creation achieved by the divine faithfulness revealed there. By holding fast even after the severest punishment to the subject who has once been chosen, it brings him to realize the shamelessness of his apostasy. Indeed, in exalting one who has been punished more severely than all other misdoers and above all others through an act of grace, this faithfulness brings him to a knowledge of God in which the tremendous distance between the unalloyed glory of divine mercy and the uncleanness of the human being is continually kept before him, freeing him decisively from all self-esteem. The central object of the whole passage is to give emphasis to the way in which such incomprehensible mercy strikes us dumb and leaves us without a word to say. The writer here saw how to unmask the self-righteous pride which he knew for the besetting sin of his own people. Did he then substitute the ceaseless torture of backward-looking remorse for the joy and freedom of forgiveness? Such an assertion can be made only by one who has ceased to experience that alternation between deep shamefulness and joyful trust which makes up even the Christian life. Not only Paul testifies to an experience of salvation rich in such tensions (cf. Gal. 1.13f.; I Cor. 15.9 with Rom. 8.31ff.; expressed in paradigm form in I Tim. 1.12–15), but Luther, too, along with his spirited panegyric of the joyousness of the Christian heart, can also state in a fundamental passage that the whole life of the believer is to be an act of repentance in accord with the will of Christ (cf. the first of the Ninety-five Theses). In actual practice, to bow in shame before the holiness of God has always proved perfectly reconcilable with an attitude of inward liberation and freedom towards the world. So we are forced to conclude that the two apparently opposed feelings are not inconsistent, but mutually condition each other.

It is striking how seldom commentators who review this chapter take any notice of one feature which does not recur in Ezekiel: the way in which he here describes divine election. Yet one cannot but admit that in the parable of the foundling child the prophet found a way of giving visible expression to the wholly unmerited election of Israel, and how it takes place as a result of the ultimately incomprehensible love of a holy God. Ezekiel expresses it in a way reminiscent of Hosea and Jeremiah, yet quite independently of them. Yahweh appears as one who is himself seized by an inward inclination, and led by it not just to forget all that is lacking in the object of his love but even in overflowing self-giving kindness to prepare it for fellowship with himself, and to bind it to him with the very strongest of links without any attempt to test its worthiness. One may feel tempted to try to explain such a far-reaching interpretation of the divine being in terms of the most powerful of human emotions, and one more remote from the nature of Ezekiel than from that of Hosea or Jeremiah, as the result of a certain constraint, arguing that his use of the folk-story compelled him to follow the motives of the plot. In this way we could rule out any possibility of inferring Ezekiel's picture of God from this passage. But the striking way in which this particular feature is underlined by an oath and the conclusion of a covenant which can only be a result of the prophet's deliberate intention rules it out of court. We must therefore take seriously the significance of this unique justification of Israel's covenant relationship for Ezekiel's picture of God. Of course, we must then also free ourselves from the diagnosis of the prophet as a cold or even cruel person, despite the almost canonical authority it has now attained: it has already become very doubtful for other reasons. Only thus is it possible to understand this portrayal of the divine love, which is expressed nowhere else. It then appears as supreme praise for the divine election evoked just by Israel's very unfaithfulness. There is no more forcible way of showing what an enigma this is, never capable of human explanation, than to attribute it to the irrational force of love. At the very point where the disgraceful entanglement of his nation in despicable self-prostitution wounds the prophet, dominated as few others are by an overwhelming impression of God's greatness and mercy, he finds in the love of God praised by Hosea and Jeremiah a counterbalance which helps him to hold out in face of extreme tension. Against the gloomy background of human guilt and disorder God's perfection dawns for him with a yet more blazing brightness, so that no word seems too strong to express the wonder of its glory.

In this light, the nature of human sin is understood completely in terms of immediate personal decision, to the exclusion of any material or legal categories. With inconceivable blindness, the courtship of the divine lover is rejected for a perverse sensuality, in which all self-respect and all understanding of the holy exclusiveness of the true I-Thou relationship must necessarily go by the board. At the root of this decision is that self-assertion which, instead of accepting its privileged position as a gift from God, grabs at it as if it were a piece of plunder it had won, and insists upon making use of it as it likes, rejecting any responsibility that is involved. From this point of view we see clearly how irreparably sin has destroyed our relationship with God, and also how hopeless it is to think of making up for it by personal effort. The impassioned fury with which God surrenders his own people to the ruthless vengeance of their enemies witnesses on his side to the frightful reality of an incurable destruction of that wonderful encounter and fellowship between mankind and its God, and appeals, even during the punishment, to the knowledge of the unique personal self-commitment made by God himself, which gave the covenant relationship its incomparable value.

There is no need to work out in detail the way in which this accusation against the chosen people impinges deeply upon the life of the covenant people of the New Testament, and reveals their faults. What the Old Testament prophet says of the criminal abuse of the divine gift of love reveals how gravely guilty the Church is of the same sin, and how often it menaces the stability of her position. The letters to the churches in the book of Revelation, many of whose phrases re-echo the language of this chapter (Rev. 2.14, 20ff.), bear witness to how God acts in exactly the same way in judging his Church. To

go still further, we cannot but recollect the collective guilt of the
nations of the West, who, in their ingratitude and blindness, have
exchanged the Gospel entrusted to them for the gospel of self-deification, which, after seeming to promise them unlimited power to
exploit life with all its riches, has finally left them at a standstill, not
knowing what to do, at the point where they anxiously face their own
self-annihilation. The prophet's indictment at this point penetrates
to the real nature of things, and discovers the reason for the hopeless
plight to which the civilized nations of today have been reduced. In
the form under which it was interpreted by the prophet's disciples, it
also points towards a creative solution for this plight, which is inaccessible to all human effort and to be effected by no other hand
than that of the God whom men have betrayed. In the statement that
the covenant is an institution which even God himself cannot overthrow, we catch a glimpse of the New Testament fulfilment by which
the covenant is to be brought into effect; it witnesses to a power of
divine love, as yet hardly discernible. In the later preaching of
Ezekiel it does, however, come overwhelmingly to the fore, so when
we do meet it we see it to be the necessary complement demanded by
his proclamation of judgment.

CHAPTER 17.1–24

The parable of the cedar and the two eagles

1 And the word of Yahweh came to me:
2 'Son of man, propose a riddle and speak an allegory to the house of
  Israel; ³say: Thus says [. . .]ᵃ Yahweh:
  The great eagle with great wings and long pinions,
  rich in plumage, brightly coloured, came to Lebanon
  and took the top of the cedar, ⁴the topmost of its shoots he broke off
  and carried it to the land of trade, set it in a city of merchants.
5 And took a shoot that sprang out of the land and set it in a cornfield.
  As a [sucker]ᵇ beside abundant waters, as growth on a river bank he
  set it,
6 So that it sprouted and grew upᶜ into a luxuriant vine, low in growth
  that it might turn its branches to him, while its roots should sink in
  beneath him.
  So it became a vine and brought forth branches and put forth shoots.

7 Now there was another[d] great eagle with great wings and thick plumage; and behold, this vine bent its roots towards him[d]
and stretched out its branches towards him that he might water it better than the bed[e] in which it was planted.

8 And yet it was planted on good soil, by abundant waters,
to bring forth branches and bear fruit and become a noble vine.

9 Say: Thus says [. . .][f] Yahweh:
Will it succeed?[g] Or will he not pull up its roots, that its grapes may rot and all its fresh sprouting twigs wither [. . .][h] when he tears it up by the roots?"[i]

10 [. . .].[j]

11 And the word of Yahweh came to me:

12 'Say then to the house of rebelliousness: Do you not understand what that means? [. . .][k]
Behold, the king of Babylon came to Jerusalem and took her king and her princes
and brought them [. . .][l] to Babylon. [13]And he took one of the seed royal
and made a covenant with him and took an oath from him.[m]
But the chief men of the land he took away, [14]that the kingdom might be humble,
that it might not lift itself up, but rather keep his covenant that it might stand.

15 But he rebelled against him, by sending [. . .][n] to Egypt, that they might give him horses and many soldiers.
Will it succeed?[o] Will he who does such things escape? Will the covenant-breaker[p] escape?

16 As I live, says [. . .][q] Yahweh, in the dwelling place of the king who made him a king and whose oath he despised and whose covenant he broke, with him in Babylon shall he die. [17]Pharaoh will not help[r] him in war with a mighty army and many soldiers, when a mound is cast up and siege walls built, to cut off many lives. [18]Because he despised the oath, by breaking the covenant, and behold he has given his hand (upon it) and yet has done all these things. He shall not escape.[s]

19 Therefore [say]:[t] Thus says [. . .][u] Yahweh:
As I live, my oath, which he despised,
and my covenant, which he has broken, I[v] bring upon his head.

20 And I spread my net over him, that he may be taken in my snare,
and I bring him to Babylon and enter into judgment with him there,
[because][w] he has broken faith with me,

21 and [all his picked troops][x] shall fall by the sword,
and the survivors shall be scattered to all winds, and you shall know that I [am] Yahweh:[y]

22 Thus says [. . .][z] Yahweh:
Now will I take a part of the top of the [towering and high][aa] cedar and break off a tender shoot from its topmost twigs and plant it myself upon a high and towering mountain, 23upon the mountain height of Israel will I plant it,
and it will bring forth twigs and bear fruit and become a noble cedar.
And all kinds of birds will dwell under it, [. . .][bb] in the shade of its branches they will nest,
24 and all the trees of the field shall know that I am Yahweh;
I bring low the high tree and make high the low tree,
I dry up the green tree and make the dry tree flourish,
I, Yahweh, say and also do it.'

[a]See BH.

[b]A contested *hapax legomenon*.

[c–g]See BH.

[h]MT: 'It will wither, but not through a strong arm and many people.' The first word seems to be dittography or a gloss on the first verb in the line. What follows seems to be a marginal note to v. 17, which has been moved back to a wrong position in the text.

[i]The Aramaic form of the infinitive is striking. Perhaps we should restore the regular infinitive form *lᵉhaśʾōt*. See BH and Köhler's lexicon.

[j]MT: v. 10: 'Behold, it was planted, will it succeed? Will it not, as soon as the east wind strikes it, utterly wither away, wither away on the bed where it grew?' The first three words are a catchword to v. 9a, so it may be a parallel version of the text of v. 9a, originally handed down in the margin. Destruction by the east wind replaces the eagle's vengeance by a direct intervention of Yahweh's; to explain that the verse gives another source of destruction besides v. 9 is in accordance neither with the sense of the allegory, nor with the phraseology of the verse.

[k]MT: 'say'; a wrong repetition of the beginning.

[l]MT: 'to himself'; to be removed as an extra stress which looks like a gloss.

[m]Literally, 'brought him under a curse'.

[n]MT: 'his ambassadors'; as in note [k].

[o]See BH.

[p]Read participle with Targum.

[q]See BH.

[r]Read *yōsiʿ* for *yāʿᵃseh*.

[s]On vv. 16–18, see explanation in commentary.

[t]Thus with LXX and in analogy with v. 9.

[u–v]See BH.

[w]For *mʿlw*, read *ʿal-*: the *m* is due to dittography.

[x]MT: 'and all his fugitives among all his troops'. For this read: *wᵉet-kol-mibḥarᵃʾgappāyw*.

[y]MT: 'have spoken'; considerations of metre demand the removal of *dibbartī*.

[z–aa]See BH.

[bb]MT: 'every wing' or 'every feather'; overfills the line, and is found elsewhere only in Gen. 7.14, where it is also a gloss.

The parable: 17.1–10

[1f.] In obedience to a command from God Ezekiel is to propound a riddle under the form of a parable. We have already had occasion to discuss the relationship between the two genres (see above, pp. 192f.). The one can easily change over into the other, if the parable deliberately requires deeper reflection on the part of the audience and, in order to secure this, employs images not intelligible at first sight. So an interpretation may be added at the end, as the solution is to a riddle, in order to prevent misunderstanding. This is the case here, though, of course, in vv. 16–18 and 19–21 we find a twofold interpretation, which can hardly have been originally intended.

One expects metrical form in a *mashal* (parable). Here, unlike ch. 16, it has been fairly well preserved. Its form is of lines of six stresses which are regularly divided into two half-lines each of three stresses. Only at the point where the prophet passes over from the parable to the interpretation can the regularity of form no longer be established. In place of two equal half-lines, we find six-stress lines, made up of four and two stresses: alternatively, there is a preference for a five-stress line which requires its caesura after the third stress, as in vv. 19–21. But even here, two half-lines of three stresses are not excluded, though we must allow for the possibility that the original metrical form has not been preserved intact.

The story of the cedar shoot and the two great eagles takes the form of a plant and animal fable, which makes no attempt to reflect nature, but treats plants and animals like persons, making them behave like human beings even when such behaviour is not in consonance with their own natural characteristics. [5] It may be true that eagles and other large birds have a bad habit of tearing the top shoots off trees. But for them to insert the broken-off shoot in a well-irrigated seed-bed is part of the arbitrary elaboration of the fable. It is not intended to instruct us about animals or plants, but about human relationships and actions. So we need not be surprised at seeing the plant and animal figures brought into the most extraordinary relationships. It matches this style that it is not characteristic of an eagle to plant a vine, or of a vine to oppose its own purposes to the intentions of its planter.

On the other hand, we must not be so trivial as to look for a feature in civilized human life answering to every single detail of the fable. In spite of the artificial layout of the points of comparison, the fable-making urge still works with freedom enough to let it insert here and there a purely pictorial detail, whose sole function is to make the whole picture more attractive. [3] Thus, the prominence given to the bright plumage has no metaphorical significance. Herrmann has demonstrated the probability of its association with the 'bright reliefs in glazed clay or other coloured sculptures' which we see not only in Assyrian-Babylonian but also in Egyptian and Hittite representations of the eagle-wings of the sun-god (who is symbolized by an eagle) or those of demons or genies.[1] Even the three different divisions of the plumage, mentioned in v. 3, can still be picked out in some representations. [4] Whether one ought to interpret the top of the tree and top shoot of the cedar as signifying the nobility and the king respectively or whether that is to read too much into the picture is also open to question. [7] Nor is it likely that the stretching out of the tendrils of the vine towards the second eagle is a metaphor for the dispatch of ambassadors to Egypt.

That the prophet may have utilized, as in ch. 16, a model from popular tradition is quite within the realm of possibility, though difficult to establish with any certainty.[2] In any case here, too, he would have adapted the material to suit his purposes. [3] As the eagle is the embodiment of strength and swiftness, it makes a very suitable symbol for a conqueror, and is thus used by Deutero-Isaiah as well (Isa. 46.11). It served well to represent the activity of the great Babylonian king Nebuchadrezzar, while a tree as proverbially regal in its pomp as the cedar of Lebanon offered a fine symbol for the house of David. This identification must have been obvious to the hearer as he followed the course of the fable, which described the replacement of the exiled ruler by a usurper not belonging to the reigning line, and his ungrateful and disloyal desertion to the rival of the above-named conqueror. If we assume that Zedekiah's plans for shaking off the Babylonian yoke with Egyptian help were known to the exiles, we can see how the apt characterization of the personages in this drama must have dawned on the exiles, too. The passive parts played by the top of the cedar and the vine not only

---

[1] Cf. Gressmann, *Altorientalische Bilder zum AT*, 1926, plates 307–11; 333; 367; 378–83; C. Bezold, *Ninive und Babylon*, 1909, plates 2; 12; 77; 78; H. Schmökel, *Ur, Assur und Babylon*, 1955, plates 81; 84/85; 96; M. Riemschneider, *Die Welt der Hethiter*, 1954, plates 37; 42; 57; 61; 86 (*Grosse Kulturen der Frühzeit*, ed. H. T. Bossert).

[2] Cf. L. P. Smith, 'The Eagle(s) of Ez. 17', *JBL* 58 (1939), pp. 43ff.

characterize the complete dependence of the little princedom of Judah upon the great powers [4] but also serve to express what Nebuchadrezzar was about when he led Jehoiachin into captivity to Babylon, that 'city of shopkeepers' (the predominant influence of economic dealings in the metropolis of the empire is well expressed thus, as is also the disgust of the Israelite at a life wholly yielded to the god Mammon). [5] Zedekiah, appointed to succeed Jehoiachin, did not originate from the reigning branch of the royal family but from a collateral line, so the prophet presents him as a mere 'shoot out of the ground', and not as a lawful representative of the dynasty (cf. II Kings 23.30f., 34, 36; 24.6, 17f.). He therefore had to make sure of being on good terms with his overlord if he was to have any hope of enforcing his rule in face of legitimist opposition. [6, 8] This task was made easier by the large-scale resources upon which he could draw: true, as a vine he could not claim to possess the proud independence of the cedar, but had to be content with a lower growth, i.e. with a subordinate position. Yet his being planted beside abundant waters shows concern that he should flourish: it is his patron's wish that he should possess all the requirements needed for the growth of a prosperous state. [7] It served Nebuchadrezzar's own interest to set up a consolidated pro-Babylonian princedom as a buffer-state against Egypt in such a perpetual storm centre as Syria. This made it all the more disappointing to him when the ruler who owed all to him tried to find a rapprochement with and support from his Egyptian rival to suit his own ends. Of course, at this point the parable makes it more or less impossible to attribute this new trend in the policy of Judah to any but purely material motives: the vine wanted to enjoy a still better soil. In actual fact, the longing for an alliance with Egypt was based, just as it had been 100 years earlier under Hezekiah (cf. Isa. 28ff.), on an ambition to be delivered from the degradation of being a mere satellite state and to win national independence, such as repeatedly led the Syrian cities into adventurous and frequent changes of allegiance towards the neighbouring empires. Ezekiel, like Isaiah, resolutely refuses to take this idealism into account as if it could justify the adventitious policy of Judah, so he simply follows his parable here. [9] He can thus portray the natural vengeance of the disappointed Babylonian by the symbol of the eagle tearing up the vine by the roots, and can insist upon the inevitability of such a result by reintroducing it under the form of a word of Yahweh,

The interpretation of the parable: 17.11–21

Apart from v. 10, what has been said so far is a complete whole. But it is otherwise with the interpretation which now follows in vv. 11–21. **[16–18]** In this, vv. 16–18 are a secondary insertion, the prose form of which makes it differ conspicuously from its surroundings. Verse 19 with its independent introductory formula is evidently intended to provide the answer to v. 15. It must also be added that these verses, apart from v. 17 with its allusion in somewhat high-flown terms to the fact that the hoped-for help from Egypt never came, do not give us any new information not already expressed in poetical form in vv. 19–21.

It has been questioned whether Ezekiel felt any wish to supply his parable with an interpretation (G. Hölscher, pp. 100ff.). This is chiefly suggested by the transparency of the parable, which does not seem to need an explanation, and by the fact that the reference to Zedekiah's broken oath (v. 19) is not supported by any feature in the parable itself. Even if one gives rein to the first consideration, it does not supply sufficient grounds for contesting the prophet's authorship; since it remains quite possible for him to have employed such a means of driving home to his audience the teachings contained in his parable as vigorously as possible, and thus have cut off every possibility of the 'house of rebellion' evading the divine threat. But above all else he wishes to show that the course proposed by Zedekiah and its failure is not just the result of immoral politics, which carry their own punishment within them, what the parable could allow, but a direct act of rebellion against Yahweh's holy will, a defiance not merely of the Babylonian, but of God himself, and which must therefore end by being judged and punished by him. In going beyond his parable at this point, as Hölscher rightly observes, he is only exercising a freedom to which as a messenger of God he has a right, as he reveals the true background to Israel's political existence, and thus necessarily confronts his hearers with the God in the face of whose inviolable demands even a patriotic Israelite policy can be an outrage. **[13]** To this end he begins with the sworn undertaking which Zedekiah had to make to his Babylonian overlord, accompanied by the invocation of the name of Yahweh, that he would be true to the treaty of alliance and would fulfil all its terms. **[19]** Yahweh calls this undertaking 'my' oath and 'my' covenant, and thus makes us deflect our attention from the great king, whom a patriot might think himself justified in resisting by fair means or foul as the enemy of his country, to himself as the guardian and keeper of the oath, who cannot leave a breach of faith unpunished, even when it involves a mere heathen. Ezekiel does not speak here as a mere formalist, using the wording of a compulsory oath as a snare in which to take his opponents, but out of a profound conviction that even such a decisive turn for the worse in the fortunes of Israel has been brought about by the God of Israel who controls history, and that her oath of loyalty to Babylon is at the same time a profession of readiness to subject herself to the will of God. In doing so he agrees at every point with Jeremiah (Jer. 27.1ff.; 28.14; 37.7ff.), [15] and takes up Isaiah's fight against a faithless policy with Egyptian backing (Isa. 30.1ff.; 31.1ff.) which Zedekiah had tried to renew by sending an embassy to Pharaoh (Psammetichus II, 594–588, or Hophra, 588–566). True, this passage is the only extant record of such a bold step in Israelite foreign policy, but it accords too well with the traditional line of Syrian politics to leave any room for doubt. An Aramaic papyrus letter found at Sakkara in 1942 contains an urgent appeal from a king Adon, apparently king of Askelon, for assistance in face of the advancing Babylonians.[1] One of the letters on broken pieces of earthenware (*ostraka*) found in 1935 in the burnt ruins of the Judaic stronghold of Lachish tells of a journey to Egypt by Kebaryahu, the commanding officer of the forces of Judah.[2] This cannot have been anything but an appeal for Egyptian assistance. According to Jer. 37.7, 11, it resulted in the arrival of an Egyptian army to relieve the siege of Jerusalem.

[20f.] The more extravagant the hopes based, according to the book of Jeremiah, on Egyptian intervention, the more severely are they hit by the prophet's threat that Yahweh himself will catch the perjured king in his net to bring him to trial at Babylon where his overlord has his palace, and will deliver his soldiers to their enemies' swords and scatter their remnants in wild panic. This pronouncement is already removed from any suspicions of being a *vaticinium ex eventu* by the fact that it does not give a word for word description of the punishment, which we know Zedekiah did suffer at the hands of the Babylonians at Riblah on the Orontes. It is perfectly obvious that the concluding assurance that Yahweh's intervention as judge will bring the exiles to the knowledge of his holy will carries its full weight. So this section does not, any more than any other, go

---

[1] H. Schmökel, *Geschichte des alten Vorderasien*, 1957, p. 315.

[2] J. Hempel, 'Die Ostraka von Lakiš', *ZAW* 56 (1938), p. 130.

to prove that the whole threat of judgment arose at Jerusalem.

Yahweh's planting: 17.22–24

[22] In effective contrast to the actions of earthly rulers comes the news that Yahweh himself takes action by planting a cedar shoot, thus displaying to all nations his power to guide the course of history. Unlike the first eagle, he plants the shoot in its native soil. [23] The high and towering mountain, further defined as the mountain height of Israel, is probably none other than Yahweh's holy mountain (20.40) with the temple of Zion, which is described in 40.2 also as an exceedingly high mountain. As in Isa. 2.2; Ps. 48.3 and Zech. 14.10, we see the ancient Eastern conception of the world-mountain taken up and transferred to Jerusalem, so as briefly to state in a new way, by a well-known term from the world of myth, the world-wide importance of the sanctuary in revealing the lordship of Yahweh.[1] In this place, with such a central position in international eyes (cf. 5.5), where Yahweh's faithful adherence to his plan of salvation has expressed itself so significantly in spite of all opposition, the tender seedling is to take root and grow up into a magnificent cedar tree. There is a deliberate insistence on the inconspicuousness of the shoot chosen by Yahweh so as to display the miracle of the divine saving work through the way in which it thrives, just as in Isa. 11.1 and 53.2f. We hear of rich fruit as well as strong branches, but this is no reason for altering the text; here, as in Hos. 14.9, the evergreen cypress is identified with the tree of life in the garden of Paradise, the cedar becomes a miraculous tree full of life-giving fruit.[2] That the birds dwell in its branches shows that it is a refuge to all who seek protection: the ruler appointed by Yahweh gains world-wide significance. True, the idea is not developed any further, and there is no attempt to give a political interpretation pointing to a world-empire; the outlines of the world-embracing salvation are deliberately left vague, a sign that the writer was aware of the danger that the picture might be misused for nationalistic purposes.

[24] The astonished recognition given by the trees of the field, i.e. the nations of the world with their rulers, to the miraculous work of Yahweh does not, as Bertholet rightly insists, involve either their 'conversion' or yet their political subjugation to a world-empire

---

[1] Cf. H. Gressmann, *Der Ursprung der israelitisch-jüdischen Eschatologie*, 1905, pp. 221f.

[2] Cf. W. Eichrodt, *Die Hoffnung des ewigen Friedens im alten Israel*, 1920, p. 93.

under the hegemony of Zion. Here we must draw on Isa. 2.2–4 for enlightenment, since in it, as in this passage, everything is centred upon religious recognition of the world-God and subjection to this righteous will, whereas the political autonomy of the nations remains quite unaffected. But whereas Isaiah sees the effects of this recognition in a new politics of peace among nations, the religious effect is incomparably more important here. The eyes of the nations are opened to the wonderful world-power of Yahweh which, by annihilation and revivification, by abasing and exalting, by the downfall of mighty empires and the establishment of an apparently quite devastated kingdom to a position of world-wide significance, shows that the world-plan announced in his word is being carried out. Just as the threat in 12.25, 28 sets up a pressure which brings it into effect, so does the word of promise; with the same certainty of inseparable conformity between the speech and action of the mighty ruler of the universe the announcement of the hope of salvation is likewise brought forcibly to a close.

As the messianic chapters, ch. 34–37, show, there is nothing here that is alien to Ezekiel's other preaching. On the other hand, we must at least raise the question whether this promise was originally part and parcel of the parable of the two eagles. In view of the undoubted object of the parable, it is unlikely that it was. We should more probably regard it as a subsequent expansion made by Ezekiel himself, when his preaching had begun to take a decided turn towards future salvation and he had come to see even the threatening words he had been charged to utter in a new light. This makes all the more impressive the way in which he refrains from any exhaustive explanation of his pictorial language, and thus preserves the mystery of the future salvation. To the observant reader of the preceding parable or anyone acquainted with predictions of salvation by earlier prophets, his word was clear enough as it was. In any case, there is no 'Jewish particularism' to be found here (Bertholet). The subtle adjustment of the thought and expression to Ezekiel's whole message, the disciplined exclusion of hopes for political empire, is hardly something that one would want to attribute to one of the prophet's anonymous followers.

The prediction against Zedekiah shows us the prophet from a new aspect, by giving us an insight into his political thought. In strong contrast to the prophets of salvation he does not let himself be carried away by patriotic enthusiasm for the independence of Judah (cf.

Jer. 28), but sees in her attempt to play off Egypt against Babylon the very thing that will set the seal upon her ruin. Attempts have sometimes been made to account for this attitude by attributing it to considerable political insight into the relative strengths of the rival great powers, but they are refuted by the consistently religious judgment passed upon Zedekiah's attempt at rebellion. The determining factor for Ezekiel is not an assessment of the political and military strength of the rival empires, but the introduction of Jewish politics into Yahweh's government of the world, which results from reverent surrender to the holy will of the Lord of the universe. The severe blows Judah had undergone, first at the hands of Egypt in the overthrow of Josiah at Megiddo in the year 609, and then eleven years later at the hands of Babylon in the first captivity of her king and nobility, are not simply failures, which might have been avoided by a better policy and more effort, or which might be made good again, but judgments pronounced by God, as he replies to the religious alienation and moral degeneracy of his people by delivering them over to the world-powers. An unrepentant nation cannot obtain his help by persistence; rather, they must start to take seriously the divine will to govern their social and political life and reconstitute the state on the foundations laid down by God for the common life of mankind, and thus attain, as a by-product of that, to a respected position in international life. That amounts to what we may call a politics of faith, which allows even the decisions of its foreign policy to be determined by the knowledge of God's will to be king and by his quite real demands, a politics like that represented by Isaiah during his bitter struggle against the pro-Egyptianism of his day. The barefaced way in which Zedekiah broke his oath of fealty is a clear example of how men refuse to conform to God's decisions, and of how, while breaking laws sanctified by God himself, they strive by false and faithless methods of their own to pursue a policy of self-willed intrigue, which has no regard for God's world-aims.

It is this profoundly serious view of politics as a decision made possible only through knowledge and real respect for the moral principles and objectives established by God himself for human community life which Ezekiel, in general agreement with his predecessors, unflinchingly maintained during a period of moral dissolution and chaos. Precisely in this way, he also causes an ultimate disquiet to the political life of our time, so that we cannot be content with *sacro egoismo* or with calculations of what means are best adapted to reach material ends as if they were the obvious principles which should guide all political practice, to which all divine and human moral commands ought to yield. Here there is a demand for an absolutely binding obedience to the direction of the eternal will of the God who rules the world, which requires us to go by the standards he has set even if it involves the sacrifice of some momentary advantage, whatever great decisive objectives of peaceful national and personal life and respect for the rights of our breathren are at stake, since that is the only road for our politics to take if they are to prove promising in the long run.

Such a type of politics becomes possible only when men are aware of a God who brings men's destiny to fulfilment, though it is imperilled by his imperfection and his sin. The concluding section of this chapter points in this direction, by describing the way in which God intervenes. It is far from describing a dark destiny dressed up in mythological embellishments. It discloses the true and real background to all human endeavour, without which those human endeavours must flag in hopeless despair under the double burden of their own responsibilities and their own failure to meet them.

CHAPTER 18.1–32

Release from imprisonment in guilt

1 And the word of Yahweh came to me: ²['Son of man],ᵃ why do you repeat [. . .]ᵇ this proverb concerning the land of Israel, saying: "Fathers eat sour grapes and the children's teeth are set on edge"? ³As I live, says [. . .]ᶜ Yahweh, you shall henceforth no longer repeat this proverb in Israel. ⁴Surely, all persons are mine! The person of the father as well as the person of the son, both are mine! The person who sins, he alone shall die.

5 If a manᵈ does what is lawful and right, ⁶if he does not eat [flesh with the blood]ᵉ or lift up his eyes to the idols of the house of Israel, does not defile his neighbour's wife or approach a woman in her time of impurity, ⁷does not oppress anyone, gives back the pledge (which he has taken) [. . .],ᶠ commits no extortion, gives his bread to the hungry and covers the naked with a garment, ⁸does not lend at interest or collect additional payments, withholds his hand from iniquity and executes true justice between litigants, ⁹in short, if he walksᵍ in my statutes and observes my

ordinances so as to carry [them][h] out, he is righteous, he shall surely live,
says [. . .][i] Yahweh.

10 But if he begets a son who does violence [. . .][j] 11 and he does none
of these things, but[k] eats flesh with the blood,[l] defiles his neighbour's wife,
12 oppresses the needy and poor, commits extortion,[m] does not restore
pledges, lifts up his eyes to the idols [. . .][n] [of the house of Israel,][o] 13 lends
at interest and collects additional payments, he shall assuredly not live.[p]
He has committed all these abominations; he must die without mercy.[q]
His blood shall be upon himself.

14 Suppose, then, that he begets a son, who sees all the sins that his
father has committed, and fears,[r] and does not do likewise; 15 he does not
eat flesh with the blood[s] or lift up his eyes to the idols of the house of Israel,
does not defile his neighbour's wife 16 nor oppress anyone, exacts no pledge
and commits no extortion, gives his bread to the hungry and covers the
naked with a garment, 17 withholds his hand from iniquity[t] and takes no
interest or additional payment, in short keeps my ordinances and walks in
my statutes, he shall not die because of his father's guilt, he shall surely
live.

18 But[u] his father, because he committed violence and[v] practised extortion,[w] and did what is not good among his fellows, he had to die because
of his guilt. 19 And now you say: "Why does the son not also join in bearing
the guilt of his father?" But the son has done what is lawful and right, he
has observed all my statutes and done according to them; he shall surely
live. 20 The person who sins, he shall die. A son shall not join in bearing
the guilt of his father nor a father bear the guilt of his son. The righteousness
of the righteous shall rest (only) upon himself, and the wickedness of the
wicked[x] shall (likewise) rest (only) upon himself.

21 But if the wicked man turns away from all the sins which he has
committed, and observes all my statutes and does what is lawful and right,
he shall surely live. He shall not die. 22 All the sins of rebellion which he has
committed shall not be counted against him; for the sake of the righteousness which he has done, he shall live. 23 Have I any pleasure [in the][y] death
of the wicked, says [. . .][z] Yahweh, and not rather in his turning from his
way, that he may live? 24 But if the righteous turns away from his righteousness and commits iniquity according to all the abominations which the
wicked commits . . . shall he do so and yet live?[aa] None of the righteous
deeds which he has done shall be taken account of. Because of the treachery
which he has committed and the sin with which he has burdened himself,
because of them he shall die.

25 Yet you say: "[Yahweh's][bb] procedure (way) is not right." Hear now,
you of the house of Israel, is not my procedure (way) right? Is it not rather
your conduct (ways) that is not right?

26 *If the righteous turns away from his righteousness and commits iniquity and*

dies [. . .]ᶜᶜ then he dies for the iniquity which he has committed. ²⁷*And if the wicked turns from the wickedness he has committed and does what is lawful and right, then he preserves his own life.* ²⁸*Because he feared*ᵈᵈ *and turned away from all the transgressions which he had committed he shall surely live, he shall not die!* ²⁹*Yet the house of Israel says:* "[*Yahweh's*]ᵉᵉ *procedure is not right."* *Is not my* [*procedure*]ᶠᶠ *right, O house of Israel? Is it not rather your conduct that is not right?*

30 Therefore will I judge you, house of Israel, every one according to his conduct, says [. . .]ᵍᵍ Yahweh. Return and turn away from all your sins of rebellion, that they may not be a snare to bring you into guilt. ³¹Cast away from you all the sins of rebellion, by which you have deserted me,ʰʰ and get yourselves a new heart and a new spirit! Why will you die, you who are of the house of Israel? ³²For I take no pleasure in the death of him who is worthy of death, says [. . .]ⁱⁱ Yahweh; returnʲʲ that you may live!'

ᵃThus with LXX, whereas MT has no address.
ᵇMT: 'to yourselves'; an assimilation to the phraseology of 12.22.
ᶜSee BH.
ᵈMT adds 'is righteous and'; the characterization of the man who acts here as righteous clumsily anticipates v. 9, and should be deleted to bring it into conformity with vv. 10 and 17.
ᵉMT: 'upon the mountains'; such a denunciation of high-place worship would be out of place in speaking to the exiles. In view of 33.25 and Lev. 19.26, the old conjectural emendation of ʿal-haddām for ʾel-heḥārīm seems worth adopting. What is meant by 'eating with the blood' is clearly shown by I Sam. 14.32–34.
ᶠMT: 'guilt'; syntactically impermissible; may be due to dittography of the first two letters of the preceding word. To change it to ḥayyāb, 'debtor', which does not appear elsewhere, is not desirable.
ᵍ⁻ⁱSee BH.
ʲMT: 'who sheds blood and does [one of these]' (see BH). Here the most severe act of violence is named before all the rest, as something about which there could be no difference of opinion. But as a capital sin it cannot possibly be set in the same category with other lighter transgressions against society. Moreover, this crime is of no importance to both what precedes and what follows. We are therefore justified in taking this to be a gloss, originally perhaps appended to 'eating along with the blood' (Bertholet¹). The second part of the phrase is an inferior variant of v. 11a, which alone has been preserved in the LXX and Syriac version at the cost of the better one.
ᵏRead kī'im for MT kī gam.
¹See on v. 6.
ᵐSee BH.
ⁿMT: 'commits abomination'; this generalization sounds out of place among particular sins; and as it also anticipates v. 13b, it may be deleted as a marginal note mistakenly inserted in the text.
ᵒNeeds to be inserted in conformity with vv. 6 and 15.
ᵖ⁻ʳSee BH.
ˢSee on v. 6.

^{t–v}See BH.

^wMT: 'robbery against a brother' has an unusual abbreviation of the word (*gēsel* instead of *gᵉsēlāh*) not usual in Ezekiel, and conflicts with vv. 7, 12 and 16. It may perhaps result from a mistaken reading of the end of the preceding word.

^{x–z}See BH.

^{aa}This intermediate question corresponds so accurately to the way the first case is constructed, in v. 21, that, in spite of the pronounced way in which it interrupts the logical sequence, and in spite of its omission in the LXX, its originality is not to be doubted.

^{bb}See BH.

^{cc}MT: 'for their sake' has arisen from a misunderstanding of the preceding consecutive perfect as indicating the establishment of guilt, whereas actually it still belongs to the protasis of the conditional sentence.

^{dd}Cf. v. 14.

^{ee}See BH.

^{ff}Read singular instead of plural.

^{gg–ii}See BH.

^{jj}For *hiphil*: 'And turn away from' (which must have occurred through dittography of the two last syllables of the preceding word), read *qal*: 'Return'.

A blasphemous proverb: 18.1–4

[1–3] God calls the prophet's attention to a winged word, which is current among the exiles. Its content is such a defiant protest against the way God treats his people that Yahweh announces with a solemn oath that he will abolish this watchword of mutiny from among the community which still bears the honourable name of Israel.

True, this mocking proverb does not actually name Yahweh. But it upsets a fundamental conviction in regard to his providential government, a conviction which Israel had so far successfully preserved inviolate in the face of all her temptations to think otherwise: the conviction that his retribution was always just. The manner in which this comes to pass reveals such a loss of all awe or reverence and expresses such a bitterly hostile criticism of God's government as to make us aware of a very dangerous dissolution of the old relationship of faith and trust in the covenant God of Israel. This is flippant cynicism, trying by a brief, bitter mocking phrase to suggest the senselessness of believing in the righteousness of God. [2] When one eats grapes that are not as yet quite ripe, but whose slightly bitter taste is all the more refreshing, one as a rule experiences a slightly unpleasant sensation as if a thin coating had come upon one's teeth— as if they had been 'set on edge', as the Hebrew word expresses it. Anyone who eats such grapes must put up with the after-effects. But it would be absurd if this were to happen to someone who had eaten no grapes. And it is equally absurd, the cynic suggests, for sons to be burdened with the consequences of paternal guilt, as they are according to prevailing belief. In spite of having done nothing to contribute to it, they must, as the German proverb says, drink the broth their fathers seethed. Can such an absurdity still be called righteousness? Can the punishment of the innocent in place of the guilty be described as conduct worthy of the divine judge?

The opinion voiced here witnesses to a profound alteration in Israelite beliefs, which came to its full development towards the end of the period of the monarchy. It calls in question a conviction which had been taken for granted and never been questioned in early Israel, and had been already given clear expression in the explanations to the Decalogue (Ex. 20.5f.; Deut. 5.9f.), that is to say, the idea of inherited guilt. Because the members of the people do not exist as isolated individuals, but stand together, being indissolubly connected by a solidarity which makes them able to fit in with and act on behalf of each other and because this association also extends to successive generations involving them in an organism extending over successive periods of time, then it must necessarily be true that the guilt of the father is avenged upon the children, and that guilt piled up in earlier generations brings later generations to ruin.

Such a conception of collective retribution was widespread in ancient times. It was kept from endangering the strong assurance of the future of the Israelite people solely by their trust in Yahweh's gracious guidance of the destiny of the nation, by which even disciplinary chastisement always turned to good. Another element was the comparative unimportance of the individual and his fortunes as compared with the community. So misfortunes suffered by those who had not directly contracted guilt were easier to accept in view of the immediacy of the link between their life and that of the whole people, and the problem spelt no threat to their faith in God's righteousness.

Changes set in, when the links by which the nation was bound together broke down from within during the seventh century. The individual lost the securities and ties which had hitherto given meaning to his existence, and saw himself thrown back on his own resources more and more. At this point the effects of collective guilt transcending the individual in the form of great catastrophes, such as the prophets had foretold their contemporaries in such vivid and frightening terms, threatened to become a fate as meaningless and heartless as in the great Greek tragedians. But it was difficult for Israel to adopt such an impersonal conception of fate, because their living faith in the divine judge saw the validity of one of its most basic principles questioned here, and reacted with a strong counter-attack. The individual had now come of age and asked questions about his own destiny, a satisfactory answer to which could not be provided by going back to the common destiny of the whole people. On the other hand, it was realized that the determining factor was not a cast-iron world-law controlling every phenomenon but the direct operation of God himself. So the threat to the individual from the common destiny of all necessarily led to the passionate question to the divine judge, how it could be consonant with his righteousness to compel the devout man to endure sufferings he had not merited. It is no mere matter of chance that we see this problem emerge in all its intensity in Jeremiah, in whom the spiritual conditions of the age so often found their expression (Jer. 12.1ff.). No direct answer was given to his question; God's freedom, even in retribution, forbade him to ask any further questions. Supposing that the quotation in Jer. 31.29 of the same mocking proverb found in this chapter is to be attributed to the prophet himself (an assumption which in any case there are good reasons for treating as doubtful),[1] then he must have had to postpone the removal of that tormenting doubt to the future period of salvation. But while he was learning how to accept in trust God's refusal to answer his question there were others whose faith had been upset by syncretistic influences and by Judah's political helplessness; consequently they became totally estranged from the faith of their fathers through the impossibility of finding a solution to their questions. They gave themselves up more and more to a negative criticism, which gave notice to the national God in view of the hopeless state in which his worshippers found themselves. They replied to assertions that his punishments were just by pointing out obvious injustices in the apportionment of guilt and responsibility. To this section of the nation the great majority of the exiles will have belonged. They felt that they had been exposed to much severer punishment than their compatriots who still remained in Jerusalem, and they felt that the real guilty parties had escaped that punishment. The poisonous proverb would thus have expressed exactly what they thought, and would have been passed on with approval, giving rein

---

[1] Cf. W. Rudolph, *Jeremia*, 1947, *ad loc.*

to an acute resentment 'about the land of Israel', as v. 2 puts it, i.e. about the destiny of the state.

In interpreting the reply which the prophet was commissioned to make to this barefaced assault upon the righteousness of God, we must note that for Ezekiel, too, the connection between the destiny of the individual and the guilt of his ancestors was and remained an undeniable fact. We must not be so hasty as to accuse him of thoughtless inconsistency when in other passages he differs from his thought in ch. 18, and presupposes almost as a matter of course a common national destiny, within which good and evil are inextricably intertwined, and where the collective guilt meets with its punishment (thus already in ch. 16, then in ch. 20; 21.3, 9; 23). But in any case he is far from defending Yahweh's acts of judgment manifest here as the universally applicable answer to the question of God's righteousness. This is because God himself has disclosed to him a second form of divine retribution, which gives the total reckoning a different complexion. [4] So the stress at the beginning of the divine address on God's absolute right as creator to deal with all men as he wills is no mere formality. He can give a man over to death, just as he called him into life. He can also decide that the son shall take the place of the father without anyone calling him to account. Here, too, God's transcendent superiority to all human complaints and attempts at self-justification, so dominant later in the book of Job, is the presupposition from which all the consequences must be drawn. And this same God now proclaims that it is his righteous will to judge each individual in accordance with his particular responsibility, 'The person who sins, he alone shall die!'

The saying thus introduces no subtle theorizing spun out of Priestly theology, in order to clear away all grounds for complaining against God's righteousness by means of a theodicy. No new doctrine is proclaimed here to serve as a basis for explaining how God acts in every case. Ezekiel rather proclaims a decision made by God for the present situation, to help those whose faith is in difficulties, and give them strength to face life afresh. That is to say, he is not speaking as a theologian, but as a prophet, whose duty it is to proclaim what God has in actual fact willed and decided to do.

Inherited guilt or personal responsibility?: 18.5–20

It seems inconsistent with the prophetic character of the following passage that the language of the law of the sanctuary is again employed, as in ch. 15, in order to elaborate the central theme. Its definitions and casuistical distinctions seem to be out of place in a prophetic vision. But we must remember that this garb for the prophetic pronouncement proved in ch. 15 to be the best possible means of expressing the absolute validity of the divine decision. That shows one reason for adopting the language of the law of the sanctuary, and the present context enables us to give another. It is that the prophet is deliberately imitating the promise of life and threat of death declared by the priest when he proclaimed the temple torah, announcing the obligations imposed upon those who frequented the temple (Pss. 15; 24.3–6; Isa. 33.14–16), or promised the aid of God the life-giver to those who sought refuge (Ps. 91), or had to proclaim the decision of the divine judge for life or death when an appeal was made to God's judgment in some doubtful case of law (I Kings 8.31ff.; Num. 5.11ff.), or else, as was customary at the great feasts, especially that of tabernacles, in conjunction with the proclamation of the law, also confronted the congregation with the prospect of life or death, depending upon their decision (Deut. 30.15, 19; Lev. 18.5, and the exhaustive promises of blessings and curses in Deut. 28 and Lev. 26). In the first and last of the instances quoted above especially, an enumeration of Yahweh's legal demands was made. There seem to have been established formulas with brief enumerations of the most important commandments. So Ezekiel now imitates such formulas.[1] His first list of demands in vv. 5–9 concludes with the solemn statement 'he is a righteous man'. It is so reminiscent of similar declaratory formulas, used by the priest to affirm the result of the examination he had made (Lev. 13.3, 6, 22 and 13.11, 13, 15f.), that the agreement cannot be merely accidental.

The prophet formulates Yahweh's new decision which he has to announce in a way which approximates as closely as possible to the old traditional pronouncements of life and death in the cultus, which he as a priest must have come to know particularly closely. He thus brings it into conformity with previous proclamations of the will of God. **[6–8]** What is new here is the selection of the divine demands and the sphere within which the promise derived from them is valid. What is enumerated by Ezekiel here is independent of any tie with

---

[1] Cf. G. von Rad, ' "Righteousness" and "Life" in the Cultic Language of the Psalms', *The Problem of the Hexateuch and Other Essays*, 1965, pp. 243–66; W. Zimmerli, ' "Leben" und "Tod" im Buche des Propheten Ezechiel', *ThZ* 13 (1957), pp. 494ff.

the soil of Palestine or the temple of Jerusalem. Out of the old covenant law, following the Book of the Covenant (Ex. 20), Deuteronomy, and the Law of Holiness in Lev. 17ff., he sets up a norm for moral and social life, which can provide a firm basis for a man's relations with his neighbour in a foreign land. First come the commands for true worship of God, including not only a demand for strict rejection of all forms of idolatry (cf. 14.1ff.), but also a prohibition of the consumption of blood; introducing a ritualistic element from Leviticus, which is evidently regarded as a fundamentally important mark of distinction from the surrounding paganism, it played an important part as late as New Testament times (Acts 15.20, 29; 21.25), which seems intelligible in view of the practices in pagan mysteries (cf. Isa. 65.4). After the prohibition of adultery, which must have constituted a particularly dangerous temptation among a crowd of exiles cut off from all traditional ties, the social and moral commandments present the obligations demanded by brotherly solidarity in the distressed state in which they all found themselves: restraint from the exploitation or extortion of poorer fellow countrymen and from exacting pledges from debtors; no trying to profit from their distress by enforcing certain conditions in every loan (as opposed to *nešek* [interest], *tarbit* [increase] means an additional charge to the sum lent which was demanded at the repayment of the loan);[1] no attempt to warp justice when a dispute is being settled. As a positive counterpart, the voluntary support of the needy with food and drink is mentioned. The list is repeated in the following sections, but not with slavish exactitude. Pollution by a menstrous woman (v. 6) and the concern for justice (v. 8) are omitted, as a sign that these things are mentioned only as illustrations, and are not intended to furnish the righteous with a complete list of all the things that he must or must not do. What would be enumerated in a similar list for the inhabitants of Jerusalem is shown by 22.6–12, where deeds of violence and bloodshed, sacrificial meals on the hills, and offences against holy places and against foreigners are mentioned.

[9] A man may fulfil all the above-mentioned commands, and as a result be termed righteous. This, as elsewhere in the Old Testament, does not mean that he is sinless, or that he has shown his virtue by conforming perfectly to a comprehensive legal system, but that he is a

---

1 Cf. C. van Leeuwen, *Le développement du sens social en Israel*, 1955, pp. 53f.

willing member of the cultic community, who conforms with the
ordinances of the community life and thus shows a right attitude
towards the covenant relationship. **[13]** Similarly, the wicked man is
the egoist who disturbs this community life by an arbitrary insistence on living his life fully.

Now the cultless congregation of exiles find themselves confronted
with either life or death according to whether they obey or disobey
the ordinances of the community, in a statement backed by the
solemn phraseology of the temple torah: 'he shall surely live' applies
to the righteous man of vv. 9 and 17; 'he shall surely die' applies to
the evildoer of v. 13. What originally had a meaning only within the
temple community and among the people of God when still living in
the promised land is here boldly transferred to the remnants of that
people, languishing in the unclean land of Babylonia, a wretched set
of displaced persons who are suffering chastisement at the hands of a
wrathful God. There is a solemn public proclamation that now the old
cultic community has been dissolved a new community is in process
of being formed by God's grace, and that the same promises are
valid for it as for the old. Yahweh now opens to those who have
fallen victims to death the possibility of new life. The exiles feel that
they are under the wrath of God, and in helpless rage can only
slander his decision as unjust, or else, as we see from 33.10 and 37.11,
in complete despair accept as their inevitable lot death in a foreign
land. Now, however, they have displayed to them a significant possibility of life. It consists in the fact that the ancient destiny of guilt,
laid on them by their fathers and delivering them over to death, has
been annulled by Yahweh and replaced by a new offer of grace.
Here and now in this heathen land everyone who believes the word
of the prophet is given room and freedom to break out of the collective guilt of past generations to a new beginning which puts him into
a personal relationship of service and loyalty to the God of his fathers.
For the promise of life to the righteous man (v. 9), and of death to his
son who has become an evildoer (v. 13), and of life again to the
grandson on his return to obedience (v. 17), all agree in what they
signify. This is nothing less than the breaking of that iron ring of
collective guilt within which all hopes die, and the opening of the
road to freedom, along which the individual, stirred by God's word
with its summons to decision, may be brought into a new association
with God and with his fellow men. All the material guarantees, such
as the temple and the kingship, the absence of which from the life

of the people of God has hitherto been inconceivable, have now lapsed. It is the community-norm of the law which is capable of being translated into life in every situation and in every period, and guarantees life and future, because it is no mere set of outward statutes, but an expression of a moral will of God which shapes history.

This is not an expression of extreme individualism, as if the collectivism of former days were to be dissolved through the operations of pure individualists, without concern for the community and striving solely after complete self-expression. The community, formed by putting into practical effect the divine standard for life, bridges the opposition between individualism and collectivism. Each individual self has become a germinating cell for that purpose through his personal encounter with God, and that encounter also admits him to a new fellowship with his fellow man. Ezekiel addresses individuals for whom exile has severed all ties by the name of 'house of Israel' (vv. 25–31), a weighty title, full of meaning. This presents a strong contrast to the other name, 'house of rebellion', by which he had formerly called them and makes it clear that they are destined to reproduce in a new form the old covenant community, which had formerly imparted its characteristic stamp to Israel. We might name that form personalism, if we wanted to state the motive power which forms its central core.[1]

Change in the life of the individual: 18.21–25 (29)

Fresh light is now thrown upon this personalism from another perspective when vv. 21–25 bring out the turning-point at which the life and destiny of each individual is decided. In the preceding passage we saw the breaking of the bonds of collective guilt. Here we see the individual man's life freed from being fettered by the sum of all the deeds he has so far done, which keep him from turning round from the course he has once begun. We find a vigorous refusal that his behaviour should be influenced by legalism, which tends to count up successful endeavours and imagines that a man's moral condition can be accurately calculated from the sum of his deeds, good or evil. The central factor in the life of the individual is not the mechanical functioning of an impersonal moral order but openness to the personal divine Lord, which leads to a personal relationship of service

---

[1] Cf. in this connection W. Eichrodt, *Krisis der Gemeinschaft in Israel*, 1955.

and loyalty. **[21f.]** Thus even the man who has already gone a long way down the wrong road may be assured of divine favour, if he responds to the prophet's call and orders his life in accordance with the God-given order of the covenant; **[24]** whereas the man who has hitherto been endeavouring to observe the law strictly is not to put his trust in the series of good works pleasing to God which he can display, as if that absolved him from all anxiety about God's decision. He, too, must be watchful and ready to respond to God's call. Where a failure to show such readiness makes him succumb in the hour of temptation, and misleads him into actions contrary to God and serving only his own selfish ends, no former merits can avail to make up for his breach of faith.

Who can deny that this appeal shows a deepened ethical understanding of the inward connection between all ethical decisions, and of how progress in the moral life can be made a real growth? The answer is that only those who no longer understand it as a call to decision and a warning against sloth and complacency at a turning-point in Israelite history, and regard it instead as a timeless piece of abstract doctrine, in which the casuistry of a legalistic ethic dissolves moral action into a series of separate efforts and thus atomizes the individual moral element, to assert free decision at each moment regardless of all former associations and habits.[1] It is evident here that the really burning question which preoccupied Ezekiel, that of the new Israel, has been quite lost to view. The actual truth is that vv. 21–25 prove beyond refutation what is meant by the previous definition of the righteous and the wicked; it is not concerned with summing up single righteous actions, which go to make up the whole of the moral life (Bertholet, *op. cit.*), but with the total orientation of a man's life towards following God's order. This state of things may be initiated or overthrown by a personal decision on the part of man, but Ezekiel does not base the possibility of such a decision upon a moral freedom of decision present at any and every time, but upon the divine offer of salvation which he knows himself called to proclaim at this particular moment. Each man must decide rightly in face of this offer of salvation. That is what the prophet is trying to bring home to his audience. To this end he also points out how it is never too late, in the life of the individual, to follow the call of God.

[1] This is the view of the older critics on Ezekiel, cf. B. Duhm, *Israels Propheten*, 1916, p. 235, and A. Bertholet, *Hesekiel*, 1936, pp. 15 and 69.

We hardly do justice to Ezekiel's promise of life leading out of the present despair into future hope if we insist on regarding it as nothing more than a vindication of the first captivity as a just judgment in face of the complaints and reproaches of those carried into exile at that time (Fohrer). If the account of the individual retribution received by righteous or wicked individuals were meant to represent an actual theory of retribution, according to which those who were deported had to recognize that they were sinners, this conclusion from the fact of deportation to the sin of the exiles would have had to enumerate a set of misdoings entirely different from those mentioned in vv. 5–17; one need only recall the prophet's previous denunciations. Moreover, the treatment of individual decision in vv. 21–25 becomes, if it is simply intended to be retrospective, just an indirect demonstration of the guilt of the exiles as the result of an *a posteriori* conclusion drawn from their reaction to past preaching, a rigid and loveless piece of formalism, such as we might expect from Job's friends, but not from a prophet who looks to the future as clearly as Ezekiel does in v. 25 and vv. 30f. Furthermore, this demonstration would inevitably recoil on the prophet's own head, since he, too, stands under the same condemnation as those against whom he brings such severe charges. Fohrer's explanations at this point are obviously too one-sided, being based exclusively on the relationship (correct enough in itself) of the whole analysis to the captivity of 598, with the object of rendering impossible any transference of it to Jerusalem.

But these explanations display their own unsoundness because they are forced to advocate an interpretation of the prophet's promise of life which cannot possibly do justice to the affirmations of life found in Ezekiel or in his predecessors. The promise of life with which we meet in Amos is a clear antithesis to Priestly reassurances (Amos 5.4, 6, 14) and already transcends the guarantee of physical life in the sense of a long happy life, pointing to a new turning of Yahweh towards his people. Similarly, what is meant in Jer. 27.12, 17; 38.2, 17 is no bare preservation of life, but acceptance into the near presence of Yahweh with all the resultant blessings. The promise of life made by Ezekiel therefore includes much more than an assurance of material life; it also includes being forgiven and blessed by Yahweh, and thus being taken out of the state of condemnation, in which the exiles feel themselves to be like men sentenced to be executed. This represents not only a revaluation of life in exile, as if

even there one could lead 'a fully effective and wholly valid existence' (Fohrer), but also a share in the coming salvation of Israel in
the new life made possible by the forgiveness of sins. Ezekiel sees with
ever-increasing certainty that the judgment upon Jerusalem takes
effect not only in punishing Israel, but also in making it possible for
Yahweh to turn once more to his people. If the promise of life to the
obedient means their preservation in time of judgment, then it also
involves a share in the future salvation. Just as Jeremiah's assurance
of the thoughts of peace which Yahweh has towards all who willingly
subject themselves to his stern judgment is linked with the sure fulfilment of the hope for future salvation (Jer. 29.10f.), so also Ezekiel's
strong affirmation of life also refers to participation in the restoration
of Israel (as is admitted by Fohrer, p. 101). That, however, means
that the exiles are at once given a fresh start in life in the service of
Yahweh and his people in the present and a sure expectation of the
eschatological blessings. That means that in this respect, too, the
saving purpose of Yahweh's retribution, as the prophet sees it, is
assured for the future.

Only in this sense can we understand properly the way in which
Yahweh twice emphatically expresses (vv. 23 and 32) his intention of
coming to the rescue. He is indeed explicitly concerned with the conversion of the wicked man, so that he can find his way through to life.
Such a conversion would be impossible, unless a new offer of salvation from Yahweh came to meet it, to set him free from the prison of
past guilt and enable him to begin life afresh. Something more than
'an impulse towards a warmer and friendlier conception of God than
is usually to be found in Ezekiel' (Bertholet[2]) is thus expressed in
these words. It is the fulfilment of Yahweh's return to those he seems
to have rejected, first hinted at in ch. 12, and then emerging more and
more clearly. He startles us by first confirming and then surpassing
the old cultic promise of life, stating that it is the aim of his holy will
to call the wicked back to life. All the shattering strokes of judgment
which have hitherto formed the main substance of the prophet's
pronouncements now begin to seem God's action 'with his left hand',
whereas his real object was the creation of a new people of God.
Indeed, as God turns to his people to ask whether it could be judged
otherwise, he recalls his loving faithfulness displayed in the earlier
days of Israel's history, and how it should have led to their recognizing him as the Lord who preferred grace to judgment. It is this same
faithfulness which finds a way of reconciling the assertion of his

judicial righteousness which shows up the ugliness and culpability of all rebellion against his lordship with the creation of a new people of God, in whom his will to love may gain its end. The course across the deadly barrier of judgment was unavoidable, in order to display the full seriousness and the unbreakable validity of the moral ordering of life, which answers to the holiness of God's being. But now these men, overwhelmed by the weight of God's retribution, see themselves met by a new offer of life at the very point at which they found nothing in front of them but death and despair, and thus at long last learn to know their divine deliverer and all the greatness of his mercy.

Before this surprising development all claims to better knowledge, all pretensions at criticizing the divine retribution, are brought to silence. [25] Yet even among the exiles there are many who are not content with this divine promise of a new order. Instead of welcoming it with joy, men go on obstinately maintaining the son's inheritance of paternal guilt, whether out of unwillingness to surrender a weapon to use again the prophet's call for repentance, or whether again because they are champions of traditional orthodoxy and feel that to repudiate the old dogma of retribution in so revolutionary a fashion constitutes a dangerous assault upon foundations which ought to stand firm. In face of this, the prophet is content simply to appeal to the sense of justice which must recognize the principle of retribution 'the person who has sinned must die' as a liberation. In solemnly insisting upon the full personal responsibility of every individual, he blocks every attempt to hide behind another's guilt in order to evade the divine reckoning. In v. 25 he goes over to the offensive. All criticisms of God's ways of executing judgment come either from a general dissatisfaction with the ways in which he acts or else in particular from resistance against being made to change one's mind. He takes all these approaches and forces them to face the question whether their total attitude, their 'way' or conduct, can stand up to thorough testing, or whether something still lies hidden, born of human desire to be in the right before God and thus bearing from the start the mark of rebellion against the divine order.

Admonition to conversion: 18.30–32

It is necessary to cleanse oneself of such a sin of rebellion in order to be fit to stand judgment. [30] So the divine offer of salvation closes with an impressive warning, to set oneself free, while the possibility is still open, from the sins of the past, and not to cut oneself off from that course by any new inclination to resist. Jeremiah was tireless in proclaiming the call to conversion as Yahweh's most fundamental demand. It must sound out clearly now, especially where human perversity is only too capable of trying to turn God's gracious purposes into a snare by which to be entangled in fresh guilt. What is required now is no mere outward assent, but an inner reorientation, a revolution in one's whole intimate inward attitude towards God. [31] That is shown by what is said about the new heart and the new spirit, and the necessary struggle to possess them. These words are not to be taken merely as a contrast to the great promise of 36.26, as if that promise were in the end the product of a doubt whether the people could ever change for the better. The truth is rather that here, just as in the New Testament, the imperative of the exhortation is a response to the indicative of God's saving action; God's gift of salvation does not leave a man alone, but calls upon him for a response to God's offer, to enter upon the new potentiality of life that has been granted him. Paul requires of believers nothing less than transformation by the renewing of their mind (Rom. 12.2), precisely because he acknowledges the all-sufficiency of the grace of God. In the same way, God has opened before the exiles a new door, leading out of certain death and into a new life. All, therefore, who claim to be of the house of Israel are to tread that path, because they are taken out of their old being by love, which keeps open the possibility of repentance for the victims of death and sets them on the way towards a new goal. All the tension that enters into human life with God's recreating grace finds expression in this heart-stirring call for repentance and change of life. [32] So even the repetition in v. 32, which once more associates conversion and life with a reference to God's saving will, is seen to be fully justified, so that the formal objections against it[1] do not prevail.

No reader of this chapter can resist the impression that at this point we have reached the climax of Ezekiel's preaching of repentance, where it breaks through to the most concentrated summary of the divine will to judge and to save which is the decisive factor for the present. First comes a ruthless uncompromising severity in the detection of guilt. Then, from ch. 12 on, we see the God of the covenant turning once more to his people. Finally we come to see in judgment the means of a new creation. A new road into the future comes into

---

[1] Verse 32 is a repetition of v. 23, and recurs in 33.11. It is partially omitted in the transmission of the Greek text.

view, illuminated by the unchanging faithfulness of God as he makes his own the people whom he has chosen. We are still in the dark as to what shape the new life of the people is to take. Yet a spell of paralysis and stubbornness which seemed to have settled upon the exile community had been broken, and a first strong impulse to a new life of faith is making itself felt. One might well wonder whether such an immense step forward in the transformation of the people's relationship with God is conceivable before the second captivity or whether the captivity did not itself create the necessary conditions for it. There are certainly several reasons in favour of this possibility. There is the way in which the proclamation of judgment still continues without reference to the turning-point reached here, the change in the prophetic proclamation which is finally achieved in ch. 24 with the news of the fall of Jerusalem, the overcoming of the inner resistance of the exiles to Ezekiel's message only accomplished through the fulfilment of the prophetic threat in the catastrophe of 587, and the problem of righteous retribution, put then with new urgency. Have we therefore a premature anticipation of a later view of the prophet's, inserted at this point by the redactors, such as we have so often encountered before? Of course, this assumption can never be a complete certainty. A first bold attack upon the barrier surrounding the exiles, consisting partly in despairing resignation and partly in vigorous hostility, is by no means out of the question. Be this as it may, however, the divine action proclaimed here is directed at the community of exiles, and not the remnant of the nation still in Jerusalem, whose case, positively or negatively, would call for a totally different set of divine demands (cf., e.g., 22.6ff.). The theory that Ezekiel's activities were exercised in both of those spheres is out of place here, and can do nothing but obscure the actual issue.

Indeed, the divine will to deliver is confined to a portion of the people which is apparently abandoned to its doom. Here, too, we see the distinguishing mark between this offer of salvation and New Testament passages which seem to echo it so strongly, such as I Tim. 2.4 and II Peter 3.9. They are concerned with God's decision about mankind and thus have already reached the final objective at the end of the road. Ezekiel announces a new beginning after the first stage of the journey had broken off in the judgment of the exile. Nevertheless, those exegetes are right who insist that there is much more here than a terminological similarity. Each time, it is the same will of God which is concerned to deliver the man who has been

condemned to death. Moreover, in the departure for the objective of a
new people of God, which Ezekiel is allowed to signify, there is already
an indication of the road which must be travelled again and again. In
all the great crises of human society it has proved to be the sole means of
salvation which God has sustained with a promise of success. We are
face to face with the collapse of human society for which today, as at
other great breaking-points of human history, the natural binding
power of human associations has proved insufficient. But here we see
the possibility of rebuilding our common life on a fresh foundation
which, while capable of manifold variations of detail, in its basic structure remains the same as the model which appeared in Israel. It is the
confrontation of atomized human society with a divine governor, whose
will has power to shape history and is devoted to bringing men together
in brotherly solidarity. Its unshakable foundation has been revealed in
the norms of moral and social life, which, in contrast to the cultural and
economic conceptions of the ancient East, protect the divine value of
every human being, and, independently of the specific historical form
taken by each national life, demonstrate the right course of action in
any given situation. These norms present man with a task. It is not the
external compulsion of law, but a direct appeal for a free decision to
the conscience of the individual. He is asked to allow himself to be
taken into a personal relationship of service and loyalty to the God
who removes man from the chain of guilt down the generations, and
gives him a new start by forgiving him, and thus guaranteeing him a
life and a future. In this perspective there is a potentiality for vigorous
action in apparently hopeless situations, but it can only become
active power where the personal encounter with the living God has
become a reality; in other words, it presupposes a revelation which
reveals the other-worldly roots of all true human fellowship and thus
imparts to the labour of bringing it into effect all the calm and sure-
ness of a river of inexhaustible power. In Israel that revelation was
made through a series of ever new acts of God in history, and through
the interpretation of them by the mouth of the prophets. Their inner
connection was always clearly present to the national consciousness
and was an assurance of the abiding presence of God with his people
and of his immutable will to achieve his aim. In taking up, recapitulating and transcending that revelation, Jesus Christ was aware
of the task which he had to perform. In his person and work he had to
show for all ages how the Old Testament God of the covenant turns
to all mankind. Ezekiel found words to express the overcoming of the

social crisis in Israel. What he said is taken up and included in Jesus' redemptive work and transposed into God's offer of salvation to all mankind. The intimate connection it has with the salvation proclaimed by the Old Testament prophets helps to guard the New Testament message against a danger. It is prevented from confining the divine economy of salvation to narrow limits—God and the individual soul, or even God and the Church, as if it had only an indirect relevance to fellowship between all mankind. When we take Old Testament prophecy as our point of departure, we keep the door open for a people of God who recognize their solidarity with all mankind, who take the problems of human life seriously as questions to which they, too, must find an answer, and who co-operate in the common endeavour to solve those problems with all the additional power of the fellowship with God which they have been given. In so doing they cannot afford to admire themselves in the mirror of their own self-satisfied superiority as if they alone possessed all the right solutions. They are still under strong tension with a future which alone will bring about a real change in the situation, just as the community of Ezekiel's day knew it had not yet reached the goal, but knew itself to be on a journey from the present world into one to come. But the call of the divine commissioner, who sets that people upon its march, also guarantees that the new age will break through in full in the end, and that the new form of life, at present only beginning to be realized, will reach its fulfilment.

Chapter 19.1–14

Death lament for the kings of Judah

1 But you, take up a lamentation for the princes of Israel
2 and say: What a lioness was your mother among lions,
   she couched in the midst of young lions, rearing her whelps.
3 And she brought up one of her whelps, he became a young lion
   and he learned to catch prey, he devoured men.
4 The nations called up hunters against him,[a] he was taken in their pit,
   and they brought him by rings in his nose to the land of Egypt.
5 When she saw her hope proved folly[b] and wholly lost,
   she took another[c] of her whelps and made him a young lion.

6 He prowled among the lions, he became a young lion;
  he learned to catch prey, he devoured men.
7 He ravaged[d] their strongholds[e] and made their cities to tremble[f]
  and the land was appalled and all who were in it at the sound of his roaring.
8 Then the nations set against him snares[g] on every side;
  they spread their net over him, he was taken in their pit.
9 And they put a wooden collar[h] about his neck and brought him to the King of Babylon,[i]
  that his voice should no more be heard upon the mountains of Israel.

10 Your mother was like a vine [in a vineyard],[j] transplanted by the water;
  fruitful and full of branches by reason of abundant water.
11 And a strong stem of it grew into a ruler's sceptre,[k]
  it towered aloft among the boughs
  and was conspicuous for its height, for the mass of its branches.
12 But it (the vine) was plucked up,[l] cast on the ground
  [. . .][m] its branches[n] were stripped off
  and its strong stem withered,[o] fire consumed it.
13 [. . .][p]
14 [. . .][q]
  So there remained in it no strong stem, no sceptre for a ruler.
  This is a lamentation, and has become a lamentation.

a–cSee BH.
dRead *wayyāraʿ* for *wayyēdaʿ*.
e–gSee BH.
h*Sūgar*, an Accadian loan-word, usually rendered 'cage', better as above following E. Vogt, 'Joiakin Collari Ligneo Vinctus (Ez 19.9)' *Biblica* 37 (1956), pp. 388f.; the following phrase 'with hooks' (rings in the nose) is an explanatory gloss.
iThe further addition: 'and they brought him with hooks' was probably originally a marginal correction to v. 8a for the word there mistaken for 'provinces'.
jA completely uncertain emendation of the unintelligible 'in your blood', in the text.
kSee BH.
lMT: *beḥēmā*, 'in wrath' is inconsistent with the allegory.
mMT: 'the East wind dried it up'; a variant in the elaboration of the catastrophe, inserted as a typical and customary turn of phrase.
nFor 'its fruit', a word which does not match the plural verb, read *pōrōteyhā* with LXXcat.
oSee BH.
pVerse 13: 'And now it is transplanted in the wilderness, in a dry and thirsty land.'

ᵃVerse 14: 'And fire has gone out of its stem, and consumed its branches, its fruit.' An amplification, intended to complete the parable by the fate of the Queen-Mother, but which only succeeds in destroying it, since a plucked-up withered vine cannot be transplanted. The destroying fire issuing from the stem is also intended to bring the parable closer to the historical event, by emphasizing the destructive influences proceeding from the King.

The funeral lament

Chapter 19 is, like ch. 17, composed in what is clearly a metrical form. It is also explicitly described in v. 1 as a *qīnā*, or death lament. This fixed verse form, consisting of a five-stress line with a caesura after the third, is one of the most indubitable, and the earliest to be identified, of the metres in Hebrew poetry. This is explained by the rite in honour of the dead. It had its roots deep in antiquity, and was stubbornly maintained, like the other old customs, whose forms had to be observed with unfailing correctitude, in order to preserve the living from misfortune.

There is, of course, no connection with any such myths as existed outside Israel about the god who died and rose again, a notion rendered totally impossible by the faith of Yahweh. This particular type of lyric is adopted by the prophet, like other forms celebrating a triumph, victory, or marriage, in order to attract the attention of his public. As well as adopting the form, he changes the contents to suit the altered design. The lament for the dead was recited by the wailing women, its most celebrated exponents,[1] who sang of the virtues and good qualities of the departed, the grief felt for his loss, possibly also cursing his enemies (II Sam. 3.34) or the place of his death (II Sam. 1.21). But the prophet aimed at exhorting and giving warning through the judgment of death executed by God on the hopes and purposes of the living. So the lament could undoubtedly become an expression of triumph at God's overthrow of his enemies (cf. Isa. 14).

Ezekiel, too, transforms the lament for the princes of Israel into a proclamation of the judgment executed upon the Davidic dynasty, who have become the prey of the powers of death. As death is not only lamented when past but held out as a threat when still to come, so also the prophet's funeral lament can take on a predictive meaning, as in Amos (5.2). Here also we must ask whether Ezekiel is

[1] Cf. the representations of wailing women on the celebrated sarcophagus of King Aḥiram of Byblos, *Altorientalische Bilder zum Alten Testament*², plate CCIV. 665, and also for more modern times the impressive description of the lament for the dead in Corsica in the famous description by Prosper de Mérimée.

referring solely to past strokes of fate, or whether he has also in view things yet to come.

The opening words 'But you' draw a contrast between what the prophet is now doing and some other preceding event. That shows the impossibility of its being an explanation of ch. 18, with which there is no internal connection. On the other hand, there may well be a hint of the fate with which Zedekiah is threatened in ch. 17 which, according to God's will, is to be the occasion for the composition of a lament, to display the event now coming to pass in its proper light. In this case one might conjecture that the two chapters came closer to one another, and were separated only when ch. 18 was inserted (Zimmerli, p. 420).

The parable of the lions: 19.1–9

This chapter contains three clearly separated strophes. The first two, in vv. 1–9, are intended to complement one another; as is evident from the wording and from their use of the same metaphor. The third, containing as it does a fresh metaphor pointing in a different direction, stands by itself and must be dealt with separately. So the interpretation must not be prejudiced by any assumption about a series of three successive kings. Two royal personages are represented by young lions entrapped by hunters with nets and pitfalls in order to bring them into captivity. We see here all the technical tricks of the huntsman, some illustrated by Assyrian and Egyptian monuments, some attested by other Old Testament passages.[1]

Nevertheless, even apart from the title, it is clear that the young lions stand for princes of Judah; for there is no one else against whom the nations could be mobilized (vv. 4 and 8). The identification of the first named is unchallenged: Jehoahaz was the only king contemporary with Ezekiel to be led into captivity to Egypt. The populace raised him to the throne as the first to succeed Josiah, who had fallen at Megiddo in battle against Pharaoh Neco (II Kings 23.29–33). He was called to become king, and his elder brother Jehoiakim

---

[1] Cf. the hunting net in B. Meissner, *Babylonien und Assyrien*, I 1920, plate 49, the wooden cage mentioned in Erman-Ranke, *Ägypten und ägyptisches Leben*, 1923, p. 275, the nose-ring or spike for human captives in Esarhaddon's bas-relief (*c.* 670) in C. Bezold, *Ninive und Babylon*, 1909, plate 1, and in the prophetic description of the punishment of Sennacherib in Isa. 37.29; II Chron. 33.11; the wooden collar on an ancient Babylonian stele: *Sumer* 10, 1954, pp. 116ff.; cf. also Ezek. 29.4; 38.4; Assurnasirpal informs us of how wild beasts were kept alive in the royal park, cf. B. Meissner, *op. cit.*, p. 73.

passed over, evidently because supporters of Josiah's great religious reform expected him to carry on his father's policy of independence better than his very differently disposed brother.

If Ezekiel's metaphor of the wild beast dangerous alike to beasts and men is to be taken as applying to his exercise of the kingly office, then he must have entered energetically on his task during the three months of his reign. But the word for word repetition of the same metaphor in v. 6 suggests that the metaphor of the lion grown to maturity is an old well-worn one and not to be pressed. So it may indicate no more than that Jehoahaz at first proved a successful king. According to the greatly abbreviated account in II Kings, he seems soon to have presented himself at Pharaoh's camp at Riblah, in North Syria, in order to be confirmed as a vassal of Egypt in his royal authority. Neco, however, preferred to arrest one chosen by the independence party in his own country and send him off as a prisoner to Egypt, and to choose Jehoiakim, who had hitherto been passed over, as more likely to play the obedient puppet prince, to take his place (II Kings 23.33f.). So the Jewish prince received a rude awakening from his royal dream.

It is much more difficult to identify the prince who is the subject of the second lion prophecy in vv. 5–9. It is, of course, certain that he is a definite historical personage. But it is stated that Jehoiachin, the son of Jehoiakim (II Kings 24.15), as well as Zedekiah underwent a captivity to Babylon (II Kings 25.7). In choosing between these two, one must not, as has already been pointed out, allow oneself to be influenced either positively or negatively by the interpretation of the parable of the vine that follows in vv. 10–14. The decisive point against its being Jehoiachin is that we cannot imagine his being preferred to his infinitely more important father, well known for his deadly enmity against the prophets, as a typical example of a king displeasing to God. Were it to be supposed that vv. 6f., which go so far beyond v. 3, are intended to describe the short period of his reign (II Kings 24.8), then we would have an empty piece of exaggeration, unless one regards the verses as an irrelevant metaphor, a mere piece of the background of the picture of these kings? But the terseness of the rest of the description does not support such an assumption, and when one recalls the preference shown in ch. 17 for Jehoiachin as the legitimate representative of the Davidic dynasty (cf. above, p. 224), then the bitterness of the present denunciation becomes inexplicable.

So only Zedekiah is left to be the person referred to in the second lion picture in vv. 5–9. His eleven years' reign (II Kings 24.18) furnishes many further reasons for saying that his rule had disastrous results. Even though he showed neither personality nor leadership, and proved only too willing a tool in the hands of his ministers, against whom, judging by the statements in the book of Jeremiah, he only succeeded in having his way very rarely and then only by stealth, it still remains a fact that he was the man who inherited the great traditions of the Davidic dynasty and who was ultimately responsible for political decisions. One has only to think of the fickle and faithless policy by which during his reign Judah so frequently threatened to break the peace, or of the violence shown by the party in power alike towards the poverty-stricken populace or towards Jeremiah (Jer. 34 and 37f.), for the features in vv. 7–9, which go so far beyond those of the first lion picture, to become intelligible, and to see the improbability of their being due to subsequent elaborations.[1]

If the parable is wholly concerned with the brothers Jehoahaz and Zedekiah, then the mother who succeeds in raising them to the throne is not the state of Judah or the Davidic dynasty (Zimmerli, etc.). Such a personification is so far-fetched as to require clearer proof. It is much more likely that, as scholars since Krätzschmar have regularly asserted, the person referred to is Hamutal, the physical mother of the two brothers, and wife of Josiah. As the Queen Mother and former Queen of Judah she held an influential position. Under the title of *gebīrā*, Lady (I Kings 15.13; II Kings 10.13; Jer. 13.18; 29.2), she was the most influential person in the court after the King.[2] Her deportation is therefore explicitly mentioned along with his (II Kings 24.15; Jer. 29.2). Hamutal must have wielded all her influence to have her sons placed on the throne in the days of confusion after the death of Josiah. That is so obvious that it cannot be dismissed as an 'unprovable assumption' (Zimmerli). Rather, the mention of it in vv. 3 and 5 as one of the contributory causes in the choice of the king has to be calmly taken account of as a given fact under the conditions that prevailed.

It may further be said, that this interpretation brings out more clearly and effectively what Ezekiel aimed at in propounding his

[1] As held by M. Noth, *Revue d'histoire et de philosophie religieuses*, 33 (1953), pp. 81ff.

[2] Cf. S. Molin, 'Die Stellung der Gebira im Staate Judah', *ThZ* 10 (1954), pp. 161ff.

parable. It names two kings, who began and ended a series of kings of special importance in the final fate of Judah. They were both sons of the same mother. We may take it that the main motive of the influence she exercised on their behalf was not only ambition but a proper concern for securing the safety of the state. But this intensified the disappointment over their both being led into deportation, and makes the more shocking the judgment of Yahweh they revealed. This is brought out still more forcibly by the fact that Zedekiah's captivity is not treated here as a historical event in the past, but as one already anticipated in the prophetic lament, and now expected in the immediate future, when Judah is overtaken and destroyed by the fate which overshadows her (so most commentators). This use of a lament to convey a prophetic warning can be observed elsewhere. That it is likely here is suggested by the close connection with ch. 17 (see above, p. 251), and by the last section of the present chapter. This portrays under a different image the whole process of the execution of judgment, and states in the postscript in v. 14c that the lament, sung before the things stated in it came to pass, was transformed by their realization from a prediction into an actual lamentation for past disaster. Thus regarded, vv. 5-9 are at once a threat and a warning to Zedekiah and his immediate associates, such as Jeremiah so often delivered. The reference to the fate of the elder brother Jehoahaz was a proof of how the dynasty was threatened by Yahweh's will to bring upon it a judgment which the efforts of the Queen Mother were seeking vainly to avert.

The fate of the two kings is thus dealt with as a real execution of judgment. Historians may not perhaps describe them as actually guilty for the terrible climax of the history of Judah, but as men who became guilty through being carried away by a fate they could not avoid or control. The lion parable may not be intended to pass any moral judgments or suggest exceptional atrocities by the wild beast which preys on and slaughters human beings, but merely to depict the glories of kingship in the ancient East in the traditional terms. At the same time, there can be no doubt that a deliberate bias is shown in the way the king and his office are depicted, and, focused as it is on the development of arbitrary claims to obedience and power, the parable contains implicit within it a criticism of kingship. It would be possible to speak in very different terms of a king who was what Yahweh meant him to be, as we see expressed in Jeremiah (cf. Jer. 22.13-17). The basic assumption taken for granted without being stated is that Yahweh takes no pleasure in a kingship founded solely on power, or seeking to justify itself by the exercise of power. Such a heathenish type of kingship cannot avert but only accelerate God's judgment upon Judah. An Israelite king, by self-willed political action, may not forget his real duty to be an instrument of the divine will, and thus destroy 'the inward significance of political events' (Fohrer) as interpreted by the prophets. His first duty, the prophets all agree in saying, is to establish law and justice; that is his fundamental God-given obligation, to avoid or despise what brings him under judgment.

Zimmerli has rightly seen in the special emphasis on the silencing of the lion's voice on the mountains of Israel in v. 9 an indication of the place of the funeral lament in the wider context of Ezekiel's message. In ch. 6, not only the people of the capital but also the land with its holy places fall under judgment (cf. above, p. 93). In the same way here the living union between people and land, with the king as its constituted guardian, whose power is nourished by it, is now, when its princely representative is led into captivity, left defence-less and exposed to dissolution. God's rejection of the king destroys also the system upon which the life of the people is based. The pronouncement of this rejection in the form of the funeral lament takes it for granted as inevitable that the house of David has been over-whelmed by the powers of death, and cuts off all hopes of the promise given to David surviving the fall of Zedekiah (Jer. 28f.).

The parable of the vine: 19.10–14

This section is not directly enough connected with what precedes it for it to form the third paragraph of the lament and thus introduce a third prince. The reference to the mother of the person addressed is the sole sign of relationship with the past two parables. But the choice of the new image of a vine gives it the character of an independent composition. To say that the occurrence of the images of the lions and the vine in ch. 19 is occasioned by their juxtaposition in the words spoken of Judah in Gen. 49.9ff. (Fohrer) is to credit the prophet with a too systematic utilization of remote literary models. It is a much more probable assumption that the images and phrases point to ch. 17 and show a connection with it (Zimmerli and see above, p. 252). Unlike the lion parable, this concluding passage speaks of the complete annihilation of the royal house, evidently so as to enhance further the ruin previously predicted.

In the parable of the lions the main emphasis was laid on the fate of Zedekiah. Verses 10–14 take up again the fate of that king, expressing it under a new image and telling of further misfortunes. The mother therefore evidently means the physical mother of the king, Hamutal. She, like a vine in favourable soil growing rankly and vigorously and forming strong branches, stood occupying an influential position in the house of David as the mother of distinguished sons. Yet only one person is mentioned as being the stem fitted to be the sceptre of a ruler, pleasant in its greatness and glory, and he is described without any metaphor as the son in possession of the royal office, conceivably at a time just after the sudden failure of the hopes set upon Jehoahaz (see above, pp. 252f.). This is Zedekiah, in whom, after his accession to the throne and the initial success of his reign, all the hopes of his mother were concentrated. But these hopes are vain: destruction attacks not only the one royal stem but the whole vine. It is torn up by the roots, its branches hewn off and the dried-up ones thrown into the fire, a fate from which its strongest and handsomest stem, the king himself, cannot escape. It is evident that, when it is torn up and thrown on the ground, the fate of the vine is finally sealed. Replanting is quite out of the question, since no one can expect a vine that has been so brutally treated to grow again after being replanted. What is intended is rather complete annihilation: the judgment stated in vv. 9–14 takes on still larger dimensions, the dynasty at Jerusalem dies out with the death of the king. Verses 13 and 14a must therefore be regarded as additions. The first agrees with 17.4 and has in view Jer. 38.22f.; it refers in metaphorical terms to the exile of the royal family. The second, under the influence of Jer. 38.14ff., asserts that Zedekiah's guilt has brought disaster on himself and also on those around him. Both of these points have no connection with the original objective of the parable.

If one asks for the reason which made Ezekiel append this second lament over Zedekiah, it is most probably to be found in the shattering events of 587, which went far beyond what is suggested in vv. 4–9 and wiped out the king and his whole family. The branches torn off the uprooted vine (v. 12a), none of which can ever again grow into a sceptre (v. 14b), make one think especially of the execution of Zedekiah's sons, carried out by Nebuchadrezzar when he punished the rebel at Riblah (II Kings 25.7).

So this parable must be regarded not as a prediction like the one preceding it, but as a subsequent record of how God carried out what he had threatened. We see a testimony to this in the way v. 12 refrains from mentioning any human agency in the carrying out of the punishment, and also in the postscript in v. 14, which states in a profoundly impressive way that the funeral lament used by the prophet to announce a coming judgment has been transformed by the course of events into a lamentation for death and ruin after they have actually taken place: 'This is a lamentation and has become a lamentation.'

One may well assume that ch. 20, which immediately follows and accuses Israel as a whole of being unfaithful to God's commission, has been inserted at this point with the deliberate object of preventing any attempt to misapply the settlement of accounts with the last representative of the monarchy in ch. 17 and 19, by claiming that they and not the people bore the whole responsibility for the disaster. The picture of the nation's history, drawn by Ezekiel, must silence self-righteousness and lead all to admit their responsibility.

CHAPTER 20.1–44

Israel's history a history of sin

1 In the seventh year, in the fifth month, on the tenth day of the month, certain of the elders of Israel came to inquire of Yahweh, and sat before me. ²And the word of Yahweh came to me: ³'Son of man, speak to the elders of Israel and say to them: Thus says [. . .]ᵃ Yahweh: Is it to inquire of me that you come? As I live, I will not be inquired of by you, says [. . .]ᵇ Yahweh. ⁴Will you tell them the judgment, son of man, tell them the judgment? Then let them know the abominations of their fathers! ⁵And you will say to them: Thus says [. . .]ᶜ Yahweh: At the time when I chose Israel [. . .]ᵈ and made myself known to the seed of the house of Jacob [. . .]ᵉ in the land of Egypt, then I lifted my hand in an oath, saying, I am Yahweh your God. ⁶On that day I lifted my hand to them in an oath, that I would bring them out of the land of Egypt into a land that I had searched out for them, flowing with milk and honey; it is a jewel among all lands. ⁷And I said to them, cast away the detestable things your eyes feast on, every one of you, and do not defile yourselves with the idols of Egypt! I am Yahweh your God. ⁸But they rebelled against me and would not listen to me [. . .];ᶠ they did not cast away the detestable things their eyes feasted on, nor did they forsake the idols of Egypt. Then I

thought I would pour out my wrath upon them, to destroy them[g] in the midst of the land of Egypt. [9]But I acted for the sake of my name, that it should not be profaned in the sight of the nations, among whom they dwelt, in whose sight I made myself known to them (by the promise)[h] to bring them out of the land of Egypt.

10 So I led them out of the land of Egypt and brought them into the wilderness. [11]And I gave them my statutes and showed them my ordinances, by whose observance man shall live. [12][. . .][i] [13]But the house of Israel rebelled against me in the wilderness: they did not walk in my statutes but rejected my ordinances, by whose observance man shall live [. . .].[j] Then I thought I would pour out my wrath upon them in the wilderness, to make a full end of them. [14]But I acted for the sake of my name, that it should not be profaned in the sight of the nations, in whose sight I had brought them out. [17]And my eye spared them, so that I did not destroy them or make a full end of them in the wilderness.[k] [15]Moreover, I lifted my hand to them in the wilderness in an oath, that I would not bring them into the land that I had destined [for them],[l] flowing with milk and honey, it is a jewel among all lands, [16]because they rejected my ordinances and did not walk· in my statutes [. . .][m] for their heart clave to their idols.[n]

18 And I said to their sons in the wilderness, do not walk in the statutes of your fathers, nor observe their ordinances nor defile yourselves with their idols. [19]I, Yahweh, am your God. Walk in my statutes and hold and observe my ordinances. [20][. . .][o] [21]But the sons rebelled against me, they did not walk in my statutes, and did not hold and observe my ordinances faithfully, by whose observance man shall live [. . .].[p] Then I thought I would pour out my wrath upon them, and spend my anger against them in the wilderness. [22]But I [. . .][q] acted for the sake of my name, that it should not be profaned in the sight of the nations, in whose sight I had brought them out.

28 And I brought them into the land, which I had sworn with uplifted hand to give them. But wherever they saw any high hill or any leafy tree, there they offered their sacrifices and there [. . .][r] they sent up their soothing odours and there they poured out their drink offerings.

29 [. . .][s] [23]So I lifted up my hand to them in an oath [. . .][t] that I would scatter them among the nations and disperse them in the countries. [24][. . .][u] [25]Moreover I gave them statutes that were not good and ordinances by which they could not have life,[26] and I defiled them through their sacrificial gifts, in which they made all their first-born pass through the fire, that I might horrify them, that they might know that I am Yahweh.

27 Therefore speak to them of the house of Israel and, say to them, thus says [. . .][v] Yahweh: In this again your fathers mocked me, by dealing

treacherously with me. [30][. . .]ʷ Will you defile yourselves after the manner of your fathers and play harlot after their detestable things? [31]When you offer your sacrificial gifts [. . .]ˣ and defile yourselves with all your idols to this day, shall I let myself be inquired of by you, house of Israel? As I live, says [. . .]ʸ Yahweh, I will not be inquired of by you.

[32] But what is in your mind, shall never happen—the thought, "We will be like the nations, the tribes of the (other) countries [. . .]"ᶻ [33]As I live, says [. . .]ᵃᵃ Yahweh, with a strong hand and an outstretched arm and with wrath poured out will I be king over you.[34]And I will bring you out of the peoples and gather you out of the countries where you are scattered [. . .]ᵇᵇ [35]and will bring you into the wilderness of the peoples and there I will enter into judgment with you face to face. [36]As I entered into judgment with your fathers in the wilderness of the land of Egypt, so I will enter into judgment with you, says [. . .]ᶜᶜ Yahweh.

[37] And I will make you pass under the rod and I will let you go in by number [. . .]ᵈᵈ [38]And I will purge out the rebels from among you and those who transgress against me; I will bring them out of the land where they sojourn as strangers, but theyᵉᵉ shall not enter the land of Israel, that you may know that I am Yahweh. [39]As for you of the house of Israel, thus says [. . .]ᶠᶠ Yahweh, go serve everyone of you his idols [. . .]ᵍᵍ if you will not listen to me, but profane no more my holy name with your gifts [. . .].ʰʰ [40]Truly on my holy mountain, the mountain height of Israel, says [. . .]ⁱⁱ Yahweh, there all the house of Israel, all of them, shall serve me [. . .];ʲʲ there will I graciously accept them and there will I require your heave-offerings and offerings of firstlings, with all your sacred offerings. [41]As a pleasing odour will I graciously accept you, when I bring you out from the peoples, and gather you from the countries where you have been scattered, and I will manifest myself as the holy one among you in the eyes of the nations. [42]Then you will know that I am Yahweh, when I bring you into the land of Israel, the country which I swore with uplifted hands to give to your fathers. [43]There shall you remember your ways and your doings [. . .]ᵏᵏ with which you have polluted yourselves, and you shall loathe yourselves for all your wicked deeds [. . .]ˡˡ [44]Yes, you shall know that I am Yahweh, when I deal with you for my name's sake and not according to your evil ways or your corrupt doings, house of Israel, says [. . .]ᵐᵐ Yahweh.'

ᵃ⁻ᶜSee BH.

ᵈ⁻ᵉMT: 'There I lifted my hand to the seed of the house of Israel and made myself known to them'; by an awkward insertion, caused by dittography, God's oath is made to precede his revelation to Israel and therefore has to be repeated a second time.

ᶠMT: 'every man', as in v. 7 is supported neither by the versions nor by the following suffixes.

gMT: 'While I spent my anger upon them'; an awkward anticipation of the intensification of the wrath of God in v. 21; it is better to make the text follow the analogy of v. 13.

hSo rightly Zimmerli, unless one prefers to delete the last clause altogether.

iVerse 12: 'Moreover, I gave them my Sabbaths, as a sign between me and them, that they might know that I, Yahweh, sanctify them' (cf. Commentary).

jMT:, v. 13b: 'and my Sabbaths they greatly profaned' (cf. Commentary).

kThe order of the verses seems to have been interfered with. Verse 17 still comes too late, which apparently has some connection with the extension of v. 16.

lSee BH.

mMT: 'and profaned my Sabbaths'.

nLiterally: 'ran after your gods'. Verse 16 as a whole, with its dragging repetitions from v. 13, among which the reference to idolatry is the only enrichment, impresses one more as being a subsequent intensification of the indictment than a portion of the original text.

oMT, v. 20: 'and hallow my Sabbaths, that they may be a sign between me and you, that men may know that I, Yahweh, am your God'. See Commentary.

pMT: 'and they profaned my Sabbaths'.

qMT: 'I withheld my hand' is lacking in the LXX. The phrase is not used elsewhere in Ezekiel, and the perf. consec. is not in keeping with the syntax.

rMT: 'presented their provoking offerings'; lacking in the LXX and suspicious as an expression not found elsewhere in Ezekiel.

sVerse 29: 'And I said to them: Why is it that you go there (read with Rothstein *bammā* instead of *mā habbāmā*)? And so its name is called Bamah to this day.' An etymological joke is made about the etymology of the word 'high place', sounding like the word 'Why?' to suggest the uselessness of such a holy place. The attempt at the play on words has been spoilt by the mistaken addition of three consonants, which also occur in the preceding and following words. One need not expect any exceptional profundity of thought in such glossatorial puns. But this gloss does avail to show that the person who made it did not have before him in v. 28 any reference to idolatry, but saw in it merely an attack against worship in high places.

tMT: 'in the wilderness'; this statement cannot have been inserted until after the removal of v. 28 to its present position.

uVerse 24: 'Because they had not executed my ordinances but had rejected my statutes and profaned my Sabbaths, and their eyes were set on their fathers' idols.' This sentence has the same dragging summary of all the charges as v. 16 and must be regarded as an elaboration.

vSee BH.

wMT, v. 30a: 'Wherefore say to the house of Israel: Thus says [. . .] Yahweh.' This is a repetition of v. 27 made necessary by the transposition of the previous verses.

xMT: 'when you make your sons pass through the fire' assumes something impossible during the exile and thus shows itself to be a later elaboration of the idolatry, which is probably a subsequent insertion.

ySee BH.

zMT: 'and worship wood and stone'; inserted by the Deuteronomic redaction.

aaSee BH.

bbMT: 'with a mighty hand and with outstretched arm and with wrath poured out'; dittography from the previous line.

ccSee BH.

ddThe phraseology of the MT has been interfered with by a dittography, 'of the covenant' having slipped in from the first word of v. 38, written with the same consonants. This first word, *bᵉmispār*, by number, has been misread as *bᵉmasoret*, often rendered by translators as 'the bond' or 'the chastisement of the covenant'. Some read for *bᵉrīt*, covenant, with different pointing, *borit*, 'lye', and think the melting pot (read *miśrat*) is named here. But this is inconsistent with the metaphor of the shepherd which dominates this and the following verse.

ee–ffSee BH.

ggMT: 'and after' or 'behind' is to be regarded as a relic of an alternative reading, which spoke of 'going after idols' and must have found its way out of the margin into the text.

hhMT: 'and with your idols' again associates the offerings with idols in contradiction to v. 28.

iiSee BH.

jjMT: 'in the land', perhaps meaning 'as far as they reached the land', is lacking in the LXX and other versions.

kkMT: 'all', see BH.

llMT: 'which you have done', not found in LXX.

mmSee BH.

An inquiry by the elders of Israel and the refusal of an answer: 20.1–4

As in 8.1 and 14.1, some of the elders of Israel (for this term, see above, pp. 121 and 179) have arrived at Ezekiel's house, in order to address an inquiry to Yahweh through him. An exact date is given for this event, showing that more than a year has passed since the great temple vision. So we find ourselves in August 591. This is the first date to be given after a long series of chapters. This plainly indicates the special importance of the inquiry addressed to the prophet and of the answer made to it, and this again is confirmed by all that follows. The reason which the prophet gives for God's refusal of an answer consists in a powerful proclamation of judgment which throws an unexpected light on the history of the chosen people. Israel was accustomed to look back proudly over the past, and point out the glory of the old heroic days, and the doings of her great leaders, which were told of by her historians and the praises of which were celebrated in her Psalms (Pss. 80.8ff.; 105.8ff.; 132; 136.10ff.). Ezekiel's forerunners, too, had felt they had a right to regard it as an ideal period, whose bright light, however, fell in judgment upon the present and brought out the full darkness of its shadows (Amos 2.9–11; Isa. 1.21; 29.1; Jer. 2.2f., 6f.). But now all this disappears, and Israel's history from its first beginnings down to the present day shows itself defiled and deformed by the abominations of unfaithfulness and rebelliousness against God's gracious will. There is nothing here of which the chosen people can boast, but all is dominated by the divine patience and faithfulness which looks down upon this history of sin.

Upon that divine patience and faithfulness the existence of Israel depends, in so far as it has any hope whatsoever of continuance. So this address goes very deep in its analysis of Israelite self-appraisement. It shows how the present generation not only passively inherits, but also actively carries on, the process of transforming God's history of salvation into a history of sin because they pollute themselves over again with the same sins as their fathers. There is only one parallel in the Bible to this declaration of judgment, Stephen's speech in Acts 7.

THE UNCOVERING OF ISRAEL'S SIN: 20.5–31

At what point is this solidarity between the men of today and earlier generations brought to light? Is it in their general rebellious attitude, which expresses itself in ever new concrete forms? One might come to such a conclusion in view of the way 'and they rebelled against me' is repeated like a refrain at the end of vv. 8, 13 and 21. But the concluding indictment in vv. 30b, 31a seems to point to a quite concrete sin, by which man shows today the same sort of will and nature as his fathers, the sin of idolatry.

The profanation of the sabbath, however, seems to have a competing claim. It is used in a stereotyped formula in vv. 12f., 16, 20f. and 24 to indict the nation during the desert wandering, and seems to imperil the whole covenant relationship at an important central point. But such a valuation of the sabbath is quite unique and occurs here only in this prophetic book. In 22.8, 26 the desecration of the sabbath is indeed referred to as an example of how holy things have been despised and profaned and associated with the disregard shown for the commands for cultic purity. The same applies to 23.37–39. On the other hand, when he names the commandments by observing which one can confess one's adherence to Yahweh even in an unclean land (18.6ff.), Ezekiel passes over that same sabbath commandment, nor does he mention it in his enumeration of the sins of Jerusalem (24.6ff.) and of the sins of those who remained in the land after the deportation (33.25 and also cf. 5.11; 7.23; 9.9; 11.6). More remarkable still, if possible, is the silence as to the sabbath in that passage where Ezekiel sees a new Israel offering her divine Lord a worship that is well pleasing to him (20.32ff.). If the prophet had really regarded the sabbath as the sacramental sign and warrant of the election of Israel to be God's own people, then that sign could not have been absent from the reconstitution of the people of God. The same holds true of the other descriptions in ch. 36f. of the new fellowship established by God with his people, where there is either a reference in very general terms either to walking in God's commandments or else to the newly constituted sanctuary as the visible incorporation of the holy presence of God. Even in the late additions like ch. 44 and 46, the references to the sabbath do not display any consciousness of the high function of that feast so emphatically stated in Ezek. 20.

This view, which cannot be proved to have been held elsewhere by the prophet himself, is stated almost in identical words in the priestly tradition of the Hexateuchal narrative in Ex. 31.13 and 17. That stratum of tradition throws a bright light on how much is meant by the brief formulas in Ezek. 20.12 and 20. For it is the priestly narrator who associates the sabbath with God's work of creation. He thus not only gives an anticipatory view of the salvation to be brought into effect by God's election of Israel, but marks that salvation as the divine gift which has basic importance for the whole created world. The sabbath is its special guarantee, the sign of grace divinely established and impressed upon it at creation, and thus included among the fundamental ordinances of the world. This gives the clue to an understanding of the whole process by which, to the priestly narrator, the sabbath was an eternally valid obligation and a sign of the subsistence of the divine covenant of grace, and explains how contempt for it came to be regarded as a symptom of the complete alienation of Israel from its sacred destiny.

A thought so alien to Ezekiel does not therefore form an original element in the denunciation in this chapter. In order to strengthen the prophetic rebuke, it has been introduced by a priestly redactor of the prophetic text who slavishly copied the phraseology of Ex. 31. Here we see a process which we have already demonstrated, when we showed how ch. 1 was filled out in conformity with priestly speculations about the cherubic throne in ch. 10 (see above, pp. 112ff.). This process can also be registered in other passages in this prophetic book. This priestly reinterpretation of the prophet's message testifies in its own fashion to strong influence exercised by Ezekiel's preaching on the life of the post-exilic community. The priestly educators could not do their work without making use of that message, while endeavouring to accommodate it to the main lines of their conception of the nature of the covenant.[1]

It seems therefore that the concrete sin of idolatry is the only one left to serve as evidence for the rebelliousness of the fathers.

The rebelliousness of Israel in Egypt: 20.5–9

In ch. 16 Ezekiel began with the history of Jerusalem, the city of God, in branding Israel as faithless; now he goes back to the deliverance from Egypt and the time when it began to be a nation. Here he uses a term never employed by him elsewhere, that of 'house of Jacob', so as to describe the people in the fullest sense of the word, as not confined to Judah as in ch. 16, but including Northern Israel. He does not therefore yield to Judah's favourite habit of ignoring the ten tribes, but insists on their claim to be an indissoluble part of all Israel, as in 37.25, to share both in being preferred above other nations and in having incurred exceptional guilt. The first status is defined by an expression common in Deuteronomy, as being 'chosen'; the word always carries with it the suggestion of being called to perform a task, so it is always closely associated with the thought of the obligations imposed on the elect. Israel is thus separated from all nations and put side by side with God as the people sanctified by him, who are specially called to be at his service and to glorify his name.[2] Ezekiel, in this one place where he uses this word, consciously takes over these connotations and puts them into effect. He does not do this with the Deuteronomic expressions 'holy people', 'people of (God's own) possession', which express God's absolute majesty and Israel's complete dependence on and close association with God. He does it using specifically priestly terminology, such as occurs in Ex. 6, according to which Yahweh makes himself known, lifts his hand in an oath, and gives himself to Israel by imparting his name in an act of theophanic self-manifestation. Israel's new destiny is therefore something derived from God alone. He has emerged from his hiddenness to make himself by an oath the Lord, the only Lord Israel can have, who is bound to him by an indissoluble oath and has given him freedom from Egyptian

---

[1] Cf., in regard to the whole problem, my article, 'Der Sabbat bei Hesekiel', *Lex Tua Veritas, Festschrift für Hubert Junker*, 1961, pp. 65ff.

[2] Cf. Th. C. Vriezen, *Die Erwählung Israels nach dem Alten Testament*, AThANT 24, 1953, pp. 51ff.

slavery and the basis of a new life in a delightful land selected from all other lands as a gift of special favour. There is thoughtfulness and concentration on the essentials in this statement, which sums up the beginning of sacred history in the words of God himself. What the prophet chiefly envisages is the mission of Moses to the enslaved people with his message of liberation, as described in Ex. 4.29ff. One cannot miss the note of love, sounded in the description of the careful choice of Israel's new home which has a parallel in 16.9–12 (cf. above, p. 206). Nor can one fail to perceive the profound earnestness of God's wish for fellowship, expressed in the double oath and in the covenant formula 'I am Yahweh, your God' (Ex. 20.2) by which Israel is called to be utterly loyal to him. This claim, already implied in the offer of salvation, to possess the chosen people is now worked out further in v. 7 in a somewhat laborious fashion in a second address by God, in order to rule out all forms, especially the Egyptian form, of idolatry. It is remarkable what few grounds for such a charge are provided by historical records. There is only Josh. 24.14 which gives a glimpse of the other gods the fathers served 'beyond the river', and then adds the laconic remark 'and in Egypt'. This remark is apparently unknown to the whole Exodus tradition, yet Ezekiel lays remarkable, if not excessive, stress upon it. Some exegetes attribute it to an impression derived by Ezekiel from the Egyptian oppression, which, by a strongly Deuteronomic process of thought, he could only account for as being a punishment for idolatry (cf. the schema developed in Judg. 2). Other exegetes deny any influence from historical tradition, and ascribe these developments to the necessity not to leave any gap as he stated a radical and systematic indictment against Israel which had to cover every period of her history.

The reaction of the people thus favoured is all the more shocking from its contrast to the rich generosity of the divine love. The description follows those in Ex. 5.19ff.; 6.9; 14.11f. To sum it up, it uses the same word-root as that used in 2.5 to make a term of reproach for Israel, 'House of rebelliousness'. So v. 8 says: 'But they rebelled against me and would not listen to me.' The unbelieving perversity in v. 8, which ignores Yahweh's word, sums up their whole inward attitude towards God. It is related to the stories that keep recurring in Exodus of the people's unbelief and their resistance towards Moses. Verse 8b gives this resistance concrete shape, by connecting it with disregard for the prohibition against idolatry. Nevertheless the love revealed in election, and thus distinguished from any

capricious momentary outburst of emotion, now shows itself as
fidelity in continuing the course once it has begun. God acts for the
sake of his name, that is, in accordance with his own divine nature as
revealed in his name. Having given himself to be Israel's own as
'Yahweh thy God', he never ceases from endeavours to arouse a
response of love and trust. But by his revelation in Egypt he has
bound himself not only before Israel but before the world. Israel's
calling took place before the nations, it must therefore be made clear
that God's will to be Lord cannot be questioned, that it is not going
to be crossed or deprived of effectiveness, but is asserting itself in the
world. Here, then, the wonder of his sparing a sinful people is brought
into the context of his revelation to the whole world, which aims at
becoming known not only to Israel but also to the nations.

Thus even the beginnings of the national history of Israel are
emptied of all ideas of merit, and based entirely on God's determination to be true to himself. Thanks to that, the first meeting between
Israel and her God did not end in rejection but led on to a new divine
act of revelation.

The first generation in the wilderness: 20.10-17

This new saving act by God consists in his giving of the law. In it the
Exodus from Egypt reaches its objective, and the wonders of the
Exodus and of the journey through the wilderness become subordinate, so as not to need any special mention. The law is divided into
statutes and judgments, in accordance with its two main aspects of
laws relating to worship and laws relating to citizenship. The value
set on the law makes it clear that it constitutes the actual divine gift of
life. The categorical statement that man finds life in these commandments goes much further than the Deuteronomic formula 'that you
may live long' which is used to intensify some of the provisions (Deut.
5.16; Ex. 20.12) or the law as a whole (Deut. 4.40). God's law as a new
order of society takes man out of the cursed sphere of sin and remoteness from God, and gives him his place in the living God's sphere of
blessing, where the powers of death cannot lay hold on him. This
seems to characterize the law of the covenant as the great gift of life
and deliverance which sets Israel's life on a new foundation. Here is
not a set of severe demands made by an arbitrary and alien will,
narrowing down life, and subjecting it to a rigid regime of reward and
punishment. It is the will of a God who is keenly interested in the life
of his people, and who takes them into fellowship so as to open the

door to life and place them under his protection. So here following the law means reaching out spontaneously and taking an inestimable gift which makes possible a life full of strength and joy. Undoubtedly this high estimation of the law, found also in the Priestly Code (Lev. 18.5), results from seeing Israel's history as a whole, so as to regard the shaping of life by law not as heteronomy, but as a primary factor in life. It is a point of view which cannot be made a target for any of the customary rebukes against nomism or legalism. [12] Verse 12, which takes the sabbath commandment, clothing it in the words of Ex. 31.13, as if it were the core and essence of the whole law, has to be excluded as a priestly elaboration.

[13] For these reasons Israel's opposition to the will of God revealed to him is in itself a rejection of life, the natural result of which should be to be annihilated by the wrath of God. [14, 17] But God's faithfulness shows itself once more towards his plan of love and salvation, in accordance with his act of election. He restrains his wrath and lets the disobedient live. [15] But now that Israel has rejected the gifts of God there is a mysterious way that must be trodden, as is impressed on Israel by the punishment of being shut out of the promised land. It is not the disobedient generation but their children who shall first enjoy the fulfilment of the promise. [16b] Here once more the reference in v. 16b to the profanation of the sabbath has to be deleted. The reference to idolatry later on in the verse is also rather unconvincing; to drag in thus a reference to idolatry only diverts attention from the main indictment of contempt for the law. We must recollect that this particular reproach has not figured hitherto among the charges.

The second generation in the wilderness: 20.18f., 21, 22

The execution of judgment might well make one hope that at least the sons of those who suffered it might be brought to their senses and take care not to offend like their fathers. But in actual fact Yahweh's earnest renewed appeals proved fruitless. [18f.] A sharp contrast is drawn between statutes and judgments manufactured by human self-will, by which man delivers himself to destruction, and the God-given statutes and judgments which help man to life. This shows what a curse is that human self-will which refuses to yield to the divine sovereignty. [20] Here once again the emphasis given to the sabbath commandment in v. 20 diverts attention from the main point, which is the opposition between man's will and God's will, and shunts us off on to the sidetrack of Priestly devotion. On the other hand, the charge of idolatry does not appear at all! **[21]** Verse 21, on the contrary, singles out the central point of Israel's inward and outward apostasy. The core of 'rebelliousness' is the completely personal act of deciding wrongly in face of the expressed will of God.

[22] God, on the other hand, is only being faithful to his plan of salvation, when, in spite of everything, he does not give vent to his just wrath, but takes yet another step in the revelation of his gracious will. In the portion of text which follows, the correct order has not been preserved. In order to have regularity of structure, v. 22 ought to be followed by a fresh declaration of grace, like vv. 10 and 18. This can consist only in the bestowal of the land, as has already been intimated in vv. 6 and 15. So it would be more than strange for this indispensable proof of Yahweh's faithfulness to be omitted here, at the point where we first get a direct view of the link between the generation now addressed and those which have preceded it. But we do not read of this highest gift of salvation until v. 28. Obviously it has been moved from its original position before v. 23 through an error on the part of some copyist.

Israel in Canaan: 20.28, 23, 25, 26

Already, in the ancient confessions of faith in the sacred history in the Israelite cultus, such as Deut. 26.5–10, Yahweh lays the foundation by making a revelation to his people, and brings it to its goal and puts the coping stone on it by the bestowal of a land comparable with the Garden of Paradise in beauty and fertility. What has Israel made out of this fresh proof of God's goodness? **[28]** Verse 28 describes the worship on the high places of Canaan taken over from the previous inhabitants of the land as a self-willed sort of worship on hills and under leafy trees similar to that described in Hos. 4.13; Deut. 12.2; Jer. 2.20; 3.6; 17.2; II Kings 16.4. The present passage seems to have been especially influenced by the phraseology of Jeremiah, and is only one instance of many which go to show Ezekiel's sympathy with his contemporary prophet. The remarkable point, however, is that there is no mention of idolatry, and that the worship practised there is regarded as offered to Yahweh. In the phrase 'then they offered their sacrifices' the LXX changes the last two words into 'to their gods', evidently noticing the absence of the usual mention of idolatry, and feeling it necessary to introduce it. Ezekiel, on the other hand, like Hosea, seems to see in worship in high place an attempt to degrade Yahweh to the level of a mere nature-god, which wishes to

falsify the image of God by means of the mystical union that is everywhere within human capacity, but which reveals a further development in the growing alienation of the people from their God. [23]
Yahweh therefore feels himself compelled to make a strong counter-
attack: in v. 23 he announces that Israel will be scattered among the
nations, and makes it irrevocable by an oath. He thus takes back the
misused gift of the homeland so as to cut off the temptation to nature-
worship. ([24] Verse 24, another prolix summary of all the charges
like v. 16, reintroducing once more that of idolatry, may be deleted.)
[25f.] At the same time he reduces the apostates, who have tried to
transform the true God who calls for obedience into the false image
of a good-natured deity who is there only to give, to such a state of
terror, as to make them realize that it is a detestable thing to divinize
the powers of nature (vv. 25f.).

We meet here with one of Ezekiel's most uniquely characteristic
statements in regard to the law of Yahweh. Seen in the light of the
divine will to chastise, that law seems to him a direct incitement to
evil, leading Israel astray into the folly of child sacrifice. There is no
doubt that here he was thinking of one passage of the Book of the
Covenant, namely Ex. 34.19f., in which the same expression as his is
to be found: *kōl peter reḥem lī* 'all that opens the womb, i.e. the first
offspring of the female animal, the first-birth belongs to me'. The
orders sound absolute, but the passage goes on to go into particulars
of how they are to be carried out in practice. Only the first-born of
sheep and cattle are suitable for sacrifice. So an ass, not being an
animal that can be offered in sacrifice, is either to be replaced by a
lamb or else killed. In the same way every first-born son is to be
redeemed by the substitution of an animal: *kōl bekōr bānēkā tipdeh*.

There is also no doubt that this further definition, even if its
present formulation is a subsequent insertion into the text of the law,
was always in force and regarded as a valid interpretation of the main
intention. The sacrifice of the first-born was never a general Israelite
custom, as is proved by the pride and joy expressed over the first-born
son in the most ancient documents, such as Gen. 49.3.[1]

The chief regulation about the offering of the first-born, such as
that in Ex. 22.28, *bekōr bānēkā titten lī* 'the first of your sons you shall
give to me', has an absolute sound, and is not further limited by any
definition, so it was likely to call for an absolute interpretation, when

[1] In regard to human sacrifice in the Old Testament, cf. W. Eichrodt, *Theology
of the Old Testament*, I, 1961, pp. 148ff.

certain definite conditions seemed to demand the giving of the first-born as a human sacrifice. According to Canaanite views this was, for example, the case in an extreme critical stage in a war. Thus King Mesha of Moab, according to II Kings 3.27, sacrificed his first-born son to the war-god Chemosh, in order to compel the god to intervene for his deliverance when his capital city was reduced to sore straits by the Israelites. A sacrifice of this sort was also thought to be justified if made in order to deliver a city from a curse that had been laid upon her. According to I Kings 16.34, the accursed city of Jericho had to be set free from Joshua's curse by the sacrifice of a first-born son at the time when she was rebuilt. Jephthah's sacrifice in Judg. 11.34-40 has no connection, not being that of a first-born son.

This Canaanite idea, however, did not begin to constitute a dangerous temptation until the eighth and seventh century BC. By that time the process of assimilating Yahweh-worship to Baalite nature-worship had been able to advance very considerably, as a result of the ever more widespread syncretism under the Assyrian overlord-ship. Under the heavy pressure of spoliation by heathen overlords and the state of misery to which most of the peasantry were reduced, it was possible for the human sacrifice of first-born sons to appear to be the most effectual means by which to purchase mercy from a wrathful deity. The best-known testimony to this attitude of mind is Micah 6.6f., where the expedient is suggested, among others, in the foolish inquiries as to how to propitiate the wrath of God:

> With what shall I come before Yahweh
> and bow myself before God on high?
> Shall I come before him with burnt offerings,
> with calves a year old?
> Will Yahweh be pleased with thousands of rams,
> with countless rivers of oil?
> Shall I give my first born for my sin,
> the fruit of my body as an atonement for my life?

According to II Kings 16.3; 21.6, Ahaz and Manasseh would seem to have offered child sacrifices. According to II Kings 23.10 there was a place of sacrifice in the valley of the sons of Hinnom belonging to Molech, where child sacrifices were offered.

At that particular period attempts may have been made to justify this appalling type of sacrifice, which is also mentioned in Jer. 2.34; 3.24; 7.31; 32.35. Appeals may have been to the apparently absolute

demand of the command of the law to offer the first-born. Such a
misinterpretation of the law seems to have been known to Ezekiel.
But the remarkable thing is that he not only does not oppose this
misinterpretation but attributes it to the will of his God to execute
punishment by deliberately giving his law a form calculated to cause
his people to fall. Here a manifestation well known to Israel, that of
God himself hardening the heart of the unrepentant sinner, is carried
to its very climax. As God, according to Ps. 18.26, reveals himself in
his purity to the pure, but gives a perverted revelation to the perverse,
thus punishing sin by sin; as according to Isa. 6.10 he piles up prophetic messages such as harden the people and make them ripe for judgment; as according to I Kings 22.22ff. he puts a lying spirit in the
mouth of the prophets, in order to ruin the rebellious Ahab, so he
lays down in his own law a stumbling-block, by means of which a
perverted mind may come to believe in the goodness and devoutness
of a sacrifice which is nevertheless a frightful abomination. The un-
merciful death-dealing commandment with which Israel insists on
tormenting herself in her state of error, and which reveals all the
hostility to life in her nature-worship, is therefore a product of the
will of God in the same way as his life-giving law. And whoever
appeals to that commandment cannot but suffer the consequences,
which God's retribution must take in the shape of a command such
as a disobedient people deserves.

Verse 26 closes by stating that the purpose of all this is 'that they
might know that I am Yahweh'—a phrase still lacking in the LXX.
This is suspicious, since the phraseology takes a form deviating from
what is usual in Ezekiel. Nevertheless it shows a profound understanding of the divine reality so unsparingly portrayed by the prophet.
Israel's faith in God, unable as it was to accept either the seriousness
of the demand for a decision or the life-giving kindness of her God,
had to experience the shock of finding herself wrong in her overconfident assumption of how God would behave, before she could be
touched by any awareness of the mysterious holiness of God.

If we look back over the four phases under which the history of the
nation has been described, we observe that sinful apostasy was concentrated round idolatry, and that that was the concrete misdeed
which is symptomatic of Israel's rebelliousness. Yet that is not kept
up here, although it alone could add decisive weight to the indictment. In fact it plays a dominant part only during the first phase,
that of the sojourn in Egypt. During the second and third phases it

serves as an unconvincing appendage to the profanation of the sabbath. In the fourth phase, the era of the settlement in vv. 27f., when
it might have been securely based on a large number of historical
examples, it disappears altogether, to give place to a totally different
set of charges. It is quite undeniable that it is rebelliousness that displays all its ruinous effects when it enters into the high-place worship
offered to Yahweh. One cannot but ask the question, whether the
energetic introductory statement in vv. 7f. does not steer the indictment in a direction inconsistent with the prophet's original aim. We
also see it is not supported by the description of the time of salvation
in vv. 39ff. with its clear recapitulations of former transgressions, in
spite of the catchword *gillulīm*, idols, having been inserted in two
places. We will see later that vv. 30f. cannot legitimately be used to
support the claim that the indictment is one of idolatry, though it may
seem so at first sight.

This forces us to suggest that, when either idolatry or the profanation of the sabbath are introduced as the main charges, they must be
regarded as later elaborations. The first should not, however, be
ascribed to the priestly transmitters of the prophetic book, but to the
Deuteronomic revision of the prophet's writings, which is recognized
as having made many such tendentious additions. Seeing that Ezekiel
does himself often name this particular crime among those committed
by his people (6.4f.; 7.20; 8.5, 10; 14.2ff.), there was a very strong
temptation to add this concrete charge (in terms otherwise usual in
Ezekiel) to the general indictment, and thus single out a transgression
obnoxious above all others to supporters of the Josian reform. This
piece of elaboration nevertheless obscures very considerably the decisiveness and the consistency of the prophet's message of judgment.
The deletion of the passages concerned restores the original simplicity
and therefore increases the impact of the prophetic piece of historical
retrospect. It also makes it at least possible to see how it is connected
with the announcement of judgment and grace that follows.

The charge against the exiles which arises out of the historical retrospect:
20.27, 30, 31
By being solemnly addressed as son of man, the prophet is entrusted
with the task of approaching the inquirers directly, and convincing
them of the self-contradictory nature of their inquiry. [27] Their
fathers have blasphemed God by being disloyal in the way just
described. But are they, their sons, not now at the point (the inquiry

shows they have not made up their minds as yet) of doing the same,
and defiling themselves after the manner of their fathers by choosing
the place of sacrifice most pleasing to themselves? This interpretation
is confirmed by v. 31, which explicitly states what is here hinted at.
'And when you are about to defile yourselves by offering your sacrifices?' you inquire of the prophet. Ezekiel therefore ascribes to the
elders the intention to organize sacrificial worship in Babylonia, the
land of exile. They wish, after the model of their fathers, to re-
establish in a self-assertive manner the access to God in the sacrament
of the altar of which they have lately been deprived, in order to evade
the excommunication excluding them from a cultic meeting with God.

[30b, 31] It is obvious that the child sacrifice and idolatry have
been imported into the lucid context of the prophet's argument in
such a way as not only to make it sound exaggerated, but to deprive
his proofs of all their force. It weighs down the exiles with matters for
which no proofs are to be found in our records about the religious
situation during the exile. However definite was the intention to
introduce regular sacrificial worship on the part of these elders who
interview the prophet, and whom he honours by addressing them as
'house of Israel', there is nothing in their attitude to suggest any rank
upsurge of nature-worship such as all the prophets condemned. That
is not what the picture of past days is intended to suggest. What it
does is to intensify the damnableness of a rebellion against God's
government capable of concealing itself behind an attitude which in
itself seems perfectly reasonable. So they are confronted by the fact
that autocratic form of worship composed by them can oppose itself
to God's order. They are thus separating themselves from God at the
very moment when they intend to make an inquiry of him. The
Deuteronomic teachers of the law insisted with increasing rigidity on
a formalistic elevation of the Jerusalem temple to a position of monopoly. That, however, is not the decisive factor here, but subjection to
God's discipline, which a man must not presume to evade by choosing
a way of worship pleasing to himself before attaining to a realization
of having been forgiven and of having become a receiver of grace.
Such a rebellious attitude must be replaced by a willing surrender to
the punishment he has deserved before a man can genuinely rid himself of the godlessness of his fathers.

Now in this closing section, which gives the practical conclusions
to be drawn from the previous historical retrospect, we cannot fail to
see the complete irrelevance of the mention of idolatry. Therefore, as

the previous sections should also lead to the same practical conclusion, the charges of idolatry there cannot come from the prophet himself, since they serve a totally different purpose. There, too, it is that self-assertive obstinacy which resists God's orders and prefers to follow self-will, which we have to recognize as the besetting sin that persists in the same way through the generations. We had felt there was something strange and suspicious in the way the charge of idolatry was stated, and now at the end we see our suspicions were thoroughly justified. It has become evident that such insertions gave a twist to the main charge in a direction totally different to that in which Ezekiel was looking.

If we ask whether the tendency to concentrate on idolatry as Israel's main sin is to be found anywhere else, we find it has long been recognized as the characteristic peculiar to the Deuteronomic historical narratives. The Deutronomic reform movement welcomed such a means of displaying visibly and tangibly how the course of past history had shown an ever-increasing degeneracy and ripeness for judgment, and thus of making it understood that the catastrophe which overtook Israel was not an undeserved stroke from an unkindly fate but the logical outcome of a course of action undertaken by men fully responsible for what they were doing.

The structure of the book of Judges is completely, and that of the books of the Kings is mainly, focused on this evaluation of the past. The pedagogic effects of such a view of the nation's history were undoubtedly profoundly searching. They gave the surviving remnant of Israel strength enough to get out of the habit of doing nothing but bewail their own hard lot, and to act like morally responsible persons ready to shoulder the burden of their own history. But it is none the less undeniable that the concentration upon idolatry as Israel's besetting sin did lead to a certain tendency to plan the historical picture so as to illustrate this point, and to overlook the underlying causes of the alienation from Yahweh. In the prophetic books, too, where its presence can be established in numerous glosses and insertions in Isaiah and especially in Jeremiah, it has led to a certain oversimplification which gives a cruder note to the indictment brought by the prophet.

The same is also true of Ezekiel. The Deuteronomic redactors must have felt themselves justified in their interference, seeing that in various passages in his book the prophet himself speaks of how his people's special sin consists in turning to the heathen gods. This sin did not, however, figure as part of the general charge in ch. 20. So it may have seemed necessary to make the prophet's accusations more definite and factual, to give point to the general charge of wilful self-assertion by adding that it culminated in the worship of idols. There was a danger in this of externalizing the actual point of the indictment, and also of obscuring the point at issue in the discussion between Ezekiel and the elders. But that never even entered the minds of those vigorous popular educationalists. Actually the Deuteronomic revision has disturbed, even if it has not altogether destroyed, the logic of the prophet's indictment, which limits itself to one charge. But when the sections in question are removed the prophet's historical retrospect regains the special characteristics and the penetrative power which distinguish it from the Deuteronomic schematization of Israelite conduct. This also makes it possible once more to see the connection with the subsequent proclamation of judgment and grace, which many commentators have been unable to find.

This will become more apparent when we deal with the second half of ch. 20, the large section comprising 20.32–44.

JUDGMENT AND RENEWAL: 20.32–44

Evidently the exiles' plans have reached maturity. We are now shown how, looked on from another side, they are dangerous and hostile to God, and a threat of judgment is added to God's refusal to listen to their inquiry. We have already come across this combination of a rebuke with a threat of judgment in 14.7 and 17.9, and it need not seem out of place here. In fact, the lengthy process of giving the reasons for the divine disapproval would fall flat if it were not developed by this threat into a vigorous attack upon Israel's rebelliousness. Verse 32 is already linked with what precedes it in a purely formal way, except that having described the concern of the elders in vv. 30f., it now moves on to an undisguised characterization of the plans considered by the exiles. So there is no justification for making a considerable break here, and then treating what follows as an independent utterance by the prophet, without any connection with the first half of the chapter. Zimmerli has also pointed out the close connection between vv. 32 and 33.

The purgative judgment in the wilderness: 20.32–38

In order to understand this section we need to recall the result stated

in the whole denunciation. It is summarized in vv. 30f. The rebelliousness of the chosen people, which we have glimpsed at four periods of
its history, is threatening to revive. This is seen in the inclinations felt
by the elders, which they have so far kept secret, but which the
prophet has somehow come to know. They intend to organize regular
sacrificial worship in Babylon, in order to regain the meeting with
God in the sacrament of sacrifice, to be deprived of which has caused
them such pain. Yet to carry out such plans will be to commit the
very same act of unfaithfulness as their fathers, setting up a place of
worship according to their own self-assertive wishes, without asking
as to God's will. Once more we see men self-assertively and defiantly
claim as a right what can only be granted as an undeserved gift of
grace by the God who made the covenant.

[32] This charge is stated with precision once again in v. 32, at the
beginning of the pronouncement of judgment which follows. The
conduct of the elders is described as assimilating Israel to the surrounding heathenism. To express this, Ezekiel puts directly into the
elders' mouths the wicked words: 'He will be like the nations, the
tribes of other countries.' The elders, of course, did not say any such
thing in their discussion with the prophet. It is a classic formula expressing the mutiny against God implicit in the plan formed by the
leaders of the exiles, which has met such a prompt rejection. Here we
find an unmistakable allusion to the story of the choice of the first
king in I Sam. 8, where the elders of the people state to Samuel their
desire to have a king in the very same words: 'We also wish to be like
all the nations.' The author of I Sam. 8 tries to capture in a single
phrase how Israel repudiates the special position ordained for her by
God, and wishes to assimilate her own sacral constitution to the profane constitution of the states in the heathen world around her.
Ezekiel makes use of this historical tradition in order to state para-
digmatically what is implied in what the exiles mean to do. What is
planned here cannot be and must not be spoken of as a sign of
dependence upon Yahweh and of turning to worship him alone,
though many of the exiles may well have been seeking for that. It
really amounts to the same repudiation of Israel's special position as
before. The situation in which the exiles find themselves serves to
bring out a new point, which is the indissoluble connection between
the special position of Israel and the temple in Jerusalem. To replace
that temple by a sanctuary in a heathen land is to give up all hope of
a return to home, and to give oneself a form of religious life in a

heathen land, by which one's faith is degraded so as to become merely one religion among many, such as one might see in exile among exiles of other nations. The notion that this also implies the worship of idols of wood and stone, as is suggested by the addition at the close of v. 32, is one we have already rejected. This addition continues the line of the polemic against idolatry which governed the Deuteronomic revision of the whole chapter, and ascribes intentions to the elders which they were far from holding. Quite apart from that, the setting up of Yahweh-worship in Babylon would have rendered it impossible for the history of the people of God to begin afresh in any real sense. That would mean a return to the old ways and a total ignoring of the special guidance and purpose of Yahweh, and the process of gradual assimilation to the heathen environment would have gone on without a break. But Yahweh is not a God who is content to let his worship figure as an optional extra tolerated alongside other cults. He is the Lord without bounds to his dominion, whose will it is to be Lord over a people set apart from other peoples to be his, and so he sets up among that people a sign of his (and their) otherness. There can be no legitimate cultic worship of him that does not take the form he himself has prepared.

It is clear that this interpretation of v. 32 rules out any possibility of seeing in it the opinion which the elders are submitting to divine scrutiny through their inquiry of the prophet in v. 1. In that case, the refusal of a divine answer, which is stressed so strongly in v. 3, would now be withdrawn, to make way for an answer at considerable length. We find ourselves, rather, in the same situation as in 14.1ff., where elders coming to inquire of Yahweh are denied an answer in exactly the same way, and then the reason for this refusal is given by exposing a heathen amulet-cult secretly practised in private houses. In the same way Ezekiel here gives as the reason for his refusal something hitherto kept hidden from him, and describes all the rebelliousness towards God which characterizes it.

[33] Verse 33 tells how Yahweh meets the menace of the exiles' plans by revealing his lordly might and by making known the unique dignity of his kingship which they have now presumed to infringe: 'I will be king over you,' he says. Those words carry with them a fresh approach by God to his people, indeed the most important one we have been able to record since ch. 11. But the present state of affairs makes it impossible for this approach to be made save in and through judgment. The bright sun of the divine grace must still go on

hiding behind that black cloud. A purgative judgment must take place in order at last to rid the people of Yahweh of those rebellious ones who refuse under the judgment of the exile to repent and be converted.

In this Ezekiel takes up words used in the accustomed liturgical language to express the first saving demonstration of God's lordship in the Exodus from Egypt 'by a mighty hand and outstretched arm' (cf. Deut. 4.34; 5.15; 7.19; 26.8). Then he combines them with 'outpoured wrath', an expression peculiar to him alone, and, in a prophetic and paradoxical manner, transforms the boastful cultic invocation of God into a threat by God to come not to show his power to save but to chastise as a wrathful judge. [34–36] At the same time the range of the visitation is extended so as to include not only the exiles in Babylonia but the Jews scattered among all nations; they, too, like those once made bond-slaves in Egypt, must be led into the wilderness, in order there to be subjected to the kingly judgment, in which God in person comes face to face with his people. But this new sojourn by Israel in the wilderness is given a depth and earnestness through this act of judgment which distinguishes it from similar pictures of the future to be found in Hosea and Deutero-Isaiah. Hosea, the first of these, thinks of Israel's new sojourn in the desert as a tenderly loving visitation, by which God will associate once more with his people as in the early days (Hos. 2.16f.). In Deutero-Isaiah, the frequent pictures of the wanderings in the wilderness serve as material to set up a permanent memorial to the triumph of God the Redeemer. The dry ground is transformed into a garden of Paradise, in a way very reminiscent of the liturgical hymns, which love to dwell on how the wanderings in the wilderness serve as a special revelation of God's providence (Pss. 105.37ff.; 114; 99.6–8; 136.16; Deut. 33.10–12; Neh. 9.12–15). In Ezekiel the recollection of the 'wilderness of the land of Egypt' leads rather to thoughts of the sentence which God executed there upon his rebellious people, as is realized and recorded also by the old tradition (Ex. 32.15ff.; Num. 11; 14.10ff.; 16.31ff.; in Ps. 106.7ff., very probably under the influence of Ezekiel, it is converted into an exhortation to repentance). The new sojourn in the wilderness serves as an antitype to these. Whether, as most scholars assume, the wilderness of the peoples specially means the Syro-Arabian wilderness contrasted with the Egyptian wilderness is a point for which we have good reason for doubt, seeing that we are not concerned only with the Jewish community in Babylonia. Herrmann, already, has described this reference to the wilderness as one with an eschatological connotation, derived from the traditional account of the Exodus and settlement in the land. Zimmerli also refuses to regard the mention of a desert sojourn as a geographical statement, and prefers to treat it as a piece of typological terminology. What is of real importance is not the place but the act, possible in the desert, of severing Israel from all other nations. [37f.] How every way of escape from the final reckoning that is to follow is to be blocked is shown by the allegory of the shepherd, who makes each animal in his flock pass under his rod, in order to count out and set together those of them which he intends to get rid of. So the new sojourn in the wilderness is like sifting with a sieve, which catches up all the dirt, so that the nation may be completely purged of all its disloyal members before it can be allowed to find its way back to its old home.

Here Ezekiel's conception of judgment has attained a profundity never yet seen. He has come to look for a third type of judgment. Along with the initiatory act of judgment in the destruction of Jerusalem and her temple, and along with the ever-repeated judicial retribution which enters into the individual lives of those who make up the nation, we find also the purgative judgment in store for all who have been spared during the national catastrophe by which they are to pass through into a new age. What previous prophets have said of God and his judgment is radicalized in a way never seen before. Here the whole history of Israel from its very beginnings is not a history of salvation in the old traditional sense but a history of sin. All Yahweh's intimations of salvation, of which the liturgical hymns loved to boast, and in the rays of which men so loved to bask, seem inscrutable miracles of divine patience, wasted on an absolutely unreceptive people, who make an evil use of every fresh manifestation of grace, turning their backs on God and refusing obedience to his lordship in an even more decided way than before. The whole traditional account of salvation thus undergoes a strange transformation; one might say that it is transposed into a story of the handing down of damnation, and of how the divine will is constantly crossed by a nation which is completely good for nothing.

No verdict could be severer. It furnishes an example so clear as to be shocking of the priest Ezekiel's emancipation from the traditional notions of election of the temple of Jerusalem.

But there are two points not to be ignored:

1. Ezekiel's conception of history is not altogether new; it only fills

in more fully outlines already traced out by those who had gone before him. Isaiah, too, knew enough to speak of Yahweh's strange work, which is the savage destruction of his own people, and sets up in contrast to saving names for Yahweh like 'Rock of Israel' or 'Mighty one of Jacob', the formidable name of 'Holy one of Israel', which spells judgment, and implies these coming developments. Jeremiah had revealed with a profundity never attained before man's incapacity of doing good, and had brought out into the open the *servum arbitrium* of human compulsion to sinfulness. Unexampled as is Ezekiel's criticism of Israel's past, he is standing on their shoulders.

2. The dark shadow provided by the history of this people's sin only serves to intensify the dazzling purity of the light that shines upon their God. It is he whose ever-enduring mercy and patience and faithfulness make the impossible into the possible again and again for his name's sake. So through all the destructive criticism there rings a hymn to the glory of God which one cannot but hear.

Indeed, this method of showing how God brings about salvation eventually transforms the history of God's judgment into a promise or rather a prediction of the salvation that is to come. The purgative judgment, despite all its horrors, proves beyond all shadow of doubt that Yahweh stands by his people still and will have his way with them in the end.

That also is why the last section of this chapter is not an irrelevant postscript but an integral part of the whole without which it is incomplete.

The new worship: 20.39–44

New worship is not possible simply through a judgment which removes the wicked; it also calls for real renunciation of the past and waiting for God to be gracious. Both of these points are to be asserted yet again in most impressive terms. [39] If they still refuse to hearken to Yahweh, it would be better for them to go over to idolatry, and become exactly like heathen. Such a consistent repudiation of the true God would at least put an end to constant profaning of his name by oscillation back and forward between contempt for his commandments and outward nominal allegiance.

This curt statement that the time for half-measures has ended, and that after this there is no fate for the man who stops his ears but final separation from the God of Israel, is followed by verses which declare the absolute certainty that God's will to create a new Israel will reach

fulfilment even in spite of the apostasy of those now addressed. [40]
Thus for the first time in the preaching of Ezekiel we see emerge an
overwhelming expectancy of a new outpouring of grace. One may
naturally ask whether here, as in similar previous passages (cf.
11.14ff.; 16.44–63; 17.22–24), the prophet adapted his denunciation
by making an addition to it at a later period. In any case the biting
denunciations and stern demands for a decision are conjoined with
friendly inducements through the offer of a new future, which is to
take shape as the result of a mighty act of God. We see the dawning
glories of a new temple in which God will look favourably upon his
own, and be well pleased to accept their offerings. The first part of
the verse speaks of Israel in the third person, as if to suggest that the
prophet's audience do not belong to it. But in the latter part of the
verse salvation is directly proclaimed to them, as if the new future
were indeed already present. God is trying to win them over in
friendly fashion, he is showing them that what they must do is to
postpone worship till it can be performed in the proper place, created
by God, and how to do precisely that is the one sure way of
putting an end to all the remoteness from God from which they are
suffering.

Here we must notice how the word 'there' is emphatically repeated
three times in v. 40 and contrasted with the similar topographical
designation in v. 28. The behaviour of Ezekiel's fellow exiles against
which he threatens judgment is thus finally unmasked as consisting
in a self-willed re-establishment of the worship of God in a heathen
land (cf. above, p. 269). Only on the high mountain of Israel, in the
place chosen and consecrated by God himself for all time, can an
offering be made with which God will be well pleased. (In 40.2 it will
be described as a 'very high mountain', and thus, in agreement with
passages like Isa. 2.2; Zech. 14.10, designated as the world-mountain
rising above all other mountains, in which the nations of the ancient
world thought that God made his dwelling place.)

[41] The restoration and rebuilding of Zion, a full-length description of which we will find in ch. 40ff., is indissolubly linked with the
act of bringing back those who have been scattered among heathen
peoples and countries, by which God shows himself to all peoples to
be the holy God of his people. For here they see that God's plan of
salvation cannot be defeated even by his people's sin, but that it has
reached its objective, and refuted all the mockery and contempt to
which God's name has been subjected. [42] Israel, too, is awakened

to a new knowledge of her God, as she witnesses the wonderful return
to the land promised to the fathers: as first the severe earnestness of
God (v. 39), so now the kindness of God reveals a new aspect of the
mystery of his being. But the main thought is of his undying faithfulness, the same words being used as in the first revelation of salvation
(v. 6), in order to recall the oath by which he promised to bestow the
land upon the fathers. [43] In the light of all this, all the hideous unfaithfulness which has characterized the history of Israel must necessarily cause deep pain and sore feelings of shame. Such a humiliating
experience, too, is the surest antidote against the unbounded pride
which has again and again led Israel to rebel against God's ordering
of salvation and which finally led her to miss that for which she was
destined. [44] She has at last broken through to full knowledge of
Yahweh, as is declared in a final repetition of the words about knowing him in vv. 38 and 42. He is the God who acts for his name's sake,
i.e. out of faithfulness to his own being, once revealed, in which
Israel's salvation is comprised; his forgiveness is not weakness which
overlooks or ignores the guilt of the breaking of the covenant, but a
creative act reshaping his people out of the depth of his unalterable
will for fellowship with his elect, in which all the wonder of his being
makes itself known. The commentator who speaks in 16.61 and 63
understood his master well, when he took up this line of the knowledge of salvation, and extended it so far in his own special terminology.

As a result of Ezekiel's method of showing his people's guilt, there
comes to view a new dimension of sacred history, not as yet attained
by other prophets with their moralizing applications of past events. It
is not found in the people's love for their God, which exists for a while
but quickly vanishes, and which by its disappointing fickleness made
the insoluble enigma of the human heart a tormenting problem to
Jeremiah. It is the faithfulness of the love of God, which does not let
itself ever be exhausted, even in face of the most unspeakable
treachery on the part of men, but again and again restores the broken
chain and imparts to past events the qualities which make them into
sacred history. It imparts to revelation that quality of historical continuity by which it serves to prepare the people of God, and never
grows old, but reconquers an effective meaning for each succeeding
generation. This is because it has instruction to give, leading to that
knowledge of the mystery of God out of which there grows a certainty
about the meaning and goal of history, even though it may also show

up the bankruptcy of human natures and human wills. So here we find
the touchstone by which to judge whether a man has fully understood
the biblical revelation. Does he try to rid theological thinking of the
offence of history? Or does he, like this prophet of ours, realize that it
is the very thing which reveals to the believer the mystery of divine
personality: 'And you shall know that I am Yahweh'?

THE AVENGING SWORD

20.45–21.32

CHAPTER 20.45–21.7

Jerusalem threatened with fire and sword

45ᵃ The word of Yahweh came to me: ⁴⁶'Son of man, set your face to-wards the south, let your words flow against the south and prophesy against the forest-land [. . .]ᵇ in the south, ⁴⁷and say to the forest in the south: Hear the word of Yahweh! Thus says [. . .]ᶜ Yahweh: Behold, I kindle a fire in you, and it shall devour every green tree in you and every dry tree. The blazing flame shall not be quenched and all faces from south to north shall be scorched by it. ⁴⁸And all flesh shall see that I, Yahweh, have kindled it, and that it cannot be quenched.' ⁴⁹Then I said: 'Oh [. . .]ᵈ Yahweh, they are saying of me, "Is he not always a speaker of riddles?" '

21.1ᵉAnd the word of Yahweh came to me: ²'Son of man, set your face towards Jerusalem and let your words flow against its sanctuaryᶠ and prophesy against the land of Israel ³and say to the land of Israel: Behold, I will go against you and will draw my sword out of its sheath and will cut off from you both righteous and wicked. ⁴Because I cut off from you both righteous and wicked, therefore my sword shall go forth out of its sheath against all flesh from south to north. ⁵And all flesh shall know that I, Yahweh, have drawn my sword out of its sheath, that it may not return back there again.

⁶Sigh, therefore, son of man! Sigh with breaking thighs and bitter grief before their eyes! ⁷And when they say to you, "Why do you sigh?", you shall say, "Because of the tidings, when it comes every heart will fail and all hands will be feeble, every spirit will be faint and all knees run with water. Behold, it comes and it will be fulfilled," ' says [. . .]ᵍ Yahweh.

ᵃ20.45–49 = Hebrew 21.1–5.
ᵇ⁻ᵈSee BH.
ᵉ21.1–7 = Hebrew 21.6–12.
ᶠ⁻ᵍSee BH.

CHAPTER 21.8–17[a]

The conjuring up of the avenging sword

[8]And the word of Yahweh came to me: [9]'Son of man, prophesy and say, Thus says [Yahweh][b] [. . .][c]
A sword, a sword is sharpened and also polished,
10 sharpened for slaughter, polished to flash like lightning.[d]
[. . .][e]
11 So it was given to the polisher,[f] that it might be handled: it was sharpened [. . .][g] and polished to be given into the hand of the slayer.
12 Cry and wail, son of man,
for it is against my people, it is against all the princes of Israel:
they are delivered over[h] to the sword with my people.
Smite therefore upon your thigh.
13 [. . .][i]
14 Prophesy, therefore, son of man, and clap your hands,
that the sword may come down twice, yea thrice;[j]
it is a sword for slaying, the great slaughtering sword, which encompasses them.
15 That every heart may fail[k] and that they that fall may be many,
at all their gates have I ordained for the sword to slaughter.[l]
Ah, it is made to flash like lightning, polished to slaughter.
16 Cut sharply into it,[m] turn to the right[. . .][n] and left where your edge is directed.
17 I also will clap my hands and satisfy my fury.
I, Yahweh, have spoken.'

[a]21.8–17 = Hebrew 21.13–22.
[b]See BH.
[c]MT: 'speak', there is no other example of it in prophetic style following a preceding commandment.
[d]See BH.
[e]A line has been inserted which has become unintelligible, the text of v. 1 goes on smoothly from v. 10 once it is out of the way.
[f]See BH.
[g]MT: 'a sword'.
[h]See BH.
[i]The present wording is very suspicious and has been remodelled more or less imaginatively by older exegetes, without producing any statement that fits in convincingly with the context. Later commentators have therefore given up all

attempts to restore it (Herrmann, Zimmerli). Fohrer accepts Bewer's interpretation which takes the text as it stands with hardly any alteration: 'For a testing is made. And why, if you despise the rod, should it not take place?' It might find a place in Proverbs, but such terminology and such meditations are derived from the teacher and pupil relationship, and constitute a foreign body among these furious threats.
ʲ⁻ⁿSee BH.

A threat against Jerusalem in a riddle and its interpretation: 20.45–21.5

[**20.45f.**] Verse 45 of ch. 20 introduces as a message coming straight from God a menacing prediction of a terrible forest fire in 'the south'. The prophet's protest in v. 49 should, however, be enough to warn us against interpreting the catastrophe too literally and forgetting the deliberate obscurity usual in mystic language. So the south cannot possibly mean the steppe south of Beersheba (Herntrich, Bertholet). Had that been so, the word Negeb would surely have been used. The word 'south' is equally common to indicate merely what lies to the south. Generally speaking this is the only sense Ezekiel uses, since he does not mention any of the particular districts of Palestine. It is also impossible to imagine his suddenly prophesying a forest fire in the treeless Negeb, even leaving out of consideration the political unimportance of the region in that particular period.

Furthermore, we are given an explicit interpretation of this first threat in 21.1–5. This is indicated by the exact parallelism of structure between 20.46 and 21.2. The extension of the disaster in 20.47 and 21.4 and the effects intended by God in 20.48 and 21.5 also point in the same direction. This shows that it is impossible to interpret the saying as though the prophet were looking south over the Negeb, thus suggesting that he is standing in Jerusalem. It is much more likely that Babylon is the place from which the threat is issued and that Israel is described as the land lying to the south. Jerusalem and her temple are therefore still intact, the land of Israel is still in existence as a state. But God's judgment is about to bring all that to an end, and is on the point of being released in the immediate future. So we find ourselves as yet in the period before the catastrophe of 589.

We have already met pictures of fires in forest in Isa. 10.17ff. and 9.18. The first passage refers to the proud Assyrian empire, to which the Holy One of Israel is like a devouring flame destroying the glory of man. In the second passage the fire represents the destructive force of godlessness in Israel, as it consumes first within, and then suddenly breaks out into an irresistibly destructive conflagration. Ezekiel follows where Jeremiah has already led (Jer. 21.14) in utilizing the image as in the first picture. **[47]** But this time he turns it against the people of God. A merciless fire blazes up in the forest, i.e. in the arrogant pride of the 'south land' of Israel. Neither green nor dry trees are spared, there is none excepted from the doom of destruction. Yahweh himself has kindled the fire. **[48]** So anyone who tries to quench it gets nothing for it but a skin scarred with burns, and is thus forced to admit that no human power can bring deliverance.

The allegorical language may use the name of the forest in the land to the south to conceal those to whom it actually applies, and present the prophet's audience with a riddle. But the interpretation given in 21.1–5 takes good care to reveal clearly what is signified. **[49]** Significantly, it is the prophet himself who asks his God to make the veiled announcement clear. Whereas Isaiah accepts without protest the duty of delivering a message which produces stubbornness (Isa. 6.9f.), and sees in the enigmatic language of his God and the flippant rejoinders it provokes a punishment well fitted to the crime of refusing to accept his warnings (Isa. 28.11, 21f.), Ezekiel is greatly troubled to see the effect of his words. Willing though he is to exaggerate the strangeness of his actions to a grotesque extreme in order to force onlookers to take notice and to ask questions, he is most unwilling to disguise the meaning of God's message in ambiguous language, and does so with great reluctance. The early church was able to admit a punitive purpose of God's in the parabolical language of Jesus, because they saw alongside the hardened multitude a circle of disciples arising who had been led on to full understanding (Matt. 13.11ff.). But that was impossible for one who preached to the exiles, and who, having given up hope of teaching anything to the people of Jerusalem, was trying to make his fellow deportees realize before it was too late what the problems were and how God had decided. To be dismissed with contemptuous mockery as a mere maker of riddles seemed to him unendurable in view of the judgment of God which they would all so soon have to face. His reverent submission to the will of God did not allow him to venture on any protest; the only objection he makes is an irrepressible sigh (21.6). Yet in that he reveals clearly enough his fear at seeing God thus hiding his gracious intentions, with all the incalculable results for the community of exiles. So here once more we see him acting as the mediator, whose chief concern is to deliver those who have been entrusted to his care (cf. 13.5; 9.8; 11.13).

[21.1] His request is granted, by his being ordered to explain his first message in words which no one can fail to understand. [2] His deliberate choice of exactly the same words as those in 20.46, 'Set your face, let your words flow, prophesy!', make the audience at once notice that the second message is closely connected with the first. The word 'flow', used of the words of the prophets, does not have the contemptuous meaning of 'dribble' or 'foam' at the mouth, as in Micah 2.6, 11, but suggests the rich and powerful surge of prophetic utterance. It is a word not used elsewhere in Ezekiel. In place of the vague suggestions of the land to the south and the forest in the south, we now find Jerusalem with her temple and the land of Israel. [3] In the place of the fire of 20.47 we find the sword of Yahweh. This also is a mythological image, but it is one so frequently employed by the prophets (Deut. 32.41f.; Isa. 27.1; 31.8; 34.6; 66.16; Jer. 12.12; 47.6; Zeph. 2.12; but cf. already Gen. 3.24; Judg. 7.20) as to be perfectly intelligible; still more, seeing how the idea of Yahweh as a warrior in battle lives on into the post-exilic period (Isa. 42.13; 59.17; 63.5f.). The green and dry trees of the allegory are now replaced by the righteous and wicked, in order to bring out how all the people without any exception are overtaken by God's judgment. This, however, apparently contradicts the statements elsewhere that the righteous will be spared (9.4, 6; 18), and leads first to an alteration of the text into 'unrighteous and wicked' in the Greek version, and various attempts in the rabbinic interpretations to explain it away or mitigate it (cf. Fohrer, *ad loc.*). Of course, if one is to regard the deliverance of the righteous from the compulsion of inherited sin, proclaimed in ch. 18, as a general theory of retribution, then there is a contradiction between this and other passages which it is not possible to overcome. But we have already rejected any such view, and insisted that Ezekiel preserves the freedom of God's retribution, a freedom which cannot be imprisoned in any doctrinaire system, even while contemplating some fresh divine act of salvation (cf. above, pp. 237ff.). So his concern for the awful seriousness of God's wrath in judgment makes it possible for him to picture all human pretensions being silenced in face of the crushing weight of this final reckoning with a rebellious people.

The fire cannot go out again, because it is the flame of God's judgment (20.48), and in the same way the sword cannot go back into the sheath, because it is settling God's final account (21.5). The exactness with which allegory and explanation correspond here forbids any attempt to shorten the text (cf. e.g., *Fohrer, ad loc.*).

[4] One should in preference let 21.4 stand in full with all its significant repetitions. It asserts how world-wide are the effects of this judgment 'against all flesh from south to north', evidently pointing to a world-judgment beginning in the punishment of Israel, and thus preparing for 21.5. The ruthless destruction of the chosen city by the God to whom she belongs serves to reveal his majesty before 'all flesh', as is shown by an exact reference back to 20.48. **[5]** Israel's ruin must open the eyes of the whole world to see who is at work here; it is the God of the whole world, who both proclaims Jerusalem's unavoidable fate and puts it into execution, in order to show that he is beginning to judge the whole world. What is happening in this little corner of the earth is destined to spread until it involves all nations and summons them to obedience to the one who is the true Lord of the whole earth. It has often been thought that in Ezekiel God's dealings with his people do not possess any universal significance. But here we see it already present in his message of judgment. We shall see more and more clearly that it does not exhaust itself in a mere demonstration of divine power.

The prophet, by sharing in the people's future sufferings, makes them present to them now: 21.6–7

Once again the prophet enters into a very deep experience of fellowship with his people by sharing their sufferings. **[6]** It has, indeed, been objected that even the expression of grief over the terrible fate in store for his fellow countrymen was enjoined upon Ezekiel, and that this manifests the complete inward cleavage between Ezekiel and his fellow countrymen, because he shows such a cold and insensitive attitude towards the misery to come and proves himself incapable of any genuine sympathy (cf. Bertholet, Krätzschmar, etc.). Such an opinion seems to us to fail to do justice to the outbreak of elemental grief and despair in 6.11; 9.8; 11.13, since it deprives the prophet of all real personality and tries to substitute for that something purely imaginary and artificial. The supreme self-discipline which keeps the natural man in him in subjection to all that God wills, assenting to it in every particular, is the exact opposite to frigidity of feeling. It is a conscious act of self-sacrifice, a willing carrying out of every duty God lays upon him, after the manner of a Calvin or an Ignatius Loyola. God's command for him to express his grief aloud breaks through this control and makes room for natural feelings, while at the same time the assertion of his humanity by the ambas-

CONJURING UP OF THE AVENGING SWORD: 21.8–17   291

sador of God is directed towards a higher objective. So it is not a self-willed departure from the usual subjection of the whole man to the higher law of his God. It is not an uncontrolled surrender to the passion of the oriental lamentation for the dead giving rise to emotions so powerful as to sever the prophet from God. The truth is rather that this painful awareness of human suffering, occasioned by man's sinful separation from God, serves to establish another and still closer link with the God who ordained that it should be so. It does this by serving as one more pledge and proof of the menacing closeness of God's judgment to his unrepentant people. The disturbance caused by the prophet's human cry becomes a symbol. [7] It is an anticipation of all mankind's unconditional surrender to whatever judgment God will impose. As a cry and no more, it knocks on the hardened hearts of the audience, so as to lead them from complacent criticism of God's messenger and his proclamation into such terror of heart that they yield at last to the hand of God, which they have ignored hitherto, but now find they cannot escape.

The prophet, groaning in anguish till he pants for breath (cf. Jer. 4.19), guarantees the truth of his tidings. What men still try to laugh off as mere empty talk is actually now beginning to approach. The threat in ch. 7 rang out like a loud alarm bell: 'The end has come, the day has drawn near.' 12.21ff. gave warning of the immediate approach of the fulfilment of the word of judgment. Now all this takes effect, the announcement of the wrath of God becomes a reality in the sufferings which the prophet undergoes before the eyes of the terrified spectators; they must perforce see that he represents what they themselves will look like when 'every heart will fail and every spirit will be faint and all knees run with water'. Here God in all his holiness, the God whose will to judge they had hoped to evade, meets them so that they cannot escape, and compels them to open their eyes and face the destruction that is to come upon them. There is no other way of removing the spellbound blindness which has hitherto prevented them from forming a true picture of God.

The song of the sword: 21.8–17

Ezekiel tried to state and solve the great problems of his age by identifying himself intimately with God's actions and proclaiming God's new dealings with his people. He did so by means of instructive descriptions and actions, and also by a considerable number of poems. Some are brief and closely woven like 15.1–7. Others rise to a greater scale and length like the threats or lamentations over Tyre in ch. 27 and 28 or over Egypt in ch. 31 and 32. They employ parable and allegory in the same way as earlier prophets, so as to attract the attention of the audience, or to arouse curiosity by purposely concealing their message. But whereas to the earlier prophets all this was no more than an improvised means to an end, whose purpose was served once the immediate objective was attained, the poems of Ezekiel attain to a weight and impressiveness that is all their own, and possess an independent significance. The impressions of the foreign land with all its striking and monumental architecture, its sculptures and traditions, impinged on an unusually gifted poetic mind. The result was that above and beyond being used to attain the immediate objective, these impressions were given shape in a poetic composition which has an originality that is quite unique in the Old Testament. Its poetic force reveals a whole new dimension in the prophet's make up: he is not only a theologian and a philosopher, but also a poet. But we can do no more than refer briefly to this side of his character.

It is, however, worth remarking here that mystery seems to have had special attractions for Ezekiel. He can give it a form full of intensity and colour, as in ch. 17, where the old animal fable of the two eagles and the vine is developed with all the freedom of a skilful narrator. The result is a picture on a large scale, the didactic aim of which at first disappears behind the bright elaboration of the detail, which evidently gave the poet himself such pleasure. When we compare it with the prophet Nathan's parable in II Sam. 12.1ff., or with Isaiah's song of the vineyard in Isa. 5.1–7, or his parable from peasant life in Isa. 28.26ff., or with the parable of the potter in Jer. 18.1ff., we see that something new has come into being, the result of an urge to give poetical expression to other feelings which have an independent power all their own. We see this most of all in the laments, which sing with tragic irony as if mourning the downfall of some enemy. Most of them are as brief as Amos 5.2, or Isa. 1.21ff. In Isa. 14.4ff. we find a lament over the king of Assyria, which may perhaps be by Isaiah himself, and it is that which best deserves to be put side by side with similar passages in Ezekiel. When Ezekiel in Ezek. 27.3ff. announces the downfall of the rich merchant-city of Tyre by means of the image of a proud ship wrecked by an east wind, this *qina* (elegy) has developed into something more than a purely incidental improvisation. It displays a pleasure taken in poetic form for its own sake, and unfolds a picture so full of rich colour that we recognize it for the work of a real poet. The same is true of the poem presenting the king of Tyre under the image of a divine cherub of wondrous beauty and wisdom, in which old myths have been melted down and reshaped with sovereign power. The representations of Pharaoh as a wonderful cedar in 31.2ff. or as the crocodile which stirs up a flood and yet is caught in a net in 32.1ff. display in full how much Ezekiel has done to develop further the old elegiac form.

In 21.8–17 we meet a poem of a particularly unusual type. It is not characterized by any epic descriptions. It is a song full of ecstatic passion and of uninhibited savagery. Yet it also is an expression of personal convictions. While linked to what has gone before by its central theme of the sword that carries out punishment, this message of menace takes on an unfamiliar form. One of the most recent commentators (van den Born) feels he can go so far as to call it a sword-dance. His theory at the very least shows how the description grows so intense as to be perceptible to the senses; the sword seems to have a power of its own as it darts and thrusts or swings to and fro to do its bloodthirsty and hideous task. It is swung as though by the prophet himself, and yet he seems to address it as a living and terrible thing. His words become an accompaniment to an event which they have directly served to introduce. Of course, it must be acknowledged that this interpretation is only conjectural; the verses alone do not suffice to prove it, even though the single lines, bubbling up and repeating the same words with powerful effect, seem well designed to serve as accompaniments to a sword-dance with its pantomimic gestures.

Yet it is well worth considering if there is not another type of activity which may help us better to appreciate the peculiar form by this composition. This is weapon-magic, a subject which deserves more attention than it usually gets. An observation by Oort[1] already points in the same direction. Quoting II Kings 13.18, he suggests that the clapping of hands in v. 14 is the gesture that accompanies the announcement that the sword shall be doubled and trebled. King Joash in the same way smote three times with the arrows on the ground at the command of the prophet Elisha, in order to represent the victory over the Syrians which the prophet had foretold. In that case, it is not sufficient to regard this action as a mere accompanying

---

[1] H. Oort, 'Ezechiël xix; xxi; 18, 19v., 24v.', *ThT* XXIII (1889), pp. 511f.

gesture; it is one which is intended actually to set a chain reaction going in the desired direction and force something to happen.

We find ourselves in the world of magic, where certain specific words and actions are regarded as invested with power, and therefore capable of compelling certain things to occur. The most recent research into prophecy has long recognized how close prophetic prediction is to this sphere of magical operation. Yet it also demonstrated how the prophets transformed the original primitive outlook by consistently subjecting the compelling words and gestures to the power of God, making them serve his purposes (cf. above p. 81). So here the clapping of the hands is to be regarded not only as an accompanying gesture but an effective action, which doubles and trebles the striking of the sword in bloodthirsty fury, and thus adds a terrifying intensity to its destructive power.

Such an explanation will be found to agree strikingly with the wording and the structure of the poem. The sharpening and polishing of the sword is at first descriptive (v. 9b), next makes it capable of slaying and sparkling (v. 10), and then makes it ready to be put into the hand of the slayer (v. 11). This is not to be regarded as a series of useless repetitions, constructed by Ezekiel or one of his disciples in order to fill out some earlier and simpler outline. Such repetitions of the same words are a characteristic and essential part of a magical formula, in which words take on compelling power. No person is named as initiating these preparations, everything takes place automatically and anonymously as in a natural process. The prophet, of course, cannot conceive of any agent but God as acting. Nevertheless, all these things are required in order to cause something to happen, and what happens is uncanny from its very intangibility. What is still more effective, poetically, is the way in which the speaker, having gone through the whole maledictory formula till it has reached its climax in the mention of the slayer, breaks into screams and cries. Here, once more, the prophet is set free by a divine command, to give vent to the natural human feelings, in face of the horror which they are to be understood as helping to anticipate and achieve by the power which they release. [12] What arouses the terror is not the mere fact of a sword being made ready to slay, or of an upsurge of war-fever in some nation or other; the prophet feels terror because, in the self-same moment that he sees the slayer take the sword in his hand, he also sees the victim upon whom it is to fall: that victim is his own people, the princes and people of Israel. And his own cry of terror at the disaster is itself one of the agencies that co-operate to bring it about. Amos cries out in the same way in his death lament over the Virgin Israel, as he sees her lying dead in the dust, long before the Assyrian has arrived to transform his vision into a reality. Some fail to see how closely all is connected. Either they say that v. 12 should be moved to a later period, in which case the whole threat-poem was not composed until after the execution of the judgment that is prophesied (van den Born, Zimmerli), or else they regard it as an elaboration of an old sword-song (Fohrer). But this happens because they fail to see the unbroken unity of the poem.

This first part of the sword-speech makes a tense incantation. The second part adds a further unexpected intensification, as the prophet himself intervenes in the operation and carries it to a climax. [14] The words about the sword's doubling and trebling the stokes, expressed in the preceding sentence as a final aim, show that the words of prophecy and the accompanying gesture of hand-clapping, which the prophet is commanded to perform, are the real means through which destruction is magically produced. The hand-clapping does not express any sadistic pleasure (Krätzschmar and most other commentators); that would indeed be extraordinary in view of v. 12! Neither does it denote the all-conquering hand that wields the sword (Zimmerli). Like similar noises made in country dances to add to the excitement, the hand-clapping sets the spell in operation which makes the sword strike twice and thrice. One must not ask how such a thing can possibly happen with a sword already in the hand of the slayer. The real point is that in this second part it is turning more and more into a demonic force of destruction which has an independent life of its own, and does not need to be guided by any man, like the flaming sword turning every way, which the Paradise story sets to guard the way to the tree of life (Gen. 3.24). That also distinguishes it from the hard and great and strong sword in Isa. 27.1 which, being the weapon of Yahweh, possesses no independent life of its own. A sword can be spoken of in saga as able to fight its own battles in this way, eventually even turning on the man to whom it belongs, and C. F. Meyer has succeeded in giving life to this whole idea in his ballad of Attila's sword ('König Etzels Schwert'). In the same way this enchanted weapon encircles the doomed nation, so that none may escape it. [16] It is even addressed as if it were a living being, and summoned to strike without mercy on every side so as to carry out completely the destruction on which God has determined. This announcement that God will bring about an attack with a cutting weapon serves to prepare the way for the effective closing lines, in which Yahweh himself is the speaker. [17] As punisher of all evil, he must satisfy his furious wrath. So he repeats the prophets' gestures in order to give them validity and to ensure that they take effect. The magic garment of poetry is thus transmuted and exalted into a divine and supernatural force. The Divine Judge appears on the scene as the owner and only real operator of the slaughtering sword.

[15] Yahweh's action as judge is anticipated in v. 15. Its aim is to humiliate all the pride of the punished by making the ruthless slaughter take place at all the gates, i.e. in every district of the holy land. One may ask if it does not spoil the effectiveness of the poem by interrupting the sequence between vv. 14 and 16, and wonder whether it was the work of the poet. Nevertheless, this verse serves to indicate that it is the Babylonian conqueror who storms the fortified cities and executes their inhabitants. That, as v. 19 shows, is undoubtedly a correct interpretation of what is meant by the avenging sword. One may therefore prefer to transfer v. 15 (apart from its last phrase) to a position after v. 16, so as to secure an uninterrupted sequence.

CHAPTER 21.18–24

The king of Babylon at the parting of the ways

18 The word of Yahweh came to me: ¹⁹'Son of man, make two ways for the sword to the king of Babylon to come; both of them shall come forth from the same land. And set a signpost at the beginning of each way,ᵃ ²⁰that the sword can come, to "Rabbah of the Ammonites" and "to Judah and to Jerusalem the fortified" (or "to Judah and to Jerusalem the impregnable").ᵇ ²¹For the king of Babylon stands at the parting of the ways, at the head of the two ways, to use divination. He shakes the arrows, he consults the teraphim, he looks at the liver. ²²Into his right hand comes the lot for "Jerusalem"[. . .]ᶜ to open the mouth with a cry, to lift up the voice with shouting, to set battering rams against the gates, to cast up a mound and build a rampart. ²³But to them it will seem like a false divination according to their opinion, after they [have sworn oaths in order to break them],ᵈ but he brings their guilt to remembrance, that they may be

captured. [24]Therefore thus says [. . .][e] Yahweh: Because you make your guilt to be remembered, so that your treacheries may be discovered, so that in all your doings your sins appear [. . .][f], therefore you shall be taken in them.'[g]

[a]See BH.
[b]The LXX simplifies this unusual expression into 'with Jerusalem in its midst'. But one must agree with Zimmerli that the peculiar expression is chosen to provide a contrast to the 'great city of the Ammonites'.
[c-e]See BH.
[f]MT: 'Because you have been denounced', exactly the same grouping of consonants as at the beginning, but pointed as the *niphʿal*.
[g]21.18–24=Hebrew 21.23–29.

CHAPTER 21.25–27

A curse against the wicked

25 'But you, [wicked one covered with shame],[a] prince of Israel, whose day has come in the time of the final punishment, [26]thus says [. . .][b] Yahweh: "Remove the turban, take off the crown, things shall not remain as they are. Exalt that which is low, [27]abase that which is high. Ruins, ruins, ruins will I make it. This also shall not exist,[c] until he comes whose right it is, and to him will I give it." '[d]

[a]It is preferable, following Zimmerli, to put both the terms of abuse in the construct state: *ḥᵃlal rāʿsā*.
[b]See BH.
[c]For *hāyā* read *hāyᵉthā*.
[d]21.25–27=Hebrew 21.30–32.

The symbolic action: 21.18–20

The sword-song states in the terms of myth that the mortal threat to Judah is on the point of being put into execution. Now the prophet feels himself summoned to convey the same message by means of a symbolic action. He is to depict two roads forking out from the same point of departure, and supply each road with a signpost, one pointing to Rabbath Ammon and the other to Jerusalem. Unfortunately no further details are supplied of how he was to execute this sketch map; the account seems unusually abbreviated, because it is wholly dominated by the interpretation which follows. The most obvious possibility is a sketch map traced on a brick, like the one described in 4.1.

This would be a more effective procedure for the purpose than a sketch plan traced in sand, or a more elaborate model carried out in wood or stone, which would have offered the opportunity for further symbolic actions like those in 12.4ff. The signposts indicating where the roads lead are a feature which we know to have been found in Babylonia. They indicate that the fate of Jerusalem will be decided by which of the two alternatives is chosen by the person using the road. There was no need to add the anticipatory interpretation referring to the sword of the king of Babylon in v. 19 (this may have been inserted subsequently, like the similar interpretation referring to Jerusalem in 4.1, or the reference to the king of Assyria in Isa. 7.17 and 20). Anyone who sees can already realize the significance of the two main roads leading to the capital cities of Ammon and of Judah. It is quite immaterial where the parting of the ways may lie. It may be the city of Riblah on the Orontes, which was Nebuchadrezzar's headquarters in his Syrian campaign, or we may think simply of Babylon herself as the point from which the great king set out on his martial expeditions. In any case it is perfectly clear that the only question for the Babylonian king would be in what sequence he should attack the centres of the resistance to his supremacy.

This undoubtedly points to 589 as the year in which the symbolic action takes place. Judah and Ammon were then allies in a coalition against Babylonian overlordship, and were its two chief supports in southern Syria. Only on that occasion did Jerusalem and Rabbath Ammon both find themselves in danger of being overtaken by the same fate, and only then was the position sufficiently clear without further explanation to anyone living at the time. Yet the Syrian resistance forces were so many-headed that each of the individual partners might well hope that the Babylonian punitive expedition might divide into separate detachments and thus give him a chance to get his head out of the noose. So the question of the direction in which the mailed fist of Babylon would strike its first blow was one of very considerable importance to Jerusalem.

The interpretation: 21.21–24

Ezekiel relieves the strain of waiting to see what Babylon is going to do by carrying the minds of his audience back to the moment when the issues were still undecided. [21] He pictures the great king busy preparing for entering on the campaign, by inquiring into the will of the gods, and engaging in the actions required for that purpose. We are

given a thoroughly realistic picture of the methods of applying oracular science in important political decisions. Its one peculiarity is that
it gives a whole series of different methods of inquiring into the future,
all belonging to different countries. The Old Testament witnesses that
the arrow oracle and the consultation of the teraphim were usual in
Syria, but they had no importance in Babylon. On the other hand,
the inspection of the liver is one of the chief departments of Babylonian augury known from its rich literature of ominology, and has
lately been shown to have been present also in Canaan. The arrow
oracle, also practised among the Arabs, seems analogous to the lots
cast in Israel by means of the Urim and Thummim. Certain marked
lots, or arrows used in place of lots, were shaken in a vessel or a quiver,
until one either leapt out or was picked out by some person previously
blindfolded. The teraphim were most probably masks covering the
face. They were used for obtaining indications in regard to the
future, and are mentioned in the Old Testament as having been an
importation from Syria in Gen. 31.19, 34f. They are associated with
stories of horseplay and practical jokes, ending in deceptions or im-
personations, Judg. 17.5; I Sam. 19.13, 16.[1]

When Ezekiel pictures the great king employing these methods of
divination as well as the others, his object is above all to indicate
what careful steps Nebuchadrezzar takes to put himself at the service
of his gods, and how he makes use of every means available to find
out what the divine will is. Of course, he may have been aware that
the great king had already marched into Syria, and may therefore be
representing him as using the methods of augury customary in that
region as well as those of Babylon. [23] Nevertheless, he still represents him as having a right recognized by Yahweh to prosecute and to
pronounce sentence upon Israel, and regards his decisions as in the
end controlled and caused by Yahweh himself. [27] His hand has
taken hold of the lot representing Jerusalem, and thus made the
decision for an attack in full force with all the weapons known to the
art of war upon the capital city of the king of Judah (cf. 4.1f.).

[23] Even when he announces the solid fact that the grace-given
respite allowed to Jerusalem has reached its end, Ezekiel finds himself
facing disbelief and disapproval. His audience regard it as a false
oracle, as would the inhabitants of Jerusalem. There cannot possibly
be a reference to the omen vouchsafed to Nebuchadrezzar, as

[1]Cf. W. Eichrodt, *Theology of the Old Testament*, vol. 1, 1961, pp. 113ff.

exegetes have lately begun ·to suggest. However false it might be in itself, there was no doubt that it would lead the great king to start in a certain direction without turning back, and that, for that moment, was the decisive point. What is being disregarded as a false oracle is Ezekiel's whole statement, which is thought fit to be ignored, like his other previous threats. The prophet calls attention to the obstinate unbelief behind such disapproval, by declaring that what he has stated is the only possible logical answer God can give in view of the godless and deceitful policy followed by Judah. Anyone who takes an oath only in order to break it cannot expect the holy God to do anything but call him to account for doing so. He makes the heathen king engaged in fitting out his punitive expedition figure as the accuser, whose duty it is to remind Yahweh that it is time for him to punish the evildoers among his own people. If the office in the Israelite court called *Mazkir*, so frequently referred to, and usually translated 'chancellor', meant originally the public prosecutor,[1] then the Babylonian is being described as one of Yahweh's highest ministers. Jeremiah calls him the Ebed Yahweh, the trusted officer of the Lord of all the world (Jer. 27.6), and Deutero-Isaiah speaks of Cyrus as Yahweh's anointed (Isa. 45.1), thus exalting him to a position otherwise reserved for the kings of Israel. Ezekiel 17.13, 19 make it the most probable assumption that the broken oaths mean primarily Zedekiah's oath of allegiance (cf. above, pp. 201f.). But the fact that oaths are referred to in the plural reminds us that Judahite diplomacy also sat lightly to its sworn obligations elsewhere. So a heathen is entrusted with the office of acting as prosecutor against God's people, and consequently of executing punishment on behalf of God.

But in order to silence all objections to the righteous judgment of God now about to be put into effect, the prophet goes still further. **[24]** He goes on in the following verse to say that there is no need for any heathen prosecutor to remind God that the condemnation is overdue. The men of Israel do nothing but call attention to their perjury, so that the sinfulness of their actions is clearly shown up, and thus serve as their own accusers. To describe the glib self-justification of his people as unmistakable self-accusation, which supports instead of refuting all their foreign accusers, is evident irony.

The curse against Zedekiah: 21.25–27

The king is the person chiefly responsible for the unteachableness of

[1] So Reventlow, 'Das Amt des Mazkir', *ThZ* 15 (1959), pp. 161–175.

the nation, and he gives strength to their unrepentant self-confidence even at this time when ruin is breaking in. It is usually said that the king can do no wrong, but he has annulled this by his wickedness, and profaned his sacred office. [25] So the curse is aimed directly at him, Israel's prince, and addressed to him with ruthless vehemence. There is no suggestion of any loss of rank in his not being given the title of king. In Ezekiel the title of king in the full sense is reserved for the great king, and all lesser rulers have to be satisfied with being entitled princes (Jehoiachin receives exceptional treatment in two passages: 1.2 and 17.12, evidently in order to assert the legitimacy of his claim). So when Zedekiah is addressed as 'prince of Israel' (v. 25) we have a strong assertion of the dignity of his position as the representative of the people of God, with a wider connotation than that of king of Judah, being associated with the part played by the whole nation in God's plan of salvation. The dignity of which he has proved unworthy serves to add weight to every blow. [26] His degradation and downfall are declared to him by loud disconnected exclamations or brief sharp commands. The turban, described by a word which elsewhere denotes the headgear of the high priest, evidently formed part of the royal apparel before it was claimed by the high priests in the post-exilic period, and the diadem, worked in precious metal, are torn off his head (cf. Jer. 13.18). He is thus completely despoiled of his dignity and royalty and cast off his throne. But this serves only as the introduction to a much more widespread tornado of destruction, which completely overthrows all respect for rank and breaks down all hitherto existent order. This is what is meant by high and low changing places with one another. It is preposterous to take this as a limitation of the execution of judgment upon Israel to the heights of Zedekiah's kingship and the lowliness of the exiles. It is much more probable that the same line is being taken as we find in the description of the day of Yahweh in Isa. 2.12ff., where the overthrow of the enemies of God among his own people seems to be closely associated with the humbling of all human pride and loftiness throughout the whole world.

[27] One must also refrain from trying to associate the first phrase of v. 27 with the destruction of Jerusalem. The allusion to that in v. 22 is too far away to be caught up again by a single pronoun. Besides, the context demands that not only the capital of Judah but the whole world, shall be reduced to ruins. Chaos is to break in once more, as Jeremiah saw in a powerful vision (Jer. 4.23–26), and as Zephaniah

also suggests (Zeph. 1.3, 14ff.). This does not contradict the hope that
new life will spring out of the ruins. It gives the character of a new
creation to the hoped-for salvation, and makes the prophet's eye see a
wide and all-embracing vision as it looks up to God. The threefold
repetition of the curse and the compulsion exercised by the magical
formula follow a line very similar to the magical curse called up by
the sword-song. By imitating such magical methods the prophet's
word has been swept into the sphere of the demonic and the uncanny,
the characteristics of which are at times akin to the operations of the
wrath of Yahweh.

Only after having reached this point can we understand the remarkable expression of the final guilt and the final punishment (the
Hebrew word ʿawōn can signify both), the time for which has come
on the day when the prince of Israel is judged. No one who gives its
full unadulterated meaning to the complete dissolution of all earthly
order, and connects it with the gruesome song of the breaking in of
the end in ch. 7, can evade the eschatological significance of the term.
One must, of course, admit the correctness of the assertion that this is
not a lecture that lays down a 'philosophical doctrine of the discontinuity of time'. Yet one must still hold firmly to the affirmation
that the final settlement of accounts which coincides with the day
when Zedekiah is judged does mark, materially speaking, the end of
the present historical phase, and say that it has run its course, and that
humanly speaking no fresh beginning is possible. Though the prophets,
including, as we shall see, Ezekiel, nevertheless see a new world
emerge, brought into being as the result of Yahweh's life-giving word,
it is not to be regarded as the further projection of a continuity inherent in the course of history as such; rather, it is one of the ever-
unpredictable miracles of God, whose power and faithfulness will
make possible the impossible. Access to this new dimension of divine
action is found only by the admission of the justice of what the holiness of God has decided, and by complete disillusionment in face of
all human panaceas and offers of salvation.

One may well question whether the final words of the threat have
brought us to the point where that divine hope begins to break
through the clouds of human despair. Up to now exegetes have pronounced themselves almost unanimously in favour of such an interpretation, irrespective of whether they see in it only a partial restoration of Judah with a covert reference to Jehoiachin, or whether they
point to Gen. 49.10 as indicating an actual messianic promise. Many

modern commentators, however, have rejected this interpretation and find here a direct prolongation of the threat. But to translate it 'There shall thus be an end to the time, for he is coming to whom judgment belongs and I hand it over to him' (Zimmerli) is still unconvincing, although grammatically possible. After the exhaustive account of the annihilation produced by the judgment Yahweh has executed, there is no room left for expecting any reference to the human executant of that judgment, who will come as an unnecessary embellishment, like a guest arriving too late for a feast. Auvray's rendering seems infinitely more apt: '(*Voilà ce que j'en ferai*) *comme il n'y en eut jamais de pareille avant que ne vienne celui à qui appartient le jugement auquel je le livrerai.*'[1]

Here the recollection of earlier and less severe judgments serves as a material and temporal motive for mentioning one whom Yahweh now commissions to be an executant of judgment. The only thing difficult to understand is why these mysterious circumlocutions should be employed in regard to the instrument that will execute God's work, seeing that this instrument has been already named and dealt with at full length. And in order to establish the unprecedented severity of the approaching execution of judgment it is impossible not to assert the hideous ruthlessness and severity of the messenger who is to act as its instrument. But in view of the utter uncertainty of how v. 27a ought to be translated, it seems that even this does not supply a satisfactory explanation.

If, however, an objection is made to understanding so controversial a word as *mišpat* as meaning 'a legal right, possessed by anyone', on the not altogether convincing grounds that no other passage is to be found in Ezekiel in which the word is used in this particular sense, then one may reply by asking if it does not refer to God's legal rights, which will be the only ones in force in the new world that will come into being after the judgment has been carried out by the one commissioned by God for the purpose.

This idea is so well known from Isa. 9.7, where the one who ascends the throne of David establishes and upholds his kingdom by justice and righteousness, to Isa. 42.1, where the one who is led by God's spirit will bring forth justice to the nations, that no words need to be wasted in discussing it. But if the coming one is the bringer of God's justice, and commissioned by God to make it effectual, then even the

---

1 '(Here is what I will do) for there has never been anything like it till he comes to whom the judgment belongs to whom I shall commit it.'

most extreme catastrophe and a world reduced to ruins still point
forward to a new establishment of God's order. We are not informed
how this is to be made possible; there is nothing more than a brief
reference which assures us of the objective aimed at by all God's
judgments. But its possibility is implied in the prophecy made in the
old words concerning Judah in Gen. 49.10, the use of which is so
obvious that no one tries to deny it in spite of the enigmatic brevity
of the wording. It has been much too readily assumed, however, that
here the words have been converted into a threat, for both the continued use of the construction with the preposition 'ad 'until', and the
promise it expresses, cannot be turned round and made to mean the
opposite quite as easily as that. What that saying in the blessing of
Jacob stated in its mysterious way is also stated by Ezekiel when he
quotes it once more; it fits in very well with the abruptness of style
employed in the words of a curse and lets it exercise all the momen-
tum, and sets no limit to it save that formed by the establishment of
the Kingdom of God.

CHAPTER 21.28–32

The sword of execution against Ammon

28 And you, son of man, prophesy and say: Thus says [. . .]ᵃ Yahweh
concerning the Ammonites and their reproach [. . .]: ᵇA sword, a sword,
drawn for the slaughter and polished to glitter [. . .]ᶜ ²⁹While they see
for you false visions, while they divine lies for you to lay [it]ᵈ on the neck
of those who are unhallowedᵉ through their wickedness, the sinners the
day of whose final punishment has come. ³⁰Return [it]ᶠ to its sheath! In
the place where you were created, in the land of your origin will I judge
you. ³¹And I will pour out my indignation upon you; I will blow upon
you with the fire of my wrath and deliver you into the hands of brutal
men, who work in the forge of destruction. ³²You shall be fuel for the fire,
your blood shall flow in the midst of the land, and none shall remember
you any more, for I, Yahweh have spoken.ᵍ

ᵃSee BH.
ᵇMT: 'and say'; a repetition of the previous order which breaks the sequence.
ᶜMT has mistaken the meaning of the word *lᵉhāhēl* 'to glitter' because of its rare
occurrence and miswritten it *lᵉhākīl*, while the following gloss *lᵉmaʿan bārāq*
restores the proper meaning (thus van den Born).

d–eSee BH.
fThe word 'it' is necessary to complete the sense.
g21.28–32=Hebrew 21.33–37.

Neither will Ammon escape judgment: 21.28–29

The context is enough to show why Ammon is pursued by the sword of Yahweh's execution. It is to cut off any hopes that survive there that she, the neighbour who has joined with Judah in rebelling against Nebuchadrezzar, may be able to escape the judgment she also deserves by swiftly re-transforming herself into a loyal vassal of Babylon. Even though Babylon made Jerusalem feel her wrath first, she will not forget to deal with Ammon as God has ordained and as rebels deserve.

In spite of this very obvious connection with what has preceded, there are, however, serious objections to this passage being original. For one thing, it undoubtedly did not originate in the same period. The statement about Ammonite reproaches against Jerusalem can only be understood as referring, according to 25.3, 6, to her mockery and sadistic joy at the fall of that city in 587. Yet all the verses immediately preceding this one have to be placed at the very beginning of the catastrophe. That this is a subsequent addition by the prophet himself is quite out of the question. What he really has to say in regard to Ammon is stated in 25.1ff.

In addition, the wording of the whole passage points, not to Ezekiel, but to one of the prophet's disciples. He tries to imitate his master's manner of expression as closely and accurately as he can. But he vouchsafes information which the author of 21.18ff. had refrained from giving. Verse 23 has spoken of a false divination. But v. 29 takes it up again and gives it a totally different sense, as if it referred to lying prophecies, declaring that the war would be a victorious one, which Ammon employed to raise her morale. Again, the Ammonites are said to be laden with guilt, and the same expression is used as is applied to the prince of Israel in v. 25. But the expression coined to suit the particular form taken by his transgression is not properly transferable to other enemies of God. Finally, the use of the second person feminine, evidently in order to address both city and people at once, leads only too easily to a disastrous confusion between it and the sword which is also addressed, although one can hardly suppose that false prophecies were addressed to it. So one cannot claim that the form given to the whole composition has been particularly successful.

The human executant of the judgment called to account: 21.30–32

Among these verses, the first three words of v. 30 form the real
stumbling-block, which makes it difficult to interpret them. Read in
immediate association with what has just preceded, a command to
sheathe the sword can only mean that the judgment by the sword of
Babylon is to come to an end. That again means that the further
judgment announced must be one against the Babylonian who carries
that sword. He is informed, as Isaiah informed the Assyrian, the rod
of God's wrath in his day, without any details of why he has deserved
it, that he is to be annihilated by fire and by violent and brutal men,
God's instruments. The artificial way in which the sword here takes
the place of the one who bears it, so that the land of its origin is
addressed (completely abandoning the mythical notion of its being
the avenging sword of Yahweh) and told that it will be blown upon
by the fire of wrath and delivered into the hands of brutal men, all of
which does not fit in with what is said in v. 32, has understandably
made its explanation of the passage doubtful. Some therefore prefer
to try to preserve the unity of vv. 28–32. They regard the sword in v.
28 as the sword of the Ammonites, who had hoped to set it at the
throats of the guilt-laden men of Judah. Now they have had to
sheathe it at the word of divine power in v. 30. So now instead they
are to experience the ruthless force of divine retribution in their own
country. But after what has been said in the introduction in v. 28 this
interpretation is totally unexpected. It makes the word-for-word
repetition of what has been said of the sword of God sink to an extraordinary bathos when applied to a thing as paltry as the sword of
Ammon. Nor does it seem to find any support in what history records
of the conduct of the Ammonites.

Others therefore prefer to maintain the unity of the passage by
rejecting the first three words of v. 30, and claiming that the text is so
corrupted that it cannot be made to supply a correct reading. Then
v. 30 can go straight ahead to accentuate the judgment with which the
Ammonites are threatened into a complete uprooting which leaves
them no further hope. The reference to the place in which the nation
was first created is meant in this case to show how the destruction
comes as a result of the way in which they have misused the grace of
the Creator.

What makes one feel suspicious of such an interpretation is the
way in which words in themselves intelligible are deleted on the plea

that the text is corrupt, in order to make the explanation run smoothly. One must prefer to follow Bewer and van den Born, who think words originally directed against Babylon have been elaborated at a later period. Originally they stated no more than that the judgment of God would be concluded by the punishment of that nation's insatiable lust for conquest, and then use was made of the hope of retribution directed against Ammon.

There is no way of securing any greater certainty than this as to which of these suggestions is preferable. Nevertheless, each in its particular way confirms how intensively the text of Ezekiel has undergone reworking by his disciples. We have already met numerous examples of it.

CHAPTER 22.1-16

The blood-guilty city

1 And the word of Yahweh came to me saying, 2'And you, son of man, will you not judge, will you not judge the blood-guilty city? Then declare to her all her abominable deeds 3and say: Thus says [. . .]ᵃ Yahweh: You are a cityᵇ that sheds blood in the midst of her, that her time may come, and that makes idols for herself, to defile herself. 4You have become guilty by your blood which you have shed, and have defiled yourself by your idols which you have made. You have brought your [judgment-] days near and the conclusion of your years has come. Therefore I make you a reproach to the nations and a mocking to all the countries. 5Those who are near to you and those who are far from you will mock you, you whose reputation is spotted and whose destruction is mighty.

6 Behold, the princes of Israel within you boast each one of them of his power to shed blood. 7Father and mother are treated with contempt in you, the sojourner suffers violence in you, the fatherless and widows are wronged in you. 8[. . .]ᶜ 9There are men in you who slander in order to shed blood, and men in you who hold sacrificial meals on the mountains, men commit lewdness in your midst. 10In you men uncover their fathers' nakedness [i.e. stepmothers], they humble women who are unclean in their impurity. 11One commits abomination with his neighbour's wife, another lewdly defiles his daughter-in-law; another in you defiles his sister, his father's daughter [i.e. stepsister]. 12In you men take bribes to shed blood, men take interest and increase.ᵈ You make gain of your neighbour by extortion, but you have forgotten me, says [. . .]ᵉ Yahweh.

13 Behold, therefore, I strike my hands together^f at the dishonest gain which you have made, and at the bloodshed^g which has been committed in the midst of you. ¹⁴Can your courage endure or your hands be strong, in the days that I shall interfere with you? I, Yahweh, have spoken and I will do it.

15 And I will scatter you among the nations and disperse you through the countries, and I will consume your filthiness out of you. ¹⁶Thus [I will profane myself]^h through you in the sight of the nations [or: you will be profaned by yourself in the eyes of the nations]. Then you shall know that I am Yahweh.'

^aSee BH.

^bThe article denoting the vocative has been lost by haplography, and must be restored to the MT, which has no article.

^cVerse 8: 'You have despised my sanctuaries and profaned my sabbaths.' The sudden shift into the second singular feminine and the insertion of such purely ritual matters among anti-social crimes make the position of the verse doubtful in its context. It must originally have been a marginal gloss to vv. 1–5, where the accusation of idolatry provided a point of connection. Its insertion in the text at the present point is anything but apt.

^{d–e}See BH.

^fLXX reads: 'Behold, I bring down my hand upon all your gain', which Heinisch prefers. But it is better to read *hikkētī bᵉqappāy*, with 6.11.

^{g–h}See BH.

The final judgment is determined: 22.1–5

This passage displays the extreme severity which has increased since 20.45. It announces that the catastrophe cannot be postponed any longer, but is on the point of breaking out. It does so by at last addressing a statement of final guilt and final punishment to the city whose faith, exaggerated into fanaticism, has asserted its own holiness and inviolability in the face of all threats. **[2]** As in 20.2, Ezekiel is ordered by God to be his mouthpiece, proclaiming the divine decision to punish her, with which the heavenly judge concludes his indictment against his chosen but now guilty city. The very name he employs brings an overwhelming charge against the city. Isaiah had already given up the honourable names 'faithful city, city of righteousness', replacing them by the shameful names 'harlot, refuge of murderers' (Isa. 1.21). Ezekiel calls Jerusalem 'the blood-guilty city', where wickedness is unforgiven and cries for vengeance. He thus equates her with Nineveh, that whore and lion's den, that centre of heathen abomination which Nahum had cursed with such similar epithets (Nahum 3.1). **[3]** He, too, sums up her hostility to God under the two fundamental sins of bloodshed and idolatry. Moral and cultic sins are thus linked together as indissolubly associated expressions of hostility to God, as the prophet had already demonstrated before (cf., e.g., 8.16f.). The prophet regards the law of God as a single integral whole. So he sees both the contempt for the ordering of the sanctuary and the ruthless denial of a neighbour's right to live as things which break up any relationship with God. The alienation from God which becomes visible in the former, of necessity leads on to the latter and weighs a man down with deadly guilt.

[4] The expressions 'made yourself guilty', 'defiled yourself' in v. 4 seem still to suggest that the law-breaker ensnares himself in an accursed world with laws which exercise their effects automatically. Yet all suggestions of any mere mechanism or determinism are transcended by the sharp opposition between the human and divine egos.[1] The people of Jerusalem have not more·or less unconsciously fallen into the net which now tightens around them. They have made a fully personal decision, and thus brought upon themselves the judgment day which will bring their life to its inevitable end. [5] Their God thus in person punishes them (v. 4c), by putting an end to their privileged position among the nations of which they were so proud, and replacing their good name by reproach and mockery, which make absurd all Israel's claim to greatness. Israel has herself profaned her own name, the name of the people of God, and by a ruin of overwhelming magnitude has given an evil meaning to the greatness of which she so arrogantly boasts. So Ezekiel ironically converts the word into its opposite (*rabbat m^{e}hūmā*, 'that which is great through destruction').

The open contempt shown for God's ordinances: 22.6–16

After the terse announcement of the final condemnation, answering to the magnitude of the sin, the following verses give a detailed statement of the crime, like a public prosecutor building up his case in court. They give such a black picture of conditions in Jerusalem, that doubts have been expressed as to the correctness of the details.

It is suggested that the statement applies a formal scheme to the many-faceted reality to be found in the capital. It may be conceded that the way in which the trespasses are enumerated is undoubtedly

---

[1] Cf. W. Eichrodt, *Theology of the Old Testament*, I, 1961, pp. 158f., 162f., II, 1967, pp. 413ff.

specially influenced by the legal style of the law of holiness in Lev.
18–20. That is not surprising in view of the prophet's priestly origin.
But the references are not schematic enough to force one to conclude
that someone living in a foreign land has simply expressed the abandoned state of the metropolis without knowledge of its details, using
legal phraseology in order to express its transgression against God's
ordinances. The enumeration does not follow any rigid order. It proceeds from deeds of violence (vv. 6f., 9) to sins of actual unchastity
(vv. 10f.), and concludes with avarice and lust for gain (v. 12).
[6f.] So there are three main headings, in all of which we see a
shocking disregard for solidarity with one's fellow countrymen. The
way in which the princes of Israel are mentioned first, as those
specially entrusted with the enforcing of the law who have yet given
the lead in breaking it, serves to bring out the special responsibility
of the court. There is an abrupt break in the context which affects
both form and matter, by the sudden charge of profaning the temple
and the sabbath. It seems to be a marginal note which has been
taken into the text (see the presentation of the text).

[9] The only ritual charge, in regard to the offering of sacrifices in
high places (v. 9b), represents a breach of the unity of the congregation guaranteed by the temple, and thus is closely related to the
other accusations. The guilty individuals are not, of course, named
nor are the concrete offences against the land given in detail as in
Jer. 34.8ff. or 22.13ff.; yet the relationship between them and the
charges brought by Jeremiah is evident. When one compares them
with the accusations in Micah 6 and 7 which are usually ascribed to
the time of Manasseh, then it seems most improbable that the royal
court of Judah has grown less degenerate during its last years. The
adoption of legal terminology here, as in other places (cf. 14.4ff.),
serves to assert the standards set by the laws of God, which cannot
lightly be broken, nor can those who break them expect by any cheap
and easy way to get rid of their guilt.

[10–12] Yet all external calculations must in the end point towards the inner alienation from God of which they are a symptom.
So now the impersonal terms are exchanged for a personal appeal to a
city which has forgotten her benefactor (cf. ch. 16) and her obligation to have personal fellowship with him. It is worth noting that
there is only another passage besides this (23.35) in which Ezekiel
adopts an approach especially characteristic of Jeremiah. He
employs this means of expression, otherwise strange to him, to show

how all these people's outward deeds show a perversion of the right relationship to their personal Lord, who in all his commandments has wanted the direct presence of his will to save and to bless them to be made known. If men forget him, instead of remembering how they obviously encounter him in every decision they make for or against their neighbours, then he must come to his people in the character of a judge, who allows no one to escape from meeting him face to face.

[13f.] God intervenes in order first of all to display the worthlessness of the powerful position the men of Jerusalem believe they have attained. The riches and the position of security and predominance, which they think they have gained by impenitently despoiling or selfishly ignoring their neighbours, have no subsistence. God himself now does what he had made the prophet do at his command (cf. 6.11 and 21.14); he claps his hands, making the dishonest gain that had been expected disappear in a second (cf. for this interpretation of the clapping of the hands the details given on p. 96 above and the similar effect of blowing in Hag. 1.9). What will then become of their courage and strength in action which they thought[1] would stand up to every danger, and enable them even to face the days of God's judgment? The section closes, like 17.24, with the remark that Yahweh's announcement of judgment is by no means empty, but inexorably brings its realization with it (cf. 12.25, 28).

[15f.] The next two verses do no more than draw out the further consequences. So they may be a later elaboration of what is already an impressive conclusion, intended to show how the days of judgment are to find their fulfilment. Israel's dispersal among the nations makes her cease to exist as a nation, and thus eradicates the uncleanness she has brought upon herself by all the wickedness of her nationalistic self-assertion. Admittedly this will also involve the profanation of her God before the nations, a thing which God's actions have hitherto striven to guard against (cf. 20.9, 14, 22). But now he will allow himself to be shamed in this way, in order once for all to put an end to the misuse of his name for the purpose of Israel's self-

[1]This internal connection between vv. 13 and 14 is destroyed by the usual explanation of hand-clapping as signifying sadistic pleasure. It is also striking how the judge in v. 13 switches over from accusation to action with 'behold', announcing a striking and unexpected action, in place of the 'therefore' usual in threats. These points, to which van den Born has rightly called our attention, are thus made much more intelligible.

glorification, and in order to bring his people to know the holiness of his being by this act of self-sacrifice.

One must acknowledge that Ezekiel's disciples, when they gave such an interpretation to the exile of Israel, showed a profound understanding of their master. Israel had hitherto closed her eyes to the way God's name was being profaned among his own people. There was no other way of making her realize the wickedness of it except for the Divine Being to be put to shame before the heathen. The way in which this shameful reproach reacts upon his people, destroying all their ambitious hopes of primacy over the whole human race, will reveal to them all the seriousness of God's 'No' to the way they have hitherto followed. At the same time it will also give them a glimpse of how ready God is to wait in hope in spite of insults and misunderstandings, and thus show them his superhuman faithfulness.

CHAPTER 22.17–22

The smelting furnace of wrath

17 And the word of Yahweh came to me: 18'Son of man, behold,ᵃ the house of Israel has become dross to me. All of them are copper and tin and iron and lead in the furnace. They have become [. . .]ᵇ dross. 19Therefore thus says [. . .]ᶜ Yahweh: Because you have all become dross, therefore I will gather you together to Jerusalem. 20As men gather silver and copper and iron and lead and tin into a furnace, to blow the fire upon it in order to melt it, so I will gather you in my wrath [. . .]ᵈ and will put you in to be melted, 21[. . .]ᵉ and will blow upon you with the fire of my wrath, that you may be melted in the midst of it. 22As silver is melted in a furnace, so you shall be melted in the midst of it, and you shall know that I, Yahweh, have poured out my wrath upon you.'

ᵃInserted, with LXX.
ᵇMT adds 'silver', but this is inexplicable as the wording now stands.
ᶜSee BH.
ᵈMT: 'and in my rage', a redundancy not found in LXX.
ᵉ'And I will gather you': to judge by what has preceded, this is a superfluous repetition and contains an expression not elsewhere usual to Ezekiel.

What Israel is like in God's eyes: 22.17–18

The prophet receives a special communication from his God,

revealing to him what his people is really made of. **[18]** They, the men of the house of Israel (notice once again the use of the honorific title of the people of God, here employed for Judah so as to bring fully to light both its noble destiny and its utter apostasy), have become dross in God's eyes. Dross can be used not only for the base metal produced in smelting silver and thrown away after the process is completed but also of litharge, the silver in which has to be extracted by a further process of smelting. In Isa. 1.21 ('Your silver has become dross') this second meaning seems to be present, since the silver is afterwards extracted from the lead and alloy by a process of smelting (Isa. 1.25). Here, on the other hand, the first meaning is the only admissible one; otherwise the mention of four metals not including silver in v. 18 is unintelligible. That is, provided that one does not accept the insertion of silver among the other metals, as is so often suggested, but regards it as an improper interference with the text. The people of God, who ought to shine like a precious metal among other nations, have been revealed by the smelting furnace as base metal, fit only to be rejected. Such is the verdict Yahweh has pronounced in regard to his people. This verdict, however, leads to further proceedings which the people must undergo and which the prophet feels it necessary to announce.

In God's smelting furnace: 22.19–22

Yahweh heaps up the dross and kindles the fire of the smelting furnace under it. It is clear that Ezekiel is recalling the words of Isaiah, who was the first to describe the Lord God as the smelter and his judgment as a smelting furnace (Isa. 1.21ff.). But he described an intelligible process which eventually purified the silver and separated it from the dross, whereas Ezekiel has no hope of any such result. Jeremiah, who knew himself to have been commissioned to exercise the function of a smelter, had already described his work of smelting as useless, saying that it was impossible to separate the silver from the dross, in order to justify God's rejection. Ezekiel states the same idea in still more radical terms by not only saying that those of the house of Israel are all useless dross, but giving it as a statement made by God himself. If, in spite of this, they are still thrown into God's smelting furnace to be melted down like silver, nothing of any value can come out. Rather, the process demonstrates the complete uselessness of the metal, and entirely justifies God's rejection of it.

At this point one can describe Ezekiel's vision of Yahweh, the smelter, as the most extreme and most radical condemnation possible of the people of God. We do not see here (as Zimmerli suggests) a mere unconscious lack of logic, but a deliberate assertion of the meaninglessness of the whole process of smelting. All thoughts of the possibility of a successful result are thus excluded beforehand. There is no single ray of hope to ease the torment of the blazing fires of divine wrath and retribution.

Viewed as an act of judgment by God, the siege of Jerusalem shows what a merciless final reckoning is in store for a faithless nation. Yahweh gathers up all the dross left by his previous attempts at smelting, forms them into the great smelting furnace of Jerusalem, and stirs up a huge fire underneath, but it is nothing more than a bonfire lit by the blaze of his rage, which will put an end to the con- tinuous contempt for his holiness. The peasant population rush into Jerusalem, seeking refuge within the city walls from the advancing detachments of Babylonians, and this is described in a horrific way as part of the preparations for the act of judgment with which the judge inaugurates his work. This statement shows that we are in the period just before the siege of the capital city began. There is nothing, however, to suggest that the passage was composed in Jerusalem (Herntrich, Bertholet). The contrary is revealed by the way in which both city and province are joined together under the term 'house of Israel' (Zimmerli).

An attempt has been made to bring one ray of light into the black hopeless despair of this prophecy. It is claimed that, as in Isaiah, dross means litharge, which contains some silver, in the hope of showing that God's smelting will separate silver from the lead and thus in the end produce something of value, though of course it is not Israel but the Gentile nations which emerge purified from God's judgment (Fohrer). This is effected by deleting *kūr sigim* in v. 18, so that we find the base metals lying 'in the midst of the silver'. But this assumption is based on a very questionable text, and such an opinion on the subject of the Gentile nations is completely isolated in the book of Ezekiel. This is enough to warn us against an interpretation of the act of smelting as he describes it, since it cannot be read out of it, but has to be read into it. It will further be shown, when we deal with 24.3–14, that there is testimony, with different imagery, of the same estimate of the results of the judgment as that characterizing this passage.

CHAPTER 22.23–31

A general description of the corruption prevailing among the whole people

23 *And the word of Yahweh came to me:* [24]*'Son of man, say to her, you are a land that was not rained upon*[a] *or watered in the day of indignation,* [25]*whose princes*[b] *in the midst of her were like roaring lions, tearing the prey; they devoured human lives, they took treasure and precious things, they made many widows in the midst of her.* [26]*Her priests did violence to my instructions and profaned my holy things; they made no distinction between the holy and the common, neither did they teach the difference between the unclean and the clean, and they disregarded my sabbaths, so that I was profaned among them.* [27]*Her men of rank in the midst of her were like wolves tearing the prey, shedding blood, destroying men's lives to get dishonest gain.* [28]*And her prophets daubed them with whitewash, seeing false visions and divining lies for them, saying: "Thus says [. . .]*[c] *Yahweh," when Yahweh had not spoken.* [29]*The citizens of the country committed violence and practised robbery and oppressed the poor and needy and treated*[d] *the sojourner in a way that is against every law.* [30]*And I sought for a man among them who should build up the wall and stand in the breach before me for the land, that I should not give it over to destruction, but I found none.* [31]*Therefore I poured out my indignation upon them, I consumed them in the fire of my wrath, their way did I requite upon their heads, says [. . .]*[e] *Yahweh.'*

[a]–[e]See BH.

The land has been withered and turned into a wilderness by the wrath of God. So now the inhabitants, whose sins have caused its plight, are summoned to appear before it. They are arranged in ranks and classes and called up in turn to be denounced for their shameless breaking of God's law. Princes, priests, nobles, prophets and citizens of the land all form one body, arranged in order of precedence, without being divided into the ecclesiastical and secular orders as in Zephaniah (3.3f.). Moral and social offences are strongly emphasized and brought to the fore. Even the priests are said to have done violence to God's instruction, having twisted the laws of the nation to win advantage for themselves. They have incurred this guilt in order to gain the favour of the upper classes in the decisions made by them as experts in difficult points of law. The transgression of the sabbath is introduced only as one example of the general disregard they show for their second main set of duties. This consists in the office of watching over the clean and unclean, so as not to let the holy shrine of the people of God suffer profanation by the irruption of heathen uncleanness. This passage shows no awareness of any such central importance of the sabbath as is asserted in ch. 20.

Zimmerli has aptly summed up the literary character of this passage by calling it 'A sermon on (the duties of each) rank', a theme we can show gradually expanding and developing in Micah 3.11, Jer. 5.31 and Zeph. 3.1–5. This passage is particularly closely related in language and material to the last of these, and the final sentence pronounced in v. 31 is close to Zeph. 3.8. Such a type of structure following lines provided by tradition is not unusual in Ezekiel. But here to a large extent earlier formulations of the prophet's message are employed, especially from ch. 13 and 18, and some of them sound like direct citations, which is unusual.

Elsewhere a sermon on ranks and duties serves to announce a judgment to come. Here, however, it gives reasons for a judgment already accomplished, asserting its justice, and warning men to take to heart the history of their past sin and to abstain from offending in the future. Passionate accusations made by Ezekiel when he was giving warning of coming disaster are now repeated in a calm didactic tone. This and other peculiarities all help to increase the impression that in this passage it is not the prophet himself but one of his disciples who is speaking. He faithfully makes use of his master's message and of the whole prophetic tradition in order to hold up the mirror reflecting the conduct of the whole nation, and to counter every attempt to transfer the guilt for the present catastrophe to others' shoulders, in order to avoid all accusations.

Such self-justification can be observed in the book of Lamentations (Lam. 1.2, 19; 2.14; 4.13; 5.7). But the only effect it can have is to hinder all classes of the nation from receiving a healthy saving shock to their complacency, and thus it must suppress any hopes of a change for the better. So it is no wonder that Ezekiel's disciples felt it necessary to make present to men the dark picture of their guilty past. They thus made it impossible to brush aside or forget unpleasant memories, and worked on lines calculated to prepare them first to face the fundamental problem of their own sin, and then to achieve an inner transformation so as to deal with the problems resulting from it in their present life.

CHAPTER 23.1–49

The parable of Oholah and Oholibah

1 The word of Yahweh came to me: 2"There were two women, the daughters of one mother. 3They played the harlot in Egypt; there their breasts were pressed, and their virgin bosoms handled.ª 4Oholah was the name of the elder, and Oholibah the name of her sister. They became mine, and they bore sons and daughters [. . .].ᵇ 5Oholah played the harlot, though she was still under my control, and she doted on her lovers, the Assyrians,ᶜ warriors 6clothed in purple, governors and commanders, all of them desirable young men, horsemen riding on horses. 7And she set her desire upon them like a harlot, all of them the choicest men of Assyria, and she defiled herself with all the idols of everyone upon whom she doted. 8But neither did she give up her harlotry which she had practised since her days in Egypt, for in her youth men had lain with her and handled her virgin bosom and poured out their lust upon her. 9Therefore I delivered her into the hands of her lovers, the Assyrians, upon whom she doted; 10they uncovered her nakedness, they seized her sons and daughters, and her they slew with the sword. So she became a bywordᵈ among women, when they had thus executed judgmentᵉ upon her.

11 Her sister Oholibah saw this, yet she was more corrupt than she in her doting and in her harlotry, which was worse than that of her sister. 12She doted upon the Assyrians, governors and commanders, warriors clothed in purple,ᶠ horsemen riding on horses, all of them desirable young men! 13And I saw that she was defiled, they both took the same way. 14But she carried her harlotry further; she saw men portrayed upon the wall,ᵍ the images of the Chaldaeans, portrayed in red lead, 15girded with belts on their loins, with flowing turbans on their heads. All of them looked like officers, in appearance like the Babylonians, whose native land is Chaldaea. 16When she saw them she dotedʰ upon them, and sent messengers to them in Chaldaea. 17And the Babylonians came to her into the bed of love and defiled her with their lust, so that she was polluted by them. Then she turned from them in disgust. 18When she carried on her harlotry so openly and flaunted her nakedness, I turned in disgust from her, as I had turned from her sister.

19 Yet she increased her harlotry, remembering the days of her youth, when she played the harlot in the land of Egypt, 20and dotedⁱ upon her paramours there,ʲ whose members were like those of asses and whose issue was like that of horses. 21[. . .].ᵏ

22 Therefore, O Oholibah, thus says [. . .] Yahweh:[1] Behold, I will
rouse against you your lovers from whom you turned in disgust, and I will
bring them against your from every side, 23the Babylonians and all the
Chaldeans, Pekod, Shoa and Koa [. . .]m with them, desirable persons,
governors and commanders all of them, officers and [warriors],n all of
them riding on horses. 24And they shall come against you [from the
north]o with chariots and wheels and a host of peoples; they shall set
against you buckler and shield and [helmet].p And I will commit the
judgment to them, that they may judge you according to their statutes.
25And I will direct my indignation against you, that they may deal with
you in fury. They shall cut off your nose and your ears [. . .],q they shall
lead away your sons and your daughters, and your survivors shall be
devoured by fire. 26They shall also strip you of your clothes, and take away
your fine jewels. 27Thus I will put an end to your lewdness and your
harlotry brought from the land of Egypt, so that you shall not lift up your
eyes to the Egyptians or remember them any more.

28 *For thus says [. . .]r Yahweh: Behold, I deliver you into the hands of those
whom you hate and from whom you turned in disgust. 29And they shall deal with
you in hatred and take away all you possess and leave you naked and bare, so that the
shame of your harlotry may be uncovered. Your lewdness and your harlotry 30have
[brought this upon you]s because you played the harlot with the nations, and polluted
yourself with their idols.*

31 You have gone the way of your sister, therefore I give her cup into
your hand.

32 Thus says [. . .]t Yahweh: You shall drink your sister's cup, which
is deep and large, [. . .]u which contains much.v

33 [It is filled with stumbling and sorrow];w a cup of horror and desolation is the cup of your sister [. . .]x

34 You shall drink it and drain it and [empty its dregs]y and tear your
breasts.

For I have spoken, says [. . .]z Yahweh.

35 *Therefore thus says [. . .]aa Yahweh: Because you have forgotten me and
cast me behind your back, therefore bear now the consequences of your lewdness and
harlotry [cf. v. 29 conclusion].'*

36 *And Yahweh said to me: 'Son of man, will you judge, yea judge [cf. 22.1],
Oholah and Oholibah? Then declare to them all their abominable deeds! 37For they
have committed adultery, and blood is upon their hands; with their idols they have
committed adultery; and they have offered up to them to be eaten by fire the sons whom
they had borne to me. 38Moreover, this they have done to me: they have defiled my
sanctuary on the same day and profaned my sabbaths. 39For when they had slaughtered
their children in sacrifice to their idols, on the same day they came into my sanctuary
to profane it. And lo this is what they did in my house.*

40 *They even sent for men to come from far, to whom a messenger had to be sent,*

and lo they came. For them you bathed yourself, painted your eyes and decked your-
self with ornaments. ⁴¹*And you sat upon a broad couch, with a table spread before it*
on which you placed my incense and my oil. ⁴²*And there was a loud tumult* [or: *and*
they sang with loud voices] [. . .] *because of the multitude that had come* [. . .]
and they [apparently the guests] *put bracelets upon the arms of the women* [the
sisters] *and beautiful crowns upon their heads.*ᵇᵇ ⁴³[. . .]ᶜᶜ ⁴⁴*And they went in to*
*her*ᵈᵈ *as men go into harlots, so they went in to Oholah and Oholibah, those lewd*
women. ⁴⁵*But righteous men shall pass judgment on them with the sentence of*
adulteresses and murderesses; because they have committed adultery, and blood is
upon their hands.

46 *For thus says* [. . .]ᵉᵉ *Yahweh: Bring up a host against them,*ᶠᶠ *and make*
them an object of terror and a spoil. ⁴⁷*And the host shall stone them and cut* [them]ᵍᵍ
to pieces with their swords. They shall slay their sons and daughters, and burn up
their houses. ⁴⁸*Thus will I put an end to lewdness in the land, that all women may*
take warning and not commit lewdness as they have done. ⁴⁹*Your lewdness shall be*
requited upon you, and you shall bear the penalty for your sinful idolatry, for I am
[. . .]ʰʰ *Yahweh.'*

ᵃMT: 'they pressed', point *pual* perfect third person plural.

ᵇMT: 'As for their names, Oholah is Samaria and Oholibah Jerusalem';
anticipating the interpretation, as later insertions usually do elsewhere.

ᶜThis also ought probably to be deleted as a premature anticipation of the
interpretation.

ᵈThere is no need for any change in the text; *šēm* = 'fame' here has a derogatory sense.

ᵉ⁻ᶠSee BH. For *kerōbîm* cf. note ᵐ.

ᵍCf. 8.10.

ʰ⁻ⁱSee BH.

ʲMT has a word elsewhere used for concubines, which must have a masculine
meaning here. Perhaps the text is corrupt. L. Köhler suggests the word Philistines
which has similar consonants; but the reference to the Philistines in 16.27 is totally
different in character. To interpret it as signifying a political association gives rise
to difficulties, cf. the commentary.

ᵏMT, v. 21: 'Thus you longed for the lewdness of your youth, when the
[Egyptians] (see BH) [handled] (see BH) your breasts, to press your youthful
bosom'; the use of the second person shows it to be an addition.

ˡSee BH.

ᵐMT: 'all Assyrians', here mistakenly added because of attributes previously
given to the Assyrians (cf. vv. 5f.). Also, a reference to them does not fit in with the
historical interpretation. *kerōbîm* here derives from *kerāb*, battle: warriors.

ⁿMT: 'and called', evidently needing to be emended to make it agree with the
stereotyped wording of previous lists. Cf. note ᵐ.

ᵒThe above reading following LXX is probably preferable to the uncertain
word of the MT.

ᵖSee BH.

ᵠMT: 'And what is left over of you (posterity?) shall fall by the sword': the

same word *'ḥarīt* is used with two different meanings in the same verse (first
'posterity', then 'survivors'), so one clause must give place. It is preferable to
delete the first, as it conflicts with what is said immediately afterwards of the
seizure of the sons and daughters.

r-tSee BH.

uMT: 'She will become a laughing-stock and derision' can be recognized for a
gloss because of the way it interrupts the sentence.

v-wSee BH.

xMT: 'Samaria'; a correct explanation, but it does not fit in here.

y-aaSee BH.

bbThe text has been so disrupted that only some portions of it can be made to fit
in with the context and give an intelligible meaning. See the commentaries for the
various emendations which have been proposed.

ccUntranslatable.

ddA remarkable instance of the use of the singular as in v. 41. Instead of
simplifying it, one must let the irregularity stand, and account for it by assuming
that different versions of the story have here been put together.

ee-hhSee BH.

The sins and punishment of the two sisters: 23.1–27

The prehistory: 23.1–4

In contrast to the closely related passage about the unfaithful wife in
ch. 16, the story which begins here is first communicated to the
prophet in a private conversation with Yahweh, without any order to
preach it. The striking feature here is that there is no attempt to tell
the story at full length or to go into much vivid detail. So there are
only a few brief phrases to give the bare essentials of the previous
history of the two main characters who are to be brought on the stage.
[2–4] Two sisters with unusual names who spent their youth as harlots in Egypt become brides of Yahweh and have sons and daughters
from that marriage. It is a manifestation quite unique in Old Testament literature. In view of the way in which sex-life is elsewhere
completely excluded from the divine realm, it is monstrous to find it
here stated bluntly how God contracted a marriage with a pair of
harlots. Where or how the wedding was celebrated, what were the
objects of the husband, what form his relationship took towards the
wives, these questions and others like them are left without an answer.
One can see from the very beginning that the narrative in which this
is clothed has no importance whatsoever; this is no parable story
full of charm and poetic beauty, like ch. 16, 17 and 19. It is an allegory, which gives no more than the bare essentials, and applies only a
few stereotyped pictorial images to bring out the point as clearly and

unmistakably as possible. The images which it employs have no life of their own; their only purpose is to reproduce in quite coarse terms the unspeakable event they convey. This renunciation of all attempts to impart any artistic adornment to the parable can, of course, only result in a completely matter-of-fact and soberly plain and realistic narrative. To criticize it for its flatness, colourlessness, prosaic frigidity, or unpoetic repetitiveness shows a complete failure to understand its nature.

Yet this also implies that what is said of the marriage between Yahweh and the two sisters cannot be made into a wild fantastic tale of sexual connections contracted by the divinity like those described in the ancient myths of the gods. The allegorical application to Yahweh's relationship to Israel, in the form it took in the two partitioned kingdoms, is so obvious from the first and so free from any mystical background that it is possible to mention how sons and daughters sprang from this marriage without feeling for one moment that this involves any essential resemblance to a nature-myth.

We have already spoken (cf. above, pp. 211f.) of how the image of marriage was applied to Israel's relationship with her God, and of the tension between it and the general character of Yahwism, whose conception of God left no room for sexuality. Ezekiel employs it here for the additional purpose of showing in a glaring light the full horror of his people's disloyalty. His treatment is quite different from ch. 16, since he confines the loving way in which Yahweh shows himself to his people to a few words about marriage, and puts all the emphasis upon the degenerate inward nature of the people who have been so highly favoured. The inclusion of both partitioned kingdoms in the married life is, strictly speaking, inconsistent with the references to the sojourn in Egypt. It has evidently been brought in, following the model given by Jeremiah (3.6–11), in order still more to humble Jerusalemite arrogance. Jeremiah was content to describe the two sisters by the epithets of 'that faithless one' and 'her false sister', but Ezekiel goes so far as to give them definite names. As his allegory is so little concerned to present a narrative, we need not expect the constituents of the names to be based on a model provided by tradition. They are more probably words with a mysterious meaning that is anything but obvious, and words which need not necessarily conform to the prophet's usual vocabulary. It is certain that the word for tent, 'ōhel, is the root word behind both the coinages. Is this intended to recall Israel's nomad period, as other similarly formed

names do (Ex. 31.6; Gen. 36.2, 5, 41, etc.)? Are we therefore to think
of a wandering unsettled population, which finds itself an alien in
Egypt (Zimmerli, van den Born)?

But such an archaeological reminiscence has no point here. It
would fit much better with the aim of the allegory that it should be
connected with the tents on the high places, which would recall the
unchaste rites practised in the Canaanite sanctuaries on high places
(Bertholet, Fohrer). The different way the names are coined would
be no more than to distinguish the two sisters by means of a play
upon the word.

There is, however, no trace in the Old Testament of any notion
that the tent was characteristic of high-place worship. Even Ezek.
16.16 cannot be appealed to in support of any such idea (cf. above,
p. 197). The older interpretation therefore still seems the most satisfactory one. What is in mind here is the sanctuary of Yahweh, for
which the term tent is found in the Pentateuch; indeed, this is a
favourite word among the priests (cf. Ex. 33.7; Num. 11.24; Ex. 27.21;
28.43, etc.). Oholah therefore means '(She who has) her own tent'
and Oholibah 'my tent (is) in her'. The pointing, in which the strong
aspirate marking the feminine suffix is softened down, is not unusual
enough to cause insuperable objections; indeed, it is particularly
likely to occur in feminine personal names. It cannot be maintained
that Ezekiel gives Judah a preferential position he denies it elsewhere. Even where he denounces the way the temple is profaned and
asserts that God himself has taken away its holiness, the original
dignity of the proper sanctuary of Yahweh over against all other
sanctuaries remains unaffected. The hint as to who possesses that
sanctuary is not meant in any way to depreciate the Northern sister-
kingdom, but to stress Judah's responsibilities, and fits in excellently
with the whole context of the allegory.

Seeing therefore that we can point to an explicit didactic tendency
which is the determining factor upon which the whole structure of the
passage is built, it is misleading to appeal to Canaanite mythology in
order to explain its chief *leit-motifs* (Hempel). It may well be possible
that the mythological motif of a divine marriage, with features
borrowed from the Canaanite cultus, is discernible in one particular
passage in this chapter, one which gives clear signs of being composite
(see below commentary on 23.40–44, pp. 333ff.). But this is only a
side issue that does not determine the whole. There is not a single hint
of goddesses with whom a divine husband enters into wedlock. The

whole stress is laid on two female figures which personify two kingdoms clearly defined politically, which are chosen by Yahweh to be his instruments and owe everything to him, but which fail to do their duty. The assumption that Ezekiel was working up an idea which he took from a profane love-song (Kuhn)—a procedure not without precedent in prophetic literature—does not lead to any better understanding of the allegory, since one has to assume also that the original model has been so altered and mutilated as to be unrecognizable. It is impossible, also, to reconstitute the whole in a metrical form in a convincing way, in spite of all the efforts made at reconstruction (Hölscher, Fohrer).

It conforms to the recollection of Yahweh's election customary in the cultus, that the wife should be said to have first belonged to Yahweh in Egypt. But nothing is said here of the people being in a sad plight and of their grateful welcome to God when he came to their help, which form the central elements there. Israel is not said to have been in any sad plight, but to have given herself away without a thought and to have led a life of shameful pleasure. The people is marked from the beginning by an indelible blemish which is the symptom of a deep urge to scorn discipline and break all rules. Ezekiel comes close to Hosea, who saw that even before her marriage the wife was actuated by the spirit of whoredom (Hos. 1.2). Nothing could express more insultingly how the history of salvation commemorated in Israel's feasts has been reduced to grim history of notorious misconduct. Here, as in 20.7, whoredom is to be taken as signifying mixing with Egyptian heathenism, now to be brought to an end by a fresh attachment to Yahweh. That this object was at first successfully attained seems to be indicated by the birth of sons and daughters, i.e. the strengthening and multiplication of the two peoples, covering the whole period from the settlement down to the days of the later kings. In the prophet's eyes this apparently was the time when the actual apostasy from God first began really to emerge to view.

The sinfulness of Oholah: 23.5-10

The Northern kingdom went in for a vacillating foreign policy. Sometimes the majority favoured a rapprochement with Assyria (II Kings 15.19; Hos. 5.13; 7.11; 8.9; 12.1). Sometimes again they sought salvation by trying to employ Egyptians and to throw off the Assyrian yoke (II Kings 17.4; Hos. 7.11; 12.1). Each time the

political dependence was associated with readiness to adopt the foreign
state cults. This state of affairs is vividly represented by the wife's
adulterous love affairs with attractive foreigners. [5f.] The description of the youthful beauty and warlike might of the Assyrians
conveys well what an impression was made by the rise to world power
of the Assyrian empire.

Cool calculations on the relativities of political power cause disregard of Yahweh's claim to exclusive possession. Not only has
Assyria the best expectations of a promising future, but that also
holds out a hope of the overthrow of dangerous neighbours like
Damascus. A price must be paid, however, for this self-surrender;
the great king makes vassals who are disloyal feel how ruthless his
vengeance can be. Or, expressed in allegorical terms, the earlier
lovers make the harlot pay for the faithless way in which she has
jilted them. The judgment executed upon her gives a picture of the
bloody overthrow of Samaria, the punishment of her leaders, the
deportation of her inhabitants, and her removal from the category of
politically independent nations.

The wickedness of Oholibah: 23.11–27

In passing on from the adulteress to her sister, the prophet is evidently modelling himself on Jer. 3.7f. [11] The sister does not im-
prove her behaviour, or take warning from seeing what results from
such misconduct, but continues to follow the same road of unbridled
lust and wanton contempt for her legitimate spouse. Ezekiel is consistent here in making the whoredom refer exclusively to a self-
willed and treacherous political policy, which makes it possible to
show how the wrong road begins with apostasy and yet leads on to
worse ill. This was not possible for Jeremiah, owing to the way he
associated adultery with yielding to Canaanite nature-religion.
Oholibah changes her allies like a prostitute cleverly changing her
lovers from motives of profit. A policy of alliance with Assyria is
followed by another with Babylon, and both lead to her giving herself
away to foreign influences. [12f.] Exact repetition of the same words
to describe the Assyrians as those used in the previous passage serves
to underline the fact that Judah was induced by similar motives and
used similar means to carry out the same self-willed policy as
Northern Israel. She was seduced into setting herself to foreigners by
the impressive embodiment of outward power. [14f.] The fascinating effect of the spectacle of martial power, which leads to total

forgetfulness of the Lord of the world, who alone has the might, and of how he manifested himself in the history of the nation, is now accentuated still more when Judah transforms herself into a vassal state to Assyria. There is no need for her actually to have a meeting with the new world-power. The sight of fresco-like wall pictures, in which the eye of the spectator is caught by the broad and probably richly embroïdered military girdle and the conspicuous headwear of the Babylonian warrior, is enough to turn the heads of the Judahites to whom everything foreign is so attractive. It is difficult to say what historical reality Ezekiel saw and described. The technique of picking out frescoes in red lead is one for which there is Babylonian evidence. According to Jer. 22.14, it must also have been employed in Jehoiakim's newly-built palace. So one may at any rate recall how foreign models were adopted for the expensive furnishings of the living-rooms of the Jerusalemite aristocracy, among whom a craze for everything foreign had set in ever since Manasseh took up a cosmopolitan policy. At any rate, one can gather from the exactness of the description that Ezekiel had himself seen wall decoration of the sort. Nevertheless, Herodotus gives a different description of the striking headgear of the Babylonian warrior, and speaks of long hair and of a band around the head (cf. Fohrer and Zimmerli, *ad loc.*). The prophet, being a maintainer of the divine prohibitions of such representations of the human figure, is already prejudiced against them, and sees in them the expression of a craving to turn away from Yahweh and fraternize with heathen neighbours. [16f.] Open as they already are to heathen ideas, people in Jerusalem are ready and eager to turn towards the rising star of Babylon, where the Chaldeans and their king Nabopolassar were engaging in an ambitious policy wide in its range. The Chaldeans were an Aramaean group whose original home was on the sea-coast beside the Persian Gulf. They gained possession of Babylon in 625 (Ezekiel therefore, to judge by the wording of v. 15, seems to distinguish them from the Babylonians proper as a people of foreign origin). In order to set up a kingdom independent of Assyria, they made common cause with the Medes and Scythians, and stormed the old Assyrian capital Nineveh in 612. In the years which followed they and their allies drove out Assuruballit, the last king of Assyria. He was trying vainly to hold on to the remaining part of his kingdom' in the region beyond Haran, in the hope of Egyptian help. They thus brought the Assyrian empire to an end. In Syria men began to believe that the hour of liberation from foreign dominance had at last arrived. In 609 Josiah of Judah tried to throw back the Egyptian army at Megiddo as it hastened to support Assyria, but met with an overwhelming defeat in which he was himself slain. Palestine and Syria had first to figure as satellites of Egypt. Then after the Egyptians had been forced to retire by the Babylonians, by the year 605 at the latest, they were incorporated into the neo-Babylonian empire under Nebuchadrezzar. It must have been during those years that Jehoiakim, who had been put on the throne by Egypt, must have been manoeuvring and intriguing, and trying to play off the Egyptians and Babylonians against each other. Secret negotiations took place once more with the king of Babylon, like those one hundred years earlier in the days of king Hezekiah (Jer. 39). In the division of the Assyrian spoils the north and north-west had gone to the Medes, while the southern portion of the Assyrian empire had been allotted to Babylon. So as Nebuchadrezzar made ready to take possession of his portion of the booty he could not but welcome every offer or promise of support from the smaller Syrian states, nor can he have been behindhand in encouraging them by promises. This competition to win the favour of the rising neo-Babylonian empire is treated with mockery by Ezekiel, and compared to a harlot's efforts to woo fresh lovers by means of presents. The result of this rapprochement, which served to give Babylonian culture and religion a right of naturalization in Judah (cf. the description of the Babylonian cult in the temple of Zion in ch. 8), was a fresh blossoming of the syncretism which Josiah's reform had tried to eradicate. The prophet represents all this in his parable of love-affairs with foreign lovers. Judah once more turns her back on her God, to whom she had sworn to be true when the covenant was solemnly made.

[17b] But she failed to gain the reward for which she had hoped. She did not, as she had hoped, obtain preferential treatment as an ally of Babylon; she found herself still in the position of a vassal which was just as oppressive as under Assyria. Disillusionment took the place of overconfident expectations, and put a sudden end to the infatuation with Babylon. The harlot turned away in disgust from her lover.

[18] But what was far worse for her than these disappointments was the fact that the soul of her husband, who had not yet repudiated her in spite of her misconduct, was now torn away from her (such is the literal meaning of the Hebrew word translated 'turned away in disgust'). Every vow of fidelity to the God of Israel was broken imme-

diately after a solemn oath to renounce all heathen things. This silent repudiation of the fundamental features of Josiah's reform, which Jeremiah terms a conspiracy in Jer. 11.9, because it takes place behind a façade of magnificent temple worship in the name of Yahweh, finally turns God's ever-hopeful love away from his people. At this very point Jeremiah shows that he has come to the same judgment as Ezekiel, regarding this as a return to the sins of the fathers and a gross breach of the covenant, which must inevitably provoke judgment and wrath (11.10f.). By breaking off all social intercourse with his fellow countrymen (16.1–9), he gives a visible sign that God has turned away from them. Ezekiel represents this inward aversion under the allegory of a husband's aversion as he turns away in disgust from a degraded prostitute, whose whole nature has ceased to be capable of true love.

[19f.] How just this condemnation is is shown by her attaching herself to fresh paramours, proving that her whorish desires are intensified and that she has no intention of changing them. After the bankruptcy of pro-Babylonian policy, political intrigue began afresh in attempts to get rid of the Babylonian yoke without any inquiry as to what God had willed. Egypt's plans for expansion towards the north had revived under Neco. So an attempt was made to manoeuvre, by means of a rapprochement with her, for a position of increased political independence and greater freedom. Ezekiel could not regard this as anything else but an intensification of the same old sinful yearnings, and describes it in contemptuous terms as revolting lasciviousness. Jeremiah had compared his people to a young heifer which breaks loose in rutting time and runs hither and thither in raging lust like a wild creature of the steppe (Jer. 2.24). Ezekiel, too, describes their obstinate alienation from the God who has elected them as like the perverse way a harlot satisfies lusts whose compulsive urges prevent her from realizing how cheap she is making herself.

There is much to be said for the application of v. 20 to the Philistines, as proposed by Köhler. But the similar rebuke in 16.26 and the explicit reference to Egypt in v. 27 turn the scale against it. Furthermore, neither Babylonian nor Israelite sources mention any coalition between the satellite states of south Palestine subsequent to Zedekiah's defection from Babylon, whereas there are repeated references to endeavours to secure Egyptian help. The Lachish letters speak of how the commander-in-chief of the forces of Judah made a journey to Egypt, and according to Jer. 37.5 the Babylonians had to give up besieging Jerusalem for a short time, while they repelled an Egyptian force which was approaching in an attempt at relieving it. So in spite of the unsatisfactory state of its text, the revolting picture of how the harlot satisfied her lusts must refer the ruinous relapse into the pro-Egyptian policy, by which Judah deprived herself of any hope of inward recovery.

[22] The unnaturalness of the process by which a whole people turn away from the God who has elected them is displayed in a series of disgusting pictures. This enables us to realize how the history of Israel's election concludes with a ruthlessly wrathful judgment. Even in it everything is calculated to move the hardened nation to feelings of their own guilt and to prepare them for a recognition of the inward necessity of the severe judgment they deserved. As in 16.37, the execution of the judgment is committed to the former lovers, and their seductive appearance is once more described in words deliberately repeated from vv. 6 and 12; but now they are not lovers but vindictive foes. Their irresistible arms and uniform, which had formerly so dazzled Jerusalem, are now turned against the treacherous city, depriving her of any way of escape.

[23] Pekod, Shoa and Koa are named as nations allied with the Babylonians and the Chaldeans, who are distinguished from the latter as the most important representatives of the northern nations, as in v. 14. Of these three names, the first certainly denotes an Aramaean tribe in east Babylonia, while the other two may be conjecturally identified as nomadic tribes on the Djala, a tributary of the Tigris. The object is evidently twofold. [24] On the one hand, it serves to suggest a host made up of many nations (cf. the host of peoples in v. 24 and their numerous weapons, as in Isa. 17.12f. and 22.6, where Elam and Kir are mentioned along with Assyria). On the other hand, the names also contain a play on words, as they sound like the Hebrew words for 'punish', 'cry for help' and 'shriek', thus recalling the fate in store for the people of Judah at the hands of these nations (the same thing happens in Jer. 50.21). God himself appoints the foreigners as judges, entrusted with the duty of pronouncing and executing the now appropriate sentence. He thus refrains from carrying out his own judgment and has Jerusalem judged according to heathen law, seeing that she has alienated Yahweh by putting herself on the same level as the heathen. So the cruel legal penalty of heathen law, which knows nothing of forgiveness, must be executed upon the city. Her exclusion from her former

favoured position justified Yahweh before the nations, who are allowed to sentence and punish Jerusalem according to their own law. [25] This leads to mutilation by cutting of the nose and ears. This was unknown to Israelite law, but a frequent custom in Mesopotamia.[1] The children are sold as slaves and all the property burnt. [26] The adulteress's clothes and ornaments are the perquisite of the executioners, while the mutilated woman has to lie naked, for anyone who wishes to satisfy his wanton desires with her.[2]

[27] It is stated in grim irony that when her apostasy has led to such results as these, it will take away for ever all the seductive attraction that Israel had always found in heathenism, so that her heart and mind will cease to feel it. Once Jerusalem is destroyed and nothing left of her there will be no more ambassadors to foreign nations to propose alliances!

This bitter conclusion may well lead one to think that Egypt, which is subjected to a still more merciless exposure than the other seducers in the north, ought to be regarded as the enemy *par excellence* of the people of God. It would also be quite explicable that the prophet conceived a special abhorrence for the Nile kingdom. It was Egypt who had filled Israel's ears with repeated instigations to rebellion against Assyria and Babylon, and who had kept her from being peaceably absorbed into the sphere of influence of the Northern Empire. Yet the basic motive behind Ezekiel's sharp attack is not so much a wish to hold Egypt politically responsible as the villain of the piece, always contestable as that was, but a theological judgment. Egypt occupied a fateful position at the beginning and the end of the history of the chosen people, and yet very different estimates could be made of that position. Israel's historical memory stamped it indeed as the house of bondage where Pharaoh had oppressed her. But that humiliating thought did not prevent, but rather kindled afresh by the very contrast, the proud compensating memory of having been liberated and chosen by a God who excelled all other powers, and that memory received fresh nourishment from every

---

[1] Cf. ancient Assyrian law, which explicitly mentions the cutting off of the nose of an adulteress, and the castration of the man, whose face was also slashed: H. Ehelolf, *Ein altassyrisches Rechtsbuch*, 1922, pp. 25, 28f., 23; also Mitteilungen aus der Vorderasiatischen Abteilung der Staatlichen Museen zu Berlin, vol. 1.

[2] This, at least, is how one must understand the present text. Yet the curious order in which the acts of judgment take place in vv. 25 and 26 points to a disturbance, which seems to be corrected in the appendix in vv. 46f., where as in 16.40 the adulteress is said to be put to death by stoning and quartering.

feast of the covenant. Ezekiel therefore takes a completely different view of the contact with Egypt. The kingdom of the Nile is not the dark background against which Israel's slavery and her liberation by Yahweh shines out brightly, providing the people as it were with a halo as the object of divine election. She is the tempter, whom Israel was only too ready to welcome, who deprived her right from the beginning not only of her natural innocence but also of the further honour imparted to her by God. So recollection of the times of bondage is also recollection of shame and scandal and brings to light a general similarity with her present condition; the history of salvation is transformed into a history of ever-increasing dishonour and loss of self-respect and self-exposure to shame. So here once more no room is left for self-glorification during the celebration of the covenant feast. The historical recollection must become a call for repentance, awakening self-accusation and thus leading to a truthful estimate of the past.

Verse 27 brings us to the natural conclusion of the story of the two sisters. It is followed by a number of postscripts, providing variations on the same theme.

A repeated proclamation of the sentence of judgment: 23.23–30

The allegorical picture-language is here totally given up. Not lovers but nations are referred to, with whom Israel has played the whore, i.e. has been false to her vow pledging fidelity to the Lord of the covenant. Her falsity is at the same time interpreted as consisting in idolatry (v. 30). At the same time there is no mention of the sin referred to in the previous passage which consisted in a perfidious policy of ever-changing alliances and coalitions, which did actually involve a relapse into heathen worship. So what we find here is a simplification in accordance with the outlook of Deuteronomy, which makes all the prophet's pronouncements refer to the particular sin which that school of thought regarded as the source of all apostasy. This passage therefore cannot come from the prophet himself.

The cup-saying: 23.31–34

As in the sword-song in 21.8–17, the preceding threat is given a concentrated form in an image, and made still more striking by being put into metrical shape. In this Ezekiel takes up an image of which Jeremiah had made use in a most striking way, and which afterwards had been used in many passages in the Old and New Testaments. The cup has been used from early days in order to represent the destiny in store for man. In the Ugaritic text II, AB, III, 14–16 this image is even used to represent the god Baal being insulted by another god.[1]

The cup filled up and handed to the guest at a feast held in his honour comes, by an easily understood association of ideas, to denote the portion anyone is destined to receive, cf. Ps. 16.5; 11.6; 23.5. It thus became a permanent feature in metaphorical language to denote the portion in life fixed by God either of good or evil. This makes it unnecessary to appeal to any mythological ideas.[2] The metaphor was itself immediately intelligible (in addition to Jer. 25, see Hab. 2.16). So it provided the prophet with a means he was glad to use to make his audience see the compulsion there is to accept destiny, the impossibility of rejecting it, the trepidation at its death-dealing effects, the bitterness of the suffering it involves, and how it has to be tasted to the full.

Jeremiah uses this image· to picture the destiny in store for the heathen nations, and proclaimed to them by God through the mouth of his prophet. But Ezekiel transfers it to the destiny that is laid upon Israel. Oholah has already been forced to drink the cup of judgment. [31] Oholibah, having gone the same way as her sister, is now also forced to drink the cup. The introductory verse, v. 31, therefore enunciates the iron law by which crime is followed by punishment. Verses 32–34 then follow. They contain three strophes each made up of three lines varying in length (with members which alternate between two and three stresses). They evoke with pungent brevity the tragic scene at which so deadly a draught is drunk. [32] The cup that is given into the hand is deep and large; its contents are as terrible as the wickedness committed is great.

[33f.] The one who is condemned to drink it shrinks back, finding it full to the brim of outward ruin and deep inward suffering. But there is no escape; the cup must be drained to the last drop, the judgment endured to the final pang. The beating of the breast, a gesture found in ancient representations to express mourning, is intensified by despair into an attempt at self-injury, and changed into a frantic tearing to seek relief from unbearable misery. Joyous feasts

---

[1] J. Aistleitner, *Die mythologischen und kultischen Texte aus Ras Shamra*, Budapest, 1959, pp. 38f. See also G. R. Driver, *Canaanite Myths and Legends*, O.T. Studies, No. 3, 1956, p. 95, III, 14–16.

[2] P. Volz, *Jeremia*, 1928, pp. 392f.

with lovers are thus transformed into the reverse with frightening effect.

Auvray suspects that Ezekiel has taken a popular song of mockery and adapted it for his purposes in this little song. Ezekiel must in that case have changed it from a song expressing pleasure in another's suffering into an announcement of judgment which tells of all the ruthlessness of the retribution.

The charge and sentence which the prophet has orders to declare: 23.35–46

According to v. 36 it seems at first as if the prophet was given the same sort of task as in ch. 20 and 22, that of acting as God's mouth-piece to sum up the charges and proclaim the sentence determined by the divine judge against the two sisters. But there we found com-bined together a series of effective compositions each with a complete structure of its own. Here we find an unorganized assemblage of details or flat repetitions of earlier words of judgment which do not carry us any further. Verses 40–44 even seem to be a fragment taken out of its original context, and inserted in a way that interrupts the sequence, and may perhaps have belonged to some lost poem of Ezekiel's. All the rest is the work of some pupil, who makes a very inadequate attempt to imitate his teacher.

[35] Verse 35, without establishing any connection with what follows, briefly defines the wickedness of Jerusalem: it consists in for-getfulness of her God, which has gone hand in hand with completely ignoring him. Only as the result of such an inward apostasy could she have come to surrender herself so completely to foreign nations in an ever-changing series of unions, to describe which the words whoredom and unchastity are now used as technical terms. One can see here the work of a redactor summing up all that has been said so far.

Verses 36–39 give a list of the iniquities of the two sisters. [37] Only the first, adultery, agrees with the description in the first half of the chapter; what follows takes a line of its own. Already we see an indi-cation of this in the fact that the lovers who seduce to adultery are said to be idols, not nations, as has been stated hitherto. But the mention of children sacrificed to foreign gods (cf. 16.20f.) creates a still more serious contradiction of vv. 10 and 25, which state that the children of the two women were seized and carried away by their foreign paramours. [38] Then this is quite unexpectedly associated with the profanation of the sanctuary and the sabbath in a way that abandons any attempt at consistency with Ezekiel's allegory. This particular item in the indictment has already been seen to be a later insertion in 22.8, 26, so here, too, it must be ascribed to some other hand than that of Ezekiel. **[39]** The association with child sacrifice is unique; it is immediately followed by a visit to the temple while the hands are still stained with blood. The complete disregard for bringing defilement upon the sanctuary shown here is evidently regarded as adding further to the sin. **[40–44]** In order to get back from that to the subject of adultery, a description of lovers visiting the two sisters is very clumsily dragged in, and the execution of the sentence is then described in the concluding passage. It is orientated towards 16.39ff. rather than towards 23.22ff., and shows inconsistency with v. 37. **[45–49]** The children sacrificed to idols according to v. 37 are here slaughtered by a company of righteous men who have been entrusted with the duty of executing the punishment. Here, once more, we see a return of the allegorical idea of a marriage between Yahweh and the two sisters (cf. v. 4), according to which the children are regarded as signifying the individual persons belonging to the two nations. **[48]** The statement of the object of the judgment is also strange: it is said to be carried out as a warning to all women to indulge in lasciviousness, thus developing an idea hinted at in 16.41. It is hardly likely that those thus warned are individual women, or that the judgment thus described is 'a narrative which teaches by typical examples' (Zimmerli) and is therefore more private in its meaning. It is more probable that the women ought to be thought of as standing for the heathen nations who see Yahweh's terrible judgment and thus become aware of their responsibility to the world-God. The comprehensive view of the judgment upon the adulterous sisters taken here, which regards it as a single act of judgment, might suggest an author who already stood at a considerable distance from the historical catastrophe (587), and who was able to see it as conveying a general verdict on the history of the nation.

To suppose that this comprehensive view forces us to assume that the writer found himself in a totally different situation from that taken for granted in the allegory, and that the two sisters must therefore be understood as standing for portions of the country or nation as they existed at a later stage unknown to us (Fohrer), seems to take much too seriously what is no more than a rather sweeping and careless summing up of past history.

[40–44] The little section formed by vv. 40–44 presents a problem in itself. In spite of the clumsy way in which it is inserted into its present context, the picture it gives is so lively and vigorous that one is tempted to think it is a fragment of what was once a more complete account of a feast, which gave still more vivid details of what heathen 'whoredom' really meant. The table set with incense and oil, the loud singing of a mighty multitude, the bestowal of the ornaments, suggest some sort of cultic act such as might accompany a festival in honour of pagan gods, and most especially a 'sacred marriage'. Is it possible that, in order to illustrate Oholibah's fall into heathenism, some reader quoted some such description in the margin and that fragments of it were later incorporated into the text?[1]

CHAPTER 24.1–14

The parable of the cooking pot

1 In the ninth year, in the tenth month, on the tenth day of the month, the word of Yahweh came to me: [2]'Son of man, write down the name of this day, this very day: the king of Babylon has laid siege to Jerusalem this very day. [3]And utter an allegory to the rebellious house and say to them, thus says [. . .]ᵃ Yahweh:
4 Set on the pot, set it on, pour in water also;
   put in it the pieces of flesh,ᵇ all the good pieces, the thigh and the shoulder; fill it with choice bones.
5 Take them out of the choicest sheep of the flock, pile the logs under it;
   boil its pieces,ᶜ seethe also its bonesᵈ in it.
6 Therefore thus says Yahweh:
   Woe to the blood-guilty city, to the pot whose rustᵉ
   is in it and whose rust has not gone out of it [. . .]ᶠ
7 For the blood she has shedᵍ is in the midst of her, she shed it on the bare rock,
   she did not pour it on the ground to cover it with dust.
8 To arouse wrath, so that vengeance may be taken,
   sheʰ set on the bare rock the blood she has shed, that it might not be covered.
9 Therefore thus says [. . .]ⁱ Yahweh:
   Woe to the blood-guilty city! I also will make a great pile,
10 will heap many logs, kindle the fire, seethe the flesh, [pour out the broth]ʲ

---

[1] In connection with such feasts cf. H. Schmökel, *Heilige Hochzeit und Hoheslied*, Abhandlungen für die Kunde des Morgenlandes, XXXII, 1, 1956, pp. 8ff.

11 And I will set it[k] empty upon its coals, that it may become hot and its copper may burn,
and its filthiness will be melted in it and its rust consumed.
12 [. . .][l]yet its thick rust does not go out of it by fire [. . .][m]
13 Because of your filthy impurity, because I would have cleansed you and you were not cleansed from your filthiness, you shall not be cleansed any more until I have satisfied my fury upon you. [14]I, Yahweh, have said it [. . .][n] and I also do it. I will not go back, I will not spare, nor shall I repent. According to your ways and doings I will judge you,[o] says [. . .][p] Yahweh.'

a-eSee BH.
fMT: 'Take out of it piece after piece [the suffix needs to be omitted], without casting any lot upon it': one does not expect anything to be taken out in this context. So the first part of the phrase may belong to v. 5 (Fohrer) and there serve as introduction to something that was done with the empty pot, but which is no longer mentioned. Alternatively, it may be an explanatory gloss which has found its way out of the margin into the wrong place in the text. It may have applied vv. 3-5 to the siege of Jerusalem and the leading of its inhabitants into exile.
gThis is what is meant by the Hebrew 'her blood'.
hRead third feminine singular, which is the only thing possible in the context, instead of the first singular.
iSee BH.
jMT: 'Let the ointment-pot anoint'. These unintelligible words can be slightly changed to produce the amended text above. The two concluding Hebrew words 'and the bones shall be burnt up' do not fit in with the context. Furthermore, the feminine form of 'bones' used here suggests the bones of dead men. So the original marginal gloss may well have referred to the defiling of Jerusalem by the burning of dead human bones.
kMT: 'Set it' could be a reference to the allegory in vv. 3-5. But here we find a point arising out of the allegory and going beyond it, which is closely connected with Yahweh's arrival on the scene as the real agent in all that is being done. So the return to the first person in v. 9 shows us what the correct reading ought to be.
lMT has two words which are difficult to understand. They may, of course, be translated 'in toil he has grown weary' (Zimmerli) or 'he has exhausted his efforts' (Fohrer). But there is a fairly widespread opinion that they are a dittography of the preceding words.
mMT: 'by the fire of its rust'; the final word must be omitted.
nMT: 'it shall come to pass' should be omitted, as it destroys the compactness of the divine assurance, often in evidence elsewhere.
oMT: 'you will be judged' the consonants admit the reading in the text above.
pSee BH.

The beginning of the siege of Jerusalem: 24.1-2

One day Ezekiel is commanded by God to record the date of the day as marking an epoch. It is the day upon which the king of Babylon has begun his attack upon Jerusalem. The prophet had seen the disaster gradually approaching. He had tried to get his fellow countrymen to realize that it must inevitably come. Now the point has been reached when it is definitely visible, and it is no longer any use to deny it or object to it. The coming storm has sent out its first flash of lightning. The glare shows how true the warnings were which the men of Israel had thought they could brush aside, and has justified the unpopular, misrepresented prophet.

Yet no one except the messenger of God has any certain knowledge of this event. His audience is contingent on the verification of his statement by a message coming straight from Jerusalem. That is why it has to be written down, so that there will be proof, when the event is confirmed in a few weeks' time. We find precisely the same procedure in Isaiah, as recorded in Isa. 8.1, 16. It is curious to see another attempt made at this point, to transfer the writing down of the day and the parable associated with it to Palestine, and to allege as a reason for it that the prophet could not have had certain knowledge of Nebuchadrezzar's attack by means of clairvoyance. But how the prophet obtained his certainty has nothing to do with the case. The fact still stands that had he been in Palestine he would have had no occasion to record the date, since everyone knew it and there was no demand for any proof of its correctness. His putting it down in writing could not have any purpose unless he was in exile, where the testimony of an eye witness was not as yet available.

The date given brings us to the end of the year 589. Among the other passages stating the day of the month on which the siege began, II Kings 25.1 is the only one which rests on an independent tradition, whereas Jer. 52.4 is dependent on the authority of the book of Kings. Fohrer's assumption that the writer of the narrative in the book of Kings took over the date from the book of Ezekiel is not a very probable one. Even though the account was composed during exilic times, the historian must certainly have had access to the exact date of so decisive an event, considering what good historical material he presents elsewhere. Zimmerli observes that the formula stating the date in Ezek. 24.1 is not in agreement with the method elsewhere employed in the prophetic book for recording dates, but repeats word for word the date as given in the book of Kings. But the conclusion he draws, that either Ezek. 24 did not give the day of the month or one originally differing from that in the book of Kings was corrected to conform with it, is not necessarily true. There is a third possibility, and one quite as likely to be true. In the form it takes in the book of Kings the date may have been inserted by some later hand into the book of Ezekiel in order to make it seem still more impressive through its word-for-word agreement with the chronology given by an official historian.

Thus, while we have no intention of suggesting that the credibility of the prophet's message is in any way dependent on the historical accuracy of the date, the assertion that Ezekiel could not have known the exact day on which the catastrophe began is as gratuitous as it is impossible to prove, lying as it does beyond the limits of what is verifiable. There is nothing to indicate clairvoyance, but it is quite in order to suggest inspiration, which is clearly implied in the formula stating how Ezekiel received the word. It is quite understandable that this particular prophecy of disaster should be further confirmed by a definite date in view of its pastoral importance.

The parable of the cooking pot: 24.3–14

The prophet is not only told to record the date. He is also ordered to proclaim a parable, which will reveal to the 'rebellious house' how deep the coming disaster will go, to shake their obstinate refusal to pay attention. An action is therefore associated with the saying, giving the word of the prophet the character of an event, which distinguishes the effectual word of God from the mere word of man.

[3–5] Verses 3–5 describe the preparations for a feast. A large cauldron, in which food can be prepared for a large number of persons, is employed (II Kings 4.38). Selected pieces of meat from the best animals in the flock and choice marrow bones are boiled up in order to serve an appetizing meal. There is nothing in this to hint at any announcement of judgment any more than there is in the elaborate description of the cultivation of the vineyard in Isaiah's famous vineyard song (Isa. 5). The description of the heated pot in Jeremiah (Jer. 1.13) is completely different, owing to its brevity, which brings to view only one detail in the whole procedure, namely the violent heating of the pot. Over-rash interpretation which tries to force our passage to follow a similar pattern has led to much misunderstanding of Ezekiel's parable. The word spoken by the inhabitants of Jerusalem in Ezek. 11.3 also has only a loose connection with the present parable. One must not jump to the premature conclusion that it describes the siege of Jerusalem and interpret the boiling of the portions of meat as signifying the sufferings of the besieged (Bertholet,

Heinisch, etc.). The sole aim of the prolix description is to lay stress
on how careful the preparations were. This is further confirmed, if
van den Born is right in suggesting that this is a working song, sung
while carrying out some particular piece of work, like the well-
digging in Num. 21.17f. This theory, to which Zimmerli also gives his
approval, would therefore include vv. 3–5 in the words of the parable
which Ezekiel is told to proclaim. Still, there is no occasion for any
doubt that the prophet performed the actions there described.

All that can at first be gathered from these words and actions is
therefore that a feast is being prepared. Is it intended to portray those
now in danger in Jerusalem triumphing over their Babylonian
besiegers? Or does it portray nothing more than the cheerfully confident optimism of Jerusalemites and exiles alike, who met the coming
catastrophe in such a careless, light-hearted fashion? The possibility
of its having more interpretations than one makes the words into an
allegory, with a hidden meaning which those who hear them must
try to find out. We must wait for what follows to see exactly where to
look and how to interpret it.

[6–8] Verses 6–8 loudly call down woe on the blood-guilty city of
Jerusalem. One feature from the allegory just heard is taken up, and
freely developed and applied in a totally different and wholly unexpected direction. Jerusalem is compared to the iron cooking pot.
Rust has bitten into it so deeply that it is impossible to get rid of it.
Obviously an idea stated in 11.3 is taken up again and given a new
significance, while at the same time it is not one that can be extracted
from vv. 3–5.

The allegory turns from the general description of the light-hearted
pleasure of life to a more deep-seated evil, imperilling the very
foundations on which the existence of the state of Jerusalem depends.
This is the remorseless bloodshed in which the ruling party have
indulged, in order to overcome those who have resisted them, which
has never been atoned for. The words of 11.6, so often called in
question, are here established beyond all doubt (cf. above pp. 137
and 141). In order to characterize the contempt thus shown for God's
commandments, Ezekiel refers to the old custom of covering with
earth blood that has been shed by violence, in order to prevent it
from crying to heaven against the murderer (cf. Gen. 4.10; Job
16.18). How great the fear was in Israel of vengenace for the shedding
of innocent blood is shown by the legal ritual of atonement in Deut.
21.1–9, as also by the impression Jeremiah made upon the people

THE PARABLE OF THE COOKING POT: 24.1-14 339

when they were incensed against him, and he reminded them of the terrible consequences it would have on them if he were to come to a violent end. **[7f.]** But, as vv. 7f. state, Jerusalem had not only not troubled to cover up the traces of the murder, but had deliberately made it impossible to do so, by pouring out the blood on the bare rock, where it could not be covered with earth. Ezekiel does not, of course, mean to suggest that those in power in Jerusalem might have protected themselves against coming under God's curse by taking a few ritual precautions. What he says aims instead at pillorying the impudent fashion that has set in at Jerusalem, of completely disregarding the divinely sanctioned law. It seems almost as if by their unabashed and unatoned-for transgression of the law they were deliberately provoking God to intervene, 'to arouse wrath, so that vengeance may be taken' (v. 8).

[9–12] It is therefore inevitable for the rust-eaten cauldron, i.e. the city stained by unatonable bloodshed, to feel the full weight of God's retribution. What was said in vv. 3–5 is repeated and given a new application in vv. 9–12. God, who himself sees to the cooking, does more than prepare the food. He empties the cauldron, stirs up the fire to a fierce blaze, and puts the cauldron on top of it, so that it must inevitably melt. As a result, not only the rust, but also the cauldron itself, will be eliminated. The state is so full of incurable rotteness that the restoration for which Isaiah could still hope is impossible. There is no way of getting rid of corruption save to eliminate it from the world.

Whether one ought to supply an interpretation for every single detail in the parable, by connecting the emptying of the cauldron with the exiling of the inhabitants of Jerusalem, and explaining the melting down of the cauldron as signifying the destruction of the city after it has been emptied of its inhabitants (Fohrer), is a very questionable point. In any case it would be preferable to follow 11.1ff. and think of the removal of the worthier portions of the population in the first exile. Ezekiel, however, is not interested in such individual details, but solely in the ultimate result after the cooking fire has been increased into a destructive conflagration. **[13f.]** Verses 13 and 14 connect this act of destruction with the sentence of the judge. The obduracy which resists the judge's will to cleanse provokes him to react by ruthlessly eliminating the offender. What was stated in 22.21f. is thus accomplished here.

Chapter 24.15–27

The death of the prophet's wife

15 And the word of Yahweh came to me: [16]'Son of man, behold, I am about to take the delight of your eyes away from you by sudden death; yet you shall not mourn nor weep nor shall your tears run down. Sigh,[17] but not aloud; make no mourning for the dead,[a] bind on your turban and put your shoes on your feet. Do not cover your beard, nor eat the bread of mourners.[b] [18a]and the next morning speak[c] to the people: [21aβb] Thus says [. . .][d] Yahweh: Behold I will profane my sanctuary, the pride of your power, the delight of your eyes and the desire of your soul. Your sons and daughters, whom you have left behind, will fall by the sword. [24]Thus shall Ezekiel be to you a sign; according to all that he has done, you shall do. When this comes, then you will know that I am [. . .][e] Yahweh. [25a]And you, son of man, in truth —, [26][. . .][f] on the day when a fugitive will come to you, to report to you the news,[g] [27]on that day your mouth will be opened to the fugitive, and you will speak and be no longer dumb, so you will be a sign to them, that they may know that I am Yahweh.'

18b And my wife died at evening. And on the next morning I did as I was commanded. [19]And the people said to me: 'Will you not tell us what these things mean for us, that you are acting thus?' [20]Then I said to them, 'The Word of Yahweh came to me: [21aα]"Say to the house of Israel: [25b]On the day when [Yahweh] takes [from you] [your] stronghold, [your] joy and glory, the delight of [your] eyes and [your] heart's desire, [your sons and daughters],[h] [22]then you shall do as I have done; you shall not cover your beard, nor eat the bread of mourners, [23]your turbans shall be on your heads and your shoes on your feet. You shall not mourn or weep and shall pine in your iniquities and groan one to another." '

[a]These two words are in the wrong order in the MT, and have to be reversed.
[b]See BH.

[c]The indicative 'so I spoke', which has arisen as a result of the phrase immediately following, must be changed back into the original imperative. Cf. below pp. 346f. and 349f. of the commentary following in regard to this and other textual changes.

[d–e]See BH.

[f]MT: 'on that day', with an insertion caused by the influence of v. 25b; read instead simply *beyôm* followed by a relative sentence without any relative particle as frequently in temporal clauses.

[g]See BH.

ʰThe third person plural masculine suffixes are here to be replaced by the second person and Yahweh inserted as the subject in place of the first person singular.

The announcement of the coming death of the prophet's wife: 24.15–17

The exiles are in a tense and feverish state at the beginning of the siege of Jerusalem. They seek reassurance, as they see their own country take arms against their Babylonian overlords. They show a great appetite for any news that comes in from the battle front, especially such items as rekindle fading hopes, like the Babylonian retreat and temporary abandonment of the siege (cf. Jer. 37.5). Who is going to prove right? Will it be that prophet of disaster, who makes one react so violently at times, and to whom one forces oneself to listen with such obstinate disapproval at other times? Or will it be the prophets of victory, who feel able to predict some wondrous deliverance for the city of God like that in the days of Sennacherib?

This time Ezekiel supported his word of judgment at the beginning of the siege by a symbolic action, calculated once again to cut all hope at its roots. What made it all the more striking was that it needed no piling up of apparatus nor any manipulation to excite attention and expressive meaning, like those of which we are told in 4.1ff. or 21.23f. It was solely accompanied by a *maggēpā*, a sudden blow struck directly by God himself, like the one referred to in Num. 16.46. It took place in the midst of the community of exiles, and was so heavy as to strike the prophet himself dumb, consisting as it did in the sudden death of his wife.

God himself informs the prophet of the terrible thing that is about to take place. No date is given. There is nothing to suggest, and everything to make it improbable, that it was at the same time as 24.1. Yet the insertion of the passage in its present position does at least serve to show that the period concerned is that of the siege of Jerusalem. However, for reasons which will later become evident one may postpone this event to a period considerably later than that recorded in 24.1ff., that is to say to approximately July 587.

[16] The imminent blow is not to strike the prophet unaware; he is to go to meet it in a state of conscious preparation. He is to know beforehand that even in so terrible an event his God is not simply delivering him to alien and destructive forces, or forcing him to undergo a punishment unintelligible to him, but firmly and fully binding him to himself. Yes, he, his God, has need of this particular

service at this precise moment. Ezekiel is thus assured that, throughout the whole course of this inexplicable happening, he continues to act as God's mouthpiece and to be taken up into God's counsels.

Admittedly, this visitation is none the less intolerably severe to the victim. And, by telling him that he is going to deprive him of this one who is 'the delight of his eyes', God conveys to him how well he knows the pain of what is to come. We must not, of course, try to utilize this terse phrase and try to draw from it biographical conclusions in regard to the prophet's marriage; these easily diverge into mere romance, and do not take into account the controlled brevity of the word of Yahweh. But we must also refrain from dismissing as 'sentimental theorizing' the suggestion that the term God uses to denote the prophet's wife is something more than the phrase employed in common parlance for a close relation (Zimmerli). *Maḥamaddim*, the plural of the same word, is indeed used in Lam. 2.4 and Hos. 9.16 to denote young men or children. But there, too, it is perfectly obvious that the expression aims at naming one especially beloved and snatched away as if by a judgment. The saying of God does not speak simply of the 'taking away of your wife'. Instead of merely calling her his wife it calls her the 'delight of his eyes'. So we would reduce this form of expression to a rather irritating blossom of flowery oriental speech, if we did not allow it to refer to the special refreshment and support which Ezekiel received through his wife. There may be some similarity here to God's command to Abraham (Gen. 22) to offer his son to him as a sacrifice. The command rises in a crescendo 'your son, your only son, whom you love', showing there, too, how very much aware God is of the severity of the sacrifice which he is demanding.

On the other hand, one must beware of trying to explain Ezekiel's clear awareness of what is to come, which he attributes to a direct divine disclosure, in a rationalistic fashion as merely meaning that he suddenly realized that an illness of his wife's would result in her death; there is no mention of sickness here, and if there was it would be inconsistent with the whole idea of God's sudden 'blow'.

Smend and Krätzschmar go further and do far worse in their attempt at a material rearrangement. In contradiction to what is actually stated they affirm that the primary factor for Ezekiel was the experience of the sudden death of his wife, and that it was the prophet's subsequent theological speculation which afterwards converted it into a divine command. Hölscher has justly termed this a falsification of the facts, and expressed surprise at the absence of ethical scruple which it displays.[1]

One may nevertheless suggest that he himself has not understood the divine communication. Agreeing with Hengstenberg, whose apologetic tendencies are ill-famed, he explains it as being sought and found in the 'why and wherefore' of the sudden death of the prophet's wife: God humiliates his servant so far as to deprive him of his wife for the sole purpose of enabling him to give as it were a mimic representation of what would happen to his people in the future. Hengstenberg softens this down by his completely baseless assumption that the story of the death of the prophet's wife was no more than a parable, but once given by the undeniable actuality of the event described, God's will is misrepresented in a way that shows extraordinary lack of taste. In any case the 'why and wherefore' of a divine intervention is not open to discussion: his sovereign freedom does not have to render any reason for what it does. The text does, however, speak of its purpose. Even in this crushing event, the prophet is to take up his stance side by side with his God and to realize that God is laying claim to him and his personal experiences and using them to touch his people's hardened hearts. Like Hosea, Ezekiel, too, realizes that with his inexplicable domestic tragedy he has been called to the service and sacrifice of bearing witness to the redeeming love of his God. At this point he, too, is a forerunner of the *kenōsis* in which, according to Phil. 2.7, Paul saw the clue to the action of Jesus Christ. All further psychological questions are, as Zimmerli reminds us, to be excluded as alien to the prophetic text.

The sudden unexpected death of his beloved wife not only throws Ezekiel into deep sorrow but also exercises a profound effect upon all around him. [17] But they must have felt additional surprise and shock when they saw the prophet who had suffered so great a bereavement completely neglecting all the usual tokens of mourning. He was doing exactly as his divine master had ordered. Such things as the raising of the impassioned death lament, or giving way to loud weeping, or along with such outbursts of strong feeling the ceremonial garb of the mourner who wore neither turban nor shoes and went barefoot and bareheaded, and—another feature which, rather surprisingly, is passed over here, but is evidently to be taken for granted—the wearing of sackcloth in place of the usual garment, and also the funeral feast, to which the relatives and friends invited the chief mourner at

[1] *Ezekiel*, p. 129.

the end of the period of fasting (cf. II Sam. 12.17): all these Ezekiel was to do without; he was to give no outward expression to his grief but speechless groans.

The explanation of the symbolic action: 24.18a, 21, 24

[18] All this leads the neighbours to ask questions and insist on an answer, as they gather next morning round Ezekiel's house (the word 'people', in the sense of 'persons', here denotes the excited crowd that collects, and only here are they described as the audience to whom the prophet spoke). The prophet is to answer them by a word from Yahweh. What is now happening is the prophecy of a bereavement that all are destined to suffer, and of a grief that will overwhelm and completely paralyse them all. [21] Furthermore, this unusual behaviour, like all such symbolic acts, is already setting in motion the event which it signifies, and causing it to come irresistibly down upon the exiles. The blow which the house of Israel is to feel at God's hand is a far greater one than that suffered by any individual man who has the 'delight of his eyes' suddenly taken away from him. For Israel possesses in her temple something that is not only a delight to her eyes but a cause for pride and an object of longing. Longing was the right word for exiles only, not for Jerusalemites, who could not have looked towards the temple with the same feeling of insatiable longing as those banished from their native land. That life-giving centre of all that Israel held precious was not to be impregnable as hitherto to the attacks of its enemies. The God himself to whom it belonged was giving it up to profanation. Once it was given up death would be able without hindrance to reap its terrible harvest. Sons and daughters must mean younger relations in general, not only direct offspring. The deportation had cut families in two. The older and more influential members of a family had been forced to set off on the route to a foreign land, whereas the younger and less experienced were allowed to remain at home, being regarded by the Great King as less dangerous. Hopes of future reunion with them had helped the exiles to endure their plight. But now they see themselves deprived of this last support, and faced with what they had always refused to believe in the person of Ezekiel: [24] God now sets him up in their midst as a miraculous sign and he prefigures in his own person the state of inconsolable depression that is in store for them. The true knowledge of God, the thing towards which they have kept their minds closed, will then assert itself invincibly.

If we are to follow the analogy of other prophetic utterances, we must assume that the word from God accounting for his behaviour in response to inquisitive questions was delivered to him along with the instructions as to how he was to mourn the departed in vv. 16 and 17. This is indicated in the first words of v. 18, though the command given there for the prophet to speak to the people the following morning has been altered, owing to a misunderstanding by a copyist, into a narrative statement in the indicative. The imperative alone is in place here, as is shown by comparison with 5.4f., where the prophet, after being instructed to perform a symbolic action, is also provided with the word from God that he is to proclaim. This shows how inadvisable it is to make v. 17 bring God's instructions to a close without providing the prophet with the interpretation which he is subsequently to proclaim. [18b, 19] It is much more probable that we ought to regard the account of the death of the prophet's wife, of how Ezekiel carried out what God had commanded, and of the resulting questions addressed to the spectators in v. 18b and 19 as a piece of material transferred to its present position from a later portion of the account, as seemed to be called for as a result of the copyist's error in v. 18a. But in reality, the command to speak was, originally, followed immediately by the interpretation of the symbolic action, as given in vv. 21ff.

[22f.] Now these verses contain a difficulty which has not received sufficient notice. Some words of the prophet's have been inserted into the words spoken by God in vv. 22 and 23, and then, without any transition, the closing words in v. 24 are again spoken by God. Here one has to choose between two alternatives. One may reject the prophet's words as a gloss or a variation of text (Herrmann, Fohrer etc.), though the wording of the closing threat does not have the character of a gloss. Or else one may ascribe to both verses some different function within the general context (so Bertholet², in part). This function may consist in giving an answer to the people's inquiries, thus making it possible to avoid a further repetition of the words spoken by God in vv. 21–24. This is not to say that Ezekiel actually suppressed what God had said; but the explicit command to proclaim it could be taken for granted and therefore omitted, as is done elsewhere, as in 5.4f., the prophet's words taking its place. Was this original arrangement of the text upset at some later date, in order that the words of the prophet might be inserted among the words spoken by God? [26f.] This is obviously connected with the function of vv. 26 and 27: they are meant to point beyond the oracles to the nations to 33.21f., thus introducing a resounding climax at the end of the last prophecy before the fall of Jerusalem. This object is equally well attained by removing the prophet's words from the conclusion to the middle of the present section, though it is done at the cost of making an almost unendurable alteration to words spoken by God. An indication of this displacement in the original order of the text is also probably to be found in vv. 20 and 21, which so pile up introductory formulas to the words spoken by Yahweh; van den Born has already remarked on them as being in their way unique. We therefore place the above-mentioned verses at the close of the whole section, where they serve to inform us how God's instructions were duly carried out (see below, pp. 349f.).

The period of silence and its end: 24.25a, 26, 27

The words spoken by God in vv. 21 and 24, assuming the correctness of what has been said above, have their direct continuation in the section vv. 25–27. The main difficulty about it is that vv. 25 and 26 contain an intolerable contradiction: on the same day that Yahweh gives up Jerusalem to her fate a survivor is to come to Ezekiel and tell him the news of it. Obviously this is impossible in view of the distance between Palestine and Babylonia. To make confusion worse confounded, we are informed in 33.21 that it was not until the fifth day of the tenth month of the twelfth year of exile, i.e. in January 586, half a year after the storming of Jerusalem, that a fugitive succeeded in making his way to Tel Abīb, who, having been an eyewitness of that terrible event, was able to confirm it in detail, whereas all that was known before was the general fact with no verification of its particulars.

Various methods can be adopted in order to get rid of the discrepancy: the most common is the deletion of v. 26 along with the mention of the fugitive in v. 27 on the score that it is a subsequent assimilation to 33.21. As a result we get two different reports of the ending of a period of Ezekiel's dumbness. According to the first, contained in vv. 24, 25 and 27, the end of the period of dumbness coincided with the fall of Jerusalem in August 587. According to the second, as transmitted in 33.21f., it ended half a year later, when the fugitive arrived with an accurate report of that catastrophe.

But it is difficult to credit that there should have been two different versions of a point so decisive in Ezekiel's life. To say that in the prophet's judgment the day of the fall of Jerusalem would be equivalent to the day on which he received the news, seeing that he did not till then feel that it had taken place (Fohrer), can hardly account for the juxtaposition of two dates with a divergence of about half a year between them, especially considering how one of them gives the exact date and thus shows an interest in fixing unalterably the exact date of such a clearly defined event. One must therefore look at some of the other proposed solutions. Bertholet's attempt at one is worthy of note. He regards v. 27 as a gloss, and therefore considers that this passage originally contained an announcement of the coming of a fugitive, who is to bring Ezekiel the news of the fall of the capital city. This suggestion does not, however, solve the above-mentioned difficulty of the relationship of this passage to 33.21. The assumption that Ezekiel was at that time residing neither in Jerusalem nor in Babylonia, but in one of the country districts of the province, where a messenger could reach him on the same day as the catastrophe, has no foundation. It also has the fatal result of making the prophet perform his symbolic acts of the war years not in the presence of the not insignificant remnant of the nation in Babylonia but in the seclusion of an unimportant country place. On the other hand, it is worth noting the remark Bertholet makes about the alleged insertion of v. 27: he says that the verse is reminiscent of what is said in ch. 3 and 4 of a lengthy period during which the prophet was struck dumb; but there are various indications showing that it belongs not to the beginning of the prophet's activity but to the period of the fall of Jerusalem.

If that is so, then the notification in v. 27 ought to be regarded as original, since it helps us to realize the full significance for Ezekiel of the coming of the fugitive. On the other hand, v. 25 seems to divert attention to the catastrophe at Jerusalem, and throws everything into confusion. As it completely coincides with v. 21, it must originally have served to introduce the prophet's words in vv. 22, 23 (so also Heinisch). When these verses were inserted into the divine words, they were adapted by means of the necessary alterations in the suffixes so as to make their introduction match the special communication to the prophet in vv. 26f. The first three words of v. 25 also belong to the original context of v. 24, along with vv. 26, 27, being directly addressed to the prophet, and form a much better introduction to v. 26 and emphasize how important it is. For obviously what we have here is a promise which is to comfort Ezekiel in face of a personal trial which is imposed upon him, and causes a sudden interruption to his preaching: with the death of his wife a long period of silence descends upon him. Yahweh has nothing more to say to his people, he preserves strict silence in the face of all complaints, petitions and inquiries, and during the trying period of waiting and of uncertainty leaves nothing but the picture of the prophet overwhelmed by his agonizing experience so that he may act as a grim symbol of a will to judge which is no longer to be postponed.

But here we arrive at the point where, with Bertholet, we must recall the time, described in 3.24ff. and 4.4ff., when Ezekiel was struck physically lame and dumb. While discussing these passages, we have already pointed out that they were first placed in their present position by the prophet's disciples and in this way were given an interpretation (cf. above pp. 75f. and 83f.). Whereas it is impossible, however much we try, to harmonize them with their present context, they fit magnificently into the set of circumstances described in 24.15–27. In that position they bring out the full meaning of the prophet's being shut up in his house and having his prophetic warnings silenced (3.24–26) and thus strengthen his parabolic action in 24.16f. Of course, the statements in this connection should not be watered down, as the gloss in 3.27 tries to do by changing words clearly intended to signify complete dumbness into a temporary silence. This painstaking attempt to correct out of existence an absolute prohibition against speaking, which could only be justified as an attempt to reconcile the discrepancy with the unceasing proclamation by the prophet at the start, only serves to minimize the prophet's utter prostration and thus makes God's act of judgment meaningless once it is transplanted into the context of 24.15ff. This is confirmed by 4.4–8, which also presupposes a long period of paralysis, and excludes any public speaking on the part of the prophet. (4.7 is secondary, like 3.27, as we saw in discussing them earlier.) Bearing the guilt of Israel and Judah is thus associated with the omission of the mourning customs in 24.16f., as a second symbolic action, in order to portray through the prophet's vicarious sufferings the impending punishment in which Judah is put side by side with rejected Israel. This period of suffering is said to last more than seven months; it must therefore have begun about two weeks before the fall of Jerusalem. The outward sign of its ultimate termination is to be the arrival of the eyewitness of the catastrophe, as is stated in 24.26f. 'Your mouth will be opened . . . and you will speak and be no longer dumb.' The triumphant experience of deliverance which is here promised to the prophet in words which are used to describe the joy of the fulfilment in the account of ch. 33, will have not only given a great feeling of unburdening and liberation to Ezekiel himself; it also points to a hope that will accompany Judah into exile. As we saw before, the numbers given in ch. 4, 5 and 6 fix a limit to the doom of punishment and thus enable the forgiveness eventually to come into sight, though not till after the expiry of a long period. Thus what we find here is not a final surrendering of the existence of the people of God to an irrevocable end, but the announcement of a divine will to forgiveness alongside the end of the period of punishment. The promise in 24.27 of a restoration of the power to speak points in the same direction: after a period of complete alienation from his people, God will once more make use of the services of his messenger and thus create the prerequisite for his word to sound forth once more. In spite of all the restraint of the language, one cannot fail to see that beyond the depths of divine retribution there is a glimpse of a new shore, and that glimpse gives courage to the prophet and to every man who joins him in humbling himself under the mighty hand of God to go forward through the darkness of the forthcoming event.

Once one realizes that this is what is meant by the promise in 24.26f., conjoined with the affliction of the prophet in ch. 3 and 4, then, despite all the difficulties of the text, one cannot accept as a satisfactory solution any out-and-out rejection of 24.25–27 as a piece of redactional elaboration, further confused by the addition of glosses (Zimmerli). In spite of the impossibility of reconstituting the original text as it existed previous to the transfer of 3.24–26 and 4.4–8 to their present position, the mutual relationship between these two passages and ch. 24 is so significant and has such clarifying effects that we would be very ill advised to give up the whole text on the plea that it is no longer possible to account for all the details of its history.

The carrying out of the divine instructions:
24.18b, 19, 20a, 21aα, 25b, 22, 23

We are told in a plain, matter-of-fact, unemotional way how God's prediction was fulfilled, and how the prophet obediently performed the task laid upon him. This report also seems to have undergone some abbreviation. There is no further reference to the omission of the mourning customs, nor are the words of God repeated over again in full. Instead, as has already been stated (cf. above, p. 345), an explanation of the symbolic action is given in the form of a statement by the prophet in the first person singular. God's words had described Ezekiel as being a token of what was in store for his fellow exiles, as he shows in anticipation the grief they are to feel, and so accordingly the words spoken by the prophet sentence them to a similar wordless and tearless grief, and to a similar forgetfulness of all the outward signs of mourning under the overwhelming weight of their visitation, like that which they see the prophet undergoing now, and which makes them shake their heads. For the last time they are warned against the un-committed attitude of a spectator, who refuses to let himself be reached by the word of God's messenger, and still imagines that what is happening before him is a mere interesting spectacle devoid of any practical importance, whereas they are actually being summoned to a repentant knowledge of their God. This prediction by the prophet is the last piece of help he can give them to prevent them from endur-ing the agony of intolerable sorrow which awaits them, and which will drain them of all the life and strength, as if it were a meaningless occurrence. He reminds them that their affliction has a higher object, which is to bring them to a new knowledge of God.

ORACLES AGAINST FOREIGN NATIONS
25-32

With ch. 25 there begins a series of chapters which stand by themselves, sharply distinguished from what precedes and follows, and forming an independent whole as compared with the rest of the contents of this prophetic book. They vary in their literary form, but form a unity, thanks to their common subject. The oracles collected here turn to threaten a number of foreign nations and proclaim to them the retribution which their guilt has brought upon them at the hands of the Lord of all the earth. We have good reasons for considering it certain that this collection is based on a set of prophecies originating from Ezekiel himself. We find seven dates. Six of these fall within the brief space of three years. This makes them stand out from the earlier dates, which are much more widely spaced. The seventh date introduces an additional item coming fifteen years later and thus helps to justify it (29.17–21). The pieces which these dates introduce and numerous other undated ones agree well in their general manner of composition with the rest of the prophetic book. The diction, too, agrees so closely with corresponding passages elsewhere in the book, such as ch. 16, 17, 19, that the most natural explanation is to assume that all are the work of the same author. In this collection Ezekiel evidently recorded in chronological order a set of his prophecies linked to one another by a common subject and thus constituted them as an integral whole.

The prophetic autograph has not, however, come to us retaining its original dimensions and wording. The collection has not preserved its original order—a prophecy against Tyre has been put first (26.1ff.), though its correct position is after the third Egyptian prophecy and in about the same period as the fourth (32.1–16). This shows that a desire to combine together material on one subject, like the oracles against Tyre, has gained a victory over the principle of arrangement according to chronological order. The little book of Tyrian prophecies (ch. 26–28) therefore only came to be formed in the course of the redaction of the whole. It was preceded in ch. 25 by the undated

prophecies against four Palestinian nations. The little book of prophecies must then have undergone numerous enrichments. On the one
hand, the number of nations addressed is increased so as to make the
favourite number of seven, whereas originally there were only two or
three. On the other hand, the individual oracles had their texts
elaborated and reinterpreted in various directions. We thus find ourselves studying the subsequent history of the prophetic text, which
helps us to realize how intensively the prophet's disciples occupied
themselves with it, and we see how they tended at some points to
carry on certain lines of the prophetic proclamation, now going further
than the prophet himself, now lagging behind him. But it must be
left to the detailed exegesis for this to be dealt with more precisely.
The condition of the material agrees so closely with the addresses to
the foreign nations in the book of Isaiah (ch. 13–23) and Jeremiah
(ch. 46–51), that these portions of these three prophetic books
mutually elucidate and support one another.

The little book against foreign nations, expanded in this way, may
have existed independently for some time after its publication; at any
rate, it did not absorb other passages similar in type, such as 21.33–37;
35 and 38f. Its insertion into the midst of the text of the prophetic
book has all the appearance of a foreign body pushing its way into an
organic whole, and in the process tearing apart things originally connected together. The announcement of the coming downfall of Jerusalem in 24.15ff. is now severed from the account, closely associated
with it, of how the prophecy came to pass, in 33.21f.; then this latter
is interfered with still more by being pushed farther back by the fresh
commission issued to Ezekiel in 33.1–20, which it was evidently
thought absolutely necessary to put at the beginning of the third part
of the book. Undoubtedly this ruthless disturbance of the organic
arrangement took place with the object of displaying three main
periods of the prophet's activity. The proclamation of judgment upon
his own nation was followed by the sentence of condemnation upon
the heathen powers, in order that this destructive action might conclude constructively with the promise of the salvation to come. How
serviceable this method of arrangement was felt to be for this particular end is shown by its being also employed in the final redaction
of the books of Isaiah and Jeremiah (in the latter the placing of the
oracles to the nations subsequently to ch. 25, as is done in the Greek
version, is preferable to the Massoretic arrangement).

Now, these collections of oracles to the nations show manifest predilection for a similar method of classifying the enemy and using the same stereotyped formulas for the threats to them. After Amos 1 and 2, the number of seven is always a favourite one for nations. It is employed in Jeremiah as well as in Ezekiel, as also in the brief enumeration in Isa. 11.14f., but the numbers in Zeph. 2 and Dan. 11.41 fall short of it. The oldest announcement of judgment to nations in Amos 1f. shows such a uniformly symmetrical structure that it poses a question whether such prophecies are not all derived from a traditional scheme, to which the prophets adhered. One may conjecture that something of the sort was most likely at the covenant feast or the celebration of the king's enthronement, in both of which the punishment of enemies was an obvious concern, cf. Pss. 97.3; 98.9; 99.1f. and Pss. 2; 45.5; 110. 2, 5ff. That this conjecture is not wide of the mark has been shown in a surprising way by the so-called Execration Texts in Egypt, dating from the first half of the second millennium BC. They were written on earthenware vessels and pronounced curses according to a conventional form against Egypt's enemies on the south, north and west of the kingdom and also against the rebels within the country itself. They were given operation and effect by the symbolical breaking in pieces of the vessels in a solemn ritual act. This justifies the assumption that a similar cultic custom existed in Israel, though, of course, we need not think that it took exactly the same shape (the smashing of a pot by Jeremiah along with a threat to break the nation and city in pieces in Jer. 19.1ff., for example, makes no mention of any inscription on the pot). Nevertheless, it may have encouraged the formation of a schema containing stereotyped formulas for such maledictions. It is easy to see how the prophets from Amos on came, all alike, to employ this same form when they wished to pronounce judgment on the nations surrounding Israel. They could count on securing the jubilant approval of their fellow countrymen, and then made use of the attention they had thus secured, in order the more unforgettably to impress upon their audience their proclamation of judgment upon Israel.

On the other hand, it is very improbable that they took over the previously existing form so slavishly that they felt obliged in every case to proclaim judgment for foreign nations, and to employ the sevenfold pattern in doing so. Their announcements were determined not by immemorial custom or by the cherished wishes of their fellow countrymen, but by the concrete situation in which they knew God had placed them and out of which they were bidden to speak.

So the sevenfold schema is not found in Isaiah. It cannot be established with any certainty for Jeremiah, owing to the conflicting assessments of Jer. 46–49. Even in Ezekiel, in whose work it is now present, most probably the schema cannot be attributed to the prophet himself, but is the final product of a number of subsequent additions. The revisers of a prophet's writings must have felt a continuous temptation to reproduce this schema, in which the number seven was interpreted as summing up the completion of all possibilities and therefore seemed to secure effectiveness for what the prophet proclaimed. The prophet did not concern himself with foreign nations in order to produce prophecies popular among his own people so that they might look on him as a genuine messenger of God. He did so only because those nations were presuming to impede God's plans for judgment, and by their whole behaviour were constituting a temptation to his nation and a danger to the realization of his own statements about the future. As with Jeremiah, the main concern is Yahweh's order for the subjection of the whole world to the king of Babylon, who has been entrusted by him with the duty of carrying out his judgment upon the nations. The apparently unconquerable adversaries of Babylon therefore occupy the chief place in Ezekiel's predictions concerning foreign nations, whereas the others only find mention in the margin.

But the surprising thing is that this commission occasioned the prophet's most important and most beautiful poems. In the magnitude of their scale, in the astonishing variety of the materials chosen, in the thrilling way in which their bright pictures are unfolded, and in the accurate characterization of all the figures appearing in them, they are without their match in all prophetic literature. We learn that the prophet, after his experiments on a smaller scale in ch. 17 and 19, has now become a poet of exceptional power, who could be so completely gripped by his subject for the time being that he is occupied with the features of common humanity in some stirring event, and the pronunciation of a judgment upon it is forced into the background. To regard him under this aspect helps to correct the traditional picture of the allegedly sober and prosaic spirit, petty minded and unable to think in any but legalistic categories!

CHAPTER 25.1–17

Oracle against the neighbouring nations in Palestine

1 The word of Yahweh came to me: ²'Son of man, set your face to-wards^a the Ammonites, and prophesy against them. ³Say to the Ammonites: Hear the word [. . .]^b of Yahweh: Thus says [. . .]^c Yahweh: Because you said Aha! over my sanctuary when it was profaned, and over the land of Israel when it was made desolate, and over the house of Judah when it went into exile; ⁴therefore I am handing you over to the people of the East for a possession, that they may set^d their encampments among you and pitch their tents in your midst. They shall eat your fruit, and they shall drink your milk. ⁵And I make Rabbah a pasture for camels and the [cities]^e of the Ammonites a fold for sheep, that you may know that I am Yahweh.

6 For thus says [. . .]^f Yahweh: because you^g have clapped your hand and stamped your feet and rejoiced with all the malice within you against the^h land of Israel, ⁷therefore, behold, I will stretch out my hand against you, and will hand you over as [spoil to]ⁱ the nations, and will cut you off from the nations and will banish you out of the countries [. . .]^j and you will know, that I am Yahweh.

8 Thus says [. . .]^k Yahweh: because Moab [. . .]^l said: Behold the house of Judah is like all the (other) nations, ⁹therefore behold, I will open up the mountain side^m of Moab and [lay bare its cities]ⁿ on its whole frontier, the glory of the country: Beth-hayyeshimoth, Baal-meon, and Kiriathaim. ¹⁰I will give it along^p with the Ammonites to the people of the East as a possession, that it may be remembered no more [. . .]^o among the nations. ¹¹And I will execute judgments upon Moab, that they may know that I am Yahweh.

12 Thus says [. . .]^p Yahweh: because Edom acted revengefully^q against the house of Judah and has grievously offended, in taking vengeance upon them, ¹³therefore thus says [. . .]^r Yahweh: I will stretch out my hand against Edom, and cut off from it man and beast and make it desolate from Teman to Dedan. ¹⁴And I will lay my vengeance upon Moab in the hand of my people Israel, and they shall do in Edom according to my anger and according to my wrath, and they shall know my vengeance, says [. . .]^s Yahweh.

15 Thus says [. . .]^tYahweh: because the Philistines acted revenge-fully and took vengeance with malice of heart to destroy in never-ending enmity, ¹⁶therefore thus says [. . .]^u Yahweh, Behold I will stretch out my

hand against the Philistines and will cut off^v the Cherethites and destroy the remnant upon the sea-coast. ^17And I will execute great acts of vengeance upon them with wrathful chastisements, that they may know that I am Yahweh, when I lay my vengeance upon them.'

^aRead ʿ*al* instead of ʾ*el*.

^b-ʹSee BH.

^gIn vv. 6f. there is a remarkable use of the masculine suffix instead of the feminine suffix second person singular which has hitherto been used.

^h-ʹSee BH.

^jMT: 'I will destroy you'; an inserted disconnected phrase, which sounds meaningless after the three preceding ones, perhaps originally a marginal gloss.

^kSee BH.

^lMT: 'and Seir'. This refers to Edom. But as it, too, has judgment pronounced in vv. 12ff., we should follow the LXX and delete this reference as a later insertion.

^mPerhaps 'the shoulder'.

^nRead with Bertholet and Bewer *meʿāreh ʿārāw* for the unintelligible MT: 'From her cities, from the cities'.

^oMT: 'The Ammonites'; erroneous addition.

^pSee BH.

^q*binqōm*, the MT reading, is an unidiomatic expression and looks like an addition, unless one takes it with Bertholet as a variant reading, changing the pointing to *benāqām*.

^r-uSee BH.

^v*hikrattī ʾet-kerētīm* a play on words.

The oracle against Ammon: 25.1–7

[1] The section is introduced by a formula with the complete structure appropriate to the introduction to a 'messenger-saying'. [2–3a] The word of God goes forth, and addresses a command to the son of man in person, bidding him pronounce a word against the Ammonites, who are summoned to attend to it.

[3b] In v. 3b the direct judgment-speech by God begins with the introductory formula 'Thus says Yahweh'. It first states the offence in the form of a threat, which makes the iniquity centre in loudly-expressed jubilation over the destruction of God's temple, God's land, and God's people. [4] Then in vv. 4f. it proclaims that the judge is just about to intervene, employing the well-known formula of judgment. [5] He will send the 'Sons of the East' as the executants of his judgment, and they will take possession of Ammon, i.e. of the territory, and drive in their flocks and set up their tents. As nomadic breeders of cattle, who despise cultivated settlements, they know only how to plunder it of such of its produce, like corn and milk, as serves their

needs, and to destroy the cities and leave them uninhabited ruins, good enough for pasturing cattle in once they are overgrown with quickly-spreading weeds.

This is a colourful picture, presented by means of a few concrete features, which depicts the fate that was always threatening to break in over those nations of Palestine who lived along the border to the east of the Jordan. The nomadic tribes who inhabited the wide desert and steppe country to the east of the cultivated territory, familiar to Israel under the name of the 'Sons of the East' (Gen. 29.1; Judg. 6.33, etc.), were under a constant temptation to force their way into the zone occupied by settled farmers every time they got a chance, and especially at times when their lives were endangered by long-continued droughts. These forays have made the Bedouin of the Hauran a plague to settled farmers all through the centuries and down to the present day. Such camel-owning nomads did not usually try to change their ways and settle down, but retired after their raids into their own native zone, which, sparse as it was, was not in danger from any conqueror. This time, however, they were going to overwhelm the cultivated land like a tide, and become the rulers of the country, forcing its former possessors to give place. Large tracts of Ammonite territory had been pasture; now the habits of nomadic life would triumph and turn even the arable land into a steppe. The glory of the Ammonite kingdom and of its proud capital Rabbah (usually called Rabbath Ammon) would be thus brought to an end once for all.

[6f.] A further formula for a prophetic word attaches a second threat of judgment to the first, and this second in vv. 6f. had noticeable peculiarities of its own. These consist not only of a change to the masculine form of the pronoun but also in the massiveness of the threats. The catastrophe to the Ammonite state will be surpassed by the elimination of the whole people, as peoples and nations now advance against them to bring about their ruin. This attempt at intensification of the judgment, however, serves to render it more colourless, the guilt being apparently reduced to contempt shown towards the land of Israel, with the object (it would seem) of bringing Ammon's fate into conformity with that of Israel, as depicted in prophetic denunciations. In view of all this, grave doubts arise whether this addition has been made by the prophet's own hand. We can better explain the peculiarities of the passage by taking it to be one of those compositions by the prophet's disciples, who, as we have already seen, often like to go further along lines suggested by what the prophet has said.

This judgment upon Ammon and the others which follow have been compared with the prophecies of disaster in Amos 1f., and all alike have been classified as belonging to the type of maledictions against foreign nations, like those known to us from the middle dynasty of Egypt. There is no doubt of the relationship from the aspect of historical development of form. Yet the saying with which we are dealing has one marked characteristic: it concentrates upon Ammon's religious guilt, and lets go all political accusations (as in Zeph. 2.8ff.). Yet plenty of the latter could be found, since the history of the enmity with Ammon was centuries old; a long list could have been drawn up of his threatening words and aggressive actions against Israel, which had endangered her settlement in the promised land as well as her consolidation as a state, and had continually broken the peace between the two nations (Judg. 10f.; I Sam. 11; II Sam. 10–12; Amos 1.13ff.). The perfidious way in which these neighbours, in spite of all their anti-Babylonian protestations, had already consented in 598 to be employed by Nebuchadrezzar on punitive expeditions against Jehoiakim (II Kings 24.2), and, above all else, the ambiguous part played by the Ammonite king Baalis in the murder of the last Judahite Governor, Gedaliah, after the conquest of Jerusalem, allowing the murderer, Ishmael, of Davidic descent, to find a safe refuge in his court (Jer. 40ff.), were all things of which Ezekiel's contemporaries were fully aware. But all such political entanglements, where the problem of who is guilty is never clear, and in which so large a part is played by the natural reaction of the weaker nation against the stronger one by whom its independence is threatened, have here completely vanished. The centre of the stage is taken up by the triumph of heathenism over Israel's religious claim to have had bestowed upon her a special revelation of God, giving a unique value to her temple and territory as well as to her existence as a nation, as guarantees of the presence of God and of her commission to a special historical task. Israel's failure to perform the duty entrusted to her gave a good enough reason for her heathen neighbour to mock at that claim of hers, as the monstrous offspring of pride and vanity, such as must necessarily lead to a heavy fall; and the message proclaimed by the Israelite prophets of doom provided a complete vindication of this opinion.

What is under discussion here is not the human right to take up such an attitude. That is only too intelligible, in view of what was unintelligible to God's own people, the obscuring of the whole revelation by a catastrophe which they thought could never happen. The subject under discussion is rather the actual blindness that does not see how God has control over the history of his people, and which rejoices at being apparently set free from this nation's intolerable claim and from its sharp criticisms of the self-assurance of heathen life. At bottom Ammon has importance only as one more example of a complete refusal to accept a specific divine sacred history which so disturbingly questions all heathen assurance of God, which has repeatedly made Israel a stumbling-block to the rest of the world in which she lives. So the prophet's announcement of judgment is directed against the suggestion that the judgment of the Holy God upon his people proves the complete nullity of any revelation that has taken place among them; for this to be proclaimed aloud will be a temporary triumph for the enemies of God, and will render insoluble the spiritual crisis into which Israel herself has been led. He holds unshakably to his belief that Yahweh has set up his royal lordship over the whole world, and promises that it will be magnificently vindicated when God intervenes also in what happens to the heathen who oppose and despise him. The prophet was able to proclaim that God was acting in the history of his people and had gone on doing so even in an unclean land. So he can also proclaim that the God of Israel who alone had majesty was asserting it in the history of the nations. Yahweh will speak later of the profaning of his name among the nations through the unfaithfulness of Israel (ch. 36) and of the necessity that his name be hallowed among them. But he is already indicating that this is the object of what he does with the heathen, when he ends his message with an announcement of this ultimate aim: 'And you shall know that I am Yahweh.' Here, as everywhere else in what the prophets foretell, Yahweh's world-wide triumph is regarded as being linked in time with the deliverance of his people. This belongs to the very nature of the expectation which looks for final fulfilment as close at hand and could be corrected only when it attained to its New Testament fulfilment. In its whole attitude this section is close to Zeph. 2.8ff.

God's word against Moab: 25.8–11

The prophecies to the nations which follow that addressed to Ammon are noticeably different from it, lacking as they do the word-event

formula and the commission to the prophet. They are introduced
merely by the messenger-saying, and this seems to mark them as
secondary additions. The introduction in vv. 1–3 limits itself to
Ammon; if anyone else is to be addressed one would expect the
prophet to receive a fresh commission. In addition, direct address of
the person denounced is given up in favour of impersonal speech in
the third person. So one may say that the oracles which follow are
arranged in a very loose order, and we find a similar looseness in their
shape and material.

The address to Moab, however, evidently stands in a closer relationship to what precedes it than either of.the two oracles which
follow it. Once more the guilt is confined to the same religious opposition to Judah, although, as in the case of Ammon, there could have
been plenty of grave political charges. Moab's encounters with Israel
went as far back, and were quite as strong. We need only recall Judg.
3.12–30 and ch. 11, II Sam. 8, and the triumphal inscription[1] of the
Moabite king Mesha (mentioned in the Old Testament in II Kings
3), in which he boasts of having succeeded in throwing off the
Israelite yoke, of having slaughtered all his prisoners to feast the eyes
of his gods, and of having occupied what had hitherto been Israelite
territory. During the Assyrian period we find the kings of Moab
joining in anti-Assyrian alliances between the smaller states of Syria,
but that does not prevent them from trying in the meantime to wipe
off old scores against their Israelite neighbours. So they let themselves
be used by Nebuchadrezzar as instruments to punish Jehoiakim, and
then a few years later negotiate at Jerusalem about taking part in a
rising against their Babylonian employer (Jer. 27.3). Zephaniah 2.8
and Jer. 48.27 also tell of their vindictive mockery of the defeated
Judahites. [8] Nevertheless, Moab's guilt is stated as consisting solely
in having triumphantly rated Judah as being on the same level as her
neighbours: 'Behold the house of Judah is like all the (other) nations.'
Hence, once more, the attack against any alliance with the neighbours of Israel, and regarding the fall of their old rival as a clear
refutation of that nation's claim to a special position as the bearer of
a message from God.

[10] Equally clear is the close resemblance of the statement of the
punishment to that of the address to Ammon. This consists of being
delivered over to the Sons of the East. It is explicitly associated with
the destiny in store for the Ammonites; but has no special concrete

[1] *AOT*[2], 1926, pp. 440–2.

feature. A commonplace like the accomplishment of judgments must suffice. Only at one point do we see a unique representation of the coming disaster. [11] This consists in the tearing away of the 'shoulder', or almost inaccessible cliff of Moab, leading to the overthrow of the three cities (v. 9) which defend it, and which are spoken of as specially important adornments of the country. These cities are mentioned in Josh. 13.15–20 and Num. 32f. as belonging to Reubenite territory, and have lately been identified with some probability. So Beth-hayyeshimoth lies in the Jordan depression at the foot of the mountain slope; and Baal Me'on (or Beth Baal Ma'on in full), which is undoubtedly the modern Ma'in, and Kiriathaim lie not too far to the south-west of it on the Moabite plateau, and are evidently mentioned as fortresses defending the northern frontier. Thus the list seems to show a good knowledge of the locality. Yet the concrete precision of this detail may be dictated mainly by interest in recovering former Reubenite frontier districts, rather than by, say, religious judgment in regard to fortresses as incorporations of human power and possession. The name of any divinely-chosen instrument of judgment is also absent, and the Sons of the East who are subsequently mentioned hardly come under that heading. So this element of the text is totally lacking in anything that can go to prove any parallelism between this section and vv. 1–5. Instead of that we must regard it as similar in character to vv. 6f. How Moab and Ammon were frequently associated together in such threats is evident from Jer. 38f. and Zeph. 2.8–11. So it seems very probable that some disciple of the prophet added the address to Moab as a later amplification, and that it was perhaps the same person who inserted vv. 6f. It is still clearer that the two sections which follow come from a similar quarter.

A word of God against Edom: 25.12–14

The word formula of the messenger-saying marks out this address, too, as an appendix loosely attached to what has preceded it. [12] It commences with a very formal and hollow-sounding argument, mentioning the inexorable vindictiveness of Edom towards Judah and the resultant guilt. But apart from repetitions of this charge, nothing concrete is brought forward, evidently because the person who has composed this passage knows that his readers are in the know right from the beginning and that he does not even have to mention the name of Edom's victim. Edom was the most fiercely hated of all Israel's eastern neighbours, and the campaigns against her ever since the time of David had been conducted with especial bitterness and with utter ruthlessness (cf. I Kings 11.14ff.; II Kings 14.7; Amos 1.11f.). Precisely because he was counted as a 'brother' (Obad. 10; Deut. 23.8) his behaviour was felt to show a still more injurious disregard for the obligations of the relationship of solidarity, and, of course, there was no thought of his having been himself a victim of Israel's encroachment. His collaboration in destroying Jerusalem, as witnessed in Ps. 137.7, seems to have brought the measure to the full, as is testified by the terrible curses applied to him in Obadiah; Isa. 34.5ff.; Jer. 49.7ff.; Joel 4.19; Lam. 4.21; he was to be made to pay for his shameful deeds towards Israel. In the similar context in Ezek. 25.12 we see a very considerable descent from the sublime heights of the preceding words of judgment on to a merely nationalist level of thought.

[13] Nevertheless the proclamation of the punishment, marked out by a separate introduction with another messenger-saying formula, and announcing how Yahweh will completely annihilate both man and beast, confines itself to the most general terms. [14] It only rises to full life with the statement that Israel is to carry out the judgment and that it will be executed with a ruthlessness corresponding to the divine wrath and fury. Consequently the object of divine judgment, which is always stated elsewhere to be the knowledge of Yahweh, is in an almost cynical manner transposed into knowledge, i.e. experience, of the *wrath of Yahweh*, without any compensating glimpse of a higher goal. This relapse into nationalistic vindictiveness seems irreconcilable with Ezekiel's attitude towards Yahweh's judgment as expressed by him elsewhere. So there has been a desire to cut it out as a later addition. Yet the value of such a partial amputation seems doubtful, in view of the fact that even after it, what is still left is at a level so much lower than what has preceded it. Both internal and external evidence combines to show that the address to Ammon has been subjected to a far wider and deeper elaboration.

A word of God against the Philistines: 25.15–17

[15] The saying has again the same type of introduction, with the same reason (confined, as before, to generalities) for the divine judgment, which does not even state explicitly who has been injured by the Philistines. Here also the repetition of the charge of contempt in v. 6 is so closely linked with the root *nākam* (vengeance), repeated three times in succession, that religious opposition seems subordinate

to national. That point is brought out by the statement that the enemy aims at destruction and is resolved on eternal enmity, but it is surprising for it to be stated of the Philistines, who are elsewhere treated with goodwill. In spite of the fact that considerable portions of the territory of Judah were given to them by Sennacherib as well as Nebuchadrezzar as a punishment for Judahite rebellions, the desire for vengeance is not as hot against them as against Israel's eastern neighbours. Amos 1.6–8 alone states that they will be annihilated for having sold into slavery the inhabitants of whole Israelite villages, a charge which is taken up again at a much later date in Joel 3.1f. Otherwise the prophecies of disaster against them follow once more the traditional formulas for such execratory texts (cf. Zeph. 2.4–7, where the threats made by Amos are repeated, and Jer. 47). In the last prophecy there is a note of what almost sounds like a little sympathy, and so Zech. 9.7 looks forward, after the destruction of their cities, which are regarded by other nations also as centres of human hybris, to the preservation of a remnant for Yahweh, which will be put on a par with the clans of Judah. This may go back to recollections of the maintenance of a brotherhood in arms, which David had kept up after driving them back behind their own frontier, but it was also due to respect for the courageous way in which they withstood the Assyrian attacks, which had generally fallen on them first. Isaiah 11.14 and Obad. 19 speak only of the victorious extension of Israelite dominions so as to include their territory. The address to the Philistines in this chapter has only two concrete features. This is the way it singles out the Cretans, the Philistine tribe situated the furthest to the south, who evidently took their name from their former home (cf. I Sam. 30.6 and the mention of them among David's professional soldiers in II Sam. 8.18, etc.) and also mentions the remnant upon the sea-coast, apparently meaning some surviving remnant now confined to a narrow coastal strip, of those Philistines who had formerly been so aggressive in the interior of the land. But both of these seem to be exceptions taken over from Zeph. 2.5, so they cannot alter the general character of the section.

The introductory chapter to the oracles of the nations thus presents us with the complicated facts of the case. There is a short oracle against Ammon which suggests, by its outward shape and also by its inward attitude of mind, that it is by the prophet. It has been subjected to amplifications by a later hand, which not only extend further the address to the Ammonites, but also append three additional oracles directed against Judah's nearest neighbours. With these additions ought also to be associated an oracle on Sidon in 28.20–25. But the fact that these additions swell the addresses to foreign nations, bringing them up to the number of seven, can hardly be taken to have been a motive which prevailed upon Ezekiel to fill up the number of his three oracles against Ammon, Tyre and Egypt, however effective one may consider the tradition of the holy number seven to have been in proclaiming such curses. On the other hand, this motive may well have had an active influence upon those who collected and completed the texts left by the prophet.

VARIOUS ORACLES AGAINST TYRE
AND HER PRINCE
26.1–28.26

CHAPTER 26.1–21

Threats against Tyre

1 In the eleventh year, [. . .],ᵃ on the first day of the month, the word
of Yahweh came to me: ²'Son of man, because Tyre has said concerning
Jerusalem:
"Aha, the gate of the peoples is broken,
it has been given over to me, but [she that was replenished],ᵇ is laid
waste",
3 Therefore thus says [. . .]ᶜ Yahweh:
Behold, I am against you, O Tyre,
and will bring up many nations against you,
as the sea brings up its waves.
4 They shall destroy the walls of Tyre,
and break down her towers,
and I will scrape her soil from her,
and make her a bare rock.
5 She shall be in the midst of the sea a place for drying nets.
For I have said it, says [. . .]ᵈ Yahweh.
And she shall become a spoil to the nations, ⁶and her daughters on the
mainland shall be slain by the sword, and they shall know that I am
Yahweh.
7 For thus says [. . .]ᵉ Yahweh: Behold I bring upon Tyre Nebuchadrezzar the king of Babylon from the north, king of kings, with horses and
chariots and horsemen and [with a levy of many people].ᶠ ⁸He will slay
with the sword your daughters on the mainland. He will set up a siege
wall against you, and throw up a mound against you, and raise a roof of
shields against you. ⁹He will direct the shock of his battering rams against
your walls, and with his iron he will break down your towers. ¹⁰His horses
will be so many that their dust will cover you. Your walls will shake at the
noise of the horsemen and wheels and chariots, when he enters your
gates as one forces one's wayᵍ into a city which has been breached. ¹¹With

the hoofs of his horses he will trample all your streets, he will slay your warriors with the sword and your mighty pillars will tumble to the ground. ¹²They will make a spoil of your riches and a prey of your merchandise: they will break down your walls and destroy your pleasant houses and cast your stones and timber and rubbish into the [sea].ʰ ¹³And I will stop the music of your songs, and the sound of your lyres shall be heard no more. ¹⁴I will make you a bare rock, you will be a drying place for nets. You shall never be rebuilt, for I [. . .]ⁱ have said it! Says [. . .]ʲ Yahweh.

15 Thus says [. . .]ᵏ Yahweh to Tyre: will not the isles shake at the sound of your fall when the wounded groan, when slaughter is made with the swordˡ in the midst of you? ¹⁶All the princes of the sea will step down from their thrones and remove their robes and strip off their embroidered garments, and will put on mourningᵐ and sit upon the ground and tremble every moment, and be appalled at you. ¹⁷And they will raise a lamentation over you and say to you:

How you have vanishedᵐ [. . .]ⁿ from the seas, O city renowned, that was mighty on the sea,
she and her inhabitants,
who [imposed your terror] on all the [mainland].º

18 Now the isles tremble on the day of your fall,
the isles in the sea are dismayed at your passing.

19 For thus says [. . .]ᵖ Yahweh:
When I make you a city laid waste
like the cities that are not inhabited,
in bringing up the deep over you,
and the great waters cover you,

20 then I will thrust you down with those who descend into the pit,
I will [make]ᑫ you to dwell with the people of old,
in the nether world, among [primeval ruins]ʳ [. . .]ˢ
so that you will not [return] and [have your place]ᵗ in the land of the living.

21 I will deliver you to the terrors of death,
so that you will be no more [. . .]ᵘ and will never be found again,
[. . .]ᵛ says Yahweh.'

ᵃThe date of the month, presumably the eleventh or twelfth, is wanting, see Commentary.

ᵇ⁻ʰSee BH.

ⁱMT: 'Yahweh', which is not to be expected according to the line set by v. 5 and is wanting in many ancient versions.

ʲ⁻ᵐSee BH.

ⁿMT: 'been destroyed': the word is not present in several versions and seems to have been introduced in conflict with the metre in order to explain the next word which had been misread.

o–pSee BH.

qDelete w^e.

rRead ḥorbat ʿōlām.

sMT: 'with those that go down to the pit'; a repetition from the first line.

tSee BH.

uMT: 'Though you be sought for'; an amplification in prose; cf. the metre.

vSee BH.

In general

One cannot fail to notice that the threat against Tyre is much more extensive than the other oracles to the nations which have preceded it. The threats against Egypt which follow are lengthier still. Yet the exceptional length of the judgments pronounced upon them is thoroughly justified by the political importance of the two states. In world-affairs revolutionized by the rise of the neo-Babylonian empire, and also in the plan of the world-God proclaimed by the prophets, they formed powerful and almost insuperable obstacles such as could cause a long postponement of Nebuchadrezzar's ultimate triumph. In comparison to them, Judah's smaller neighbours were like wretched little curs, which could be rendered harmless without much effort. Tyre and Egypt, on the other hand, impressed by their power and were exercising and developing political forces which people in Jerusalem had good reason to hope would soon put an end to the series of Babylonian successes.

Both of these great powers therefore had an important part in the political calculations of the diplomats at Jerusalem, and they on their part regarded the kingdom of Judah as an ally valuable enough to be worth courting. Even during the last days of Jerusalem, Tyre was trying her utmost to resist the extension westwards of the neo-Babylonian empire, and took a really vigorous part in the attempts at revolt by the smaller Syrian states, just as she had done earlier against Assyria. According to Jer. 27, she took part in the negotiations of the year 594 for a Syrian coalition against Babylon. That these negotiations actually took place at Jerusalem shows Judah's prominence among her neighbours, which had assuredly been further intensified by Josiah's success in extending her territory to the north (cf. II Kings 23). Tyre, of course, generally knew how to withdraw her head from the noose, when a revolt misfired, escaping severer punishment by a prompt payment of tribute. Thanks to her incomparable situation

EZEKIEL

on a rocky island (hence the name of the city, which means 'rock'), she could, even when such manoeuvres were unsuccessful, have very good hopes of withstanding any attack by an enemy. The enormous difficulties of investing her deterred most conquerors from pinning down their forces. Only a few, like Sennacherib and Nebuchadrezzar, engaged on sieges, which lasted for years, and did not meet with the success which was first attained by Alexander the Great.

Beside this central political importance there was also an inward cause for the great length of the prophecy against Tyre. It consisted in the inner widening of the prophet's mental horizon. The message of judgment at first confines itself to punishment for malicious joy over the misfortunes of the chosen people. But it gains a higher perspective when it brings an indictment against the mistaken faith which the merchant city puts in her world-famed riches (ch. 27). Finally it soars to sublimity when it proclaims the overthrow of a human *hybris*, which tries to put itself in the place of God (ch. 28). Tyre thus becomes a typical enemy of God, in whom the powers that resist God concentrate themselves and try to dispute his sovereignty. This is a criticism very similar to that made of Assyria by Isaiah.

The nations attack Tyre: 26.1–6

This first section of the chapter is marked out by the date and correct formula introducing the word of God at the beginning, by the prophetic concluding formula in v. 5, and by the definition of the object of the judgment by the formula about the knowledge of Yahweh in v. 6.[1] The statement of the date has suffered damage. However, the careful method of construction of the whole section in forms found elsewhere in Ezekiel is a clear indication of composition by the prophet's own hand.

[1] Some discussion is called for by the dating. It gives the eleventh year of Jehoiachim, i.e. the year 587/86. But the form of the word for the number eleven is not the one usually found in Ezekiel (cf. 30.20; 31.1). So it may easily be a misreading of the number twelve, which is also found in Greek manuscripts. The censure of the malicious joy of Tyre in v. 2 seems directly evoked by the storming of Jerusalem, so it cannot be far removed from the arrival of the fugitive in the tenth month of the same year (33.21). So anyone who wants to bring it into

[1] For the conflict between these two formulas see below in the Commentary on vv. 5f.

close association with that event will prefer to choose the eleventh or at any rate the twelfth month of that year, rather than the first of the following one. None the less, that still leaves undecided the reasons which caused the word giving the date to take such a peculiar form. But in any case we find ourselves between February and April in the year 586.

As in 25.3, the word of God commences by naming the sin. [2] Here, too, it consists in mockery and malicious joy over the fall of Jerusalem, which arouses God's displeasure. Yet they assume a special character, since there is behind them a triumphant feeling of all the riches Tyre will gain by assuming a position that has hitherto been occupied by Jerusalem. This position is indicated by the peculiar expression 'gate of the peoples'. It is not at first clear what this means. One is tempted first of all to think of a central trading market, which the neighbouring nations cannot do without. That presupposes, however, a much better position on the traffic routes than that held by Jerusalem, which does not lie at the junction of a number of trade routes, and does not allege anything like as favourable a position as Samaria. Its strategic position, on the other hand, is exceptionally good, especially when it is combined with the mastery of the south as far as Elath and the Egyptian frontier, and used to the full thanks to an energetic policy such as Josiah had carried out so capably. In addition to this it controls some of the trade routes connecting Arabia and Egypt with the north. Certainly, one is led by the term 'gate of the peoples' to think of it in the sense of a closed gate (Fohrer), which hinders free trade by means of tolls and charges. In this case, however, it is hard to say what gain would arise for Tyre as a result of Jerusalem's exclusion from the manoeuvres for political power. The transformation of Judah into a province of Babylon was not calculated to open the way to freer trade. The political importance of Jerusalem was not, however, transferable to a Phoenician city, so there was no possibility of Tyre figuring at this point as the joyful heir. Evidently this interpretation of the triumphant boast is a much too narrow one. One must give it up for a wider view, and see it more in the satisfying of an ambition not to have any rival with whom to share political importance in Syria, now that the proud corner-pillar of Southern Syria, with its special claim to act as a counterpoise to the Phoenician power in the north, has been overthrown and broken to pieces.

[3] The world-God sets his face against such shameful joy at the liquidation of one of the competitors for dignity and influence. [4] He

lifts his menacing hand against the island fortress and launches a host
of nations against it, who surge against it like a spring tide and cast
down its walls and towers. What yet survives is swept away by the
Divine Avenger till nothing remains, as when a gigantic tidal wave
bares a naked rock. [5] Its reduction to complete desolation is unforgettably expressed by the picture of a bare shore in the midst of the
sea, used by no one except the fishermen who still dry their nets there.
The term used to describe the place with its almost impregnable
situation, which was also employed by the Egyptians and Assyrians
(one expression from an Assyrian war communiqué 'in the heart of
the sea' is used again word for word by Ezekiel, cf. 27.4; 28.2), is now
employed to express extreme desolation and unimportance. The protection which the sea gave to the proud city is transformed into the
opposite by its divine overlord and possessor, who makes its waves
surge into it with terrible force. In spite of its resemblance to Isa.
17.12 and Jer. 47.2, this is a completely unique and newly-invented
image. The threatening words come to a significant close with
Yahweh's personal guarantee of his word and with the prophetic
formula of conclusion.

The continuation, which is very loosely attached by means of the
last three words of v. 5, cannot be regarded as anything but an
additional insertion. [6] It adds a further act of divine retribution,
consisting in the plundering of the conquered city and the slaughter
of her daughter cities on the mainland. To strike a blow against these
satellite cities of Tyre was a very effectual method of weakening the
dominion of Tyre, which no attacker failed to strike. But after the
metropolis has been totally annihilated, this feature, like the plundering of its treasures, comes too late, and only serves to weaken the
effect of vv. 3–5 with their large-scale vision of judgment. The concluding formula about the knowledge of Yahweh, which must of
necessity refer solely to the daughter cities, thus becomes superficial
and is in any case ruled out by the other concluding formula preceding it. All this indicates an amplification by one of the prophet's
disciples.

The details of the storming: 26.7–14

This war-song has the same object as the appendix in vv. 5b and 6.
It is mostly in short lines of three or four feet, with longer *stichoi* here
and there between them. It takes up the task of describing the assault,
which has been thrown into the background by the great stroke of

retribution in vv. 3–5. What that threatening word has left, shrouded by the dark grey of a half-concealed future, is now revealed down to the smallest detail. **[7]** The place of God as sole agent is taken by his instrument Nebuchadrezzar, king of Babylon, under his full title 'king of kings'. His powerful military levies replace the many nations of v. 3. **[8f.]** His attack on the daughter cities is made to proceed out of the circumstances given in v. 6. How he applies his military science in the siege and with what results is partly described in words from 4.2. **[10–12]** This is followed by a full-length description of a thundering attack by war-chariots through the breaches made in the city wall, and the subsequent thorough plundering and destruction of the city. This is quite regardless of the fact that Tyre's position on an island made all such events hardly conceivable. **[13f.]** Finally, Amos 5.23 is quoted (v. 13) and v. 4 repeated again in v. 14a in order to point to God as ultimately the sole agent of all this. In the words prohibiting any attempt to rebuild, Yahweh's self-authentication and the prophetic concluding formula are linked together after the model supplied by v. 5. It may be correct to conjecture that vv. 9–11 quote an old battle-song, and are not without some poetic power. Nevertheless, the difference of level between this elaborate description of how the judgment is executed and the few terse words in which it is announced in vv. 1–5 is so great that it is impossible to entertain the idea that it was composed by Ezekiel himself.

Now, of course, the words of God in 29.17–21 mention the king of Babylon and presuppose that it is he who plunders and destroys Tyre. During the fifteen years which have passed since Ezekiel spoke his threatening word against Tyre, further elaboration took place, as we have repeatedly proved. The meaning of the prophet's words was brought out by means of further elaboration of what it depicted, stronger following up of its consequences, and concretization of matters left indistinct. This work was taken up by the prophet's disciples along with that of the transmission of the text. It had already commenced and had an effect on the reception of the prophet's message by the community of exiles.

This is a momentous conclusion to draw, and some may think it too daring. So they may point to 17.11ff., and suggest that the prophet himself supplied his first threat of judgment, of course by a much briefer specification, naming the human instrument by which the judgment was to be executed. This might be confined to vv. 7, 12 and 14b, reduced by a few minor excisions. The fact that it is precisely at v. 12 that the description of the avengers is transposed from the singular into the plural, and that this makes it easy to connect it up with v. 7, may be taken as a still-present outward sign of this first briefer form of the prophet's words. In its present form the brief oracular utterance could then be expanded into a detailed description of a massacre, and we have already indicated that this really means that it has been weakened down. But as the rest of the matter contained in ch. 26 is characterized by his compact style and would be considerably impaired by such an assumption, this alternative does not seem a likely one.

The death lament: 26.15–18

Two short sections are now introduced by the formula 'thus says Yahweh' in vv. 15 and 19. They simply follow one another and bring out so effectively the full meaning of the judgment upon Tyre announced in vv. 1–5 that it is difficult to find any reason for doubt of Ezekiel's authorship. By the death lament, prophets again and again present a threatened disaster as equivalent to an already accomplished fact, and do so in such a way as to be able to call on the audience to join in the lament for the dead (cf. ch. 19 above, pp. 251f.). But here the prophet puts the death lament into the mouths of others, who have hitherto stood in a close relationship to the mistress of the sea whom God is threatening, and they mourn for her fate as they would for that of a near relative. **[15]** At the commencement God himself addresses Tyre, informing her of the effect her ruin will have on the commercial cities associated with her, so the lament becomes like the writing on the wall, and makes it dreadfully visible to the eye that the city that is so certain of her own impregnable strength is already actually under attack from a superior power.

Sober and restrained as it is in form and content, in contrast to the related passage in 27.28ff., this death lament makes a lasting impression for that very reason. The isles, i.e. the coastlands of the Mediterranean, feel a shudder go through them as they witness the terrible overthrow of the allegedly impregnable island fortress. **[16]** The princes act as their spokesmen, and on hearing the sad news are deeply disturbed and begin the funeral lament. **[17]** We see a company of mourners as in a vision lay aside the signs of their power and join together with mourning rites. They climb down from their lofty thrones to sit in the dust, put on mourning garments in place of their sumptuous robes, and strike up the lament, going through all the prescribed gestures expressing how much it excites and affects them, beginning with the long-drawn-out lamenting cry 'How . . .' and following the strict conventional movement of the *qinah* (cf. in this connection II Sam. 1.22ff.). Just as the good qualities of the deceased are proclaimed, and his seizure by all-levelling death lamented, so the city is directly addressed as the bringer of good fortune, which brought her much praise, and made her glorious with terror-inspiring power, so as to be feared by sea and by land. [18] Her downfall calls for no malicious jubilation, since all see themselves menaced by her fate; her disappearance from the sea reminds them that the same may soon happen to them. Yet what is here bewailed in mere uncomprehending grief as a fate full of dark menace is what Israel must regard as a proof of the power of her God to bring all men to his feet.

The mistress of the sea's descent to hell: 26.19–21

This section has an introduction similar to the previous one declaring it to be said by God. Tyre is informed by a word of God that the glory that was Tyre has come to an irrevocable end. The metrical form with its short trisyllables (which, however, often form longer lines through the conjunction of two verses) is remarkably clear. Only in v. 20 is the restoration of the line of verse hypothetical.

[19] Tyre is laid utterly desolate, and her ruins rendered uninhabitable. The Primal Deluge is brought upon the scene. God had set limits to it at Creation (Gen. 1.2–6f.). It had broken out of them again only at the Flood (Gen. 7.11). [20] But God now causes its mighty waters to cover the city, and in v. 20 we see the mistress of the sea cast into the realm of the dead with her inhabitants, whence none can ever return. Most commentators regard the unusual way in which the statements are linked together as a somewhat laboured recapitulation and expansion of the threats issued in vv. 3 and 4. In v. 19 they are further accentuated, becoming the wreaking of total annihilation, with the old chaos myth occupying the background. In v. 20 comes a further attempt to deepen and interpret what this means by employing a fresh image, which now shows the judgment to be really irrevocable. This is done by a casting down into the realm of the dead which is derived from a totally different complex of mythical imagery. But such a view fails to recognize the inner connections which link all these statements together, and turns them instead into a sort of artificial jigsaw puzzle. The varying elements that are united together

here all have common roots. One does not see this clearly, till one realizes the Old Testament conception of Sheol.[1] We will try to give a brief sketch of it, and to relate it to the closely allied conceptions current in Babylon.

Sheol or the realm of the dead (there is probably an Accadian loan-word here) is already associated on the earliest occasions on which it is mentioned (Gen. 37.35, etc.) with conceptions of a subterranean place to which one descends after one's death. According to Job 10.21f. and Pss. 88.11f.; 143.3, etc. it is situated within or beneath the earth, a localization probably resulting from the influence of a thought-association with the grave, since to 'go down to the grave' means the same as 'to go down to the realm of the dead' (cf. Job 33.24; Pss. 13.10; 28.1; Prov. 1.12; with Ps. 55.15; Job 7.9; Num. 16.30). Since, however, the 'depths of the earth' (Ps. 63.9) were washed round by the *tehom* or primitive ocean, the subterranean sea on which the earth rests, it was also possible to localize those depths in the waters under the earth (Job 26.5; 38.16; Ps. 18.4f.; Jonah 2.3f.). Anyone therefore who must go to join the dead must pass over the subterranean waters with their currents and whirlpools, which separate the other world from this world, and must take his abode in the subterranean ocean. Yet the man who experiences the threat of death feels as if he had already been caught by the torrents of the underworld (Ps. 18.4f.) by which the realm of death throws its snares around him. Only when God strikes fear into those floods, so that the bed of the sea is seen and the foundations of the world are laid bare, can he take hold of him and deliver him from his peril (Ps. 18.15f.). The closeness of the association between the world-sea and the subterranean ocean is shown by the Psalm of Jonah, in which Jonah, when cast into the heart of the seas with its waters closing in over him, realizes that he is now in the underworld (Jonah 2.4, 6f.). This does not, of course, mean that any clear or unequivocal conceptions existed in regard to the depths of the earth or their connection with the primal ocean; these conceptions may be said rather to have included the various manifestations of the powers of death, which were not combined into a coherent system, but employed all alike so as to provide parallel descriptions of the realm of the dead.

When therefore one tries to picture the realm of the dead, one may think of a house, or of a city, or again of a wide-stretching country.

[1] Cf. in this connection, W. Eichrodt, *Theology of the Old Testament* II, 1967, pp. 95f. and 210ff.

The provision of doors and bars is necessary to, and characteristic of, the former two ideas. So doors and bars play a special part in the Babylonian myth of Ishtar's journey to hell, and are also referred to in Jonah 2.7. They serve to make the underworld into a prison, from which no one can find release, unless whoever is in control of the realm of the dead consents to order him to be set free, as Ereshkigal did for Ishtar, and the world-God Yahweh for his unfaithful messenger, whom he cast down into the underworld, but whom he also brought up out of it again (Jonah 2.7f.; I Sam. 2.6). The second conception is usually associated with wasting and destruction, and takes its images from the desert, or from ruined cities which have been forsaken by their inhabitants. So in Babylon the God Nergal is not only the lord of the grave but also the king of the desert. In Israel Isaiah sees how the whole tumultuous city of Jerusalem is to be swallowed up by the underworld, and gives an impressive description of how the stillness of death covers her earthly ruins, and is like the stillness that reigns in Sheol. According to the Gilgamesh Epic, the heroes and sages of ancient days dwell there, along with priests and courageous warriors, and according to Ezek. 32.18ff. there are resting places there awaiting whole nations. But existence there is a sorrowful one, and so Enkidu, the friend of Gilgamesh, whose ghost is brought back by means of magic to the upper world, at first hesitates to give any information on the subject, since the ordinances of Sheol can occasion nothing save woeful weeping for those who come to understand them. For the dead pine without peace or joy in the dust-covered world of the dead where there is nothing to eat but dust. Only a small relief is enjoyed by the most highly privileged. For example, those slain in battle may repose upon couches and drink clean water. On the other hand, those of the dead whose corpses still lie unburied must wander restlessly to and fro, and gather round the gutters for the leavings of the meals eaten by the more favoured ones.

Once they are seen in this light, the remarkable statements in Ezek. 26.20, about the primeval ruins and the people of old, who are situated in the underworld, now become intelligible: that which has had its being on earth in the pride and strength of earthly life, in magnificent palaces and towering fortresses, now finds itself in the realm of the dead in a state of powerlessness and ruin. The proud mistress of the sea must go the same way as all the others who go down to the pit; that is to say, she, too, must vanish into the 'nether world', the spacious dwelling of the dead. There she is seized by the terrors of death, the horrifying dissolution of existence which is a part of the woeful ordinance of the underworld and cuts off all hope of a fresh life.

This also makes it evident that these statements and those in v. 19 are homogeneous. The acts of judgment which are then briefly introduced, by which the city is reduced to ruins and plunged into the *teḥom*, are certainly not without some connection with 26.3–5. These verses do not, however, expand and enhance the earthly event in such a way as to bring about a transposition of it into a mythical catastrophe on a cosmic scale. The statements give expression solely to the global conceptions of things which in Israelite thought were always associated with earthly disaster as its ever-present substratum. In this way the exclamations in the Psalms and Wisdom literature of men who have fallen into affliction and peril serve to show how in all forms of suffering they felt threatened by death and had already a real experience of death's actual presence and power, so that experience is described in terms of being laid hold of by the realm of death in its various forms. That shows that there is no fixed boundary separating the realm of death from the realm of life. Rather it reaches out its menacing and conquering hands into all the regions of the living to secure its victims, who, while still amid the joys of life, feel themselves suddenly exposed to its assault. So the man who is overwhelmed by severe affliction is conscious of encountering the terrible power of death and of being dragged down into its dominion, in such a way that he can already feel himself to be a dweller within the realm of death.[1]

This complex view of death in all its manifestations can find verbal expression on each occasion when there is a desire to go behind the scene of some earthly catastrophe and to uncover its ultimate significance. In individual cases this finds expression in the laments of the afflicted or in admonitions by sages telling of how to avoid the menacing fate of death. But the prophet either makes use of it to warn his own people of how the powers of death lie in wait for them or else employs its terrors to threaten the enemies of God.

When, therefore, Yahweh brings up the primal deep to overwhelm Tyre, that can be taken as it is in v. 3 as an image for the approaching

[1] This concept of death has been described in a particularly impressive way by J. Pedersen, *Israel, its life and culture*, I. II, 1926, pp. 453ff., and by C. Barth, *Die Errettung vom Tode in den individuellen Klage-und Dankliedern des A.T.*, 1947.

hosts of enemies. But it can also easily be understood to mean, as it does in v. 19, the mythical reality of the subterranean river, of the *tehom* which reaches from this world into the realm of the dead, which carries those seized by it into Sheol, and severs them for ever from the living world. The kingdom of death is enclosed by gates and bars, but it also appears to be a wide country where the torrents of perdition roar (Ps. 18.4). This leaves plenty of room for the ever-lasting desolation in which dwell the people of old, or where in Babylonia the heroes of ancient times are assembled (cf. in this con-nection Ezek. 32.26f.). In Israelite thought the connection between the destructive powers of this life on earth and the underworld region where death has its dominion is so close that when one is experiencing the one, one sees the gates of the other opening so that one feels one has been delivered over to it.

Regarded under this light, Ezekiel's announcement that the great commercial metropolis is on its way to hell does no more than lay bare associations between earthly disaster and the dominion of the realm of the dead expressed in the symbolic terms that were current among the ancient people. It is easy to understand how a line runs from earthly destruction (26.1-5) through the death lament by the victim's friends (26.15-18) on to the announcement that she has been cast into the underworld, so as to recognize how the earthly judgment involves her being finally rejected and cast out of the world of the living, and deprived of all hope of any return to life. Yet the final warrant for this does not come from the world of the dead as an autonomous power with laws of its own, but from the decision by the world-God, since even Sheol is under the control of his power.

Aim and period of composition

As the result of these considerations, we may decide that the first, third and fourth sets of threatening words are closely and solidly con-nected with each other, and are characterized by a terseness and vigour of form which is conspicuously absent from the second. The primary object of this proclamation is evidently to provide an assurance that the hitherto unbroken resistance to God's authorized executor of judgment will be brought to an end by the destruction of the island fortress of Tyre. It was undoubtedly composed during the period immediately after the fall of Jerusalem, in the beginning of the year 586, as 26.2 already suggests. As regards the siege of the city, all we know is that Nebuchadrezzar was not long before he started it, and that according to Josephus it lasted thirteen years, which, if we judge by the length of the reign of Itobaal who was then king of Tyre, may be dated between 586/85–573/72. This may or may not apply to the second set of threatening words, which was not introduced into the collection till a much later date, but which may have been already in circulation from quite an early period. For Ezekiel, however, it was important that just before Nebuchadrezzar came to his final decision, belief that the divine plan for the world was continuing to be carried out, and which had received such strong support through the fulfilment of the prophecies against Jerusalem, should be established beyond all doubt by the assurance that even the most powerful opponents of the Babylonian king were going to be overthrown by God. The sentence of judgment proclaimed by Ezekiel, it is true, was not fulfilled as completely as he had announced, though Tyre did surrender, as is stated in the Babylonian records for that year (for further details see Zimmerli *ad loc.*), accepted a Babylonian commissioner, and had to subject itself to the domination of the Babylonian empire. This led to the interesting postscript in 29.17–21 which is written by the prophet's own hand.

CHAPTER 27.1–36

The wreck of the gallant ship of Tyre

1 The word of Yahweh came to me: [2]Now you, son of man, raise a lamentation over Tyre[3] and say to Tyre, who dwells[a] at the entrance to the sea,[b] merchant of the peoples on many coastlands:
Thus says [. . .][c] Yahweh:
O Tyre, you [are a ship perfect in beauty].[d]
4 [You were made great][e] in the heart of the seas, you were made perfect in beauty,
5 they made all [your] planks[f] of junipers from Senir;[g]
they took a cedar of Lebanon, to make [. . .] the mast.[h]
6 Of the tallest oaks of Bashan they made your oars,
your cabin walls they made [of ivory][i] and cypress wood from the coasts of the Citeans.[j]
7b Of bluish purple [. . .][k] from the coasts of Elisha[l] was your awning,[m]
7a of fine embroidered linen[n] from Egypt was your sail [. . .].[o]

8 The inhabitants of Sidon and Arvad[p] were your rowers,
   [skilled men of Zemer][q] were in you, they were your pilots.
9a The elders of Gebal (Byblos) [. . .][r] served as your stewards.[s]
9b All the ships of the sea with their mariners were in you, to barter for your wares. [10]Paras[t] and Lud[u] and Put[v] were in your army as your men of war. They hung the shield and helmet in you, they gave you splendour. [11]The men of Arvad were [in][w] your army upon your walls round about; and they were watchmen[x] upon your towers; they hung their shields upon your walls round about, they made perfect your beauty. [12]Tarshish[y] trafficked for you because of your great wealth of every kind, for silver, iron, tin and lead they sold your wares. [13]Javan,[z] Tubal and Meshech[aa] traded with you, they exchanged your wares for slaves and vessels of bronze. [14]As for Beth-togarmah:[bb] they exchanged your wares for draught-horses, saddle-horses and mules. [15]The men of [Rodan][cc] were your merchants, many coastlands were your own special markets, they brought you in payment ivory tusks[dd] and ebony. [16]Edom[ee] trafficked for you because of your abundant goods, they exchanged your merchandise[ff] for turquoise, purple, embroidered work, fine linen, coral and rubies![gg] [17]Judah and the land of Israel traded for you; they exchanged your merchandise for wheat and laudanum and wax(?), honey and oil and mastic. [18]Damascus, she trafficked for you [. . .][hh] because of your abundant [goods: wine][ii] of Helbon[jj] and wool from Zachar [19][. . .][kk] they gave for your wares. From Uzal[ll] came [wrought][mm] iron (in bars), cinnamon and calamus in exchange for your wares. [20]Dedan[nn] traded with you in saddle-clothes,[oo] [21]Arabia and all the princes of Kedar[pp] acted as dealers for you in lambs, rams and he-goats. For these they trafficked for you. [. . .][qq] Saba[rr] and Ra[c]mah[ss] traded for you: they exchanged your wares for all kinds of spices and all kinds of precious stones and gold. [23]Haran,[tt] Canneh[uu] and Eden[vv], [. . .][ww] these traded for you; [24]for choice garments, mantles of bluish purple and embroidery, for carpets of two colours and for woven and twisted robes, for these they traded for you. [25]The ships of Tarshish brought you the goods in exchange for your wares.[xx]

   And you were filled (with wares) and heavily laden in the heart of the world-sea.
26 Your rowers have brought you into the high seas,[yy]
   the east wind has wrecked you in the heart of the world-sea.
27 Your riches [. . .],[zz] your mariners and your crew [. . .][aaa] and all your men of war [. . .][bbb]
   sink into the heart of the world-sea in the day of your ruin.
28 At the loud cry your crew tremble [. . .][ccc]
29 And down from their ships come all that handle the oar,
   the mariners, and all the crews of the sea stand on the shore.

30 They cry aloud over you and wail bitterly,
and cast dust on their heads and wallow in ashes.

31 They shave themselves bald for you and gird themselves with sackcloth
and weep over you in trouble of soul in bitter mourning.

32 And they raise over you [. . .]ᵈᵈᵈ a lamentation and lament over you.
Who is to [be compared]ᵉᵉᵉ to Tyre in the heart of the sea?

33 When your wares came from the ocean, you satisfied [. . .]ᶠᶠᶠ peoples
with your abundant wealth,ᵍᵍᵍ [. . .]ʰʰʰ you enriched the kings of
the earth.

34 But now you are shattered, (vanished) from the ocean, in the depths of
the waters
your merchandise and all your crew have sunk within you.

35 All the inhabitants of the coastlands are appalled at you, the hair of
the kings stands on end, their faces are convulsed.

36 The merchants among the people whistle [together]ⁱⁱⁱ over you;
you have become terrors of death and are gone for ever.

ᵃThe consonantal text reads *yōšabtī*, closing it by the *ḥireq compaginis*, but this
has been ignored by the pointing.

ᵇ⁻ᵈSee BH.

ᵉThe verse-line in its present state is excessively long. So it should be lightened by
deleting 'your builders', which seems to be derived from the following line.
Instead of 'your borders' make a slight emendation and read 'you were made
great'.

ᶠSee BH.

ᵍA part of Mount Hermon.

ʰInstead of *ʿalayiq*, which is metrically superfluous, read *ʿelyōnē* with Bertholet
at the beginning of the following verse, so as to get the accent lacking there.

ⁱMay be deleted as a dittography.

ʲInhabitants of Kition, a city of Cyprus, later extended to signify the southern
part of Cyprus.

ᵏ MT: 'and reddish purple'; as a result of the similarity of vv. 6b and 7b to the
description of the tabernacle, the purple often referred to there seemed to be called
for to add to the elaboration, but it overloads the line.

ˡInterpreted as meaning Cyprus, but this is uncertain.

ᵐSee BH.

ⁿByssus.

ᵒMT: 'serving as your ensign'; to be deleted as an isolated portion of a line of
doubtful importance.

ᵖA Phoenician city north of Sidon, the modern Ruād, whose inhabitants were
regarded as bold sailors in ancient times.

�q A probable emendation for 'your wise men, O Tyre' in the MT. Zemir is a
little north of Arvad, cf. Gen. 10.18.

ʳDelete 'and their wise men' of MT.

ˢZimmerli; literally 'repairers of your damages'.

ᵗThe context, of nations in a region near Egypt, makes the interpretation

'Persians', following Ezra 1.1, an unlikely one. The name seems to have behind it that of some still unidentified African tribe.

ᵘLud should not be identified with the Lydians in Asia as in Gen. 10.22, but sought in Africa as in 30.5; Jer. 46.9; Gen. 10.13; Isa. 66.19.

ᵛPut is to be identified either with Punt (Babylonian Puta) on the African coast of the Red Sea, perhaps that of Somaliland, or with a region of Libya in North Africa, to which the name is also applied.

ʷ⁻ˣSee BH.

ʸThe identification with Tartessus, a Tyrian colony in Spain, is still the most likely one, although many at present try to prove it is Tunis.

ᶻThis means the Ionian Greeks.

ᵃᵃTubal and Meshech are the names used by the Assyrians and Greeks for the nations dwelling in Cappadocia between the Black Sea and the Taurus Mountains, whose chief products were iron and bronze.

ᵇᵇTo be identified with Armenia.

ᶜᶜRodan = Rhodes, to be inserted (following LXX) instead of Dedan, which does not appear till v. 20. The list moves over to the Greek islands.

ᵈᵈLiterally 'horns of ivory'.

ᵉᵉSee BH.

ᶠᶠDelete the *bᵉ* before *ᶜizᵉbōnāyik*.

ᵍᵍThe translations of *rā'mōt* (coral) and *kadkod* (rubies) cannot be any more than conjectures, and in any case the text of the verse seems uncertain.

ʰʰMT: 'because of the abundance of your products'; evidently a variant of the following phrase, which is absent from the LXX.

ⁱⁱSee BH.

ʲʲTo the north-west of Damascus, and celebrated for its wine also among the Assyrians, Babylonians and Persians.

ᵏᵏThe first two words of v. 19: 'And Dan and Javan' seem to be a gloss which has become unintelligible. The following word 'from Uzal' introduces a new phrase and needs to be transferred.

ˡˡThe modern *Sanᶜa* in Yemen or Izallah between Haran and the Tigris.

ᵐᵐSee BH.

ⁿⁿA tribe in north-west Arabia, cf. Gen. 25.3.

ᵒᵒLiterally 'for riding'.

ᵖᵖAn Ishmaelite tribe in the 'Arabian desert', cf. Gen. 25.13.

 qqMT: 'the merchants of'; evidently a misreading of a proper name, perhaps Havilah, which is situated in the same district as the places which follow (Gen. 10.7).

ʳʳIn south Arabia.

ˢˢRagmat, today *Uḥdūd* (Fohrer) in south-west Arabia.

ᵗᵗThe well-known junction within the upper arm of the Euphrates.

ᵘᵘCuneiform inscription *kannū*—perhaps Nisibis.

ᵛᵛCuneiform inscription *bit adini*, half-way down the Euphrates.

ʷʷMT: 'The merchants of Saba, Assyria and all Media traded for you.' Part of this is inconsistent with v. 22, and the conclusion conflicts with v. 24a. Assyria and Media are hardly to be expected amid a list of individual towns of Mesopotamia. So it should probably be regarded as an insertion.

ˣˣThis sentence resumes from v. 9b after the insertion of vv. 10–24.

yyLiterally 'among mighty waters'.

zz'and your wares, your goods for exchange.'

aaa'Your stewards and they who exchanged your wares.'

bbb'Those that are with you, with all your levy, in the midst of you.' The words of notes zz, aaa, bbb should be deleted as superfluous lengthenings of the line.

ccc*migrᵉšōt*, pastures, does not fit here. The word remains unintelligible.

dddMT: 'their sons' or 'with their cry'. See BH. The word overloads the verse and must be regarded as a gloss.

eeeSee BH.

fffMT: 'many' destroys the structure of the verse, not found in LXX.

gggSee BH.

hhhMT: 'wares for exchange' must be deleted, as the additional word from the trading list added to complete 'trade-goods'. It is hardly proper to delete the whole verse as an elaboration on account of this connection with the trading list. The praise of former greatness is an indispensable part of every lament for the dead.

iiiNecessary in order to supply a verse-foot which is wanting.

A prophetic lament over Tyre: 27.1–9a, 25b–36

As in 19.1, the prophet receives an order from God to raise a death lament over Tyre. This represents the downfall of Tyre as if it has already taken place, and thus expresses strikingly the certainty of the prophet that God's threat of judgment against the city will be fulfilled.[1] Just as ch. 19 is orientated towards the foregoing threat to Zedekiah in ch. 17, so ch. 27 looks back at the threat uttered in ch. 26, describing the event threatened there under the image of the wreck of a magnificent ship.

Yet, since the messenger-formula in v. 3 explicitly describes this lament as a word of Yahweh, the reader's attention is drawn from the very outset away from its artistic form to what underlies it, a decision by the world-God, which must be taken seriously; there is no question of being lulled to sleep by the masterliness of the poetry. It looks as if this was intended to serve as an antidote against lack of seriousness on the part of his audience, who took a purely aesthetic pleasure in the prophet's preaching and thus closed themselves up to all deeper impressions (cf. 33.30ff.).

This is the more easy to understand, in view of the fact that this poem rises to a high level of poetical perfection, and that as it proceeds to unfold the tragic event it does not give any hint that God himself is intervening in the affairs of the world. **[3]** When Tyre is herself addressed in v. 3, the attributes there conferred upon her are

[1] For a general account of prophetic laments for the dead see Commentary on ch. 19, pp. 251ff., above.

expressive not of any reproach but solely of admiration of her favourable situation and of her attention to her business. The city so often personified as a woman lives in a place with access to the sea, so her position makes her an unrivalled market for trade between coast and coast. This is true of Tyre with her two magnificent harbours even more than it is of most other seaside cities. Situated as she was, she could engage in international trade in innumerable havens, and make such good use of these favourable circumstances as to win a dominant position in world-trade in her day. So the first half of the poem (vv. 3b–9a) is given up to a description of all this pride and greatness. The poet deliberately lets himself be carried away by his subject and inspired by the city's maritime situation into comparing it to a splendidly equipped merchant ship, whose proud beauty he is well able to portray in glowing colours. He weaves the list of all her advantages into a lifelike picture of the building of the ship, building up the details skilfully as the subject develops and thus, instead of dry statistics, presenting us with a glimpse of an enterprise deliberately engaged in and carried to a successful climax.

There is already a note of suppressed admiration in the way the city is addressed as a ship perfect in beauty. (The Massoretic reading: 'Thou hast said, I am . . .' which introduces a rebuke for self-admiration, is metrically, stylistically and materially objectionable, and must be derived from a misreading of *'nyh*.) **[4–7]** Yet the following vv. 4–7, which describe the industrious labours of the shipbuilders, inform us that there was no skimping in the selection of the materials, and that only the best was thought good enough for use in such a magnificent vessel. Planks, mast, deck, sail, and awning are constructed out of timber of the highest quality or brightly coloured fabrics, an eloquent image expressing the size and splendour of the sea-girt city. Even the crew is not composed of slaves of alien origin and doubtful reliability. **[8–9a]** Instead, the oldest and wisest men of the neighbouring Phoenician cities esteem it as an honour to serve in this capacity; which is a slightly exaggerated metaphor expressing how the richest maritime cities of Phoenicia were her vassals.

[9b–25a] At this point the poem is suddenly interrupted, to make room for a lengthy insertion. It gives an enumeration in prose of Tyre's multifarious trade connections throughout what was then the known world, and describes the wealth in costly goods of every kind that poured into the merchant city. One can see how this extensive elaboration aims at showing the wide-reaching power and importance of the trading city from this additional aspect. Nevertheless it causes such a disturbance to the beautiful structure of the lament that it becomes imperative to set it aside. Even after this has been done, the text of the poem is left so disturbed in some places that it can only conjecturally be restored.

[25b] One can establish with reasonable certainty that the lament recommences in v. 25b. Whereas before that the rich commercial city is spoken of without any use of metaphor, that line of verse deals once more with how the ship, its construction finished, is filled with wares of all sorts, in order that it may set off upon a profitable voyage. It is indispensable that such a transition to the following sector should be made, and the assumption that it was at one time fuller is a more probable one than that it ought to be totally deleted. [26] Only this valuable cargo which has been put on board gives the reason for the ship to take to sea; the oarsmen operate for a while until they are out on the high sea where a fresh breeze can fill the sail.

But it is there, in the heart of the seas, in that very place in which Tyre has achieved greatness, that ruin breaks in. This takes the form of a stormy east wind, which according to Ps. 48.7 constituted a well-known danger to ships voyaging to Tarshish, and was also feared inland for its destructive power, as the desert wind (Jer. 4.11; Job 1.19). [27] It seizes the ship and shatters its firmly built hull, so that it is swallowed up by the sea along with its costly cargo and its picked crew. At this point the poet is extraordinarily quick and brief. He uses only four lines, describing not the nature or cause of the catastrophe, but merely stating its occurrence and its results. [28] The terrified cry that goes up into the air from the men who sink into the depths is the one expression of distress which comes to touch the hearts of the listeners. It is no wonder that in v. 27 a later hand has tried to atone for that reticence by means of additions drawn from the manifest of the cargo. One may also ask the question whether the prophet had experience enough to know what a voyage was like and to be able to describe what it was like to be on board a ship in distress, or whether he deliberately refrained from attempting to do so. The description of the storm at sea in Ps. 107.25–27 shows how another Israelite poet was capable of doing full justice to such a theme. Ezekiel gets over this shipwreck quickly. But he strikes a special note by thrice repeating in vv. 25, 26 and 27 the words 'in the heart of the world-sea', thus underlining the three chief moments of the event. Destruction and downfall are seen to be closely associated with the element from which this maritime and mercantile city draws its life; we see the connection between the attractiveness and adventurousness of the sea and its capriciousness and dangerousness. It is a bulwark of defence against attacks by enemies, it is a road to unheard-of riches, yet it is also capable of suddenly shattering to pieces those whom it has hitherto protected. Stress is thus laid on the transitoriness of any success attained upon such a stage. Yet the poet of set purpose abstains from giving any hint of the deep causes of this transitoriness. So he presents the helpless perplexity of the rest of the world in face of the unexpected catastrophe without softening it down in any way.

[29–31] What a shock seizes the sailors, as they stand and witness the ruin of the greatest and most successful exponent of their calling! They break off all their voyages, and break out in excited manifestations of woe as soon as they learn of the terrible event. We were struck before by the brevity, now we are struck by the lengthiness of the description as it enumerates in three whole strophes the mourning rites and manifestations of grief which must necessarily strike the reader. [32–36] After that we are told the lamentation struck up by the mourners, and that takes up still more space. This puts the greatest stress on the second part of the poem. The prophet gives a main place in his own lament to the lament by the sailors. Now, as in ch. 26, he lets the centre of the stage be occupied by the irreparable loss, which is directly and convincingly expressed by the mouth of those affected by it. [33] The people of the coastlands get their living, and their kings their riches, out of the world-wide trade of Tyre. [34] So the disappearance of the city that had ruled the waves spells a catastrophe for them all, with profound effects on their life. [35f.] This forces them to give free expression to their dismay. Here the whistling by the merchants must be interpreted as a protective gesture engaged upon in order to ward off the threat from the powers of ill luck (so Fohrer). [36b] The repetition of 26.21 in a slightly altered form may be regarded as a deliberate recollection which brings about a weighty conclusion, once more expressing helplessness in face of the all-destroying power of death.

One may indeed admit that this final conclusion is the logical consequence of all that has preceded, and that the consistent way the allegory is kept up makes the poem unusually effective. This is intensified by the very fact that it limits itself severely to the feelings immediately felt by the heathen sailors, and resists the ever-present inclination to draw upon personal convictions and faith. In face of this high poetic quality it is not advisable to interpret the details allegorically as signifying daring political manoeuvres on the part of Tyre, or showing how the seafaring nations have taken to heart the lesson they have been taught by her fall. One must rather follow what is indicated by the actual construction of the poem and recognize the whole point of what the poem means to convey as it piles up the horror of the history in a way motivated by pure human sympathy, and thus reveals the ultimate insignificance of even the very greatest human achievements. Undoubtedly the explicit way v. 3 attributes the whole to a word of Yahweh serves as a sign-manual which makes Israelite listeners aware of the Lord of the world even while fixing their eyes on this mighty picture of ruin. But that only renders more remarkable the renunciation of all indictments or vindictive appeals for punishment, making the terrible events that take place in this world an ever-inexplicable mystery, inaccessible to man and shut away in the counsels of divine wisdom, in face of which all human calculations are confounded. The view Ezekiel takes of earthly events recalls that of the poet of the book of Job, who expresses similar ideas in a still more powerful way and leads Israelite and heathen alike to bow humbly before him who alone possesses power and glory and bestows and resumes possession of them as it pleases him.

The world-wide trade of Tyre: 27.9b–25a

We are here given a list of the regions who engage in trade with Tyre or who trade on her behalf. [9b] The first half-verse makes use of the image of the sea-going ships which run into the Tyrian harbours with all their rich wares. [10f.] Then a long list is appended of the places they come from and the goods they carry. This is interrupted by the insertion of two totally different verses, which tell of the armed might of the sea-girt city. However, v. 10, at any rate, can be salvaged by means of a few deletions as a piece of the lamentation, which not only enumerated the members of the crew, but also mentioned the marines who were stationed upon the gallant ship in order to protect it against pirates. Yet in its present position this verse, like v. 11, is there for the sole purpose of describing the military strength of the merchant city which employs mercenaries from every country and allegiance to guard her walls and towers. The accompanying reference to the perfect beauty of the city is borrowed from the lament (cf. v. 4) and can serve as a clear symptom of the confusion between city and ship, reality and metaphor, which facilitates the transition to what follows next.

The geographical survey in vv. 12f. of Tyre's trade connections is a learned piece of work. Its composer displays an astonishingly accurate knowledge of the commerce of the world in his day. It is confirmed by various pieces of information from other ancient sources. As the practice of drawing up such lists of objects of a similar nature is known to be specially characteristic of Egypt,[1] it has been conjectured that a list derived from that country was used as a basis. This assumption is confirmed when we observe that Egypt is the one country which does not figure among the countries and cities enumerated. This suggests that the list was originally drawn up to be used in that country and was subsequently adapted and corrected so as to refer to Tyre.[2] According to another interpretation, the basis has been furnished by some Persian system of streets devoted to trade.[3] Attractive though such conjectures may be, they are so full with gaps and unsolved problems that one cannot regard them as anything more than hypothetical in spite of their cleverness. The omission not only of Egypt but of all the regions named in the poem about the shipwreck, e.g. Cyprus and the cities of Phoenicia, seems to show that the redactor is consciously recalling the lament which he has in front of him, and which he has taken upon himself to supplement, and thus arouses doubts whether this is not really a foreign body with an autonomous structure of its own which has been introduced from the outside world.[4] The manifold associations with the table of nations in Gen. 10 makes the problem of the possibility of traditions of the kind being of purely Israelite provenance one that should not be evaded. Also the accurate knowledge of the goods used in trade makes one conclude that it was composed by a Jew with an intimate acquaintance with all the many branches of Phoenician trade who probably wrote at the beginning of the exile.

From the geographical aspect the list stretches from the farthest west (Tarshish in Spain), going east through the Ionian trading cities, to the north-west corner of Asia Minor (Tubal, Beth Togarmah, Meshech), and adding further the islands of the Aegean (vv. 12–15). This line from west to east is set against a line from south to north,

---

[1] Cf. G. von Rad, 'Hiob 38 und die altägyptische Weisheit', *VTS* III (1955), pp. 293–301.

[2] Cf. G. Fohrer, *ad loc.*

[3] So H. P. Rüger, *Das Tyrusorakel, Ez. 27*, dissertation, Tübingen, 1961.

[4] This is rightly asserted by Zimmerli, *ad loc.*

which in vv. 16–18 brings in the region of Syria and Palestine, including Judah and Israel (we notice how they are put into their place without any special exclamation mark!). Then the Arabian region is appended in vv. 19–22 and in vv. 23f. some Mesopotamian cities provide a conclusion.

This is a systematic assemblage of material of purely practical interest. The style is achieved from a few frequently repeated variations. So it forms a strong contrast to the poem that forms the setting into which it has been introduced. None the less it supplies a wide geographical frame for the picture of the merchant city and shows Tyre's importance to the civilization of that day, and does so in a sober matter-of-fact shape which is yet clothed in iridescent colours.

CHAPTER 28.1–19

A threat and death lament for the prince of Tyre

1 The word of Yahweh came to me: ²'Son of man, says to the prince of Tyre: thus says [. . .]ᵃ Yahweh:
Because your heart was proud and you have said: "I am a God,
I sit in a seat of the gods in the heart of the seas";
yet you are but a man and no god and nevertheless think yourself to be God.
3 You are indeed wiser than Daniel
and nothing hidden is a secret to you;
4 by your wisdom and understanding you have gotten wealth for yourself
and have gathered gold and silver in your treasuries,
5 [. . .]ᵇ and your heart has become proud because of your wealth.
6 Therefore thus says [. . .]ᶜ Yahweh:
Because you think yourself equal to God,
7 therefore, behold, I bring strangers upon you, the most terrible of the nations,
who will draw their swords against [you]ᵈ and defile your gleaming splendour.
8 They shall thrust you down into the pit, so that you will die
the sad death of those that are pierced through in the heart of the seas.
9 Will you still say, "I am a God", in the presence of [those who slay you],ᵉ
when you are but a man and not God, in the hands of those who [pierce you through].ᶠ

10 You shall die the death of the uncircumcised by the hand of foreigners,
for I have said it, says [. . .][g] Yahweh.'
11 Moreover, the word of Yahweh came to me:
12 'Son of man, raise a lamentation over the king of Tyre and say to him:
Thus says [. . .][h] Yahweh:
You were a [perfect signet][i] [. . .][j] and of perfect beauty;
13 You were in Eden, the garden of God, every precious stone was your covering [. . .][k]
and wrought in gold were your [ear rings][l]
and your [settings][m] which you wore, in the day that you were created [. . .][n]
14 with[o] the guardian [. . .][p] cherub I placed you;[q] you were on the mountain of God,[r] in the midst of the stones of fire you walked.
15 You were blameless in your ways from the day you were created,
till iniquity was found in you.
16 In the power of your trade you filled yourself within[s] with iniquity,
and when you sinned, I cast you from the holy mountain of God
and the guardian cherub extirpated you[t] from the midst of the stones of fire.
17 Your heart was proud because of your beauty, you corrupted your wisdom for the sake of your splendour.
I cast you down to the ground,
I exposed you before kings to feast their eyes on you.
18 By the multitude of your iniquities[u] in the unrighteousness of your trade you profaned [my sanctuary].[v]
So I made fire come forth from the midst of it,[w] which consumed you,
and I turned you to ashes upon the earth in the sight of all who saw you.
19 All who knew you among the peoples are appalled at you;
you have come to a dreadful end and shall be no more for ever.'

[a]See BH.

[b]MT: 'By your great wisdom in trade you have increased your wealth', which is to be regarded as a variant of v. 4.

[c]See BH.

[d]Thus in place of MT: 'against the beauty of your wisdom'.

[e–h]See BH.

[i]The meaning of both words is contested.

[j]MT: 'full of wisdom' is not in the LXX and is not an expression applicable to a signet.

[k]MT: 'ruby, chrysolite, jasper, tarshish, carnelian and jade, sapphire, turquoise and beryl'. These are the precious stones of the first, second and fourth rows in the high priest's breastplate, Ex. 28.17ff., but arranged in a different order. The details of the transmission are uncertain: the suggestions by L. Köhler have been introduced here. It is generally recognized as a later insertion.

[l]This is only a conjectural version.

^mSee the above note.

ⁿMT: 'they were prepared'; superfluous as regards metre and context, and not in the LXX.

^oSee BH.

^pAn unintelligible word.

^{q–v}See BH.

^wRead third person, masculine singular suffix instead of second person, masculine singular.

The threat: 28.1–10

Threats have been addressed by the word of God to the city and then to her king. But this is not because Itobaal II, the monarch then reigning, had drawn the eyes of the world towards him by any exceptional wickedness. The reproach addressed to him does not reveal any personal details about his character or his political policy, but is couched in terms so general that any Tyrian king might have served as its target. It is rather that the kingship *per se* is being prosecuted and sentenced in the person of its representative.

[2] The indictment precedes in the form of a causal clause, as in 26.2. It has not the remotest connection with any act of injustice committed against Israel, but operates entirely in the dimension of that reverent awe before the divine majesty which is obligatory upon all men. The Tyrian king is capable of describing himself as a god, who has set up his impregnable divine dwelling in the heart of the sea, and has thus broken down the eternal boundary between the Creator and the creature (we catch an echo here of the same opposition between man and God as in Isa. 31.3). It is that which brands him as a rebel who is bringing down divine judgment upon himself. This is no lightly-delivered rebuke, provoked by dislike for the heathen. It is astoundingly verified by the Syrian expression of the ideology of ancient Eastern kingship, and it is this which has undoubtedly lent colour to the prophet's rebuke. The Ugaritic documents testify to the king's claim to receive worship and to be in his own person the guarantee of his people's salvation, as being the earthly embodiment of the god who dies and rises again, whose fate he represented in the cult. This divinizing of the king has worked itself into the Israelite psalms, and made it possible to address the prince as *'elohīm*, God, in singing his praise (Ps. 45.6, according to the most likely interpretation), even though his exaltation was not based upon any physical apotheosis, but upon his election to be God's earthly representative. But what there secured an entry only among

certain circles within the nation, and was unable to influence the king's subjection to the law of God, was in Syria, as in Egypt, a deeply rooted idea exercising a real material influence on the value attributed to kingship. The centralizing of the political existence of the nation in the king was thus given an anchor in the divine realm which gave it an absolute value, and claimed such unlimited authority for its human guarantor, that he could not let himself be subjected to any criticism.

[3] This exaltation of human caprice into a divine right creates powerful supports for itself in claims to superhuman wisdom and in the attainment of the power of wealth. The provoking assumption of superiority, by which Tyrian diplomacy regarded its plans and decisions as the only right ones, and was able to back them up by all the weight of its huge resources, is mentioned also in Zech. 9.2 as a habit characteristic of Phoenicia, and in that passage, as in this, we find an ironic emphasis placed upon it. There is no other way in which the almost admiring language of vv. 3 and 4 can be interpreted. This would be still more impressive if, as Van den Born conjectures, we are here meeting a fragment taken from a Tyrian royal hymn. When Daniel is named in it as a proverbial manifestation of wisdom, then some figure of the past known throughout the whole Syrian region must be referred to. This excludes the Daniel of the Old Testament book bearing that name. It is very probably the king of that name known from Ugaritic testimonies who is also named in 14.14-20 (cf. above, pp. 189f.) and belongs to that class of hero who is also a sort of demi-god. [4f.] The complacent way in which the men of Tyre speak of the wisdom of their prince, and appeal to the piling up of huge riches as a proof of its genuineness, is reproduced in caricature leading to a brief statement of the conclusion: 'and your heart has become proud' (v. 5). Man has gone beyond the limits set for him by his self-glorification. The combination of earthly advantages, the impregnable situation of the island fortress, the cleverness of its policy and the astounding success of its commerce, have blinded its eyes to the limitations of human nature and misled it into laying claim to divine honours. This reveals the brittleness of the foundations of the claim to political importance and the excessive self-esteem, and displays all the inward weakness of such a piling up of political power.

[6] The excessive self-exaltation which calls down God's judgment is completely refuted by the divine sentence now pronounced upon it.

[7] Proof will be given that the divine dwelling in the sea is not impregnable when the divine judge calls in the Babylonian hosts so notorious for their ruthlessness, whose sword will not shrink before the gleam of a non-existent divine majesty, [8f.] but put it to shame before the whole world and make its would-be wearer die the painful death of one overtaken by the vengeance of God. Blasphemous self-equalization with God is thus put to silence, and the distinction between man and God brought to light. [10] The abysmal fall into the realm of the dead is even combined with the special disgrace destined for the uncircumcised, whose lot is described in 32.17ff. Thus the very highest of all is stripped of his usurped majesty.

The death lament: 28.11–19

The threat is once again followed by the death lament (cf. 26.15–18 following 26.1–6). The execution of the sentence is treated as if it had already been carried out, and its irrevocability revealed by a retrospective glimpse of the former glory now cast down into the dark night of destruction. The present text, however, does not consistently preserve the well-known metrical form of the dirge, which can only be restored by radical interferences with the words in their present form, for which it is difficult to find reasons.

The whole lament is presented as being a word of God. This adds impressiveness to the recollection of how its subject has been singled out and distinguished by God and makes his misbehaviour all the more serious and disappointing. This effect is heightened further by the peculiar form of the lament. It makes use of a myth telling of the primal man and how he dwelt on the mountain of God, in order to bring out all the wickedness of the king of Tyre. This myth is evidently closely related to the old Israelite story in Gen. 2f., but bears still clearer indications of its heathen origin. This goes to suggest that the Paradise story was not the only tradition current in Israel in regard to the beginnings of the human race, but that it was told in all sorts of variations conforming, some strictly, some more loosely, to Israelite thought.

The variant chosen by Ezekiel is one which puts into specially high relief the greatness and the worth of the first man in his intimate relationship with God. [12] Admittedly the description of him as a 'carefully-worked or perfect seal' is hard to understand. It is hardly possible to justify its correctness by explaining it as reflecting the divine image. On the other hand, the emphasis placed on its beauty

puts beyond all doubt that the seal is to be regarded as a mar-
vellously-worked piece of ornament. Yet the particular metaphor can
hardly have been chosen merely to emphasize that feature. Now, the
same image, applied to the sons of David, is used in Jer. 22.24 and
Hag. 2.23 in order to show how closely the person thus entitled
belongs to Yahweh and how great is the authority imparted to him.
It may well be taken for granted that God had some similar object
when he created the primal man: he was to be the executor of his
plans. So the passage that next follows describes him as dwelling in
the immediate presence of God. [13] He has his dwelling place in
Eden, the Garden of God, and gleams adorned with precious stones
of all kinds which cover his garments (the actual words state in
exaggeration that he is actually clothed in precious stones), and also
with golden ornaments. This probably stands for the protective
powers attributed to such jewels, and is also intended to signify the
special blessedness of the person thus distinguished. [14] His companion and protector is the cherub. We know this figure out of the
heavenly realm from Gen. 3, where the cherubim are installed as
guardians of the Garden of Paradise. We know from other passages
how they figure as members of Yahweh's heavenly court, as bearers
of his throne from Ezek. 10 and as protecting genii of the ark in the
holy of holies in the temple from I Kings 8.6f., as ministrants which,
according to Ps. 18.10, bear Yahweh himself through the air. Here,
therefore, he is put at the service of this highly-favoured created
being. The latter is further described as having a glorious dwelling
place upon the mountain of God with its fiery stones, a locality which
also seems to be presupposed in Gen. 2.10-14, and which ought therefore not to be thought of as contrasted to the Garden of God, even
though the two descriptions may originally go back to different conceptions and traditions. In Isa. 14.13 it bears the name of 'Mount
of Assembly', i.e. the place where the gods gather together, and is
thought to be in the furthest north, raised higher even than the stars
of God. Psalm 48.2 boldly takes up this image and applies it to Zion,
in order to distinguish it as the true abode of God from all heathen
mountains of the gods. Seen from this point of view, it is legitimate to
interpret the fire-stones (with or without emending the 'stones' into
'sons') as the stars, i.e. the star-gods. This may be preferable to
explaining them as the lightning-stones or thunderbolts of the storm-
god or as precious stones employed to build a palace for the gods, such
as are referred to in Ugaritic mythology. Yet it is worth taking

notice of the description in Enoch 18.6–9, 23–25, according to which seven mountains of different precious stones appear at the end of the heavenly firmament, one of which supports the throne of God and is covered with sweet-scented trees, while day and night a blazing fire appears which feeds the lights of heaven. Here we may be meeting the same tradition as that which Ezekiel followed. Not quite as close is the description of the grove of the gods with its trees of precious stones which Gilgamesh came upon according to the ninth tablet of the Epic on his journey to Utnapishtim (*AOT*², pp. 169f.). God's chosen place for his dwelling seems to occupy a position similar to that of the Babylonian Adapa in Eridu, the residence of the god Ea, whose command has the same authority there as that of Anu (*AOT*², pp. 143ff.). Yet this passage does not indulge in any similar naïve description of the activities of this major-domo of the gods, who is also termed the seed of the human race, meaning the first man. Like Adapa, he dwells on the mountain of the gods and walks faultlessly, until the day when he becomes guilty of a sin and loses his special position. [16] The description of the trespass is a little unexpected, since trade is here suddenly represented as the source of iniquity. [17] Whereas the subsequent mention of overweening pride in his own beauty, which evidently expresses itself by an attempt to become equal to God, is in conformity with the preceding description, a foreign element seems to have been blended in at this point, which many commentators regard as an insertion coming from some secular quarter. Yet one must at the same time remember how the description of the angelic being on the mountain of God is employed merely as an allegory for the king of Tyre and did not carry with it any force to compel Ezekiel to follow slavishly the lines of the myth. All that he was aiming at was to portray the unique position of the prince of the glittering commercial city in the colours of the myth, so as to display the enormity of his sin and the terrible change in his destiny. That he now stresses, with reference to the earthly city of Tyre, whose importance depended upon its world-wide trade, both the deeds of violence which so often accompany commerce, and also the whole commercial policy which has no scruples about injustice, but concerns itself only with heaping up gains, and claims that this is the source of all error, is sufficiently justified by the concrete object of the lament. Beauty and wisdom, according to v. 17, also give occasion for error. They are more closely connected with the traditions about the primal man, but at this point are not so central. The deceitfulness of riches is the actual reason leading to contempt for the will of God, and that again turns beauty and wisdom into a snare. So the profaner of the mountain of God is spoiled of his dignity by God himself and expelled from the heavenly sphere. As in the Paradise story, the protecting cherub performs the act which finally separates him from the shining divine abode (v. 16). God casts him down to earth from the heights of heaven, i.e. he reduces the king who enjoys such high regard to a miserable helpless creature, whom the kings who used to fawn upon him now treat with contempt.

[18f.] In v. 18 the description of guilt and punishment is repeated once again, but under the impulse of new motives, not at first sight compatible with the previous ones. Yet in spite of the inconsistency these do in their negligent way serve the divine will to reject evil and help to give it a richer expression. The wickedness incurred through trade profanes the sanctuary of the mountain of God. So out of its brightness only destructive fires of punishment can come forth, which consume and reduce to ashes the evildoer, as a warning to all nations who have let themselves be blinded by seeing injustice triumph, but who now have their eyes opened (v. 19). It would be perverse to assume, in view of the new formulation of the punishment, that the description departs from its subject in order to deal with the fate of the city of Tyre. For an evildoer to be annihilated by a fire proceeding from the holy precinct profaned by him is a common idea, cf. Lev. 10.1, 2 and Num. 16.35. The refrain which occurs in 26.21 and 27.36 is also employed here to conclude the description of God's judgment.

CHAPTER 28.20–24

Threatening word against Sidon

20 *The word of Yahweh came to me:* ²¹*'Son of man, set your face against Sidon and prophesy against her,* ²²*and say: Thus says [. . .]*ᵃ *Yahweh: Behold I will go against you, O Sidon, and I will glorify myself in your midst. And [you]*ᵇ *shall know that I am Yahweh when I execute judgments in you and manifest my holiness in [you].*ᶜ ²³*And I will send pestilence out against you and blood into [your] streets and [the slain shall fall in the midst of you]*ᵈ *by the sword that is against [you]*ᵉ *round about, and [you]*ᶠ *shall know that I am Yahweh.* ²⁴*And for the house of Israel there shall be no more a painful thorn or a hurting briar among all that dwell about*

them and have treated them with contempt. And they shall know that I [. . .]ᵍ am Yahweh.'

ᵃ⁻ᵍSee BH.

The proclamation of disaster for Tyre is large in scale and varied in its literary forms, and concentrates on human self-divinization as the worst sort of apostasy from God. The threat against Sidon that follows it seems brief and uninformative with its commonplace generalities, and seems an unnecessary piece of padding without any reason for its existence apart from an external urge to give completeness to the list of the nations to be put under God's judgment. No special sin on the part of Sidon is mentioned; the only object of punishing her is the glorification of Yahweh as the world-judge. He displays his destructive holiness at the expense of the city, and gives it up to be destroyed by pestilence and blood, which is a partial reproduction of the threefold pattern of pestilence, famine and sword found elsewhere in Ezekiel (5.12; 6.12). Obviously that city had little importance in Israelite history, during which it did not share with Tyre in the hegemony over the Phoenician cities. But after Tyre had been deprived of her position of leadership as a result of being weakened by the long years of the Babylonian siege, Sidon had begun to flourish once more, and that is all the reason to be found for numbering it among the powers of the past age that have been rejected by the Divine Lord of the world, since in the Persian period it stood at the head of the Phoenician cities. But as the threatening oracle can hardly have originated as late as that, it is more likely that this prophecy of disaster was inserted as the result of an urge to bring up to seven the number of the neighbours of Israel given over to judgment. Accordingly, the accentuated association between holiness and glory in the judicial revelation of Yahweh may be influenced by a similar juxtaposition to that in Lev. 10.3, and therefore may owe its origin to the priestly recension of the text of Ezekiel, since the priestly narrator in Ex. 14.17f., when telling of Pharaoh's overthrow, connects a reference to the divine glory with the formula about knowledge of God in the same way as in the phrase we find at the end of v. 23. The reviser has thus, in fact, summarized the meaning of the previous threatening prophecies against the nations in a way agreeing closely with Ezekiel's conception of how God judges the world, and has proclaimed the way in which God asserts his will to save in world history.

[24] There follows in v. 24 an announcement of salvation for the house of Israel, closely associated with this divine utterance, yet envisaging not only it but also all the preceding oracles to the nations. Verses 22f. state that the nations learn to recognize Yahweh as the holy one, but what that means for Israel is the revelation of his mercy to his people by freeing them from the ceaseless aggressions of hostile neighbours. All the miseries and injuries will be replaced by cheerfulness and prosperity. One significant feature here is that the most painful feature of a misfortune encountered on suffering was felt to be the malicious joy it caused (cf. 25.6–15). The more thorough the conviction of election, the more profound was the feeling that mockery was an inexplicable contradiction to the task and mission as declared by God. Yet now, after the cup of hatred and contempt has been, as it must be, drained to the dregs, Yahweh can allow his people to appear in the eyes of the world also in their true stature. The use of the word 'painful' (v. 24) only here and in Lev. 13.51f. and 14.44 shows that the composer of it came from the same circle and had the same idea, the presence of which we have shown in the preceding section.

CHAPTER 28.25–26

The gathering of Israel to dwell in peace

25 'Thus says [. . .]ᵃ Yahweh: When I gather the house of Israel from the peoples among whom they were scattered, and manifest my holiness in them in the sight of the nations, then they shall dwell in their own land which I gave to my servant Jacob. 26And they shall dwell securely in it and shall build houses and plant vineyards and dwell securely, while I execute judgments upon all their neighbours who have treated them with contempt. And thus they shall know that I am Yahweh, their God.'

ᵃSee BH.

[25] The way in which this promise is provided with a fresh introductory formula testifies to its independence from what has preceded it. It interprets Yahweh's manifestation of his holiness in the sight of the nations as the final fulfilment of his promise of the land to the patriarchs, of whom Jacob is named. This shows that the primary aim

of God's exercise of judgment is not merely to prevent injury by neighbours, but to gather together the Diaspora scattered all over the world, so that they may once more be united as one definite nation in full possession of its own territory. Here the visions of the exilic prophet Deutero-Isaiah and of his disciple who composed Isa. 60 come to life, but there are also echoes of words of Jeremiah; the corresponding promises in Ezek. 34.25, 27f. also seem to have exercised some influence, while at the same time a clear agreement is expressed with vv. 22 and 24. All of this points to an interpretation of the prophecies of Ezekiel dating from at least half a century after his time. Whereas the fresh replanting of the people in their native land and their undisturbed enjoyment of its gifts had hitherto been rendered uncertain by encircling enemies, these latter now have their own right to exist put into question. In this way is experienced the act of fulfilment performed by the covenant God, as he once more gives himself wholly to his own people (cf. the concluding covenant formula) and makes known his imperishable faithfulness.

Undoubtedly this concluding interpretation of the oracles to the nations does bring to life some of the fundamental ideas which served to maintain the Old Testament covenant relationship. Nevertheless their horizon is a very narrow one as compared with Ezekiel's much broader view of sacred history. They take the wide prospects of his prophecy to the nations and narrow them down into a small glimpse of the earthly consummation of the covenant people. The later chapters of Ezekiel will show how much further the prophet's hopes for his people reached, so as to transcend all this.

THREATENING WORDS AGAINST PHARAOH AND EGYPT
29.1–32.32

Egypt was singled out along with Tyre to be the object of lengthy prophetic threats, whose dates extend a full year before and after the fall of Jerusalem. We have already tried to show how this arose out of the decisive part which these states played in the political power-game of the seventh and eighth centuries, and have tried to assess their direct or indirect contribution to the elimination of Judah (cf. preliminary remarks to ch. 26, pp. 367f. above). Once Egypt, at the beginning of the new kingdom in the sixteenth century, had brought all Syria as far as the Euphrates under her sway she held on to it for centuries. As each period of decline was followed by a resurgence under an energetic dynasty, she had to take measures to protect herself against the rival great powers to the north by the re-establishment of this protective outwork. This was clearly her object when she intervened in the eighth century in opposition to Assyria's wars of conquest. The campaigns of Asarhaddon and Assurbanipal, which in the seventh century moved in still further towards Egypt, serve to show how right she was in her estimate of the danger spelt by that aggressive power. It is perfectly plain that she could find useful allies among the Syrian states who were trying to defend their freedom against Assyria as she attempted to re-establish her former hegemony in Syria. So her policy was to support resistance to Assyria in that area as far as she could, or, wherever Assyrian dominion had already been established, to encourage every effort at rebellion by promises of help and offers of alliance. But since Egypt did not really possess military power sufficient to put a stop to Assyrian aggression, the small states of Syria again and again found themselves disappointed in their trust in Egyptian assistance. There was a particularly flagrant exhibition of this in relation to Judah in the Palestinian revolt against Sargon in 713–711, against which Isaiah had given warning (Isa. 20), and it was still worse in the comprehensive revolt against Sennacherib after 705. When Sennacherib was threatening Jerusalem in 701 an

Egyptian army did actually march out to the relief of the city, but nevertheless suffered a reverse and had to abandon Judah to her fate. In Isa. 28–31 we see the campaign conducted by the prophet Isaiah against a policy of independence which an endeavour was made to put into effect against Assyria with the help of Egypt. So those chapters are full of appeals and warnings against her as a people that cannot profit (Isa. 30.5f.), but brings shame upon those who trust in her (Isa. 30.3, 5; 30.16f.; 31.1–3).

A similar grouping of powers recurred once more when, after Assyria's sudden downfall at the end of the seventh century, Egypt revived her old plans and tried once again to re-establish her over-lordship in Syria. Pharaoh Neco (609–593) succeeded in 609 in advancing the whole way to the Euphrates and in making all Syria an Egyptian province. In Judah, after Josiah had marched out against him and lost the battle and his life, he replaced Jehoahaz, the king chosen by the nation, with Jehoiakim, who was favourably disposed towards him. But the undertakings begun under such hopeful auspices were crushed after a few years by Nebuchadrezzar's advance in about 605. Egypt was again confined to her original boundaries, whereas Syria as far as the Egyptian frontier passed into the posses-sion of the Babylonian king (cf. II Kings 24.7). This did not prevent Pharaoh from provoking Babylonian vassals to throw off the Baby-lonian yoke by offering them his assistance. Both Jehoiakim's revolt in about 602 and that of Zedekiah in about 589 were based upon their confidence that they would be able to break the Babylonian yoke with the help of their southern ally. The fact that Nebuchadrezzar had temporarily to give up the siege of Jerusalem in order to repel an Egyptian relieving force shows that these hopes were not altogether unfounded (Jer. 37.5; 34.21). None the less the warnings of the prophets Jeremiah and Ezekiel were proved right (cf. Jer. 2.16–19; 46; Ezek. 17; and for the last, pp. 224f. above); Egypt once again proved to be a staff made of reed, which does not supply any reliable support and causes the person who depends on it to fall down.

So Egypt, along with Tyre, is seen to be the chief supporter of the resistance to the prophet's preaching of repentance and judgment. Their appeals to yield to Yahweh's will and accept foreign overlord-ship as what he had decided upon in judgment and to wait in faith for his forgiveness could not deprive the attempts at achieving a self-willed freedom which proceeded from Egypt of their power to attract. In Jerusalem and also among the exiles it was thought possible to ignore the prophets' warnings, and it was this which took away the last chance of deliverance. The prophet of the exile, who sees that those for whom he is responsible are necessarily hardened against his appeals because they have been seduced by the world power, raises his voice in a pastor's distress. He speaks in order that during the very moment of Jerusalem's death agony and the complete spiritual confusion that follows, his hearers may get a clear picture of the world power that is at enmity with God. He thus teaches them to recognize in the coming disaster the inexorable will to judge of his God, who forces himself to be recognized not only among his own people but before the eyes of the nations of the world, as the Lord and sole controller of history.

CHAPTER 29.1–16

A sentence of guilt against the king of Egypt

1 In the tenth year, in the tenth month, on the twelfth day of the month, the word of the Lord came to me: 2'Son of man, set your face against Pharaoh, king of Egypt, and prophesy against him and against all Egypt 3[. . .]ᵃ and say: Thus says [. . .]ᵇ Yahweh:ᶜ

Behold, I will come over you, Pharaoh, king of Egypt,
the great dragon,ᵈ that lies in the midst of the currents of his river,
that says:
"The currents of my Nile are my own and I myself have made . . ."ᵉ
4 I will put hooks in your cheeks [and will draw you upᶠ out of your streams]
and make the fish of the streams of your Nile stick to your scales [. . .]ᵍ
5 And I will cast you forth into the wilderness, you andʰ the fish of your streams,
you shall fall upon the open field, and none will gather you [. . .].ⁱ
To the wild beasts of the earth and to the birds of the air (I give you) as food.
6 And all the inhabitants of Egypt shall know that I am Yahweh.

Because [you]ʲ have been a staff of reed to the house of Israel when they grasped you with theᵏ hand, you broke and tore their [hand]ˡ . . . 7and when they supported themselves upon you, you broke and [made their loins to shake]ᵐ . . . 8Therefore thus says [. . .]ⁿ Yahweh: Behold I bring the sword upon you and will cut off from you man and beast; [9]*and the land of Egypt will become a desert and a ruin, and they shall know that I am Yahweh.*

Because you said, "The Nile is mine and I made it," [10]*therefore, behold I will come over you and your streams and I will make the land of Egypt a ruin and a* [. . .][o] *desert from Migdol to Syene and to the border of Kush.* [11]*No foot of man shall pass through it, and no foot of beast shall pass through it, it shall be uninhabited forty years.*

12 *And I will make the land of Egypt a desert in the midst of desolated countries and her cities shall be* [ruins][p] *among ruined cities for forty years, and I will scatter the Egyptians among the nations, and disperse them among the countries.*

13 *For thus says* [. . .][q] *Yahweh: At the end of forty years I will gather the Egyptians from among the peoples among whom they were scattered,* [14]*and I will restore the fortunes of Egypt, and bring them back to the land of Pathros,*[r] *the land of their origin, and there they shall be a lowly kingdom.* [15]*It shall be the most lowly of the kingdoms, and never again exalt itself above the nations. And I will make them so small that they will never again rule over the nations.* [16]*And they*[s] *shall never again be the reliance of the house of Israel, recalling their iniquity when they turn to them for guidance, and they shall know that I am* [. . .][t] *Yahweh.'*

[a–b]See BH.

[c]Verses 3–6 display the Kina metre, which can be reconstituted by a few slight emendations of the text. But this metre stops at v. 7, and only the first three lines can be forced into metre.

[d]See BH.

[e]So with LXX.

[f]Moved forward from v. 4b from considerations of metre.

[g]MT: 'and all the fish of your streams will stick to your scales'; a repetition of what has preceded, cf. Cornill, Herrmann.

[h]Delete: 'all'.

[i]MT: 'and gathers'.

[j]MT: third person plural.

[k–l]See BH.

[m]Abbreviated from the awkward reading of the MT: 'and make all the loins of them to shake'.

[n–o]See BH.

[p]MT: 'desert'; as the word has already been used for the land and is not so suitable for destroyed cities, it is most probably best replaced by *ḥorbōt*, ruins, cf. vv. 9 and 10.

[q]See BH.

[r]The Egyptian name for the 'land of the South', i.e. Upper Egypt, as also in Isa. 11.11; Jer. 44.1, 15.

[s–t]See BH.

The execution of the death-sentence on Pharaoh: 29.1–6a

This passage is the earliest of the prophecies against Egypt, as is shown by the date in the superscription. It comes at the beginning of 587, the same year in which Israel's catastrophe took place six months later. There are no concrete allusions to contemporary events, but that does not justify removing it from that fateful year and putting it in some later year when Egypt would have found herself at peace. The picture that is being painted is not one of security from every danger, but of Pharaoh's proud consciousness of his own strength. This is the ultimate cause of that complacent assurance in face of all dangers, which keeps him from having any feeling of being responsible to a higher authority than his own.

So here we see exactly the same thing as in 28.1ff., the hybris of a human potentate, with full control of power so great that it makes him give way to the dream of being equal to God and makes him refuse to recognize any as Lord over him. [3] Whereas in the case of Tyre it was the divine dwelling with its riches which constituted the chief temptation, here it is the rich produce of the low-lying valley fertilized by the Nile, and its skilful system of irrigation, which gives solid reasons for believing that it will flourish economically and be guaranteed against disaster, and this again is regarded as a sign of exceptional cleverness and leads to ambitious self-exaltation. The indolent pride of possession, which here grows so great as to imagine it can disregard all the blows of fate which threaten the other nations, is strikingly conveyed by the picture of the crocodile which rests indolently in the water in proud consciousness of its inviolability and superiority to all attack. Actually this metaphor was a favourite one in Egypt itself and used there in the hymns in praise of Pharaoh. The word *tannūn*, sea monster, is used, which is so frequently identified with Rahab, Behemoth or Leviathan that it seems related to the terrible chaos monster, in which all the powers hostile to God concentrate themselves (cf. Ps. 74.13f.; Isa. 27.1; 51.9; Job 7.12). So the prophet uses it to suggest not only the savage uncontrollable strength of the crocodile but also the characteristics of the mythological power of chaos in its opposition to the Creator of the world, as a revelation of the real nature of the heathen world-power.

[4] But *vis-à-vis* the power of the world-God this apparently irresistible dominating power shows its real colours and is seen to be mere blinded self-deceit. Job 40.25f. may picture a battle with the crocodile as an adventure almost too great for man, but Yahweh can come even where he appears in all his might, and tame him by a mere play of power. In a way described in ancient accounts of crocodile hunts

(the latest is Herodotus II.70), he is pulled by means of hooks put in his jaws out of his native element on to dry land, and then slaughtered. The curious picture of the fish which stick to his scales and share his fate is meant to convey how the coming destruction will include not only Pharaoh but his subjects. **[5f.]** The carcass lying in the desert is eagerly seized by birds and wild beasts which complete the work of destruction, thus shattering human pride. Israel's God, who judges his own people with such severity, also shows the Egyptian that he is the Lord of the world, and that any challenge of his supremacy will feel his death-dealing stroke.

Few words are wasted in telling of this mighty act of Yahweh's. The verse is a five-stress one, like that we have already met in the death lament. Here only a few minor emendations of the text are needed to restore it. A few strokes produce a fully rounded picture, too concise and powerful to endure any superfluous features, and that is enough to mark it out as an original piece of creative poetry. The interest is never allowed to swerve, but is always focused on the central point of the opposition between worldly and divine power which provides a vigorous prelude to the anti-Egyptian poems.

Fresh grounds for Egypt's guilt: 29.6b–9a

We note here the presence of something similar to what we saw in the successive patchwork of the pieces in ch. 25 and in the inconsistencies between ch. 26 and 27f. When we turn to the second threatening utterance against Egypt we find different reasons given for her being punished: hitherto everything has concentrated on the hostile atti- tude towards God which is of the very essence of that world-power, but now, instead, her relationship to Israel occupies the centre of the stage. Egypt has shown herself to be a broken reed to Israel, arousing great hopes which ended in shameful disappointment. We meet with the same picture of Egypt as a staff of reed in Isa. 36.6. But it takes a simpler form, and speaks only of an injury to the hand, caused by the bending or breaking of the apparently solid reed which has become useless because of an unnoticed crack. Here, on the other hand, there is not only the injury to the hand owing to the reed being split, but also shaking of the loins when the reed breaks and suddenly ceases to give firm support, an elaboration which makes the metaphor more complicated. In each case what is being pilloried is the unreliability of any alliance with Egypt. In earlier prophets, disillusionment with Egypt is attributed to the fact that God smites her power (cf. Isa.

30.2–5; 31.2f.; Jer. 2.17f., 36f.) and appears to be the result of Israel's apostasy from her Lord. But here it is the unreliability and internal weakness of the apparently compact world-empire that is counted as guilt on the part of Egypt, because it was that which made her a deceitful temptress to Israel and led her subsequently into disaster. It cannot be said that Ezekiel gives any evidence elsewhere of such an opinion; at any rate, ch. 17 is in totally different terms. One may think the prophet was giving a very secondary reason for punishing Egypt, and dwelling on all the power a state which trusts in its own strength and unscrupulous policies must have had to mislead a neighbour like Israel. Or, if not, one may prefer to think this is a supplement to the prophet's original words about the punishment which has been added by one of the prophet's disciples in order to soften down Israel's responsibility. The way in which direct address is discontinued, metrical form given up and v. 6a repeated again for a conclusion may be regarded as supporting this latter opinion.

Egypt humbled and shown grace: 29.9b–16

Clearer light is thrown here on what the statements in the previous section were intended to mean. As v. 16 shows, the ideas expressed here about Egypt's guilt towards Israel regard it as consisting mainly in Egypt's prompting Israel to rely mistakenly on the help of a world-power, although the introductory phrase in v. 9b explicitly establishes a connection with the charge stated in v. 3, the first section. [10] Its writer is interested above all in the way such a secure and fertile piece of territory has been laid waste, which he has found stated just before this, and he accentuates the scene once more by making it stretch from the north (of the various place names given, Migdol, found in Jer. 44.1, is probably the most suitable) to the furthest south, where Syene (at the modern Assouan, by the first cataract) and the border of Kush (probably lying still further south) serve to show that Upper Egypt is also involved in the great catastrophe. He adds that the inhabitants will be carried into exile among nations outside Egypt, so that Egypt's fate seems like a repetition of that of Judah, but on a gigantic scale. In this, as in the second section, Pharaoh totally disappears behind his people. Retribution, however, takes on the character of the exact equivalent of the damage inflicted on Judah, following the principle of the ancient *lex talionis*.

[11–13] The parallelism in the judgment of the two countries is now —and this is the startling feature—also extended to their restoration.

The sentence of forty years' imprisonment, fixed for Israel in 4.6, is also applied to Egypt. Once it has elapsed, those deported to foreign lands are to be repatriated. This will not, however, in any case lead to the renewed existence of any greater Egypt. [14] Apart from the Delta, only Pathros or Upper Egypt will be reconstituted as a kingdom. According to other witnesses (cf. Herodotus II.4.15), it was regarded as the original home of the Egyptian race. [15] The reason given for this is the divine intention to provide against any renascence of the all too mighty empire which had in the past been the cause of war and of the enslavement of other nations.

Obviously we find a different attitude towards the Nile kingdom here, as compared with that in the preceding sections. [16] The concluding phrase asserts that the knowledge of Yahweh is the fruit of his judgment, acknowledging the common objective of all prophecy in the same terms as in vv. 6 and 9. Yet we do not find any further reference to the indissoluble opposition on the part of the heathen empire or to the corresponding severity of the judgment executed upon it. This undoubtedly suggests that it comes from a later period, when Egypt had given up her position as a great power and had ceased to be a menace to Israel. It even expresses a certain sympathy towards the southern neighbour in the glimpse it gives of the day when she will have grace shown to her, very similar to that in Isa. 19. 18ff., which forms so obvious a contrast to the threats preceding it. But whereas there the interest is entirely in Egypt's conversion to Yahweh, which leads to her reception into the congregation (of his people), here the emphasis is on the carrying out of Yahweh's will in the common political life of the nations. His judgment has as its objective the subjecting of the nations to his plan for peace, for which the disarmament of the great empires is the obvious prerequisite. Here ideas of Ezekiel's have been taken up and thought out further by an independent mind and then by means of the concluding verse connected with his wide view of the extending of the knowledge of the Lord of the world. Even though it does not attain to the magnitude of the hope expressed in Isa. 2.2–4 or Zeph. 3.7, the assimilation of Egypt's destiny to that of Judah is a sign of how prophetic universalistic ideas of the pattern to be assumed by the nations of the world are breaking through, and of how all political vindictive feelings must be subordinated to those principles.

CHAPTER 29.17–21

Egypt as a reward for Nebuchadrezzar

17 In the twenty-seventh year, in the first month, on the first day of the month, the word of Yahweh came to me: 18'Son of man, Nebuchadrezzar, king of Babylon, made his army labour hard against[a] Tyre; every head was made bald and every shoulder rubbed. Yet neither he nor his army got anything from Tyre to pay for the labour that he had performed against it. 19Therefore thus says [. . .][b] Yahweh: Behold I will give the land of Egypt to Nebuchadrezzar, king of Babylon, and he shall carry off its wealth and despoil it and plunder it, and it shall be the wages for his army. 20I give him the land of Egypt as his recompense for which he laboured [. . .],[c] says [. . .][d] Yahweh.'
21 In that day I will cause a horn to spring forth to the house of Israel, and I will open your lips among them, and they will know that I am Yahweh.'

[a–b]See BH.
[c]MT: 'because they worked for me', not in LXX. The siege of Tyre is described as a service performed to Yahweh.
[d]See BH.

This utterance of the prophet, shown by its date to be the latest dated one (it is separated by a period of about sixteen years from the previous date given in 29.1), falls at the end of April 571. Nebuchadrezzar's campaign against Tyre, after having lasted thirteen years, had come to an end two or three years previously, without having had the result expected by the prophet in his pronouncement of judgment against Tyre: Tyre was not destroyed or even plundered. Still, one cannot say the prophecy was completely unfulfilled. True, Tyre had to surrender to Babylonian overlordship, as is witnessed by inscriptions of the years 570 and 564. She escaped with a black eye, so to speak; but from that time her power seems to have been broken, and she never recovered her former greatness. Nevertheless, it was apparent to all that she was far from being overtaken by the utter annihilation Ezekiel had foretold, and there was a danger that those who had heard the threats uttered beforehand might be tempted to feel doubts. Had Yahweh failed to stand by his word, had he failed to ratify it in full as a genuine revelation of his will? The doubts

aroused on earlier occasions in regard to predictions the prophet had
made (cf. 12.22) must have revived and been still stronger than
before, and added to the difficulty of his work. So it must have been
a great relief from accusations from outside and questioning within
when, on New Year's Day in the twenty-seventh year of Jehoiachin,
a word of God came to the prophet announcing what God had determined upon, and providing an explanation for the hitherto unsolved
perplexity.

First of all it expresses in almost pitying terms how disappointing
the result of the many-years-long siege has been to the Babylonian
king; his army has indeed so worn itself out that he would be granted
some reward for his trouble. Yahweh, too, on his side regards
Nebuchadrezzar's investment of the island as a task performed for
him, and is not so unjust as to withhold payment. He, the rich Lord
of the whole world, has means enough at his command, to be able to
compensate his servant in full. And he is going to do this on the most
generous possible scale, by granting him the riches of Egypt. By this
means he will be able to pay up his arrears and reward his troops in a
way that will transform their dissatisfaction with his field-marshals
into good cheer. There is no word of Egypt's annihilation or permanent incorporation into the Babylonian empire; words like those
of Jer. 43.8ff. seem rather to suggest a punitive expedition. So one
may ask if a certain softening down of the previous threats to the
Nile kingdom is not already beginning to become visible.

It is unlikely that Ezekiel was already aware then that the Babylonians were mobilizing in haste for an Egyptian campaign and that
that aroused hopes in him which were subsequently confirmed by a
word from Yahweh. The earliest Babylonian expedition to Egypt of
which we know did not take place till 568–567, so one could hardly
yet venture on any reliable forecast of what Nebuchadrezzar was
going to do in 571. Yet the general direction of aggressiveness in
Babylonian policy after the fall of Tyre must have been perfectly
plain to every spectator of world-events, since the Babylonian world-
empire knew of nowhere save Egypt whence a threat could come. The
earlier threatening utterances against Egypt had long focused attention on the south. So the disclosure made to the prophet was well in
keeping with the political situation of the day, and could be sure of
arousing close attention.

Its fulfilment by a campaign by Nebuchadrezzar a few years later
is confirmed by what—it must be admitted—is only a fragmentary

Babylonian clay tablet. The opponent named in it is Amasis, who after a long revolutionary struggle had succeeded in overthrowing and killing Pharaoh Hophra, who had ruled since 588 and taken part in the last battle for Jerusalem. According to the fragmentary text, there seems to have been a vigorous encounter between the Egyptian and Babylonian armies, though we have no information as to its place or its outcome; nevertheless, Nebuchadrezzar was evidently able to claim to have been the victor. Amasis also was henceforth no longer capable of engaging in active intervention in Palestine and Syria, and of going any further with the policy of conquest like his predecessors. So everything goes to prove that Ezekiel's prediction was verified by the course of history.

Offence has been taken at the way, unique in prophetic literature, in which attention is called to the fact that a prophetic prediction was not fulfilled word for word, and the transference to Egypt of the threat not fulfilled upon the city of Tyre has been called a 'cynical performance' (Van den Born), unworthy of Ezekiel. Yet the date which is placed before it makes it difficult to assume that it is a later piece of fiction. Above all, the scapegoat chosen is not altogether innocent or free from all complicity. Egypt had for a long time been under a threat of punishment fully as severe as that of Tyre. Also, the judgment in store for Tyre does not fall on its head; the unpaid reward of the plunder which should have been won by the struggle to reduce the rich city, but long since used up by its defenders, has now to be paid out of the riches of Egypt.

The genuine cause of offence, which some readers may find at this correction to the threats against Tyre, is much more likely to be found in the apparently cool self-assurance with which the prophet brushes aside his earlier pronouncement of judgment in its literal meaning, and feels himself commissioned to announce that Yahweh is free to alter it if he likes and has actually done so. This makes the alteration sound almost ludicrous, since all the emphasis is placed on the money owed by Yahweh for the purpose of paying Nebuchadrezzar's troops, making it look as if righteous divine retribution could no longer be mentioned. Can Ezekiel really have believed that Yahweh had incurred the legal debt of wages to the instrument he had employed, like an earthly monarch who has to pay the mercenaries he has hired? Does this anxiety about minor monetary matters distinguish Ezekiel's work from the lofty manner in which Isaiah and Jeremiah take for granted God's right to make use of earthly monarchs in whatever way he likes? Or ought we rather to regard all this as an ironical critique of the difficulties which disturbed the faith of his contemporaries, and the way they became excited over the far from literal fulfilment of the threat against Tyre, as if it was their bounden duty to see that Nebuchadrezzar was fairly treated? At any rate, such a piece of irony would assert in a most effective way the sovereign freedom of God to fulfil a prediction of a prophet in whatever way seems good to him, and would bring out still more strongly the cool and nonchalant way in which the Lord of the world can control the mightiest of nations by merely moving a finger.

Of course, this cannot obscure the fact that we find here a decision with regard to a problem of really crucial importance; the uncertainty whether a prophecy ought to be regarded as an infallible disclosure of divine truth, if it falls short of being literally fulfilled. It is plain that Ezekiel is far from indulging in any anxious effort at reappraisal. His predictions have another object than that of anticipating beforehand the exact details of the course history is going to take, since like all other prophetic utterances they are subordinated to their general object. This is to make his contemporaries aware within their concrete situation of the Lord of all history's unshakable will to reign, in order to make them capable of taking up the right attitude towards the powers of their age. The prophecies look up and out to the central fact of God's revealing act, which is the accomplishment of his lordship, and in describing the road to it they make use of the means available in their time and in their world.

There we see their greatness and their limitation. We see their greatness, in so far as they, in contradistinction to heathen prophecy, regardless of its undoubted capacity to give genuine predictions of future events, are not dependent upon single events, which at the very best furnish only a sort of miraculous proof, but do not supply any further guidance in regard to the mysterious developments of history. The predictions of the prophets, on the other hand, are always associated with that to which the prophets testify, a direct awareness of the whole control of providence, so they subordinate each single historical event to its context in the activity of God which makes the whole development of history serve his kingdom. Their limitation consists in the fact that they are trying to show the way along which God is leading, whereas that God is always transcendent and far above all human capabilities, and so his march through history cannot be imprisoned in human words. He carries his plans home and attains his objective with all the freedom of the Creator; so, while prediction can make statements clarifying the plan and assuring us of its existence, it can never determine the exact line it will take or calculate beforehand its individual stages. So prediction demands humble obedience to the mystery of the divine work of realization and, like the rest of what prophets preach, it confronts the hearer with the question of a faith which refuses to let itself be led astray by unexpected delays, changes of front, or reconstructions. Thus Deutero-Isaiah, though he above all others felt himself called to proclaim completely new dispensations of providence, is completely decisive in the way he repels all human claims to know better and to meddle in displeasure with the divine plan. And the post-exilic prophet Zechariah is firm in his insistence that he is to be recognized as a true messenger of God, in spite of considerable transformations in his picture of the future (Zech. 2.9, 11; 4.9; 6.15). Ezekiel, too, speaks out of a certainty of being right in his interpretation of God's will to judge, even though in the wider perspective of historical events, some opinions as to the points at which divine control of history seemed to be emerging have had to be scrapped and replaced by others. It remains true that the Lord is on the march to set up his kingdom throughout the whole world, to humble the powers of this world, and prepare his salvation for the believing people of God.[1]

[21] The accomplishment of the judgment by Nebuchadrezzar, regardless of how it works out in detail, opens up the way to salvation for Israel. The judgment is not the final one; God is guiding the decisive political events of the world in order to accomplish his plan of salvation. In that plan Israel has the premier place now, as always. Do the words of v. 21 point towards the coming of the great son of David, in whom God sets up his new covenant with Israel (34.23ff.), as the use of the same image in Ps. 132.17 and the mysterious allusion in 21.26 seem to suggest? Or is the springing forth of the horn to be given a more general application as referring to the expectation that Israel's destiny will reach a final saving fulfilment? One cannot decide with complete certainty which interpretation is right. It is enough to say that the darkness of the divine judgment does not quench but stirs into fresh flame the old messianic hope of his people. In any case one cannot imagine that there is any sort of political calculation, or any expectation that Nebuchadrezzar might feel

[1] For the whole problem see E. Jenni, *Die politischen Voraussagen der Propheten*, AThANT 29, 1956.

favourable to the idea of restoring the kingdom of Judah once Egypt
had been rendered powerless, thus making it unlikely that there
would be any more conspiracies against Babylonian overlordship.
Such reckoning of the probabilities, in which the prophet would
conform to the line of thought followed by the diplomats of Jerusalem, is totally alien to his hope: on the contrary, as ch. 34ff. clearly
show, he recognized only one reason for hope, Yahweh's zeal to
sanctify his name. He thus takes over the 'nevertheless' of faith, of
which the older prophets spoke in their announcements of salvation.
But when salvation arises again the prophet's mouth must also over-
flow once more with appeals to advance in faith to meet the God who
is coming. In his struggle for the fulfilment of his prophecies to the
nations, the prophet has so far kept silent and left the decision to his
God. But now he receives a promise that his mouth will be opened,
in order that he may testify to God's victory.

As far as we can see, he did not live to see that day and hour; the
utterance of 571 seems to contain his last piece of public preaching.
So he, like so many of his predecessors and successors, has joined the
company of the forerunners, who in the words of the Epistle to the
Hebrews, 'did not receive what was promised, though they did
through faith succeed in testifying to God, since God had foreseen
something better for us: they shall not be made perfect apart from
us' (Heb. 11.39f.).

It is obvious that the present position of this section, among the
dated oracles to the nations in ch. 25–32, is not original. It should
in fact have been put in its proper place as a last word at the conclusion of the prophecies to the nations. In its present position,
attached to the first utterance against Egypt, it brings it into connection with Tyre, and intensifies the threat to Egypt as one not as
yet fulfilled, but already due for fulfilment, since it will serve to add
the final touch still required to complete the judgment upon Tyre.

CHAPTER 30.1–19

The day of Yahweh upon Egypt

1 The word of Yahweh came to me: 2'Son of man, prophesy and say:
thus says [. . .]ᵃ Yahweh: Wail: "Alas for the day!" ³For the day is near,

yea, the day of Yahweh is near, it will be a day of [the end]^b for the nations!

4 A sword shall come upon Egypt and trembling will fall upon Kush, when the slain fall in Egypt [. . .]^c and her foundations are torn down.

5 [. . .]^d

6 [. . .]^e Those who support Egypt shall fall and her proud might shall come down;
from Migdot to Syene they shall fall within her by the sword, says [. . .]^f Yahweh.

7 And [it] shall lie^g desolate in the midst of desolated countries and her cities in the midst of cities that are laid waste [. . .]^h

8 And they shall know that I am Yahweh, when I set fire to Egypt and all her helpers will be broken.

9 [. . .]ⁱ

10 Thus says [. . .]^j Yahweh: I will put an end to the proud behaviour of Egypt by the hand of Nebuchadrezzar, king of Babylon.

11 He and his people, the most terrible of the nations, shall be brought in to destroy the land,
and they shall draw their swords against Egypt and fill the land with the slain.

12 And I will dry up the currents of the Nile and will sell the land into the hand of evil man.
I will bring desolation upon the land and its abundance by the hand of foreigners. I, Yahweh, have said so.

13 *Thus says* [. . .]^k *Yahweh:*
I will destroy [*the mighty*]^l *and will put an end to the* [*strong ones*]^m *from Noph*ⁿ
and the prince [*in the*]^o *land of Egypt shall no longer exist, and I will put fear in the land of Egypt.*

14 *I will make Pathros*^p *a desolation and will set fire to Zoan*^q *and will execute acts of judgment upon No.*^r

15 *And I will pour my wrath upon Sin,*^s *the stronghold of Egypt and cut off the multitude of No.*^t

16 *Yea, I will set fire to Egypt, Sin*^u *shall writhe in convulsions*
and No shall be breached [*and its walls broken down*].^v

17 *The young men of On*^w *and Pi-beseth*^x *shall fall by the sword, and they (the cities) shall go into captivity.*

18 *And at Tahpanhes*^y *the day shall be dark, when I break there the* [*sceptre*]^z
of Egypt, and her proud might shall come to an end.
The city shall be covered with a cloud and her daughters shall go into captivity.

19 *Thus I will execute acts of judgment upon Egypt and they shall know that I am Yahweh.*

^aSee BH.

[b]MT: 'a day of cloud, the time of the nations'. The above translation follows the LXX reading which is supported by ch. 7.

[c]MT: 'and her wealth shall be carried away'; not in LXX and not in accordance with the metre or the style of the neighbouring verses.

[d]Verse 5 reads in the MT: 'Kush and Put and Lud and all the mingled people and the Libyans (reading *lūb* with LXX in place of *kūb*) and the sons of the land of league shall fall with them by the sword.' This list of nations included in the catastrophe along with Egypt is given in prose and interrupts the whole sequence. The verse was originally a marginal gloss to Kush in v. 4 and gave the names of the allied and tributary nations of Egypt who were involved in the disaster: Ethiopia, Punt which is either on the Red Sea or a part of Libya in Cyrenaica, see on 27.10; the Lydians (auxiliary troops from Asia Minor); some unnamed mercenaries; the Libyans and mercenaries from Judah, also known to us from the military colony from Judah at Elephantine on the southern border of Egypt. The original order seems to have been interfered with.

[e]MT: 'Thus says Yahweh'. This fresh introductory formula is to restore the sequence broken by v. 5.

[f-g]See BH.

[h]MT: 'they shall be' must be deleted to preserve the metre.

[i]Verse 9: 'On that day messengers shall go forth from me in ships to terrify the unsuspecting Ethiopians, and trembling shall come upon them in the day of Egypt, for lo it comes.' The phrase forms an appendix to what precedes it, by repeating v. 4b word for word, and attributing the terror of Ethiopia to messengers sent by Yahweh with news of the occurrence. Its author has evidently been stirred up by Isa. 18.1ff., where the messengers sent from Ethiopia to Jerusalem, crossing the Nile on swift ships, are told by the prophet Isaiah to go back, and take home with them an oracle from Yahweh telling of the imminence of judgment. What Isaiah prophesied during the Assyrian crisis is applied in this passage to God's acts of judgment upon Egypt. The verse is an interesting testimony to how the prophetic circles made use of older prophecies that could be adapted to the circumstances of the new period. Yet at this point in the context it comes too late, and fails to realize how in the great day of Yahweh the terror will be directly felt.

[j-m]See BH.

[n]In the Old Testament also *mōph* = Memphis, south of Cairo, on the southern edge of the Delta, a very ancient city which has always been representative of Egypt.

[o]See BH.

[p]A name for Upper Egypt, cf. 29.14.

[q]The Greek Tanis in Lower Egypt, on the second Eastern Channel of the Nile Delta, already a political centre under the Hyksos, as well as the residence of Rameses II in the thirteenth century, and also a royal residence during the twenty-first dynasty (1113–945) which received from it its name of Tanite. Being a commercial city and a fortress on the eastern frontier, it retained its importance till a late period.

[r]In full, No Amon = 'the city of Amon', Nahum 3.8. In Greek 'Thebes', in Upper Egypt, famous as a royal residential city especially during the New Kingdom (1580–950), during the period when Egypt was growing into a world empire, the city where the greatest of the Pharaohs had their tombs, a priestly city after

1085, but which then gave up its importance to the cities of Lower Egypt.

sUsually identified with Pelusium, the commercial city on the eastern frontier, which is regarded as the bulwark of Egypt. In the Greek version, however, it is interpreted as meaning Sais, which being the residence of the twenty-sixth Saite dynasty (663–525) was the one which first came to view during the very period when this passage was written.

tLXX instead reads Noph (see above, note n, p. 414), which would thus be mentioned twice over.

uLXX instead reads Syene, a place on the southern frontier of Egypt.

vA brilliant but rather doubtful conjecture by Cornill for the text which is unintelligible in its present state.

wThe Greek Heliopolis in Lower Egypt, north-west of Cairo, metropolis of sun-worship since the third dynasty c. 2800 bc and possessing a celebrated temple of the sun-god Re.

xGreek Bubastis, 'house of the goddess Bastet', at the western entrance to the Wadi Tumilat, widely renowned for the great feast of the cat-headed goddess, residence of the twenty-second dynasty from 950.

yGreek Daphne, south-west of Pelusium, probably wrongly conjectured to be the Hanes of Isa. 30.4, but named in Jer. 2.16 along with Noph in order to represent Egypt. It was the frontier fortress to the East which received parties of refugees from Judah in 587–586, who had compelled the prophet Jeremiah to join them in taking refuge from the wrath of Nebuchadrezzar with their neighbour and ally (Jer. 43.7; 44.1). It was also the place where Jeremiah delivered a threatening word against Egypt, which he confirmed by a symbolic act in front of 'Pharaoh's palace'.

zSee BH.

This passage differs from its surroundings, in being the only one without any exact indication of its period, whereas the others are all precisely enough dated. Its structure recalls ch. 26 and 30: a word of judgment moving in brief phrases, and held together by one dominant idea. Then, loosely attached to it by the formula announcing prophetic words in vv. 10 and 13, there follow two loosely built sections which are controlled by different concerns and seek to complete the main oracle in a particular direction, partly by a historical interpretation of the pronouncement of judgment that is still hidden (cf. 26.7), partly by further extension of the power of destruction as it overthrows all obstacles (cf. 26.8ff.; 29.9bff.). So here only the first section (30.1–8), which is marked out by the full introductory formula and command from God to proclaim it, is an original saying of Ezekiel's which has been taken as a basis to which disciples of the prophet's have appended further variations on the same theme.

The day of Egypt's doom: 30.1–8

No one can miss seeing that the theme of ch. 7, the day of the end determined for every nation, recurs here (cf. above, pp. 101f.), this time with a special application to Egypt. The theme is connected with the day of Yahweh which formed so marked a feature in proclamations of judgment by earlier prophets, and as a result the idea that fate will take a final decisive turn, which also enters into heathen expectations of a coming day of damnation full of terrible punishments, now loses its impersonally inevitable character, and is seen as the judgment day appointed by the king of the world, on which he will deliver his enemies to well-deserved retribution. [2] The Egyptians are bidden to cry out in terror at the day of disaster which will suddenly fall upon them, and like the phrase in 7.2: 'An end comes, the end comes', so here the prophet's certainty clothes itself in three phrases which move forward from the general to the particular: 'The day is near, the day of Yahweh is near, it will be a final day for the nations' (v. 3). [4] What is at first a vague undetermined terror reveals itself as the world-wide day of reckoning which awaits all nations. The judgment upon Jerusalem was always viewed by the prophets against the background of the judgment of the whole world, and the same is true now of the punishing of Egypt. Like a destructive force growing into demonic independence, a sword begins to exercise its fury upon Egypt, so that the news travels to the furthest south, striking terror into the neighbouring land of Ethiopia. [6] The sword mows down all the inhabitants, and the depopulated country loses all power to revive, since all law and order disappears and the 'foundations are torn down'. What help are the numerous allies and tributary nations which the wealthy land has at her disposal, a list of which is given in v. 5 by a well-informed reader! They, too, fall victim to the fury of the sword, as it wipes out every living thing from furthest north to furthest south. Every reader must be reminded of the sword-song in ch. 21. As it raged then in Israel, so it rages now in the much richer and mightier land of Egypt [7] It was a country that had seldom seen a foreign foe carrying all the horrors of war inside its own boundaries. As a result of its favoured position it had suffered only partial war damage while its neighbours underwent all the disasters of defeat, but now it is to be reduced to the same condition as the others, a desolation amid desolations (v. 7). [8] Thus Yahweh will administer the *coup de grâce* to this apparently invulnerable world-power, which had so far been able to defy him, and show himself, amid the ruins of the nations, to be the one in whose name the mystery of who is the true master of the world is revealed.

This announcement of the great judgment day, which only outlines it in the most general terms, may originally have served as an
introduction to the great prophecies of judgment upon Egypt, which
afterwards worked out and dated more precisely each of the separate
strokes of judgment. Its removal to its present more out-of-the-way
position may be connected with elaborations which have obscured
the original character of the passage. This suggests that it, along with
the majority of the anti-Egyptian prophecies, originated previously
to the fall of Jerusalem. The inclusion of their much-renowned ally
in the world-judgment that now rises to its climax serves to intensify
the inexorability of the threat to the people of God itself, and is to be
regarded as well in keeping with the pastoral correction of the congregation of the exiles and the warnings against blindness to those in the
homeland.

Historical interpretation of the preceding threat of judgment: 30.10–12

As so often happens, the concealed threat in vv. 1–8 has light thrown
on it by connecting it with contemporary historical factors. **[10f.]** The
unnamed power of destruction, which rushes like a terrifying tornado
through Egypt from north to south and turns it into a depopulated
desert, is Nebuchadrezzar and his warriors, here as in 28.7 described
as the most terrible of the nations; they carry out a campaign of merciless annihilation. **[12]** To strangle all life, the Nile, the source of the
wealth and fertility of Egypt, along with the system of many branch-
ing canals in its Delta, is to be dried up, as the divine overlord attacks
nature itself. This sober and somewhat commonplace comment does
not succeed, save by the clumsy lumbering confusion of its sentences,
in associating together the historical and the cosmic aspects of the
disaster. It must have originated during the period after the end of
the siege of Tyre, when expectations turned towards an Egyptian
campaign on the part of Nebuchadrezzar.

The doom of the proud power of Egypt as seen in the fate of
its most famous cities: 30.13–19

Anyone who looks over the list given here of cities with their proud
history, and recalls what centres of wealth and power they were,
and how more than once they were sources of ruling dynasties and
political movements, will admit that they provide a very suitable
means of representing the almost inexhaustible resources of the
kingdom on the Nile.

[13] From the beginning this is emphasized and the object made plain by the references to the great and mighty ones of Egypt, and to Pharaoh himself, the most outstanding of them all. But the whole plan has been executed in such a feeble way that it must be admitted that the capabilities of the writer were not sufficient to give shape to what was in itself a happy conception. [13–16] At the beginning a city in Lower Egypt seems to alternate with one in Upper Egypt, as if to suggest that both kingdoms will suffer the same fate. But this scheme peters out in v. 16 at the latest, and probably in v. 15, if one refuses to accept the threefold repetition of the name of Thebes in vv. 14–16 and the twofold reference to Sin or Pelusium in vv. 15 and 16. With the help of the Greek version these pointless repetitions may be removed; but once that is done it is still more difficult to discover any intelligible principle in the way the whole list has been drawn up. So we may conjecture that three different Egyptian lists of names have been adapted by the writer (so Fohrer), or alternatively we may regard vv. 13–15 and vv. 16–18 as two parallel texts, only the second of which offers a reliable text (so Herrmann). On the top of all this, the writer is unable to produce in the statement about each city something with a suggestive connection either with the sound of the name or with the particular fate of the city, such as we find in similar lists in Isa. 10.27b–34 or in Micah 1.10–15, which may perhaps here have been taken as models. Instead, most of the statements fall flat, and some are partially repeated (cf. vv. 14 and 19; 14 and 16), and could easily change places with each other. [16–18] Verses 16 and 18 show the best text, and if Sin is replaced by Syene, they name at least two cities in Upper and three in Lower Egypt. Perhaps they were those best known to the writer. The usual results of an unsuccessful war: terror, the tearing down of fortress walls, the slaughter of the young men, the making captives of the women, follow in succession. [18] The author connects the climax of the judgment with Taḥpanhes, the frontier fortress to the north-east of the Delta, where the first refugees after the destruction of Jerusalem, of whom Jeremiah was one, found a reception. This is the place at which the sceptre of Egypt, the dominion of Pharaoh, will be broken, but whether it is through the loss by Egypt of a decisive battle[1] or by some other means we are not told. It is also the place where the darkening of the sky, which covers the city like a cloud, will give the cosmic sign of the

[1] At Pelusium to the south-west of Taḥpanhes, Psammetichus III lost his power and his freedom in 525 BC, in an unsuccessful battle against Cambyses.

end of Egypt, thus repeating the second to the last of the plagues brought upon Egypt by Moses (Ex. 10.21), which will inevitably be followed by God's final blow. This does not exclude the additional possibility of Jeremiah's threatening words (Jer. 43.8ff.) being re-echoed here.

As all the centres of Egyptian defensive power fall one after another, the writer sees all human resistance disappear before the sole supremacy of the world-God, and thus provides his own people, who are also included in the judgment, with a guarantee that their fate does not depend on the right of the stronger, that pitiless root-principle of this worldly order, but that it is controlled by the Lord of the world, as he brings his plan for history to its fulfilment.

CHAPTER 30.20–26

God breaks the arm of Pharaoh

20 In the eleventh year, in the first month, on the seventh day of the month, the word of Yahweh came to me:

21 'Son of man, I have broken the arm of Pharaoh, king of Egypt, and lo it has not been bound up, to heal it, by putting on a bandage [. . .]ᵃ so that it may become strong and wield the sword.

22 Therefore thus says [. . .]ᵇ Yahweh: Behold, I will go to Pharaoh, king of Egypt, and will break his arms [. . .]ᶜ and will strike the sword out of his hand. 23And I will scatter the Egyptians among the nations and disperse them throughout the lands, 24and I will strengthen the arms of the king of Babylon and put my sword in his hand, [that he may bring it over Egypt and win his booty and carry his spoil away from it].ᵈ 25Thus I will strengthen the arms of the king of Babylon, but the arms of Pharaoh shall fall, and they shall know that I am Yahweh, when I put my sword into the hand of the king of Babylon, that he may stretch it out against the land of Egypt. 26[. . .].'ᵉ

ᵃMT: 'in order to bind it'; omit with Hebrew MSS and LXX.
ᵇSee BH.
ᶜMT: 'the strong one and the one that was broken'; an unsuccessful attempt by a commentator to harmonize the apparent inconsistency between the broken arm of v. 21 and the two arms still to be broken in v. 22.
ᵈMT: 'but the arms of Pharaoh will I break, so that he howls before me, as a smitten man howls'. This repetition of v. 22, to stress the personal suffering of

Pharaoh, must presumably be inferior to the better text of LXX, which we have reproduced above.

ᵉVerse 26 reads in the MT: 'And I will scatter the Egyptians among the nations and disperse them throughout the lands, and they shall know that I am Yahweh.' This word-for-word repetition of v. 23 with the acknowledgment formula appended to it is stylistically impossible immediately after the conclusion. But one may well ask if this marginal gloss with its catchword does not preserve the hitherto forgotten acknowledgment formula of v. 23, which ought therefore to be reinserted at the end of the verse.

These words are dated April 587, about three months before the fall of Jerusalem. Verse 21 clearly refers to a past event, whereas vv. 22ff. look into the future, but to conclude that the first word originally stood alone, and that afterwards as time went on various additional statements were successively attached to it, is to adopt too superficial an attitude towards the inward relationship between the prophet's retrospective and perspective view of events. We must prefer to regard the news of what has happened in the past as furnishing the basic presupposition, from which a tense expectation of further action on the part of Yahweh can realize the consistent measures he will take to put his plan for history into execution.

[21] There can be little doubt as to the event alluded to in v. 21 as the breaking of Pharaoh's arm. It refers to Hophra's attempt to intervene in the Babylonian siege of Jerusalem by going with a relieving force to try and dispute with the Babylonian king the possession of the final fruit of his Palestinian campaign. Jeremiah 37.5, 9 and 34.16, 21f. give quite a vivid description of how high the hopes of those in Jerusalem rose when they saw the besiegers retiring to drive off the attacking Egyptians. The light-hearted way in which they broke a solemn pledge wrung from them by the urgent necessity of the hour (Jer. 34.8–11) shows how the former insolent complacency of the governing class of the capital city came once more into full bloom. But the arm of Pharaoh upraised in battle was broken by Yahweh; this is a favourite image (cf. Jer. 48.25; Pss. 10.15; 37.17) asserting direct divine intervention by which the complete defeat of Egypt is described. The Babylonian besieging force resumes its work and the last phase of desperate resistance by the besieged begins. They refused to the end to give up their hopes that Egypt would succeed in relieving them, and many of those interned with Ezekiel in Babylon shared their outlook. But the broken arm of Pharaoh has not been bound up or made strong once more by curative treatment, or, to

express it directly, the results of the defeat render it impossible for Egypt to renew the attempt at relief. Ezekiel is thus resuming the same warnings that Jeremiah was giving within Jerusalem, and dismissing all further hopefulness as folly and self-deceit.

[22] Yet he feels authorized to interpret this warning, in view of the way his God is now executing judgment, as only the first beginnings of a thorough-going settlement of accounts with the power of the world. In the same way, in 30.4 he connects the Day of Yahweh upon Egypt with the general judgment of all the nations, in which the world-God prepares the end of all earthly power. The promise in 29.19f. takes as its point of departure a previous statement about a past event, and the same is true of the glance into the future in vv. 22–25. As a result of Pharaoh's elimination from present events, his future power will also be so reduced as to put an end to his part in world-politics. It is once more emphasized that it is God who really acts in this, even though he employs the king of Babylon as his instrument. Verse 22 adds to the blow to Pharaoh's sword arm the further breaking of both his arms, i.e. the complete overthrow of Egypt, and the leading into captivity of its inhabitants, so as to share the fate of Judah (v. 23). [24f.] Verses 24f. depict the same event as the victory of the king of Babylon over his obstinate opponent; God strengthens his arm, puts his own avenging sword into his hand, whereas he weakens the arms of Pharaoh, so that they fall before the Babylonian assault. So the invader is able to plunder and despoil Egypt, though nothing is said of any permanent occupation or incorporation of the country. In repeating the statements of v. 24 with a slight change, v. 25 concentrates the whole interest on illustrating how Yahweh alone controls the power of the world. The eyes of the Egyptians are to be opened to that, so the formula about knowing him, as in 12.15; 20.44; 33.29, is connected with a retrospective glance at the actions of the Lord of history which alone decide matters.

The close connection between the various constituent parts of this section is a presupposition for any satisfactory elucidation of its meaning, and also serves to show at what an early stage God's vengeance upon Egypt was determining the prophet's message, and how inevitable it was for him to proclaim this judgment in the course of his struggle against the mistaken political calculations of those who led his nation. The folly of putting their trust in the kingdom of the Nile as if it were a strong ally and helper is very effectively brought home, by including that kingdom in God's future judgment of the whole world. Hopes that are disappointed by the present may try to appeal to the future, but that way of escape is blocked by God's decision to have a final settlement of accounts with the world-empires which resist him, and leads to the conclusion that all attempts to go on resisting Nebuchadrezzar are sinful folly.

CHAPTER 31.1–18

The fall of the proud tree of Paradise

1 In the eleventh year, in the third month, on the first day of the month, the word of Yahweh came to me:

2 'Son of man, say to Pharaoh, king of Egypt, and to his pomp:
Whom are you like in your greatness?

3 Behold, a *te'ašūr* tree,[a] a cedar on Lebanon, with fair branches
[. . .][b] and of great height;
its top reached among the clouds.[c]

4 The waters nourished it, the deep[d] made it grow tall;
it made its rivers flow[e] round the place of its planting[f]
and it sent forth its channels into [all its region].[g]

5 So it towered high above all the trees of the forest,
its boughs became many and its branches long [. . .].[h]

6 All the birds of the air made their nests in its boughs
and under its branches all the beasts of the field brought forth their young [. . .][i]

7 So it was beautiful in its greatness, in the length of its branches,
for its roots went down to abundant waters.

8 The cedars in the garden of God could not rival it, nor the fir trees equal its boughs;
the plane trees were as nothing compared with its branches,
no tree in the garden of God was like it in beauty,

9 [. . .][j] and all the trees of Eden envied it, that were in the garden of God.

10 Therefore thus says [. . .][k] Yahweh:
Because it towered high[l] and set its top among the clouds
and its heart was proud of its height,

11 I gave[m] it into the hand of a prince among the nations
who dealt[n] with it as its wickedness deserved [. . .][o]

12 And foreigners, the most terrible of the nations, drew it up

and cast it on the mountains, and its branches fell in all the valleys
and its boughs lay broken in all the watercourses of the land [. . .][p]
13 Upon its fallen trunk all the birds of the air descended[q]
and upon its boughs lay all the beasts of the field,
14 So that no trees by the water might grow to lofty height or set their tops among the clouds
and their mighty ones should not stand there in their height, all that could taste water.
For they are all given over to death, to the nether world
among the (common) men, along with those who have gone down to the pit.
15 Thus says [. . .][r] Yahweh:
In the day when it went down to Sheol, I made the deep mourn [. . .][s] for it
and restrained its rivers and the great waters were stopped.
And I clothed Lebanon in blackness for it and all the trees of the field were veiled[t] because of it.
16a I made nations quake at the thunder of its fall, when I cast it down to Sheol with those who have gone down to the pit.
17b And they were scattered,[u] who dwelt[v] in its shadow among the nations.
16b And all the trees of Eden were comforted [. . .],[w] the choicest [. . .][x] of Lebanon, all that drink water.
17a [. . .][y]
18 Whom are you thus like in strength,[z] glory and greatness among the trees of Eden?
Yet you are brought down to the nether world [. . .][aa]
You lie among the uncircumcised, with those slain by the sword.
This is Pharaoh and all his pomp, says [. . .][bb] Yahweh.'

[a]In place of *'ašūr* in MT, the above name of a tree should be read, adding a *t* in the first syllable. We also meet the word in 27.6, though it cannot be identified with certainty (cypress or spruce).

[b]MT: 'and shading forest', which does not fit into the context or agree with the other epithets. So its omission by LXX seems justified. If the words are transposed, however, it would produce 'and shading the forest'.

[c] MT: 'thickness, thick branches' is a reading similar in consonants and pronunciation, but not in place here.

[d]Cf. Deut. 33.13b.

[e–f]See BH.

[g]MT: 'to all the trees of the field'. But the concern here is not that this one tree should be like others, but that it should be superior to them. Instead of replacing the phrase by 'to it', it is less of an interference with the text simply to omit 'trees'.

[h]MT: 'from abundant waters in its outreach' is an incomplete line inserted

among a set of regular verses, repeats what has been said at length in the first part, while its last word is unintelligible and is omitted by the LXX. These three words must be deleted.

ⁱMT: 'and in its shadow dwelt all kinds of numerous nations': does not fit in with the allegorical language and can hardly be justified by the translation 'all great nations'.

ʲMT: 'I had made it beautiful in the mass of its branches'; this transition to creation by Yahweh is unexpected here, and leads to superfluous repetition of what has already been said, perhaps with the object of excluding independent action by the deep in v. 4.

ᵏSee BH.

ˡRead third person for second person of MT.

ᵐThe perfect tense should be read for the future to conform with tenses in adjoining lines.

ⁿAs in note ᵐ.

ᵒMT: 'I cast it out'; unintelligible in the context.

ᵖMT: 'And all the peoples of the earth went from its shadow and condemned it'; connects with v. 6b, and is therefore similarly an addition.

 q–rSee BH.

ˢMT: 'have veiled'; not in the LXX, probably a reference to the mourning custom of veiling the head.

t–vSee BH.

ʷMT: 'in the nether world' should be deleted, cf. above, note ᵈ.

ˣMT: 'and best', not in LXX and weakens the previous expression.

ʸVerse 17a reads in MT: 'They have also gone down to Sheol with it, to those slain by the sword.' This phrase can only be regarded as a marginal remark arising from a misunderstanding on the part of a reader, which has forced its way into the text. It robs the thorough-going comparison between the *teʾašūr* tree and the other trees of the garden of God, or Lebanon in its splendour and in its humiliation, of its meaning in order to be able to damn not only Pharaoh but all the mighty ones of earth to the same death. Verse 17b is to be placed after v. 16a. So 'the nether world' must be deleted in v. 16b.

ᶻSee BH.

ᵃᵃMT: 'with the trees of Eden'; an impossible adaptation following v. 17a. See above, note ʸ.

ᵇᵇSee BH.

[1–2] As in the previous sections, a word of God goes out to the prophet, directing him to address the political leader who is conscious of his power. Yet the pronouncement he is commissioned to deliver is not clothed in the form of a sentence of judgment like 28.1f. or 29.1f., nor described as a death lament as in 27.1 and 28.11f. [3] It launches into an almost admiring description of the royal power of Egypt under the image of a magnificent tree, just as the beauty and wealth of Tyre is indicated in 27.3ff. under the image of a magnificent ship. The immediate mention at this point of Pharaoh's pomp along with his name as the addressee introduces a note of criticism into the background of the brightly coloured picture that now follows.

It is perfectly clear that the magnificent tree, described in vv. 3–9, is not just an ordinary tree of unusually large dimensions, but is identical with the great world-tree, known not only to Mesopotamian religion as the Kishkanu tree in Eridu, and to Teutonic religion as the world ash-tree in the Edda, but also to the Vedas and Upanishads in India, and playing an important part even in China and in the religion of the Arctic tribes. Its top reaches to heaven; [4] its roots are nourished by streams and channels from the great primal deep which lies under the earth. The deep, which sends its water out to it, is still known in the Babylonian Creation Epic by the name of Tiamat (Hebrew: $t^eh\bar{o}m$) as the great anti-divine power. In this passage, however, there is hardly any suggestion of this hostile power of chaos left, but only of the beneficial forces of the realm of the deep flowing out to favoured ones, as in Gen. 49.25 and Deut. 33.13. It thus connects together the great cosmic zones, and, possessing as it does inexhaustible life, can figure as the representative of the whole living cosmos, and be thought of as situated at the navel, or central point of the earth. It is not surprising that such a symbol of cosmic life should be credited with possessing forces of divine life, and find another manifestation as the tree of life. [5f.] So the birds of the air make their nests in its strong, wide-spreading branches, and it provides a protective roof over the wild beasts of the field, which make it their refuge. A gloss at the end of v. 6, apparently by someone still well acquainted with the association of ideas that open up here, even speaks of the nations which seek shelter under it.

It is clear that this is not the simple plant fable out of the world of folk-tales, which it was thought to be in earlier days. The tree described here is a mythical feature, a favourite means of expression of primitive beliefs about life, so from the very start it has an inward affinity with other means of expressing religious longings for life, and can enter into association with them in a great variety of ways. Its association with the dwelling place of the gods, or with a garden of God, which in Babylon was that of Eridu on the Persian Gulf, the favourite dwelling place of the God Ea, was a widespread idea going back to a very early period. King-worship also adopted it into its circle of ideas as an image expressing the importance of the king.[1]

---

[1] M. Eliade, *Die Religionen und das Heilige*, 1954, ch. VIII, pp. 299ff. He offers

Only when the original mythical meaning has grown faint can the myth be transferred to the sphere of fable and folk-tale and shed its numinous characteristics. It seems doubtful if this process has yet set in in Ezek. 31 or in the narrative in Dan. 4.7ff. which shows such a close resemblance to it. It may be granted that in vv. 1–24 the elements of fable are more prominent than the mythology in the background; but nevertheless the latter does furnish various details which still stand out in the whole picture. The tension between them and the story of the fall of the magnificent tree which occupies the foreground is the result of the prophet's evident intention to employ the traditional material for an allegorical description of a historical occurrence. So this allegory derives some of its profundity from the mythical elements contained within it and shining out through it, as we have already seen in vv. 4 and 6.

[8] So it is not surprising when v. 8 mentions the garden of God whose trees are so inferior in beauty to the world-tree and tree of life, and which are so envious of its proud splendour. [9] Yet one cannot conclude from this minor detail that there was a tradition in the background about rivalry between the trees or interpret it as signifying rivalry between the great powers of the earth. At any rate, vv. 10–14, the second part of the poem, follows a way of its own, and after reasserting that God is speaking goes on to speak of Yahweh's sentence of judgment and of its execution. What was hinted at in v.2 is here briefly described as the proud self-exaltation of the mighty one who does not accept that his rise comes from the hand of one mightier still, but makes an ill use of it in order to satisfy his own ambition. That makes his impressive appearance on the scene a disaster and puts him under the judgment of God.

The catastrophe which breaks in upon the tree at this point might very well have been depicted as caused by a terrible storm, like the one introduced in 27.26. But evidently the intention is to lay strong emphasis on the righteousness of the retribution accomplished by the overthrow of the tree, and also on the historical reality of it. This leads to a further development in the allegory here that is alien to the traditional view of the world-tree. In the tradition, the symbol of the whole cosmos survives all catastrophes. In the Edda, while shaken by the flood which brings the world to an end, it is not brought to a

the most convenient access to a wide variety of material, and also provides an exhaustive account of the literature on the subject.

fall. But in the prophet's vision something quite different happens to the world-tree. [10] Even though we see in its form an expression of the divine power and vitality which exalt the king of Egypt above all his fellow trees, i.e. rulers, there is someone who brings him to a fall, the God who arraigns his self-exaltation before his judgment. [11] He does indeed hand him over to a ruler of a nation chosen by himself, who is to execute sentence upon him for his wickedness, and cut down and lay low both him and the terrible nations under his sway. [12] Comparison with 28.7 shows that the Babylonian king there, chosen by God as his instrument, is also referred to here. This world-tree is brought crashing down like any ordinary tree of the forest, its exceptional magnificence cannot deliver it. What contradicts the original content of the myth is highly significant when applied in the allegory. Verses 12 and 13, in a picture full of originality and poetic power, describe the operation of judgment, in which the claims to invulnerable might and divine power to bestow life are broken against the Almighty's will to judge. [13] As in Isa. 18.6, the way in which the swarms of birds alight on the fallen giant and the wild beasts lie on it is no more than a temporary acceptance of a crude resting place. It shows the worthlessness to which the tree's fall has brought it, as does the gloss mentioning how the peoples flee from and curse the giant they once admired. [14] A warning is given to all trees growing to a lofty height, which like the one they admired are nourished by the waters of the deep, i.e. all the rulers who indulge in dreams of world-empire and aspire to being worshipped like gods are reminded that their power exists only by divine permission, and that it cannot conceal their creaturely transitoriness, or shelter them from the death which awaits all men alike.

Undoubtedly in this free application of old traditional material there are still some incongruities, which the prophet did not overcome, and for which we cannot find any rational solution, owing to their being derived from a tradition which existed in many different strata and was not in itself a unity. So we must not try to make out that the cedar on Lebanon is really a cedar on the mountain of God, seeing that Lebanon never figures as a divine dwelling place; nor should we assert that the position of the tree on the mountains conflicts with its being abundantly watered by the streams of the great deep. Nor can we try to identify the streams from the primal ocean with the rivers of paradise, which water the garden of God. Obviously the poet is employing the various motifs of the myth with complete freedom, without thinking it important that his allegory should be completely consistent. And he does in reality succeed in conveying the impression at which he aims, of how superior the power of the world-God is when he judges, and how human power at its very highest falls far below it, and he conveys it very forcibly.

As in 26.19ff., a third section, vv. 15–18, which is freshly introduced as a word of God, seals the ultimate destruction of the condemned prisoner by casting him down into the realm of the dead. One must nevertheless admit that excessive demands are made here on the allegory of the world-tree, since an idea which has to be illustrated by means of men, peoples, and eventually cities, begins to become somewhat grotesque. **[15]** Details from the allegory are still employed at the beginning; the separation of the tree from the sources of its strength is associated with the grief of its nursing mother, the primal deep, when God himself holds back her streams. It is in keeping with the cosmic significance of the world-tree, also, for Lebanon and all the trees to be covered with a black cloud, as if they were wearing mourning garb. **[16]** Furthermore, the way in which the nations shudder at the thunderous fall of the mighty one does still indicate that the cosmos has been shaken. **[17f.]** On the other hand, the world-tree's descent into the underworld, in which it has to lie among the uncircumcised and those slain by the sword (cf. 32.20ff. for the meaning of this feature) goes far beyond the potentialities of the allegory, and subsequent elaborations of this statement which make the trees of Eden also go down to hell at the same time only serve to strengthen this impression. It is solely because at this point the image of the tree of life and the trees of the garden of God has lost its original character, and retains no function save that of denoting certain known figures that the introduction of the scene in the underworld can become intelligible. It is really Pharaoh, who goes down to the world of the dead, and it is really the princes of the earth who are comforted at it, i.e. who are now relieved of their fear of the excessively mighty one, who behaved like a god, and are able to ask exultingly what has become of the power, glory and greatness of him who was once without his equal. **[18]** For whoever once falls into the power of Sheol can never rise again. Separation from the world of the living, sinking down into the twilight darkness of a world of gloom and contempt (this is what is suggested by the reference to the circumcised and those slain by the sword, cf. 32.20ff., and what has been stated above in regard to 26.19ff.) is the equivalent of utter rejection.

One may describe this threatening poem as Ezekiel's most power-ful piece of testimony against Egypt's world-power. First, with the help of the myth he greatly heightens the importance of this adversary of the Lord of history which interferes so mysteriously in the history of his people. Then he makes his downfall a judgment already execu-ted by God to serve as a word written on the wall by a mighty hand for all the mighty ones of this earth to read. The full significance of this is seen still more, when we recall that when this word of God was proclaimed, Jerusalem's desperate resistance to her besiegers had already entered upon its final phase. By June 587 Jerusalem had been reduced to her most desperate straits and was to hold out only a few more weeks and then fall. The exiles in general kept their eyes fast shut to the inevitably approaching end. But Ezekiel puts it in the setting of the world-wide judgment his God is now carrying out. By this means he tries to get his people to look to the only one who has the might, and see how it is he who is putting into effect with un-shakable strength and consistency his plan for the whole world. Once one can see the destiny of Israel against that wider background, one sees the obvious senselessness of giving oneself up to despair over the downfall of the nation, as if it meant that the heathen gods had established their dominion, and as if not only the glory of Yahweh's people but the glory of Yahweh himself was buried under ashes and fallen masonry. On the contrary, national history and world-history together must be helping this one God to attain his objectives and to establish his dominion over all the nations of the world. The history of the nations struggling for world-power is written in blood, but it is not meaningless: Nebuchadrezzar, who is treading Israel underfoot, is the instrument selected by God to carry out his orders. The apparently unconquerable kingdom of the Nile falls victim to him, when God carries out his plans. The oracles of the nations, among which ch. 31, in view of the time of its composition and the nature of its constituents, occupies the key place, serve to hammer the certainty of this into the heads of Ezekiel's fellow countrymen during the days of Judah's death struggle, and to prepare them for the terrible thing that was to happen.

CHAPTER 32.1–16

The catching of the sea-monster

1 In the eleventh year,[a] in the twelfth month, on the first day of the month, the word of Yahweh came to me:

2 'Son of man, raise a lamentation over Pharaoh, king of Egypt, and say to him:

You are like[b] a young lion among the nations,

but yet you were like a dragon[c] in the seas and blew with your nostrils[d] and troubled the waters with your feet and stirred up its streams.

3 Thus says [. . .][1] Yahweh:

I will throw[e] my net over you

[. . .][f] and will haul you[g] up in my dragnet

and will cast you on the ground and fling you on the open field.

4 And I will cause all the birds of the air to settle on you

and will gorge all[h] the beasts of the earth with you.

5 And I will strew your flesh upon the mountains and fill the valleys with your carcass.

6 And I will make the earth drink what flows out of you [. . .][i] and the watercourses will be full of your blood.[j]

7 When you are blotted out, I will cover the heavens and make their stars dark,

I will cover the sun with clouds,

and the moon shall not give its light.

8 All the bright lights of heaven will I make dark over you,

and put darkness upon the earth,[k] says [. . .][l] Yahweh.

9 And I will trouble the hearts of many peoples, when I carry your captives among the nations, into countries you do not know.

10 And I will appal many peoples, and their kings shall be filled with shudderings, when I brandish my sword before them, and they shall tremble every moment, every one for his own life, on the day of your downfall.

11 *For thus says* [. . .][m] *Yahweh: The sword of the king of Babylon shall come upon you.* 12 *I will cause your pomp to fall by the swords of mighty ones—all of them the most terrible among the nations. And they will deal violently with the pride of Egypt and all its pomp will perish.* 13 *And I will destroy all its beasts out of many waters, and no foot of man shall trouble them any more nor shall any beast's hoof trouble them any more.* 14 *Then I will make their waters clear and cause their rivers to run like oil, says* [. . .][n] *Yahweh.*

15 *When I make* [. . .][o] *Egypt a desolation and the land lies waste,*[p] *and stripped of all that fills it, when I smite all who dwell in it, then they will know that I am Yahweh.*

16 This is a lamentation, and [you shall strike it up][q] and the daughters of the nations shall chant it, over Egypt and all her pomp shall they chant it, says [. . .][r] Yahweh.'

[a]See BH.

[b]The accused is described with the same imagery as in 19.10 and 27.32. So the translation 'you are destroyed' or 'you must be silent', while linguistically possible, is not confirmed by any of the ancient versions, and remains questionable. The statement is in any case difficult owing to the juxtaposition of such conflicting objects of comparison as a young lion and a dragon.

[c]Cf. 29.3.

[d–e]See BH.

[f]MT: 'by means of the levy of many peoples', see BH. The historical interpretation of the preceding phrase is clumsily introduced, in order to avoid an excessively crude representation of Yahweh as a warrior.

[g]MT: 'and they will haul you up': the person is changed after the previous gloss has found its way into the text, but it is not present in the LXX.

[h]See BH.

[i]MT: 'of your blood upon the mountains'; the first word is a proper marginal correction of the last words of the verse 'of you'; the second has slipped in from v. 5.

[j]See BH.

[k]MT: 'upon your land'. However, the cosmic manifestations just mentioned suggest rather that it is the whole earth that is darkened.

[l–r]See BH.

The slaying of the chaos-monster: 32.1–10

This poem is similar in its subject-matter to 29.3ff., where Pharaoh is also described as a sea-monster (*tannīn*), which is slain by Yahweh. The main portion from v. 3 on deals entirely with the future, in which God will destroy the monster, so in view of its constituents it must be classified as a poem of threat. This is contradicted by v. 2, where it is explicitly announced to be a lamentation, and by v. 16, where orders are issued for its recitation by the prophet and by the daughters of the nations. Isolated features which suggest a lamentation are not, however, entirely absent, such as the comparison to the young lion, also found in the lamentation in ch. 19, and also the description of the monster's awareness of its strength, and how its rage disturbs the waters, in which the verse-form of the lamentation is also employed. But these few elements are hardly sufficient to justify giving the name of a lamentation to the whole composition, unless it is argued that this poetic form of speech has already begun to disintegrate, or vv. 3–8 are regarded as a denunciatory poem which has taken the place of the original poem; the new introduction by means of the messenger formula could be an indication of this. [2] In any case, the present introductory strophe in v. 2 seems to have suffered severe damage, since the abrupt juxtaposition of the two animal metaphors and the unsatisfactory form of the wording cannot be attributed to the original poem.

If one deals with each one of the images by itself, each will be found to contain a thoroughly meaningful comparison. The description of the king as a young lion is a very fitting metaphor for a newly-crowned warlike young man like Pharaoh Hophra who had come to the throne in 588. In contrast to the minor kings of Judah in ch. 19, he is called 'a young lion among the nations' because of the various nations united together in his empire. It can hardly be demonstrated that the metaphor had by this time become a well-worn royal title.

The picture of the sea-monster which stands so starkly beside it without any transition is here as plain and intelligible without further explanation as in ch. 29, in view of the position of the Egyptian delta with its great channels and canals. At first, as in 29.3, it seems as if the crocodile is intended, which raises the waters into a foam and swell as it snorts and wallows, and stirs up mud and troubles the water—an excellent picture of the Egyptian, whose policy is so mysterious and so productive of uncertainty, because it aims at keeping things in permanent unrest. But someone stronger than he is preparing to put an end to his disturbances.

[3] As in ch. 29 (see above, pp. 402ff.) the description proceeds to the tying up and slaughtering of the chaos-monster, so closely related to the *tannin*. The battle scene, which starts afresh with the words marking a message from God, rises to a cosmic scale. The catching in a net no longer fits the crocodile. Yet that ought not to make us think of some other gigantic aquatic animal such as a hippopotamus. The use of such equipment in a battle ought rather to recall to us one well-known combat out of Babylonian mythology, the duel between Marduk, the Babylonian god of creation, and the terrible primitive monster, which the god first binds up with his hunting net and then kills and cuts into pieces. [4] In the same way this monstrous creature, whose home is in the water, is bound by Yahweh, drawn up on land and cast out for the birds of the air and the beasts of the field to devour. Its size is represented as being so enormous that its decaying masses

fill mountains and valleys and its life-blood floods the earth and causes a spate in the watercourses. **[5f.]** In this picture, bloodthirsty descriptions in inscriptions by Assyrian kings speaking of how the corpses of the enemy lie piled up and how their blood fills the clefts of the mountains, which were typical elements of style in the literary tradition, seem to have exercised some influence. **[7f.]** The accentuation of the event to a world catastrophe reaches its climax in vv. 7 and 8 in the darkening of the stars, and this particular feature serves to introduce the typical features of the well-known prophetic descriptions of the day of Yahweh in the judgment upon Egypt (cf. Amos 5.18, 20; 8.9; Isa. 13.10; Joel 2.10). This again sets it in the wider framework of the world-judgment which establishes the divine sovereignty over all nations.

This individual judgment is clearly and explicitly linked with God's general reckoning with a rebellious world even more than in other similar passages (cf. 29.3; 30.3; 31.1–9). The date perhaps throws some light upon it. The first day of the twelfth month of the eleventh year brings us to March 586, only two months after the arrival of the fugitive from Jerusalem, of which we are told in 33.21. The words against Tyre in 26.1–5, which are of uncertain date owing to the absence of the month, may very possibly belong to the same time as it. In this case both utterances give testimony of how when the exiles were overwhelmed by the news that Jerusalem had at last fallen, Ezekiel tried to restore the balance by giving them an assurance that his God was taking action in judgment on a still wider field. The end of Jerusalem was not the end of the history of God or of his people, nor did it spell any permanent or irrevocable victory for heathen gods and forces. Thus to repeat and intensify the threats against Egypt and Tyre is to assert with a certainty which defies all doubt that the Lord of the world has now really begun to act, and is making the world move on to that great day when all the kingdoms of the world will lie at his feet.

The established formula concluding a prophetic utterance at the end of v. 8 brings about a significant caesura. Then, without any attempt at connection with what has preceded, vv. 9f. add some further thoughts, in which the allegorical language is abandoned, and the historical events referred to begin to be conveyed by words directly addressed to the king or the country. This involves stepping back from the lofty hopes of the preceding passage, in order to assimilate Egypt's fate to that of Judah, whom she has so misled, by speaking, in similar terms to 29.12, of the exiling of her inhabitants, and portraying the panic caused to the neighbouring nations by the catastrophe which comes on the Nile kingdom (cf. 30.7f.; 31.16). Here the eschatological horizon has evidently retreated; the emphasis is on giving a warning to kings and nations of the one Lord of the world who alone is mighty.

The historical interpretation: 32.11-16

The regular formula introducing the word of Yahweh marks out the beginning of another section. The great mythical picture is given an interpretation, by being applied to an attack on the Nile kingdom by the king of Babylon and his irresistible hosts. The author, probably one of the prophet's disciples, conforms, even in individual phrases, to 30.10ff. [13f.] The final words about the devastation of Egypt by a direct intervention by Yahweh were already present in that passage. One may therefore conclude that they are by the same redactor who edited the prophet's works. In a direct reference to v. 2, the waters of the Nile stirred up by the aquatic monster are reinterpreted to denote the devastation of the land. Hitherto, it has been disturbed by beasts and men that wallowed in it, but now, when all life disappears, it will cease to be stirred up and will flow smoothly like oil. [15] Yet this uncanny silence will proclaim to all who have survived the disaster that the God of Israel is revealing himself as the Lord of the world.

[16] The words concluding the original lamentation have been preserved in those now summarizing the whole section: the death lament for the swiftly vanished glory of the ruler over nations is to pass everywhere and travel from land to land as the women chant of how all the mighty deeds of men come to nought in face of the Lord of all life. This serves in actual fact to take all the widely varying components of the chapter and recapitulate them in the one leading thought, which bids its audience not to indulge in the tragic pride of the would-be hero or yet in despairing resignation, but to recognize that human history centres upon the revelation of what God is doing on behalf of the realization of his objective.

CHAPTER 32.17–32

Lamentation over the descent to hell of Egypt's pomp

17 In the twelfth year, [in the first month],[a] on the fifteenth day of the month, the word of Yahweh came to me:

18 'Son of man, wail over the pomp of Egypt and send it down [. . .][b] to the nether world, to[c] those who go down to the pit.

21[d] The godlike heroes shall speak to it out of the midst of Sheol: [. . .].[e]

19 Whom do you surpass in beauty? Go down and be laid with the uncircumcised.

22 Assyria is there and all her levies [. . .],[f]

23 whose graves are set in the innermost part of the pit, and her muster lies round about her grave, all of them slain, fallen by the sword, who spread[g] terror in the land of the living.

24 Elam is there and all her pomp about her grave; all of them slain, fallen by the sword,[h] who went down as uncircumcised into the nether world, who spread their terror in the land of the living and must bear their shame with those who went down to the pit.

25 They have made her a bed among the slain with all her pomp [. . .],[i]

26 Meshech-Tubal[j] is there and all her pomp round about her grave, all of them as uncircumcised and judged, for they spread terror in the land of the living.

27 And they do not lie with the heroes, the giants[k] of old,[l] who went down to Sheol with their weapons of war, whose swords were laid under their heads and whose shields[m] are over their bones, for the terror of the heroes was in the land of the living.

28 But you shall lie among the uncircumcised [. . .][n] with those who are judged.

29 Edom is there, her kings and her princes, who for all their might were laid with those who are slain by the sword. They lie with the uncircumcised, with those who have gone down to the pit.

30 The princes of the north are there all together and all the Sidonians, who have gone down with the slain, in spite of all the terror which they caused in shame with their might, and they lie as uncircumcised with those that are judged with the sword, and must bear their shame with those who go down to the pit.

31 These will see Pharaoh and comfort him for all his multitude [. . .][o]

32 For I spread terror of him in the land of the living; therefore there shall be laid among the uncircumcised with those who are slain by the sword Pharaoh and all his pomp, says [. . .]ᵖ Yahweh.'

ᵃIn the MT the number of the month is not given; that inserted above is derived from the LXX, but even it is peculiar in its phraseology. No more reliable statement of the date being available, we must make the best of what we have. That brings us to April 586.

ᵇMT: '[You] and the daughters of majestic nations'; amplification influenced by v. 16 (the second person masculine of the personal pronoun has been erroneously read as 'otāh in the MT).

ᶜSee BH.

ᵈIn the LXX, v. 19 follows 21. Verse 20 reads in the MT: 'They shall fall among those that are slain with the sword, the sword is destined, its camp (for the unintelligible moško read miškabō) is with her and all her multitude'; a line reduced to a state of complete confusion, a heap of meaningless words.

ᵉIn the second part of v. 21, MT gives a very corrupt text, which seems originally to have formed a doublet to v. 19.

ᶠMT: 'his graves round about him, they are all slain, fallen by the sword'; an inferior version of v. 23b.

ᵍ⁻ʰSee BH.

ⁱVerse 25b is a repetition of v. 24 with only minor variations '[round about her grave] (emendation following vv. 22a and 26c), all of them uncircumcised, slain by the sword, for terror of them was spread in the land of the living and they had to bear their shame with those who went down to the pit; they were placed among the slain'.

ʲMoschi and Tibareni familiar to the Greeks, and already to the Assyrians, who wandered from northern Asia Minor southwards and threatened Assyria in the seventh century.

ᵏFor nopᵉlīm, 'fallen', of the MT it is better to point nᵉpilīm 'giants'; cf. Gen. 6.4.

ˡ⁻ⁿSee BH.

ᵒMT: 'Slain by the sword is Pharaoh and all his army, says Yahweh': repeated almost word for word from v. 32, but correctly placed only there.

ᵖSee BH.

A dance of death: 32.17–32

All the preceding denunciations conclude in the powerful picture of that human greatness which has itself sat on the judgment seat and endeavoured to be an object of fear upon earth being now banished to the underworld and there delivered over to contempt. The new piece of information additional to what we have heard on this subject is not only that Sheol is a power which treats all alike and reduces them to comfortless shades, so that the mightiest pride of man apparently built to last for ever is overcome by it and dragged down into final decay and extinction, but the fact that Sheol also executes a particular sort of punitive justice, in which unforgiven guilt meets with its retribution. This is a development of the genuine Israelite conception of the world of death, by which it gains a new significance. Ezekiel thus finds himself able to appeal to features characterizing heathen beliefs about the dead, while at the same time transferring them to another context, that of Yahweh's just retribution as seen by a prophet's eye, and thus giving them a new significance.

The ancient Eastern conceptions of Sheol current in Israel as well as elsewhere have already been discussed in the commentary on 26.19–21 (cf. above, pp. 373ff.). They already recognized certain differences in the lot of the dead, bound up with their position during their earthly life or with the way the corpse had been treated. Thus, for example, there were the mitigations enjoyed by a valiant warrior, or by a person of high social rank, and the shame and disgrace of those whose corpses lay unburned, or had been mutilated and deprived of a proper funeral. Yet at this stage, as in the earlier one of primitive religions, we see no moral retribution, but only a general vague notion that the conditions of earthly life, and especially the treatment accorded to the corpse, serve either to mitigate or to add severity to the lot of the human ghost. The ghost merely continues its former existence in a more shadowy form. In Israel the high value given to circumcision resulted in all, especially children, who died uncircumcised being severed from their families in the realm of the dead and only allowed to associate with other similarly unclean persons in a separate place of shame. The higher the sacramental value attributed to circumcision, the more the guilt was of rejecting it, and that guilt was regarded as operating even in the underworld. Those who had been executed or murdered were only too likely to suffer a similar lot, since they seldom enjoyed an honourable funeral, and were hastily hidden away in some inconspicuous corner. Here, parallel to the morally neutral way in which their position was determined, we find some sort of putting of guilt to a person's account, guilt which the deceased had incurred during his lifetime.

This outlook Ezekiel now brings into conformity with the established standards of retributive justice. So when he speaks of a shameful place on the outermost edge of the underworld which is the dwelling of the uncircumcised and of those slain by the sword, he means by these latter not men who have fallen honourably on the battlefield, but men who have been executed by means of the sword, and regards both groups as consisting of dead persons condemned to

such an evil lot as the result of guilt. But belief in retribution finds a
deeper expression even than that. We find along with them the man
whom the righteous God has found guilty and placed along with
them, in spite of being, according to the old beliefs about the dead,
entitled to honourable treatment in Sheol (cf. Isa. 14.18) by his influential position during his life and by an honourable burial, and
even though he may have known of and carried out the custom of
circumcision. It is only because the old conceptions of the realm of
the dead have thus come to be permeated by moral principles that it
becomes possible for such a dance of death to evolve in this chapter.

[17f.] God's instructions to Ezekiel tell him to wail over the pomp
of Egypt. They do not specifically name the *qīna*, the typical funeral
lament, but refer more generally to the cry of woe, not identical with
the *qīna*, which, as in Micah 2.4; Jer. 9.10, 19f., may be raised over the
desolation and depopulation of the land and the leading into captivity of its inhabitants. Actually the circumstances are different from
those in 26.17; 27.2; 28.11, etc. The lament is raised here not for the
annihilation of earthly glory by sudden defeat and devastation. The
object with which it is concerned is the final disappearance of worldly
power into the depths of Sheol, whence none can return. And the
prophetic wail of woe actually serves as an effectual means of bringing down that final punishment upon proud Egypt. 'Send them down
to the nether world': [19] the prophet's word is full of God's mighty
power to act, so it brings about the event in which Egypt duly goes
to that land whence none can return. But v. 19 ought not to come in
its present place as the fate-fraught word of power. It is better to
follow the Greek version, and the model by which in Isa. 14.10 the
king on his arrival in the underworld is greeted by those who already
share his lot. [20] So v. 19 is to be placed after v. 20 and understood
as an ironical welcome from the godlike heroes who, according to v.
27, have a preferential position in the underworld. According to
Gen. 6.1–4, they have been sentenced to death, yet, although their
deeds spread terror in the earth, they belong to that heroic age celebrated in widely known epics as standing at the beginning of man's
history, and some of its glamour still clings to them. It is impossible
to know whether in Israel that age was regarded as superior to a
subsequent iron age of ruthless violence, following old pagan patterns,
or whether the position they enjoyed was based on some other form
of merit. It was not till a late period in Judaism that they came to be
regarded as the originators of bloodshed upon earth, from whose

bodies evil spirits came forth and wrought destruction everywhere
(Jubilees 5 and Enoch 6–11; 15).[1] This conception, also found in the
Qumran writings, is still alien to Ezekiel. [27] Here, on the contrary,
the giants appear as the aristocracy of the underworld, as godlike
heroes, who occupy a place of honour and lie there with all their
arms and armour (v. 27).

At this point Pharaoh, who concentrates in his person all the
glamour of Egypt, does not receive any admission. He, as the representative of all the Egyptian refinement and cult of the body, has a
bitterly ironical question addressed to him. He is asked, when corruption has already impressed its terrible brand upon him, what has
become of the beauty by which he sought to distinguish himself
above others. Then with a gruff command to 'go down', he is dismissed to the lowest regions of Sheol, where the uncircumcised and
the executed are gathered in a place of shame and occupy the lowest
stratum in shadowy and comfortless life of the dead. [22–26] Yet
there he encounters celebrated conquerors, overtaken by a like fate
previously to him: the Assyrians, the Elamites, the members of the
tribes of Meshech and Tubal who dwelt in what was later Cappadocia and in the Taurus districts of Asia Minor, the peoples on the
northern border of the Babylonian plain. All these nations had carried
on continuous warfare of aggression and conquest into the fertile
plains to the south and south-east of them. They have graves in this
place as well as upon earth; here we see once again the association
between the grave and the underworld. He who was once king stands
for the people as the chief bearer and representative of the name of
each particular country. His grave therefore is in the middle, and
round about him lie the members of his company, his warriors and
officers. Yet these ghostly correspondences to things upon earth are
stationed in the outermost corner of Sheol, where the outcasts and
the accursed, condemned to a most miserable existence, are placed.
The rude violence, which heaps up the wealth of other nations and
abolishes their frontiers, and treats them as mere objects of plunder or
subjects to be incorporated in one's own empire (cf. Isa. 10.13f.), is
destined to be punished by being deprived of that last shadowy
refuge, for which even the meanest of men may hope in peaceful
times, namely the final resting place among the dead with its surroundings of religious awe.

Monotonously repeated, we hear one description after another of

[1] Cf. W. Eichrodt, *Theology of the Old Testament*, II, 1967, pp. 206f.

the shame which has overtaken the conquerors who did nothing but spread disaster and terror upon earth. [28] We see row upon row of phantom-like figures of dead men go down into the depths on the way they are destined to go according to the iron law of the underworld, and we hear the sentence directly addressed to Egypt compelling her to go on that same path without any effort to resist.

It is tempting to assume that this ghostly death dance which concludes the prophet's denunciation of Egypt came not very long after his denunciation of Pharaoh under the image of a chaos-monster. According to the Greek version it was composed in April 586, only a few weeks after the preceding section. The fact that while Jerusalem had fallen the Babylonian king had not yet come to a decision at close quarters with his elusive Egyptian rival does not prevent the prophet from proclaiming that his God has irrevocably willed the complete annihilation of that uncanny chaos-force. For in this, as in the severe punishment suffered by Israel, what is involved is the execution of his divine world plan by the Lord who makes all nations serve his purposes.

The denunciation against Egypt comes to a powerful conclusion, the effect of which is interfered with, not accentuated by, the other verses that come after v. 28. [29] The account of how the same fate is suffered by Edom, the kings of the north and the Sidonians is put in very similar words, though with a few characteristic variations; but their influence upon world-history has no connection and cannot be compared with that of those named before them. As 25.12–14 states, it had been continued to a pettily vindictive campaign against Israel. So they appear like dwarfs among giants. [30] The association of the kings of the north with the Phoenicians seems intended to magnify the importance of these latter. But it does no more than repeat what has been said in vv. 24 and 26 without adding any fresh information on the subject. The guilt incurred by the Phoenicians is also left in obscurity. [31f.] Verses 31 and 32 are furnished with the customary conclusion of a prophetic message, in the words 'says Yahweh'. They make the first mention of how Pharaoh is consoled by the sight of such distinguished companions in his adversity, which sounds odd as well as being unjustified by anything similar in the death song. We may regard v. 32 as more in line with prophetic ways of thinking, stating as it does that Yahweh himself is the author of the terror which Pharaoh exuded, just as Isa. 10 speaks of Assyria as being the rod of the Lord's wrath. But the allusion is too ambiguous, and also too brief, to add any new or striking note to the whole poem. So one must regard these passages as elaborations by various different hands.

Yet all the statements in the chapter taken together indicate that Israelite beliefs about retributive justice have taken a new line: they are now beginning to gain control of the conceptions of the land beyond death, so that earthly guilt finds itself expiated through the sentences of the world-judge being put into effect in a sphere beyond that of earthly life. Nevertheless this takes place within the limits of the old imaginative ideas of the shadowy existence led by the dead, without drawing any further conclusions in regard to individual lives, or developing any fresh evaluation of the life in the next world. Still, the mere fact that the land of the dead, elsewhere not thought worthy of Yahweh's notice, and kept completely separate from his realm of the living, is now laid open to his retributive intervention, amounts to a new step forward in what prophecy has to say about God, which cannot fail to have momentous effects.

CHAPTER 33.1-9; 3.20-21

The office of a watchman

1 The word of Yahweh came to me: 2'Son of man, speak to your people and say to them: If I bring the sword upon a land, and the people of the land take a man from among them, and make him their watchman, 3and if he sees the sword coming upon the land and blows the trumpet and warns the people, 4then if any one who hears the sound of the trumpet does not take warning, and thea sword comes and takes him away, then his blood shall be upon his own head. 5He heard the sound of the trumpet, and did not take warning, his blood shall be upon his own head. But the other gave warning:b he has saved his life.

6 But if the watchman sees the sword coming and does not blow the trumpet, so that the people are not warned, and thec sword comes and takes any one of them; then that man will be taken away because of his iniquity, but his blood will I require at the watchman's hand.

7 Now you, son of man, I have made a watchman for the house of Israel, so whenever you hear a word from my mouth, you shall give them warning from me. 8If I say to the wicked [. . .];d you shall surely die, and you do not speak, to warn the wicked of his way, then he,e the wicked man,

shall die for his iniquity; but his blood I will require at your hand. [9]But if you warn the[f] wicked to turn from his way, and he does not turn from his way, then he shall die because of his iniquity, but you will have saved your life.

3.20 And if a righteous man turns from his righteousness and commits iniquity, and you do not warn him, he shall die for his sin, but his blood I will require of you. [21]Nevertheless if you have warned the righteous man not to sin, and he does not sin, he shall surely live, because he took warning, and you will have saved your life.'[g]

[a-f]See BH.
[g]For reconstruction of text see above, pp. 74f.

The parable of the watchman: 33.1–6

Ezekiel, by order of Yahweh, is to draw a picture for his fellow countrymen showing what a watchman is like and what he is expected to do. He starts by sketching a picture with which they are all acquainted: Yahweh brings the sword upon a land, or, in other words, a war breaks out. The inhabitants of the land therefore choose from among them a watchman, whose duty it is to keep a look-out for the approach of the sword, i.e. for the approach of the enemy, and in any such event to blow a blast on the trumpet, in order to announce his arrival. This warning sign makes the inhabitants of the land aware of the danger which threatens them. So anyone who is going out to his work in a field or vineyard will try as quickly as he can to seek a safe refuge behind the walls of some city.

It may, however, happen that someone has not been taking notice at all, or else has heard the blast of the trumpet but not taken it seriously. The result is that he is surprised and struck down by the enemy. In this case the watchman incurs no guilt, he has done his duty: he has given due warning. It is the duty of each individual citizen to act accordingly; if he fails to do so, he bears the responsibility for whatever harm ensues, and no one will hold the watchman responsible for it.

It is obvious, on the other hand, that if the watchman neglects giving the prescribed signal of warning he may then be regarded as responsible for the death of those whom he failed to warn.

So far all has been based on well-known circumstances, accessible and familiar in habitual experience. Only the closing words diverge from the account of objective facts: instead of saying at the end of v. 6 'His blood will be required of the watchman's hand', Yahweh for this once appears as the person who carries out the transaction and announced 'His blood will I require at the watchman's hand'. This gives us the first clear sign of where this parable is leading: it is going to depict one particular way in which Yahweh acts. So this tiny phrase already serves as a transition to the sequel, where Ezekiel is represented as a watchman of Israel and the resultant conclusions are drawn.

Appointment of the prophet as watchman: 33.7–9: 3.20–21

The parable presented above is of itself incapable of revealing the teaching contained in it. This is already shown by v. 7. In the parable, the inhabitants of the land choose and appoint the watchman to his office, whereas now Yahweh himself appoints the prophet to an office, making him a watchman for the house of Israel. So at this point it already becomes evident that the interpretation transcends the parable and cannot be attained simply by applying the various details to Ezekiel or to Israel. For the fact that the watchman is appointed by Yahweh introduces a peculiar tension into the picture. The enemy of whom Ezekiel is to give warning is not any foreign foe but—no room is left for any doubt about it—Yahweh himself! It is from Yahweh that the danger threatens Israel; it is his action as judge that overhangs the nation and constitutes the most genuine and most menacing of dangers. Yet that same God appoints a watchman, evidently in order to give warning of himself and of the deadly danger he brings with him.

This interpretation, full as it is of tension, obviously cannot simply be read out of the literal meaning of the parable of the watchman, depending as it does on the further announcement of Ezekiel's call to the office of a watchman. This renders impossible from the outset any interpretation insisting on following the parable according to its obvious matter-of-fact meaning and regarding the subsequent appointment of Ezekiel as a watchman as superfluous. It is obvious that this treatment is inadequate, and that the image must be taken in the same way as in the prophet's other parables: since what the prophet means to convey transcends the image and adds new features to it. This shows that the attempts which are sometimes made to separate vv. 7–9 from what precedes them constitute a grave error. A similar error has been committed in ch. 15, the parable of the vine, where attempts have been made to sever the interpretation in vv. 6–8 from the parable in vv. 1–5 (cf. above, pp. 193f.). We shall see that realization of this point has important consequences for the understanding of the whole parable of the watchman.

But we must go a step further. In the section 3.16b–21 (cf. above, pp. 75ff.) the first verses reproduced 33.7–9 word for word apart from unimportant differences. But the two last verses, 20 and 21, contain an additional statement which takes a further step. It places as a pendant to the wicked man who because of his wickedness must receive a warning from the prophetic watchman, the righteous man who must also receive warning because he has turned away from his former righteousness. We see a similar opposition of wicked and righteous in 18.21–24, emphasizing the decisive importance of their present attitude in face of God's requirements. We will probably therefore be right in assuming that the words in 3.20f. referring to the righteous originally also stood in ch. 33, but that when the words came to be inserted at the beginning of the book they were also accidentally omitted from their place at this present point. We may therefore reclaim these two verses and use them to provide a conclusion to 33.7–9.

Fohrer agrees in setting a higher valuation on the wording of 3.16bff., but regards 33.7–9 as a deliberate effort to cut down the original conception made by the redactors of the prophetic book, because they already regarded the righteous as an ideal figure not in need of any warning. This makes it still more surprising to find that, although he regards Ezekiel as the author of 3.16bff., he does not introduce it here to supply an interpretation of the allegory in 33.1–6, but makes it stand in complete isolation.

Zimmerli, on the other hand, thinks that 33.7–9 is the genuine original wording and 3.17–21 a piece of filling in by a redactor. He explains the two verses about the warning to the righteous as being a subsequent extension of the description of the watchman undertaken under the influence of 18.24, and introducing an alien theme. But this way of arguing does not seem to us to show sufficient regard for the difference of theme between ch. 18 and ch. 3, and so it does not seem to carry conviction. We will return to this attempt at explanation later, when we deal with the interpretation.

[7] How, then, is the image of the watchman interpreted in the section which follows it? At first sight it seems undeniable that there we find the prophet approaching his fellow countrymen and Yahweh approaching his people in a new and intensive way. [8f.] We no longer hear of general proclamations of judgment to the nation as a

whole; we hear instead of an explicit word spoken by Yahweh to the wicked, to announce to him that he is to die. When Ezekiel hears this threat, he is to add weight to it by his own warning, informing the wicked of the ruinous results for himself which his behaviour has had hitherto. It is clear that this is intended as a παρακαλεῖν, an address of promise, appeal and admonition, a word of warning to an individual among the people, and this supplies a new element in Ezekiel's activities that has not hitherto been present in this particular form. It would probably not be correct to call this type of speech a sermon: the word paraenesis or admonition is more apt to fit such a thing. All this undoubtedly both refines and individualizes the picture of the watchman with his trumpet blast. But here also Yahweh himself is seen to be the menacing adversary who comes in a man's way. His threat, 'You shall surely die', seems like an enemy attacking a city or a country. But his threat does not strike at people in general, but one wicked man among them, and the prophet is not told to deliver a general sermon to a congregation, but to address an appeal to this one threatened person among the people, in order to rescue him from the danger to which he is exposed.

[3.20f.] Exactly the same applies to the righteous man, who turns from his righteousness and commits iniquity (3.20f.). Here, instead of a divine threat telling him to expect death, what is mentioned is a mikšōl which Yahweh puts in his path, over which he is to stumble, fall and die. mikšōl, literally 'that which causes to stumble', 'obstacle', 'offence', certainly does not mean here a stimulation to sin, in order to render the people ripe for judgment. Such a concrete temptation leading man to fall and coming from Yahweh is already known in the Old Testament, as, for example, in David's numbering of the people in II Sam. 24.1. But this uncanny, almost demonic, force that drives a man into a ruinous act of sin would come too late at this point, since the righteous has already turned from his righteousness and is committing iniquity. In this case Yahweh prepares ruin for him by a mikšōl in the same way as one may make a blind man fall by means of some obstacle placed in his path (Lev. 19.14). What is threatened in Isa. 8.14 under the image of the rock of stumbling for the whole nation, and what is seen in Jer. 6.19, 21 as mikšōlīm, stumbling-blocks causing both fathers and sons to stumble because they have not heeded the trumpet blasts of the watchmen God has appointed for them, is here applied to the devout individual and is the divine act of chastisement, which brings him to ruin. But when Ezekiel sees this being prepared (how he becomes aware of it we are not told; perhaps the self-assured attitude of the disloyal member of the nation was sufficient), then he is once again coming up against his duty as watchman to sound a blast on the trumpet, i.e. in this case to give warning, in order that the thoughtless sinner may change his attitude before it is too late. So once again it consists in addressing a purely personal appeal, in which the watchman appointed by God points out the disaster which threatens, and calls for conversion.

It is perfectly clear that this explanation of what is to be done by the prophetic watchman goes far beyond what is implied by the literal meaning of the imagery of the political watchman in a land threatened by some danger. It is, of course, impossible for it to be otherwise, seeing that what is being dealt with here is a spiritual office, for which the political office can only furnish an intuitive approximation. We will not be doing justice to the aim of the imagery if we try to apply it too forcibly, in such a way that each one of its details must stand for something. While, therefore, it is perfectly correct to call attention to the fact that the political watchman does not direct his warnings to individuals, but to the general mass of the inhabitants of his country, it is incorrect to conclude from that that Ezekiel's warning needed only to reach two large groups of righteous or wicked among the whole people, and that after that he could let the responsibility fall on the individuals composing these groups to decide whether they would or would not obey his warning. Such a conclusion does not do justice to the completely individual way in which the prophet is described as meeting the members of his people. The image and the reality do correspond in two points: in the watchman's obligation to give warning and in his responsibility for the conscientious execution of this duty. But the reality transcends the image in the case of the persons to whom the paraenesis is addressed, since the paraenesis is varied to suit the needs of the hearer. It is therefore something totally different in kind, and much more complicated than a loud trumpet blast. There can therefore be no objection to our seeking aid from the concept of the pastor or adviser in order to throw light on the prophet's new duties. Only when we do so does Ezekiel's task really begin to contain 'something that stands by itself and is characteristic of him' (Fohrer). Otherwise he would still remain at the same stage as in Jer. 6.17, where the prophets are compared to watchmen whom Yahweh has appointed for his people, along with a warning to 'give heed to the sound of the trumpet'. It is also stated there that their refusal to give .heed to the prophetic message is the reason for the downfall of the nation.

Thus the order given to the prophet, as we understand it, is to become one who gives warning to the individual wicked man or lapsed pious man. It is also closely connected with the new situation in which the prophet finds himself, as compared with his predecessors. The group of exiles belonging to his people confronted him in a different way from that in which the people of Judah confronted Jeremiah. The little group had been uprooted from the homeland and cut off from the protective framework of national co-existence and fixed family tradition. It found that the continuance of life in a foreign land required labour and effort. So it could for that reason alone no longer be compared to the proud people of Judah and Jerusalem who, despite all inward disturbance, were still capable of forming a compact body and moving forward to meet the prophet's attack. We have already come across the flippant, who ignore all threats, the sceptics, who are doubtful of the very existence of any prophetic authority, the conservative defenders of the outworn dogmas of the faith, and also those who have undergone a complete breakdown and been reduced to such despair through being unable to reconcile themselves to the severity of their plight. So we already recognize that the company of exiles was composed of such varying elements, and that this alone called for greater differentiation in the prophetic message. The individual had grown up so as to claim independence and assert his rights against the community, and that produced a general mental attitude which either rejected or else failed to understand any message which was not couched in personal terms and which spoke of a divine law capable of possessing validity within a closed community. This undoubtedly laid down the presuppositions which rendered personal appeals to individuals not only possible but also necessary, and which made the old method of prophetic preaching appear ineffective. A man as conscientious as Ezekiel could not ignore this state of affairs.

He could not possibly ignore it, knowing as he did of the necessity of a decision which at that time and in that place God was demanding that each individual should make, and which had to be brought home to him. In ch. 18 we have already encountered a sermon by the prophet which tried to produce a decision occasioned by a fresh offer of grace. He stated that the acceptance of that offer of grace was the one act of obedience that was necessary and pleasing to God which could make it possible to move forward from being imprisoned and reduced to despair by the past. In 20.37f., also, we found the prophet expecting a judicial act of separation in which Yahweh would test each individual in the immediate future, like a shepherd making each animal in his flock pass under his rod, and would thus gather a new people of God. So Ezekiel realized that he had been placed within a period of decision, in which every individual was required to take up a position in full consciousness of what he was doing, and needed to have some words addressed to him on the subject. A mere general message, which left the individual to apply it by himself and took his goodwill for granted, of the sort characteristic of past prophetic activity, was no longer sufficient.

We do not know to what extent considerations of this kind had already occupied the prophet since the beginning of his work. But they can hardly have been new and strange, in view of the fact that he was a priest concerned with instructing the people. However, his mind first began to reach clarity when Yahweh called him to the new office of a watchman whose duty it was to bring home to each individual a warning of how God was threatening to intervene in his life.

There is no reason for surprise at finding that this appeal is expressed in the language of sacral law. We have already observed how frequently the prophet employs this form of speech, especially in ch. 18. A study of it in minute detail has recently been made by Reventlow.[1] These researches are especially important and valuable in view of the way in which they display how narrowly related were the prophetic preaching, with its close connection to the sacral law, and the exposition of the law at the covenant festival. In what Yahweh himself says of his revelation in Israel, we see the objective which this preaching is endeavouring to attain. It announces that God is taking action to win recognition for his revelation and his sovereignty, which have presided over the history of Israel from the very beginning. The conferring of the office of a watchman over Israel was closely connected with the special character of the whole period and with the course of action already put into execution by Yahweh. Only in so far as we keep this in mind will we be able to see clearly what the danger was of which Ezekiel was to warn his fellow countrymen. The threat to their existence was not spelt by their being incapable and unwilling to follow the law fully, and therefore

[1] *Wächter über Israel. Ezechiel und seine Tradition,* 1962.

delivered over to suffer retribution at the hands of an account-keeping deity who measured their devotion in accordance with the number of the works demanded by the law. Such a representation of the law worked out in terms of reward and punishment as a consistent system by which to live can only be read out of the words of the prophet if one makes him proclaim a timeless doctrine of divine retribution for the actions of the individual. But here, as in ch. 18, the matter takes on a totally different complexion, if what is at stake is saying yes or no to what God is *now* doing to establish a new covenant nation. Wherever the individual opens himself to what God is offering, to what raises him out of past imprisonment in guilt and calls him to a fresh beginning, he will give expression to his solidarity with all the other members of the people called in the same way by actions particularized for him in the law of the covenant. Wherever, on the other hand, the same individual closes himself up in face of what God offers, one of the two things happens. Either he goes on with the thoughtless and godless behaviour into which he had been misled by the dissolution of discipline and morality amid the difficult conditions of a heathen land, or else, in so far as he has hitherto kept up the morality brought with him from the home country, he is in danger of throwing it overboard as useless and, in view of the hopeless state of affairs, letting his behaviour be determined purely by considerations of his own selfish pleasure or profit. Contempt for the law is not itself the matter at stake; that is the decisive point at which we have arrived; it is only a symptom for the deeper-seated ill of obstinate opposition to the call of God that is now being issued. It is this opposition that God must necessarily doom to death if his seeking and saving mercy is disappointed by it.

[7f.] The prophet is to feel this death-sentence ringing in his ears every time he sees before him either a wicked man who thoughtlessly ignores it or a devout man who has gone astray in his faith. He cannot simply stand by and watch that man go on to meet what is destined for him, and calm his own mind by reflecting that he has already announced sufficiently audibly and publicly what his God is offering and what are the consequences of rejecting it. On the contrary, at the same time, a 'second sphere of activity'[1] is being introduced, in which God's calling and demands are strengthened and made fully effective by appeals addressed to individuals by his ambassador. In ch. 18 God's offer could still be announced in the impersonal style of the

[1] See G. von Rad, *Old Testament Theology*, II, 1965, p. 230.

system of sacral law, but we see Yahweh, in appointing the watchman, turning in love to his people and feeling it worth while to give
a particular warning to each individual, so as to make him feel
through it the mercy of the God who seeks him.

This new and intensified approach by Yahweh is specially marked
off by the severe responsibility it imposes on the watchman whom it
appoints. He must answer for it; it may even cost him his life, if he
neglects to give warning as commanded. The man who for lack of
warning goes on in his forgetfulness of God will indeed come under
judgment, but that will bring blood-guilt upon the prophet and
bring him under God's sentence. 'A solidarity therefore exists between watchman and people, which finds outward expression in
their joint liability for seeing that God's command is observed. Only
when the transgressor ignores a warning and thus breaks away from
the community of action of the people of God does he destroy the
fellowship that binds together all the members of the people and with
it also the liability of the watchman. Otherwise the fact that they are
bound together by the common bond of the will of Yahweh revealed
to the whole people creates mutual fellowship between prophet and
people. The prophet (watchman) cannot work himself free of that
by any unilateral process' (Reventlow).

It is clear that this provides the presuppositions which demand the
choice of new objectives for the prophetic office. A totally changed
situation demands a change in the message, such as can be observed
in the earlier history of the prophets as well as now. Mere recital of
sacral law in the form it has taken so far, which identifies a prophet's
whole activity with that of the old pronouncer of the law at the
covenant festival, has lost its meaning in the new situation, even
though one may freely grant that an appeal calculated to charm and
court the audiences provides an inner enrichment to a mere proclamation of the law. For this sacral law, which forms part of what
the priests proclaim at the covenant festival, takes for granted that the
bond between the God of the covenant and his people is unbroken.
It is part of the covenant with God, which the message of the prophet
declares to have been abolished by the judgment. The covenant,
once destroyed, cannot be restored by a general proclamation of the
law of the covenant in the style of the old formulations, as if nothing
had happened; it demands the establishment of a new covenant, and
for that again the people must be prepared. In this, preaching can be
carried out effectively only by applying it to each individual member

of the people of God and issuing an appeal to suit each case, so as to convince him of the importance of the decision demanded of him, since only by such a decision can he gain a share in the coming salvation. Form criticism has shown that Ezekiel's prophetic speech has close links with the style of sacral law. But this ought never to blind us to the totally new thoughts contained in that style.

Here we see a wedge being driven through the dominant inclination among the people of God in all ages, to acquiesce in an impersonal fashion in delivering God's message to the congregation, and to forget the embarrassing position in which God's offer of grace places every individual. The fact that anonymous common membership must yield place here to personal commitment, involving inevitable personal decisions, makes a direct appeal by the bearer of the message to the individual member of the congregation an unavoidable necessity for the completion of the preaching, and the preacher is seen to be responsible for making such an appeal. In this way, God's offer testifying to the way in which he is seeking to be merciful at last finds its way into the commonplace actuality of individual life so as to transform it. But that means that such 'pastoral care' as this does not claim to provide an ever-ready panacea for all imaginable human ills, but aims at continually reminding men of the decisive encounter in which a reorientation of one's whole life can be carried out and which therefore contains within it a guarantee of complete salvation.

This new task of being the watchman for Israel thus committed to Ezekiel may be described as pastoral care, provided that it is rightly understood, and not confined to a so-called spiritual inwardness. It must take a wider view so as to embrace the whole man. Or one may prefer to call it *paraklesis* (von Rad), in accordance with the New Testament word *parakalein*. What term is used is comparatively unimportant as long as it is clearly realized what we are talking about, the appeal to the individual, informing him of how the people of God is being reconstituted at this moment, and of the responsibility of his own which arises from that. Yet in so far as such an appeal leads towards mutual liability and responsibility for each other, between prophet and people, it brings fully to light the mediatorial and representative office which we have frequently seen illuminated in those passages where the prophet seemed almost a reincarnation of the dying nation in the severe bodily and mental suffering by which he took upon himself the burden of the judgment that he saw being laid upon his own people as a whole. He has been a sign and a wonder to his contemporaries (12.6b; 24.24), as he bore symbolically the guilt of the house of Israel and was the first to suffer the coming chastisement with his whole being. Such active participation in the chastisement and suffering of his people is the most intense possible way of assenting to his vocation to be a watchman. As a consequence, he himself described it as the task of the genuine prophet to stand in the breach and form a protective wall against Yahweh's attack upon his people (13.5). He is therefore the first, in the faithful exercise of his office of admonisher and watchman, to suffer that attack and, united to the uttermost with his people, to surrender himself to the chastisement, so that by saying yes to God's just retribution he may not betray, but establish, his fellowship with Israel. Here he goes far beyond Jeremiah's posture of defence in face of the sufferings which his vocation involved, but is yet not far removed from the joyful endurance of suffering in consciousness of victory which we meet in the servant of God in Deutero-Isaiah. The veil of mystery which God has spread over the representative sufferings of his messenger is not yet lifted; yet in the obedient way in which the messenger of God unites himself with his guilty people we can see something preparing itself that makes ready the way leading on to the profundities of the knowledge of vicarious suffering. At the same time, this suffering bound up with vocation reminds us for all ages that that fundamental law of solidarity with the guilty remains valid even for those who follow the perfect mediator and representative under the new covenant, and that it alone lends credibility to the delivery of the message which refers to him.

CHAPTER 33.10–20

Yahweh's new offer as the basis of pastoral care

10 'And you, son of man, say to the house of Israel; Thus you say:[a] Indeed our apostasies and our misdeeds weigh us down and we waste away because of them; how then can we live furthermore?[11]Say to them: As sure as I live, says [. . .][b] Yahweh, I have no pleasure in the death of the wicked, but that the wicked turn from his way and live. Turn back, turn back from your evil ways! For why will you die, O house of Israel?

12 And you, son of man, say to your people: the righteousness of the

righteous shall not deliver him in the day of his apostasy, and the wickedness of the wicked shall not make him fall in the day when he turns away
from his wickedness [. . .].ᶜ ¹³Though I say to the righteous,ᵈ You shall
surely live, yet if he trusts in his righteousness and commits iniquity,
none of his righteous deeds shall be remembered, because of the iniquityᵉ
which he has committed, on account of it he must die. ¹⁴Again, though I
say to the wicked, You must die without mercy, if he turns from his sin and
does what is lawful and right, ¹⁵restores the pledge [. . .]ᶠ and gives back
what he had taken by extortion, and thus walks in the statutes of life, so as to
commit no iniquity, then he shall surely live and not die. ¹⁶None of the
sins that he has committed shall be remembered against him. He has done
what is lawful and right, he shall surely live.

17 Yet your people say: "The way in which Yahwehᵍ acts is not right",
when it is their own way that is not right.

18 When a righteous man turns away from his righteousness and commits iniquity, then he must die because of them (his misdeeds). ¹⁹And
when a wicked man turns away from his wickedness and does what is
lawful and right, he shall live because of them (because of the righteous
deeds). ²⁰Yet you say, "The way Yahweh acts is not right." I will judge
you, each one according to his ways, O house of Israel.'ʰ

ᵃMT: 'as follows'.
ᵇSee BH.
ᶜMT: 'And the righteous shall not be able to live by them in the day when he
sins': a variant of v. 12b, which has made its way into the text from the margin.
ᵈMT third person, but v. 14 points to the address.
ᵉ⁻ʰSee BH.

An appeal to the despairing: 33.10–11

A cry full of profound despair passes round the house of Israel, i.e.
in this case among the exiles. The 'house of rebellion', which has so
far maintained such an obstinately closed attitude in face of the
charges brought by the prophet, at last comes to confess its own guilt.
This confession of sin is brought about by a feeling of faintness, like
that which a man feels when his body is covered with festering
wounds which will inevitably cause death. It is the hard blow which
has struck the men speaking in this way, by which their eyes are
opened to see the full seriousness of what they have stiffly refused to
admit, the sin against a holy God, the sins of apostasy, which have
transgressed his holy will, breaking his ordinances and putting the
dominion of man in the place of God's sovereignty.

Yet this confession, in the style of the popular penitential lament
(cf. Jer. 3.22–25; Hos. 6.1–3; Lam. 3.42–48; 5.16, 22; 4.6, etc.), does

not rise into a petition for mercy and forgiveness. It is no more than a
cry of lament. The name of God is not mentioned, even though it is
implied by the strong words about the sin of apostasy; it seems as if
there were a fear of mentioning the wrathful judge, so as not to arouse
further disaster (cf. Amos 6.10). That is because judgment by him
implies utter annihilation, unlit by a single gleam of light. What
Ezekiel had kept hammering into the ears of his hearers, the utter
ruthlessness of the execution of the judgment by which the chosen
people, having repudiated their own destiny, must be totally wiped
out (24.33f.), now came before their eyes in the full horror of its
reality. Only now, when the last hope of having a home to return to
was extinguished, did it become clear to them how hopeless their
position was. They might indeed be able to hold on to their lives.
But it was no longer possible to delude themselves. There was nothing
left for them but to die in an unclean land, now that everything that
had made life worth living, their nation and home, their state and
family, their worship of God and faith in the future, lay buried
beneath the ruins of Jerusalem. There was nothing left but a long-
drawn-out process of withering up and fading away. 'How then can
we live furthermore?'

But it is exactly at this point, at the nadir of all natural hope, that
this same prophet, whose threatenings have been so frighteningly fulfilled, has to proclaim afresh the promise of life, in which the incomprehensible miracle of divine judgment shines out brightly. It
was first stated in 18.23. The possibility of a new life was opened to
those who were destined for death. At that point, the shape in which
it appeared was that of the majestic measures taken by the Lord of
humanity in face of doubts as to his righteousness. But now it comes
confirmed by an oath in an impassioned expression of the will to
redeem, shown to these broken men, awakening their dead will to
live by the irresistible force of merciful love. Even where they can see
nothing but death, God's will is still directed towards life. So the
inconceivable happens; in the presence of the terrible harvest of
death it is not his wrath, but his favour, that is directed towards the
wicked, opening to him a last access to life by turning away from
the apostasy that leads to death. This has already been called for in the
admonitions in 14.6 and 18.30, 32. But now it is particularly forcibly
proclaimed as being the last possibility of deciding in favour of life.
The section which follows is devoted to working out what that
possibility means.

The turning from death to life: 33.12-20

The thoughts are those of 18.21-25. Often they are repeated in much the same words, but there are some significant alterations. Here, as there, the learned exposition is in legal style, but it is significantly interrupted over and over again by references to the direct speech and action of Yahweh. His promise of life and death invades the daily life of the exiles (vv. 13f., cf. 33.8), calling them to responsible action; his decision accompanies that action and changes life into death, death into life. How do those thus called upon react towards this divine will which is on so overwhelming a scale and which yet at the same time comes so alarmingly close to them? Do they realize the unique importance of this present moment? [12] No appeals to previous attitudes towards God's ordinances are any help towards standing in it, whether these attitudes have deserved praise or blame. All sentences are repealed, all left undecided. [13] To have shown piety hitherto confers no right to the grace that God offers, if that piety lets itself now fall into despair and gives up its faith by refusing to obey the call to be awake and ready. [14-16] On the other hand, careless lawlessness that has become habitual need not be any obstacle to laying hold upon the grace of God, provided that a man now lets himself be reached by the living word and moved to conversion. God's readiness to begin afresh with his people at once gives them a clean sheet and opens up all the possibilities of entering into a new fellowship with him. The only thing that matters is whether or not the man opens himself to this affirmation of the will of God, and does not let himself be put to sleep by reliance on his own piety and thus come unexpectedly to a fall, or, again, does not go along the way of disobedience light-heartedly because he has hitherto been able to do so with impunity. For then, in both these cases, he will suddenly find himself facing the judge and hear himself sentenced to death without any appeal. If, however, he lets himself be stirred up by God's offer of grace, then his willingness to be converted will not find its external expression in beautiful words and resolutions, but will give proof of its genuineness in everyday life by a closer approach to his neighbour, taking him seriously as a bearer of the same offer of grace and showing towards him in complete simplicity the brotherliness commanded in the law. That sounds sober, almost banal, but it is what a right response to God's call must seem like. It is as far removed from the narrow-minded legalism that tries to merit salvation as the admonition in I John 3.3: 'Everyone who thus hopes in him purifies himself, even as he is pure.' Believing acceptance of the promise effects an inward transformation from unbounded selfishness to solidarity with the other members of the new people of God. This can be illustrated by picking out as examples the prohibitions against keeping a pledge and against extortion (cf. 18.7), since the matters they concern make them statutes which lead to life (cf. 20.11, 13, 21) and deal with what is lawful and right, i.e. with the recognized foundations of a brotherly communal life. The inward connection between the commandment and God's gracious will to institute a new fellowship is here expressed with the same life and power as in the New Testament.

The inward change of direction towards the goal promised by God which is given here is thus the content of conversion, which God means to make possible by his offer of grace. It changes the death-sentence into a promise of life, whereas to say 'no' to it is to exclude oneself from life. [17] So here, as in 18.25, stiff-necked criticism of God's surprising decisions and the way in which they put the godless on the same level as the godly, and take away from the godly that feeling of superiority to sinners that they find it so very hard to do without, must be met simply by a completely serious declaration of its wrongness.

[18-20a] Whether vv. 18-20a, repeating as they do the decisive phrases in exact agreement with 18.26-29, are to be regarded as a mere postscript emphasizing and illustrating what has just been said (Zimmerli), or whether, on the other hand, one ought to regard such repetitions as part of the governing style in proclamations of sacral law, the influence of which the prophet could not resist (Reventlow), is a matter which must be left open. In any case, one would not want to be without the concluding phrase in v. 20b, which is a repetition of 18.30: whoever rejects the redeemer finds himself face to face with the judge (cf. above, p. 246).

CHAPTER 33.21-22

The fulfilment of the divine promise

21 In the eleventh[a] year of our exile, in the tenth month, on the fifth day of the month, a man who had escaped from Jerusalem came to me

with the news: 'The city has fallen'.[b] [22]Now the hand of Yahweh had been upon me the evening before the fugitive came [. . .][c] till the time the man came to me in the morning. So my mouth was opened, and I was no longer dumb.

[a]See BH.

[b]Literally, 'smitten', 'overthrown'.

[c]MT: 'and he opened my mouth'; an insertion which has a disrupting effect on the statement about the time. It anticipates what is stated in the next verse, in order to assert that the prophet was set free by divine action. But 24.27 tells of his mouth being opened in the same impersonal way.

It is obvious that this piece of narrative no longer stands in its correct position. Originally it was closely associated with 24.25–27, but it has been detached by the prefixing of vv. 1–20. Most of the blame for this must certainly fall on the editors who reconstructed ch. 33. They were concerned about finding a suitable introduction before the third main division of the prophetic book, so they used Ezekiel's appointment as a watchman for Israel in order to provide an effective description of this new phase in his activities. As we have already seen, this was, in substance, correct enough. But their insertion of vv. 21–29, which undoubtedly belong to an earlier period, into a position after 33.1–20 also contributed to the confusion in the wording of 24.15–27, which, as we saw earlier, was caused by the displacement of 3.24ff. and 4.4ff. to their present positions. We must therefore study these reports of how the prophet was struck dumb for more than half a year with some attention.

The fixing of the date in the MT at the twelfth year of the exile seems, on the basis of a comparison with the statements in II Kings 25.2f., 8f., to reckon upon a period of about a year and a half for the fugitive's journey from Jerusalem to Babylon, which is far too long for the actual distances involved. It has therefore been assumed that the date of the year was subsequently altered from the eleventh year to the twelfth. This is supported by the way in which the Hebrew and Greek traditions alternate between the two numbers. So the time taken must have been half a year, as originally stated. One can actually find an illuminating reason for this alteration: this is the date of the twelfth year which occurs previously in 32.17 and which, as a result of the editorial rearrangement of the whole book, seems to render it impossible for 33.21 to date an apparently subsequent event in the eleventh year, expecting as one does a strict chronological succession in all the dates. The hypothesis of a correction in the date of the year made for some such reasons has the advantage of simplicity, over against the various theories of a confusion of Israelite and Babylonian chronology, which would also make it possible to suppose that the fugitive's journey took apparently half a year (Steuernagel, Hölscher, etc.).

But is not perhaps even this shorter period far too long for a journey by a single individual from Palestine to Babylonia? This assertion has frequently been made, to be followed either by considerable abbreviation of the traditional text (Bertholet, etc.) or its total rejection as an unhistorical addition (Van den Born, etc.). But these scholars fail to realize the utter impossibility of obtaining certain dates for the fugitive's journey, which is described with two words. In spite of being well provided with all necessities, Ezra took three and a half months to make the journey from Babylon to Jerusalem (Ezra 8.31; 7.9); one may therefore allow six months at the very least for a Jew who had to be circumspect on the journey and would inevitably have been forced to take circuitous routes or to lie in hiding in order to avoid being surprised by the catchpoles (see Fohrer's thorough considerations). If the conjecture is correct that the reference here is not to a fugitive but to a survivor of the catastrophe journeying with the others to Babylon as a prisoner (Zimmerli), then there is no reason left for finding fault with the text as it stands.[1]

In actual fact, however, it is hard to shake off the impression that here a piece of narrative which is free from any inconsistency has been subjected to criticism solely for the reason that it establishes, in a way that is hard to refute, that Babylonia was Ezekiel's sphere of operation. In view of the promise he had received (24.26f.), it was only to be expected that the prophet would set such a high value on the arrival of an eyewitness of the dismal happenings in the home country. But it was also a convincing confirmation of the fulfilment of his prediction of judgment, which made an important direct contribution towards demonstrating the truth of what he prophesied, in a way already present in Isaiah (8.1ff.),[2] to which Deutero-Isaiah supplies a far-reaching theological basis. The importance of this event to Ezekiel is also seen in the form under which it is expressed,

---

[1] This assumption is not, however, a very probable one in view of the elliptical use of the article, denoting the fugitive who is to be expected under the circumstances.

[2] Cf. W. Eichrodt, *Der Heilige in Israel*, 1960, pp. 93ff.

since we find here a report which confines itself to and is solely interested in the material facts, and there are none of the formulas introducing a prophetic utterance, which are never omitted elsewhere. This also serves to throw light on the beginning of the whole book—but that is another question (see above, p. 51).

On the other hand, this matter-of-fact report demonstrates in a most vital way what a profound impression the event made upon the prophet. The first sentence drops all the accompanying details and goes without ceremony to the main point of the news brought by the fugitive: 'The city has fallen!' It is certain that other important pieces of news came to be known as a result of the arrival of the fugitive. But what was now transmitted, the indubitable assurance that Jerusalem had met her fate, fills the prophet's ear like a loud trumpet-blast, which leaves no room for noticing anything else. Verse 22 indicates the extreme state of inward tension in which he had waited for that moment: during the preceding night, as on a former occasion after the vision in which he had received his call (3.14), the hand of Yahweh had come upon him and had once again reduced him to a state of ecstatic paralysis, in which he divested himself of all volition of his own and felt himself to be nothing but the instrument of a higher power. After the preceding month-long paralysis of body, by which he was made a speechless messenger of the judgment of his God who portrayed the fate of Israel (cf. p. 72), he had a last experience of severe suffering as his body broke down again and again under its trying task, which made him look all the more longingly for the promised deliverance. The morning brought it, and he recovered not only the free use of his limbs but also his power of speech, so that he was able to speak to the fugitive and was no longer dumb. The narrator adds this here, though it was a later fact which he had to tell in advance. In these few words we hear the expression of a tremendous feeling of liberation, of a man who can breathe again now that the heavy burden of death has been removed and the realm of death has set its victim free. Yet at the same time he had experienced something totally transcending his own destiny. Although in the announcement of this event in 24.26f. God's act of judgment still occupied the foreground, we have now reached a point where the eye can look forward to a fresh approach by Yahweh to his people, and catch a glimpse of the further side of the period of judgment, the point where a new hope and a new obedience may take shape. And, bound up with the power of speech bestowed anew upon the prophet, comes the certainty that his mouth is now to transmit new messages from Yahweh, messages which will not have to proclaim the wrathful retribution exacted by the Holy One, but which will be able to do service in building up a new people of God.

CHAPTER 33.23-33

The danger of false security

23 The word of Yahweh came to me: [24]'Son of man, those who dwell amid the ruins[a] in the land of Israel say:[b] "Abraham was only one man, yet he got possession of the land; but we are many, the land is surely given us to possess." [25]Therefore say to them: Thus says [. . .][c] Yahweh: You eat flesh with the blood[d] and lift up your eyes to your idols and shed blood and would you possess the land? [26]You have resorted to the sword and have committed abominations[e] and have defiled everyone his neighbour's wife and would you possess the land? [27]Say this to them: Thus says [. . .][f] Yahweh: As I live, surely those who dwell amid the ruins shall fall by the sword and those that stray in the open field I have given to the beasts to be devoured[g] and those who have found safety on the hill tops and in the caves shall die by pestilence. [28]And I will make the land an utter waste and its proud might shall come to an end, and the mountains of Israel shall be so desolate that no one shall pass through them, [29]and they shall know that I am Yahweh, when I have made the land an utter waste because of all their abominations which they have committed.

30 As for you, son of man, your people who talk together about you by the walls and at the doors of the houses say to one another:[h] Come and hear what sort of word comes forth from Yahweh. [31]They keep coming to you, as people come together, and sit before you [. . .][i] and hear your words, but do not do them; for [lies][j] are in their mouth [. . .][k] and their lust is for their unjust gain.[l] [32]And of a truth, you are to them like one who sings[m] a love song with a beautiful voice and plays well on a stringed instrument; they hear your words, but do not do them. [33]When this comes to pass—and come it will—then they will know that a prophet has been among them.'

---

[a]MT: 'these desolations'; the demonstrative pronoun does not occur in the LXX and must be a subsequent gloss.

[b-c]See BH.

[d]A slight emendation makes it possible to read 'you eat upon the high places of

sacrifice'; the resumption of the old high-place worship and its licentious practices
would correspond to the outbreak of depravation.

e-hSee BH.

iMT: 'my people'; apparently a marginal correction of the previous ʿam, which
has slipped in at the wrong place.

jSee BH.

kMT: 'they themselves act'; out of keeping with the construction and not in
LXX.

lThe text of v. 31 in the MT cannot be translated without emending it, and
shows many variations in other versions. Probably there have been considerable
insertions, and the last half of the verse should be deleted (so Zimmerli).

mSee BH.

The superscription explains the point of view which makes the
redactors place side by side the two passages which they give us here.
Yet we still have to discover whether they were doing full justice to
the passages by treating them thus.

The excessive self-valuation of the survivors in Judah: 33.23-29

As in 18.2, the prophet's message is called up by a winged word. This
time the word comes from those in Judah who have survived the
catastrophe of 587, since 'those who dwell among the ruins in the land
of Israel' can have no other meaning. That the fugitive mentioned in
v. 21 was the particular source from which information in regard to
the watchword they proposed (Herrmann) is not quite impossible,
but it is most improbable, since it seems to suggest some sort of
improvement in conditions in a land devastated by war after the
temporary destruction of all order, and after the first attempts at
reconstruction had broken down two months after the burning of
Jerusalem, as a result of the assassination of Gedaliah, the governor
appointed by Babylon. However, we cannot exclude the possibility
that during the months when Gedaliah was endeavouring to repopu-
late deserted villages with displaced and landless persons still in the
country (II Kings 25.12) and to induce the settlement of the scattered
soldiery of Judah who were still roaming about the land (Jer. 40.9f.),
some sort of watchword like that quoted here may have arisen, in
order to make the heavy labour of reconstruction more attractive as
being the will of God. That is what the words are intended to mean,
no matter in what period we may think them to have originated.
They do more than cast a religious cloak over the theft of ownerless
property when men in the devastated country recollect the promise to
Abraham, which promised that a landless cattle-breeding nomad

should have Canaan as his possession. The promises to the patriarchs had been asserted over and over again, even by the reform of Josiah, as strong supports for faith in God's election (Deut. 1.8; 6.10; 9.5; 30.20; 34.4), because they were able to express the wonderful works of God in their paradoxical greatness by what he had done for one of the weakest nations. So if God had already shown how great his power was in his dealing with one man, how much more would he do so by replanting the many who had escaped the sword of the enemy, in the land and making them grow up again into a new Israel, in order to fulfil his promise that the seed of Abraham would become an innumerable multitude! The main emphasis of this saying is not, therefore, on justifying those encroaching on others' titles to property —they had been sufficiently legitimized by the Babylonian conqueror (cf. Jer. 39.10): but on providing encouragement for those who had decided to start life afresh amid all the dangers of a disordered land.

But even when thus understood, the appeal to Abraham could have undesirable results. For in it there survived something of that obstinately wilful self-assertion which tries to force even God himself to serve it, and which replaces a pure trust in God by a fanatical belief in a divine election which retains its validity under all circumstances. What the popular prophets had promised to the defenders of Jerusalem to the very end, the certainty of deliverance through Yahweh's miraculous power, still exercised its effect. Their unexpected preservation in the common downfall was ascribed to the special favour of God, who after cutting off the guilty would show special favours to the humble and needy and would bring them to honour. Promises by the great prophets pointing in that direction were sufficiently well known (cf., e.g., Isa. 14.32; 17.14; 28.5; 29.19; 30.29, etc.). Faith's deceiving double is once more lifting up its head and trying to identify national reconstruction with the will of God, by giving an absolute value to isolated prophetic words and ignoring the totality of God's message, the only context in which they receive their true significance. This is the method employed by human self-will in every age, in order to make sure of having a divine ally in their own concerns.

There is no longer any trace here of the mighty call of the prophets for the whole people, without exception, to repent. There is far too much readiness to regard those swallowed up by the fury of war or led off into exile as sinners who have received their just punishment, and far too little room left for considerations of how one has conducted one's own life. The information that Ezekiel has received from the home country throws a shockingly clear light on the moral degeneracy of these men who united in this new religious watchword. They have fallen back into old heathen practices in the sacrificial high places, they are given to violence which indulges in every sort of bloodshed, their unbounded sensual lust has ceased to respect the sanctity of marriage (in ch. 18, which is sometimes referred to for comparison, bloodshed and reliance on the sword are conspicuous by their absence). This gives us a glimpse of a class of the nation who have grown depraved and indisciplined during the long war years, and who no longer know or want to know of the unconditional moral ordinances of a people of God. So anyone who insisted on seeing the germ of a new Israel in such elements as those was only serving by fanaticism and exaggeration to allow a fresh error to grow, which would completely block the way to that knowledge of God which Ezekiel had again and again proclaimed to be the object of all the chastisements. [25f.] The prophet shows up the hollowness of this religious watchword to the problem by an indignant question, which twice goes into the attack by asserting the incompatibility of the lofty claims with the actual behaviour of those who make them. [27f.] Then he solemnly proclaims God's answer to this blasphemous misuse of his name. This caricature of a new people of God will be eradicated from the land of promise by calling in the three providential plagues, war, wild beasts and pestilence, so that God's true nature may be made known (v. 29). He would prefer to turn the land into an uninhabited desert rather than let the holy aim of his judgment be twisted out of his hand and made unrecognizable by the deceitfulness of pseudo-piety. No man is to carry out the reconstruction of Israel according to any specifications of his own; it is reserved for the mysterious creative power of God to put it into execution in what everyone regards as the one impossible place, the unclean land of exile.

It is evident that this utterance of judgment was of great importance to the exiles. The news from the homeland seemed to indicate something quite different from what the prophet had been saying hitherto about Yahweh's re-creating action in the congregation of exiles. It was the homeland which, in spite of the burning of the temple and the massacre, still seemed, as always, the sole right and guarantee of the nearness of God. The former landowners who had been led into exile might be strongly opposed politically and socially to the miserable remnant in Judah, and disapprove violently of their pretentious conduct. To the prophet it was not a governorship which existed by the favour of Babylon which stood in the way of the rights of the Davidic dynasty, nor was it the new dividing up of the land which aroused his disapproval, but adherence to ancient sins united with impudent appeals to the ancestral God. This attitude leads to the sentence of judgment that he proclaims, and it always comes into actual effect once more wherever men are not led by divine chastisement to a repentant surrender to the judge and lord, but instead appeal proudly to the 'blessing of the Almighty' and lay claim to the preservation and further security which knows nothing of any inward transformation and thinks it can maintain a long outdated right to live by living on the old life and claiming to have enlisted the name of God in its service.

The barrenness of uncommitted hearing among the exiles: 33.30–33

With sound consideration during the composition of this chapter, the present section, which forms a counterpart to the picture of the men of Judah in the preceding verses, has been inserted at this very point. It serves to prevent the portion of the nation living in exile from joining all too unanimously to condemn their fellow countrymen in Judah, without applying any test to their own behaviour in face of God's purposes of salvation.

The section takes the shape of a direct communication by God to Ezekiel, speaking of the exiles solely in the third person, and calling the prophet's attention to their behaviour. There are other instances of the occurrence of this form in the book of Ezekiel (cf. 12.26f.; 14.3, etc.), but in them the statement of the facts is followed by a word of judgment to be proclaimed by the prophet. Here this latter element is missing, and we are left with what God says to his messenger, which approximates to a word of judgment only when it looks into the future and suggests what the exiles will realize when it is too late.

The uniqueness of the content matches the uniqueness of the form. [30] First of all, God refers to the undeniable stir caused among the exiles by the preaching of this prophet whom they have hitherto regarded with such animosity. Wherever men meet in Tell Abīb and stop for a moment to talk, in the scanty shade of a wall or in the shelter of a doorway, the conversation at once turns to the extraordinary man of God and his strange and often eccentric manner of appearing. And each encourages the other to pay him another visit, to hear the latest word from Yahweh. [31] The prophet has become the sensation of the hour; the people crowd around him, to catch every word of his frequently obscure utterances, and wait patiently also while he sits there and does not speak a word.

There is no doubt that a perceptible change has come over the attitude of the people towards Ezekiel. There is hardly any trace left of what he called 'dwelling among scorpions' (2.6). The prophet can count on an increase in the numbers and attentiveness of his audience every time he opens his mouth.

We are not informed of what has led to this state of affairs. It is quite conceivable that it was already beginning to take shape before the fall of Jerusalem, especially in view of the contrast between the attitude described here and that of which we are told in 33.10, 17. Yet when one thinks of the opposition kept up by Ezekiel's audience, according to ch. 24 until the last few months before the fall of Jerusalem, one will agree with the views taken by the editors of the prophetic book as correct, in indicating that an outlook is represented here which was frequent in Tell Abīb after 587, but which did not become dominant immediately after the disaster—rather, at a somewhat later period. This seems to be confirmed by the severe criticism which now follows.

It may be asked why God gives his trusted servant a description of the change in the attitude of his audience of which he cannot himself have been unaware. The way seems purposeless, as no message is given on this occasion. As the sequel shows, it happens in order to prevent Ezekiel from drawing any false conclusions from the striking improvement in his position. How, indeed, could Ezekiel not have been provoked to joy at having at last secured recognition? Would not expectations have been aroused of a change from defensiveness to receptivity, from reservedness to understanding and from impenitence to conversion? Did it not seem as if the seed that he had sown with such immensely heavy labour, that had caused him so much pain, was at last beginning to ripen into fruit?

But he who can 'search the mind and try the heart' (Jer. 17.10) can see below the surface; so he lets his messenger know the real state of things in blistering terms, so as to save him from illusions and disappointments. [31b] That is why no communication is given to be passed on, and there is nothing more than a conversation with the 'son of man'. This superficial appearance of interest and of a new attentiveness is far from being a symptom that the audience is really being stirred within by the prophet's word, or of readiness to be led off on the march towards new objectives. The interest now being awakened marks, rather, a revival of the old creature of the twilight which wants to have a share in the divine salvation without going so far as to be converted. Acceptance of God's offer with all its conse- quences means less to this man than living on as before in applying all intrigues and ruses, as he is determined to do in order to assert his personality amid all the hardships of exile. As a result, all the pious words of the people are seen to be lies; the self-assertion which thinks solely of self-advantage and cares nothing for the rights of a neighbour acts as destructively now in the exile as it formerly did in the homeland upon a brotherly community life under the control of God, and pre- vents God's insistent call from entering this man's ear so as to reach his heart.

[32] This attitude is portrayed by a bitter simile. The crowds gathering in front of the prophet's house are exactly similar to those who would be there if his place were taken by some itinerant minstrel showing his skill in performing light frivolous love lyrics and accom- panying them on his lute or harp. It is not the messenger of God whose word confronts his audience with the choice between life and death whom they rush to hear, but the master of words, who has done with his grim preaching of judgment and now speaks of all sorts of attrac- tive possibilities of a new life, and of an hitherto unimagined national future that may perhaps be on the verge of appearing, and who thus provides something interesting to talk about. The fact that the reality and intimate nearness of the holy God is reaching out for them in order to take them into his service is one that they take great care not to see. So they still refuse to let themselves be dragged away from the non-committal attitude of the spectator: they 'hear your words but do not do them'.

[33] Yet the messenger of God need not fall into doubt; Yahweh is not bringing him face to face with the unvarnished truth in order to drown him in a deep abyss of pessimism in regard to the success of his work. God's communication concludes with a promise that never- theless a breakthrough to a real knowledge will take place. What was affirmed when he was first called is still true (2.5): 'they shall recog- nize that a prophet has been among them', i.e. not only that an extraordinary man has provided them with all sorts of entertainment that does not commit them to anything, but also that the word of the living God has proceeded from the mouth of Ezekiel.

God, of course, refuses to let himself be forced to fix any set time for this much-to-be-desired event. 'When this comes—and come it will!' Here we are no longer concerned with a word of judgment like that in 12.25f., 28, but with a new approach of Yahweh to his people, which the word of the prophet indicates with increasing insistence before and after the fall of Jerusalem. It is now time to keep one's eyes open for this wonderful event, of which God himself has given a guarantee. What Ezekiel keeps impressing upon his audience applies also to himself: to wait in faith is assuredly the fulfilment of the divine promise, so it can endure the present disillusionments, however bitter they may be. What matters here is not the success or failure of the human messenger, but his obedience in carrying out what he has been commissioned to do (cf. 2.5): God has reserved to himself the demonstration of his truth.

Thus once more we have a picture of the presuppositions of the activity of a prophet, and how it replaces all calculations about success by calm reliance upon the God who is already at work. But this piece of instruction originally intended for the prophet alone has been taken up very properly by the prophet's disciples when constructing this present chapter, and has been employed by them as a word of warning to the exile community. What had already been proclaimed in 20.33ff., and had been revived again in the office of the watchman in 33.1ff., the thorough-going measures taken by the creator of the new covenant to screen and sift those who have survived the catastrophe, is now made real in actual practice in the ruthless way in which all their sordid and selfish motives in regard to his promise are uncovered. After the judgment upon Jerusalem there can be no such thing as comfortable repose in certainty of receiving grace, but only the 'working out of one's salvation with fear and trembling' (Phil. 2.12), by the man who lets 'God's kindness lead him to repentance' (Rom. 2.4). The creation of the new Israel is not brought about by any magical process done over men's heads, but through genuine fellowship between God and man in which both listen and answer. So if anyone refuses to let himself be drawn into this mighty event, then God's mighty act has no fruit for him.

THE GOOD SHEPHERD
34.1–31

CHAPTER 34.1–16

Liberation from the false shepherds and
proper shepherd's care

1 The word of Yahweh came to me: 2'Son of man, prophesy against the shepherds of Israel, prophesy and say to them: You shepherds,[a] thus says [. . .][b] Yahweh: Woe to the shepherds of Israel, who have been feeding themselves. Should not shepherds feed the sheep? 3You eat the milk,[c] you clothe yourselves with the wool and you slaughter the fatlings, but[d] you do not feed the sheep. 4The weak[e] you have not strengthened and the sick you have not healed; the injured you have not bound up and the strayed you have not brought back, the lost you have not sought and the strong[f] you have violently[g] trampled down. 5So my sheep[h] were scattered, because there was no shepherd, and they became food for all the wild beasts of the field [. . .] 6[. . .][i] My sheep were scattered over all the mountains and all the high hills and over all the land, and none cared for them or sought for them.

7 Therefore, you[j] shepherds, hear the word of Yahweh! 8As I live, says [. . .][k] Yahweh: Because my sheep have become a prey, and my sheep have become food for all the wild beasts of the field, since there was no shepherd, and because the[l] shepherds did not care for my sheep, but the shepherds fed themselves and did not feed my sheep, 9therefore, you shepherds, hear the word of the Lord! 10Thus says [. . .][m] Yahweh: Behold, I will come down[n] upon the shepherds and will require my sheep at their hand and will put a stop to their being shepherds over my sheep,[o] and the shepherds shall no longer feed themselves, and I will rescue my sheep from their mouths and they shall no longer be food for them.

11 For thus says [. . .][p] Yahweh: Behold, I myself will take charge of my sheep and will care for them. 12As a shepherd cares for his flock [when it has been overpowered, and his sheep scattered],[q] so will I care for my sheep and rescue them from all places where they have been scattered in the day of clouds and of darkness. 13And I will bring them out from the peoples and gather them from the countries and will bring them into their own land and I will feed them on the mountains of Israel, in the valleys

where brooks flow and [in the best places of the land].[r] [14]I will feed them with good pastures and upon the mountain heights of Israel shall be their pasture; there shall they lie down on good grazing land and on fat pasture shall they feed upon the mountains of Israel. [15]I myself will be the shepherd of my sheep and I will make them lie down in quiet, says [. . .][s] Yahweh. [16]I will seek the lost and will bring back the strayed and bind up the injured and strengthen the sick and [. . .][t] the strong will I watch over and pasture, in the right way.

[a]MT: 'to the shepherds'; the vocative is better.
[b–h]See BH.
[i]'My sheep were scattered and wandered': this has arisen through a marginal gloss finding its way into the text.
[j–p]See BH.
[q]The text as given here has been considerably disrupted in MT, but can be reconstructed by transposing some words to make sense.
[r]MT: 'in all the inhabited places of the country'; here both the form and content of the noun are strange.
[s]See BH.
[t]MT: 'the fat and', rightly omitted by LXX.

The false shepherds and their punishment: 34.1–10

Ezekiel does not employ a new image, but a very old one, to reveal the change to a new mode of action on the part of Yahweh. The representation of ruler and subject by means of the image of shepherd and flock is well known through all the ancient East. At the beginning of his celebrated laws, Hammurabi already describes himself as the 'shepherd of men', the 'supplier of pasture and water', who has been appointed 'to destroy the ruthless and wicked and to prevent the weak from being robbed of his just rights by the strong'. The same note is struck in royal inscriptions down to Merodach Baladan II (*c.* 710), who expresses consciousness of his duty as a shepherd to collect those who are scattered. The oldest of the Egyptian royal hymns also speaks of the duty of earnest love for the king, the shepherd, through whom his subjects live and breathe. Alongside power, the ancient oriental ideal of kingship includes the protection the true shepherd gives to his flock, by leading the needy to pasture, providing food and drink, and establishing pasturages and places of safety.[1]

[1] Cf. the painstaking collection of statements about shepherds in ancient oriental royal writings by Lorenz Dürr, *Ursprung und Ausbau der israelitisch-jüdischen Heilandserwartung*, 1925, pp. 116ff.

[2] So when Ezekiel addresses the shepherds of Israel, there is already a very definite picture of the true shepherd in the background, as in the previous appeal by Jeremiah, cf. 23.1f. In Ezekiel, however, the picture is once more on a grand scale and broadens out into a conspectus of Yahweh's control of history in the past and future.

[3] That is because it is from him that the shepherds of Israel and their power are derived. Verse 3 describes this power in completely objective and realistic terms as consisting in having command over the consumption of the milk and meat produced by the flock and the use of its wool for clothing. But the enjoyment of this right must go side by side with the duty of caring for the flock and faithfully providing for its pasture, otherwise that right becomes a crying injustice.

[4] In v. 4 the prophet arranges the sheep that need to be cared for in six groups. The first five consist significantly of the sheep which have suffered some injury or have fallen into danger. There are the weak, the sick, the injured, the strayed (i.e. probably those driven away from the flock by a storm or by an attack by wild beasts), and the lost, those which have fallen behind during a night journey and have been unable to find their way back, or those which have been lost in pathless regions while out at pasture. In contrast to them, the strong or vigorous form only the one group. So the office of a shepherd is represented to us as a very onerous and responsible vocation, requiring unwearying vigilance and readiness for sacrifice. Yet the shepherds of Israel have not only failed to show self-sacrifice in protecting and providing for those in need of their care, but have violently trodden down the stronger sheep, which would otherwise be the pride of the flock, i.e. they have atrociously overworked them and taken advantage of them for their own profit. [5f.] The natural result was that, according to v. 5, the sheep were scattered and became food for wild beasts, or, as stated in v. 6, they wandered unprotected all over the land. We find in this description the same compassion for those who have no rights and are subjected to their rulers as we see in the words of the Gospels, where Jesus looks at the people and sees them to be 'harrassed and helpless, like sheep without a shepherd' (Matt. 9.36).

This image does not need to be explained in detail; it is transparently obvious and immediately applicable to the way in which the proletariat are taken advantage of, denied their just rights and treated with injustice.

[7f.] Verses 7–10 therefore issue a threat, once more recapitulating the charges to account for it (v. 8). [9f.] They then state that the actual owner of the flock is going to intervene: the shepherds will be cashiered and the sheep torn out of their greedy hands. Or, in non-metaphorical language: the ruling classes of Judah are to retire from the scene, since they will no longer have power to control the flock.

Ezekiel thus supplies the final climax of the protest against the political leaders of Israel which his predecessors had raised so repeatedly. The mismanagement for which the ruling classes in Judah were responsible had, especially at this point in the closing days of the kingdom, increased to a terrifying extent, as other sources of information also tell, leading to the final rejection of the whole section of the nation responsible for it. One need hardly ask if there were not some exceptions: obviously there must have been, but not enough to postpone the radical change which is now to take place. So such few exceptions as there may be are of no interest to the prophet. Nor need one ask whether temporal authority was not in any case completely abolished, so that no rule was conceivable except a spiritual one. Isaiah spoke in a similar passage (1.26) of judges and counsellors, whom Yahweh himself would once more establish in Jerusalem after his judgment had been completed. Ezekiel says nothing of them, since he is already looking beyond them to the new shepherd, who is to take the place of those who have been dismissed.

The rescue by the true shepherd: 34.11–16

Wrathful retribution concludes with the brief threat in v. 10; after that, all the emphasis falls on the promise of salvation which follows next: [11] v. 11 says that Yahweh himself will take charge of his flock and be the true shepherd who will put an end to all the misrule. [12f.] So now we see the scattered sheep gathered together, which had been driven apart and destroyed in the 'day of clouds and darkness', i.e. in Yahweh's day of judgment, here as so often represented by features portraying cosmic disaster. [14f.] So now they will be collected from all directions and be cared for in good pasture-land, where they will be protected from every enemy and able to recover and to thrive. [16] Thus v. 16 brings into view, in reverse order to what we saw before in v. 4, the lost, strayed, injured and sick (omitting the weak), so as to colour in the picture of the true shepherd's care for the flock; he also watches over the strong in the right way. Quite possibly the 'pastor's pattern', as Ziegler terms it, is derived from a well-known theme in folk-tales, and perhaps it had also come to be well known through being used in occasional songs. If so, we find the prophet taking up a well-known motif and adapting it to his special purpose.

It is also striking how the interpretation is already incorporated in the imagery in the features which refer specially to Israel: the sheep are brought out from the peoples and gathered from the countries and brought into their own land. Here, too, the interpretation transcends the imagery.

In this parable of the shepherd, as a whole, we see again the verdict on the history of the nation, to which we were first introduced in ch. 20. Yahweh's endeavour to build up a people of God has broken down through human failure. But here it is not the whole nation that is judged worthy of condemnation and rejection, but only the leaders responsible. This is not to say that this means that the people are acquitted, but in Yahweh's retribution the different degrees of responsibility are seen and taken into account. What is all-important is that Yahweh's original plan should be successfully carried out: man's betrayals only make his faithfulness shine out more brightly, and serve to display how his personal intervention is the sole means by which deliverance is effected. The new intimate fellowship between God and people cannot be more vividly expressed than by the love with which the shepherd approaches the stunted, smitten remnants of the people. Jesus himself recognized this passage as furnishing him with a model of his own task. The great shepherd discourse in John 10 undoubtedly regards him as the fulfiller of this prophecy, and invests him with the office which Ezekiel sees being assumed and exercised by God. Indeed, even this interpretation is not without its association with Ezekiel himself, as we shall see when we deal with the last section of the present chapter.

Chapter 34.17–22

The sifting judgment

17 'As for you, my flock, thus says [. . .]ª Yahweh: Behold, I will judge between sheep and sheep [. . .].ᵇ 18Is it not enough for youᶜ to eat up the best pasture that you must tread down with your feet the rest of your pasture, or to drink of clear water, that you must foul the rest with your feet? 19So my sheep must eat pasture you have trodden with your

feet and drink water that you have fouled with your feet. [20]Therefore thus [. . .]ᵈ says Yahweh [. . .]ᵉ: Behold I myself will judge between the fat sheep and the lean sheep. [21]Because you push with side and shoulder and thrust away all the weak with your horns, till you have scattered them abroad, [22]I will save my flock, so that they shall no longer be a prey, and I will judge between sheep and sheep.

ᵃSee BH.

ᵇMT: 'concerning rams and he-goats'. According to this, the judgment is once more directed against the leaders of the nation. But to suggest that is to misunderstand what follows. So both these words are best deleted as a subsequent piece of exegesis.

ᶜ⁻ᵈSee BH.

ᵉMT: 'to them', rightly omitted by LXX.

In the preceding passage, Ezekiel was not searching for a scapegoat to bear all the blame for the disaster, as is shown by the fresh aspect of God's activity as a shepherd that is brought out here. At this point the imagery is, of course, in process of becoming a parable, since one cannot stand in judgment upon sheep. So each of the details refers to the people.

God's retribution is not limited to the rulers, but also includes the people themselves. For his people has not formed a community based on solidarity, to which it was called, but has become guilty of unbrotherly behaviour. The image of the strong animals of the flock, which push away the weak from grazing and water, in order to arrive there first and have all the best, but which nevertheless do not leave the remains of the available food for the late-comers, but want only to spoil it wantonly and render it unusable, gives us a picture of the propertied classes in Israel. Anti-social guilt is here sketched in living colours. Ezekiel explicitly restates the same burning convictions as his predecessors, who had recognized and combated the lack of social righteousness as a cancerous sore of Israel. Matters already noted at various points are now brought into the open: it is quite impossible to hold that Ezekiel concerned himself solely with the cultic offences of Israel; he regards the unpropertied and unprivileged classes with the same sympathy as Amos or Micah, and calls to account those who have been guilty of wronging them. When Yahweh assumes his office as shepherd, his judgment will not fail to reach the men of violence and the plunderers among his people.

The way thus leads to the complete re-establishment of Yahweh's

flock by means of judgment, so we can put this section side by side
with the purifying judgment of 20.33ff. The downtrodden classes are
not regarded as altogether sinless, yet the prophet seems to speak of
them as if they were more accessible to his demands and invitations
than the representatives of property and culture. Here once more we
find an outlook similar to that of Jesus, whose parable of the sheep
and goats in Matt. 25 is obviously derived from this present picture of
judgment.

Only after such a thorough-going removal of the guilt of the past
can we come to the full unfolding of the blessings which Yahweh's
shepherding brings with it.

CHAPTER 34.23–31
The kingdom of peace

23 'And I will [. . .]ᵃ set up one single shepherd to feed them, even my
servant David [. . .]ᵇ and he shall be their shepherd, ²⁴and I, Yahweh,
will be their God, and my servant David shall be prince among them. I,
Yahweh, have spoken. ²⁵And I will make with them a covenant of salvation, and banish the wild beasts from the land, that they may dwell
securely in the wilderness and sleep in the woods. ²⁶And I will giveᶜ
showers in due time and cause the rain to fall in its season, they shall be
showers of blessing. ²⁷And the trees of the field shall give their fruit, and the
earth shall yield its increase, and they shall dwell securely on their own
soil and shall know that I am Yahweh, when I break the bars of their
yoke, and deliver them from the hand of those who enslaved them. ²⁸And
they shall no more be a prey to the nations, nor shall the beasts of the land
devour them, and they shall dwell securely and none shall make them
afraid. ²⁹And I will provide for them a plantation of prosperityᵈ and they
shall no more be consumed with hunger in the land, and no longer suffer
the reproach of the nations. ³⁰And they shall know that I, Yahweh, am
their God, and that they, the house of Israel, are my people, says [. . .]ᵉ
Yahweh.' ³¹[. . .]ᶠ.

ᵃMT: 'over them'; the alternation between masculine and feminine suffixes in
v. 23 points to an alteration in the text which introduced prematurely the masculine
suffix into the image of the flock. So the words 'over them' (masculine) must be
omitted, and also the second suffix form 'ōtām, which is also absent from LXX.
ᵇMT: 'he shall feed them'; not in LXX.

c-eSee BH.

ᶠMT: 'And you, my sheep, will be the sheep of my pasture (men); and I will be your God, says (the Lord) Yahweh.' This sentence, which ought not to be expected after the prophetic concluding formula, supplies no new information, but by using the image of the sheep harks back to the first half of the chapter and fits that image into the covenant formula: 'You my people, I your God.'

It can hardly be said that this passage is remarkable for definitiveness in division or for clarity of construction. Familiar features expressive of prophetic eschatological expectation come one on top of another, without any effort at completeness or systematic arrangement. They none the less throw some significant light on what was contained in the old traditions, and show how the prophet made use of them to express his deeper feelings.

[23f.] So in vv. 23f., the messianic hope of the pre-exilic prophets is taken up, yet depicted in a peculiar shape. The special problem in this passage consists in the unique way in which, once the full reasons have been given for Yahweh's decision himself to take over the office of being shepherd over his people, we are next informed of his intention to appoint his servant David as the one shepherd, who shall feed his people. Some regard this as a more or less outward accommodation of Ezekiel's fundamentally quite differently orientated hope of a deliverer to the traditional prophetic hope for a prince of peace from the house of David. The prophet himself would then have put him in a sort of bureaucratic striving after completeness, to conform on paper to official requirements, and the prince would really be a mere formality, or administrative measure, seeing that the one thing that really matters, the establishment of the new people, has been accomplished by God alone. Others find in the word *hēqîm*, employed for the setting up of the prince, the expression of the idea of the resurrection of king David from the dead. This may be accounted for by the general feeling in Israel of longing for an ideal ruler after God's own heart, such as David was. It is similar to the German people's expectation of the return of Barbarossa. After the fall of the Holy Roman Empire, the longings for its restoration clothed themselves in the shape of the return of the emperor Barbarossa from where, according to legend, he sat in the Kyffhäuser.

A third group tries to prove what renders these unconvincing suggestions superfluous by roundly denying the messianic character of the 'servant David' referred to here, and maintaining that all that is asserted here is the reinstatement of the old Davidic dynasty. As a result, the expression 'my servant David' is to be understood not individually, but collectively. Yet these recalled sons of David will have to content themselves with a much more modest station than the pre-exilic royal house.

To speak frankly, it is quite impossible to read all this out of the title *'ebed*, 'servant'. In the temporal order of precedence in a princely court, to begin with, the *'ebed* is a minister and trusted adviser to some king. But in the religious sphere the word denotes a specially preferential position among Yahweh's counsellors. Like Moses and other great leaders of the sacred community, David bears this title. But that does not make him the *'ebed par excellence*, in whom, at least for certain circles, Yahweh's past graciousness to Israel was to culminate, in a way never subsequently to be surpassed. Ever since the word spoken by Nathan in II Sam. 7, the Davidic dynasty had begun to be an integral part of Israel's hope of salvation, and the Davidic kings were always greeted at their accession as kings bringing salvation and distinguished by messianic attributes, as is clearly to be seen in the royal psalms, especially 2, 45 and 110. Every new son of David who succeeded to the throne could potentially be the messianic king who would bring salvation, if it should please Yahweh to choose him for that purpose. Isaiah and Micah did indeed predict in very harsh language the rejection of the Davidic house, but they still held on to the house of David's father, Jesse, and thought that the future deliverer would come from some contiguous branch of that house, so as to humble the pride of the Davidic dynasty and preserve God's freedom as to how the word spoken by him was to be fulfilled. Nevertheless, Jeremiah harked back to the old line, and felt able to speak of the *zemah zaddîq*, the righteous or genuine scion of David, whom Yahweh himself would raise up, Jer. 23.5f., where he chooses the same word as Ezekiel for the setting up of this king. Ezekiel, too, on his part shows how closely he agrees with Jeremiah in the way he takes up and accentuates this line of thought. 'My servant David' is therefore equivalent to 'my servant of the family of David', and has no connection whatever with any resurrection of the original David, a notion which is in any case completely alien to Israelite ways of thinking.

While, therefore, the title *'ebed* does not limit in any way the dignity of the expected ruler, the second title of *nāsî'* or prince is much better calculated to assert that dignity. Ezekiel usually reserves the title *melek* for the great king of Babylon, and gives the title *nāsî'* to the kings of smaller states, with the exception of the banished Jehoiachin, whom he always terms *melek*, evidently to emphasize the legitimacy of his claim to the throne of David, whereas Zedekiah, whom Nebuchadrezzar substituted for him, is in Ezekiel's eyes an illegitimate usurper. When, however, he employs the word *nāsī'* for the king of salvation bestowed by Yahweh upon the new people of Israel whom he has called into life, he does it to avoid using the title *melek*, which is similarly avoided by all his three predecessors, Isaiah, Micah and Jeremiah. The Canaanite origin of the title and its associations with despotism and absolute rule evidently created too strong a prejudice in the minds of these prophets against it to allow them to use a word so full of associations with an accursed past to denote the chosen of Yahweh, in whom all things, and with them the office of the ruler, were to become new.

Thus when one recollects the previous history of the word used to denote the coming king of salvation, then the word *nāsī'* in its present context does not in any way suggest anything lower in rank than king, but does suggest that the office of the ruler in the newly created fellowship of the people of God is something totally different in nature. Recollections of the tribal representative of the Israelite amphictyony are not entirely to be disregarded, since he bore the same title and officiated as the guardian of the divine covenant. But after the de-. scription we have just heard of how the true shepherd is to act, it is only too easy to see why there is such reluctance to speak of it in the language of political power. This future ruler is called to the laborious and responsible office of being a shepherd, one which he cannot fulfil without a great deal of self-sacrifice.

It is in harmony with this that the messianic ruler is to abstain from war or bloodshed in overcoming his enemies. As we have seen, this is a very characteristic feature of the whole of the future hope of the prophets. So in Ezekiel the future David does not appear on the scene until after Yahweh has accomplished the judgment and thus taken the decisive step to bring in the new age. Here the prophets have consciously gone back to the lines of the old popular hope, which described the future as a return to paradise, and so was able to speak of a king of paradise, who brings about paradisal peace not by figuring as a bloodstained warrior but by being the bringer of the garden of God, full of the rich products of nature and the peaceful pleasures that they afford. Genesis 49.8–12 and the utterances of Balaam in Num. 23.21; 24.6f., as also the Immanuel passage in Isa. 7.14ff., give eloquent testimony of this ancient ancestral hope. So the one who is here named the servant David does not act as a leader in battle carrying out judgment upon the nations in the way described in the royal psalms. The duties of his office as a ruler consist in the establishment and preservation of justice and righteousness, and that not only does not surprise us but serves rather to confirm his messianic character.

Seeing, then, that what Ezekiel promises is so largely in conformity with previous prophecy, this renders probable a totally different interpretation of the, at first sight, surprising installation of a prince of peace after Yahweh's emphatic assertion that he himself will be the shepherd of his people. No bureaucratic shift in administration is being resorted to here, nor is a subordinate shepherd being installed to play a necessarily superfluous part as compared to the supreme shepherd. On the contrary, he who is to come is much more intimately associated with Yahweh, and more definitely taken into his divine being than any other has been hitherto. All the things previously stated about help and deliverance by Yahweh are now carried out by his servant as his earthly plenipotentiary and representative. One can see Yahweh himself at work in this servant, and thus be assured of his effectual and saving nearness among his people. So the whole of the stress is laid on the way in which the other-worldly God actually approaches his own, in his real presence. This God expresses his humanity, his will to have the most intimate personal fellowship with his people, by the very fact that he exercises his own office of shepherding through his servant. So at this point one needs to recall one isolated passage in the Priestly writing, Gen. 1.26f., which speaks of man as being the image of God. Consequently, what Ezekiel chiefly means by this servant David is that he is to be regarded as the fully reconstituted image of God, in whom the will of God, already expressed in creation, for the very closest fellowship in nature with the most excellent of all his earthly creation, is finally brought into effect. The closer one finds Ezekiel in this and other respects to the great principles of the priestly interpretation of the world, the more one should feel inclined to credit him with such a view, even though he may not state it in set terms.

In any case, one cannot invalidate the unique majesty of the coming one either by appealing to 21.32, an enigmatic passage on the interpretation of which opinions still diverge greatly (see above, pp. 306ff.), nor yet by bringing in the *nāsī'* mentioned in ch. 44–46 in order to supply an explanation. What is actually referred to there is not an individual, but a whole succession of rulers of the Davidic dynasty, so if one refuses to recognize that the present passage is a messianic prophecy, then an explicit or implicit appeal to that passage must serve as the chief determining factor. But we shall be ignoring the great material differences between ch. 34–37 and 44ff. and putting completely heterogeneous matters on one level if we insist on identifying the ecclesiastical figure of the *nāsî'* who has become a hierarch of the last chapters of the book of Ezekiel with the one whom we find here and in ch. 37. We shall return to the subject later.

Our interpretation of v. 23 is confirmed by the way in which v. 24 inserts the installation of the 'servant David' in the words of the old covenant formula, thus showing it to be an integral part of the new covenant: 'I, Yahweh, will be their God, and my servant David shall be prince among them.' The second half of the covenant formula 'and they shall be my people' has evidently been omitted deliberately, because the only matter of principal concern is the supreme blessing conferred by the personal presence of the prince of peace. So at this point all that is added is the 'I, Yahweh, have spoken', which affirms that such is Yahweh's will. The full covenant formula is therefore used in v. 30 to conclude the whole section. The new shepherd is the only one who is installed. That is thoroughly in keeping with his duty to act as the accredited representative of the sovereignty of God, but it also serves in addition to express how entire the unity of the new Israel will be, as we see from 37.22.

For the blessings enumerated in vv. 25–29, parallels can be found at every point in the future hope of earlier prophets. Evidently Ezekiel has no intention of adding anything fresh, yet once more his formulations are of special interest. [25] Verse 25 tells of the concluding of the new covenant, the content of which is for the moment limited to the destruction or driving out of wild beasts by v. 26b. Naturally the covenant mentioned in Hos. 2.18 between Yahweh and the beasts, as a result of which they put away their wildness and become friends with mankind, furnishes an attractive parallel to this limitation of the covenant here. But it is a misleading one! For if one translates the expression whose wording is identical with that in Hos. 2.18 as it is translated there, 'I will make a covenant in favour of you', then the partner with whom God is to conclude the covenant is wanting here. Hosea names as partners to this covenant 'the beasts of the field, the birds of the air, and the creeping things of

the ground', so he raises the beasts to the same level as men as par-
takers in a covenant, by which they lay aside their wildness. This is
undoubtedly a primitive idea, not invented by Hosea, but taken
over from tradition. The same idea recurs in Gen. 9.9f., where men
and beasts are the contracting parties in the covenant with Noah;
we certainly must admit that here the priestly author was going back
to an ancient tradition.

Ezekiel evidently refrains from naming any such partner in the
covenant, because it does not accord with his thought. It also sounds
very extraordinary to make a covenant with the beasts which leads
to their being driven out of the land. In the event of a covenant being
concluded with them, one would rather expect the beasts to retire
from the land of their own accord, or else to change their nature
and become man's play-fellows in the way depicted in Isa. 11, 6–8.
The consideration carries still more weight, seeing that the covenant
that is concluded is entitled a $b^e r \bar{\imath} t$ $\check{s} \bar{a} l \bar{o} m$, a covenant of salvation: the
beasts, if partners in this covenant, would feel very little of the said
salvation; their banishment by the power of Yahweh does not, however, require any covenant, but is a sovereign act on the part of God
the Creator. If anyone appeals to the fact that immediately before
the covenant with beasts Hosea speaks of the new betrothal between
Yahweh and Israel, and that therefore an exhaustive picture of all
the aspects of the new covenant is to be unfolded, then it is most
probable that the covenant of salvation must be limited to Israel and
that the mode of speech employed here and in other passages (I Sam.
11.2; II Sam. 5.3) refers to the members of the people of God as
partners in the covenant: 'I will make a covenant of salvation with
them.' One may find an indirect confirmation of this in Deutero-
Isaiah, where the servant of God chosen by God is described as himself bringing in a new covenant with Israel. So the sequence 'servant
David—covenant of salvation' is seen to be quite appropriate.

Here we should notice the mode of expression chosen by Ezekiel.
He imploys the old form $k \bar{a} r a t$ $b e r \bar{\imath} t$, whereas the Priestly writing in
the Pentateuch has as one of its well-known distinguishing points its
use of the alternative term $h \bar{e} q \bar{\imath} m$ $b e r \bar{\imath} t$, to set up a covenant, by which
the covenant is transformed out of a mutual contractual relationship
between God and man into an institutional relationship, which puts
man from the outset in the position of a receiver who is graciously
treated apart from any co-operation on his part. So Ezekiel's avoidance of a phrase so thoroughly in keeping with his modes of thought

gives us yet another example of his remarkable independence in regard to the priestly forms of speech with which he so often complies on other occasions.

Verses 25b–28 speak of dwelling securely in the land, and of its wonderful fertility, as among the blessings resulting from the making of the covenant. These features of salvation are also found in Hos. 2.21f.; Isa. 29.17ff.; 32.15ff.; Jer. 31.4ff.; 32.40ff. as an integral part of the future hope, except that in Hosea it is seen to be an action by heaven and earth in obedience to God's manifestations of grace, while in Isaiah it takes the form of the transformation of the earth into the garden of paradise. These images of salvation clothed in the language of myth are already regarded by Jeremiah as no longer suitable for use; he speaks in much more sober terms of the fruitfulness of a land that is to be resettled and repopulated after a period of desolation. **[26f.]** Ezekiel, too, refrains from following Isaiah, and speaks of the seasonable showers of rain which fertilize the land so that the trees of the field yield their fruit and the earth its increase (v. 27). **[28]** The same applies to his description of how the people come to dwell securely in the land; it is not brought about, as in Isa. 2.4 and Hos. 2.18, by the destruction of weapons and their transformation into implements of peaceful labour, but by the breaking of the bars of their yoke (an image known to Isaiah also, cf. 9.4) and deliverance from the hand of their oppressors, that is to say the removal of their present state of slavery. If one takes along with that the previous mention of the banishment of wild beasts from the land, then the mythical picture seems to be replaced by a highly nationalistic description of a peaceful and fertile homeland in which the sudden disappearance of the wild beasts and the reduction to harmlessness of foreign foes seems like a direct miracle performed by God. **[25b]** Yet the complete transformation of nature, of which Isaiah speaks, is re-echoed in the assertion that men will dwell securely in the wilderness and be able to sleep in the woods, which seems to involve the terrible thirsty wilderness becoming a fruitful field and the woods with their dens of wild beasts turning into vegetable gardens, in the way already described in Isa. 32.15.

It is, however, significant that Ezekiel, simple as are the lines of his picture of salvation, does not accord with Jeremiah, but to a large extent expresses himself in the form of speech of the priestly law, and in particular that of the Holiness Code in Lev. 17.26. The statements coincide, often word for word, with Lev. 25.18f. and Lev. 26.4–6, 13,

22, and the context shows that they describe the sort of blessings that will fall on a people who are faithful to the law. Far-reaching conclusions have been drawn from this: some regard the association between the proclamation of salvation and an act of judgment by Yahweh, such as is undoubtedly described in the first half of ch. 34, as proving that Ezekiel has adopted a formula similar to that in Lev. 26, which was customarily used at the covenant festival. The blessings and curses regularly repeated afresh at every covenant festival would then have been given a fixed shape in the words of a fixed liturgical office. It must be realized, however, that there are no curses in the prophet's announcements of salvation, but words of blessing nullifying the corresponding curses. Take, for example, v. 28: 'You shall no more be a prey to the nations, nor shall the wild beasts of the land devour you', answers to the old curses: 'You shall be a prey to the nations, and the wild beasts of the land shall devour you.' The phrases are actually found in Leviticus, but the prophet converts them into the opposite. Yet it is impossible to find a malediction in Leviticus to correspond to each of the prophetic benedictions, and one of Ezekiel's favourite and most frequently used expressions, 'the reproach of the nations', does not occur there at all. All this goes to show that Ezekiel's movements here are free and unencumbered, in spite of wearing the garb of priestly speech.

That does not mean, of course, that we ought to make little of the agreements which are proved actually to exist. They are one further indication of the prophet's inclination to use the language of the law which had been familiar to him from his youth. But to admit that does not involve the conclusion that proclaiming salvation meant to Ezekiel nothing more than 'a prophet's commission bound to and formed by the historical conditions', which demanded that, after proclaiming the demands of the law at the covenant festival, he should also announce the decision of the covenant God in his capacity of divine judge in the form of an act of execution of judgment, after which Ezekiel, as the official pronouncer of law and judgment at the covenant festival, would state the rewards for obedient members of the covenant in the old traditional forms.

It seems to us that here, as when the prophet was commissioned to act as a watchman, his intensely personal prophetic speech, which tries to let the newly imposed commission give shape to the words, and makes use of earlier forms of preaching in a characteristically autocratic way, is suddenly seized and pressed into an antique suit of armour, that of an official formula, which robs him of all freedom of movement and does not allow him to say anything that has not been said already. It is a poor consolation to be informed that this silenced once for all the doubts that were so usual over the prophet's message of salvation. The price thus paid seems too high. It seems so indubitable that a completely independent type of preaching cut through all the traditional forms and threw out to the audience the hitherto unheard of news of the new way in which God was moving to create a new covenant people, that we are compelled to make a completely different estimate of what is signified by the use of the legal terminology. We need only recall how Ezekiel takes for granted that Israel will be totally and ruthlessly exterminated. That one simple fact puts an end to all ritual, however venerable; one could not when in a state of exile just go on reading out the old formularies as if nothing had happened. That ritual belonged to the covenant with God which the judgment had invalidated. What can it mean to say that God is now going to conclude a new covenant, when the priestly law regards the eternal covenant as a contract between God and Israel which cannot be set aside? To a priestly judgment any talk of a new covenant must necessarily appear to be nothing short of a blasphemy. The priestly redactors who worked over ch. 16 would not have had to make such a frantic effort in v. 60 to interpret the inauguration of the new covenant as being a re-enactment of the eternal covenant had it not been so.

Accordingly, while one may give all due attention to the traditional forms of speech employed by the prophet, one ought not simply to ignore, but should do justice to, the freedom with which he departs from the priestly vocabulary. We cannot enter into detail here, but we may mention one additional example, which occurs in v. 29 in connection with the *maṭṭaʿ šālōm*. **[29]** This plantation of salvation, or peace, this garden in which *šālōm* dwells and which has a correlative in the *berīt šālōm* of v. 25, presents an exact parallel to Isa. 32.15–18, where the wilderness is represented as being changed into a fruitful field. There, says Isaiah, justice and righteousness will dwell, and their fruit will be peace and everlasting safety; then he adds, 'My people will dwell in a peaceful habitation in secure dwellings and in quiet resting places.' It is hard to find anything which better illustrates what is meant by Ezekiel's 'garden of peace' than this passage. Deutero-Isaiah has once more taken up the same thought and must be replacing it in its original context when he says of Zion in 51.3: 'Yahweh will make her wilderness like Eden and her desert like the garden of Yahweh. Joy and gladness shall be found in her, thanksgiving and the voice of song.' So it is the old, old expectation of paradise regained which still lives on in Ezekiel's brief catchword *maṭṭaʿ šālōm*, and clearly shows his links with prophetic hope, in spite of his frequent echoes of the sacral law.

[30] The whole series of rich blessings reaches its climax in the recognition that the covenant between God and people is once more established; v. 30 therefore concludes with the full covenant formula. This recurs in various other passages in Ezekiel, especially in 36.28; 37.23, 27; but also as early as 11.20 and 14.11. This formula is, of course, found in Lev. 26.12, but it also occurs in Jeremiah, and no less than seven times. That makes it hardly a sufficient proof of a connection with the language of the priestly formularies; it is much more probable that it is a product of the striking popularity and wide extension of the idea of the covenant after the Josiah reform of 621, when the king, as a result of the finding of the book of the covenant in the temple, entered along with the whole people into a solemn vow to observe the covenant. What was not effected on that occasion, the revivification of the old covenant by a reformation in head and members, is what Yahweh is going to bring about under a completely new form at the turning-point of the times. So in stating this the words 'my people' are solemnly completed and explained by the words 'house of Israel': the house of rebelliousness having ceased to exist, the old honorific title regains its validity.

[31] Verse 31 with its various explanatory glosses, which are not yet present in the LXX, must be an addition, since the preceding 'says Yahweh' prohibits all additional elaborations. The object of the insertion was evidently merely to identify the flock of the parable in the first half of the chapter in an explicit way with the people of God and thus to safeguard the unity of the whole chapter.

CHAPTER 35.1–15

The threat against Mount Seʿir

1 The word of Yahweh came to me: 2ʿSon of man, set your face against Mount Seʿir and prophesy against it 3and say to it: Thus says [. . .]ᵃ

Yahweh: Behold, I will come to you, Mount Se'ir, and will stretch out my hand against you, and will make you a terrible waste. ⁴I will turn your cities into ruins and you shall become a desolation and you shall know that I am Yahweh.

5 Because you cherished perpetual enmity, and gave over the people of Israel to the sword at the time of their calamity, at the time of their final punishment, ⁶therefore as I live says [. . .]ᵇ Yahweh [. . .]:ᶜ of a truth you have been guilty of blood,ᵈ so blood shall pursue you. ⁷[. . .]ᵉ ⁸And I will fill yourᶠ mountains with the slain, on your hills and in your valleys and ravines, those slain with the sword shall fall. ⁹I will make you a perpetual desolationᵍ and your cities shall be uninhabited and youʰ shall know that I am Yahweh.

10 Because you said, "These two nations and these two countries shall be mine and Iⁱ will take possession of them", although Yahweh is there, ¹¹therefore, as I live, says [. . .]ʲ Yahweh, I will deal with youᵏ according to the anger and rage in which you dealt with them in your hatred, and I will make myself known to youˡ when I judge you. ¹²And you shall know that I Yahweh have heard all the revilings which you uttered against the mountains of Israel, saying they are laid desolate, they are given us to devour. ¹³And you magnified yourselves against me with your mouth and spoke impudent wordsᵐ against me. I heard it. ¹⁴Thus says [. . .]ⁿ Yahweh: "As you rejoiced over my land, because it was desolate, so I will deal with you."ᵒ ¹⁵[. . .]ᵖ You shall be desolate, Mount Se'ir, and all Edom shall be a destruction. Then they will know that I am Yahweh.'

ᵃ⁻ᵇSee BH.

ᶜMT: 'therefore into blood will I make you and blood shall pursue you', is not a suitable continuation of the adjuration; it anticipates the second half of the verse, and is not found in LXX and other versions.

ᵈSee BH.

ᵉMT: 'And I will make Mount Se'ir a terrible waste and will cut off from it all who come and go.' Noticeable for the switch to the third person plural and the word-for-word repetition of the close of v. 3. The verse could only properly be placed after v. 8, but there it is rendered unnecessary by v. 9.

ᶠ⁻ⁿSee BH.

ᵒ⁻ᵖThe phrase which is mutilated and thus meaningless in the MT has been displaced by a correction which probably originally stood in the margin, but has made its way into the text in 15a. So it may be corrected as follows: ¹⁵As you rejoiced over the inheritance of the house of Israel, because it was desolate, so will I deal with you.

At first sight it may seem surprising that a somewhat lengthy threat against the neighbouring country of Edom on Mount Se'ir should be seen here apparently interrupting the proclamation of the salvation of the future. But this threat has a definite function of its own within the context: it eliminates the opponent who may try to prevent the new creation of the house of Israel, by trying to occupy and seize possession of the temporarily ownerless territory which Israel is to inherit. In 33.24 those who had remained in the land claimed the right to possess it, and refused to recognize that those deported to Babylon any longer had a right to dwell in their ancestral home and had their claim refuted. Now the same treatment is given to the threats of violence from this neighbouring people, who claim that they are to inherit what Israel has left. The faithfulness of the Lord God to his chosen people is shown also by his giving them as their own that same land which they had made use of in order to apostasize from their liege lord, so he now gives it back to them, in order that it may now realize the purpose he determined for it.

[1-4] So this utterance, which is constructed in three sections, first addresses Mount Se'ir and recalls the enmity between the two neighbouring nations. Verses 1-4 announce, without giving any why or wherefore, that the mountain homeland of the Edomites which lies to the east of the rift of the Arabah stretching from the Dead Sea to the gulf of Akaba will be reduced to complete desolation. Its cities will be laid in ruins and its arable lands reduced to desert, so that Yahweh may be recognized for what he is, the sole controller and determiner of the destinies of nations.

As it seems implied by this that this aspect of his activity has been hitherto ignored, the second section, vv. 5-9, affirms that Yahweh's control over the nations is not exercised capriciously, but according to the principles of justice. [5] The long-standing enmity between the two nations had led Edom, in the very time when Israel was suffering a terrible disaster as a final retribution for her iniquity, to give free rein to her passionate feelings and to take every opportunity to deliver the hated foe to the Babylonian sword. In Obadiah 10ff. this is told in greater detail, and Ps. 137.7 refers to the way in which Edom co-operated in the destruction of Jerusalem. [6] Since blood that is unjustly shed cries for vengeance (Gen. 4.10), these blood-thirsty deeds cry for retribution, or the blood pursues the person guilty of shedding it, as the bold phrase puts it. [8] It brings about the onset of bands of warriors bent on slaughter. They move down upon Edom, and fill her mountains and valleys with the slain. [9] But the divine avenger will make sure that no one is left to dwell in the de-populated land and that it remains a perpetual desolation. In distinction to the ill wishes expressed in 25.12–14, which these words recall, not only is the perpetual enmity recalled here, but also the especially shameful act of betraying her ally to their common foe, yet the vengeance for it is not left to Israel, but reserved to the only just judge.

The third section, vv. 10–15, goes still deeper, in describing Edom's crime as consisting in an act of trespass upon the property of Yahweh. [10] They believe that they may take possession of Israel's home as being one ownerless piece of land, which means that they may also commit aggression on the territory of north Israel, but they forget that Yahweh has not given up his claim to possess the land, even though he has sent his people away into banishment from it. [11] The God of Israel is still holding out his hands to guard the deserted land, therefore he will make Edom feel his mighty presence by bringing her under his judgment. [12] The words in which the men of Mount Seʿir expressed their contempt for the desolate territory of Israel still stand to witness against those who spoke to them that they showed little regard for what belonged to God, as if the laying waste of the mountains of Israel gave them a right to take free seizure of whatever appealed to them. Ezekiel may have been informed by the fugitive of these evidences of Edomite arrogance, when he brought him the first detailed account of conditions in the homeland. [13] These arrogant boasters are like wild beasts about to rush down on their prey, but the real owner of the land has heard their revilings and has a suitable response ready for them. They have mercilessly driven out God's own people from the promised land, but they have totally misinterpreted his holy will and his judgment if they think this means that the God of Israel is powerless to protect his own possession. In this Edomite arrogance rises to blasphemy, and their attempt to enrich themselves shows open contempt for Yahweh's control over his own land. [14f.] So this piece of aggression will be rebutted in such a thorough way that the men of Mount Seʿir will recognize that even in executing his judgments Yahweh reserves to himself the right to deal with what is his own. Palestine is still Yahweh's land, which he alone can give away, and which he does not allow to be seized by any plunderer. Anyone who dares to lay hand on it will bring destruction upon himself.

CHAPTER 36.1–15

The promise to the mountains of Israel

1 'And you, son of man, prophesy to the mountains of Israel and say: You mountains of Israel, hear the word of Yahweh. 2Thus says [. . .]ᵃ Yahweh: because the enemy said of you: "Aha, a perpetual desolation!ᵇ It is given to us for a possession", 3therefore prophesy and say: Thus says [. . .]ᶜ Yahweh: Because they rejoiceᵈ and lay traps for you on all sides, so that you may become a possession for the rest of the nations, and become the talk and evil gossip of the people 4[. . .]ᵉ 5therefore thus says [. . .]ᶠ Yahweh: I speak in my hot jealousy against the rest of the nations and against Edom, against all who have given my land to themselves as a possession in whole-hearted joy and utter contempt [. . .]ᵍ 6Therefore prophesy concerning the arable land of Israel and say to the mountains and hills, to the ravines and valleys: Thus says [. . .]ʰ Yahweh: Behold I speak in my jealousy and wrath because you must suffer the reproach of the nations¹ 7[. . .]ʲ I lift up my hand in an oath: of a truth the nations that dwell about you shall themselves suffer their reproach. 8But you, O mountains of Israel, shall shoot forth your branches and yield their fruit to my people Israel, for they will soon come home. 9For behold I draw near to you and turn to you and you shall be tilled and sown. 10[. . .]ᵏ 11And I will multiply upon you man and beast [. . .]ˡ And I will make you populous as in your former times and will do more good to you than at your beginning, and you shall know that I am Yahweh. 12And I will let men walk upon you, my people Israel, they shall possess you and you shall be their inheritance and you shall no longer bereave them of children, says Yahweh,'ᵐ 13–15[. . .]ⁿ

ᵃ⁻ᵈSee BH.

ᵉMT: 'Therefore, you mountains of Israel, hear the word [. . .] of Yahweh: Thus says [. . .] Yahweh, about both mountains and hills, about the ravines and valleys, the desolate ruins and deserted cities, which have become a prey and derision to the rest of the nations round about.' This fresh interpolation into the announcement of the word of Yahweh stated in v. 3 once more sums up the thoughts in the surrounding verses and attempts to describe the land as a whole.

ᶠSee BH.

ᵍMT: 'because of their banishing for plundering'; the text is unintelligible here.
ʰSee BH.

¹Verse 6, which actually only repeats v. 5 without developing any further ideas, looks suspiciously like a repetitive gloss.

ʲMT: 'Therefore thus says (the Lord) Yahweh' should not be retained in view
of the immediately preceding announcement.

ᵏMT: v. 10, 'I will multiply men upon you, the whole house of Israel all of it,
and the cities shall be inhabited and the waste places rebuilt.' An inferior variant
of v. 11.

ˡMT: 'And they shall be fruitful and multiply'; a quotation from the blessing
at creation in Gen. 1, not found in LXX.   ᵐEnding as in v. 15.

ⁿMT: ¹³'Thus says (the Lord) Yahweh: because men say to you, you devour
men and deprive your nation of children, ¹⁴therefore you shall no longer devour
men and no longer bereave your nation of children, says Yahweh. ¹⁵And I will no
more hear of the reproach of the nations against you, and you shall no longer have
to bear the mockery of the peoples, and you shall no longer bereave your own
people of their children, says (the Lord) Yahweh.' A double addition which turns
the last words of v. 12 into the theme of a special promise. Verse 12, which is often
deleted instead, contains the two expressions 'people Israel' and 'inheritance' which
are affirmations indispensable for a promise to the mountains of Israel, and form
the proper climax to all that has gone before.

The fate of the mountains of Israel forms a contrast to that of Mount
Seʿir, and is equally unexpected and contrary to all human calculations, such as could be observed in the neighbouring country. On the
one side is the proud self-assurance of one who has had the good fortune to come unscathed through all the perils of war, and now fancies
that he is secure and contrives elaborate plots to bring the helpless
victims of the war under his dominion, and thus secure the increase
of power which seems at this moment ready to fall into the lap of
anyone who is cunning enough in his calculations. On the other side
we see a country depopulated and to a large extent laid waste by war,
with its villages burnt down and its cities in ruin. It seems defenceless, and given away to its neighbours, seeing how the Babylonian
rulers of the province have allowed them to make use of whatever
districts they covet, in order to bring them once more under cultivation. It seems quite obvious what the natural result will be of a
defeat so destructive to Israel, but what does happen is entirely unexpected. The highlands of Seʿir, which seemed to be beginning a
period of prosperity, will lose all the trump cards they think they hold
and suffer devastation through war, which will deprive them of all
power of recovery. The highlands of Israel, which seemed to have lost
all power of recovery, will survive to enjoy a period of unexpected
prosperity, to the disappointment of her adversaries, and to the
incredulous amazement of her exiled inhabitants.

In this intense contrast between what happens to the two neighbouring countries, Ezekiel sees the work of the unseen controller of

history. He acts by laws totally different to those taken for granted by
political calculators, as he brings his sovereign plans to accomplishment amid the turmoil in which the nations encounter each other.
The prophet is fully aware of how incredible such an announcement
is, so in the first half of 36.1–15 he piles up instances of what the
neighbours have said with all the cocksureness of their calculations, in
phrases which follow so hard on each other's heels as almost to prevent those expressing the will of his God from being heard. That is
because it is precisely this habit of taking for granted the obvious
truth of purely worldly calculations which has to be unmasked as the
chief error of man in the face of this God. If one takes 36.1–12 as the
staging of a trial and the pronouncing of a sentence, then many of
what seemed at first sight objectionable repetitions will be seen to
form part of the 'ceremonial of an official court of law' (Reventlow)
with its solemn proclamations, repetitive descriptions of the parties
and of their legal pleadings, a renewed announcement of the intervention of the judge, and then the concluding formulation in v. 7 of
the 'verdict' in the language of sacral law.

Scholars have long been struck by all the details given of the
mockery to which Israel's old homeland is subjected by the 'rest of
the nations' (v. 3), i.e. the states that survive after the severe devastation by war which Palestine and Syria have undergone. They mock
at it with uninhibited self-assurance, and Edom, of course, plays the
chief part (v. 5). [2f.] They speak joyfully of the perpetual desolation
of the land, which they believe to lie wide open to their attack; they
refer to the land in their mockery and their plotting, they are full of
joy at seeing its misery, and show the greatest contempt from Israel's
once proud possession. But the point of this is taken away if one
thinks that this reproach repeated in so many variations has no
motive except Israel's sensitive honour, which pride in her great past
caused to react violently against the shame cast upon her name. The
ugly reality which stands behind the mockery is the wish to see Israel
destroyed and reduced to final and utter hopelessness, so that, having
been uprooted and deprived of all reconstructive power, it might be
left as a ruin of no value on the battlefield of history. So the words of
mockery are so many maledictions intended to evoke and intensify
the destructive powers so that disaster may lay all level with the
ground.

[6f.] But such a wish to eradicate Israel from her place in the
common life of the nations amounts to trespassing on the limits of

vengeance permitted to man and to attack God's majesty as judge. So his justice, following the severe *jus talionis*, the foundation principle of which we can read in Ex. 21.23–25, will lay upon these same neighbours of Israel's the heavy load which they had hoped to see overwhelming the people of God.

[5, 12] From another aspect also, the ill-wishes against the devastated land bring guilt upon those responsible for them: they are fundamentally opposed to God's own rights. It is not in vain that God speaks of Palestine as 'my land' (v. 5), and therefore to covet the possession of it is an intrusion upon his property rights. This thought is forcibly expressed in v. 12, which contains the decisive words 'my people Israel' and 'their inheritance'. Human enmity and vengefulness is setting itself into opposition to God's plan for the history of his people. It is his will to be gracious to his people and to reinstate them, and so he is keeping this land ready for that purpose. He had indeed put it under the same curse as its people and had cut off the roots through which it received life from the gifts and forces of nature, but he accepts it once more as his and reopens the full stream of life from his gifts of creation. Here we see the second contrast, that between this passage and the curse pronounced in ch. 6 upon the mountains of Israel, which put an end to the misuse of the divine forces of life in nature. The reinstated people is granted a new foundation for their life in their land, where they are to have experience of how serving their God involves a new communion with the Creator.

[8–11] Verse 8 therefore describes how the law shoots up and bears fruit, so as to put on festive decorations to celebrate the return of its inhabitants; v. 9 describes how it is tilled and sown; v. 10 how men and beasts flourish, and v. 11 how they are fruitful and multiply. Yet in all these events it is God himself who is the subject; it is his drawing near which makes the forces of fertility flow out of the land, in such a way that they no longer constitute any temptation to serve nature-gods, but form a picture, never to be blotted out, of the goodness of the one Creator of all. The new knowledge of Yahweh which is declared to result from this blessing is very much in place here. Not until after this connection has been made between the land and the people will those who are spoken of in ch. 34 as being brought back from exile know themselves once more to be the new 'house of Israel', who have taken possession of their 'inheritance', out of which no one may drive them again (v. 12).

[12] At the end of v. 12 the words 'and you shall no longer bereave

them of children' sound out, and directly express a very grim view of
the land, regarding it as a sort of monster which devours its own
inhabitants. This view is referred to in a derogatory sense as coming
from the mouths of those who returned from spying the land (Num.
13.32) and in the covenantal cursing (Lev. 26.38); it is associated
with the land of their enemies, to which the breakers of the covenant
are to be banished. **[13–15]** So here, in the position where one would
least expect to find it in view of all that has preceded it, it seems to
serve as a transition to vv. 13–15, in which the statement that the
land devours men is carried to a fresh climax in the mockery of the
nations, but is wholly to vanish as a result of the new relationship
between people and land. As the verses referred to fail to conform to
the attitude shown throughout the whole promise and do not address
the mountains, but the land as if it were a feminine personification,
they must necessarily be regarded as an addition, which has interfered with the original conclusion of v. 12, where the prophetic concluding formula, 'says Yahweh', might be expected.

CHAPTER 36.16–38
The new creation of Israel

16 And the word of Yahweh came to me: 17'Son of man, when the
house of Israel were still dwelling in their own land, they defiled it by their
ways and their doings; their conduct before me was the monthly uncleanness of a woman. 18And I poured out my wrath upon them [. . .]ª 19and
I scattered them among the nations and [dispersed]ᵇ them through the
countries, in accordance with their conduct and their deeds I judged
them. 20But wherever theyᶜ came among the nations, there they profaned
my holy name, in that men said of them, "These are the people of Yahweh,
and yet they had to go out of his land." 21But I had concern for my holy
name, which the house of Israel caused to be profaned among the nations
to which they came.

22 Therefore say to the house of Israel: Thus says [. . .]ᵈ Yahweh: It
is not for your sake, O house of Israel, that I am about to act, but for the
sake of my holy name, which you have profaned among the nations to
which you came. 23And I will vindicate the holiness of my name, which
has been profaned among the nations [. . .],ᵉ and the nations will know
that I am Yahweh [. . .],ᶠ when I shall be sanctified in you before their
eyes.

24 And I will take you from the nations and gather you from all the countries and bring you into your land. 25And I will sprinkle clean water upon you that you may become clean. From all your uncleanness and from your idols will I cleanse you. 26And I will give you a new heart and a new spirit I will put within you, and I will take out of your flesh the heart of stone and give you a heart of flesh. 27And I will put my spirit within you, and cause you to walk in my statutes and to observe and fulfil my laws, 28and you shall dwell in the land which I gave to your fathers, and shall be my people, and I will be your God.

29 And I will deliver you from all your uncleanness and I will summon the grain and make it abundant and lay no famine upon you. 30And I will make the fruit of the tree and the increase of the field abundant, that you may never again suffer the disgrace of famine among the heathen. 31Then you will remember your evil ways, and your deeds that were not good, and you will loathe yourselves for your iniquities and your abominable deeds. 32It is not for your sake that I will act, says [. . .]ᵍ Yahweh, let that be known to you. Be ashamed and bear your disgrace for your ways, O house of Israel.

33 Thus says [. . .]ʰ Yahweh: On the day that I cleanse you from all your iniquities, I will cause the cities to be inhabited and the ruins shall be rebuilt, 34and the land that was desolate shall be tilled, instead of being the desolation that it was in the light of all who passed by. 35And they will say: This land that was desolate has become like the garden of Eden. And these cities that lay in ruin and were deserted and destroyed are now fortified and inhabited. 36And the nations that are left round about you shall know that I, Yahweh, rebuild the ruined places, and replant that which was desolate. I, Yahweh, have said it and will also do it.

37Thus says.[. . .]ⁱ Yahweh: This also I will be moved by the entreaties of the house of Israel to do for them: I will increase them like a flock of sheep [. . .]ʲ, 38like the flock for sacrifices, like the sheep at Jerusalem during her appointed feasts, so shall the cities that now lie in ruin be full of [. . .]ᵏ men, and they will know that I am Yahweh.'

ᵃMT: 'Because of the blood, which they had shed in the land, and with their idols had they defiled it.' This short sentence, in a bad style, is not found in the LXX and gives a brief and late characterization of the besetting sins of Israel.

ᵇIt is better to restore the first person singular, following LXX, instead of the plural passive.

ᶜ–ᵈSee BH.

ᵉ'Which you had profaned among them'; intensifies the previous statement, but is a superfluous repetition.

ᶠ–ⁱSee BH.

ʲMT: 'Men'; a gloss intended to prevent misunderstanding, as is shown by its position in the sentence.

ᵏMT: 'Sheep' cannot be justified either by translating it 'human sheep' or 'flocks of men', as it is the result of an ugly attempt to include the metaphor in the newly created reality.

The basis and aim of the new divine creation: 36.16-23

In order to introduce the central divine act of the new creation, the prophet once more looks back over the hopelessly disastrous history of his people. What the more despairing of his fellow countrymen say (cf. 24.23; 33.10) is right: if Yahweh only is the righteous judge, then nothing can be expected to happen but for the nation to disappear in a heathen land. The greatest blessing bestowed upon the chosen people, their being provided with such a glorious country, has been defiled and made valueless. [17] For the defilement and destruction of this gift of God, Ezekiel employs the word *ṭimmē*', 'to make unclean', which is derived from sacral law. He thus takes a cultic term and applies it not only to cultic sins, as, for example, in 20.30f., but also in the more general sense of showing contempt for God's holiness by breaking his commandments. [18] The inheritance of Yahweh, the land, being the place where he is present in Israel, ought to have been treated with special reverence, but as a place in which disgusting sin has been committed it has become an object of loathing to God, a part of the accursed world on which he turns his back.

It is very interesting to note the shape which the retribution for the profanation and defilement of the holy land is described as taking: it does not take the form of self-destruction automatically following sin, proceeding by its own autonomous rules, in the way stated upon occasion in the old laws, which declare that a defiled land vomits forth its inhabitants (Lev. 18.25, 28; 20.22) or devours them (Num. 13.32; cf. Lev. 26.38), or refuses to yield them its produce (Gen. 4.11f.; Deut. 28.39ff.; Lev. 25.2, 4; cf. 26.34). Much attention has been paid to this 'synthetic view of life', which has its origin in primitive taboos, and it is at times appealed to so as to cast doubt on whether there is any such thing as judicial retribution by God in the Old Testament.[1] In Israel, however, it was replaced at a very early stage by Yahweh's personal action of carrying out punishment, in a way which is expressed with particular distinctness by the prophets. So in the connection between sin and punishment we do not find any impersonal judicial process, but a completely personal reaction on the

[1]K. Koch, 'Gibt es ein Vergeltungsdogma im Alten Testament?' *ZThK*, 1955, pp. 1ff.

part of Yahweh against the injury and dishonour committed against him. [19] He pours out his wrath upon Israel (v. 18) and scatters her among the nations. We even hear in 20.26 that it is he who on his part profanes the wicked people and casts it out into that accursed part of the world which it had hitherto been able to avoid, thanks to being situated in a land which had been consecrated by God.

[20] As a result, of course, God is forced to allow his name to be put to shame by the heathen, as it is when they witness what he has done to punish his own people. For there is no way in which they can explain his abandonment of his own people except by saying that it only serves to show the helplessness of Israel's God in face of the heathen nations, in whose names the heathen world empire has triumphed. To feel that this throws shame upon the holy name of God involves taking for granted as a premiss the universality of God's sovereignty, a point which is much too often overlooked in Ezekiel. Evidently it was originally the will of God that he should have a prosperous and blessed people, the name of whose God the heathen would pronounce with awe and reverence. Here, as in 5.5ff., we meet with a world-wide obligation imposed upon Israel according to Yahweh's plan; her fellowship with God was to throw a bright light out into the world around her. Israel's sanctification of the name of God by her obedience to this obligation was to witness clearly to God's life-giving election and thus to establish the knowledge of God in the heathen world. But now the history of God's dealings with Israel, instead of moving towards this objective, had moved in the opposite direction: profanation had taken the place of sanctification, and clear witness to God had been replaced by the scandal of a God reduced to helplessness.

[21] Here something more is at stake than the mere misfortunes of man, who is so inclined to put himself at the central point of world events and to look on his own ill luck as providing him with the halo of a hero of tragedy. Israel for her part needs to learn that she is not God's spoilt darling to whose complaints God is always ready to give an indulgent hearing; she must realize that there are other and higher objects than her own feelings of well-being. She has indeed been chosen in preference to all other nations, and has had unique experience of God's love. Yet, although that divine love is higher, more faithful and more steadfast than mothers love, it is still always a corrective love, i.e. it cannot help man except by drawing him back out of the wrong paths he takes to the proper position designated for

him by God's creative will, the place in which he will serve towards bringing about God's world-wide kingdom, in which for the first time he will really rediscover himself and realize the meaning of his life.

This means that all his salvation, liberation and redemption does not consist in satisfying his own desires but in surrendering himself to the holy will of God, which rises over him in its overmastering greatness. [22] This is the fundamental orientation which is implied by the sharp opposition in v. 22, 'It is not for your sake, O house of Israel, that I am about to act, but for the sake of my holy name, which you have profaned among the nations to which you came.' God's compassion for his guilt-laden people, his efforts to bring them into a new fellowship of love, is not repudiated by this statement. What is now at stake is to ensure that the profound seriousness of this love should not be obscured by egotistic self-pity, and that human wishes should not prescribe involuntarily to that love what way it ought to take, since such notions would lead to a complete misunderstanding of its deeper nature.

[23] So it is not sadistic cruelty, with which Ezekiel is sometimes credited, but sincere compassion which leads him at this most decisive of moments, when Israel's restoration is at stake, to insist that the compass must be carefully set in the right direction, since only then can one comprehend the way in which God is acting, and since otherwise he will cease to be the Lord God and be turned into a mere idol. In all such realization of salvation, the main thing that matters is that God should be given the honour due to him, i.e. that he should have such a place in man's thought and action as will lead to the recognition that he alone is mighty and that he alone is Lord, in a way which rules out every form of idolatry.

This clear determination of where the centre of gravity lies, and of how in the effectuation of salvation the outward transformation of the national destiny has as its objective the restoration of God's honour, may at first sight seem 'a hard saying'. Indeed, to many Christian exegetes it is only conceivable when contrasted with the New Testament message of the love of God. Yet to the exiled nation, being mistaken in themselves, it offers a new hope which, in contrast to their own deep despair and their helpless notions about God's dealings, gives them an indissoluble guarantee of a continued historical existence amidst the chaotic history of the nations. If Israel can still possess any sort of hope, it must have as its sole basis the certainty that God's fidelity to his own intrinsic nature (and that is precisely what is ultimately meant by the hallowing of his name) must necessarily lead to his sanctifying and renewing the people whom he has rejected. With absolute consistency in this way, all expectations of salvation are given a basis beyond human expectation. God's honour demands that he shall sanctify his name in the eyes of the whole world. In other words, his will to reveal himself cannot capitulate to human resistance, since to do so would be an admission of helplessness, but his holiness must receive recognition and honour and the worship that is its due. In this way his promise transcends and stands high above all human questionability. What is at stake is not an impressive position for Israel, but the justification of God's claim to reveal himself to the world as its God. This has no connection whatsoever with the sphere of national sensitivity, in which God's honour is mistakenly identified with the honour of Israel and requires the intervention of God because of the contempt to which Israel is subjected by the surrounding nations. We see this expressed in such psalms as 74; 83; 92; 109, etc., and it looks dangerously like favouritism towards his own people on the part of the divine party to the covenant. But here it is transcended by the vision we are given of the world-wide objectives at which God's sovereignty is aiming, and of the part which Israel is to play in serving these purposes. After the chosen people has so shamefully failed to perform its duty, it is left, as v. 19 asserts, without any rights or claims in face of the covenant God's right to give a just punishment. All human arrogance and all human security are thus guarded against; no appeal to the covenant at Sinai is possible any longer, the new salvation which is coming is totally unmerited.

So now that it has been established from the very beginning that God's turning to his people is a pure act of grace, the following section brings us to the actual new creation of Israel.

The actual new creation of Israel: 36.24-28

[24] Here it is immediately made evident that the bringing home of the nation from its dispersion does not hold the centre of the stage; it is only a preliminary to the essential bestowal of salvation. This so penetrates into the depths of personal existence that it fulfils all that has been said hitherto about the way in which the new people of Yahweh demands the participation of all its individual members.

[25] The first act of inward renewal consists in the cleansing from all defilement which is portrayed in v. 25. It is represented under the

image of cultic sprinkling, such as occurs in Ps. 51.9. We find both simpler and more complicated sprinklings in the Priestly writing, e.g. Ex. 12.22; Lev. 14.4, 49ff.; Num. 19.4ff. The preparation of the purifying water employed for the sprinkling plays an important part here; some of the blood is directly sprinkled upon the houses, as at the Passover. Yet no special purifying water is mentioned either here or in Ps. 51, which clearly shows that there is no attempt here to portray an actual rite performed by a priest, but that, regardless of what particular form it may take, that well-known rite is used as a means of representing the cleansing action of Yahweh, using a symbol immediately intelligible to every Israelite. In other passages, cultic actions are similarly taken and used as symbols; Ps. 141.2 compares the prayer of a devout man to an offering of incense and evening sacrifice, while Isa. 30.29 compares the community's song of triumph at the destruction of the Assyrians to the cultic hymn the night before the festival, that is on the vigil of the Harvest and New Year Festival. It would be absurd to think that Ezekiel's mention of purification refers to some actual rite to be performed in the new temple at Zion. Its main object is to give an assurance that the uncleanness will really be removed, and so the cultic act seen under its symbolic aspect provides him with a suitable means.

The priestly term *ṭum'ā* is once more used for sin, but this does not mean any approval of purely external Levitical purity. This is rendered improbable by the way this term is also applied to anti-social sins, as we established at the beginning. The uncleanness which seizes and disfigures a man and must be washed away by the waters of purification, serves rather to provide the prophet with a suitable symbol for the inward disturbance to which the nature of man is exposed by desires which pull him away from God and drive him towards other lords and other powers. It destroys the relationship of mutual trust that ought to serve as a link between God and the man whom he has exalted by grace to be his partner. This is the real source of opposition to God's commandment, and this is the place of origin of the uncleanness which defiles his whole being and separates him from the Holy One and abandons him to the accursed sphere of evil. This shameful defilement of a man's whole inward life through a disregard for the will of God which has grown into an enslaving habit was a mystery which had always given Ezekiel a profound shock, and what he says on the subject agrees with Jeremiah's statements in regard to the *servum arbitrium* of man (cf. esp. 16.20, 23). Only the purifying power of the divine nature into which God's forgiveness lifts a man is capable of annulling this defiling power and thus laying the foundation for inward transformation and conversion.

In ch. 18, Ezekiel had been authorized by God to break external connections with past guilt, and now it is his duty to speak also of liberation from its inner effects. No curse is to extend out of the past over a man's nature like an unbreakable fetter which will make any hope of deliverance from his guilt into a mere illusion. The writer of the gloss in Isa. 52.15, who, by a slight alteration in a single word, describes the suffering servant of God as the one who sprinkles many nations, i.e. relieves them of that same fetter of guilt, has, it is clear, understood all the deep meaning of this present passage in Ezekiel. When Paul, in I Cor. 6.11, describes God's great act of deliverance as consisting in the washing, sanctifying and justification of the sinner, and connects it not only with the name of Jesus but also with the Holy Spirit, he is in a surprising way touching upon the chief element contained in this passage of the prophet's writings.

[26] Verse 26 takes a further step towards a second act of renewal: Yahweh, it says, will bestow a new heart and a new spirit. The parallel passage in 11.19, and the demand in 18.31 where the indicative of promise is transformed into the imperative calling for a decision, make it clear beyond all doubt that the spirit named side by side with the heart cannot be regarded as additional to it. The word heart is used here, as it is in many other places, to denote the human will, even though it may include the personality as a whole.[1] The term rūaḥ is more inclusive still; it suggests a man's whole inner life as moved by strong and often overmastering passions, which can easily rob the individual man of his independence and drive him in a certain direction almost as if he had no will of his own. In Ezekiel, however, rūaḥ has already come to mean an organ of spiritual life in general, synonymous with 'sense' or 'disposition', the activity of which is to a very large extent concerned with the ethical determination of the human spirit.[2] We may therefore define the renewal of heart and spirit more precisely by saying that it is brought about by the bestowal of a new will and a new attitude of spirit towards things. This gives point to the way in which v. 26b says the new heart is a heart of flesh in contrast to the one which has hitherto been a heart of stone. It is made abundantly clear that the new creation is related to

---

[1]Cf. W. Eichrodt, *Theology of the Old Testament*, II, pp. 142ff.
[2]*Ibid.*, pp. 134ff.

Israel's real central sin, her insensitiveness, as a result of which she
has completely closed herself up in face of all God's declarations of
his love and all his appeals, so as to become a house of rebelliousness.
This attitude of inaccessibility, which has developed into actual
obduracy, cannot be cast off by any mere momentary decision, or by
any transitory upsurge of emotion. A creative intervention on the
part of God is required, in order to make possible any fresh hearing
or acceptance of God's promptings.

[27] This new turn in the inner life of man is brought about by the
outpouring of the spirit. In the spirit, God imparts to man a motive
power pervading all that is within him and bringing him into union
with God's nature and will. This statement of Ezekiel's is important
for the way it enlarges the meaning of the word 'spirit' beyond its
former limits. In doing so he was able to build on foundations supplied by the preaching of Isaiah, who had already recognized that
the spirit was the power of God's being and the transmitter of all the
moral purity and sublimity he saw in his God (Isa. 30.1), and as
the power through which God could lead those he called to guide the
people, especially the messianic king of a nation alienated from God,
into religious submission and moral obedience (Isa. 11.2). Along
with the deepening of the nature of the spirit went a continuity of
its activity. That activity was not a mere sudden flaring up and
dying down which by its discontinuity served to stand out as an
unusual event; it was a continuous act, which could be described by
saying that the spirit continually rested (Isa. 11.2) or was poured out
upon a man so as to be a permanently effective power (Isa. 32.15;
28.6). Ezekiel's promise develops the conception of how the spirit
works still further along the same line, and makes it the central point
of God's renewal of his people in the new age. The spirit of God
permeates each individual member of the people of God so as to
carry out an inward transformation through which the regenerative
power of God's purity and holiness lays hold of the most intimate
part of man's nature and assimilates it to the nature of God. Here
we see the new importance of the individual member of the people
to the coming people of God, and how he is aroused to a feeling of
responsibility for realizing God's plan of salvation. It is a subject
which comes up in ever new forms in the message of Ezekiel, but
here we see its most powerful proof and display. The human will is
fully united with the will of God through being brought into permanent contact with the might of his spirit, which gives man power

to shape his life in accordance with God's commandments. By this means, genuine fellowship between God and man is guaranteed in such a way that it is impossible to fall back to the former nature. By this means also, the new covenant between God and people is transformed from a new institution into a spiritual reality, making the covenant formula, once again solemnly repeated in v. 28, serve to describe a direct connection between the covenant God and every single member of his people.

When regarded from this point of view, the giving of the spirit is put in its right place in the message of Ezekiel and is protected against misinterpretation. It is a misinterpretation to associate it with the people as a whole as if it meant that they have to be trained in the outward regulation of obedient conduct. Any such thing is impossible, however, in view of what we understand uncleanness to mean.

The same may be said of the assertion that the transformation of the members of the people by God's spirit shows that Ezekiel had been mistaken in preaching the law so far, and that the only source from which it can have arisen is from the prophet's disillusionment over his own activities. That could be correct only if Ezekiel had wished by his preaching in ch. 18 to bring the people into a totally new and unchangeable state. But what we actually saw there was a breakthrough of Israel's state of paralysis and a fresh beginning, and that the problem was solved by God's offer of grace. This brought out clearly to us the provisional character of the national community of which we were vouchsafed a glimpse, and how it was summoned to set off on the march towards a great objective. So one might counter that assertion by saying that the thing striven after in that chapter was crying out to be fulfilled in a totally different dimension, and that without such fulfilment it remains a mere torso.

Finally, it has been suggested that the purifying of the people from every stain contradicts the promise in ch. 18, that once the wicked man is converted his sin will no longer be remembered. But forgiveness must on no account be limited to a forensic acquittal from guilt, as if that exhausted its whole meaning. Within the context of ch. 18, such an acquittal was the main point at stake, without which there could be no certainty of a new future. But acquittal did not exclude either the enslaving effects of habitual alienation from God nor the possibility of backsliding. And so the marvellous deepening of fellowship with God as a result of the implanting of the divine nature in man's heart means the revelation of the full extent of God's action of forgiveness, by which the will which decides in faith is assured that it will reach its goal in spite of all human weakness.

The outpouring of the spirit is thus seen confirming and fulfilling in every direction all the prophet's previous work. The watchman over the house of Israel in caring for souls was certainly not free from disappointments due to all sorts of setbacks, but the glimpse he was thus given of the certainty of divine fulfilment prevented them from ever crippling him.

His message at the same time displays once again its independence of priestly modes of thought. To the old covenant it opposes a new one, which means a great deal more than the re-establishment of the old. In the same way, it moves on past the return of the nation to its newly prepared homeland and the assurance of prosperity and peace under God's servant David, and reaches its object in the freedom of a new union of life between God and his people. Here the priestly institutions become tangible images and ministerial helps towards a communion between man and his God in which human life is determined by direct divine action working out from within. This covenantal conception of being upheld and permeated by God's supernatural power keeps clear of any sort of mystical deification, or fanatical enthusiasm, preferring rather to insist that joyful fulfilment of the commandments is the outcome of the bestowal of the spirit which best accords with the covenant. In spite of Jeremiah's avoidance of the idea of the spirit, the over-all agreement with Jeremiah's promise of a covenant is at this point complete (Jer. 31.31ff.).

It is plain that here Ezekiel is anticipating in the form of a promise what the New Testament is to make the basis of the inner life of the Christian, and contributing towards an understanding of the mode of life mediated through Jesus to his disciples by providing the appropriate form in which inward transformation and outward service are fused into a living unity. But it is equally clear what limitations exist at this stage; they consist in the lack of the closer links between the spirit and the God-sent mediator which are so characteristic of the New Testament gift of the spirit. Yet the effectual anticipation at essential points of the New Testament gift of life, through which the Old Testament is already incorporated in the life of the Church, makes clear at this point the powerful movement of life passing from the Old Testament into the New.

The third section of our picture of salvation extends the effects of the new inward creation of Israel into the outward form of the nation.

Yahweh's new creation under its bodily aspect: 36.29–38

Verse 29a describes Israel's inward renewal as consisting in 'being completely brought out of the sphere of influence in which uncleanness is dominant'. Here this appears to be closely bound up with a renewal of the earthly shape taken by the life of the people of God and with a transformation of the old homeland into a garden of God. An impressive description takes up and recapitulates 34.25ff. One who is schooled in the shape taken by that future hope in the New Testament may feel disposed to identify all this with a very earthbound remnant of a national culture religion, and to condemn the prophet for sinking so low here after having attained in the previous passage to an inward and spiritual treatment of redemption. There can also be no doubt that this portrayal of the fulfilment of salvation is not to be regarded as forming the centre of the prophet's message, and that its isolated details are not to be taken as portraying God's work of salvation in a way that has to be taken literally. What we are given here can only be regarded as an attempt to describe a state of things which is quite beyond actual description and which can only be suggested by means of symbols. The eschatological shape of life is something other than an improved version of natural and earthly conditions. Pre-exilic prophets like Amos, Hosea, Isaiah and Micah expressed this by means of a mythical picture of the return of paradise, in which the qualitative otherness of life in the new aeon was revealed in a way that was not open to misunderstanding. Jeremiah and Ezekiel to a large extent avoid making any use of this mythical element, so they may seem to convey an impression that all they expected was a gradual improvement on their present life.

But here, as in 34.25f., there are indications enough to show that the miracle-world of myth was by no means forgotten (cf. the reference to the Garden of Eden in v. 35, and above, pp. 481f., 483f.). When we reach ch. 40 and 47, we will also realize how much this world of miracle is taken into Ezekiel's hope. Consequently, vv. 33–36 and 37f. are seen to be supplementary statements successively added in order to develop a good deal further some statements actually present in Ezekiel. They represent special longings on the part of the later generation, such as the erection of fortified cities and the increase of the diminished population (cf. Lev. 26.9, Gen. 17.2), things which

the returned exiles were particularly disappointed to see withheld,
and which were therefore brought into the picture of the future. The
awkward way in which words of Yahweh are introduced in vv. 33
and 37 supplies a clear indication that it is a later addition. For
Ezekiel himself, on the other hand, Israel's material reinstatement in
Palestine is entirely determined by theological considerations. So he
is concerned not with giving Israelites what they most want, but
with sanctifying the name of Yahweh in the eyes of the nations, i.e.
public testimony to the power of Yahweh to bring to its goal, in spite
of all opposition, the plan of salvation once for all for the chosen people.
That Israel should be mocked because of the helplessness of her God,
who lets his people starve in their own country or gives them up as a
prey to their foreign enemies, is a sign of failure to know the world-
God himself, and must be refuted by a tangible demonstration to the
contrary. Hence comes the repetition of the insistent 'not for your
sake' at the beginning of v. 32.

A second aspect under which the restoration acquires a special
importance for Ezekiel is its effect upon the favoured people themselves, as described in vv. 31f. The very richness of the gift of God
leads to unrestricted self-condemnation. In face of God's unfailing
faithfulness in carrying out the promise already given to their fore-
fathers, the nation at last comes to realize how deep their own disloyalty has been, and cannot receive the divine gift except in the
most profound humility and the bitterest of repentance. Here once
more we must not allow any coarse simplification, as if the sole
object of God's act of redemption were to humble man in this way.
The object is rather that they should finally be delivered from all the
self-glorification and self-righteous pride which had led them so often
to misuse the good gifts of God, and had rendered Israel incapable of
performing her duty towards the world (cf. above p. 217).

A third aspect of Ezekiel's portrayal of salvation, finally, consists
in making due allowance for the way in which the whole Old Testament hope forms a contrast to all false spiritualization. Here God's
created world is not light-heartedly dismissed as a thing of minor
value in comparison with a purely spiritual relationship with God.
On the contrary, creation is brought in so as to form part of the new
world-harmony; the inward and outward fulfilments mutually
correspond, as the acts of the Creator and the Redeemer. The
deeper the realization of man's alienation from his Creator, which has
led creation away from the objective intended by God, the more indis-

pensable does it seem that the glory of the original designs should be brought out in all their fullness and clarity in a new creation, without which no real fulfilment of salvation can be conceived. The Old Testament message here is distinctly re-echoed in the New Testament (Rom. 8.19–22; II Peter 3.13: 'A new heaven and a new earth, in which righteousness dwells'; Rev. 21.1–4, 23–27). Israel's material recreation is in this way brought into association with her recreation from within. Undoubtedly we must repudiate any attempt to give a literal interpretation to the symbolism. Yet in its deeper significance it serves as a pointer, and helps us to understand the cosmic breadth of God's redemption. A petty-minded reduction of it to merely human notions of existence only leads to a caricature of biblical beliefs about creation.

CHAPTER 37.1–14

The vision of the dead bones

1 The hand of Yahweh was upon me and Yahweh brought me out in the spirit and set me down in the midst of the plain which was full of bones. 2And he led me round among them, and behold there were very many upon the face of the level valley and they were all dried up. 3And he said to me, 'Son of man, can these bones become alive again?' And I said: [. . .]ᵃ 'Yahweh, thou knowest.' 4Then he said to me: 'Son of man,ᵇ prophesy over these bones and say to them: O dried up bones, hear the word of Yahweh. 5Thus says [. . .]ᶜ Yahweh [. . .]:ᵈ Behold, I will bring the breath of life into you that you may come to life, 6and I will make sinews to come in you and cause flesh to grow upon you and will cover you with skin and put the breath of life into you that you may come to life and know that I am Yahweh.'

7 So I prophesied as I was commanded, and as I prophesied, there was a noise, and behold there was a rush, and the bones came together one with another. 8And as I looked, behold sinews came over them and flesh grew up and skin covered them, but there was not any breath of life in them. 9And he said to me: 'Prophesy concerning the spirit, prophesy, son of man, and say to the spirit of life: Thus says [. . .]ᵉ Yahweh: Come from the four winds, O spirit of life, and breathe upon these slain, that they may come to life.' 10So I prophesied as he commanded, and the spirit of life

came into them, and they came to life and stood up upon their feet, and became an exceedingly great host.

11 And he said to me: 'Son of man, these bones are the whole house of Israel. Behold, they say, "Our bones are dried up and our hope is gone, we are given up to death." ¹²Therefore prophesy and say to them: Thus says [. . .]ᶠ Yahweh: Behold, I will open your graves and bring you out of your graves [. . .]ᵍ and bring you into the land of Israel. ¹³And you shall know that I am Yahweh, when I open your graves and bring you out of your graves [. . .]ʰ ¹⁴And I will put my spirit within you, that you may come to life, and I will place you in your own land, and you shall know that I, Yahweh, have spoken and am doing it, says Yahweh.'

ᵃ⁻ᶜSee BH.

ᵈMT: 'To these bones'; a further piece of information added by someone who did not realize that we have just been told to whom the words are addressed.

ᵉ⁻ᶠSee BH.

ᵍMT: 'as my people': this anticipation of the final aim of Yahweh's act is out of place here, so the words are not found in the LXX.

ʰThe MT reading 'as my people' at this point cannot be regarded as anything but a repetition of the phrase in v. 12.

The parabolic event: 37.1–10

We find in Ezekiel's announcement of salvation, inserted between the promises of the inward recreation and of the national restoration of Israel, a vision so full of dramatic power that one must put it beside the great visions described in ch. 1–3; 8–11; 40ff. One automatically tries to discover the date of an occurrence that was evidently so important, not only to the prophet himself but also to his community. But one encounters at the beginning of the narrative nothing but a perfect form of the verb in the absolute state, of the kind as a rule found elsewhere after a statement of the date, but standing here in isolation. We may probably assume that this, like the similarly constructed clause in 40.1, was preceded by a statement of the date, which later came to be omitted here for some necessary reason, perhaps editorial, which is no longer perceptible to us. We must therefore try to fix the date of the occurrence by the relation between the passage and its context, a process in which obviously only a certain approximation to probability can be attained. The utter despair expressed in the words of the exiles cited in v. 11 to which the words in 33.10 present a parallel may indicate a period still fairly close to the fall of Jerusalem during which the prophet's office of administering consolation had not as yet been able to take effect. That is about all one can say. Yet the obvious allusion in v. 14 to 36.27 should nevertheless warn us against giving this present passage a position antecedent to the promise expressed there. It is in any case impossible to fix dates for the composition of the major promises, and to try to determine the period of time during which they exercised the strongest influence on Israelite mentality is a piece of experimentation which can follow only the uncertain lines of psychological conjecture. The experience of the vision begins with Ezekiel being seized by the hand of Yahweh as in 1.3 and 8.1, i.e. by an ecstatic trance in which the prophet's mind is made to serve a reality other than itself. This brings about a movement from one place to another, like that brought about by the spirit of Yahweh in 3.12, 14. Both passages speak of his being carried in a particular manner: the prophet is carried away from Tell Abīb into the valley-plain, the place towards which 3.22f. similarly speaks of his being transported. As has already been observed (cf. above, pp. 75ff.), the passage just referred to transfers the period during which the prophet was reduced to a state of paralysis from the period immediately before the fall of Jerusalem to the period when he first began to prophesy. This was done in order to impress upon the reader the way in which he was a sign and a warning which again and again con-fronted the people, and also by its connection with 4.4–8, to show how from the very beginning of his period of activity the prophet was participating in the same way towards death as his people (cf. also 24.15ff.). What occurs in 37.1ff., however, now forms a complete contrast to all that. The valley-plain, which has been a place where judgment had to be suffered, now becomes the place where Yahweh triumphs over death and serves as an impressive symbol in which to cloth the great turning-point in Ezekiel's message. So the points of emphasis put by the redactors who edited the prophetic book serve to bring out the central importance of this vision within the whole context of Ezekiel's activity.

In contrast to 3.22f., the prophet finds the whole plain strewn with dead bones. [2] Their condition visibly demonstrates that the bodies of those once slaughtered here (v. 9) have long been reduced to decay. The prophet is led around the plain, and can see nothing but dry bones, which leads him to an overwhelming realization that this is the place where death holds triumph. [3] But then he hears his God asking him a surprising question, 'Can these bones come to life again?' His answer is compatible both with the hopeless condition,

humanly speaking, of these withered remnants of once vigorous forms
and also with the illimitable potencies of divine power. No words are
wasted on any human hopes of resuscitation; responsibility for
answering the question is shifted on to God's shoulders. Even death
does not set a limit to the manifestation of his power, although it is a
limit which he does not as a rule cut across (I Kings 17.17ff.; II Kings
4.31ff.; I Sam. 2.6). But this resignation in face of the human aspect
of death, which accords with the attitude towards death hitherto
current in Israel, is now shot through by the certainty bursting all
the limitations of human thought, of a miracle performed by God
which he, the Lord over life and death, makes known to his messenger by drawing him into the first beginnings of this unheard-of
event and giving him a decisive part to play in it. [4] For he is to
speak the authoritative prophetic word by means of which the bones
are to be once again transformed into living men. Will he shrink back
from this duty, and thus reveal that that first word of his was really
meant to conceal his lack of faith, or will he do honour to that power
of God's which he acknowledged, and obey his God by giving the
word of command which will bring the dead to life? He succeeds in
passing the test, and has experience of the effectiveness of the divine
word of power which he has been ordered to proclaim. [5f.] The
words in which he calls on the dead bones and tells them of the
coming of the spirit of life give occasion to a stupendous event, the
resuscitation of the earthly bodies, now carried out in a series of acts
which follow each other in exact sequence. [7f.] The bones arrange
themselves together; they are covered with sinews which evidently
also connect them to each other; they are provided with flesh and
clothed with skin. As in the account of how the first man was made,
this leads to the production of complete human forms, but without as
yet bringing them to life. God must, once again, breathe in the
breath of life, before they can really be brought back to life on earth.

[9] The decisiveness of this moment is brought out by a fresh
command to the prophet to proclaim it: his word is to summon the
spirit of life from each of the four winds to come in its full power to
flood the lifeless bodies, breathing into them and awakening them
into life. The underlying idea here, that of a spirit of life, is a very
ancient Israelite conception, though Ezekiel does not refer to it
elsewhere. His words suggest that he thinks of the spirit as being a
sort of invisible fluid which pervades the whole world and communicates life to it as God commands, so as to import life and growth

everywhere in the created world. He is in actuality going back to an ancient Israelite notion, according to which the mystery of natural life is comprised in spirit and the created world is assured of being kept alive by the ever-renewed pouring out of this breath of life from God, whereas death and corruption seize upon it whenever God withholds his spirit from it (Ps. 104.29f.; Gen. 6.3, 17; 7.15, 22; Num. 16.22; 27.16; Job 10.12; 12.10; 17.1, etc.). This is the same life force which the prophet recognizes as having again and again lifted him up out of his helplessness and made him ready for carrying out God's commissions (cf. 2.2; 3.12; 11.1, 4; 43.5). This conception of spirit is completely related to the natural aspect of divine activity, and clearly distinguished from what is stated in regard to the spirit being the organ of sacred history and the inward power of God's being. The conception which emerges so powerfully here and shows its special characteristics is one which always plays a large part in priestly thought. It is very closely related to the breath of life in Gen. 2.7. There, however, to have had the breath of life imparted to him is a peculiarity distinguishing the first man from all other created beings. [10] Here the way in which the concentration of spirit inundates the field where the dead lie evidently constitutes a major offensive against the forces of death, which must result in a victory for life. Those who lay there and seemed to be dead stand up upon their feet and become an exceedingly great host.

The interpretation: 37.11–14

Up to this point, the reader may have been thinking that this is a presentation of belief in the resurrection of the dead. This, however, is not the case, as we see from the ensuing interpretation and the promise to Israel included within it. [11] God himself equates the dead bones of the vision with the house of Israel as seen in its representatives now living. It is not dead Israelites who are to be resurrected to partake in the consummation of salvation. The house of Israel, with whom the prophet now has to deal and whose despairing complaints he must hear, is to experience liberation from the power of death, by which it is at present dominated. Only now do we begin to realize that the vision has come as a mighty answer from God to the despairing laments of the exiles. They had regarded Jerusalem as the ultimate guarantee of their survival as a nation, so the effect of its fall had been to make them feel as if they had been given up to be the prey of death; that is, they could describe themselves as already given over to death, their bones already dried up, i.e. deprived of the last remnants of life. Elsewhere, too, the bones can stand for man himself in his vitality and his expression of it;[1] the statement by the men that their own bones are dried up is therefore perfectly intelligible. In Ezekiel, however, this idea takes solid shape as an objective fact, so that he employs the image of actual dead bones to represent the present condition of his people. As a result, the people's lamentation can be followed by the event which displays the overwhelming power of the victory of divine salvation. Here, then, we find a most effective symbol of the way in which every despairing refusal to live may be overcome by the consoling forces of the divine promise.

[12] A remarkable thing here is the way in which the original form of this symbol retreats into the background in the words of promise which next follow, so that the revival of the nation now resembles that of a corpse made to rise out of its grave. Here the land of exile has become a grave, the dwelling place of death, in a way which could be seen as a reality at the end of each individual life and on a large scale in the fate of deported nations. In the portrayal of Yahweh's action, the exodus of the people from Babylon, the great graveyard of the nations, is evidently easier to realize, because it can be directly connected with the return to the home country, the land of life. [13f.] The opening of the grave is the breaking through of the prison door of Babylon, while the bringing forth of those imprisoned in the tomb and their revivification by the spirit already leads straight to the hour of departure. In this way, the remaining words of the lamentation in v. 11 are contradicted: for according to this promise, hope must live once more and death set free its captives. All the immeasurable might and boundless compassion of the divine Lord will go forth to the desperate in this miraculous act. Thus, like his previous acts of judgment, this present act leads to a fresh knowledge of his nature and therefore to inward fellowship with him; twice over it is formally stressed that this has always been the fixed objective he has sought on the way of his salvation.

The despair of the exiles meets here with something much more than a mere superficial word of comfort. Ezekiel does not see any less sharply or realistically than the rest of his fellow countrymen the utter ruin to which Israel has been reduced. He therefore demonstrates to them that under such conditions the sole basis for hope lies in the superhuman and miraculous power of his God, who is calling

[1]See W. Eichrodt, *Theology of the Old Testament*, II, 1967, p. 146.

the lost to a new fellowship with him. All that he has so far said about the way in which such a God will accomplish salvation must be seen against the background of well-justified desperation on the part of man. That desperation can only admit itself to have been overcome when it meets with the Lord of life in all his mysterious power. Viewed from this aspect, the vision becomes an indication of the decisive breakthrough beyond the forces of death by which the mediator of fellowship with God is presented as king of kings and lord of lords not only to Israel but to the whole human race.

CHAPTER 37.15-28

The reunification of Israel and Judah

15 The word of Yahweh came to me: [16][. . .][a] 'Son of man, take a stick and write on it: "Judah" [. . .],[b] then take another stick and write upon it: "Joseph [. . .][c] and all the house of Israel, associated with him", [17]and put them together [. . .],[d] so that they may become one in your hand. [18]And when your people say to you: "Will you not show us what you mean by these?", [19]say to them: Thus says [. . .][e] Yahweh: Behold, I take the stick of Joseph [. . .][f] and the tribes of Israel associated with him and put [it with the stick of Judah][g] and make them one stick, that they may be one in my hand. [20]When the sticks on which you write are in your hand before their eyes, [21]then say to them again: Thus says [. . .][h] Yahweh: Behold, I will take the people of Israel from the nations among which they have gone, and will gather them from all sides and bring them back to their own land. [22]And I will make them one nation in my[i] land, upon the mountains of Israel, and they will have one prince over them all [. . .],[j] [23]and they shall not defile themselves any more with their idols [or with their detestable images or with all their apostasies],[k] and I will save them from all their backslidings[l] in which they have sinned, and will cleanse them and they shall be my people and I will be their God. [24]And my servant David shall be prince over them, so they shall all have one shepherd, and they shall walk in my ordinances and observe and follow my statutes. [25]They shall dwell in the land that I gave to my servant Jacob where their[m] fathers dwelt. They and their children and their children's children shall dwell there for ever, and David my servant shall be their prince for ever. [26]And I will make a covenant of salvation with them, it shall be an everlasting covenant with them [. . .][n] and I will set my sanctuary in the midst of them for evermore, [27]and my dwelling place

shall be with them. And I will be their God, and they shall be my people.
²⁸And the nations shall know that I am Yahweh, who sanctifies Israel,
when my sanctuary is in the midst of them for evermore.'

ᵃSee BH.
ᵇMT: 'and the children of Israel associated with him'; evidently a variant of the
following phrase, as it is lacking in v. 19.
ᶜMT: 'the stick of Ephraim'; an attempt to make the definition as unmistakable as possible.
ᵈMT: 'into one stick for you', anticipating what follows.
ᵉSee BH.
ᶠMT: 'which is in the hand of Ephraim'; shows the same tendency as is noticed
above in note ᶜ.
ᵍ⁻ʲSee BH.
ᵏThese terms are not altogether compatible, and are absent in LXX, so they
may be a later expansion.
ˡ⁻ᵐSee BH.
ⁿMT: 'and I will give them and multiply them' is rightly absent in LXX.

The symbolic action

The first half of ch. 37 portrayed Israel's restoration from exile as a
miracle of resurrection from death and as an irrefutable certainty
willed by God. The second half goes one stage further and describes
this restoration as a reunion into one kingdom of the two kingdoms
partitioned during the days of the kings. This happens through a
symbolic act, the performance of which introduces and helps to bring
about the actual event. The description is so vivid that it is impossible
to understand how it could be described as literary fiction. [16] The
prophet is to take two pieces of wood, evidently like staves, to judge
from their later usage, and write a different inscription on each. The
inscriptions assign one to Judah and the other to Joseph. The latter
cannot, however, represent the northern kingdom by itself, so the
'tribes of Israel' associated with it have to be added, keeping the
name 'Israel' for the whole people. [17] The two sticks or tribes are
to be fitted together in such a way that both their ends are out of
sight in the prophet's hand, so that they can be presented as one staff.

[18] Here, as in other symbolic actions, the spectator is expected
to ask what these things really mean. [19] This question leads to the
announcement in vv. 19–22 of the interpretation, given in a twofold
word of Yahweh. The first contains a divine assurance that God himself is giving effect to what his prophet is doing, and is uniting the
sceptre of Joseph and the other tribes with the sceptre of Judah so as

to form one staff in his hand; i.e. he wills the reconstitution of the two divided nations and kingdoms into a single unity. [20] So in what he does the prophet appears before the people as a representative of Yahweh himself. When he has finished carrying out the sign and stands before the spectators with the reassembled staff in his hand, he is to proclaim to them a second word of God, which now discloses the whole act of salvation suggested by that symbol: [21] Yahweh is taking all who belong to Israel from among the nations among whom they have been scattered and is bringing them back to their former homeland. [22] There they are to be brought together so as to form one nation indissolubly united under a single prince.

In this way we come to see a new factor in the future salvation which has not so far been mentioned, as all that has been announced hitherto could very well be interpreted as signifying no more than the restoration of Judah alone. It has rightly been pointed out that so far the northern kingdom has not featured in Ezekiel's message. But we ought not to overlook the one occasion where it is actually mentioned, in 4.4–8, where the prophet represents in his own body the way in which the guilty brother nations of Israel and Judah are bound together, and shows his expectation that the periods during which both are to be punished will end at the same minute. If, as we have suggested, this happening is originally to be associated with the prophet's state of dumbness and paralysis immediately before the fall of Jerusalem, then even at that time he was already contemplating how the nation was to exist once again with all its twelve tribes, as of old.

One reason for this that is sometimes suggested is that the prophet came to know some surviving exiles from northern Israel or their descendants. It may be agreed that such meetings cannot altogether be excluded, but it would almost certainly be reading too much into them to make them the foundation on which a new hope for the northern tribes is to be built. It would be better to think of an influence from Jeremiah's extension of the new period of salvation to include the former northern kingdom, in Jer. 3.6ff., 31, since there are other points where it can be demonstrated that Ezekiel has taken up some of the views of his contemporary. On the other hand, we must regard the inward reasons as those which contributed most decisively towards broadening the prophet's future hope. Once again, we should remember that God's saving act would not be complete unless it restored Israel as a whole. The election of that people, once made, must inevitably come to its goal. In turn, the calling of a second David made it a likely presupposition of his rule that the two long-divided parts of the nation should be reunited. So far as Judah was concerned, such a reunion on equal terms of the formerly divided brother kingdoms was the best antidote against any national self-righteousness on the part of the people of Judah against their northern brethren, who had been overtaken so much earlier by God's judgment. Like the entire religious development of the past, so, too, its political development is to be reversed as being a ruinous mistake, so that God's original saving purpose in his election of David can be put into effect.

[23] As part of this new creation through which Israel exists as a nation, the following verses produce a series of promises which have often been dismissed as an afterthought or even as an ideal for the future (Van den Born). In this context, however, they evidently serve a special function over and above the mere repetition of statements already made. They reveal the special nature and object of the newly existing state and people in such a way as to prevent misunderstanding. First and foremost, the new state is never again to thrust itself between God and his people and to assimilate its way of life to that of neighbouring nations, so as to give occasion for apostasy to other gods. Instead, it is to be a humble instrument of God's projected purification of the people from its sins of apostasy, so that the covenant newly made by God, indicated by the covenant formula at the end of v. 23, may come into full operation. [24] To guarantee this, the new David is to exercise this office and preserve the new order by obedient observance of the divine commandments. [25] He is also to guard the newly-bestowed territory of Israel from all defilement, so that there need be no more judgments to throw doubt on the old promises made to the patriarchs. [26] When it stands on a basis like this, the covenant of salvation, authorized by God, can be an everlasting covenant, and have a better right to that claim than the one described by the same title in the Priestly writing (Gen. 17.7, 13, 19; Ex. 31.16; Lev. 24.8; Num. 18.19). The actual seal will, however, be set on this new order when the building of the new temple in the midst of this grace-filled people has been completed. [27] For this sanctuary, described as a dwelling place, guarantees the presence of God with his people which brings into full effect the contents of the covenant formula cited at other points. Just as, in the great temple vision of ch. 8–11, the temple was robbed of its status as the place of meeting between God and

people by the general alienation of princes and people from God, and made into an assertion of the dominion of other gods, so in the time of salvation it is to fulfil its supreme purpose and mediate the realization of communion with God, the communication of God himself in abundant fullness. [28] This will finally lead to the sanctification of God's name among the peoples; when they see the strict judge of his people now doing his work as one who has compassion on them and being hallowed by his people, they will recognize the nature of the God of Israel whom they misunderstood and blasphemed. They will see him revealing himself as a newly-created reality in their midst, and bow down before him. With this description, Ezekiel is undoubtedly following a similar line to the glimpses of the future in Isa. 2.2–4 and Zeph. 3.9. Like them, he postpones missionary work by the chosen people until after the will of God has fully been put into effect, for, like a lighthouse, this will throw out the bright beams of the true knowledge of God into the heathen world. What he had indicated in 5.5ff. as the duty originally set before Israel, and which she had failed to carry out, is now to be fulfilled. He as it were encloses the people of salvation with a political and national shell, which does material service towards making God's new creation visible among the nations of the world. Basically, however, it is the community founded in God and sanctified by God which is here described as giving light to the Gentiles. This is brought out in ch. 40–48, in which we are given a picture of the temple with its worshipping congregation.

CHAPTER 38.1–39.29

Gog's attack

1 *The word of Yahweh came to me:* 2*'Son of man, set your face towards Gog* [. . .],[a] *the chief prince of Meshech and Tubal,*[b] *and prophesy against him* 3*and say: Thus says* [. . .][c] *Yahweh: Behold, I will come to you, O Gog, chief prince of Meshech and Tubal,* 4*and I will turn you about and put hooks in your jaws, and I will bring you forth, you and all your army, horses and horsemen, all of them clothed in full armour, a great company with bucklers and shields, all of them skilled swordsmen.* 5[. . .][d] 6*Gomer*[e] *and all his hordes, Beth-togarmah*[f] *from the uttermost parts of the north with all his hordes, many peoples are with you.* 7*Be ready and keep ready, you and all your host that assembles about you, and be ready for me*[g] *to call upon.* 8*After many days you will be mustered, in the latter end of the year you*

shall come to a land that is restored from the violence of the sword, where people are gathered from many nations, upon the mountains of Israel, which have been a waste [. . .]ʰ *but now all its people dwell in security.* ⁹*And you will ascend like a storm, you will come like a cloud covering the land* [. . .]ⁱ *you and all your hordes, and many peoples with you.*ʲ

¹⁰*Thus says* [. . .]ᵏ *Yahweh: On that day thoughts will come into your mind, and you will devise an evil scheme* ¹¹*and say to yourself: "I will go up against a land of unwalled villages, I will fall upon quiet people who dwell securely: all of them dwell without walls and have no bars or gates,* ¹²*to seize spoil and carry off plunder to lift up my*ˡ *hand against waste places which are now inhabited and a people who are gathered up from the nations, who have gotten cattle and goods, who dwell at the navel of the earth."* ¹³*Sheba and Dedan and their merchants, Tarshish and its traffickers*ᵐ *say to you: Have you come to carry off spoil, have you assembled your host, to carry off plunder, to carry away silver and gold, to take cattle and goods* [. . .]?ⁿ ¹⁴*Therefore prophesy, son of man, and say to Gog: Thus says* [. . .]ᵒ *Yahweh: you will be awakened on that day, when my people Israel are dwelling securely,* ¹⁵*and come from your place out of the uttermost parts of the north, you and many peoples with you, all of them riding on horses, a great host, and a mighty army.* ¹⁶*You will come up against my people Israel, like a cloud covering the land. In the end of the days I will bring you against my land, that the nations may know me, when through you, O Gog, I vindicate my holiness before their eyes.*

¹⁷ *Thus says* [. . .]ᵖ *Yahweh: You*�q *are he of whom I spoke in former days through my servants, the prophets of Israel, who in those days*ʳ *prophesied that I would bring you against them.* ¹⁸*And on that day* [. . .],ˢ *says* [. . .]ᵗ *Yahweh, shall my wrath rise into my nostrils.* ¹⁹*And in my jealousy, in my blazing wrath I declare: Behold, on that day a great earthquake will come upon the land of Israel.* ²⁰*Then the fish of the sea and the birds of the air and the beasts upon the field and all creeping things that creep on the ground, and all the men that are upon the face of the earth shall quake at my presence; and the mountains shall split asunder, and the cliffs shall fall, and every wall shall tumble to the ground.* ²¹*And I will summon every kind of terror*ᵘ *against him, says* [. . .]ᵛ *Yahweh, every man's sword will be lifted up against his brother.* ²²*And I will enter into judgment with him with pestilence and bloodshed, torrential rains and hailstones, and fire and brimstone will I rain upon him and his hordes and the many peoples that are with him.* ²³*So I will show my greatness and my holiness and make myself known in the eyes of many nations, that they may know that I am Yahweh.*

39.¹ *But you, son of man, prophesy against Gog and say: Thus says* [. . .]ʷ *Yahweh, Behold I will come to you, O Gog, chief prince of Meshech and Tubal,* ²*and I will turn you about and drive you forward and bring you up from the uttermost parts of the north and lead you against the mountains of Israel.* ³*And I will strike the bow from your left hand and will make your arrows drop out of your right hand.* ⁴*You shall fall upon the mountains of Israel, you and all your hordes and the many*ˣ *peoples that are with you; I will give you to the birds of prey of every sort and*

to the wild beasts of the field to be devoured. ⁵You shall lie in the open field, for I
have said it, says [. . .]ʸ Yahweh. ⁶I will send fire against Gogᶻ and against those
who dwell securely on the islands, and they shall know that I am Yahweh. ⁷And
my holy name will I make known in the midst of my people Israel, and I will not let
my holy name be profaned any more, and the nations shall know that I, Yahweh, am
holy in Israel. ⁸Behold, it is coming and it will be brought about, says [. . .]ᵃᵃ
Yahweh. That is the day of which I have spoken.

9 Then those who dwell in the cities of Israel will go forth and [. . .]ᵇᵇ
make fires with the weapons and shields and bucklers, bows and arrows, hand-pikes
and spears, and they will kindle with them a fire lasting seven years. ¹⁰And they will
not need to take wood out of the field or collect fuel out of the forests, but will keep up
their fires with the weapons and thus despoil those who despoiled them and plunder
those who plundered them, says [. . .]ᶜᶜ Yahweh.

11 On that day I will give to Gog a celebratedᵈᵈ place as a burial place in Israel,
the Valley of [ᶜabārīm], east of the seaᵉᵉ and they will stop the valleyᶠᶠ and there Gog
and all his pomp will be buried, and it will be called the valley of the pomp of Gog.
¹²For seven months the house of Israel will be burying them, in order to cleanse the
land. ¹³And all the people of the land will help to bury them, and it will redound
to their honour on the day that I show my glory, says [. . .]ᵍᵍ Yahweh. ¹⁴And they
will set apart men continually appointed to pass through the land and [. . .]ʰʰ
bury those remaining upon the face of the land, so as to cleanse it. At the end of seven
months they are to make their search. ¹⁵And when these pass through the land and
anyone sees a man's bone, then he shall set up a sign, till the buriers have buried it in
the valley of the pomp of Gog. ¹⁶[. . .]ⁱⁱ Thus shall they cleanse the land.

17 As for you, son of man, speak to the birds of every sort and to all beasts of the
field: Thus says [. . .]ʲʲ Yahweh: Assemble and come, gather from all sides to my
sacrifice which I have slaughtered for you, a great sacrifice upon the mountains of
Israel, and eat flesh and drink blood! ¹⁸You shall eat the flesh of the mighty and
drink the blood of the princes of the earth: rams, lambs, and he-goats, bulls and
fatlings of Basham are they all. ¹⁹And eat fat till you are filled, and drink blood till
you are drunk at my sacrifice which I have slaughtered for you. ²⁰At my table you
shall satisfy yourself with horses and ridersᵏᵏ with mighty men and all kinds of
warriors, says [. . .]ˡˡ Yahweh.

21 Thus I will bring forth my glory among the nations, and all the nations shall
see my judgment, which I have executed, and my hand, which I have laid on them.
²²And the house of Israel shall know that I am Yahweh their God from that day
forward. ²³And the nations shall know that it was for their iniquity that the house of
Israel went into captivity, because they dealt so treacherously with me that I had to
hide my face from them and give them into the hands of their adversaries, so that they
all fell by the sword. ²⁴I dealt with them according to their uncleanness and their sins
of apostasy, and hid my face from them.

25 Therefore thus says [. . .]ᵐᵐ Yahweh: Now I will restore the fortunes of
Israel and have mercy upon the whole house of Israel and be jealous for my holy name.

²⁶*And they shall forget their shame, and all the (effects of the) treachery they have
practised against me when they dwell securely in their own land with none to make
them afraid.* ²⁷*When I bring them back from the peoples and gather them from their
enemies' lands, and through them vindicate my holiness in the sight of the* [. . .]ⁿⁿ
nations, ²⁸*then they shall know that I am Yahweh their God, not only because I sent
them into exile among the nations, but also because I gather them into their own land,
and do not leave one of them behind.* ²⁹*And I will not hide my face any more from
them, because I have poured out my spirit upon Israel, says* [. . .]^{oo} *Yahweh.'*

^aMT: 'in the land of Magog' separates the name Gog from the title appended to
it, so this further description can hardly be original. It is probably derived from
Gen. 10.2, where Magog is named as one of the sons of Japhet. In Ezek. 39.6, the
LXX reads 'Gog' instead. Magog could possible mean 'land of Gog'.

^bFor these nations see Ezek. 27.13.

^cSee BH.

^dMT: 'Paras, Cush and Put with them, all of them with shield and helmet.'
According to 27.10, Paras and Put are to be taken as nations of North Africa, and
it is very improbable that they or Cush (= Ethiopia) would be among the followers
of Gog, whose kingdom was in the far north.

^eReferred to by the Assyrians as Gimirrai, and by the Greeks as Cimmerians.
They emerge in the eighth century as conquerors of Urartu (Armenia) in Asia
Minor and then as invaders of the territory of the Phrygians and Lydians.

^fAccording to Gen. 10.3, a son of Gomer, cf. Ezek. 27.14; in Assyrian, Til-
garimmu.

^gSee BH.

^hMT: 'continually, but it was gathered from the nations'; a repetition from
the beginning of the verse.

^{i-m}See BH.

ⁿMT:'in order to carry off much spoil'; dittography from the beginning of the
verse.

^{o-r}See BH.

^sMT: 'in the day when Gog comes upon the land of Israel'; an explanatory
gloss.

^{t-y}See BH.

^zMT: 'Magog'; read 'Gog', with LXX, but the whole verse, which suddenly
includes the dwellers on the isles in the judgment on Palestine, looks suspiciously
like an addition.

^{aa}See BH.

^{bb}As the LXX only reads one verb here, the first of the two expressions meaning
'to kindle' should be deleted.

^{cc-dd}See BH.

^{ee}Undoubtedly this means the Dead Sea, where the north west part of the high-
lands of Moab is called ʿ*abarim*.

^{ff}A conjectural emendation of the impossible reading in the text, see BH.

^{gg-hh}See BH.

ⁱⁱMT: 'And also the name of one city is Hamona' (i.e. pomp); an archaeological
note, explaining the name of a city, Hamona, by the 'pomp of Gog'.

ⁱⁱ⁻ᵐᵐSee BH.
ⁿⁿMT: 'many' is rightly omitted by LXX.
ᵒᵒSee BH.

In ch. 38 and 39 we meet with what, in spite of its generally well-preserved text, is one of the most difficult parts of this book. The most important of the subjects of which it speaks are unknown, and the names of various places, which at first sight impress us as being historically accurate, cannot fully be elucidated. The order of the fairly clearly defined sub-sections has been interfered with, and finally there is a dispute about the real object of this passage which describes itself as a prophecy. This has led to various explanations of why it has been inserted at this point in the prophetic book. More than anything else, it should be possible to reach a clear view of the main purpose of these two chapters. Once this has been done, we can move on to deal with many of the individual problems and either solve them or, at least, see what limits there are to their importance.

The overriding objective that determines the whole prophecy is the hallowing of the name of Yahweh before the nations, which is emphasized again and again as a result of the divine judgment now to be executed. This is a theme well known to the prophet Ezekiel, and one about which he has much to say in his oracles to the nations. Furthermore, ch. 37 ended with the promise that the nations will know that Yahweh dwells in Israel when the new temple is set up among his people. The mention of this theme undoubtedly points towards ch. 40ff., where it is developed at length. In this context, however, there is clearly no reason why the prophet should once again assert the superiority of Israel's God to the nations by any terrible acts of chastisement. The salvation of the new Israel, described in ch. 34–37 and carried to its conclusion by the establishment of the new temple and the transformation of the land in ch. 40ff., is complete, and stands in need of no further addition. From a purely literary point of view, the disruption of the connection between 37.28 and ch. 40ff. by the insertion of ch. 38 and 39 is contrary to the prophet's intentions. It is equally incomprehensible that he should describe a great campaign by the peoples of the north, to whom by common admission he never gives any dominant role, and which takes place quite a long time after Israel's return to the land of her fathers, a campaign reaching right to the hills of Judah, which has the sole purpose of annihilating the invaders by a miraculous divine intervention, so as to bring the

nations into humble subjection to this mighty God. The suggestion
that this was done to supply an interpretation of Jeremiah's prophecies about the northern enemy in Jer. 4–6 and some other passages,
and that this was the sole motive for such an extensive picture of the
future, is quite incredible. The reference to early predictions, the fulfilment of which is depicted here (cf. 38.17; 39.8) indeed seems most
likely to refer to the enemy from the north so strikingly mentioned in
the proclamation of Jeremiah, though it does not completely exclude
other prophecies of a similar kind (cf. Zeph. 1.14ff.; 3.8; Isa. 10); on
the other hand, the manner in which they are mentioned: 'in former
days', 'my servants the prophets', does not suit Ezekiel, indicating as
it does someone separated from them by a much longer stretch of
time. Furthermore, this reference is merely incidental, and its only
object is to ensure trustworthiness for what it states by connecting it
with earlier prophecies, as is done also in Zech. 1.4; 7.12; Dan. 9.2.
Ezekiel never even thought of making any such references, as he did
not need any supports for the authority of his word.

One may now ask when the prevailing desire that we have mentioned above, the overriding concern for the justification of Yahweh
before the nations, could have grown so strong as to look for a fresh
intervention of Yahweh, although the return of the Israelite people
had already taken place and lay a considerable distance back in the
past (as is indicated by the way in which the nation is pictured living
peacefully and prospering upon the mountains of Israel, after having
rebuilt the dwelling places destroyed in earlier days; cf. 38.11f.). The
answer must necessarily be that we see here expressed in words the
thoughts of a generation which had seen it all come to pass, but which
felt that it fulfilled only one side of the prophet's promise of salvation,
whereas the other equally important side, the setting up of God's
dominion over the nations, still remained unfulfilled. The tormenting
question as to why the two movements had not taken place in association with each other, in the way promised and foreseen by the prophet,
and why Israel's restoration, regarded by Deutero-Isaiah as the sign
for the emergence of the new age, had left the Gentile world exactly
what it was before, cried out for an answer; and it received one in the
description of the great drama of Gog and his destruction. Their
author presented these, feeling convinced that he had helped to do
justice to prophecies hitherto left unfulfilled, and had thus found a
firm support for his future expectations. The language all indicates
that the author came from the school of disciples who gathered

themselves to Ezekiel. The longing which he expresses is also to be found in Isa. 63.1–6; Zech. 9.11ff.; 14.1ff. and other such passages, whereas Isa. 60 and 66.18ff. see the same objective being reached by peaceful means. When a place had to be found for the prophecy in the book of Ezekiel, the only one of which the final redactors could think was immediately before the great self-contained block of chapters describing the new temple and the new land.

In the event, this proved to be a decisive step in the transformation of Old Testament prophecy: what had hitherto appeared to be the final turning-point introducing the new aeon now took on the character of a merely provisional objective, beyond which the attack by powers hostile to God would once again enforce the final decision. Not until after this dark storm cloud could God's world rise up in its final form. This line has its New Testament continuation in the picture of the millennium in Rev. 20, and there, too, the objections that may be made to the unorganic insertion of the Gog prophecy into Ezekiel's description of the future still retain their force.

A closer examination shows that this Gog prophecy is far from possessing any dramatic unity of conception. It is a series of individual visions, impossible to combine with one another into an organic picture, even if they are complementary to one another, and describe an action on the part of Yahweh, seen developing to a large extent in a series of events. So, provided one does not make excessive demands for complete logical consistency in the way in which events develop, one may take ch. 38 as giving a general picture of the coming danger to Israel and of how it will be averted. Out of ch. 39, however, only vv. 17–20 and 21–24 fit with this passage. Verses 9f. and 11–16 give individual pictures which differ so widely, and are determined by such dissimilar traditions, that they must be regarded as additions. In 39.1–8, on the other hand, all the matters so far dealt with in care-free length are recapitulated tersely and concisely, so that one is tempted to find here the original core of the Gog prophecy, which a later redactor took and adapted to his requirements by extensions and elaborations. Finally, in 39.25–29 we find a portion of text clearly dissimilar to all that has preceded it, which shows no acquaintance with the main concern of these chapters and differs linguistically. It is certainly directed towards a different historical situation and towards a different objective, which are on exactly the same line of thought as ch. 34–37. One may therefore feel inclined to regard it as the original transition from 37.28 to 40.1ff.

The first announcement of the summoning of Gog: 38.1–9

The solemn commission takes the same form as 25.1 and (apart from the date) as 29.1ff. It summons the son of man to turn his face against the lord of the northern nations, that is, evidently, towards the north, and to prophesy concerning Gog, the paramount prince of Meshech and Tubal. We know the geographical situation and even something of the historical emergence of these nations, among whom we must include Gomer and Beth Togarmah mentioned in v. 6 (see the textual notes). This makes it clear that we are concerned with well-known figures among the nations in the seventh and sixth centuries. Their campaigns in Asia minor and the way in which they and other northern peoples had from time to time threatened countries to the south and west had left a strong impression on the minds of those they had so threatened, with the result that it was still possible for Herodotus in the fifth century to gather some fairly reliable information about them. The author of this passage is therefore moving on historical grounds. This makes it all the more surprising that no historical equivalent has so far been found for the name of Gog, who gives the nations their orders.

The name of king Gyges of Lydia, supported by Assurbanirpal in about 676 BC against the attacks of the Cimmerians (Gomer) and referred to by Assyrian writers as 'Gugu of Lydia' does indeed correspond exactly. But this king of Lydia was continually at war with the Cimmerians, the enemies who sacked his capital in about 630. The Lydians, to be sure, succeeded half a century later in refounding a powerful empire, but anyone who tries to identify Gog with the Gugu just mentioned must realize that this is inconceivable without assuming that the real historical circumstances were transposed into legendary memories for a later generation. The naming of the land as Magog points in a similar direction, since it is not to be found in any ancient records. References to an otherwise unknown Median city prefect of the time of Assurbanirpal named Gāgi, or to Gaga, the name of a country which occurs in the Amarna letters, are completely unsatisfying, as there is no sign of either of them having any connection with the biblical Gog. It is therefore impossible to say any more than that the name of Gog is derived from legendary accounts of campaigns by northern nations and may in some way unknown to us have come to be the name given to their commander-in-chief. What an important part is played here by such legendary elements is shown by some of the other names in this chapter.

[3–6] The author of the Gog prophecy had free access to a rich body of tradition about that leader of the northern nations, but drew only on what seemed most important to him. This is shown by the way in which Gog is conscripted into the service of the Lord of the world; he has to be dragged by violence like some wild beast towards the goal willed by Yahweh. The model followed here was probably provided by 29.4. This, however, suggests that he had originally set another plan in motion and had to be turned away from it. What this plan was can only be conjectured: as the author is elsewhere seen to follow the prophecies in the book of Jeremiah, we may well think of some connection with Jer. 50f., in which the overthrow of Babylon is expected to take place at the hands of a nation from the far north (Rothstein, Herrmann). In that passage, too, ancient traditions, coming perhaps from Babylon itself, may be drawn upon. As we see no glimpse of any judgment on Babylon elsewhere in Ezekiel, it is quite conceivable that this Gog prophecy may make use of this method of introducing the northern nations as instruments of Yahweh's judgment. [7–9] Whether he was executing judgment on Babylon or on some other object, Gog is in any case told in strong words of a fresh goal, for which he must prepare, so as to be ready when his master calls him up. His new destination is the hills of Israel, now newly inhabited after having lain waste for a long time, and which now seem to be safe and sheltered. As to the time when he is to be summoned, only a hint is given, as we have an eschatological terminus, in respect of which it is impossible to state accurately whether it is immediately about to come, or whether a long period must first elapse. In any case, it is something that is to happen in 'the last days', as is shown by the picture of the messianic state of peace in v. 11, following closely upon v. 8, and by the piling up of cosmic catastrophes in vv. 20ff.

Gog's own plans: 38.10–13

It may well seem at first sight like a contradiction to Yahweh's express command, to come up against the holy land like a thunderstorm (v. 9), when we hear of wicked and rebellious schemes of Gog which are, surprisingly, introduced by the formula which marks the word of Yahweh. [10–12] He has apparently been given full authority to chastise, but he intends to employ it to satisfy his own selfish lust for loot and desire for gain. Here, the author probably has in mind

Isaiah's anti-Assyrian prophecy in Isa. 10.5ff., in which the world-conqueror, whom the Lord of the world has employed as the rod of his wrath, recklessly misuses his power, and offends against all divine and human law by trying to gather the riches of the world as a boy does the abandoned eggs of some bird. Gog now acts as the Assyrians did of old, in contradiction to his divine commission. He has no regard for the dignity of a people 'who dwell at the navel of the earth' (v. 12), i.e. who have a unique and unrepeatable importance for the nations of the world, as is clearly conveyed by the allusion to 5.5ff. [13] The slave-traders are already prepared to see that there is a market for the profitable human merchandise which will become easily available as a result of the campaign. The contradiction between the walled cities of Ezek. 36.35 and the emphasis laid here on the complete defencelessness of Israel's centres of population shows that the author of this passage is following all the typical messianic features, such as are found also in Zech. 2.8.

An additional proclamation of the divine purpose: 38.14–16

The introduction by the formula denoting the word of Yahweh in v. 10 showed that Gog's self-will had been taken into account long before in God's plan. [14f.] So in v. 14, as in v. 2, the prophet is again given orders to deliver God's command to Gog, in obedience to which he is to mobilize all the forces of his native land in order to go up against Israel and cover the whole land like a thundercloud (v. 15), i.e. occupy it with his troops. [16] The latter days have come, when Yahweh himself is to lead him into his own land, since it is his will through him to vindicate his holiness before the nations, that they may be led to knowledge of him. What was therefore viewed in the first section as a future event is now brought to fruition by the word of the prophet.

The destruction of Gog: 38.17–23

What greater contrast can be found than between the heavily armed masses of the army now in the attack (cf. vv. 4 and 15) and the multitude of defenceless peasant villages who rely on the prevailing peace and expect no evil to happen to them? This contrast has been deliberately built up by the seer in order to bring out as strongly as possible how contradictory to all human possibilities is the result of the encounter between so unequally matched a pair of contestants. [17] He even introduces a second factor to add further assurance to this incredible event: a declaration made by Yahweh himself to Gog that he has long since forewarned the people of his coming. This shows that the enemy from the north, who plays so large a part in Jeremiah's first prophecies, but whom Jeremiah himself in ch. 19 interprets as meaning Babylon, is regarded as a force which has not as yet entered history and is to materialize for the first time in the shape of Gog. Such a transference was possible only because behind the anonymous northern foe through whom Yahweh is to settle his final reckoning with his people is seen first one historical adversary and then another, first Assyria, in the time of Isaiah (Isa. 5.26ff.; 14.31), then Babylon, in the time of Jeremiah, in whom the terrors of the end seemed to be approaching. To the author of this chapter, the conditions prevailing in his times seemed capable of being explained only if he assumed that those prophecies had not as yet really been fulfilled, and were still waiting their consummation. Now, however, no judgment is to be executed against Israel, and the sole task left for this still remaining foe is to act obediently and in so doing to serve as a stock illustration of the power and glory of Yahweh. So Israel can face him with calm confidence, whereas the Gentiles will regard him with fear and terror. [18] His appearance signifies an outpouring of the wrath of Yahweh, whose rage in the holy war had been so often described by the Israelite narrators (cf. Josh. 8.14ff.; Judg. 4.14ff.; 5.4, 20; I Sam. 7.7ff.; 14.15ff.; II Sam. 5.20ff., etc.) and also by the prophets (e.g. Isa. 28.21; 30.27ff.; Zeph. 1.2ff., 15ff., etc.). [19f.] Both the cosmic powers and the destructive forces of history are enlisted in the service of this God. So first of all a terrible earthquake (cf. Jer. 4.24–26; 10.22), such as is often mentioned as an accompaniment to a manifestation of the divine wrath, shakes the land of Israel and brings terror to birds, fish and creeping things. That the returned people of God would also necessarily fall victim to it is overlooked by the author, his picture of the judgment being motivated by the scheme of the last plagues. [21f.] The panic aroused as a result of the earthquake leads to suicidal strife in Gog's army, which is wiped out all at once by pestilence and bloodshed (also named together in the list of all conceivable plagues in 5.16f.), by terrible torrential rain, and even by fire and brimstone (these features of a volcanic eruption are referred to in connection with the destruction of Sodom and Gomorrah in Gen. 19.24, but seldom mentioned elsewhere—cf. nevertheless Isa. 30.33; Ps. 11.6). The schematic accumulation of these images of destruction, too extreme to allow any clear picture of them, is characteristic of the style of this prophecy, closely akin to that of apocalyptic. [23] But the way in which horror is piled up without discrimination is wholly calculated to serve the object stated at the conclusion, that all the nations will now no longer be able to close their eyes to the greatness and holiness of Yahweh, but will have to acknowledge it with fear and trembling. This, the central concern of this whole vision of the future, has already been mentioned in v. 16, and is now once more declared to be the real key towards understanding the whole event.

The invitation to the birds and beasts of prey to the feast: 39.17–20

Out of the confused heap of fragments of various kinds in ch. 39 only vv. 17–20 can be regarded as immediately linked with the preceding passage. What was anticipated in an ugly fashion in v. 4 of the passage 39.1–8 is here placed most effectively after the destruction of Gog's mighty host. The prophet himself is to invite the birds and wild beasts by the order of the God of battle to be present at a feast of unprecedented sumptuousness. If this is regarded as a sacrificial banquet after the slaughter of an immense victim, the metaphor means no more than that the creatures feast in joy to celebrate their Lord's day of victory. All attempts at drawing further conclusions lead to abnormalities, as in Isaiah's picture of the Assyrian sacrificed on a huge pile of wood (30.27–33) which derives its significance solely from the contrast it presents to the poverty of the sacrifices offered by men. The similar exaggeration in the description of this present sacrificial banquet serves to heighten our awareness of how very different it is from Ezekiel's message of judgment. The accumulated horrors filling the scene in which this author takes such pleasure are omitted in Rev. 19.17f., which is itself a reminiscence of this passage.

The sections discussed so far have been introduced either by a command to the prophet to prophesy (38.1, 14; 39.17) or else by the formula denoting a word of God (38.10, 17); they thus claim to be a series of words of God addressed to Gog or, in the last section, to the birds.

The original conclusion of the whole picture of judgment: 39.21–24

This is most probably to be seen in 39.21–24. Once more, but this time without any special introduction, it is stated at length that the dominant object of the destruction of Gog and his hordes is that the judgment of Israel may be justified before the nations, and a statement is added mentioning the new knowledge of God in Israel (v. 22). This was also stressed in 36.20f. as the misunderstanding of the divine action among the heathen that led to the profanation of God's name. It is meant here to be transformed into a new insight into the inward necessity of a holiness expressing itself in judgment. But what totally different roads lead towards this objective in these two passages! Instead of undergoing inner conversion in view of Israel's new creation, the heathen are forcibly compelled to bow down before an uncanny destructive power. A dangerous corollary for Ezekiel's disciples to draw from his promises!

The sections of ch. 39 still remaining require only a few more words. As we have already seen, *the terse summary in 39.1–8* contains within it all the essential elements in the long-drawn-out picture of judgment as seen so far. [6f.] The sanctification of the name of God both within and outside Israel is the strongly emphasized concern of the prophetic vision, even here. [3] It is striking to see how the enemy is óvercome by Yahweh in person, knocking the weapons out of his hand and rendering him defenceless. On the other hand, we are not told who it is who actually destroys him. [8] The appeal to the fact that the event has already been announced by Yahweh is carried to a most effective conclusion by the introduction of the words of Ezek. 21.12.

Yahweh's order to his prophet to speak is conspicuously absent from the two following sections, *39.9–10* and *39.11–16*, which are concerned with *the burning of the weapons and the burial of the corpses of the mighty army from the north.* Here, in spite of the sonorous concluding formula in v. 8, there is a continuation of the narration of events which could only appear important to an attitude of a very superficial type, which was concerned above all with the Levitical purity of the holy land. [9f.] For the war material to be accumulated in such quantities that it provides fuel for seven years is, of course, one further testimony to the mightiness of the host which has fallen victim to the wrath of the Lord of the world. There may, however, also be an allusion to the idea of the eternal peace now dawning, such as originally belonged to the Golden Age, as is to be seen in Isa. 9.5; Hos. 2.20; Zech. 9.10.

Here, then, the great event is playfully caused to vanish into humdrum usefulness for the citizens of the new era. In the following section it arouses concern about the Levitical purity of the land. [12] The great numbers of unburied corpses of the fallen were inevitably defiling the holy land (Num. 35.33), as well as exposing the inhabitants

to continual defilement (Num. 5.2; 19.16), as is presupposed also
in Ezek. 36.18; 22.2–13. The people have to be ordered to bury
these corpses in a place chosen by God, and this takes seven months
to do. [13–16] Meritorious as this work is, however, it is not enough to
cleanse the land thoroughly. A permanent commission of men has to
be appointed to inspect the land and set up signs wherever any
remains of corpses are still to be found, so that they, too, may be
buried and eventually the land may be completely cleansed. These
prescriptions, made in juridical language and with all the circumspect
exactness of priestly injunctions, also, in their own way, contribute
towards illustrating Yahweh's mighty victory over his last adversary.
On the other hand, they diverge so far from praise and thanksgiving
for the glorious exploit of God into the bathos of the meritorious
human contribution of burying the dead that they lose all connection
with the story of what God has done, which has been the main object
in all that has been said so far. Here we see the predominance of a
spirit completely alien to the previous wide sweep of prophecy.

Nevertheless, its emergence seems not solely to be due to concern
for proper observance of the laws of ritual purity, but also to be determined by certain more or less legendary traditions associated with
the figure of Gog. The very figure of seven years and seven months
already points to a background of this kind, and still more do the
geographical names, which cannot be explained from their present
context. [11] Among these is the valley selected by God as the burying
place of Gog, which is called, depending on the vocalization, 'valley
of travellers' or 'valley of *ᵃbārīm*'. The proper reading cannot be
established with any certainty, as the first name may contain some
play on words referring to a legendary item in the Gog-tradition
which is no longer preserved for us (its connection with the commission who 'travel' through the land is a word-play introduced at a
secondary stage). The second name denotes a portion of the land of
Moab lying between the *wadi Hesbon* and the river Arnon, in which
Mount Nebo constitutes the chief landmark, which in actual fact is
not 'in Israel' (v. 11) at all. One cannot find any reason in the present
context for the choice of this locality. [16] If, however, we also bring
in the city of Hamona (v. 16), mentioned in an appended gloss,
despite the fact that the name is applied to the 'pomp' of Gog, we
seem to have a glimpse of an independent tradition, no longer
accessible to us, which prescribed to the narrator the line he was to
follow. The same holds true of the remarkable role played by the

corpse-filled 'valley of the pomp of Gog' (v. 11), through its being blocked by burials or rendered impassable to travellers. This is made the more remarkable by the fact that Zech 14.5 also speaks of the stopping up of a valley which plays a now obscure part in the trans-formation of Jerusalem in the last days.

It has been claimed that these peculiar details of places are of Egyptian origin (Gressmann), but the references to Egyptian tradi-tion that we have are insufficient to establish this. So we must rest satisfied with what was stated at the beginning, that the name of Gog had long been connected with a cycle of more or less legendary stories, before the author of this chapter made him the central figure in his prophecy. The legendary nature of the material evidently constituted a temptation to him to weave some further details into his picture here and there, and thus to have a mysterious background to the additions which he had himself provided.

The last of these pieces, which cannot be brought into conformity with the original outlines of the Gog-prophecy, is the concluding section.

Retrospect on the merciful restoration of Israel: 39.25–29

[25] Here the spectral manifestation of Gog has vanished, to be replaced by the imminent change in Israel's destiny, thanks to the complete assembling and return home from their dispersion in foreign parts of all those who belong to the nation, so that they may be settled on their native soil under the shelter of God's power. This is the way in which Yahweh shows his jealousy for his holy name (vv. 25, 27), and by which he produces profound shame (v. 26) and a new know-ledge of God (v. 28) among his people. The outpouring of the spirit, however, serves as a guarantee of their being continual objects of divine favour and of the future unbroken fellowship between God and his people (v. 29). This shows that the coming of salvation still lies in the future, and that God's action is not directed towards the nations, but concentrated upon Israel alone. So this section must be regarded as in the main a retrospect or summary of God's accomplishing of salvation described in ch. 34–37. It may from the first have served as a connecting link between those chapters and 40.1ff., or may have been composed subsequently to the insertion of ch. 38f. in order to re-establish the connection with ch. 37. The very loose order, in which the chief constituents of the salvation promised to Israel are put side by side with their consequences for its inward transformation, points in all probability to the second of these alternatives.

THE TEMPLE AND ITS ORDINANCES; THE LAND AND THE PEOPLE IN THE NEW ISRAEL OF THE TIME OF SALVATION

40.1–48.35

In the series of chapters with which the book of Ezekiel ends we meet with a part separated from the rest so as to form a self-contained whole. In it, a number of pieces of different types have been put together, representing contradictory tendencies. But in spite of that they provide a picture of the temple, land and people in the time of fulfilment with features all its own, forming a clear contrast to the promises of salvation in the preceding chapters. We do not learn anything more here about the Messiah of ch. 34 and 37, nor is anything said about what happens to the foreign nations. The land and the people in the time of salvation have their centre and the justification of their existence in the presence of the temple and the worship there. It is thus from this all-dominating perspective that the restored Israel is to be seen.

At the same time, when we begin to look more closely at this remarkable entity, it is seen to be anything but a figure cast in a single mould or a creation by a single writer free from self-contradiction and logically developed in all directions. Pieces of widely different origins are combined together within it. These pieces in turn have been enriched by additions and elaborations, the work of a whole series of different hands, which shape and develop them further in many different directions. This makes it difficult to determine the real significance of this set of chapters. What does it mean, for example, that soon after the beginning in ch. 40 the whole seems to take on the character of a great vision, a prophetic glimpse of God's act of fulfilment in the midst of his people, and then that as this vision continues further it is interrupted in long or short stretches, by descriptions with a character of their own quite independent of it, or by proclamations of divinely ordained statutes which depart from what is seen in visions and come down to earthly realities with all their sins and imperfections? It is inevitable that, even when we believe we are

nevertheless confronted with a self-contained whole, we should come
upon widely varying opinions as to what it means, according to
whether we let ourselves be mainly influenced by this or that part of
it. Do we have here a sketch of a constitution for the new Israel,
which is merely waiting for the turning-point in history, at which it
can be translated into realities? Or are we to say that there are at
least certain problems about which Ezekiel's earlier pictures of the
future have vouchsafed no information, problems, that is, concerning
ministry in the promised temple and the organization of the temple
staff, or problems about the distribution of the old homeland to the
tribes and their prince, or problems about the rights and duties of the
king, and that we are told how these problems may be or should be
dealt with—at least in a few of the main points? Or are these not
prophetic counsels at all here, counting on the obedience and co-
operation of men for their realization, but rather a prophetic vision
of a future which the divine Lord of the people will bring into effect
in his own time in complete independence from man, something
therefore which we must not set down in detail, since it is enough to
describe the general aims of the divine action without wanting to
anticipate the divine freedom in his creation of the new people? The
interpretation will have to show whether any one of these various
explanations is capable of accounting for this picture of salvation as a
whole, or whether they are all upset by the basic contradictions in the
way in which it is constituted, so that it is an illusion to think of its
having any ultimate unity as a whole. This again must lead to the
recognition that in it totally different elements have been temporarily
linked together so as to form a single whole, and yet in any thorough-
going examination they reveal themselves to be independent bodies of
tradition, each following its own autonomous rules.

CHAPTER 40.1–42.20

The vision of the temple

40.1–37 *The outer and inner gates*
1 In the twenty-fifth year of our exile, at the beginning of the year, on
the tenth day of the month, in the fourteenth year after the city was taken,
on that very day the hand of Yahweh came upon me and brought me

[. . .]ᵃ ²in the vision of Godᵇ [. . .]ᶜ into the land of Israel and set me down upon a very high mountain, on which was a structure like a city opposite me.ᵈ ³When he brought me there, behold, there was a man, whose appearance was like bronze, with a line of flax and a measuring reed in his hand, and he was standing in the gateway. ⁴And the man said to me: 'Son of man, look with your eyes and hear with your ears and set your mind upon all that I shall show you, for I have come here in order that I might show it to you.ᵉ Declare all that you see to the house of Israel.'

5 And behold, there was a wall all around the outside of the temple area, and the length of the measuring reed in the man's hand was six cubits long, each cubit measuring a cubit and a hand breadth in length, so he measured the thickness of the wall: one reed, and the height: one reed also.

6 And he went into theᶠ gateway, which faced east, and went up seven steps. And he measured the threshold of the gate: one reed deep [. . .].ᵍ ⁷And every niche was one reed broad and one reed in depth, and the pillarʰ between the niches five cubits, and the threshold by the vestibule of the gate at the inner end one reed. ⁸And he measured the vestibule of the gateway [. . .]ⁱ ⁹[. . .]ʲ eight cubits and its pillars two cubits. And the vestibule of the gate looked inwards. ¹⁰And the niches of the east gate: three on the one side and three on the other side, all three of the same size, and the pillars on either side were of the same size. ¹¹And he measured the breadth of the opening of the gateway: ten cubits, and the breadth of the gateway: thirteen cubits.ᵏ ¹²There was a barrier before the niches, one cubit broad on each side, on the one and the other side, and the niches were six cubits on either side. ¹³And he measured the gate from the beginning of the roof of one niche to the beginning of the roof of the other: twenty-five cubits, from the opening of one niche to the one opposite to it.ˡ ¹⁴[. . .]ᵐ ¹⁵And from the front of the gate at the entrance to the end of the inner vestibule of the gateⁿ was fifty cubits. ¹⁶And there were windows with frames to the niches and then pillars inside the gate on both sides, and likewise the vestibule had windows on both sides [. . .]ᵒ and on the pillars were palm trees.

17 And he brought me into the upper court, and behold, there were chambers, and a pavement round about the court: thirty chambers fronted on the pavement. ¹⁸The pavement ran along the side of the gates corresponding to the length of the gates. This is the lower pavement. ¹⁹And he measured the breadth of the court from the inner front of the lower gate to the outer front of the inner gate: a hundred cubits.

Then he went before me to the northᵖ ²⁰and behold, there was a gate�q which faced towards the north in the outer court, and he measured its length and breadth. ²¹And its niches, three on either side, and its pillars and its vestibule were of the same size as those of the first gate, its length was fifty cubits, and its breadth twenty-five cubits. ²²And its windows and the windows of its vestibule and its palm trees were like those of the gate which faced towards the east. And seven steps led up to it, and its vestibule was on the inside.ʳ ²³And opposite the gate to the north was a gate to the inner court as on the east,ˢ and he measured from gate to gate: a hundred cubits.

24 And he led me towards the south, and behold there was a gate on the south, and he measured its niches,ᵗ its pillars and its vestibule; they were of the same size as the others. ²⁵And there were windows on either side in it and in its vestibule like the windows of the others. Its length was fifty cubits and its breadth twenty-five cubits. ²⁶And there were seven steps leading up to itᵘ and its vestibule was on the inner side. And it had palm trees on its pillars, one on either side. ²⁷And there was a gate on the south of the inner court. And he measured from gate to gate [. . .]ᵛ a hundred cubits.

28 And he brought me to the inner court by the south gate, and he measured the south gate; it was of the same size as the others. ²⁹Its niches and its pillars and its vestibules were of the same size as the others, and there were windows on either side in it and in its vestibule; its length was fifty cubits and its breadth twenty-five cubits. ³⁰[. . .]ʷ ³¹And its vestibule faced the outer court, and palm trees were on its pillars, and its stairway had eight steps.

32 And he brought me to the inner court at the gate facing east.ˣ And he measured the gate which was of the same size as the others. ³³And its niches and its pillars and its vestibule were of the same size as the others, and there were windows on either side in it and in its vestibule. Its length was fifty cubits and its breadth twenty-five cubits. ³⁴And its vestibule faced the outer court, and palm trees were on its pillars on either side, and its stairway had eight steps.

35 And he brought me to the north gate and measured the gate; it had the same size as the others. ³⁶And its niches and its pillars and its vestibule were of the same sizeʸ as the others. And there were windows on either side in it and its vestibule. Its length was fifty cubits and its breadth twenty-five cubits. ³⁷And its vestibule faced the outer court, and it had palm trees on its pillars on either side, and its stairway had eight steps.

40.38–43 The tables for slaughtering

38 *There was a chamber with its door in the vestibule of the gate; where the burnt offering was to be washed.* ³⁹*And in the vestibule of the gate were two tables on either side, on which*ᶻ *the burnt offering and the sin offering and the guilt offering were to be slaughtered.*⁴⁰ *And outside on the side wall of the vestibule of the north gate*ᵃᵃ *were two tables and on the other side wall of the vestibule of the gate were two*

tables. ⁴¹*Four tables were on the inside and four tables on the outside of the side wall of the gate, altogether eight tables on which the sacrifice was to be slaughtered.* ⁴²ᵃ*As for the four tables for the burnt offering, they were of hewn stone, a cubit and a half long and a cubit and a half broad, and one cubit high.* ⁴³ᵃ*And the shelves*ᵇᵇ *were a span high, firmly fastened round about within.*ᶜᶜ ⁴²ᵇ*On them were laid the instruments with which the burnt offering*ᵈᵈ *was slaughtered.* ⁴³ᵇ*And on the tables the flesh of the offering was laid. And over the tables, above, were roofs to shelter from rain and heat.*ᵉᵉ

40.44-46 The priests' chambers

44 And outside at the inner gate there were two chambers in the inner court, one at the side wall of the north gate facing south, and the other at the side wall of the south^ff gate facing north. ⁴⁵And he said to me: This chamber, which faces south, is for the priests who have charge of the temple. ⁴⁶And the chamber which faces north is for the priests who have charge of the altar. (These are the sons of Zadok, who alone among the sons of Levi may come near to Yahweh, to minister to him.)

40.47-41.15a The inner court and the temple house, with side building

47 And he measured the court, a hundred cubits long and a hundred cubits broad, foursquare, and the altar was in front of the temple.

48 And he brought me to the vestibule of the temple, and he measured the pillars of the vestibule, five cubits on either side, and the breadth of the entrance was fourteen cubits and the side walls of the gate were three cubits on either side. ⁴⁹And the breadth of the vestibule was twenty cubits and the depth twelve cubits, and ten steps led up to it, and there were columns beside the pillars, on either side.

41.1 And he brought me to the nave and measured the pillars; six cubits on either side was the [depth of the pillars].^gg ²And the breadth of the entrance was ten cubits and the sidewalls of the entrance were five cubits on each side. And he measured its length forty cubits and its breadth twenty cubits. ³And he went on inwards^hh and measured the pillars of the entrance: two cubits; and the breadth of the entrance six cubits, and the side walls¹¹ of the entrance seven cubits on each side. ⁴And he measured its depth twenty cubits and its breadth twenty cubits ahead of the nave, and he said to me: this is the most holy place.

5 And he measured the wall of the temple house: six cubits thick *and the breadth of the side building, four cubits, round about the temple.* ⁶*And the side chambers, side chamber above side chamber three times,*ʲʲ *and there were supporting beams on the wall of the house for the side chambers all around to support them, but there were no supports in the wall of the house.* ⁷*And the passage*ᵏᵏ *from storey to storey became broader in the side chambers [. . .].*¹¹ *And one went up from the lowest storey to the middle storey and up to the top storey.* ⁸*And round about the temple house there was a raised pavement, and the foundations of the side chambers*

measured a full reed of six cubits high (?).[mm] *9The thickness of the outer wall of the side chamber was five cubits, and an open space* (Hebrew: munnāḥ) *between the side building of the house,10 and between the chambers had a breadth of twenty cubits round about the temple house. 11And the doors of the side building opened on the open space, one door towards the north and one door towards the south. And the breadth of the wall[nn] of the open space was five cubits round about. 12And the building* (Hebrew: binyan), *that was facing the enclosed space* (Hebrew: gizrā) *on the west side, was seventy cubits deep, and the wall of the building* (binyan) *was five cubits thick round about, and its breadth was ninety cubits.[oo]*

13 And he measured the temple house, its (total) length was a hundred cubits, and the enclosed space and the building (*binyâ*) and its walls were a hundred cubits long. 14Also the breadth of the front of the temple and the enclosed space to the east was a hundred cubits. 15aAnd he measured the width of the building (*binyan*) beyond the enclosed space [. . .][pp] and its walls[qq] on either side: a hundred cubits.

41.15b–26 Internal decoration
And the inner nave of the temple and the outer vestibule[rr] 16were panelled, and the window frames and the door frames all around in their three parts[ss] over against the threshold were covered over with wood round about. And from the floor to the windows the walls were panelled. 17[. . .][tt] 18And there were made cherubim and palm trees, a palm tree between two cherubim, and every cherub had two faces. 19The face of a man was turned towards the palm tree on one side and the face of a lion towards the palm tree on the other side; they were placed thus on the whole temple round about. 20From the floor to the lintel of the door the cherubim and palm trees were placed on the wall.[uu] 21And the doorway[vv] of the temple had a fourfold frame. And in front of the holy place[ww] was something resembling 22an altar of wood, three cubits high, two cubits long and two cubits broad; it had corners, and its base and its sides were of wood. And he said to me: That is the table which stands before Yahweh. 23The nave had a double door and also the holy of holies 24had a double door, and the doors had swinging leaves which could be drawn back to the wall; two swinging leaves for each side of the door. 25And on them, on the double doors of the nave, were placed cherubim and palm trees, such as were placed on the walls. And there was a wooden lattice[xx] in front of the vestibule outside. 26And there were arranged windows and palm trees on either side on the side walls of the vestibule. [. . .][yy]

42.1–20 The priests' chambers and the overall measurements of the temple area
1 *And he led me out into the outer court towards the north and brought me to the chambers which were [opposite][zz] the enclosed space[aaa] and opposite the binyan[bbb] on the north 2[. . .][ccc] Their length was a hundred cubits on the north and their breadth fifty cubits. 3Opposite to the twenty cubits (space) which belonged to the inner court, and opposite the pavement which belonged to the outer court, was slope in*

front of slope in three storeys.^{ddd} ⁴*And before the chambers*^{eee} *was a passage inwards*^{fff} *ten cubits wide and a wall one cubit (thick).*^{ggg} *And their doors were on the north.* ⁵*And the upper chambers were narrower, for [slopes took away room from them and from the middle and lower storeys].*^{hhh} [. . .]ⁱⁱⁱ ⁶*For they were threefold in construction*^{jjj} *and they had no pillars like the pillars of the courts. [Hence from the lower and middle ones was taken room beginning from the ground.]*^{kkk} ⁷*And there was a wall outside parallel to the chambers towards the outer court; and its length along the chambers was fifty cubits. So [its total length]*^{lll} *was a hundred cubits.* ⁸*For the chambers on the outer court were fifty cubits long. So [its total length]*^{mmm} *was a hundred cubits.* ⁹*And below these chambers was the entrance on the east side, for someone wishing to enter them from the outer court* ¹⁰*at the head*ⁿⁿⁿ *of the boundary wall of the court. And on the south, along the enclosed space and the binyan, there were also chambers,* ¹¹*with a passage in front of them (cf. v. 4a); they were similar to the chambers on the north, of the same length and breadth,*^{ooo} *with the same exits and arrangements and entrances.* ¹²*And below the south chambers was an entrance at the head of the passage, leading in front of the boundary wall towards the east, for anyone wishing to go in.*^{ppp} ¹³*And he said to me: The north chambers and the south chambers alongside the enclosed space are the holy chambers, where the priests who approach Yahweh shall eat the most holy offerings. There they shall put the most holy offerings—the cereal offering, the sin offering and the guilt offering, for the place is holy.* ¹⁴*There the priests shall go in*^{qqq} *and they are not to go (straight) out of the holy place into the outer court; they shall lay down there the garments in which they minister, for they are holy. They shall put on other garments and (only then) shall they approach the place assigned to the people.*

15 And when he had finished measuring the interior of the temple area, he led me out in the direction of the gate which faced east, and measured round about. ¹⁶He measured the east side:^{rrr} five hundred cubits with the measuring reed.^{sss} And he turned ¹⁷and measured the north side five hundred^{ttt} cubits with the measuring reed. And he turned^{uuu} ¹⁸and measured the south side: five hundred^{vvv} with the measuring reed. ¹⁹And he turned and measured the west side: five hundred^{www} with the measuring reed. ²⁰He measured it on all four sides, five hundred long and five hundred broad.^{xxx} And it had a wall around it, to make a separation between the holy and the common.

^aMT: 'there'; not in LXX.
^bSingular for plural, following LXX.
^cMT: 'had brought me', not in LXX.
^dInstead of 'in the south', 'opposite me' is to be read, following LXX, unless one prefers to delete the expression as a gloss.
^eMT has a mixed wording which also allows the translation 'you have been brought here'.
^{f–h}See BH.
^{i–j}A lengthy dittography: see BH.

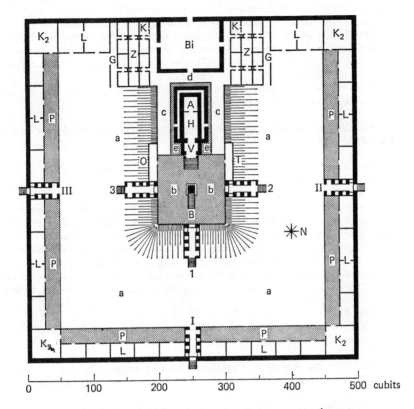

Ezekiel's Plan of the Temple. An attempt at a reconstruction

I, II, III: gates of outer court
1, 2, 3 : gates of inner court
a: outer court
b: inner court, 100 cubits square (40.28,44)
c: munnāḥ
d: gizrā
e: terrace of temple
P: pavement (40.17f)
L: chambers for visitors to temple (40.17)
Bi: binyan

O, T: chambers for priests (40.44)
Z: 'chambers' or cells with changing
   or dining rooms for the priests
   (42.1,4, 7–13)
G: passage with dividing wall between
   it and outer court (42.7)
B: altar (40.47)
A,H,V: temple hall (40.48–41.4)
A: holy of holies; H: holy place (nave);
V: vestibule
K_1 kitchens for the priests
K_2 kitchens for the people (46.21f)

[k]The two different measurements of the breadth of the gate are produced by first measuring the gateway opening from one hinge of the door to the other and then measuring the whole gateway without taking these into account.

[l]As the whole width of the vestibule cannot be measured along the floor because the barriers would be in the way, the measurements have to be taken from the top of a niche at the point where the roof begins to the same point on the opposite niche, across the openings of the other niches.

[m]This verse seems to have originated through corrections to the next verse; it has mistakenly been inserted at this point (Gese).

[n]See BH.

[o]MT: 'facing inwards'; a superfluous repetition of the same detail from the first part of the verse.

[p–v]See BH.

[w]This verse needs to be deleted. It arises from a mistaken insertion of dittographies which have no connection with the context.

[x–z]See BH.

[aa]This translation is preferable to the alternative: 'and on the outside as one goes up to the entry of the north gate there were two tables'. We thus avoid the difficulties of what is frequently taken for granted, that this refers to the inside of the east gate, whereas there is nothing to indicate any such change of position.

[bb]An uncertain word, which Galling takes to mean 'hooks'.

[cc]Probably better than the conjectural insertion of 'on the pegs', as it would be most likely that the instruments for slaughtering the sacrifices would be kept inside the chamber.

[dd]See BH.

[ee]This last statement, found only in LXX, can refer only to the tables standing in the open air, and seems to be a subsequent addition.

[ff]See BH.

[gg]MT: 'the depth of the tent', probably a scribal error.

[hh]This restrained mode of expression is used to indicate entry into the holy of holies.

[ii–jj]See BH.

[kk]Read *hamm^{e}sibbā.*

[ll]An unintelligible line. Gese: 'And the side chambers had a broad stairway leading up, for the house was surrounded by it leading upwards round about the house; therefore the house grew broader as it rose.'

[mm]An unintelligible word.

[nn]For *m^{e}qōm* read *geder* (Gese).

[oo]In vv. 9–12 the 'open space' between the temple and the neighbouring chambers on the north and south sides should evidently be distinguished from the 'enclosed space' on the west designated by the word *gizrā*. It was therefore at the back of the temple, and separated it from what was now a newly erected building, called the *binyan* (Cooke would restore everywhere the form *binyā*, used here in v. 13).

[pp]'Which strikes against its back'—unintelligible.

[qq]See BH.

[rr]The singular should be read for the plural here.

[ss]That is the two doorposts and the lintel.

ᵗᵗAn assemblage of words which cannot be given any meaning, see the commentaries.

ᵘᵘSee BH.

ᵛᵛInsert *ūpetaḥ*.

ʷʷThis probably refers to the holy of holies.

ˣˣThe word *'ab* is unknown, so the translation is only conjectural.

ʸʸThe last three words of the verse are unintelligible.

ᶻᶻThus, with Elliger.

ᵃᵃᵃAccording to 41.12f., 15, the space twenty cubits broad and a hundred cubits long between the temple and the *binyan*. The open space to the east of the temple is given the same name (41.14). The open space around the long sides of the temple is given a different name, *munnāḥ* (41.9f.).

ᵇᵇᵇCf. 41.12f., 15.

ᶜᶜᶜSee BH.

ᵈᵈᵈAn alternative translation (Elliger) is: 'There were "ledges?" ledge on ledge all along in three stages.'

ᵉᵉᵉThe plural is evidently occasioned by the triple division of the building. Presumably it also alludes to the form of the building erected on this steep slope, as the narrow side at the edge of the roof also displayed a line rising in two stages, cf. v. 6.

ᶠᶠᶠThat is on the longer side to the south, opposite the *binyan*.

ᵍᵍᵍThis wall shields the passage on the east from the ledges or slopes of the site.

ʰʰʰAlternative translation: 'the ascending site reduced the area of these and the middle and lower ones'. On the other hand, Elliger has, 'Projecting rocks penetrated into them. From the lower and middle ones/steps led to the upper ones and to the passage beside/the *binyan*.' The section between the strokes is a new piece of text, conjecturally reconstructed to accord with the general description of the building.

ⁱⁱⁱMT: '*binyan*', i.e. building or wall, has no connection with what precedes.

ʲʲʲThat is 'in three divisions' or 'in three rows'. Elliger: they were constructed in three storeys'.

ᵏᵏᵏAnother translation is: 'Hence they were shorter as compared with the lower and middle ones.' Elliger: 'Hence the lower and middle ones were in terraces from the ground.' The idea seems to be that the whole building, because of the irregularity of the site, fell into three divisions, each of which had a piece rising from the ground below the next. This step-like gradation of the building could have been avoided by substructures of pillars, in a way apparently employed in many places in the court (though it must be admitted that the present description of the court supplies no information). Instead of this, the base of the north wall was set back a little deeper at each storey to correspond to the ledges. This, of course, meant that the ground floor of these sections of the building was reduced in size by the ledge projecting inwards, so 'from the lower and middle ones was taken room beginning from the ground' (v. 6).

ᵐᵐᵐMT: 'in front of the temple', which cannot be correct. The LXX text is followed above. The wall referred to in vv. 7–9 has the purpose of protecting the priests' chambers, which projected beyond the terrace between the outer and inner court into the outer court, from the people's chambers at the western outer wall of the outer court and from the traffic in the outer court. So it not only runs along the fifty cubit long wall of the nearby dining-rooms, but another fifty cubits beyond, so as to protect the whole length of the priests' chambers and shut off their entrances from being viewed from the outer court.

[mmm]See the previous note.

[nnn–ooo]See BH.

[ppp]Thus, following MT with a few slight alterations. There is therefore to the south of the *binyan* a priests' chamber exactly similar to that on the north, which does not need to be described at length, since that has already been done in detail for the northern one.

[qqq]MT: 'When they go in, the priests' is rendered intelligible by this slight alteration.

[rrr–www]See BH.

[xxx]The measurements should precede the mention of the wall.

Ezekiel is transported to the place of his vision: 40.1–4

When in 8.1 Ezekiel was transported to Jerusalem in order to see in a vision the destruction of the temple, the happening was given a date. The same holds true of its counterpart, his transportation to view the new temple, last mentioned in 37.27f. The twenty-fifth year after the exile brings us to 573/2, i.e. more than twelve years after the last oracle to the nations in 32.17ff., and two years previous to the last date in the book, in 29.17. The curious way in which the month is stated here is not found eslewhere and is open to various interpretations. Only here in the Old Testament do we find the beginning of the year termed *rōš-haššānā*, literally, the head of the year. Opinions differ as to whether this means the beginning of the cultic year in the seventh month (cf. Lev. 23.24f.; 25.9; Num. 29.7) or whether it is more likely to refer to the beginning of the civil year in the first month. No importance should be attached to the fact that the date is given as 'on the tenth day of the month', as it is to be found with the first as well as the seventh month (cf. Ex. 12.3 and Lev. 23.27; 25.9; Num. 29.7). It therefore seems to have been the usual one in the priestly terminology. As the tenth of the month was never the first day of the year, it is in any case impossible to translate *rōš-haššānā* by 'New Year's day'.[1] This expression can only be taken as referring to the month, which was evidently the first month of the year. This also corresponds to the way in which the year is given according to the civil calendar used throughout the book of Ezekiel. It is, however, striking that in 29.17 and 30.20 this month is denoted by the custo-

[1]The terminology of the Mishnah on this subject is better ignored in the interpretation of the Ezekiel text.

mary ordinal number 'in the first month'. Consequently it is hardly possible to adduce any convincing reason for the choice of a different expression here.

This brings us, then, to the month of Nisan, i.e. March/April 573, as the time when the hand of Yahweh came upon the prophet, i.e. his self-control was overpowered by a divinely caused ecstasy (cf. 1.3; 3.14; 8.1) and, to receive a divinely inspired vision, he was transported to the holy land, being set down on a very high mountain. It is quite obvious that the mountain intended can only be Zion; yet in view of the way in which the mountains around it tower above it, the assertion of its great height is a strange piece of poetic licence. To be sure, we have here the influence of the idea, widespread in the ancient East, including Israel, that the mountain of God is the highest of all mountains (cf. Isa. 2.2; Ps. 48.2; Zech. 14.10) and that the river of paradise had its source in it (Zech. 14.8; Ps. 46.4; Ezek. 47.1ff.). The transference of these primitive mythical conceptions to Zion gives vivid expression to the claim of the God of Israel to the sole possession of majesty and world dominion.[1] At this point the prophet sees something before him like the towering shape of a city; this is the first impression made by what is later seen to be the temple area with its mighty gateways and its successive terraces each rising above the other. He is led on towards this castle-like temple by the hand of God, and sees a man standing in the eastern gate. The man gleams like polished bronze, and by this outward appearance shows himself to be a heavenly messenger. On the other hand, his instruments, as in the case of the seventh man in 9.2, in the linen coat with the writing instruments at his thigh, show what service he is to perform: he has a linen tape in his hand and a measuring reed, the length of which, as subsequently specified in v. 5b, is six cubits and a span. It is therefore the 'long cubit', to be distinguished from the normal cubit, as was the 'royal cubit' of Babylon and Egypt. II Chronicles 3.3, too, seems to know that a different unit of measurement was used for the temple (cf. also the 'writing of man' in Isa. 8.1, which is apparently different from 'writing of God'). These two instruments for measuring larger and smaller distances show that he has been given the task of measuring the sanctuary, and the figures he gives are to be taken as *ipso facto* binding expressions of the will of

---

[1]The seer of the book of Revelation still clearly perceived the significance of these images and applied them to the new Jerusalem, cf. Rev. 21.2, 10. The angel with the measuring reed is also to be found there (Rev. 21.15).

EZEKIEL

the divine architect. He therefore conveys to the prophet a command from God to pay close attention to his measurements and to remember them, so that he may pass them on to the house of Israel.

This has led to the conclusion that what follows was intended to provide the returning exiles with a set of building instructions binding upon them in all details. But even apart from the very obvious gaps in the description which follows (e.g. no particulars at all as to height are given), and apart from the fact that economically speaking the new temple congregation was bankrupt and in possession of very limited resources, too little allowance is made here for the purely visionary nature of the building represented here. The temple makes its appearance as a heavenly reality created by Yahweh himself and transplanted to stand on earth. Its appearance is inseparable from the complete transformation of geographical conditions, producing the towering world mountain with its encircling plain and the miraculous river proceeding from it. There is nothing to suggest that it should have a human builder. The entirely miraculous character of the dwelling place of God described in the following passage must therefore be kept in view in estimating its significance as a whole; the same is true of it as of the descriptions scattered through Isa. 40–55 of the miraculous journey home across the wilderness by the returning exiles, or the statements made about the new Jerusalem in Isa. 60. Already they all shine with the colours of the new age, and are images of the future blessedness which transcends all the limits of history. In this way they are better fitted to represent the magnitude and steadfastness of the divine compassion than some course of events which can be measured and expressed by the petty inadequacies of earth.

This does not rule out the possibility that, by and large, Ezekiel's picture of the temple is modelled on that of the pre-exilic temple at Jerusalem, while reproducing it in ideal proportions. That temple, too, was the copy of a heavenly archetype, the plan of which, according to I Chron. 28.19, had been delivered to David in a writing attributed to the hand of Yahweh. Before that the tabernacle, the prototype of that temple, had been constructed after the form of a heavenly original which had been shown to Moses. This priest, whose every thought and concept was rooted in the sanctuary of Jerusalem, could not draw any ideal picture save along the lines of the memories which haunted him day and night and were confirmed in an hour of holy rapture as the newly existent, ideal dwelling place of Yahweh.

The outer and inner gates:[1] 40.5–37

In Ezek. 40–42 the main concern is to bring out the special characteristics of the vision to which the prophet was led by an angel. It has evidently lost its original simplicity and clarity as the result of a number of subsequent insertions. So it must be reduced once more to its original dimensions if it is to reveal the basic principle underlying it.

The prophet is first of all struck by the wall enclosing the temple area,[2] only the thickness and height of which are given; both of these are the exact length of the measuring reed, that is, six cubits and a span, i.e. a little more than three metres (ten feet). Thus the structure is regarded not as a fortification but as a sort of massive enclosure, separating the holy area selected by God from its secular surroundings and making it recognizable to all. This is in conformity to the new age, to which any sort of military defences are unknown.

[6] After that the angel, followed, of course, by the prophet, who has to keep a close watch on all that he does, climbs the seven steps of the stairway which rises to a height of about two metres (six and a half feet) and leads to the outer entrance of the eastern gateway, so

---

[1] We cannot go into the structural details of the temple here. This commentary does not provide enough space to deal with them exhaustively. Such archaeological matters require an expert archaeologist, sufficiently acquainted with the religious architecture of the ancient East to be able to master the various problems which arise, and therefore able to deliver pronouncements based on a comprehensive view of Israelite architecture in the context of its associations with neighbouring states. Bertholet's and Fohrer's commentaries were able to verify their conclusions in regard to these matters by the co-operation of a biblical archaeologist as distinguished as K. Galling. In this department, however, repeated re-examination and reappraisal of the frequently obscure description of the building has led here and there to important progress towards a better understanding of it, as is shown by the monograph by K. Elliger, 'Die grossen Tempelsakristeien im Verfassungsentwurf des Ezechiel (42.1ff.)', *Alt-Festschrift*, 1953 (Beiträge zur historischen Theologie, no. 16), pp. 79ff., and the exhaustive treatment by H. Gese, *Der Verfassungsentwurf des Ezechiel (Kap. 40 bis 48) traditionsgeschichtlich untersucht* (Beiträge zur historischen Theologie, no. 125, 1957). The present commentary has gratefully made use of the knowledge provided by these basic studies, which at many points have made a definitive contribution towards the understanding of the text. These works are referred to by the author's name only. But obscurities which still remain are not glossed over, nor are other possibilities of elucidating the text excluded.

[2] In Rev. 21.12 this becomes the city wall of the new Jerusalem, so it is described as being great and high, whereas the temple wall here is more modest in its measurements.

that he can first walk the whole distance to the back of the gateway and take its measurements. **[7, 10, 12f.]** On both sides of the passage behind the threshold lie three large niches or side rooms separated by pillars and each about three metres (ten feet) square, which are separated from the central passage by a barrier so that they can serve as a post from which superintending priests or guards can keep watch, and exercise control over those who enter, or stop unauthorized persons. **[8f.]** An inner door gives access to a vestibule about four metres (thirteen feet) long with an open gateway giving on to the fore-court of the temple. **[15]** The total length from the outer gate to the pillar-flanked exit of the vestibule amounts to twenty-five metres (eighty-two and a half feet). **[11, 13]** Hence the breadth measurements conform to the length measurements, in that the average breadth of the gateway represents exactly half its length; thus the proportion preferred is 1:2.

[19] Opposite the gateway of the vestibule and fifty metres (165 feet) away lies the east gate leading to the inner court, so the width of the outer court, including the outer and inner gate projecting into it amounts to a hundred metres (330 feet). **[17f.]** Along the sides of this spacious court, surrounded by a broad stone pavement, rise thirty chambers, which are most probably used for sacrificial meals, and also serve as meeting-rooms for small groups (cf. Jer. 35.2, 4).

[20–27] The inner eastern gate is not as yet entered; instead, the guide goes across to the northern outer gate and then, after it has been inspected, to the southern outer gate, and each of them is more briefly described as having the same measurements as the eastern outer gate. **[28]** Only after reaching the outer southern gate does their path take them through the inner southern gate, which begins in the outer court and leads to the limit of the inner sanctuary. **[31]** Eight steps lead up to its open vestibule which faces the outer court; so the inner court is not quite two and a half metres (eight feet) higher than the outer one. The dimensions of the gate correspond exactly to those of the outer gates. **[32–37]** The prophet and his guide pass through it and reach the inner court and then proceed to the east gate and then to the north gate, establishing that they, too, are exactly the same size.

Tables for slaughtering and priests' chambers: 40.38–46

After this deliberately progressive tour through the gates and courts one would now expect to be led to the temple building itself. Instead, we find that a section giving details about additional furnishings to the northern inner gate has been inserted here. [38] It first mentions a room on or in the vestibule for washing the burnt offerings; [39–43] and secondly eight slaughtering tables in and outside the vestibule for preparing the sacrifices, along with shelves on which to keep the utensils; and thirdly, perhaps by way of a subsequent addition, protective roofs over the tables which stand along the outer wall of the vestibule, evidently out in the open air. These details are in a completely different style from that of the vision narrative; and nothing is said of any measurement or guidance by the angel. The purpose of the objects listed, which are not mentioned elsewhere in the whole narrative, is at times stated in the style of a legal regulation.

[44–46] Equally out of keeping is what is said in regard to two priests' chambers, one at the north and the other at the south gate; here, too, nothing is said about any visit by the prophet under the guidance of the angel; instead, we get more of the information as to their purpose which is withheld elsewhere. [45a] This information is indeed imparted to the prophet by the mouth of the angel, but we must regard it as a very superficial attempt at accommodation to the account of the vision. Thus the whole section must be regarded as a subsequent elaboration, made when the account of the vision was edited to lead over into instructions about how men were to restore the sanctuary. [46] Only the final sentence of v. 46, insisting on the right of the sons of Zadok to minister at the altar, seems not to have belonged in this context originally, but to have been inserted by a glossator, who already had 44.6ff. in front of him and who insisted on regarding what had gone before in the light of it.

Inner court, altar and temple building: 40.47–41.4

The inner court is now approached through the northern inner gate. [47] In direct conformity with what is stated in v. 37, it is found on measurement to be a square of fifty metres by fifty (165 feet by 165). As before, the measuring is carried out by the 'man', and he also conducts the prophet from each place to the next; this shows that we have here a continuation of the main vision. In the middle of the court, and therefore opposite the temple proper, stands the altar, about which, curiously enough, no further details are given. This gap is filled by a later appendix in 43.13–17, in which the prophet is no longer the speaker. [49] The angel now leads on towards the temple proper, which is elevated up ten steps (v. 49) and is therefore about three metres (ten feet) higher than its surroundings. The building, along with the open area on either side of it, also occupies a square the sides of which are fifty metres (165 feet) long, and which abuts on the western side of the square inner court.

[48] Here, too, the prophet is first led into the vestibule: through an open doorway with wall pillars and two columns probably standing in front of it (cf. I Kings 7.15–22) he crosses the chamber, which is ten metres (thirty-three feet) wide and six (twenty) deep, [4.11f.] to enter by a door five metres (sixteen and a half feet) wide into the temple proper, the so-called holy place, which is the same width, but twenty metres (sixty-six feet) in length. Here in the older temple stood the altar of incense, the golden lamps and the table for the shewbread (I Kings 7.40f.) which are probably omitted deliberately; only the last of them is mentioned later in an additional note (41.21b, 22).

[3] A further door, three metres (ten feet) wide, opens into the holy of holies. Here the angel alone enters to take the measurements, while the prophet reverently waits outside; [4] the measure is that of a square ten metres by ten (thirty-three feet by thirty-three). Not a word is said about the ark of the covenant (I Kings 8.6–9). The whole account resembles an outline design which confines itself to the bare essentials and, with the utmost economy of detail, seeks to convey a clear picture of its proportions, while treating all other points as of no importance. This makes it all the more surprising to find the side building of the temple described as fully as it now is.

The side building of the temple: 41.5–12

The description of this portion of the temple, paralleled in I Kings. 6.5f., 8, 10, is hard to clarify in its details. It is enough to say here that we have a three-storeyed annexe adjoining the side and back walls of the temple, containing thirty chambers the purpose of which is never stated. (Were they to hold vestments and utensils and perhaps also votive gifts, and to serve therefore as storechambers or something of the kind?) As II Chron. 3ff. does not mention any such part of the temple, it would seem no longer to have existed in the post-exilic temple.

The nature of the description shows plainly that here once more the prophet's account of his tour has again been interrupted by an intrusive narrative: nowhere is the prophet said to be led. The earlier remarks about the measurements made by the 'man' in v. 5 have no influence over the following verses; here the phrases change, rather, into a bare description of the parts of the building and briefly catalogue the measurements. So v. 5a, with its measuring of the temple wall may perhaps be regarded as belonging to the previous passage; but on the other hand, it may have been added to provide a quite superficial link between the preceding passage and the section which follows.

The overall measurements of the temple area: 41.13–15a

Following on 41.4, 5a, this piece of information is to be expected at this point. Forming a rectangle with sides of 100 cubits (fifty metres, i.e. 165 feet), the temple area in the narrower sense of the temple building and its immediate surroundings corresponds exactly to the inner court. Verse 13b, which anticipates v. 15, may owe its present position to the carelessness of a copyist. Verse 15, which mentions the front side of a building to the west of the temple building beyond an enclosed space (gizrā), a building which was already introduced without explanation in v. 12 under the name of binyan, as though it were already known, may have been included here from the preceding section. In these verses, however, the measurement by the 'man' is introduced once again. The omission of the formula by which his guiding is described may be explained as a result of the process of elaboration of the passage.

The internal decoration of the temple: 41.15b–26

The holy of holies is, as we might expect, omitted from the description, but the ornamentation of the holy place and the vestibule, as well as the appearance of the table of shewbread and the double door are described at considerable length. In view of its contents, the passage might have been expected to come immediately after 41.4, 5a. But the simple description shows itself to be completely unconcerned with any guidance of the narrator or taking of measurements by the 'man'. The insertion of this intrusive narrative into the account of the vision has nevertheless given rise to a communication made to the prophet in v. 22b, which calls the table of shewbread 'the table which is before Yahweh' (I Kings 7.48: 'the table on which the shewbread lies'). We might regard this as a remnant of the original briefer description of the vision given by the prophet himself, which has been displaced by the present more exhaustive description.

The priests' chambers on either side of the western building (binyan):
42.1–14

This passage is introduced by a formula referring to the guide, but it is not clear to what it is connected. We are shown two buildings, each of them comprising three priests' chambers and situated on the northern and southern sides respectively of the large building which lies to the west of and behind the temple. The description given of them forms one of the most difficult sections of this description of the temple. In particular, only a conjectural explanation of the architectural structure of these chambers can be given (cf. the footnotes to the text). The style characteristic of the account of the vision is also absent here apart from the opening words; nowhere is there any reference to measuring or guidance. The purpose of the chambers, that they are to serve as refectories, or changing-rooms, to prevent the holy garments used for priestly ministry from coming into direct contact with the people (vv. 13f.), is stated in words ostensibly addressed to the prophet in v. 13a, but their style is that of a legal code, and agrees ill with the manner in which the 'man' speaks on the other occasions.

The overall measurements of the whole temple area: 42.15–20

Here we undoubtedly have the concluding passage of the prophet's visionary. guiding. We are told of the way in which he is led and how the 'man' moves at regular intervals from one place to the next to take measurements. This is reminiscent of what is said at the beginning of the narrative. But even here there are at least some alterations by another hand, as is shown by certain peculiarities of style which give the section a colouring all its own.

According to the account, the whole temple area is a square with sides of 500 cubits (about 250 metres, i.e. 825 feet), corresponding exactly to the measurements of the sides as previously given. The whole therefore conforms to a complete plan, into which the separate parts harmoniously fit. It summons up a clear picture of a temple compound which forms a most imposing structure. The outer court makes a terrace higher than the level of the ground surrounding it. Its outer walls enclose a great outer quadrangle approached by three great gateways on its north, east and south. Above it rises an inner court also provided with three gateways, standing about two and a half metres (eight feet) above the level of the outer court. It, together with the temple proper, forms a rectangle, the narrower side of which is about fifty metres (165 feet) long and faces east. So the person who has come in from that direction first arrives in a square court the sides of which are about fifty metres (165 feet) long, in the midst of which there stands the altar of burnt offering. On the western side of this court a stair with ten steps leads up to a podium about three metres (ten feet) high, on which the temple itself stands. So the whole complex of buildings is constructed on three successive terraces each raised above the other, with the house of God standing on the uppermost. It catches the eye of the beholder through its dominating position and turns his thoughts to God enthroned above the universe as the Lord in all his glorious majesty (see the illustration in Fohrer, p. 264).

The surprising feature of this picture is its purely two-dimensional geometrical arrangement which, without a word about the elevation of the buildings, produces its effect solely through the symmetry of the plan. Nothing at all is said about any of the internal ornamentation, and the work of the craftsmen in painting, panelling and coating with gold and other metals, apart from a few not very informative statements about palms being carved on the pillars (40.16, 22, 26, 31, 37). Nor is anything said about the purposes of the chambers and open spaces, with all their breadth and spaciousness, permitting the joyous activities of a great festival to develop to the full and impressing the invited guests with the riches and graciousness of the divine host. Nor are we told of the very adequate accommodation provided by the thirty chambers in the outer court for the holding of sacrificial meals and committees, or how their great, easily barred, doors help to guarantee the strict enforcement of order and exclude all forms of undisciplined irreverence. Even the most important of the sacred objects within the temple (cf. above, pp. 545f.) are not mentioned so much as once. The description continually concentrates on the one point, that is to guarantee the dwelling of God among his people; it resists every temptation to portray elaborate detail or to stress individual features in order to excite admiration (one need only compare the description in I Kings 6f., which lays such emphasis on the ostentatious costliness of everything in the temple). In this central mystery resides the guarantee of Israel's well-being and the establishment of the kingdom of God. As the earthly abode is to bear the divine presence in a completely new actuality, there is no longer need of any symbol of that presence. In the old temple there was no way for men to hold back the fire of destruction, once the glory of God had withdrawn from the deconsecrated site. Now, the age of salvation will not pass away, because it depends solely on the new indwelling of this glory, recognized and revered in its towering sublimity, cleansing and purifying, creating peace and giving life among the people of God, and through their mediation to all nations (see also below, pp. 586f.).

The sober unembellished portrayal of this miracle of the divine presence, pervaded once again by an implicit criticism of the old temple, appears altogether in keeping with Ezekiel's whole method of describing man's relationship with God and concentrated entirely on the cleansing power of God's action on his people. To large circles among his people, however, and especially to the priesthood, it was intolerable. They could not envisage a new sanctuary without associating with it the performance of a cult pleasing to God, and this gave rise to various attempts to introduce at suitable points some, at least, of the things which seemed most important from their point of view. The first insertion in 40.38–46 provides for the introduction of the main activities of sacrifice and suggests a numerous body of priests, describing as it does the places for slaughter at the inner north gate and the priests' chambers at the north and south gates. 41.15b–26 tell of the ornamentation, always kept within modest bounds. 42.1–14 are concerned with various measures to ensure the strict maintenance of priestly purity. We will become acquainted with further developments in this direction in the chapters which follow, in connection with the altar of burnt sacrifice and the sacrifices there, as also with the privileges of priests and kings.

With these practical concerns are associated others of a more constructive nature. They find expression in the detailed description of the side building adjoining the temple on three sides, and are evidently mainly due to recollections of an important part of Solomon's temple. They reappear once more in the last chapter.

Once we have learnt to recognize the guiding principle behind the vision narrative, we shall develop a sharp eye for insertions containing matter extraneous to it. This serves to establish that here, as in earlier chapters, later hands have interfered with the original structure of this prophetic book, in a concern to express their particular interests. This has happened here and in the succeeding chapters on an hitherto unprecedented scale. The reason is obvious. One has only to recall how important the temple vision must have been in the eyes of all who were interested in preparing for the building of a temple in Jerusalem.

To suppose that the passages we have set aside are really expansions from the prophet's own hand would not only ignore the differences in vocabulary and style, but would also make the author responsible for such an ineffective and incomplete expansion of his first version as not merely to ruin its original form but also to distort its real purpose so much as to make it unrecognizable. Ezekiel's vision of the future had a character all its own, and was wholly unsatisfactory to the priestly interest. So to assume it to have been subsequently adapted for the purpose of putting into effect actual arrangements for congregational worship seems to us to furnish the most natural explanation. It provides a satisfying understanding of this last portion of the book, unhampered by preconceived opinions about Ezekiel the priest.

CHAPTER 43.1–27

Yahweh's entry into the temple
The altar of burnt offerings and the sacrifices offered on it

43.1–12 *The appearance of the glory of God*

1 And he brought me to the gate [. . .]ª facing east, 2and behold, the glory of the God of Israel came from the east, and the thunder of it was like the thunder of mighty waters,ᵇ and the earth shone with his glory. 3[. . .]ᶜ and the vision I saw was [. . .]ᵈ like the visionᵉ that I had seen by the river Chebar, and I fell upon my face. 4And the glory of Yahweh entered the temple by the gate facing east. 5And the power of the spirit lifted me up and brought me into the inner court, and behold the glory of Yahweh filled the temple. 6And I heard one speaking to me out of the temple, while the man was standing beside me, 7and he said to me: 'Son of man, do you seeᶠ the place of my throne and the place of the soles of my feet, [where I will make my name to dwell]ᵍ in the midst of the people of Israel for ever? And the house of Israel shall no more defile my holy name [. . .]ʰ 8[. . .]ⁱ by their abominations which they have committed so that I have had to consume them in my wrath. 9Now let them put away their harlotry [. . .]ʲ far from me, that I may dwell in their midst for ever. 10But do you, son of man, give the house of Israel the information about the house [. . .]ᵏ and its measurement and pattern,ˡ 11[. . .]ᵐ the image of the temple and its arrangement and its exits and entrances, [. . .]ⁿ

and make known to them all its ordinances and all its laws and write them down in their sight, *so that they may observe and perform all its laws*[o] *and all its ordinances.* 12 *This is the law of the house: the whole territory round about upon the top of the mountain shall be most holy. Behold, this is the law of the house.'*

43.13–17 The measurements of the altar

13 *And these are the measurements*[p] *of the altar in cubits, the cubit being reckoned with a handbreadth added: its excavated depth*[q] *shall be one cubit and its breadth one cubit with a rim of one span round its edge. And this shall be the height*[r] *of the altar:* 14 *from the excavation on the ground to the lower rim two cubits and the breadth one cubit,*[s] *and from the smaller rim to the larger rim*[t] *four cubits and the breadth one cubit.* 15 *And the* 'ari'el[u] *four cubits and from the* 'ari'el *projecting upwards four horns on its four sides.*[v] 16 *And the* 'ari'el *shall be square, twelve cubits long and twelve cubits broad* 17 *and the* [*large*][w] *rim shall be fourteen cubits long and fourteen broad on its four sides* [*and the smaller rim sixteen cubits long and sixteen broad on its four sides*][x] *and the border around it half a cubit broad and its excavated depth one cubit round about. And its steps shall face east.*

43.18–27 The sacrifices at the consecration of the altar

18 *And he said to me: 'Son of man, thus says* [. . .][y] *Yahweh: These are the ordinances for the altar in the day when it is erected for offering burnt sacrifices upon it and for sprinkling blood upon it.* 19 *You shall give to the levitical priests of the family of Zadok who may draw near to me, says* [. . .][z] *Yahweh, to minister to me, a young bull from among the cattle for a sin offering.* 20 *And you shall take some of its blood and put it on the four horns and on the four corners of the rim and upon the border round about and thus cleanse it from impurity.*[aa] 21 *And you shall take the bull of the sin offering, and it shall be burnt in the* mipqad[bb] *belonging to the house outside the sacred area.* 22 *And on the second day you shall offer a he-goat without blemish for a sin offering and the altar shall be cleansed, as it was cleansed with the bull.* 23 *And when you have finished cleansing it, you shall offer a bull without a blemish and a ram from the flock without blemish.* 24 *And you shall present them before Yahweh, and they shall sprinkle salt upon them and offer them up as a burnt offering to Yahweh.* 25 *For six*[cc] *days shall you provide daily a goat for a sin offering, also they shall provide a young bull from among the cattle and a ram from the flock, beasts without blemish.* 26 *Seven days shall they make atonement for the altar and purify it and so consecrate it.* 27 *And when they have completed*[dd] *these days, then from the eighth day onward the priests shall offer your burnt offerings and your peace offerings, and I will accept you, says* [. . .][ee] *Yahweh.'*

[a]See BH.

[b]This comparison is secondary in 1.24 and may be so here. As, however, 3.12 also mentions the noise when the throne of Yahweh was in movement, one cannot regard it as impossible that the same is thought to happen here.

cSee BH.

dMT: 'like the vision which I had seen when he came to destroy the city'; an insertion based on such secondary passages as 8.4; 9.3; 11.23; cf. above, pp. 105f., 108ff.

eLXX: 'and the vision of the chariot'; no chariot is ever spoken of in connection with the earlier appearances of the glory of God, even though the large insertions in ch. 10 may have been occasioned by the idea of a chariot (cf. pp. 115f.). The LXX therefore provides a subsequent explanation of the difficult MT: 'and visions like the vision', the first word of which must be deleted.

fSee BH.

gThus LXX instead of MT: 'where I will dwell'.

hMT: 'they and their kings by their harlotry and by the dead bodies of their kings in the midst of them' (see BH) g'by setting their threshold by my threshold and their doorposts by my doorposts, so that there was only the wall between me and them': this is a more detailed description, not to be expected here, of the profanation of the name of God, which, however, concentrates in preference on 'harlotry' (v. 2), sufficient examples of which are provided by ch. 8.

iSee the previous note.

jMT: 'and the dead bodies of their kings'; inserted from the previous verse.

kMT: 'that they may be ashamed of their iniquities'; secondary insertion.

lThus instead of MT: 'and they measure the pattern'.

mMT: 'and, if they are ashamed because of all that they have done'; an insertion at an unsuitable point.

nThe second half of v. 11 has been seriously disturbed by copyists' errors and corrections which have crept from the margin into the text.

oSee BH.

pConjecture: 'foundations' (Galling).

qThis refers to the channel running round the altar which was left open by those who constructed the altar's base. Its depth and breadth require a rim which, according to v. 17, is half a cubit high and, according to v. 13, a span wide, to prevent anyone falling in.

rSee BH.

sThe first step of the altar, a square of sixteen by sixteen cubits (cf. v. 17b), is two cubits high and projects a cubit beyond the step above it. It is called the lower or smaller border.

tThe second step of the altar, here called the large border, is a square with sides fourteen cubits long (v. 17a), four cubits high and also projects a cubit beyond the step above it.

uThe name of this uppermost step of the altar should not be translated 'lion of God', but interpreted as meaning the 'burning place' or 'hearth' of God, taking the root as being 'rh, to burn. It is the actual hearth on which the sacrificed animal is burnt, a square with sides twelve cubits long (v. 16); it is also four cubits high and has the four horns, well known from pre-exilic tradition, at the four corners, which are especially holy and are used in sprinkling of blood.

vTo be inserted here from the end of v. 16.

wInserted as the sense demands.

xInserted as the sense demands.

y–zSee BH.

ᵃᵃMT: 'and make atonement for it' is not in LXX.

ᵇᵇUncertain in meaning, perhaps 'appointed place'. As in Neh. 3.31 a *mipqad* gate is also mentioned, the above-mentioned burning place may be expected to have been situated near it.

ᶜᶜAs the sacrifice of the second day mentioned here can only be offered on six days, the 'seven' of MT must be altered. On the other hand, this number is in the right place in v. 26, since it speaks in general terms of the whole ceremonial of consecrating the altar.

ᵈᵈRead the perfect: the phrase is not found in LXX.

ᵉᵉSee BH.

Yahweh's glory fills the temple: 43.1–12

[1] The measurements have concluded by establishing the dimensions of the total area (42.15–20). Then the angel leads the prophet back to the outer eastern gate, to the very point outside the gate at which the whole tour had started (40.3–6), so that he may witness the spectacle of Yahweh ceremonially taking possession of the temple. As the whole temple complex faced east, that was the direction from which the solemn entry might be expected to take place. [2] The appearance in glory of the God of Israel (cf. 1.28) had been described at length in ch. 1, [3] so the prophet does no more than refer back to the appearance at the Chebar by which he received his calling. There the vision had drawn near in a storm wind (1.4) and then vanished (3.12); so, too, here it is preceded by a mighty roaring sound. Just as earlier the appearance of the one who sat in indescribably shining splendour of colour on the cherubic throne had blinded the prophet's eye (1.26–28), so now it shines even more brightly and fills the whole earth with its light (cf. Isa. 40.5). [4f.] Only to look upon such blazing splendour throws a man to the ground (cf. 1.28), so that after the vision has disappeared into the temple through the two eastern gates the power of the spirit has to lift Ezekiel up again on to his feet (cf. 2.2) and bring him into the inner court, whither the angel accompanies him, as a sign that he has yet to complete his task. [6] Now, from the temple illuminated by the theophany,[1] Ezekiel hears words addressed to him. Extreme reticence is shown, and the speaker is not explicitly named, as he points to the importance of the event which has taken place so suddenly and so strikingly: God has taken up his dwelling in the midst of his people by preparing a perpetual place for his name, i.e. his revealing presence, henceforth in the temple. [7] He uses the same expressions as those that are to be

[1]An evident counterpart to the description in 10.3f., 5.

found in the prayers of the old temple, speaking of the temple as his throne (cf. Jer. 14.21; 17.12) and as the place of the soles of his feet (Lam. 2.1; Ps. 99.5; 132.7), using these anthropomorphic expressions to exclude all doubt about the reality of his presence. He combines this mode of speech with the Deuteronomic use of the name of God as a synonym for his direct presence with his people, and at the same time refers, as was most usual in priestly circles, to glory as the mode in which the supernatural God appears in earthly spheres. [7-9] Thus while guarding against any crude localization of the world-God in a single building like the temple, such as had been a constant threat to temple-worship in pre-exilic days, he expresses in compelling terms what faith wants and needs for its vitality: the direct encounter with God, and his penetration and control of earthly phenomena. As the central point for a believing people who have once for all left behind them the horrors of apostasy to alien powers along with all its social consequence in their new life of communion with the holy God, the temple makes possible that fellowship between God and man which can never again be imperilled, in which the fulfilment of his commandment is taken for granted as one element of the life of faith; and God's lordship on earth is thus effectualized. It must be shown as realistically as possible that this is the object of the divine economy of salvation. In this way the outward forms of temple worship are to be penetrated, and their inward meaning laid bare. This is the purpose of this sober yet irresistibly logical structural outline of the buildings of the temple and the account of how God takes possession of them as he returns to his people. It provides us with an apt delineation of the objective at which the prophet aimed in his whole life work.

[10f.] It also makes immediately intelligible the command, repeating a direction already given in 40.4, to give information to the people in writing about the form and arrangements of the temple. Yet at the same time, it is plain that this command has undergone expansion, in order to adapt it to a different description of the temple which we have recognized already in some isolated additions, but which does not find its full expression until ch. 44ff. The prophet's vision is reinterpreted and made into a set of directions as to how worship is to be conducted in the new temple. This has led to the inconsistency which strikes us in this series of chapters and, at the end of God's injunction, to the insertion of those laws and regulations without which the prophet's vision appeared to be incomplete in the eyes of disciples who were priests by profession. This alien element added to the original wording is intended to make a bridge over to the following chapters. It therefore needs to be indicated in different type.

[12] Verse 12 also seems to be connected with this purpose. This proclamation of the law of the temple is not a conclusion drawn from what has preceded (Herrmann). We can see that from the impossibility of describing ch. 40–42 in such terms, as also from the direct way in which v. 12 is connected with the laws and ordinances mentioned in v. 11. On the other hand, the temple laws given in ch. 44ff. do need to be introduced by some such ceremonial heading as this. Here we, in fact, have a conventional introductory formula of the Priestly Code, cf. Lev. 6.9, 14, 25; 7.1, 11, etc. The formula is, of course, also employed at the conclusion of a proclamation of the law, cf. Lev. 11.46; 13.59; 14.32, 54. In the latter passage, the formula is also repeated at the end of the same verse, as it is in Ezek. 43.12. But in the Priestly Code the concluding formula is always used to wind up a preceding legal text which, as has already been remarked, is not the case here. This means that v. 12 must be paving the way for a proclamation of the law which is to follow, and which will be proclaimed in the customary form of the Priestly Code. In that case, however, a transition is being made here with all due form from, on the one hand, the vision of a temple which comes down to earth as a heavenly reality and signifies God's dwelling with his people as the highest fulfilment of all the expectations of salvation to, on the other hand, practical directions in regard to the use of the temple by priests and people.

The declaration that the whole of the temple area is most holy is therefore put at the beginning as the presupposition of all the laws that are to follow: their aim is to preserve and assert the special character of the area. But it must be admitted that the following chapters do not form a complete code of law. It might be possible to ask whether v. 12 did not originally introduce a much ampler body of law, much of which has either been lost or deliberately suppressed out of regard for the Priestly Code in Leviticus. That is, however, unlikely. Like the additions in ch. 40–42, the chapters which now follow do not look as if they belonged to a systematic corpus of law, but possess all the marks of a very heterogeneous set of amplifications, which seemed important to those who composed them and which were attached to each other as well as circumstance allowed.

The altar of burnt offering: 43.13–17

It is generally recognized that this passage cannot originally have been one of the laws of the sanctuary. It contains only the dimensions of the altar, which are not stated in juridical style but in the form of the description of a building. In content it is undoubtedly connected with the account of the temple measurements in ch. 40ff., and must have its proper place there, after 40.47. But it is quite impossible to maintain that it was once removed from that position to its present one. This is because there is no reference at all to the prophet's being led or to the angel's taking measurements; there is a successive enumeration of the measurements of the various parts of the altar. The introductory heading 'these are the dimensions of the altar' does indeed recall the style of the law, but this is not maintained in what follows. It is impossible to regard the section as anything other than an appendix of independent character inserted here during the redaction of the book, since it was possible in this way to go from the temple to a single part of the temple and on from there to the outer eastern gate.

The description is easy to understand in itself and remarkable for the fact that what it contains disregards the old law concerning the altar of Ex. 20.25f., according to which no hewn stone is to be used in constructing an altar, and an altar is not to have steps leading up to it. After Solomon had already ignored this in constructing his bronze altar (II Chron. 4.1; I Kings 8.64) and building a temple according to the taste of his time, King Ahaz, according to II Kings 16.10ff., constructed another altar in its stead, following an Assyrian pattern. According to I Macc. 4.47, the Jews erected an altar of unhewn stones in accordance with the old law after the expulsion of the Syrians. Here great blocks of hewn stone rise like a tower one on top of another so that the altar grows narrower as it rises. The question has been raised whether this has not been modelled on a Babylonian ziggurat. In that case, the author of this account would be contrasting a 'cult-requisite for the worship of the God of heaven' with the 'imposing idol-monuments' of heathendom (Fohrer-Galling, pp. 238ff.). It is also interesting to see an illustration of a stepped altar of similar type in the synagogue at Dura Europos (*ibid.*, p. 338).

The consecration of the altar: 43.18–27

According to vv. 18f., the prophet himself is told by Yahweh what abundant sacrifices are to be offered to cleanse the altar, and then he together with the priests puts the orders into execution. So we find him taking the same position as that ascribed to Moses in Ex. 29.31ff., in the sacrifices for the consecration of the priests. It is, however, clear that there was never any question for Ezekiel himself of his taking up this sort of position as arch-priest. On the other hand, supposing that what was aimed at was the subsequent attachment of the law of the altar to the temple vision, then the only way to achieve it was to make Yahweh entrust the prophet with the task, and to make it a continuation of the directions given in 43.1–11. Now it can be demonstrated that the third person plural which first appears in vv. 25bff. in reference to the priests who carry out the rite of sacrificial cleansing was originally the characteristic pattern of the whole rite. So we have here an independent account of the ceremony of purification which was accommodated as far as necessary, through v. 18, to fit in with the temple vision, without being completely assimilated (as is clear, for example, from the fact that in v. 24 God is twice spoken of in the third person). The enhancement of the sacrifice of a young bull on the first day and a he-goat from the second to the seventh day as a most holy offering, of which nothing but the blood comes to the altar, while all the rest is burnt up outside the temple, is quite unparalleled in any of the propitiatory sacrifices of the great Day of Atonement in Lev. 16 and shows that the priestly ritual has developed further.

LAWS OF THE SANCTUARY
44–46

CHAPTER 44.1–3

The use of the outer east gate

1 *And he brought me back towards the outer gate of the sanctuary which faces east, and it was shut.* ²*Then [he]*ᵃ *said to me: 'This gate is to remain shut. It shall not be opened, and no one shall enter by it; for Yahweh, the God of Israel, has entered by it, therefore it shall remain shut.* ³*Only*ᵇ *the prince*ᶜ *he alone may sit in it in order to take bread before Yahweh. He shall enter by way of the vestibule of the gate, and shall go out by the same way.'*

ᵃMT: 'Yahweh', but Yahweh does not speak here; he is mentioned in the third person in v. 2. The speaker is the guiding angel.
ᵇ⁻ᶜSee BH.

[1] We notice a certain carelessness about the way in which the prophet is led and addressed in the introduction to this small section. Whereas in the previous passage the prophet was led by the spirit into the inner court (43.5) in order to hear Yahweh address him, we find here that the same formula about leading is used as before, but without any precise delineation of the agent; this is intended to recall 43.1 and simply imply the 'man' with the measuring reed. [2] This lack of clarity has led some reader to think that the words that follow (v. 2), like 43.6, are words of Yahweh, and so he has inserted the divine name. In actual fact the explicit mention of Yahweh in the third person in vv. 2 and 3 serves to demonstrate that the author was thinking here of the 'man' as the speaker. The pattern of guidance has therefore been reintroduced here without any reference to ch. 43, merely in order to effect a smooth join between the measuring of the temple and what now follows. The sequence of leading, vision and explanatory address during the measuring of the temple automatically begins again here.

The angel who is leading the prophet next brings him out of the inner court and back to the east gate, to inform him that it is to be kept closed in the future. The reason is that it was through this gate that the glory of God passed in returning to his people, and so this holy place must be preserved from every profanation. The further corollary of this precaution, either emphasizing the continuity of God's presence henceforth with his people or ruling out any retrogression into sun worship, because the opening of the eastern door at the equinox would allow the rays of the rising sun to penetrate into the temple, is not so readily suggested by these words; in the case of the latter, there are doubts about its physical possibility which cannot be overcome, in view of the fact that the temple stood at a higher level than the gate.

[3] The one person counted worthy of treading on such a holy spot is the reigning prince of Israel, who is allowed to consume his sacrificial meal within the gate-building by going into it from the outer court through the vestibule and out again by the same route, in order that the eastern gate may remain closed. As the future prince, as will later be made plain, possesses a number of other definite cultic privileges and duties, it is quite intelligible that an exception should be made in his case. This is confirmed by 46.1ff.

In communicating these instructions, the angelic guide of ch. 40–42 evidently takes on a new role which did not originally belong to him, that of serving as an intermediary for laws applying to the temple area. This task has already been prepared for by the enrichments made to the word of Yahweh in 43.11; but now the Lord who spoke directly to his prophet retires behind the divinely-sent interpreter of his command; his transcendence is thus perceptibly heightened.

CHAPTER 44.4–31

Regulations for Levites and priests

4 *And he brought me by way of the north gate to the front of the temple, and I looked, and behold the glory of Yahweh filled the house of Yahweh, and I fell on my face.* [5] *And [he]*[a] *said to me: 'Son of man, mark well and see with your eyes and hear with your ears, what I say to you*[b] *concerning all the ordinances of the temple of Yahweh and all its laws, and mark well those who may go into the temple and all*

those who must be excluded from the sanctuary.[c] [6]*And say to the house*[d] *of rebelliousness, to the house of Israel, Thus says* [. . .]ᵉ *Yahweh: Now let there be an end to all
your abominations, O you of the house of Israel.* [7]*You have admitted foreigners
uncircumcised in heart and flesh to be in my sanctuary and to profane it* [. . .],ᶠ
*when you offer my food, the fat and the blood, and thus you have broken my covenant
to add to all your abominations.* [8]*And you have not kept charge of my sanctuary, in
appointing them*ᵍ *to do service to me in my sanctuary.*

[9] *Therefore*ʰ *thus says* [. . .]ⁱ *Yahweh: No foreigner, uncircumcised in heart
and flesh, shall enter my sanctuary, of all the foreigners who are among the people of
Israel.* [10]*But the Levites, who went far from me, when Israel went astray, who went
astray from me after their idols, they shall bear their guilt* [11]*and shall minister in
my sanctuary as watchers at the gates and shall serve in the temple: they shall slay
the burnt offering and the sacrifice for the people and shall attend on them, to serve
them.* [12]*Therefore because they have*ʲ *ministered to them before their idols and thus
become a stumbling block of iniquity to the house of Israel, therefore I have lifted
my hand (in an oath) against them, says* [. . .]ᵏ *Yahweh, that they shall bear their
guilt* [13]*and not come near me, to serve me in the priesthood, or to come near any of my
holy things nor to that which is most holy. Yes, they shall bear their shame because of*ˡ
the abominations which they have committed. [14]*And I appoint them to keep charge of
the temple, to do all its service and all that is to be done in it.*

[15] *But the Levitical priests, the sons of Zadok, who kept the charge of my sanctuary when the people of Israel went astray from me, they shall be permitted to come
near me to minister to me and to attend on me to offer me the fat and the blood, says*
[. . .]ᵐ *Yahweh.* [16]*They may enter my sanctuary and approach my table to minister
to me and keep my charge.* [17]*When they enter the gates of the inner court, they shall
wear linen garments, but no wool shall touch their bodies, while they minister at the
gates of the inner court and in the temple.* [18]*They shall have linen turbans upon their
heads and linen breeches upon their loins; they shall not gird themselves with anything that causes sweat.* [19]*And when they go out into the outer court* [. . .]ⁿ *to the
people, they shall put off the garments in which they have been ministering and lay
them in the chambers of the sanctuary and put on other garments, lest they communicate holiness to the people with their garments.* [20]*And they shall not shave their heads,
nor let their locks grow long, they shall only trim the hair of their heads.* [21]*No priest
shall drink wine, when he enters the inner court.* [22]*They shall not marry a widow or a
divorced woman, but only a virgin of the stock of the house of Israel or the widow of a
priest.* [23]*And they shall teach my people the difference between the holy and the
common and show them how to distinguish between the unclean and the clean.*
[24]*And in a controversy they shall act as judges, and they shall judge in the criminal
court according to my judgments. They shall keep my law and my statutes in all my
appointed feasts, and they shall keep my sabbaths holy.* [25]*They shall not defile
themselves by going near a dead person; only for father or mother, for son or daughter,
for brother or unmarried sister they may defile themselves.* [26]*And when such a man is
clean again, he*ᵒ *shall count for himself seven days* [27]*and on the day that he goes*

again [. . .][p] *into the inner court, to minister in the sanctuary, he shall offer his sin offering, says* [. . .][q] *Yahweh.* [28]*And* [*they shall have no inheritance*][r], *I am their inheritance. And* [*no*] *possession* [*shall be given*][s] *them in Israel, I am their possession.* [29]*They shall eat the cereal offering and the sin offering and the guilt offering, and every devoted thing in Israel shall be theirs.* [30]*And the best of all the firstborn of every kind, and every heave offering of every kind from all your offerings*[t] *shall belong to the priests, and the best of your mingled dough you shall also give to the priest, that a blessing may rest upon your house.* [31]*The priests shall not eat of any carrion or of anything torn of bird or beast.'*

[a]Here MT once again mentions Yahweh as the speaker, as in 44.2. It is for the same reasons to be regarded as an incorrect definition of the subject of the verb in a later interpretation.

[b]See BH.

[c]With a slight alteration of the obviously corrupt MT reading 'in regard to the entrance to the house through all the exits of the sanctuary' (cf. Fohrer).

[d–o]See BH.

[p]MT: 'into the sanctuary', which the sequel shows to be an over-exact gloss which should be deleted, as it is not found in LXX.

[q–s]See BH.

[t]In Num. 18.26–29 this means a tithe of the tithe.

At the beginning of this section the formula about leading is used in the same way as in 44.1, once again placing the prophet in the inner court, as in 43.5. The course followed through the outer court to the inner north gate so as to arrive in the temple filled with the glory of Yahweh is prescribed by 46.1, according to which the inner east gate must remain shut on weekdays. At the sight of the glory which appears in the temple, the prophet again falls on his face; no notice of this, however, is taken in the following passage (cf., on the other hand, 2.1ff.), which begins at once with words spoken by the angelic guide, who goes on to announce further temple regulations in the name of Yahweh. Here the introductory exhortation in v. 5 can be seen to be verbally identical with 40.4, apart from a few changes in the order of the phraseology, except that it concludes by calling the prophet's attention not to what he is to be shown but to what he is to be told. Thus 40.4 forms the model according to which the new exhortation to pay attention is deliberately and carefully constructed. This utilization of ch. 40 and 43 serves to confirm what has already been concluded from other indications, that the regulations about the temple are a later insertion, which is now being put into the mouth of the angel. The introductory title applies well enough to all the

sections which follow as far as 46.19, where we once more find the
formula about leading. This merely provides the framework necessary for fitting into the actual vision the other additional material
alien to it, so as to combine all the heterogeneous material into an
integral whole.

This, of course, cannot obscure the fact that the appendix has no
connection whatsoever with what Ezekiel originally wrote, and that
it betrays its totally different origin by its form and content. The form
of these sections shows that the traditions they convey have a history
of their own, embracing as they do passages of earlier and later dates.
It is obviously very difficult to distinguish what is original and what is
a later addition in material of such a legal type, as our requirement
of logical sequence and systematic development of the material
belongs to our way of thinking, and cannot be expected from ancient
writers. Attempts to separate earlier and later ingredients are therefore more a matter of conjecture than an assured result of research.
At the same time, it is impossible to deny the general fact that there is
a mixture of pieces of varying provenance.[1]

In addition to this, there is a totally different estimate and valuation of the first chapters of the temple vision, which diverges in
essential points from that made by the prophet himself. To Ezekiel,
the temple which he is shown is a miraculous creation of Yahweh's,
done without the co-operation of any human hand, and thus a manifestation of the new aeon. It is quite out of the question for the old
features of Solomon's temple to be transferred to it. In addition, the
picture shown to him earlier in ch. 34-37 presented a people inwardly and outwardly transformed. For them the ideas of reverently
keeping their distance under external restraint from the holy God
now dwelling among them no longer apply, since the God of their
salvation has become a reality to them through a fellowship no longer
disturbed by any guilt. No room is left here for rebukes for past sins
or for sins that still threaten, any more than there is room for human
precautions taken in order to prevent any backsliding into the former
sins. Only a retrogression from this time of fulfilment to a cultic
community which, while idealized, is still menaced by the old conditions of human imperfection and error, can render intelligible the
juridical system presented in the passages which follow, in which
ancient legal prescriptions, in a form similar to that of the Priestly

[1] For the details, we can only refer here to the researches by H. Gese, cf. below,
p. 543, note 1.

Code in Exodus, Leviticus and Numbers, are given a new application. The totally different atmosphere which prevails in ch. 40–43 is no longer present here. Instead of the sight of the divine miracle which is still continuing in ch. 40–43, the temple vision becomes the means of giving energetic completion to a new constitution for the community returned from exile, in which the priestly ideals of purity and holiness are reflected in every detail. Attempts to make light of this distinction must in time be seen to be impossible; their sole effect is to make it difficult, if not altogether impossible, to understand Ezekiel's prophecy. They change the prophet, boldly moving forward to a new future, into a petty-minded man who takes refuge in the old-fashioned forms of the priestly ideal of holiness, who becomes false to his own vocation, and uses the prophetic ecstasy in which he felt himself uplifted above all earthly sources of knowledge as a literary form by means of which he can bestow on his flight the mantle of divine revelation which may lend it the necessary authority.

A recognition of the real nature of the legal content of ch. 44–46 liberates us from forming such a contradictory picture. These chapters present the outline of a legal system similar to that which underlies the Priestly collection of laws in Exodus, Leviticus and Numbers. But in spite of the closeness of the relationship, it differs from the latter in the independent character of its formulation, which is of a sort which would never have been adopted there. No self-contained composition can be recognized in this collection of legal material. At the most, vv. 6b–16 can be regarded as a consistent systematization of temple worship, with which some individual provisions in the following section, such as vv. 17, 19, 21 can be connected, while the rest of this material is concerned with other aspects of priestly purity which needs to be guarded in various directions.

[6–8] Verses 6–8 contain a word of reproach addressed directly to the people of Israel. First it finds fault with the employment of non-Israelite slaves for menial services in the temple, an arrangement apparently taken over from usual Canaanite practice, as there is evidence for a similar custom in Phoenicia. [9] In v. 9 a threat seems to be beginning with the usual introductory prophetic formula, but it turns out to be the proclamation of a legal enactment in which Israel is no longer directly addressed. [10–14] Here a demand is made for the total exclusion of heathen from services in the temple; their place is to be taken by the Levites, i.e. in the linguistic usage of this passage, the former priests of country high places, who are to carry out their duties as guardians at the temple gates and assistants to visitors to the temple in slaughtering animals for sacrifice, but who are always strictly excluded from actually ministering at the altar. The reason given for this degradation is the idolatry in which they formerly indulged, and by which they misled the people.

[15f.] The sons of Zadok, here called 'Levitical priests' according to a favourite expression in Deuteronomy, are appointed as the offerers of sacrifice and guardians of the inner sanctuary. This is allegedly because they held steadfastly to the rightful worship of Yahweh in the days of Israel's apostasy. This reason, which has little connection with historical fact, is an astonishing one, and would have been totally unimaginable from the mouth of Ezekiel. The state of affairs in the temple of Zion described in ch. 8 and the threats and accusations in 7.26 and 22.26 show clearly what Ezekiel thought. The legislator who speaks here must, of course, be sought among the Zion priesthood, who claimed to be descended from the Zadok, who exercised his priesthood under David in the royal sanctuary. As a result of the banishment by Solomon of Abiathar, whose name is given along with his (I Kings 1.26f.), Zadok evidently became the sole high priest of the Jerusalem sanctuary, and his successors naturally tried to preserve this privileged position in the sanctuary when its importance continued to increase after the fall of northern Israel. When, shortly before or after the exile, the Zion temple won a position of monopoly, the problem of the country Levites, whose sanctuaries had been laid waste during the political catastrophe and owing to the reform by king Josiah, became a burning one. The Zadokites showed a tendency to evade the provisions of Deut. 18.1, 6f. and to push the Levites down into a subordinate position in temple ministry, whereas actual ministry at the altar and in the temple was reserved for themselves. In our chapters it is possible to follow the gradual sharpening in the formulation of this tendency; in 40.45f., two classes of priests are named, one of which serves within the temple precinct whereas the other takes over the ministry of the altar. Yet neither of these classes is denied the title of priest. The gloss in 40.46b, evidently under the influence of 44.6ff. is the first to describe the class designated to minister at the altar as Zadokites. The distinction between Levites and priests comes out clearly in ch. 48, in which different portions of land are assigned to the two groups, yet even there the confining of the priesthood to the Zadokites does not force its way in until the gloss added to 48.11. Only 44.6ff. states any clear separation between Levitical 'ministry in the house' and Zadokite 'ministry in the sanctuary' as a legalized system; 45.1ff. and 46.19ff. already take this separation for granted.[1]

On the other hand, the statements that non-Zadokite priestly families were accepted for ministry in the sanctuary, while all legitimate priestly families had to be descendants of Aaron in the wider sense, shows that this legal decision was not finally enforced after the exile without the successful resistance of some individual Levitical families. The Zadokites claimed to be descended from Elezar, the elder son of Aaron (I Chron. 6.4–8) and laid claim to a leading position by this right of primogeniture, while other priestly families claimed that they went back to Ithamar, the younger son of Aaron (cf. I Chron. 24; Ezra 8.2; Neh. 7.61ff., compared with I Chron. 24.10). So the regulation in Ezek. 44.6ff. is modified in the Priestly Writing into the form of a distinction between sons of Aaron and Levites (Num. 18.1–7) and in this way becomes determinative in regard to the form of priestly service.

[17–22] The list of commandments for priests enumerated in vv. 17ff. deals with such matters as clothing (cf. Ex. 28.42f.; Lev. 16.4), coiffure (cf. Lev. 21.5, 10), wine drinking, forbidden to priests when ministering (the same prohibition occurs in Lev. 10.9, and one may see its importance brought out by Isa. 28.7), regulations about marriage (cf. Lev. 21.7, 13ff.). [23–31] It also gives a short summary of priestly duties in relation to the people, including instruction in the laws about purity (cf. Lev. 10.10), judicial decisions in difficult cases (cf. Deut. 17.8ff.), provisions to ensure the sanctification of the sabbath and the proper celebration of festivals (cf. Ex. 31.12–17, where the importance of the sabbath is considerably increased, and again Lev. 23.4ff.), the avoidance of uncleanness through contact with a corpse (cf. Lev. 21.1–3; 15.13, 28; Num. 19.11ff.), the conditions under which priests might hold property (cf. Num. 18.8ff.; Deut. 10.9; 18.1ff.), the avoidance of unclean meat (cf. Lev. 22.8; extended to all Israelites, Lev. 7.24). No fixed order can be discerned in this list and the items often have no connection with ministering in the sanctuary. Evidently the original text has been enlarged and elaborated.

[1] Gese, *op. cit.*, p. 67, can even claim that there is a secondary Zadokite stratum in Ezek. 40–48.

CHAPTER 45.1-8

The portion of land set apart from the holy land as a gift
consecrated to Yahweh and the land assigned to the city
and the prince

1 '*And when you allot the land as an inheritance, you shall set apart for Yahweh
an oblation of the land, a holy district twenty-five thousand cubits long* [. . .]ᵃ *and
[twenty thousand] broad. It shall be holy in all the border thereof round about.*
²[. . .]ᵇ ³*And in the holy district [you shall]*ᶜ *measure off a section twenty-five
thousand cubits long and ten thousand broad, in which shall be the sanctuary; the most
holy place* ⁴[. . .]ᵈ *of the land it is. It shall be for the priests, who minister at the
sanctuary, and approach Yahweh, to minister to him. And it shall be a place for their
houses [and pasture for their cattle].*ᵉ ⁵*Another section, twenty-five thousand cubits
long and ten thousand cubits broad, shall be for the Levites, who minister at the
temple* (cf. 44.11, 14); *it shall be assigned to them as a possession [with cities to live
in].*ᶠ ⁶*Alongside the portion set apart as the holy district* (cf. v. 1) *you shall assign
for the possession of the city an area five thousand cubits broad and twenty-five
thousand cubits long; it shall belong to the whole house of Israel.*

7 *And to the prince shall belong the land on both sides of the holy district and of
the property of the city, alongside the holy district, and the property of the city, on the
west side towards the west and on the east side towards the east corresponding in
length to one of the (tribal) portions from the western to the eastern boundary of the
land.* ⁸*It shall be his property in Israel, so that the princes [of Israel]*ᵍ *may no more
oppress my people, but let the house of Israel have the land according to their tribes.*'

CHAPTER 45.9-17

Regulations for the princes

9 '*Thus says* [. . .]ʰ *Yahweh: Enough, O princes of Israel! Put away violence and oppression, and execute justice and righteousness! Cease your evictions of my
people, says* [. . .]ⁱ *Yahweh.* ¹⁰*You shall have just balances and a just ephah and a
just bath.* ¹¹*The ephah and the bath shall be of the same measure, the bath containing
one tenth of a homer and the ephah one tenth of a homer; the homer shall be the
standard measure.* ¹² *The shekel shall be twenty gerahs; [five]ʲ shekels shall be five
shekels and [ten]ᵏ shekels shall be ten shekels, and your mina shall be [fifty]ˡ shekels.*

13 *This is the offering which you shall make: one sixth of an ephah from each homer of wheat and [one sixth]*ᵐ *of an ephah from each homer of barley.* ¹⁴*And the fixed portion of oil: [. . .]*ⁿ *one tenth of a bath from each cor (the cor contains ten baths) [. . .]*ᵒ ¹⁵*and one sheep of the flock from every two hundred [from the families]*ᵖ *of Israel for cereal offerings, burnt offerings and peace offerings, to make atonement for them, says [. . .]*�q *Yahweh.* ¹⁶*All the people [. . .]*ʳ *shall give this offering for the prince in Israel.* ¹⁷*It shall be the prince's duty to furnish the burnt offerings*ˢ *and the cereal offerings and drink offerings at the feasts, the new moons and the sabbaths, at all the appointed feasts of the house of Israel.*

18 *Thus says [. . .]*ᵗ *Yahweh: In the first month, on the first day of the month, you shall take a young bull without blemish and cleanse the sanctuary.* ¹⁹*And the priest shall take some of the blood of the sin offering and put it on [the]*ᵘ *doorposts of the temple and on the four corners of the border of the altar and on [the]*ᵛ *posts of the gates*ʷ *of the inner court.* ²⁰*You shall do the same on the seventh day of the month*ˣ *for anyone who has sinned unintentionally, and for anyone who has sinned unwittingly; and so shall you make atonement for the temple building.*

21 *In the first month, on the fourteenth day of the month, you shall celebrate the feast of the Passover: for [seven]*ʸ *days unleavened bread shall be eaten.* ²²*On that day the prince shall provide for himself and all the people of the land a bull for a sin offering,* ²³*and during the seven days of the festival he shall provide as a burnt offering to Yahweh seven young bulls and seven rams without blemish, on each of the seven days, and a he goat daily for a sin offering.* ²⁴*And he shall provide as a cereal offering an ephah for each bull and an ephah for each ram and a hin of oil to each ephah.* ²⁵*In the seventh month, on the fifteenth day of the month and for the seven days of the feast, he shall make the same provision for sin offerings, burnt offerings, cereal offerings and for oil.'*

ᵃSee BH.

ᵇMT: 'and of this a square plot of 500 by 500 cubits shall be for the sanctuary with fifty cubits for an open space around it'. The verse is not presupposed by v. 3, which follows immediately on v. 1; the measurements given are already known from 42.15–20, except that in this one a strip of fifty cubits of untilled land is made to surround the sanctuary. The insertion of v. 2 has led to a misunderstanding of v. 1 and to textual alterations in vv. 3f.

ᶜSee BH.

ᵈMT: 'holy'; the insertion of this word (not in LXX), in order to make it easier to connect with v. 1, compels us to associate the last word of v. 3 wrongly with the sanctuary, whereas it is actually applied to the district which is measured off.

ᵉ⁻ⁿSee BH.

ᵒMT: 'for a homer contains ten baths': a note describing the homer and cor as identical in quantity.

ᵖ⁻qSee BH.

ʳMT: 'the land': this probably points to the reading 'the people of the land'.

ˢ⁻ʷSee BH.

ˣThe LXX gives another date: 'in the seventh month on the first day of the month.' The MT therefore refers to the seven days of the feast mentioned in v. 18, whereas LXX is thinking of a second festival of purification in the seventh month. This second reading departs very noticeably from the way in which the Priestly Code fixes only one feast of atonement in the year (cf. Lev. 16 and 23.26ff.), on the tenth day of the seventh month.

ʸSee BH.

The oblation of land destined for Yahweh: 45.1–8

This section is not a direct continuation of the preceding one, even though Israel is addressed directly in both places (in fact, the rule is not strictly adhered to in this section). As is shown by the beginning, with its reference to the allotting of the land to the tribes, 47.21ff. is presupposed here, the first passage in which we are given explicit details about the distribution of the land. Many commentators therefore insert the present section before ch. 48, where 48.9ff. forms an exact parallel to it. But it seems, rather, to repeat in terser form what is stated in ch. 48, and in this respect it appears already to be influenced by 44.6ff.[1] Its connection with that passage is shown by its use of the same word and idea once again: of the portion of consecrated land which plays a part in 45.1ff. and is employed to provide a loose connection with the priestly laws, to pass on from that to deal with the duty of princes.

[1] Verse 1 requires that in the redivision of the holy land a piece of consecrated land, bearing the stamp of exceptional holiness, shall be assigned to Yahweh. [3f.] For it is here that, with the temple there lies the holy of holies of the land. The section of land consecrated to Yahweh consists of a rectangle twenty-five thousand cubits long and twenty thousand cubits broad: it is divided lengthwise into two great strips of equal size, each ten thousand cubits broad and assigned to the priests and to the Levites. The strip of land allotted to the priests has the temple precinct at its central point, while the remainder provides sites for dwelling houses and pasture for cattle. This conforms to 44.28 in so far as the land is not stated to be the inheritance or property of the priests; it does no more than provide them with a means of support. [5] This does not apply to the Levites' strip of land which lies to the north; this is explicitly called their property, and also supplies sites on which cities are to be built.

[1] Cf. 45.4 with 44.28.

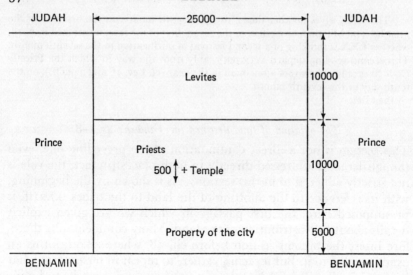

[6] To the south of these two sections is attached a similar section only five thousand cubits broad, which is reserved for 'the city', i.e. Jerusalem, which in the future, as in the past, is to be closely connected with the sanctuary. This gives a square with sides twenty-five thousand cubits long, the measurements of which evidently witness to the perfection of the region thus marked out. The shape taken by the land allotted to the city is far from suitable for its natural expansion. But this does not occur to the author. In his eye, geographical considerations are outweighed by the theoretical perfections of geometrical measurements. Chapter 48 then proceeds in the same cavalier fashion, ignoring all previous historical conditions and geographical possibilities, to measure out areas for five tribes to the south and seven tribes to the north of the city. This is a corollary derived from the new messianic form given to Israelite life as seen by the prophet in his vision. That is a point to which we shall have to return later.

[7] The prince is to receive his estate from land lying on both sides of the piece of consecrated land set apart as a gift for Yahweh. It has the same breadth of twenty-five thousand cubits as the central square, and stretches west and east, to the frontiers of the holy land at the Mediterranean and the Jordan valley. The fact that the prince's land lies next to that consecrated to Yahweh is undoubtedly meant to give him an advantageous position, just as in what follows he is the mediator of the sacrificial gifts of the people.

[8] This makes it the more striking that v. 8 should conclude this allotment of the land by a sharp rebuke. It is stated that he has this amount of land assigned to him in order to protect the people against all oppression, consisting in their being forcibly deprived of their lands by the princes. Here Yahweh himself suddenly begins to speak. This was forgotten in the preceding passage, in which Yahweh was referred to in the third person (v. 4) and the princes are now spoken of in the plural. This version must therefore be regarded as an insertion disturbing the original wording of the section, and made in order to introduce the severe reproaches against princes in vv. 9ff.

The cultic duties of the prince: 45.9–17

As in 44.6, the series of commandments addressed to the prince is introduced by the prophetic formula 'thus says Yahweh', and the words of reproach also commence with these same words. We could only conclude that they were by the same writer if the words which follow could be understood as a deliberately planned elaboration of the law for the priests. But this is not the case, as vv. 13–15 and 18–20 can be seen to be prescriptions for sacrifices, originally intended for the people or the presiding priest, which have been worked over at a later date in such a way as to make them accentuate the importance of the prince. **[9]** Verse 9 is therefore seen to be a deliberate imitation of 44.6, made in order to make an originally independent law fit in better with the context.

As in the transition in v. 8, the arraignment is not against the prince, as in v. 7, but against the princes of Israel. This makes it perfectly clear that here we are no longer presented with the figure of the servant David, the good shepherd who is to put into effect God's purposes of blessing his people. What the writer is thinking of is the restoration of a ruling dynasty among the people after their return, and he does not show any interest in its Davidic descent. But this new institution suffers from the same faults as the old one; it is possible for the old selfish attempts to extend the powers of royalty and to infringe the laws of God to revive even here. So its representatives receive vigorous admonitions to preserve law and righteousness, couched in the manner of the old prophets. Instead of arbitrary oppression of the people by all sorts of excessive taxes and tributes, for the purpose of securing a means by which the government may indulge in an ambitious foreign policy at the expense of neighbouring nations, a return is to be made to discipline and moderation. This is the point of view which suggests the provisions that follow, even though they may not be calculated to further it. The taxes to be paid by the people are to be settled in a way which is to be binding in the future.

[10–12] These regulations are preceded in vv. 10–12 by the establishment of a fixed standard for measures, weights and coinage, with no explicit mention of who is to be responsible for enforcing it. However, the context makes it clear that the writer intends to name one of the important duties to be performed by the prince, in view of the clear association between it and the collection of tribute. For weights and measures the connection is obvious. For the question of money being up to weight, we have only to recollect how money might be substituted for payment in kind, and how its purity is determined by its weight, which gave plenty of opportunities for cheating (cf. Amos 8.5; Hos. 12.7; Micah 6.10f.). We therefore find similar warnings in Deut. 25.13ff.; Lev. 19.35f. The destruction of the solidarity between all the members of the nation through secret interference with the means used to pay wages and prices, and also any enrichment of the state treasury by such manipulations, is not accepted as an inevitable evil in the Old Testament, but is met with threats of punishment by the God of the covenant.[1]

[13–15] Verses 13–15 state the tribute to be paid by the people; it is very moderate in quantity, is paid in kind, and goes to the sanctuary to provide the regular sacrifice for the congregation. It therefore does not serve to swell the state treasury or to add to the riches of the prince, who must draw his income from the land assigned to him; it is used to finance the worship of God in his holiness by his people. [16f.] Verses 16f., which, in contrast to vv. 8b and 9, again use the singular in referring to the prince, appoint him as the one who receives the tribute and passes it on to the sanctuary. This duty committed to him of providing for the worship of the temple certainly makes him seem to be an important cultic official, a sort of patron of the Church, who, as the representative of the nation, brings into the house of God the sacrificial offering by which the congregation is reconciled, and thus incorporates in his own person the nation's obedience and willingness to maintain the great institution of atonement upon which their fellowship with God depends. But any active

[1] For weights, measures and money in ancient Israel, cf. Kurt Galling, *Biblisches Reallexikon*, 1937, cols. 174ff., 366ff.; B. Reicke and L. Rost (eds.), *Biblisch-Historisches Handwörterbuch*, vol. I, 1962, cols. 546f.; vol. II, 1964, cols. 1159–69.

intervention in the cultus by new regulations, the power to make which was taken for granted as belonging to the king in pre-exilic times, is not even considered here. As far as the performance of the priestly ministry is concerned, he is in exactly the same position as any other individual among the people, even though his rank is taken into consideration so far as to permit him to be present at the solemn sacrifices in a preferential position (46.2) and to take his sacrificial meal at the outer eastern gate (44.3).

[18–20] A priestly torah on the purifying of the sanctuary has found its way into vv. 18–20. The duty of carrying it out is assigned to an unspecified 'thou', perhaps addressed earlier to the high priest, but which, judging from the present context, is probably meant for the prophet, who, according to 44.6, is to make known the regulations concerning the sanctuary. The sanctuary is to be purified before all the great festivals, a feature which shows the tendency of the post-exilic cultus to concentrate on removing all guilt which may deprive the nation of God's grace. According to the Massoretic text, this means not only two purificatory ceremonies at the beginning of every half-year, but also the first and last days of the same festival week. This also adds importance to the offerings which are made for the same purpose of purification. The argument for the celebration, that it is performed because of the erroneous sins of the congregation, is unexpected and cannot refer solely to the second ceremony, seeing that intentional sins cannot possibly be atoned for in such a way. The last sentence seems to connect the atonement made by the second ceremony with the whole temple area by its naming of the temple building; this marks a distinction from the purification of the sanctuary (v. 18), i.e. the inner court, made by the first ceremony (Gese). But perhaps the sentence is no more than a summary post-script.

In contrast to these arrangements for the festival, the Priestly Writing in Lev. 23.26ff. and Lev. 16 lays down that the festival is to take place on the tenth day of the seventh month.

[21–25] Verses 21–25 name the Passover and Harvest Thanksgiving as the two great annual feasts for which the prince is to provide sacrifices of a specially solemn character. The Passover on the four-teenth day of the first month is followed by the seven-day-long feast of

Mazzoth, marked by the eating of unleavened bread. Here, as in
Deut. 16, it seems to be a part of the Passover feast, and its earlier
independent existence is totally forgotten. The Harvest feast or Feast
of Ingathering, here called simply 'the Feast', because it does, in fact,
mark the climax of the year, is to be celebrated by the offering of the
same sacrifices. Nevertheless this does not entirely match what is
prescribed by the Priestly Writing in Lev. 23.33ff. and Num. 29.12ff.
Yet the date given for both feasts is the same there and in the present
passage.

It is significant that the expression 'people of the land' is used in
v. 22 as a term for the lay people as distinguished from priests,
Levites or princes. As compared with its old meaning, of full citizens
of Israel, and its post-exilic one, which served to distinguish the
portion of the people who stayed in the land during the exile from
those who had returned from banishment, it has here evidently
become a technical term of cultic terminology, and one which is not
to be found elsewhere in Ezekiel.

CHAPTER 46.1–24

Further cultic obligations of the prince and provisions regulating his hereditary property

1 *'Thus says [. . .]*[a] *Yahweh: The gate of the inner court that faces east shall
be shut on the six working days; but on the sabbath day it shall be opened and on the
day of the new moon it shall be opened.* 2*The prince shall enter by the vestibule of the
gate from without, and shall take his stand by the post of the gate; then the priest shall
offer his burnt offerings and his peace offerings, while he worships at the podium*[b] *of
the gate and then goes out. And the gate shall not be shut until evening.* 3*The people
of the land shall worship before the entrance of that gate before Yahweh on the
sabbaths and new moons.* 4*The burnt offering that the prince offers to Yahweh on the
sabbath day shall be six lambs without blemish and a ram without blemish.* 5*And the
cereal offering with the ram shall be an ephah, and the cereal offering with the lambs
shall be as much as he is able, together with a hin of oil to each ephah.* 6*On the day of
the new moon he shall offer a young bull from among the cattle without blemish, and
six lambs and a ram, which shall be without blemish;* 7*as a cereal offering he shall
provide an ephah with the bull and an ephah with the ram and with the lambs as
much as he is able, together with a hin of oil for each ephah.*

8 *When the prince enters, he shall go in by the vestibule of the gate and he shall*

go out by the same way. [9]*When the people of the land come before Yahweh at the appointed feasts, he who enters by the north gate to worship shall go out by the south gate, and he who enters by the south gate shall go out by the north gate. He shall not return by way of the gate by which he entered, but shall go out straight ahead.* [10]*But he that is prince among them shall go out again[c] by the door by which he came in.*

[11]*And at the feasts and the appointed seasons the cereal offering with a young bull shall be an ephah, and with a ram an ephah, and with the lambs as much as he is able to give, together with a hin of oil to an ephah.*

[12]*When the prince provides a freewill offering, either burnt offerings or peace offerings* [. . .][d] *to Yahweh, the gate facing east shall be opened for him, that he may offer his burnt offerings or his peace offerings, as he does on the sabbath day, and he shall go out, and after he has gone out the gate shall be shut.*

[13]*You shall provide a lamb a year old without blemish for a burnt offering for Yahweh; morning by morning you shall provide it.* [14]*And you shall provide a cereal offering with it morning by morning, one sixth of an ephah, and one third of a hin of oil to moisten the flour, as a cereal offering for Yahweh. This is the continual ordinance (the continual offering[e]).* [15]*And they shall provide the lamb and the meal offering and the oil morning by morning for a continual burnt offering.*

[16]*Thus says* [. . .][f] *Yahweh: if the prince makes a gift to any of his sons out of his inheritance, it shall belong to his sons, it is their property by inheritance.* [17]*But if he makes a gift out of his inheritance to one of his servants, it shall be his till the year of liberty and then it shall revert to the prince. Only the inheritance[g] of his sons shall continue to be theirs.* [18]*The prince shall not take any of the inheritance of the people, thrusting them by force out of their property. He shall give his sons their inheritance only out of his own property, so that none of my people shall be dispossessed of his property.*

[19]*And he brought me through the entrance, which was at the side of the gate, to the north row of the holy chambers for the priests,[h] and behold there was a place at the extreme western end of them.* [20]*And he said to me: 'This is the place where the priests shall boil the guilt offering and the sin offering and[i] where they shall bake the cereal offering, in order not to bring them out into the outer court, and to communicate holiness to the people.'* [21]*And he led me forth to the outer court, and led me to the four corners of the court, and behold in each corner of the court was a court;* [22]*thus in the four corners of the court were small courts, forty cubits long and thirty broad; the four were of the same size* [. . .].[j] [23]*On the inside, round each of the four courts, was a row of masonry, with hearths made at the bottom of the rows round about.* [24]*And he said to me: these are the kitchens[k] where those who minister at the temple shall boil the sacrifices of the people.*

[a]See BH.
[b]See above the commentary, p. 113, on ch. 8–11.
[c]This follows Herrmann's proposal, after the Syriac version. MT: 'When they go in, the prince shall go in with them; and when they go out he shall go out.' It is

difficult to see how he can do this at the same time as the whole multitude of visitors to the temple, who may keep on coming and going all day long.

ᵈ⁻ˡSee BH.

ʲThe closing word of the verse, distinguished in MT by Massoretic points, and thus contested, can be translated 'made into corners'. But it seems to be the result of a copyist's error and is not supported by the other witnesses to the text.

ᵏSee BH.

Regulations about the sabbath and new moon: 46.1–10

Here, alongside rules for the offering of sacrifices, regulations for the behaviour of those who celebrate festivals in the temple area play an important part. **[1f.]** As before, the prince enjoys privileges not possessed by the congregation: the east gate to the inner court, closed on workdays, is opened on sabbaths and new moons so that he may go in through its vestibule and stand by the doorposts of the gate which encloses the vestibule on a raised step (podium), and witness from there the offering of the sacrifice. **[3]** The people, on the other hand, may only stand and worship in silence in front of the gateway. After the prince has left his position and gone back the way he came into the outer court, the door is left open until the evening. In view of their subject, the rules about conduct in vv. 8–10 should follow at this point, but instead they are preceded in vv. 4–7 by an enumeration of the sacrifices for the two festivals, for the provision of which the prince is responsible. **[4f.]** The sabbath with its six lambs and one ram is allotted as many animals for sacrifice as the seven days of the week; **[6f.]** the new moon receives an additional young bull, which is perhaps an expression of the greater age and dignity of that feast. The association between the moon and the bull is a primitive one, as the Babylonian cultic hymns show. In addition to this, there are the accompanying offerings of corn and oil. The Priestly Writing, in Num. 28.9–15, strengthens and refines the new moon sacrifices, but has a simpler sacrifice for the sabbath.

[9] In order to control the movements of the festive crowd in the temple precincts, v. 9 arranges that only the north and south gates shall be used for access, and that each person entering shall make his exit by the opposite door, so that two streams of visitors to the feast will meet each other. **[8, 10]** The prince alone, as has already been said in the comment on v. 2, uses the inner east gate as both entrance and exit. We are not informed by what gate he enters the outer court. The pre-exilic positions of the palace and temple would suggest the south gate.

Two postscripts: 46.11–12

[11] Verse 11 gives an isolated regulation about meal offerings on feasts and holy days. We may perhaps take it as a correction to 45.24, which does not mention any meal offering with lambs. In that case, it must have found its way into the text at the wrong place. [12] Verse 12, on the other hand, arranges that at freewill sacrifices by the prince, which are not tied to festivals, the east gate is to be used in the same way as at feasts, except that the gate is to be closed again immediately after the sacrifices.

Regulations about the daily sacrifice: 46.13–15

This section differs from the preceding ones in that it gives an independent priestly ordinance in regard to the daily burnt offering, and omits all mention of the prince. [13f.] The regulations issued in regard to the provision of sacrifices are made in the second person singular, in conformity with 45.18–20 and 43.18–27, which blend elements from priestly tradition with instructions to the prince. The insertion of such material is perfectly explicable by reason of its content, but the way in which it retains stylistic peculiarities shows that the author of this chapter was not aiming at producing a unified composition. Instead, he tried to secure his object by loosely assembling together traditional material, and treating its special characteristics with respect. This can still be seen in this passage from the way in which the directions about meal offerings differ from 46.5 and 7.

Whereas the Priestly Writing prescribes a daily morning and evening burnt offering (Ex. 29.38–42; Num. 28.3–8), here all that is spoken of is the morning burnt offering called the *tamīd* (continual offering). [15] Following a favourite expression of the Priestly Writing, it is described emphatically as an everlasting ordinance, and in the concluding phrase is brought into conformity with the priestly requirements (Ex. 29.42; Num. 28.3, 6) by means of the technical term *'ōlat tamīd*, 'continual burnt offering'.

The conditions under which the prince is to hold property: 46.16–18

This section explicitly refers back to the regulations for the prince. Externally it has nothing to do with the cultic obligations of the prince, but it is not entirely unrelated to them, since it tries to prevent any permanent alteration in the property holding of the prince as a result of gifts of land. This is to obviate the temptation to appropriate the ancestral land of the tribes and thus to maintain a healthy basis for the system according to which tribute is paid. [16] So the prince is empowered to transfer the ownership of his property to one of his own sons, and the one to whom it is given is approved as the successor in ownership of the land. [17] On the other hand, gifts of land to any of the prince's servants are allowed only as a temporary lease, which terminates at the year of liberty. It has been thought that the year of liberty occurs every seventh year, since the proclamation of freedom for Hebrew slaves in the seventh year is described in Jeremiah (34.8, 15, 17) by the word *derōr*, the same term as that used in v. 17, whereas it does not occur in the relevant laws (cf. Ex. 21.2; Deut. 15.12). However, a period as short as this so reduces the value of such a gift that a better possibility may be the land law of Lev. 25, where the word *derōr* is used for the return of all landed property that has been sold to the original owner in the fiftieth year, called the year of Jubilee (Lev. 25.10). Perhaps the formulation of Lev. 25 took place at the same time as that of the composition of the present regulation.

[18] The concluding verse, basing the foregoing regulations on a prohibition relative to members of his people being dispossessed by the prince, is filled with a similar distrust of the newly re-established dynasty to that expressed in 45.8. One may ask whether this ought not to be regarded as a late addition to the regulations for the princes, in view of the more benevolent terms generally used to describe this privileged status. It is in keeping with the nature of the cultically based community ideal that, seeing that the protection of the congregation is ensured by the presence of Yahweh, the prince should not be allowed by the new age to develop political power.

The section is constructed in a way answering to the division of land described in 48.1ff. and 45.1–8, so that it is probably one of the later additions to the appendices to this prophetic book. The transposition from the land laws to the cultic regulations also suggests a subsequent elaboration of the latter.

An appendix to the description of the temple: 46.19–24

Here, with the regulations fixing the place in which sacrifices are to be cooked, we find an appendix to the description of the temple given in ch. 40–42. The way in which the formula of the prophet's being led precedes the account also brings out its connection with that passage. The main concern of its author is evidently to make a precise division between the sphere of the holy and that of the profane,

FURTHER CULTIC OBLIGATIONS OF PRINCE: 46.1–24   579

the point which was also the determining factor in 42.13f. **[19f.]** The kitchens for preparing the meals destined for the priests are situated at the back of the priests' chambers described in 42.1–13, so they ought really to have been referred to at that point. Their purpose is to prevent the food from especially sacred offerings from being allowed to communicate its holiness to the outer court and thus to the profane multitude. **[21–24]** Spacious cooking places in the four corners of the outer court are allotted for the preparation of the people's sacrificial meals. There the duty of preparing those portions of the sacrifice which they are allowed to consume is undertaken by the Levites, who are described as 'those who minister in the temple', a title already known to us from 44.11 and 45.5.

Had these been indispensable parts of the description of the temple, then they would already have had to be inserted in 42.14 and 40.17 respectively. But they are evidently supplements, and so an attempt has been made to try to fit them in among the numerous directions about sacrifices in the more loosely arranged section, ch. 45f.

So we notice that ch. 46 has the same structure as ch. 45. Cultic laws explicitly concerned with the prince appear in conjunction with ordinances relating to priests, the style and structure of which, like 45.18–20 and 46.13–15, shows them to belong to an independent stratum, while on the other hand their style points to a connection with 43.18ff. This material was eventually assembled under the main aspect of the prince's cultic duties and attached to ch. 44 by a number of different links (cf. 45.8f. 5; 46.24). It absorbed some further additions at a later stage (cf. 45.2; 46.11f., 16–18, 19–24). All the constituents of the chapter serve to confirm the observation made in connection with 43.10f., that the command given by God at his entry into his temple have been subjected to further elaboration, and that this in turn has led to the setting down of the laws for the sanctuary, according to which a cultic type of worship, conducted in the earthly sanctuary, may develop. The formula describing the way in which the prophet is led is employed upon occasion, as are words directly spoken by Yahweh, but this cannot conceal how totally different the subjects here are in themselves and in the motives which have given rise to them, because they have grown on other ground than the actual description of the temple with which they have been blended. It is a documentary expression of the same priestly type of piety that is developed still more exhaustively in the Priestly Law. We must certainly not overlook the great service it performed in imposing

strict discipline on the cult-community: great emphasis is placed on
the way in which the holiness of God's person provides the unity for
his commandment, and there is a concern throughout for a purity
which embraces all of life and mirrors in all spheres of human
existence the purity of the divine nature. Yet even so, it must necessarily seem completely alien to the clear assurance of the prophetic
visionary, in whose eyes all the details of cultic worship become unimportant and fade away in the light of the divine act by which the
chosen people is created anew. The hope of the prophet's faith was on
such a sublime scale that it could regard the legal community simply
as an interim measure between one age and the next (cf. above, p.
243), but it was taken up by priestly interpreters and once more
contained within the limitations of actual earthly conditions, in which
the eternal archetypes of divine grace were once again to assert themselves in the old way as forces to renew and preserve life. The exegete
must regard it as his duty to do full justice to the different types of
faith manifested in different contexts, without trying to harmonize
away the oppositions between them, and thus depriving them of the
fruitfulness of their mutual tension.

CHAPTER 47.1–12

The temple spring and the river of paradise

1 *And he led me again* to the door of the temple, and behold, water was
issuing from below the threshold (podium) of the temple towards the
east, for the front of the temple faces east. And the water flowed down
[. . .]ᵃ from below the south front of the temple [. . .]ᵇ 2Then he brought
me out by way of the north gate, and led me round on the outside to the
outer gate that faces towards the east; and behold, the water was gushing
from below the wall on the south side. 3And the man [led me out]ᶜ east-
ward [. . .]ᵈ and he measured a thousand cubits and led me through the
water, and it was ankle deep. 4Again he measured a thousand and led me
through the water, and it was knee deep. Again he measured a thousand
and led me through the water and it was up to the loins. 5Again he measured a thousand, and it was a river that I could not pass through, for the
water was so deep [that one had to swim],ᵉ a river that one could not
wade through. 6And he said to me: 'Have you seen this, son of man?'
And he led me back along the bank of the river. 7And as I went back, be-

hold there were very many trees upon the bank of the river on the one side and on the other. [8]And he said to me: 'This water flows towards the eastern region and goes down into the [Arabah][f] and flows into the sea, into the [salty waters],[g] and the water will become fresh.

9 And wherever [the river][h] goes, every creature which merely moves shall live, and there will be very many fish. When this water comes there, then it[i] shall become fresh [. . .][j] [10]And fishermen will stand beside it from En-gedi[k] to En-eglaim.[l] And there will be many drying places for nets there; the fish [of it][m] will be after their kinds like the fish of the Great Sea, exceeding many. [11][. . .][n] [12]And on the banks of both sides of the river there will grow all kinds of fruit trees, the leaves of which shall not wither nor shall their fruit fail. Every month they shall bear first-fruits; because the water for them flows from the sanctuary. Their fruit therefore will serve for food and their leaves for healing.'

[a]See BH.

[b]MT: 'south of the altar'; seeing that the south side of the temple has just been referred to, this is rather unintelligible. In addition, the use of a different word for 'south' from 40.24 casts doubt on the mention of this new fixed point.

[c]MT: 'at the going out of the man', which is stylistically unusual and difficult to connect with what follows. It seems to be originally a correction intended to rule out any notion that the passage is concerned with going through the east gate.

[d]MT: 'and there was a measuring line in his hand': subsequently inserted in view of the process of measuring, but using a different term for the line from the usual one.

[e]Literally 'water for swimming'.

[f]The name for the low-lying steppe-like land on both sides of the Jordan above the Dead Sea.

[g]See BH.

[h]MT: 'the two rivers'.

[i]That is the salty water referred to in v. 8.

[j]MT: 'and everything will live wherever the river goes'; originally a marginal correction to the beginning of the verse.

[k]At about the middle of the west shore of the Dead Sea: now 'ain dšidi.

[l]Cannot be identified with certainty; supposedly near the mouth of the Jordan.

[m]See BH.

[n]MT: 'But its swamps and pools shall not become fresh; they are to be for collecting salt from.' In view of the way in which it provides for the maintenance of the important industry of salt-collecting, this verse should be regarded as a gloss. It has no connection with the preceding sentence.

The first part of ch. 47 returns once more to giving an account of a vision of the same kind as that in ch. 40–43. Once more the same man acts as guide, takes measurements, and furnishes explanations of what is seen. The introductory phrase, telling how the prophet is 'brought back' to the front of the temple, is not, of course, original. It can only be accounted for by assuming that there is a connection here with 46.21, and that an attempt was made here to link this new piece to that secondary element in the text. As we left the prophet waiting for the proclamation of the temple regulations in the inner court (cf. the remarks on 43.10f.), there is no need to say anything about an alteration in his position.

The original introduction seems to have been displaced by this redactional formula. What follows, however, agrees so strikingly with the former description given by the prophet of the miraculous change in Israel's fortunes, and brings it to a conclusion so characteristic of him, that one would need to have very convincing reasons before one could treat it as being on the same level as the regulations found in ch. 40–48. The further additions which have found their way into the text here are confined to comparatively modest limits and do not exceed the average number seen to occur elsewhere in the book of Ezekiel.

[1] At the eastern front of the temple, in the place where Ezekiel has received the command to make a written record of his temple vision, a wonderful event takes place to display what fullness of blessing is beginning to operate now that God has entered the holy of holies. Before the entrance, and significantly from under the podium there, which supposedly was an essential feature of a temple, being the place where the authorized representative of the invisible God took his stand (cf. above, p. 113, n. 1), he sees a spring well out. This proves to be a messenger of salvation sent directly from the Lord of the temple. It trickles first from below the south wall of the temple and thus vanishes from the prophet's sight. [2] Only when the guiding angel leads him on through the north door (the only route left after the closing of the east outer gate) and along the outer wall of the temple precinct to the closed east gate does he realize that it has turned in its course towards the east and is flowing from below the south wall of the eastern temple gate. [3] Not until after the 'man' has led him away to the east of the temple area does he see that the trickle has grown into a brook which flows in the same direction and now very rapidly increases in depth and abundance of water. [4f.] Four times the guide measures a length of a thousand cubits along it in order to call attention to the sudden increase in the depth of the waters which in just over a mile have grown from a brook no more than ankle deep to a great river which can only be crossed by swimmers. [6] At this point

the angel-guide makes him turn round and come back, after calling his attention to the inexpressible abundance of water in the desert of Judah, which was formerly known for its drought. **[7]** Now he sees a second wonder: in what was formerly bare ground bordering the watercourse there stand innumerable trees, transforming the barren desert landscape into a field gleaming with verdure. **[8]** Of the further transformations produced by the stream as it goes along its way the angel informs the prophet by word of mouth, rather than showing him. The river flows out with undiminished force down into the cleft of the Jordan, to debouch into the salty waters of the Dead Sea. Even in the absence of further descriptions we can ourselves imagine what a transformation of the wilderness is thus effected, in the way twice outlined by Isaiah as a picture of the future (Isa. 29.17; 32.15ff.), and in the way used on such a scale in Deutero-Isaiah to describe the future salvation. **[9f.]** The dead landscape of the Dead Sea, which seems under a curse, the secret of which old narrators knew and told (Gen. 19), undergoes a complete transformation, and, thanks to the strong health-giving properties of the temple spring, the salt water is turned into fresh water, in which living creatures can disport themselves and where fish can become as varied and numerous as in the sea. Numerous villages full of fishermen come into existence and the uninhabited region becomes a place in which men make their homes. To simplify this comparatively exhaustive description by eliminating alleged additions does not really do justice to the intention of the narrator to make his audience aware of the full wonder of it all. **[12]** The concluding phrase calls attention to a special quality in the trees growing on the river banks: they are to display inexhaustible fruitfulness, bearing new fruit every month, so that as in Amos 9.13 the harvest goes on all the year round. The leaves of the trees drive away sicknesses and so the fortunate inhabitants of the blessed land do not suffer from them.

The wonderful effects produced by the waters that flow from the temple leave us in no doubt as to the source on which this chapter has drawn for its images and its colours: it is from the stories of the river of paradise, whose streams make glad the city of God (Ps. 46.4), the city which stands upon the highest of all mountains (Ps. 48.3), and may be compared to the world-mountain, on which the dwelling place of God stands, and from which the four world-rivers issue forth (Gen. 2.10-14). The psalmists can tell of the river of pleasures and the well of life (Ps. 36.7), with which Yahweh provides drink for his people in his house. This is the language they use when they seek to give praise to the refreshment bestowed by the communion with God which is found in the temple. It is insufficient to refer to the well of Gihon, which springs up in the valley of Kidron, below the temple, to account for the notion of a well of life associated with the temple, despite the importance of this source for Jerusalem. Just as we have already found the myth of the world-tree and of the world-mountain recurring in Ezekiel (31.1ff.; 40.2, cf. above, pp. 424f., 541f.), so, too, the river of paradise and the images of the marvellous blessings associated with it now appear. This is what the prophecy of Joel means by the well proceeding from the house of Yahweh and watering the mythical vale of acacias, and what Zech. 14.8 signifies by the living waters which will flow out in the time of salvation to the eastern and western seas, in summer as well as in winter. At the same time, a comparison between Gen. 2 and this passage in Ezekiel makes it clear that this conception could take many different forms and was not confined to any single systematized shape (compare what is described here with Gen. 2). The features selected by Ezekiel surely represent only one of the numerous variations of the mythical conception which seemed to the prophet to be especially appropriate for his purpose.[1]

Here, too, a myth has been employed in order to express spiritual realities which grew up on totally different soil. God's saving acts in Israel contain an affirmation of a fulfilment which is to become a reality in history, to make it an abode for the fellowship between God and man. This cuts the ground from under the feet of pagan conceptions which are still tied to the influences of the powers of nature. At the same time, the myth now serves to produce awareness of the total otherness of God's new world by the element of the miraculous contained in it. But the decisive feature is not limited to an earthly manifestation of how salvation takes a bodily form among the chosen people corresponding to the daily experience of earthly happening, important as is the rejection of all attempts to spiritualize this away. It may be called a this-worldly happening (Fohrer). But it is to be understood that it takes place in a transformed world, and that the forms taken are not a mere natural development from present earthly

[1] In Rev. 22.1f. we find the symbols of the river of water of life with its trees of life suggesting the return of the former paradise. Evidently it has been taken from this passage in Ezekiel and employed in order to portray the salvation to come in the last days.

history, but are a result of a radical and creative new-shaping of it all. For the river of paradise and the marvellous effects brought by it signify the transformation of this world into the garden of paradise, whence not only the hosts of earthly diseases, but also sin and guilt have been banished, and God's good pleasure in his creation comes to full effect and works a complete inward and outward transformation of the whole shape of human life. It is therefore quite legitimate to call this state of salvation eschatological, seeing that it marks the end of what has hitherto been known as history, and prepares the way for a new event.

The remarkable thing about this is the way in which the old mythical expressions lose their earthly grossness in this new context, and grow transparent so as to let the spiritual re-creation of the people of God shine through. They no longer have any importance of their own, but serve to portray a salvation corresponding to the God who has revealed himself in history. These myths originally emerged to embellish a reality limited and finite. But they are brought into association with a God who not only transforms men inwardly, but also builds up a reordered world, an interplay and interweaving of moral and spiritual reality and outward corporeality. So the mythical expressions are made to symbolize a new relationship with God, in a way conceivable only within the context of the historical revelation experienced in Israel. Here all the features of the image of salvation point towards the holy will of a God who himself shares in the suffering of humanity and in so doing opens hearts to his compassion, which creates new life beyond and after judgment. This symbolic power of what the prophet says reveals under a new aspect how the eschatological fulfilment can only be portrayed by means of images which point beyond themselves and which set a personal relationship with God at the centre of God's redemption and bestowal of grace.

The same may be said, finally, about the breadth of the picture outlined here. The return of paradise, apparently at present limited to Palestine, is of its very nature a universal event embracing the whole world. So we may take it for granted without further demonstration that Palestine is a part that stands for the whole. Other prophecies of the same kind (Hos. 2.18; Isa. 9.3; 32.15ff.) give confirmation of this, coming to a climax in the universalism of Deutero-Isaiah. The constant formula: 'They shall know that I am Yahweh', which keeps recurring in Ezekiel, and applies to the nations as well as to Israel, therefore implies a great deal more than a mere theoretical recognition of the truth of the prophet's message. Rather, it expresses how the light of the new fellowship with God bestowed upon Israel also shines out over the Gentile world. The reason why this is not worked out fully is connected with the central importance of the chosen people, whom God has destined to be the carriers of his saving purposes and the witnesses of his redemptive power. What happens here spells a decisive change for the whole human race, as has already come to view in Gen. 12.3. But the prophets realize that if this is to happen at all it must first happen in Israel, and that they have been called for the main purpose of helping to bring it about.

Nor, however, can one fail to see how free Ezekiel's predictions of the future are of priestly limitations. The many insertions and elaborations in ch. 40–48 are enough to prove the point. They show what seemed indispensably necessary, and therefore in need of being added, in the eyes of disciples of the prophet who belonged to priestly circles. But they only succeeded to a very limited extent. Ezekiel himself was fully conscious of what he had done. His description of the new temple provided the complete frame for a fully developed cultus, but he deliberately left it empty. He does not confound the supernatural reality revealed to him with the portrayal of the way in which men will make use of it. This does not, of course, mean that he disapproved of the joyous pomp of temple festivals, or that he took no pleasure in the thought of the new sacrificial worship that could now be offered to the giver of full salvation. He had already described it as the homage pleasing to God presented by his redeemed people (20.40ff.), through which both Israel and the Gentiles are to come to a knowledge of how Yahweh has sanctified and glorified his holy name. But his eye is ever fixed upon what his God is giving, and so the way in which he speaks of the temple as the place where God dwells with his people puts the whole emphasis on the personal presence of the Holy, through which a decisive transformation of the inward and outward life of his people comes to pass. It is not the temple congregation celebrating the festivals, but the continual nearness of the redeemer and fulfiller who has taken up his dwelling in the most holy place, that constitutes the central point and the guarantee of the new form which the life of his people is taking. An immediate grasp of the self-comunicating divine nature, which finds its full expression in the shaping of an inwardly renewed community of men, is seen to be the reality most characteristic of God's new world. So the

paradise image of ch. 47, transparent as it is to the total transformation of earth which proceeds from the holy being of God, is thoroughly
in keeping with the outlook of Ezekiel.

<h1 style="text-align:center">CHAPTER 47.13–48.35</h1>

<h2 style="text-align:center">Boundaries and division of the promised land</h2>

47.13–20 The boundaries of the land

13 *Thus says* [. . .]ᵃ *Yahweh:* '[*This is*]ᵇ *the boundary within which you shall
divide the land according to the twelve tribes of Israel* [. . .]ᶜ *as an inheritance;*
¹⁴*and you shall take possession of it, each having as much as another, for I swore to
give it to your fathers, and so this land shall fall to you as your inheritance.* ¹⁵*And
this is the boundary of the land: from the Great Sea by way of Hetlon*ᵈ *to the entrance
of Hamath,*ᵉ *Zedad,*ᶠ ¹⁶*Berotha,*ᵍ *Sibrayim,*ʰ *which lies on the border between
Damascus and Hamath, to* [*Hazar-Enon*],ⁱ *which is on the border of Hauran.*ʲ
¹⁷*So the boundary shall run from the sea to Hazar-Enon, and the territory of
Damascus shall continue to lie to the north*ᵏ [. . .]ˡ *This shall be the north side.*
¹⁸*And the east side:* [*from Hazar-Enon*]ᵐ *which lies between Hauran and Damascus, and between Gilead and the land of Israel the Jordan*ⁿ *shall be the boundary, and
it shall run to the Eastern Sea*ᵒ *and as far as Tamar.*ᵖ *This shall be the east side.*
¹⁹*And the south side towards the midday sun: from Tamar as far as the waters of
strife at Kadesh*�q *by way of the Brook*ʳ *to the Great Sea.* [*This*]ˢ *shall be the south
border.* ²⁰*And on the west side: the Great Sea shall* [*be the boundary*]ᵗ *to a point
opposite the entrance of Hamath. This shall be the west side.*'

47.21–48.35 The division of the land

21 '*And you shall divide this land among you according to the tribes of Israel.*
²²*And it shall be that you shall allot it as an inheritance for yourselves and the aliens
who reside among you and have begotten sons among you. And they shall be to you as
natives among Israel. Like you they shall attain an inheritance by lot among the
tribes of Israel.* ²³*In whatever tribe the alien resides, there you shall assign him his
inheritance.*

48.1 *And these are the names of the tribes: further to the north from the sea*ᵘ *by
way of Hetlon to the entrance of Hamath as far as Hazar-Enon, so that the territory
of Damascus lies to the north over against Hamath* [. . .]ᵛ [*from the east side to the
west*]:ʷ *Dan, one portion.*

2 *And adjoining the territory of Dan*　　*from the east side to the west,
　　　　　　　　　　　　　　　　　　Asher, one portion.*

3 *And adjoining the territory of Asher*　*from the east side to the west,
　　　　　　　　　　　　　　　　　　Naphtali, one portion.*

4 *And adjoining the territory of Naphtali*   *from the east side to the west,*
                                                 Manasseh, one portion.
5 *And adjoining the territory of Manasseh*   *from the east side to the west,*
                                                 Ephraim, one portion.
6 *And adjoining the territory of Ephraim*   *from the east side to the west,*
                                                 Reuben, one portion.
7 *And adjoining the territory of Reuben*   *from the east side to the west,*
                                                 Judah, one portion.

8 *And adjoining the territory of Judah, from the east side to the west, shall be the oblation which you shall set apart as a consecrated gift, twenty-five thousand cubits in breadth, and in length equal to one of the portions from the east side to the west, and the sanctuary shall be in the midst of it.* 9 *The oblation which you shall set apart as a consecrated gift to Yahweh shall be twenty-five thousand cubits in length and twenty thousand*^x *cubits in breadth.* 10 *And to these shall be the allotments of the holy portion: the priests shall have an allotment measuring twenty-five thousand cubits on the northern side and ten thousand cubits in breadth on the western side, ten thousand in breadth on the eastern side and twenty-five thousand in length on the southern side, and the sanctuary of Yahweh shall be in the midst.* 11[. . .]^y 12 *It shall belong to them as a special oblation from the oblation of the land, a most holy place adjoining the territory of the Levites.* 13 *And the Levites (shall have) corresponding to the territory of the priests (an allotment) twenty-five thousand cubits in length and ten thousand in breadth. The whole therefore shall be twenty-five thousand cubits long and twenty thousand broad.*^z 14 *And they shall not sell or exchange*^{aa} *any of it nor alienate the best portion of the land. For it is holy to Yahweh.* 15 *And the remainder, five thousand cubits in breadth alongside the twenty-five thousand in length, shall be for ordinary use for the city for dwellings and for open country. In the midst of it shall be the city.* 16 *And these shall be its dimensions: the north side four thousand five hundred and the south side four thousand five hundred and the*^{bb} *east side four thousand five hundred and the west side four thousand five hundred.* 17 *And the city shall have open land on the north two hundred and fifty and on the south two hundred and fifty and on the east two hundred and fifty and on the west two hundred and fifty.* 18 *The remainder of the length alongside the holy portion, ten thousand to the east and ten thousand to the west [. . .]*^{cc}*: its produce shall be food for the inhabitants of the city.* 19 *As for the inhabitants*^{dd} *of the city, it shall be inhabited by men from all the tribes of Israel.* 20 *The whole oblation which you shall set apart shall measure twenty-five thousand cubits by twenty-five thousand cubits; you shall make the holy portion together with the property of the city to take the form of a square when you consecrate it.* 21 *The remainder shall belong to the prince: the land on both sides of the holy portion and of the property of the city along the twenty-five thousand cubits [to the east]*^{ee} *as far as the east border, and to the west along the twenty-five thousand cubits as far as the west border, parallel to the tribal portions, shall belong to the prince. The sanctuary of the temple shall lie in the midst of the holy portion.* 22 *And from the property of the Levites and from the property of the city,*

which lies in the midst of that which belongs to the prince, the land between the territory of Judah and the territory of Benjamin shall belong to the prince.
23 *And the rest of the tribes: from the east side to the west: Benjamin one portion.*
24 *And adjoining the territory of Benjamin from the east side to the west,*
    Simeon, one portion.
25 *And adjoining the territory of Simeon   from the east side to the west,*
    Issachar, one portion.
26 *And adjoining the territory of Issachar from the east side to the west,*
    Zebulun, one portion.
27 *And adjoining the territory of Zebulun from the east side to the west,*
    Gad, one portion.
28 *And adjoining the territory of Gad on the south the boundary shall run from Tamar as far as the waters of strife at Kadesh along the Brook towards the Great Sea.* 29*This is the land which you shall allot as[tt] an inheritance among the tribes of Israel, and these are their portions, says [. . .][gg] Yahweh.*

30a *And these shall be the exits of the city,* 31a *and the gates of the city shall be named after the tribes of Israel.* 30b*On the north side[hh] which is to be four thousand five hundred cubits by measure* 31b*three gates [. . .][ii]: one the gate of Reuben, one the gate of Judah, one the gate of Levi.* 32*And on the east side, which is to be four thousand five hundred cubits by measure, three gates: one the gate of Joseph, one the gate of Benjamin, one the gate of Dan.* 33*And on the south side which is to be of four thousand five hundred cubits by measure, three gates: one the gate of Simeon, one the gate of Issachar, one the gate of Zebulun.* 34*And on the west side, which is to be of four thousand five hundred cubits by measure, three gates:[jj] one the gate of Gad, one the gate of Asher, one the gate of Naphtali.* 35*Its circumference shall be eighteen thousand cubits. And the name of the city henceforth shall be "Yahweh is there".'*

[a–b]See BH.
[c]MT: 'Joseph two [read dual for plural] parts': an over-careful correction, since Levi is included among the twelve tribes in 48.30ff.
[d]According to Heinisch, ʿadlun between Tyre and Sidon; a more exact position is unknown.
[e]This point between Lebanon and Antilebanon is often referred to as forming the northern boundary in ideal conditions: Isa. 13.5; I Kings 8.65; Amos 6.14, etc. Hamath, situated on the Orontes north of the territory of Lebanon, was a celebrated fortress.
[f]Zedad, also named in Num. 34.8, south-east of Homs, on the way from Riblah to Palmyra, 100 kilometres (sixty-two miles) north of Damascus. But as Damascus is not included in Israelite territory, one may ask if it is not preferable to make a slight emendation and read Zerada, the ruins of which are situated south-west of Mount Hermon.
[g]= Bereitan, a little to the south-west of Baalbek.
[h]Not as yet identified.
[i]Also mentioned in Num. 34.9f.; perhaps situated, like Banias, at one of the sources of the Jordan (Cooke).

[j]A mountainous district of volcanic origin in Transjordan, with a plain before it, and then the name of the district south of Damascus, a part of which, Bashan, is well known as a very fruitful plateau on the upper reaches of the Jarmuk, cf. Deut. 3.1ff.; Num. 33–35; Josh. 9.10.

[k]See BH.

[l]MT: 'And the territory of Hamath', a gloss following 48.1.

[m]Must be inserted at this point.

[n]See BH.

[o]Meaning the Dead Sea.

[p]Tamar, also referred to in I Kings 9.18, must be somewhere to the south-west of the Dead Sea, and perhaps may be identified with the ruins at Kurnub.

[q]Num. 27.14, also known as the waters of Meribah: Num. 20.13; Ps. 81.8; 106.32.

[r]Otherwise called the Brook of Egypt: Num. 34.5; Josh. 15.4, 47; I Kings 8.65, etc., identical with the *wadi el arish.*

[s–t]See BH.

[u]Thus with 47.17 instead of MT: 'at the side'.

[v]MT: 'and they shall be his'; a statement which does not fit in with the context.

[w–x]See BH.

[y]v. 11: 'For the consecrated priests, the sons of Zadok, who continued in my service, who did not go astray, as the Israelites and also the Levites went astray.' An addition, since here Yahweh speaks in the first person. What is contained in 44.6ff. has to be added as an appendix in ch. 48. We find similar additions in 40.46b and 43.19 (Gese).

[z–hh]See BH.

[ii]MT: 'towards the north'; a gloss which became necessary when vv. 31a and 30b got out of place.

[jj]See BH. The twelve gates of the new Jerusalem are also named after the tribes of Israel in Rev. 21.12f.

The fixing of the frontiers of the new Israel: 47.13–20

The chief point to be noticed in the fixing of the frontiers to the north, east, south and west is the abandonment of Transjordania, in spite of the fact that a considerable part of it was genuine Israelite territory. By this, the writer shows that historical and geographical factors are of no account to him in securing the old home of his nation. We can hardly be mistaken in holding that this attitude is due mainly to theological considerations: only the land to the west of the Jordan was the object of the promise in the histories of the patriarchs. The memories of the great sanctuaries and their history, which had played so large a part in the ancient and sacred traditions, and had shaped the whole being of Israel, had their home there. In the light of later events, the territory east of Jordan had held latent within it from the very beginning the menace of schism and apostasy, as is shown at length in Josh. 22, a piece of priestly tradition (cf. also Num. 32). In addition, it was easier to establish a clearly marked boundary line there than where Transjordania gradually merges into the eastern wilderness.

A loose link with the preceding sections is provided in v. 13 by the formula marking a divine utterance. But the word of God is not indispensable in stating what follows, since vv. 15–20 do no more than list the places along the line of the frontier. The northern boundary is seen to be the most difficult, as there are no river courses or mountain chains to mark it. Starting at an undefined point on the Phoenician coast, perhaps at the mouth of the *nar el kasimiye* immediately north of Tyre (Cooke), a frontier is described from west to east. The most definite of the data is the entrance to Hamath, which must be located somewhere in the depression between Lebanon and Hermon, although its exact situation cannot be defined. The northern frontier of Israel was located there in the time of Solomon (I Kings 8.65), and later references show general agreement. After that, the frontier seems to run across south of Baalbek to the sources of the Jordan, the Hauran being named as one of the boundaries, so it must include in its territory the district of Dsholan which stretches as far as Hermon, and was the subject of frequent conflicts between Israel and Damascus. Starting at Hazar-Enon, the most easterly point of the northern boundary, the eastern frontier follows the course of the Jordan as far as the Dead Sea, stretching beyond it to Tamar, situated to the south-west in the Negeb. The southern frontier, commencing there, makes a wide sweep to the south-west to reach the oasis of Kadesh, well known in the stories about Moses, and then describes a sharp bend to the north-west until it arrives at the Mediterranean sea at the brook which forms the boundary with Egypt. This line clearly expresses awareness that the southern frontier ought not to run in a straight line from east to west, but this is not in agreement with the ideas usually prevailing in the lists of the divisions of the land. The western frontier coincides with the Mediterranean coast as far as the point where the northern frontier begins. This statement of the boundaries agrees to a large extent with Num. 34.1–12 and Josh. 15.2–4 which belong to the priestly tradition. So it has probably made use of the same traditional sources as those two passages.

The division of the land: 47.21–48.35

Before the beginning of the allotment of the various tribal territories, an important statement of basic principle has been inserted in vv. 22f., correcting what has been said in vv. 14 and 21. This means that whereas v. 21 has said that the process of dividing the land among the tribes may begin, v. 22 comes in and clearly brings it to a stop. The words 'and it shall prevail' interrupt by laying down an incisive appointment which has no direct connection with the determination of the frontier, and which must therefore be regarded as a later addition. Neverless, this appointment is of great social importance. The words of Yahweh are taken up again from vv. 13f. and a class of persons whose right to hold land is not recognized elsewhere in the Old Testament is named as having equal rights to ownership of land with the native-born Israelites. This class is that of the aliens, i.e. the people belonging to foreign nations who have settled in Israel. Of course, it takes into consideration only those aliens who have sons to succeed them to whom they can bequeath their land. But this is a principle with wide implications. Aliens had, of course, been well treated hitherto and protected against oppression (Ex. 22.21f.; Lev. 19.33; Deut. 24.17); they might own houses (Gen. 19.9) and become rich (Lev. 25.47). This meant that they were to a large extent regarded as members of the congregation and increasingly expected to observe the ritual commandments (Ex. 12.19; Lev. 18.26; Num. 19.10) and, if circumcised, were admitted to take their part in festivals (Ex. 12.48) and sacrifices (Num. 15.14, 26). Thus their status gradually kept approaching that of proselytes. Nevertheless, they did not enjoy full rights of citizenship, nor could they hold any property in land (Isa. 22.15ff.). But now at this point the admission of aliens to the right to hold property in land in 47.22f. is a great and daring step forward towards putting the alien on the same footing as the native born. The provision may have been contested for a long time, since special regulations were appealed to at various periods excluding particular aliens (Deut. 23.4–9; 25.17–19). Yet such exceptions serve logically to develop the existing right for aliens.

The accomplishment of the apportioning of land to the tribes which follows in 48.1ff. moves in a series of short sentences of similar structure, which provide each tribe with a strip of land, all evidently of equal size and each running from the western to the eastern border, succeeding one another from the northern frontier to the south. The width of these strips of land is not stated. Levi does not count as a secular tribe here, and is replaced by the division of Joseph into Ephraim and Manasseh. Between the territory of the seventh and eighth tribes lies the holy portion of land for the temple and the colony of priests and Levites, as well as for the holy city; the details about it are repeated at somewhat greater length, but in complete agreement with 45.1–8. The prince's land lies on either side.

In the arrangement of the tribes, it is significant that seven of them lie to the north and five to the south of the city and temple. Here the geographical position of Jerusalem, south of the centre of the land, seems to have been taken into account, whereas all other historical or geographical presuppositions about the settlement of the tribes are completely disregarded. So tribes which had had their homes in the north, like Issachar, Zebulun and Gad, are transferred to the extreme south; those formerly settled in Transjordania have to be removed to the west; Judah takes her place north of Jerusalem, contrary to her context in history, whereas Benjamin finds itself occupying Judah's place to the south of the city. The deciding factor for the general order of precedence seems to have been the distinction between full-born and half-born tribes; the latter are placed furthest to the north or south and therefore furthest from the sanctuary (Dan, Asher, Naphtali, Gad), the former are in two groups nearer to the temple, four to the north and four to the south. Verse 29 concludes the list by a double summary of what it contains and the final formula denoting the word of Yahweh.

There is appended without any formula to attach it a final passage in vv. 30–35 about the holy city, which in view of its subject should belong to v. 16. In agreement with v. 16, it states that the city is a square with sides four thousand five hundred cubits long, having three gates on each side. They bear the names of the twelve tribes, among which Levi is once more included, while Ephraim and Manasseh are jointly represented by Joseph. This seems to suggest that this section is independent of the preceding one. It is not possible to account for the order taken by the names.

The section concludes with the short phrase speaking of the name of the city. It gets a new name, answering to the new state of salvation, i.e. 'Yahweh is there'. The name recalls 'Immanuel', the old name that tells of salvation, and like it points to the nearness of Yahweh, who has not taken up residence in the city in the same way as before, but in still greater closeness. This gives a correct definition of what was the essential content of the age of salvation in the eyes of Ezekiel and also of his disciples, and those who transmitted his writings. However differently they may express it in detail, they all agree that full fellowship with the God of election is the deciding factor in the fulfilment of Israel. For in that alone lies the guarantee that this people will reach the goal for which they are destined: to be freed of all sin and imperfection so as to be a credible witness to the Holy One, their God.